ONLY THE MAKER'S NAME

Ray Blyth

ISBN 978-1-905553-92-1

Printed by Dolman Scott
www.dolmanscott.com

A CHILD'S DREAM.

I lay down in a field of gold
and looked up to the sky,
In warm sunlight I fell asleep
and dreamed that I could fly.

I stood up in my field of gold
and held my arms out high,
I felt the wind caress my face
as I began to fly.

The whispering wind then
spoke to me
and softly said 'One day,
when you're man you'll fly again
and I will guide your way.'

I woke up in my field of gold,
my eyes held tears of joy,
I knew God's hand was guiding me,
a lonely little boy.

RMB

I would like to dedicate this book to my dear friend Rex Smith OBE.

I knew Rex for over 56 years, from the time when I was learning to fly, and later as my boss when I instructed at Oxford Air Training School.

Throughout my forty years employment in aviation, Rex remained a firm friend and valued advisor.

Rex was a fighter Pilot during the Second World War. Later he joined CSE and was the key figure in building Kidlington Flying Club up into Oxford Air Training School, renowned at the time as the finest Commercial Pilot training facility in the world. Rex became Chairman of OATS, and was awarded the OBE for his contribution to the world of professional Pilot Training. At one stage of his career Rex Smith was appointed Director of Flying Training for the Civil Aviation Authority.

Rex was a treasured friend whom I turned to for advice many times during my career in aviation.

Sadly Rex Smith passed away on Saturday the 14th April 2012.

I miss him terribly.

CONTENTS

PART ONE

PART TWO.

PART ONE.

PREFACE

I first considered writing a book when I was hospitalised for a period of two years following an aeroplane accident in 1968. The idea was to record the hilarious, as well as more sombre events that took place during my childhood and the years that followed. However, on my release from hospital in 1970, all thoughts of writing a book had to be set aside as I needed to concentrate on the serious matter of getting fit and finding another job. Nevertheless I was encouraged by friends and colleagues to write a book about my experiences many years later when I retired as a pilot.

I have tried to be as accurate as possible about the events recorded in this book concerning my life during the period from 1931 to 1996. The script was compiled with the help of notes accumulated over many years as well as entries in my diaries and pilots log books. For the rest, I have had to rely on memory.

Unsurprisingly, with the passing of time, it has been impossible to recall various conversations with complete accuracy; therefore I have attributed words that were most likely to have been spoken. If I have mistakenly ascribed words or deeds to people who did not say or do them, I am sorry. However all the actual situations, circumstances and events are, to the best of my knowledge, perfectly accurate.

The book is in two parts. You will see that events recorded in Part One are not in chronological order because they are memories of the past as I recalled them during my lengthy stay in hospital. All the events in part two however, are in order that they actually occurred.

The title of the book, "Only the maker's name" is derived from conversations frequently overheard at the end of the day in the pilot's crew-room.

'There I was old boy, upside down with nothing on the clock bar the maker's name.'

CHAPTER 1.

In the beginning.

I lay on my back unable to move any part of my body with the exception of my right arm. Although heavily sedated I could still feel the waves of pain that surged up my legs and through my body with monotonous regularity. The drugs had the effect of detaching the pain in some way, it was still there, but somehow didn't seem to matter. I had been in hospital for three months, and virtually unable to move, I had memorised the number of bricks, windowpanes, and every countable detail of the small ward I was in.

The first six weeks, or thereabouts, had been spent in the intensive care unit of the Radcliffe Infirmary Oxford. Memories of that period were blurred and confused: Kind faces, sympathetic voices, bottles of red and clear liquids hanging from odd shaped structures over my head, severe pain, and the relief that came shortly after periodic injections somewhere in my back. Day and night seemed jumbled into one, and I had little idea of what was happening.

But now, in the small ward adjoining the main section of `C` ward in the Radcliffe Hospital, I was able to think more clearly. Of one thing I was certain, I had been in a serious aeroplane accident, and was lucky to be alive.

Several surgeons had taken a look at me since my arrival, and to date I had undergone two major operations on my legs. I wasn't quite sure of the full extent of my injuries at that time, but I did remember with crystal clarity that I had been mentally prepared for the possibility of having one, or maybe both of my legs amputated. The ward sister assured me that the surgeons would do everything possible to avoid amputation, and I would now be in the hands of Mr J.D. Morgan who was one of the finest consultant orthopaedic surgeons in the country, a man whom, over the next two long and painful years, I grew to respect and trust implicitly.

It wasn't long before my confused mind cleared sufficiently for me to comprehend the unthinkable: I would probably never fly again. From then on that single thought was foremost in my mind. In reality, I should have been more concerned with the possibility that I may never be able to walk again, which was probably much nearer the mark!

Drugs play peculiar tricks on a person's mind: terrific highs, devastating lows, depressions and hallucinations, but today I felt a kind of calmness, and I was able to think a lot more clearly than at any time since the accident.

Prior to the crash I had been the Chief Flying Instructor of 'E' flight at Oxford Air Training School where we trained pilots for many of the worlds airlines.

Having been born in a very poor area of King's Lynn during the slump of the 1930s, it had been a long arduous struggle over many years for me to realise my childhood dream of becoming a pilot. Now it seemed that all had been taken away from me in a matter of seconds.

How had all this begun? My thoughts wandered back in time to my earliest childhood memories…

I was born on the 30th January 1931 in a small terraced house on the outskirts of King's Lynn in the county of Norfolk. My earliest memories were of the very narrow cobbled street where I lived, and the smell of freshly baked bread from the small bakery on the corner. I clearly remember the old gas lamps that lit our tiny street in Winter when the frost sparkled on the windowsills and heavy snow deadened the sound of horse drawn vehicles busy about their business as Christmas time approached. Those happy times were indeed my earliest cherished memories.

Number five Wellington Street was a small terraced house with two very small rooms on the ground floor known in those days as the "front room" where no-one was allowed to set foot except on Sundays and Christmas Day, and the living room.

A small outhouse had been attached to the rear of our house that served as the kitchen and doubled as a bathhouse when required. Upstairs there were two tiny bedrooms, each with a real fireplace. The joy of a coal fire in the bedroom was a luxury that made being ill much more endurable.

The street itself was very narrow, ending in a cul-de-sac. In fact Wellington Street was so narrow that tradesmen delivering coal, bread, and milk etc., had to back their horse- drawn carts out of the road as there was insufficient room for them to turn.

My interest in aeroplanes first began when my mother brought me a cut-out aeroplane book back from the local grocers shop where they were given away to customers who purchased a certain brand of biscuits. One seldom saw or even heard a real aeroplane in those days, nevertheless I was fascinated with the idea of flying. Then one day in the Summer of 1934 things changed forever.

I sat with my father and mother in the railway carriage of the early morning train bound for the seaside town of Hunstanton, some twenty miles southeast of Lynn. We always spent our annual day out by the sea, it was our one and only highlight each Summer, and it was there that my interest in aeroplanes was first kindled.

On arrival at Hunstanton station we left the train angrily hissing spurts of steam into the air, and made our way to the beach, mother clutching a case of banana sandwiches, and me armed with a bucket and spade. It was a beautiful calm summer's morning with clear blue skies, perfect for a day by the sea. As we reached the concrete steps that led down to the sandy beach, we were startled by an ear-splitting roar that caused us to look up and see a brightly coloured aeroplane flash low over our heads as it climbed out over the sea. It looked fantastic with its light green fuselage and silver wings silhouetted against the pale blue of the sky. I stood there gazing in amazement when a sudden jerk brought me back to my senses as my mother took my arm and said…

'Come on my boy your fathers leaving us behind.'

Before long I was busy building a sandcastle. Dad lent a hand by digging a channel from the castle moat towards the incoming tide. At Hunstanton the sea goes out a very long way, so far in fact that when it's fully out you can barely see it.

We ate our sandwiches and drank lemonade from the tin mugs mother had carefully packed away in her little case. It's funny, but one of the things I remember is that we always had banana sandwiches when we went to the sea-side, at any other time we never set eyes on a banana.

As the day progressed, dad left us and strolled over to read a poster that was propped up in the sand near to the sea wall. He returned moments later looking quite excited about something.

'They are giving joy flights in that little green aeroplane we saw earlier, apparently they're taking off from a field near to the beach, would you like to go up Mag?' he said.

He always called my mother Mag. Maggie was her real name, Maggie McKenzie, before she married Dad.

'Oh my god, never,' I heard my mother saying, 'you'll never get me up in one of those things Len!'

'I'll go Dad.' I said almost unable to contain my excitement.

'No you're too young son.'

'I'm three' I argued.

'No definitely not, they'd never let you go, besides it's an open cockpit aeroplane and you'd fall out' he said, no doubt hoping that would be the end of it.

It didn't put me off at all, but one thing I knew for certain was that dad was not the sort of chap to argue with. So defeated, my eyes filled with tears, I slumped down onto the sand to enter the unplumbed depths of sheer misery.

Dad stared at me for a moment then, seeing I was heartbroken, he said...

'Let's take a walk over to the aeroplane old son and see what they say, but don't go building your hopes up.'

Dad's words brought me instantly to my feet, and I found myself in one of those odd circumstances when happiness overtakes distress, and I was laughing with my eyes still bubbling over with tears.

We started off down the beach in the direction of the arrow on the notice board, the immediately forgotten sand castle left to its ultimate fate against the incoming tide.

After walking for a short time the landing strip came into view. My feelings were a mixture of exhilaration and anxiety, worried in case I wouldn't be allowed to go up after all. The bi-plane zoomed over our heads again as we arrived at a small wooden office mounted on large cart wheels where "Joy Flight Tickets" were on sale for five shillings each. A small section of the field had been fenced off to prevent the public from straying onto the take-off and landing area.

'My son is three and a half years old, do you think he could be taken up for a Joy Flight?' father was addressing a tall smiling lady in the ticket hut.

'Well he's definitely too small to go up on his own sir, but perhaps the pilot will let him sit on your lap' the lady answered.

The whole thing was far too much for me...another agonising wait. Not knowing where to put myself, I ran round in circles until I became dizzy and sat down with a plonk! My mother said something about not acting silly, and when I pulled a face at her, she snatched my cap off and swiped me with it.

Two or three hundred yards away the aeroplane had landed and was snarling it's way towards us. It turned around just short of the safety fence and came to a standstill. When the propeller stopped turning my father told me to stay where I was for a moment whilst he went to speak to the pilot. Those few moments seemed like a lifetime as I waited for the verdict. Mother looked very worried indeed, and no doubt we were each hoping for opposite results. The pilot turned out to be a very pretty young lady. Her name was Miss Pauline Gower. Miss Gower later became very famous as the commandant of the ladies section of the Air Transport Auxiliary that flew service aeroplanes on positioning flights throughout World War Two.

My father returned beaming from ear to ear with his hands outstretched towards me.

'It's O.K old son, you can sit on my lap, and I only have to pay for one ticket.'

I jumped up and down with excitement. My mother however couldn't have looked more upset and began to fuss round me tucking my shirt into my trousers, pulling up my socks and issuing endless instructions on what not to do.

'Come on Ray' my father was waving the ticket and walking towards the aeroplane.

'Now be careful and don't do anything silly' were my mother's final words.

She kissed me and gave me a hug that almost suffocated me. I'm sure that she was convinced she would never see either of us again.

The pilot sat in the rear cockpit of the aeroplane, which I have since discovered was a Spartan Three, built by the Spartan Aircraft Company of Southampton.

Whilst my father was being helped into the front cockpit by the lady who sold the tickets, the pilot smiled at me and said something which I cannot remember, but years later my father told me that I had asked her to promise not to "loop the loop" as I would be sitting on my dad's lap and would probably fall out!

The ticket lady lifted me up, lowered me onto dad's lap in the front cockpit and strapped us in together. She then went to the front of the aircraft and began turning the propeller by hand until the engine burst into life.

My first ever flight was a wonderful experience that made a lasting impression on me. During the take-off run I kept my eyes tight closed because there was lots of dust swirling around inside the cockpit.

'We're up now old son open your eyes.'

It was at that moment I discovered the indescribable grandeur of flight, a magnificence that would one day be my privilege to experience as part of my everyday working life. I saw the light blue sky in contrast with the darker blue sea beneath. I could hear the powerful roar of the engine, and felt the wind blasting on my face. Then, as we passed over the coast heading towards the town, I could see tiny houses and cars and miniature trees that seemed for all the world that they were toys. There was very little impression of height or speed, it just seemed that everything had shrunk to a beautiful miniature-sized world, a world that made such an impression on me that it would stay with me for the rest of my life. My father held me tightly, I felt secure and happy…that's one thing about dad, anything could be happening, but so long as I was with my father I always felt safe. It's hard to believe that twenty four years later that same little boy sitting on his father's lap would grow up to become a flying instructor and take his father up for flying lessons.

Although I was only three years old, the experience of flying reached through to the very heart of me, and even though there were very few private cars and even fewer aeroplanes around in those days, I somehow knew, that however difficult it may be to achieve, I would one day fly an aeroplane myself, I never once doubted that I would.

The next moment we were touching down on the grass, and rolling to a halt. I could see my mother, her expression had changed completely, beaming from ear to ear, as if to say she knew flying was perfectly safe all the time, and never had the slightest worry about it whatsoever. If only my dear mother had lived to see her son's later success in the world of aviation.

The tall lady reappeared, undid our straps and lifted me down. I looked up admiringly at the pilot smiling down at me and thanked her. From that moment onwards my obsession with aeroplanes was a permanent part of my existence.

When I was five years old I was taken to attend my first day at school. On the way my mother met up with a friend who was also taking her little son to attend his first day at school. That was how I came to meet Eddy Baldock who was to become my dear friend for life.

Eddy came from a good honest working class family that lived in Holcombe Avenue. We met every day at the entrance to "The Walks", a long avenue of trees in the centre of King's Lynn, and sauntered off to school together.

Everybody's first day at school is a memorable occasion; mine was no exception although I seem to remember more of the journey to school than the rest of the day.

The smell of damp freshly fallen leaves from the tall chestnut trees that formed Lynn Walks filled the air. It was a magic place to be at any time, but Autumn brings with it a special beauty. To this day whenever I smell wet fallen leaves, no matter where I am, it always reminds me of those happy journeys to school along that tree-lined path. On our way we past a circle of tall Birch trees known as the "Seven Sisters", then over a little river bridge and through an archway in the remains of the old town wall. Clutching my mothers gloved hand, we would journey on further, passing the Red Mount Tower with its mystic tales of a torture chamber and underground tunnels. Crows always circled overhead calling to one another, then the occasional sound of a crack would denote a badly executed treetop landing that sent twigs hurtling downwards. We also had to pass close to the railway station. Black puffs of smoke would sometimes billow high into the clear air on the far side of a tall safety fence signifying the 8.30am train to London was about to leave.

'That's enough' my mother said as I stooped to pick up just one more conker, 'You'll be late on your first day at school if we don't hurry.'

Every shiny horse chestnut that lay partly hidden by the crimson leaves seemed bigger and more collectable than the last one. But my dear mother was making sure I would not be late for my first day at school, so conker collecting was over for that day.

As we approached the gates of St James Junior School, the ancient red brick building didn't seem quite so welcoming as it had when my mother took me to view it from the outside a few days earlier!

Miss Wright was a kind looking lady who smiled a lot. She picked me up, gave me a gentle shake, as if to see if anything would drop off, and put me down again.

'Miss Wright is going to be your teacher, now be a good boy, mummy will be back to collect you after school.'

She bent down, kissed me, and hurried away looking quite upset. I was whisked off and shown where to hang my hat and coat. Eddy received similar treatment, and before long we were sitting at a desk in a tiny, dimly lit classroom, but sadly not together. Each desk was shared by two children; I had to sit next to a plump girl with jam-jar bottom spectacles and short straight hair. Her name was Muriel Whittaker...We didn't speak!

I can't remember exactly what we did on my first day at school, but it passed quickly and without fuss. At midday I was given a bottle of milk that had been warmed by the classroom radiator, and sucked it up through a straw that passed through a cardboard milk bottle top. Such bottle tops would no doubt be considered as a collector's item these days.

8

CHAPTER 2.

Volunteers.

The rain lashing down outside the hospital ward brought back more memories of my childhood. I remembered that it had been raining when my parents and I moved to our new home in Holcombe Avenue during the Winter of 1937.

At first I didn't want to leave Wellington Street, but I could hardly believe my luck when my mother told me that our new house, number twenty-one was just a few doors away from No 14 where my new found friend Eddy lived.

Everything small enough had been packed into tea chests and cardboard boxes including most of my toys. Mother spent the whole of the final day cleaning number five Wellington Street so that it would be spotless for the next tenants to move in.

It was still raining when the removal men arrived with their horse drawn cart to take our possessions to our new home. Tarpaulins were stretched over the cart to protect our treasured belongings, but we were all soaked to the skin by the time we arrived at our destination. The houses on either side of No. 21 were still empty, but my friend Eddy was there to greet us, and Mrs. Baldock (Ed's Mum) arrived with a thermos flask of tea and some freshly cut sandwiches. Fortunately the rain eased off and it was not long before the task of unloading the cart began. Dad was giving instructions to the removal men, and mother was busy unpacking the tea chests as they were brought into the house.

Number twenty-one was infinitely bigger and brighter than our old home. It had a large dining room, and a spacious sitting room (Referred to as the front room). The kitchen was much better than the little out-house we had been used to, and we rejoiced in the pure luxury of actually having a real bathroom. The one and only toilet was downstairs in a small brick-built extension adjacent to the back door, its slanting tiled roof was just below the window of the smallest of the three bedrooms, which incidentally was destined to become my bedroom.

My father was very proud of our few possessions, he had worked very hard for everything we owned, and like most fathers in those days he was also a very strict man. I loved him dearly, but one certain kind of look from him would terrorise me because I knew what usually followed. Moving in day unfortunately was not without tragedy for me.

It all started to go wrong when I was bringing in one of my toys that had been packed into a very large cardboard box, almost too big for me to carry. It contained my second hand Hornby Train-Set that had been given to me by my Uncle Mac. Staggering under the weight of the box, I entered the front door and started to climb the stairs with the intention of putting the train set under the bed in my newly designated bedroom. I was gripping the box firmly under my left arm. I'm hardly likely to forget which arm I had the box under as that was the key factor resulting in the disaster that followed. It happened that the stair banister rail was also on the left, so instead of supporting myself with the rail, I steadied myself against the wall with my right hand. As I neared the top of the stairs a voice immediately behind me thundered out…

'Bloody Hell, look at that!!'

The words were undoubtedly directed at me and the voice was unmistakably my father's. I froze on the spot, hardly daring to turn round to see what was wrong, but when I did my heart sank and I was left in no doubt that the incident had by no means been fully dealt with. To my horror I saw a clearly marked set of grubby little fingerprints stippled on the newly distempered wall tracing my progress up the stairs!

Unfortunately my problems didn't end there. The sight of my black fingerprints coupled with the fury in my father's voice served to activate one of my unfortunate weaknesses, and a yellowish puddle began to form at my feet. In seconds it reached the edge of the step on which I was standing, dripped gently down onto the next step, and from there on proceeded to bounce joyfully down the stairs like a half-hearted waterfall.

Dad was speechless, as his eyes traced the trickle on it's way down towards him! What followed is a memory far too painful to recall… suffice to say that the excitement of the day ended in tears.

We soon settled in at No. 21, and within a few days the houses on either side had also become occupied.

First to arrive were the Canham family who moved into No.19 the other half of our semi-detached house. I remember they were more fortunate with the weather as it was quite a sunny day when they appeared on the scene with a horse and cart containing their belongings. My father had been struggling for most of the morning trying to make a start on our medium sized garden, which at the time resembled a builder's tip more than a garden. He went out to greet the Canham's, and in no time they were all standing in our kitchen sipping tea from Mum's best cups! (Normally only brought out at Christmas) and talking about the merits of our new homes, all except Brian that is.

Brian, their son, was about my age. He stood peering at me from behind his mother's skirt, rather like a cat eyeing up a mouse. It was obvious that we had taken an instant dislike to one another on sight.

Before long all the grown-ups were helping to unload our neighbour's furniture from the horse and cart that stood patiently outside.

Brian and I were soon to become very good friends, but at this moment in time we never took our eyes off each other whilst our parents carefully carried furniture from the cart to the house.

It was during the unloading of the cart that I first met Mr. Hewitt, a neighbour from the opposite side of the road. Mr Hewitt was a Chemist by profession, he was also a keen gardener who loved children and was very much a boy at heart himself. He appeared from nowhere carrying a shovel and bucket, and quickly scooped up a large pile of horse manure almost before the last steaming lump had plopped to the ground. Smiling he patted the horse's rear, and without a word to anyone whisked the valued contents of the bucket back to his garden.

'Who the hells that?' I heard my father say,

'Sshh', mum said 'He'll hear you.'

'Well I could have done with that on my garden,' dad mumbled.

'What garden?' mum asked 'it's just a jungle.'

Mrs. Canham seeing the likelihood of an argument interrupted with...

'Don't worry, he'll probably do some more before we've finished unloading!'

At that moment the horse leaned forward slightly and started to pee. It seemed to go on forever; ejected with some considerable gusto it steamed and splashed several inches high before streaming down towards the roadside drain. All four grown-ups watched in silence, then Dad, determined to have the last word, said in a loud voice...

'I notice he didn't put his bucket under that.'

With that mum went into the house and slammed the door. I looked at Brian and he stuck his tongue out... Instant hate reigned!

A few days after the Canham's had moved in, Mr and Mrs Waters together with their dog Tony arrived to take over their house at number twenty-three and became our other neighbours. Mr Waters turned out to be a policeman, a very friendly man who adored children and loved to play practical jokes. In short our neighbours on either side were lovely people, and unbeknown to us, with world war two looming up, we were to share many happy and sad experiences together.

A week or so went by. We were still trying to sort out where to put our possessions in the new house.

'That will have to go soon Ray,' mother was pointing to my little pedal car.

'You're far too old for that, and I doubt if you can get in it now anyway.'

I recalled just how much I loved that red pedal car. As far as I can remember it was the only time in my life when a car took precedence over an aeroplane. In the 1930s it must have been difficult for my parents to find the money for such an expensive toy, and of course Father Christmas quite undeservedly got all the credit!

I was eight years old when World War Two broke out in 1939. My father was called away so I spent all five years of the war living with my Mother.

Norfolk soon became inundated with military airfields, and the drone of highflying aeroplanes was commonplace.

A few months after the war had started, I was playing in the garden when suddenly the loud roar of an aeroplane engine made me jump out of my wits! I looked up to see a Spitfire skim overhead just a few feet above the rooftops. The impressive sight of that sleek aeroplane added to my keenness to fly when I grew up.

Most Saturday mornings my friend Eddy and I would walk around Lynn town centre looking in shop windows, or on occasions stroll down to the docks to take a look at the ships. We always used to take Tony with us. Tony was the black Labrador belonging to the Waters family that lived next door. He was a lovely old dog that never had to be on a lead, he would just trot along with us, and apart from delicately sniffing the occasional lamppost he never left our side.

It was one such Saturday morning when Eddy and I set off accompanied by Tony to visit the RAF Recruiting Office in King's Lynn High Street.

Smartly dressed with well-polished shoes, we entered the office confidently where we were confronted by a very tall RAF Sergeant with a large bushy moustache that curled up at the ends.

'How can I help you lads?' he said.

All my courage drained away at this point and I just stood there in silence. Eddy gave me a firm poke with his elbow urging me to get on with my planned speech.

'I...er... that is we, would like to join the RAF and become Spitfire Pilots please,' my voice tapering off to a whisper.

The Sergeant's eyebrows shot to the top of his forehead. With no sign of a smile he leaned forward and said quietly...

'I see.'

Eddy finding a smidgen of courage suddenly blurted out...

'Yes that's right, my brother is in the RAF so we know all about it ....er.. sir.'

The Sergeant scratched his head.

'And how old might you young men be?' He addressed his remark to Eddy.

'We're nearly eighteen sir' he said unconvincingly.

Looking back now this might have been a little more believable if we hadn't been wearing our school caps and short trousers!

The RAF man smiled warmly, thought for a moment then gesturing with his finger for us to draw closer to him, said...

'This being wartime, we have to be very careful that we don't allow enemy spies to join the RAF.'

He fumbled around in the drawer of his desk and produced a couple of complicated looking forms.

'Now I want you two to take these forms to your mum and get her to fill them in for you, we must also have a letter from her, and another from your school teacher to say you are "nearly" eighteen, that you are very courageous, and definitely brave enough to become a Spitfire Pilot. Now you do that for me and bring them back here, and I will see what can be done.'

He held out his large hand and gave us both a warm handshake. As we left the recruiting office feeling quite miserable, the RAF Sergeant called after us...

'What about the little dog?'

'His name is Tony and he will be joining up as our mascot.' I said, now almost in tears.

Full of disappointment, we didn't say very much to one another on the way home.

Perhaps it was a bit too soon I thought, after all he may have spotted that we were only nine, but one day maybe we will be more successful.

Not long after the war started, the children in our avenue formed a gang, and I somehow became the undisputed leader of the unimaginatively named "Holcombe Avenue Gang".

There was a large building site at the end of the avenue where more houses were planned to be built, but all construction work ceased immediately when war broke out, consequently the building site, with all the builders huts and materials still in place, formed a wonderful area for our gang to play in.

A dyke separated the land from an area known as the Lynn Chase. There were several boys at our school that belonged to the "Chase Gang". So seeing that Great Britain had declared war on Germany, we thought it right and proper for the Holcombe Avenue Gang to declare war on the Chase Gang.

I decided that all the members of my gang would have army ranks, as leader I elected myself to be a Major. Second in command was my mate Eddy, who held the rank of Captain. Third in command was Brian Canham from next door who was also a Captain, mainly because he wouldn't play unless he was! The oldest member was David Brinn who was nearly twelve. David was much bigger than any of us, and was considered an excellent front line soldier in the event of dealing with the enemy at close quarters.

Other members of the gang were Brian Garwood known as "Gizzy", he was a policeman's son, Alan Giles who's father owned a garage and petrol station, Terrence Michael Hugh Anthony Smith, not only did he have this amazingly long name but he also had a seven year old sweetheart called Diana who unfortunately kept him from active "Gang" matters on most days as he would sit in our observation tree near to the dyke and complain that he was too love-sick to play! Unfortunately Terry's dad was an Officer in the RAF and was later to be reported as missing. There was also Richard Baker who I think was about seven years old and the son of a schoolteacher, and Adrian Brown, better known as Flop. Flop had beautiful "Jug-Handle" ears, which made him an easy target for torture practice....
He also happened to be the smallest and youngest member of the gang. The nursing section consisted of Meg Davidson, Jill Pooley, Glenna Hanton, and Terry's sweetheart Diana Back, who's mum kept a fish and chip shop.

As a gang we were more regimental than most. The appearance of our uniforms depended on what scraps of clothing and material our mothers could muster up. They were all slightly different, which technically I suppose meant they were anything but uniform. Nevertheless, we all tried to dress like soldiers of one kind or another. For instance, "Gizzy's" mother made him a beautiful kilt out of bright green Scots Plaid material and his sporran was constructed from two fluffy hand brushes tied together. Sadly my mum didn't have any Scots Plaid material, so I had a kilt made of pink material that looked strangely like a dress! My sporran was made out of an old piece of white linen. The rank of Major caused a little problem because I couldn't get hold of two matching "crowns". So on one shoulder I had a brass crown, and on the other was a beautiful guilt padded badge from an RAF hat. Brian Canham had a Postman's uniform that his mum bought from Woolworth's, very smart. I can't remember what the rest of the gang wore, but although we were all dressed differently; we looked a fine body of men!

The war with Germany was increasing in its intensity. The Prime Minster, Mr Winston Churchill, made frequent speeches on the radio, his inspiring words left no-one in any doubt about the seriousness of the situation, or that, in the end, we would win. Posters appeared everywhere warning us that "Careless talk costs lives", the idea being that there could be spies working amongst us. The Holcombe Avenue Gang were convinced that the Chase Gang were definitely spies, so we made up our minds to knock *"seven bells out of em"* every Saturday afternoon with possibly a short break for tea of course.

Fortunately for the Holcombe Avenue Gang the builders had left hundreds of old bricks and rubble lying around the site, which was now our battlefield, and such materials could be used in our war against the Chase Gang. It wasn't long before we built ourselves a very respectable looking fortress as our gang headquarters. The walls were two bricks thick, and although not cemented together, provided a very secure structure. We also dug out a slit trench a few yards in the front of the Fort, but because the members of the Chase Gang were bigger than us, our trench proved to be difficult to climb out of in a hurry when events frequently called for a "strategic retreat".

Wars continued to be fought on Saturday afternoons. The Chase Gang would suddenly appear climbing over the close boarded fence that separated the building site from the tree lined dyke, an area we called no-mans land, in other words the boundary between Chase Close and Holcombe Avenue. Some parts of the boarded fencing were completely missing which could have been a great advantage to us had it not been for the dyke itself being too wide to cross at certain points.

Usually, at the commencement of battle, both sides would charge screaming out their gang's war-cry, hurling stones and anything up to the size of half a house brick at the opposing side whilst protecting themselves effectively with the aid of a dustbin-lid which made a very good shield. Homemade catapults were sometimes used, but in the main stone throwing was more effective. A battle could be won or lost by a carefully aimed pebble. The Chase Gang had to retreat when they ran out of stones, whilst our gang being on the building site, had an inexhaustible supply of ammunition.

We did have a few casualties of course; the first to fall in the line of duty was Flop, the smallest member of our gang. One Saturday morning, we were preparing for war when I had the idea of constructing a couple of very nasty booby traps for the enemy to fall into. One of these traps was situated in front of our fortress and the other in the centre of a path that led from the entrance of the building site to our fort.

We dug two large holes about a couple of feet deep. Each hole contained a barrow load of reasonably fresh horse manure sprinkled with a few sundry lengths of dog muck mixed up with a modicum of dyke water and builder's lime found on the site. The texture came down to a sort of jelly wobbliness that smelt terrible! The holes were then covered with pieces of roofing felt scattered with a covering of grass and small twigs. Great care was taken to make sure that there were no telltale signs that would give away the position of our traps. We did however take the wise precaution of marking each trap with a small stick placed upright in the ground alongside the holes so that our gang knew where the traps were.

There was one very nasty moment when we saw a policeman, who turned out to be Gizzy's father, walking up the path and heading straight for the booby trap. We all ran out to greet him just managing to stop him before he reached the edge of our latest defences! His purpose was to collect Gizzy and take him back home to have his dinner.

Flop however was not so lucky. Being the youngest member of the gang he had been posted on guard as lookout. He was sitting in the small slit trench outside the fort, the rest of us were inside filling up old paint tins with suitable stones for ammunition. Suddenly we heard high-pitched screams from Flop.

'They're here, they're here the Chase Gang are here.'

We ran out to see Flop desperately struggling to drag himself out of our slit trench. He was wearing his school cap back-to-front because he said he looked more like a pirate, and that would undoubtedly frighten the enemy. Two of the Chase Gang were climbing over the fence and heading our way. I immediately gave the order to 'CHARGE.' Eddy, Brian, Terry, Gizzy and Alan all started to run with me, each of us brandishing our dustbin lids and hurling stones for all we were worth at the enemy. Flop in a mood of sheer panic, having extracted himself from the slit trench, initiated a personal retreat, passing us like a rocket running in the opposite direction!

The Chase Gang, probably more frightened by Flop's screams, than our attack, fled back to the fence. At that moment we heard a terrific CRACK SPLOOSH sound that emanated from the general direction of our booby-traps... Flop had disappeared altogether. We all stood in wide mouthed astonishment waiting for Flop to reappear. A small dripping ghost-like figure slowly emerged, emitting strange gurgling noises and smelling very nasty, from the cesspool depths of our newly constructed booby-trap. The staggering little figure tried to stand up, but on the first attempt slid gracefully down to the bottom again and disappeared in a crescendo of bubbling sobs. As there was a definite danger of contaminating our own clothes, and subsequently being in serious trouble with our mothers, I ordered my men to stand back. We watched in amazement as first one hand, then the other, followed by a cap-less dripping head with jug handle ears appeared from the hole in the ground. Sobs turned to screams, and screams to sobs. Flop was covered from head to foot in a fudge-textured blend of lime, horse-muck and dog-crap. No more the brave pirate of moments earlier. The brownish-grey mass was now requesting the presence of his mother, a thought that struck fear into the hearts of all the members of our gang. I looked back toward no-mans land to see the Chase lads climbing the fence, giggling as they disappeared over the far side.

I was not happy with Flop, who in his state of panic had turned his back on the enemy and run full speed into our own booby trap. He would have to be dealt with for desertion in the face of the enemy of course, a crime that warranted limitless torture. But for the time being, taking into account the safety of my men and myself when Flop's mother discovered the state he was in, I considered it wise to get him into the Field Hospital where our nurses could hopefully clean him up a bit.

In the event it turned out that we couldn't catch him. Flop had taken off propelling his smelly little body as fast as he could for home. Eddy, my second in command, suggested that it might be a good idea for us to spend the rest of the day practising the art of camouflage, in addition to posting a lookout for Flop's mother of course.

Adrian Brown (Flop), was really a lovely little chap bless him. Looking back now I am ashamed at the things we put him through, but Flop was a little hero and always wanted to be with us. He was therefore a handy sort of chap to assist in trying out new inventions! His finest asset was he trusted us implicitly and volunteered for everything.

I recall that there was one particular experiment in which dear Flop was called upon to play a very important part...

One section of the dyke that separated Lynn Chase from Holcombe Avenue was difficult to cross because of the width of the water at that point. As it was the closest point to Chase Close, home of the Chase Gang, it was important for us to find a method of crossing the dyke at this point. So my third in command, Brian Canham and I got our heads together and thought up an ingenious invention that would assist our gang in crossing the dyke at any point that was too wide to jump. This contrivance called for a volunteer to act as a sort of test pilot, and Flop was once again ordered to volunteer!

In our search for suitable materials to construct our invention, we found part of a heavy metal lawn roller completely rusted up without its handle. It had been dumped with lots of other rubbish on the edge of the building site, no doubt destined to remain there for the duration of the war. Without too much difficulty we managed to manoeuvre the roller near to the edge of the dyke at its widest point. Brian, who was good at sums, worked out that if we put a long scaffold plank over the roller so that it balanced rather like a see-saw, we could have one "man" (Flop) stand on one end of the plank, whilst the heaviest member of the gang could jump onto the opposite end from the top of a step ladder, this would undoubtedly catapult our volunteer over the dyke with ease. Excellent thinking.

Eddy brought along a tall step ladder that his father used for decorating, whilst the rest of us sorted out a strong looking scaffolding plank from a pile left on site by the building contractors. The 25ft plank was so heavy that it took four of us some time to manoeuvre it into position. We placed it on the roller so that it balanced nicely with one end just on the verge of the dyke. The stepladder was positioned at the opposite end so that Brian, who happened to be the heaviest member of the gang, could jump from the top of the ladder onto the end of the plank.... All was ready. Our hero, little Flop, came prepared wearing his rubber boots, school blazer, short grey trousers and a large scarf wrapped twice round his neck. His school cap was replaced by the toy tin hat he had been given for Christmas. When he first arrived on the scene the little chap took one look at our contraption and made a run for it! But he was captured, and after a minimal amount of persuasion re-volunteered! There followed a short briefing so that everyone knew exactly what they were expected to do.

Flop, almost apologetically mentioned that he'd like to change his mind, that is if we didn't mind of course. This cowardly state of affairs could not be tolerated. I told him that he wasn't entering into the spirit of things and that he needed to alter his frame of mind right away. With that two of us lifted Flop onto the end of the plank closest to the dyke…. Flop turned rather pale, and wasn't his usual chirpy self. Brian, brave as ever, climbed the step ladder and stood poised at the top looking down at his intended landing area six feet below, which incidentally had been carefully marked with a white chalk cross to avoid confusion. Eddy, erring on the side of safety, moved further away and sat down on the grass.

It had been decided that on the count of three, Brian would leap from his position at the top of the ladder onto the plank, and the rest should be plain sailing.

Being the head of the gang, I unflinchingly took on the tricky job of the count-down! I looked around at my men. Brian was in a crouching position ready to jump, Eddy, still sitting on the ground, was now sucking a long stem of grass and looking intently at our volunteer. Flop, his large ears protruding from under his toy tin hat, looked at me with a forced grin on his face and terror in his eyes. I ordered him to brace himself. "ONE.. TWO..THREE..JUMP", my words came out confidently without any sign of nerves or concern for my own safety! Brian hesitated for a moment, obviously considering his own well-being, then bravely leapt into the air landing spot on the white cross.

We all looked on in stunned amazement as Flop's knees almost hit him under his chin, then like a rocket he shot up into the air with a most impressive blood-curdling scream! reaching a height of about eight feet.

Our mouths wide open with astonishment; we followed Flop's progress as he came crashing down through an overhanging bush just missing the end of the plank and straight into the dyke with an enormous splash. The depth of the water at his point of impact was about eighteen inches deep. There he sat, head and shoulders out of the water, his tin hat cocked over one eye, and to our utter amazement still managing to force a smile! True character building stuff.

Eddy ran forward as Flop pushed his tin hat onto the back of his head, and threw him the special rope with rescue handles at each end (Meg Davidson's skipping rope), and together we dragged Flop out of the mud to safety.

We dried Flop's clothes as best we could in front of a hastily prepared bonfire. Then our brave volunteer staggered off home steaming a little and looking strangely different to the smart little boy who turned up for the experiment. He had however been very carefully briefed that his mission had been TOP SECRET, and under no circumstances should he tell his mother!

I remember there was also a funny incident concerning an anonymous lad, believed to be one of the older members of the chase gang, and our neighbour Mr Hewitt. This, to the best of my memory, is how the incident was recorded in story form. ...

Mr Hewitt paused for a moment to relight the dead embers of his much-admired "Sherlock Holmes" type pipe. Pleased with the progress he had made on his vegetable garden, he felt that he owed it to himself to take a short break, straighten his aching back and enjoy a few well-earned puffs of his pipe.

The very end of the garden where he had been digging, was separated from the chase dyke by a six-foot high close-boarded fence which was well weathered and treated regularly with generous amounts of creosote. He had been preparing his potato patch near to the fence, and took little notice of the noise coming from members of the Chase Gang who were playing out of sight on the far side. The ditch itself was well camouflaged by bushes and small trees, and a plank had been placed across the ditch at its narrowest point to make a bridge, thus providing a wonderful secret place for children to play, their imagination turning the area into anything from a fairy glen to a Japanese Jungle. Also the fence being pitted here and there with knotholes of various shapes and sizes, provided excellent spy holes and gun positions for the imaginary wars being fought on the far side. As it turned out however, some of the older children had more imagination than others!

Mr Hewitt heard the clink of cups in the kitchen signalling that Mrs Hewitt was preparing a much-welcomed cup of tea.

Life had been kind to Mr Hewitt, although the country was at war he had escaped call-up due to his exempt occupation as a chemist. Although he sometimes felt a twinge of guilt, he was grateful that he was able to stand in the peace of his garden whilst many of his friends had gone to war and were experiencing a far from peaceful time.

Still admiring his handy work, Hewitt noticed that he had missed a small clump of stinging nettles that lay close to the fence and needed removing. He knew that Mrs Hewitt was meticulous by nature, and would point out the weeds in a flash, that certainly wouldn't do.

Stooping down to pick up the nettles he suddenly stopped dead, his pipe struck the ground as his mouth opened wide in astonishment at the sight before his eyes.

There, not six inches away from his face, was a small erect penis pointing directly at him through a conveniently placed knothole in the fence. At the same instant he heard the jingling of a cup and saucer accompanied by the unmistakable footsteps of Mrs Hewitt coming up the path behind him, she had decided to inspect the work done so far on the potato patch and reward her husband with a hot drink and a digestive biscuit.

Mr Hewitt quickly reflected that his wife, being of a religious nature, would probably get the wrong idea and not take too kindly to the sight of her husband's face being close to the offensive object poking through the fence.

There was little time to spare. Hewitt's weekend training in the Home Guard (Dad's Army) came immediately to the fore. Totally disregarding any pain to himself, he grabbed the freshly dug nettles from the ground and swiped the unsuspecting penis a deadly blow. "Little Willie" shot back through the knothole with the speed of light accompanied by a muffled scream from its owner on the far side of the fence.

A gentle voice from behind Mr Hewitt whispered…

'What's the matter dear, are the wasps troubling you?… I've brought you a nice cup of hot tea and two of your favourite biscuits.'

Further investigation revealed that some adolescent lad had made a gruesome life-sized chalk drawing of his idea of a naked female body on the far side of the fence, and I would imagine that he was left with a tingling memory of his imaginary sexual experience.

CHAPTER 3.

The Old Tobacco Tin.

My father had been posted away leaving me to spend the war with my mother. The first bombs to fall on Kings Lynn during the 1939-1945 war fell at the end of August 1940; the town was visited by the Luftwaffe on the 28th, 30th and 31st of the month. Prior to that the air-raid sirens had sounded on numerous occasions, each time nothing significant happened, consequently everyone had become complacent about air-raid warnings, and we probably kidded ourselves that Lynn would never feel the wrath of the enemy. The fact that all the students from the Hackney Downs Secondary School had been evacuated to Kings Lynn from London gave most people the impression that the British Government considered East Anglia to be safe from German air attacks, consequently when bombs did finally drop on the town it came as a shock to everyone.

The sirens sounded as they had many times before. As usual my mother and I got dressed in order to take cover in the Anderson Shelter we shared with the Canham family. There was certainly no hurry to get down there as we all felt sure it was just a repeat performance of all the other uneventful air-raid warnings we had experienced over the last twelve months.

As we walked out into our back garden we paused to look up at the gleaming white shafts of light from the searchlights that lit up the ghostly patterns of a few small clouds. There was no Moon, and when the sirens ceased their morbid wailing, the ominous drone of aircraft engines could be heard in the distance.

The noise from the aircraft engines gradually died away. Mrs. Canham's soft voice broke the silence…

'Fred says there's a red alert at the A.R.P. Station, he's just gone back there, this could be it Maggie, Fred thinks they're definitely coming tonight.'

'O.K. Nora' mum replied taking my hand. 'Come on Raymond dear, we'd better get down into the shelter.'

We walked cautiously in the darkness of the blackout, feeling our way down the unlit path towards the air-raid shelter.

As Brian and his mother entered the hatchway, we again heard the distant drone of aircraft engines, this time they seemed to be getting nearer. We followed on into the shelter. The entrance hatch was extremely heavy, far too heavy in fact for any of us to lower from inside. So the strong prop was left in place awaiting the return of Mr Canham.

I peered at the sky through the open hatch and saw that many more searchlights had joined in the hunt for enemy bombers. It now seemed certain that the aircraft we could hear approaching the town were hostile.

Safely inside the shelter my mother drew the thick black anti-gas curtain across the opening and struck a match to light one of the tiny "Night-Lights". These specially made wartime candles were about an inch and a half in diameter and about an inch high, they were designed to stand in a saucer of water where they could float around in safety giving off a dim flickering glow. Mum was just about to light a second candle when we heard a distinct whistling sound, almost immediately it was joined by a second slightly higher pitched whistle. Everyone in the shelter stood in petrified silence as the whistling turned into a full-blooded scream. The ground shook violently to a muffled CRUMP, a split second later there was an ear-splitting BANG that jolted the shelter like a boat colliding with the bank. Small chunks of earth fell to the floor through cracks that appeared in the corrugated iron roof-joints of the shelter, and the dim light from the candle grew dimmer as the air became polluted with fine particles of dust. There were about three further explosions, followed by an eerie silence broken only by the throbbing sound of distant aeroplane engines.

Mother put her arms around me, holding me very close to her trembling body and whispered....

'Oh my God.'

The shelter hatch was still open, but there was no sign of the gas-curtain that had previously covered the entrance. Fearing the light may be seen from outside, my mother blew out the candle. Instantly we saw the sky had turned golden red reflecting flames from the fires where the bombs had fallen. In the distance, someone was repeatedly blowing a whistle; the inauspicious drone of aircraft engines could still be heard, whilst the four of us crouched in the shelter, each with our own thoughts of what the future held.

The war for many young schoolboys was an exciting time. Up until now all we really knew about death and destruction were the stories we heard on the radio or read about in the newspapers. It was something that always happened to other people, never to us. But the real facts were very different. Practically every street and avenue in the town would sooner or later be visited by the dreaded telegram boy who had the unpleasant task of handing over that fearful message from the War Office. A trembling hand would take the telegram, and behind closed doors a terrified mother would read the heartrending message that always began…. 'The war office regrets to inform you that…..' Curtains would be drawn, and neighbours would call to offer sympathy and comfort.

One Saturday morning, such a telegram was delivered to the door of number fourteen Holcombe Avenue.

'Eddy is here' my mother said, having seen him pass our kitchen window.

I ran to greet him thinking he was calling to see if I was coming out to play with the gang, but when I opened the door I instantly knew something terrible had happened. Eddy stood there unable to say a thing, his eyes swollen from crying. My mother saw the state he was in and instantly put her arms around him guiding him into the house. Ed sat down on the chair beside our fireplace; my mother knelt beside him cupping his head in her hands trying to comfort him. For a long time he was unable to speak. Then between sobs Eddy told us that his mother had just received a telegram informing her that Lewis, Eddy's eldest brother, had been shot down over Germany and killed. One could hardly begin to imagine the heartbreak and misery that such terrible news brought to his family. Eddy was so proud of his brother, always telling me about the letters he received from him, and his escapades in the RAF where he flew as a Flight Engineer in Lancaster Bombers. My mother continued to cuddle Eddy whilst the three of us cried together. From that moment on I began to appreciate the true horrors of war.

It was not long after when my mother, who had been out shopping, rushed into the house, dropped her bag of groceries, and flung herself face down onto the sofa bursting into torrents of tears. My first thoughts were that my father had been killed, but my panicky attempts to find out seemed to fall on deaf ears.

'Is it Dad? Is he dead?' I screamed repeatedly.

But mum just couldn't speak. Panic began to set in. I tore at my mother's coat.

'Answer me Mum, please answer me.'

My mother appeared to be close to fainting when she finally turned towards me, put her arms around me and managed with great difficulty to tell me that my Uncle Jim had been killed during the bombing raid on Lynn the previous night. Jim was my mother's eldest brother and without a doubt my favourite and most loving Uncle. I cuddled my mother and we both sobbed our hearts out. The full awfulness of war had certainly come home to us.

During the 1914-1918 war my Uncle Jim had been wounded in France by a shell that had exploded close to the trench he was in. His injuries left him severely deaf, although he could still hear with the aid of a hearing device that incorporated a microphone that hung from a thin black cord around his neck. He was locking up his shop when a high explosive bomb hit the Eagle Hotel on the opposite side of the road. The terrific blast from the explosion carried him through the wall of his shop and killed him. Forty-one other people were killed by the bomb that fell on the hotel that night.

My mother lost her father during the First World War when she was seventeen years old, and her brother Jim had replaced him in many ways. Whenever my mother had a serious argument with my father, which sometimes got out of hand, she would turn to her brother Jim for comfort or advice.

Uncle Jim and Aunty Daisy never had children of their own, but it was obvious they both loved children very much.

That evening mum and I set out despondently to visit my Aunty in her little cottage on the far side of town. The thought of never seeing my uncle again was so painful that I dreaded entering their house. I expected Aunt Daisy to be in floods of tears, but she seemed to be more in a trance than anything and showed little signs of emotion. Inside the house everything was in its place, the lino shone with polish and there were freshly cut flowers on the dining room table. The windows facing the street had their curtains discreetly drawn. Daisy was about five feet tall, her doll-like face, with bright pink cheeks, was perfectly framed by shiny jet-black hair. For some reason that evening I took note of how immaculately dressed my Aunty was in her spotlessly white blouse, black skirt and glossy-black high-heeled shoes. My mother always used to say she was just like a little doll.

I was very upset to see my Uncle's belongings, a hat on the hall stand, his pipe rack on the wall, and his bookshelf full of books about clocks and musical boxes. Would I really never see him again?

There were several other people in the house whom I had never seen before, they were drinking cups of tea and fussing around my Aunt. It all seemed wrong somehow, and I was glad when it was time to go.

'Before you leave Raymond dear, there is something I want to give you.'

Daisy was groping in one of the drawers of her sideboard. She pulled out an old battered tobacco tin and passed it to me.

'Jim would want you to have this' she said, 'it was his hobby you know.'

I studied the box for a moment, and couldn't help wondering if my Aunt had cracked up altogether and was trying to get me to take up smoking.

'Go on open it' she said.

I fumbled for a moment or two trying to remove the lid, it was very tight indeed. Eventually when it opened there was the smallest of musical box movements you ever did see. Immediately it started to play, it's tiny metal keys tinkling out a sad little melody, one that I had never heard before. I fought to hold back the tears that began to fill my eyes; somehow it felt like my Uncle Jim was standing there beside me with his hand on my shoulder as he so frequently had done in the past.

'He makes them himself you know, er…well he used to.' Aunt Daisy faltered… I think the catchy little melody that chimed out from the old tobacco tin had upset her too.

By this time over one hundred civilians had been killed or seriously injured by the bombing raids on Lynn. The air raid that frightened me more than any other occurred on the 17th September.

I'm not sure what time it was, but I was in bed and fast asleep when I was awakened by the mournful wail of the air-raid sirens. My mother rushed into the bedroom and told me to put my clothes on as quickly as possible. I certainly didn't waste any time because I could hear the sound of aircraft engines and the anti-aircraft guns on Lynn recreation ground were already firing at something. As we ran towards the shelter the sharp rapid cracking of machinegun fire could also be heard and tracer bullets started to streak across the night sky.

'It sounds like we're in for it again tonight' Mrs. Canham said.

'I do wish Len was here, I always feel much safer when he's around' my mother replied.

The sound of aircraft engines grew louder, and the crump crump of anti-aircraft gunfire increased. Mum caught hold of my hand.

'You'll be alright dear.'

She was trembling and the anxious look on her face portrayed her true feelings. At that moment we heard the formidable sound of a bomb screeching down, the whistle turned into a deafening howl and a tremendous explosion rocked and twisted the shelter like a broken shoebox, the blast immediately followed by a sudden rush of air that lifted the entrance hatch up and slammed it down again filling the shelter with clouds of dust and blowing the candles out. In pitch darkness I held on tight to my mother as bits of earth sifted into the shelter from the roof. Everybody was silent for a few seconds then someone found the torch. The corrugated iron roof of the shelter was badly cracked, allowing sand, earth and rubble to fall on us. Brian and I struggled to lift the hatch and finally managed to wedge it open. Outside the whole of the sky flickered red and orange. Showers of sparks were floating about and the smoke filled air was full of the sounds of people shouting and screaming. Some relief was gained by the fact that our two houses were still standing and appeared to be undamaged apart from glass missing from most of the windows.

Brian's mother began to scream out at him to get back into the shelter. My poor mother was strangely quiet, I knew for sure that she too would normally be concerned to get me back with her but she never spoke a word.

Brian and I clambered back into the shelter, searched around for the matches and lit the candle. I found mum with her head buried in her hands. She wasn't crying or anything, but when she lifted her head to speak to me I saw that her face was bleeding, even in the light of the flickering candle I could see her terrified expression. I dabbed her face with my scruffy old handkerchief, the cut, just above her left eye was fortunately no more than a scratch. But it was obvious that mum was in shock. Then, just as I was wondering what to do, my mother, to my amazement said…

'We had better get out of here and see if we can help.'

Mum never ceased to amaze me, I knew she would always do anything to help anyone in trouble, but I could hardly believe that she was prepared to risk her life out there whilst the air raid was still in progress.

It was agreed that Brian should remain in the shelter with his mother whilst I went with mum to see what had happened and if there was anything we could do to help.

A few yards further along from our house we were horrified to see that the house belonging to Mr and Mrs Curtis had received a direct hit and was ablaze. Several of the neighbours were forming a human chain, and started to pass buckets and bowls of water from a nearby kitchen tap to the blazing house. At the head of the column ARP Wardens and NFS Volunteer Workers were already busy trying to extinguish the raging fire.

I joined the chain of bucket passers, and mum was asked to go into one of the houses and help fill the buckets with water. I managed to get near the head of the queue and soon realised that the warden I was passing the buckets to was Brian's father.

Margaret Curtis, her clothes still smouldering, was carried from the burning house in her father's arms. Mrs Curtis was nowhere to be seen. Margaret was twelve years old, and had been a member of our Gang acting as a nurse, but all that seemed so unimportant now.

It was difficult to see properly but I had noticed that the person in the chain handing buckets of water to me was quite small, he was puffing and panting and seemed to be rapidly running out of energy. When there was a suitable lull in the supply of filled buckets, I turned to speak to the person beside me and couldn't believe my eyes. A grinning little face looked up at me, it was Flop, as brave as punch doing his best to help out!

'Good Lord, does your mother know you are out here?' I asked.

'She sent me next door to get in their table shelter, but I thought I would come and see what was happening here first' he said.

'How long have you been here?' I asked.

'I followed you and your mum up the road' he said.

I couldn't believe what I saw, brave little Flop, helping to put out the fire of a bombed house whilst the air raid was still in progress. His grubby little face, black from where he had wiped the sweat away with his equally black little hands, and of course, he was wearing his toy tin hat. What a star!.... But I had to get him back home before his mother realised he was missing.

The Fire Brigade arrived at that point and took over from the helpers.

The sirens were sounding the all-clear when I caught up with my mother who was on her way back home. I told her about Flop, who still stood next to me grinning away.

'What a brave little fellow' mum said giving him a cuddle.

Flop struggled a bit to get away from my mother's affections, obviously thinking that this didn't look too much like the stuff of heroes! Alas, we didn't quite make it. Mrs. Brown, Flops mum, came running down the road towards us. Before I could say a word about Flop's brave deeds, she ripped into me saying that sometimes the Holcombe Avenue Gang went too far, and did I realise that Adrian was far too young for this sort of thing?

Flop tried to tell his mother that it wasn't my fault, but Mrs. Brown swiped him hard on his bottom, and dragged him off broken hearted.

I walked slowly back to our house. My mother, who was now busy sweeping up the glass from the smashed windows, promised to go and see Mrs. Brown the next day, and explain how courageous her little son had been.

1942 arrived. Fortunately I passed the scholarship examination and my first day at King Edward V11 Grammar School remains a treasured memory.

Dressed in my new school uniform and clutching my government issued gasmask, I left the house in good time to walk the mile and a half to the school gates.

On the way I came across the Co-op Milk Cart standing by the railway crossing. I knew Stan the Milkman very well because he had taken me with him on his rounds to help him deliver the milk on several occasions during school holidays.

'My word you look smart lad, you'll soon be too proud to talk to the likes of me.'

I patted his faithful old horse; he knew exactly which way to turn, and where to stop without a word from Stan. As I hurried off Stan shouted...

'Good luck lad, I wish I was your age again.'

Approaching the school I decided to follow a bunch of lads who appeared to be old hands and seemed to know what they were about. We passed through the impressive main gates and into the courtyard where lots of boys stood around in small groups chatting away studiously. I couldn't help noticing that most of the boys appeared to be considerably older than myself. I wandered around not knowing exactly what to do when a very tall gentleman with thick horn-rimmed glasses came over to me and said...

'You look lost boy, I take it this is your first day with us?'

Addressing him as sir, I said that it was indeed my first day at grammar school.

'Welcome to the school young man, I'm head prefect; we will undoubtedly meet again in the future. In the meantime you need to get yourself over to the junior assembly area which is through that door in the wall over there and turn left into the small courtyard.'

I wasn't sure how to address the young man who I had at first mistaken for one of the masters, so I played safe and addressed him as sir again, thanking him rather timidly for his help, and hurried off.

Through the door in the wall I turned left. Just as I was thinking what a wonderfully sophisticated bunch of chaps they all were, my brand new school cap was snatched from my head and hurled into the air with the enthusiasm of an Olympic discus thrower! My heart sank. Any illusion of gentlemanly conduct that I may have had about Grammar School boys was dispelled in a flash.... Boys rolled over on the ground in mortal combat. Screams and shouts echoed throughout the courtyard, it seemed that all hell had broken out. I tried to retrieve my cap from a tall boy who was holding it high above his head and sneering at me. I kneed him in the crutch and collected my hat from the hand of the lad who was now doubled over in agony. I've always been of the opinion that chaps who are considerably larger than ones-self deserve to be brought down by any means available.

At that moment a bell rang out and the whole scene miraculously transformed to one of order. Cases, caps, gasmasks etc., were soon retrieved by their owners and an orderly column of boys filed their way into the impressive building. So began my first term at Grammar School.

I loved the atmosphere of learning at King Edward's School, the whole ambience of this beautiful building reeked of knowledge and sophistication. The masters looked regal in their gowns as they swished their way along the corridors and into the classrooms where we would stand in silence until given permission to sit. Discipline was strict, but I loved every minute of it.

As our School didn't have an A.T.C. Squadron, I decided to join their Army Cadet Force and proudly wore the uniform and badges of the Royal Norfolk Regiment. Mother was a bit upset the first time she saw me in uniform, no doubt she thought that if the war lasted much longer I'd be in the real thing.

Rifle drill at the school came in quite handy, as I was able to pass this on to members of my gang. They all had home made wooden rifles of one sort or another, so I was now capable of teaching them how to slope, order and present arms with the precision of a guardsman, roughly speaking! Strangely enough Eddy Baldock and Brian Canham did not join the cadet force, my mum said it was because they had had enough of it being ordered about by me

My father, as well as being in the cavalry, was also a drummer during the 1914-1918 war. He taught me quite a bit about military drumming with the aid of a couple of knives and a large biscuit tin. So I joined our cadet force band as a kettle-drummer. Every Thursday evening we met for band practice in the assembly hall at school. I also practiced regularly at home but unfortunately my enthusiastic banging was met with considerably less enthusiasm from my mother.

Drumming, and the Army Cadets did however provide me with a couple of embarrassing moments. Both of these incidents involved my mate Eddy's next-door neighbour, Meg Davidson. Meg was about twelve years old when I joined the army cadets. She was a member of the Holcombe Avenue Gang, and as one of our nurses she had played an important part bandaging many a head split open by an accurately propelled stone from a Chase Gang catapult.

Anyway, to get back to my embarrassing moments. The committee of the Local 'Toc H Club' had asked Meg's mother, if her daughter would like to play the piano in a charity concert being given in aid of raising funds for the war effort. Meg played the piano quite well having been taught by her mother who also happened to be a schoolteacher.

Mrs Davidson had bright red hair, I always thought she looked like a witch and she made it quite clear that she didn't think much of me either.

Before accepting the invitation for her daughter to play, Mrs Davidson took Meg over to have a short practice on the Toc H Club piano. When she returned, Meg called in at our house to tell me that there was also a full set of drums on the stage in the 'Toc-H' Club. Knowing how much I loved playing the drums in the Cadet Band, Meg asked if I would like to accompany her when she played her piano piece. I was a little dubious about the whole thing as I had never played a full set of drums before; in fact I wasn't at all sure what a complete drum-kit looked like! But in the end I agreed providing we could get permission from the Toc H Committee for me to use their drum kit. And so it was that my first public appearance on the drums was arranged.

The day finally arrived. My mother, proud as punch, fussed around getting me ready for the great event. She polished my shoes and dressed me up in my best Sunday suit complete with a large bow tie that she borrowed from a neighbour. I looked ridiculous.

Meg and I never got the opportunity to practice playing anything together, in fact I had no idea what she intended to play and just assumed it would be a march of some kind!

When we arrived at the Toc H Club the show had already begun. A large woman in a bright yellow dress was screeching her way through "Oh for the wing's of a Dove" accompanied by a red faced gentleman playing the mouth organ. Eventually the woman stopped screeching and everybody clapped loudly. Next a skinny little man with a large moustache and glasses played the spoons to a record of "Run rabbit run". His performance came to an abrupt end several seconds after the record had finished. Then, God forbid, it was our turn.

An official looking lady climbed onto the stage and announced…

'We are now going to be entertained on the pianoforte by pretty little Meg Davidson, please give her an encouraging round of applause.'

What about me? There was no mention of me at all ! That put me off a bit as I wasn't sure whether or not I should be there.

Loud applause erupted from the audience as Meg walked nervously up to the piano and placed her music on the stand. Then Meg's mother appeared announcing that she would be turning the music pages for her daughter. Feeling somewhat embarrassed I crept onto the stage looking as though I had no right to be there at all and stood behind the mass of drumming equipment, most of which I had never seen the like of and had no idea what it was for! Worse was to follow.

On the count of her mothers whispered 'one, two, three' Meg began to thump away with her rendition of 'Bless this house,' I felt weak in the knees… I ask you, how could anyone be expected to play the drums to bless this bleeding house?

As Mrs. Davidson, quite unconcerned about me, turned the first page of the music for her daughter, the man who had been playing the mouth organ came to my rescue with a chair, until then I had been standing up. I sat down with a plonk and disappeared completely behind the base drum. I had learned my first lesson in dance band drumming….drummers have to sit on tall stools. I detected a certain amount of sniggering from the audience, so in a way it was a blessing to be hidden from sight whilst I still searched desperately for the drumsticks. Eventually I found them tucked behind one of the brass tightening rods of the base drum.

Time was creeping on. I had to do something before Meg came to the end of her piece and finished playing altogether. I took a deep breath and started off with a rousing march tempo. Rat er tat tat Boom Boom, Rat er tat tat Boom Boom….. The audience practically leapt out of their seats with surprise, and glared at me in savage astonishment. Meg stopped playing abruptly as if she had been shot, and her mother glared at me in horror. One nasty individual in the audience shouted 'Be quiet drummer.' That did it for me; I crouched down even lower behind the drum-kit and seriously considered crawling out on my hands and knees. Meg cautiously started to play again and finally fizzled out. I carried on a few seconds finishing in my own time with a rousing smack on the cymbal which shot off it's stand and fell to the floor with a loud clang.

Everybody applauded loudly, Meg looked as if she was about to burst into tears at any moment. Her mother had a savage look on her face, so, in the interests of self-preservation I decided not to hang around. As I crept off the stage I caught a glance of Eddy who was sitting in the front row of the audience. His eyes were red with tears of laughter.

A year or so had passed when I plucked up enough courage to ask Meg if she would like to accompany me to the School Army Cadet Force's Christmas Dance, to be held in the assembly hall in the Grammar School.

Meg's mother wasn't too keen but agreed that Meg could come with me providing she was back home by ten o'clock.

Neither of us had been to a proper dance before, and at the age of thirteen I was pretty naive about what I should wear at an army cadet dance. After some consideration I came to the conclusion that the occasion called for me to wear my army cadet uniform, complete with boots and gaiters!

The day of the dance arrived. At seven o'clock precisely I marched smartly down the avenue to collect Meg and take her to the ball. Mrs. Davidson would have to be the one that answered the door. Her first words to me were…

'You're not going to a dance looking like that are you?'

I thought I looked very smart indeed, so did my Mum.

Having assured Mrs. Davidson that all the Cadets would be in uniform, she invited me in whilst her daughter finished getting ready. Then Meg came down the stairs looking quite nice I suppose.

She was wearing a bright pink party frock, thick black woollen stockings, and white plimsolls. Her hair was in pigtails tied up with large pink ribbons. We set off rather ominously for the Christmas Ball with me dressed up as a soldier holding hands with the first date I had ever had.

I felt quite proud until we arrived at the school. The chap on the door looked alarmed when he first saw us, then he asked if we were taking part in some sort of entertainment during the evening. Not fully understanding what he meant we laughed and strolled into the hall…..What a shock!….I felt the blood drain from my face when I realised that I was the only prat in uniform. All the boys were in suits whilst the girls wore long elegant evening dresses that swished majestically as they danced around the room.

With mounting nausea I whipped my army cap off, grabbed Meg by the arm and crept into the hall like a sniper! We sat down at the side of the dance floor feeling very uncomfortable and conspicuous. I'll never know what made me think I should go to a dance wearing boots and gaiters. And having seen how the other girls were dressed, I must admit that poor old Meg didn't look so good either.

Neither of us could dance a step so we just sat there silently watching the others. Then to my horror I noticed that my French Mistress together with the English Master were making their way across the hall directly to where we were sitting. Before we could escape one of them said...

'Come on you two lets be having you.'

With that we were dragged protesting onto the dance floor. Poor old Meg staggered onto the floor with the English Master, whilst I clumped around the dance floor in hobnailed boots desperately trying to avoid trampling on my French Mistress's delicate toes.

Needless to say the whole evening was an embarrassing disaster. We left the dance early and, apart from the sound of my army boots echoing down the streets, we headed for home in silence.

Meg's mother, who had never forgiven me for the drumming escapade at the Toc H. Club, took one look at her daughter who had burst into tears, and suggested that I should stay away from her in future.

So much for my first date, it would be many years before I asked a girl out again.

As a small boy I was destined to have my second flight in an aeroplane at the age of twelve. The year was 1943 and war with Nazi Germany was at its peak. My father, knowing I was mad about flying, offered to take me with him to visit RAF Tempsford Aerodrome.

I never knew exactly what my father did during the Second World War. He sometimes wore an officer's uniform, but most of the time he was in civilian clothing when he came home on leave. He never spoke to me about his job, but my mother told me that he held a highly responsible and covert position concerning high explosives and gas warfare. Later I learned he was also responsible for the safety of the Royal Family when they stayed at Sandringham House in Norfolk.

My father became acquainted with several members of the staff and officers who were directly responsible to His Majesty. One of these gentlemen was Group Captain Fielden MVO. AFC. Air Equerry to the King and Captain of the Kings Flight.

My flight from Tempsford Aerodrome took place when my father was organising a military exercise involving both military and civil defence personnel. It concerned the likelihood of an invasion by German forces and the defence against the use of poisonous gas in East Anglia. On this particular day my father was to fly over certain areas in Norfolk. Group Captain Fielden, who was the Commanding Officer of RAF Tempsford, arranged for my father to fly in an American B24 Consolidated Liberator. Knowing how mad I was about aeroplanes, dad somehow managed to obtain permission for me to visit the airfield with him. He collected me early one morning from our home in King's Lynn and arranged for me to stay in the Air Traffic Control building whilst he was airborne. I hoped that I would be allowed to fly with him, but was told in no uncertain terms that it was definitely out of the question for any unauthorised person to fly in military aircraft, and certainly not in wartime. So I was deposited in the Air Traffic Control building under the care of a very kind RAF officer to await my fathers return.

Ten minutes later the most unbelievable, almost miraculous, thing happened. My father reappeared in the Tower and said that the Canadian Flight Commander in charge of the flight had given my father permission to take me with him. Dad had to sign a special indemnity document to say that he agreed to allow me to fly. (Can you imagine that ever happening in wartime these days?)

There were no seats in the fuselage, so I had to stand with my father clinging to the fuselage frame throughout the flight.

The noise from the four massive 1,200 hp radial engines was deafening. My father was busy most of the time looking at maps and discussing details with an Army Officer who came with us. The flight lasted about an hour. I couldn't believe that I was actually flying in a Canadian bomber aircraft in wartime. When we returned to Tempsford we circled for several minutes as there was some trouble with lowering the undercarriage. In the end we landed safely.

When we got back home to Kings Lynn that evening, my mother didn't believe me when I told her I had been flying.

'What have I told you about telling lies my boy?' she said

Then, when my father confirmed that it was true, mum burst into tears.

'What if you had been shot down?' she said.

Then poor old dad got it in the neck for taking me!

So if anyone ever asks me 'did you fly during the war?' I could answer, tongue in cheek, that I did, even if it was just the once. Best not mention I was only twelve years old at the time!

I adored my mother and was very proud of my father. On the whole I had a wonderful childhood that lasted until the end of the war, then unbelievably, our happy home life and my enjoyable schooldays came to an abrupt end.

My father never returned home to live with us at the end of the war. I didn't really understand what was going on until my mother told me that she would have to divorce my father. She became very ill with a nervous breakdown and cried endlessly. I remember lying in bed at night with my head buried under the pillow so that I couldn't hear the mournful cries of my mother in the next room. I had no idea what a divorce was, and just couldn't believe it when I was told that our home was to be sold and I would have to leave the school I loved. Neither of my parents would remain in Lynn and there was insufficient money for me to become a school boarder.

The final shock came when my poor mother sobbing her heart out said that I would have to make my mind up about which of my parents I wanted to live with. I was inconsolable, at the age of fourteen it was an impossible decision for me to make.

Things turned from bad to worse. A few weeks later I stood in our house waiting to be picked up by my father. That morning my mother left in floods of tears to live with her cousin and her husband in Feltwell. It would be difficult for me to find work in the small village of Feltwell, so it had been arranged that my father would pick me up the same day and take me to stay with him at his lodgings in Hertfordshire until I could find work.

Mum and I had packed everything up in boxes that my father said would be collected and taken into storage until things were sorted out. I was waiting for my father to arrive when several people I had never seen before in my life turned up and walked into the house. I questioned a man that was putting numbers on all our boxes and furniture, and to my horror I was told that the contents of our house was to be sold that morning by auction. Neither my mother nor I had any idea that my father had apparently arranged for this to happen. By the afternoon my father had still not arrived and I just stood there watching the contents of our house being auctioned off. Even my box of toys that contained my much-loved teddy-bear was sold off to strangers.

It was all too much for me, so without considering the possible consequences I decided there and then to run away.

Not having sufficient money for the fare to London, I bought a ticket for as far as I could go with the few shillings pocket money my mother had given me, and finally landed up in the small town of Biggleswade in Bedfordshire. With the help of a very kind policeman I found lodgings for the night in a lorry driver's pull-up. The next day I managed to get myself a job sweeping factory floors for Weatherly Oilgear Ltd., an engineering company in Biggleswade, and continued living in the roadside pull-up that was called Mrs Gee's Lodge. I slept in a bleak room that had seven beds in it. So every night I shared the room with various long distance lorry drivers. I was heart broken and very lonely. Over a period of time I found better lodgings, and eventually was offered an apprenticeship as draughtsman with the same company.

My dear mother sadly died three years later. She was only 45 years old. She loved my father dearly and never really recovered from the shock of him leaving her and our home breaking up. If anybody ever died of a broken heart, my mother did.

Time passed, and in 1949 I was called up for National Service. I wanted to join the RAF as a potential pilot, but there was no chance of that happening, and in the end I was conscripted into the REME. What a cock-up that was. I passed my machinist tests on both a lathe and a shaper, then, to my surprise, I was sent on a sixteen-week vehicle mechanic's course. I passed, only to find myself posted on a clerical course. After all that I was transferred to the Northants Yeomanry and became a tank driver. My demob was delayed by six months due to the Korean crises.

When I left the army I had to find somewhere to live. With my fathers help I found lodgings in Hitchin and got a job selling Britvic fruit juices to the licensed trade.

In 1954 I married Mary, a lovely girl who I first met at a dance five years previously when I was stationed at Turweston. We were fortunate enough to be allocated a council house in Brackley, my wife's hometown, just a few weeks before we planned to get married.

After several years selling various alcoholic beverages to public houses, I became a representative for Bell's Distillers Ltd., selling whisky to breweries and the licensed trade throughout the Midlands.

All this time I never lost sight of my childhood ambition to become a pilot, but in the early 1950s civil flying was a difficult and very expensive career to get into.

Then the headline of an advertisement caught my eye in the local press. It read.

"LEARN TO FLY AT KIDLINGTON AERODROME"

CHAPTER 4.

Hospital life continues.

'How are we then?'

The doctor's sharp voice ended my reminiscing about my past and brought me back to reality with a jolt. He was on his early morning ward rounds and paused at my bed to look at my notes which apparently revealed that I had incurred no less than 27 major fractures.

'Are you in much pain?' he enquired.

He only needed to take a glance at me to see that I was obviously in trouble.

'Yes Doc' I answered, 'I am in considerable constant pain, the drugs give some relief but can you please give me something to relieve the excruciating pain in my right leg?'

The House Doctor stared at my notes for a moment then with a fixed smile on his face said...

'Well done, that's progress.'

I wondered if he had heard a word I had said or even cared. His next words were a little more encouraging.

'Our senior consultant surgeon Mr Morgan is coming to see you tomorrow, I think he plans to operate on you before the end of the week.'

The houseman nodded vigorously as if to agree with himself and moved on to the next bed where I heard him say again...

'How are we then?'

I forced a smile: 'He means well' I thought: 'Just doing his job.'

'That's progress' I heard him say again as he moved to another bed.

The pain, which had mercifully been deadened to some extent by an injection three hours earlier, was now beginning to intensify. Sweat was forming on my forehead and trickling down past my ears to the back of my neck. A sudden, almost unendurable, jab of pain in my left leg momentarily replaced the agonising red-hot burning in the back of my right thigh where my broken femur had torn a gaping hole. The palms of my hands became moist, and a feeling of panic began to take over. I had been through this sequence so many times before, each time I wondered how much more I could stand before losing control and screaming. Another sudden jab of pain in my right leg, this time the surging agony was so intense that it made my body lurch in a spasmodic reaction. The agony did not subside, I felt desperately sick as the convulsive movements became more frequent. I closed my eyes tightly whilst trying to stifle a scream, and began to break down uncontrollably.

I heard the screens being drawn around my bed. Sister was saying something comforting as I felt the merciful sting of a needle in the side of my bottom... very soon voices faded and peace returned.

I awoke later to the storm-darkened ward with the distant rumblings of an approaching thunderstorm. The sudden brightness of the ward lights made me wince as Sister switched all sixteen tubes into action. If only I could turn onto my side to avoid the glare, but the heavy plasters, steel cables and plastic tubes attached to my body made even the thought of movement seem quite ridiculous.

It started to rain, slowly at first, large drops splashing down, then within seconds developing into a heavy storm with rain and hail stones hammering at the windows of the ward in a thunderous roar. I have always loved the rain, even as a child I was enchanted by the sky in all its guises. It was great fun to watch rain lashing down from the storm filled sky onto the street where I lived, and I found it fascinating to see the raindrops strike the puddles and bounce up to form narrow pyramids of water that looked similar to a pawn in a game of chess, only lasting for a split second before disappearing forever. The effect of another morphine injection held the pain off to some extent. In the peace of the moment my mind returned again to my early flying training.

CHAPTER 5.

Tiger Moth.

I arrived at the rusty gates of Oxford Aerodrome rather late in the afternoon. It was a dull day, miserable in fact, which didn't do very much for the general ambience of the place. My first impression of the airfield was that it appeared to be disused and derelict, but I knew this was not the case as the advertisement clearly stated, Learn to fly at Kidlington Aerodrome.

Driving along the very rough road surface towards a group of large World War Two hangars was like taking a journey into the past. Rain had fallen earlier, adding to the depressive atmosphere of the place. It even felt a little ghostly as there was no sign of life whatsoever.

I parked the car on an area of muddy ground close to a hangar. Nearby there was a sign that looked as if it had seen better times, with the words "Visitors Car Park" painted in faded white paint. There were no other cars to be seen. I began to wonder if I had entered the airfield by the wrong entrance.

As I walked towards the nearest hangar, all that could be heard was the sound of Jackdaws squabbling inside, and my own footsteps echoing back to me off the metal walls. A small side door was partly open. I peered inside, but apart from a bicycle propped up against the far wall, and piles of bird crap, the building appeared to be completely empty.

'Anybody there?' I shouted.

My voice echoed around the empty hangar to no avail. I shouted again just to make sure, but no one replied.

I was about to give up when I heard the faint sound of a light aeroplane approaching the airfield, but I was unable to see it from where I was standing. I ran round the end of the hangar in time to see a little red and silver biplane very low, obviously about to land. It passed directly over my head, and I recognised it at once as a TIGER MOTH. The engine cut as it crossed over the airfield boundary and I could hear the wind whistling through the wing-struts as it rounded out to make a perfect landing. Wow! this was more like it. The presence of an aeroplane changed the whole atmosphere of the aerodrome completely.

I watched as the aircraft turned and started to taxi towards me, weaving from side to side as it did so. The person in the rear cockpit, who was wearing a leather flying helmet and goggles pushed up onto his forehead, stared at me for a second as he passed then gave a friendly wave of his hand.

Looking back at the situation now, it seems silly that I could get so excited at just seeing a Tiger Moth on the ground. But I was beside myself. Even now, to this very day, with over forty years of flying experience, and eleven thousand hours in command, I still get a feeling of excitement just to be near aeroplanes, and consider it a privilege to have been fortunate enough to earn my living as a professional pilot and flying instructor. I frequently look back unable to believe it all happened, it just seems like a wonderful dream.

I started walking in the same direction as the aeroplane appeared to be heading, losing sight of it as it passed behind the end of one of the hangars. Alongside the hangar I discovered a small, almost derelict looking hut, with smoke curling lazily out of a tin chimney at one end of its rusty corrugated iron roof. Outside was a very smart hand painted sign which read "Welcome to the Oxford Aeroplane Club".

I popped my head around the door, but there was no one to be seen. The coke-burning stove at the end of the building glowed red-hot. A large trestle table in the centre of the room was strewn with maps, navigational instruments, a couple of tin mugs and a rather battered old pipe which rested on a coffee tin lid that was obviously used as an ashtray. The walls were decorated with maps, notice boards and a coat rack that held a couple of fur lined leather flying jackets, with helmets, goggles etc. on a shelf above. The little hut had an atmosphere of real cosiness. Nothing appeared to be new. Old comfortable chairs with large cushions, a well worn piece of carpet and a model Tiger Moth hanging from the ceiling, all seemed to be just right, and somehow I instantly felt this is where I belong. But where had everyone gone?

Another short walk took me to the entrance of the second hangar. The large doors at the far end were wide open, and bright lights lit up the inside. The two men had climbed out of the Tiger Moth and were busy pushing it inside for the night. I was amazed to see how light the aircraft appeared to be. One of the pilots had lifted the tail up and was hauling the aeroplane backwards on his own, whilst the other chap stood by one of the wing tips guiding him into the hangar.

Neither men saw me waiting by the door, and after putting the chocks (Wooden blocks) under the wheels to stop the aeroplane from moving, they stood by the rear cockpit obviously discussing the flight they had just completed.

'Excuse me' I said, surprised at feeling a little nervous.

Both men turned round and looked in my direction.

'How can I help you?' the taller of the two men was speaking, his voice sounded very cultured, which made me feel even more uncomfortable.

'I...err...well I wondered if it would be possible for me to have flying lessons?' I burbled.

'Anything's possible' the man with the cultured voice was smiling as he walked towards me holding his hand out.

'My name is Coburn' he said, 'Spelt Cock-Burn, but the less said about that the better.'

We shook hands warmly, and I immediately began to feel a lot more at ease.

'So you want to learn to fly do you Mr er....?'

'Blyth, Ray Blyth' I interrupted.

'Well you would like to learn to fly would you Ray?'

'Yes sir, but I'm not certain if that is possible, education, cost, all that sort of thing?' I said.

Mr Cockburn indicated to his student that he would be back in a few minutes; he then strolled back to the flying club with me.

'I will introduce you to my assistant Eric Stowe; he will be able to answer your queries and supply you with all the relevant bumph. That's the trouble with aviation these days, you can't do a damn thing without filling in a stack of forms, usually in triplicate!

We entered the hut, passing through to the far end and into a small room that I had failed to notice earlier. The door was clearly marked with the letters CFI which I soon learned stood for Chief Flying Instructor.

'Sit down dear boy and make yourself comfortable whilst I find out what mischief young

Stowe is up to.'

With that Mr Cockburn left.

I only had a few minutes to wait, when a young man of medium build and height with brown wavy hair and piercing blue eyes, crashed through the door completely out of breath.

'Stowe's the name. Sorry to keep you waiting, I was working on something in number

three hangar' he said.

Before I had time to answer, a very attractive young girl, equally out of breath, followed him into the office looking very red faced and embarrassed. She was obviously the little something he had been working on in number three hangar! I couldn't help smiling. Eric winked at me, and from then on we hit it off very well together.

We had a long chat and consumed several mugs of hot tea. I was given an application form to apply for a student pilot's licence, and an appointment was made for me to have a medical in Oxford the following day.

Having booked my first flying lesson for the following week, I left the airfield feeling very excited at the prospect of learning to fly. At last my dream of becoming a pilot was coming true. In fact, although there was no way of me knowing at the time, this was the beginning of a long and successful career in aviation.

At last things were looking good on all fronts. It had been around September time when Mary started to suffer from bouts of early morning sickness. A visit to our local Doctor soon confirmed that she was expecting our first, and as it happened, only child.

It was January, and there were some months to go before Mary was due to give birth. In the more immediate future I somehow had to get through another week's work as a representative before the day of my first flying lesson arrived.

The first hurdle had been to pass the pilot's medical. Then, as the time drew nearer to my first lesson, I began to worry about the weather. Would it deteriorate so that my booking would have to be cancelled?

It was Saturday the 19th of January 1957, the morning my first flying lesson was due to take place. Fortunately it turned out to be a typically fresh crisp January morning; the sky was crystal clear, not a cloud in sight.

There was no rush, so I took my time to enjoy every minute of the journey to Kidlington. A watery sun lit up the Oxfordshire countryside completing the picture of a perfect day to fly.

As I entered Langford Lane, the road leading to the airfield, I saw a young man walking along the side of the road carrying a leather flying-jacket. Presuming he was on his way to the airfield, I stopped and offered the chap a lift. He introduced himself as Nils Bartleet, and told me he was about to have his third flying lesson in a Tiger Moth that morning. Although we had no way of knowing it at the time, this was the beginning of a great friendship that lasted many years, a friendship that almost came to an abrupt end as the result of a serious aeroplane accident eleven years later when we were both severely injured and lucky to escape with our lives.

We entered the gates of the airfield and parked outside the Flying Club. Nils got out of the car and strolled over to the Club entrance, his flying jacket slung over his shoulder looking for all the world like a veteran Pilot!

Inside the clubhouse we were greeted by a young lady who introduced herself as Sandy.

'Eric's flying at the moment' she said, 'he should be down at a quarter to ten, so you've just got time for a nice cup of tea.'

Sandy was the club's official receptionist, tea maker, and secretary. She was a very pleasant young lady who's natural friendly attitude made us couple of sprogs feel at ease the moment we met her.

From the window I could see one of the Tiger Moths parked on the grass verge in front of the Club. The dark red fuselage of the Moth contrasted beautifully with its silver wings that reflected the light from the early morning sun. I gazed in awe at this super little aeroplane. Both front and rear cockpit hatches were open, and the leather harness straps hung down over the sides of the fuselage. The letters on the side of the aeroplane were G-AMEY. I wondered if this would be the first aeroplane I actually flew myself? It turned out that it wasn't, the Tiger Moth that I was destined to fly was airborne at the time.

Having consumed a cup of tea, my attention was suddenly drawn to the sounds of an aeroplane droning overhead.

'That will be Eric' Sandy said.

I couldn't help noticing that there was a distinct tone of admiration in her voice whenever she mentioned his name.

Having landed, Eric booked in, and whilst consuming a mug of hot tea, debriefed the student he had just flown with. Nils was sent off to carry out the ground checks on G-AMEY.

Eric handed me some notes about the Tiger Moth and said that he would be flying with Nils first and should be back in an hour to fly with me in the Tiger Moth he had just landed in. With that he signed out and left the building to join Nils at the aeroplane.

I sat by the window watching Nils strap himself into the rear cockpit of EY, wondering what it would be like when it came to my turn.

Flying as a hobby was very expensive and still very much an out of the ordinary thing to do. Flying lessons, to the best of my memory, were about £4.10s per hour, and the average working wage at that time was between £6 and £8 per week.

The young man who had just returned from his lesson stood by the coke burning stove for a while trying to thaw out. He introduced himself to me as Ken Scott, Scotty to his friends. Ken told me that he had already gone solo and completed over twenty flying hours and was now on map reading and navigation exercises.

I heard the engine of G-AMEY start up, and from the Club window I watched as Eric climbed into the front cockpit, strapped himself in, and with a loud burst from the aircraft's engine, taxied off across the airfield.

Whilst I was waiting for Nils to complete his lesson, the door opened and a very smartly dressed middle-aged gentleman entered the clubhouse. He went straight over to the reception desk, picked up a few documents and left as quickly as he had arrived. I was told that his name was Peter Clifford, the Chairman of Oxford Flying Club. The airport itself apparently belonged to Oxford County Council and was leased by Goodhew Aviation Ltd., who owned the Flying Club.

I later learned that Peter Clifford also had his own aircraft sales company that operated from Kidlington Airport. During the war Mr Clifford had been a test pilot flight-testing service aircraft, and I was told that he had also won the Kings Cup Air Race in a Percival Mew Gull aeroplane in 1959. A few years later Peter was to become a close friend and I would be privileged to fly many of his aeroplanes.

With time to spare before Eric and Nils returned, I asked Sandy if it would be OK to take a look at the Tiger Moth standing on the dispersal area outside the Clubhouse. She told me not to touch the propeller and got me to sign the standard company indemnity form before letting me loose.

The morning continued to stay bright and crisp. There were no sounds of aircraft engines, only the chirping of distant birds, and the occasional echo of far off laughter from inside the hangar. I approached the red and silver Tiger Moth feeling a little emotional. I had dreamed of this day ever since my first flight at the age of three. I stood for several minutes admiring the aircraft, amazed by its smallness and feeling of frailness when I ran my hand affectionately over its smooth fabric covered fuselage. I looked at its registration letters, G-ALNA, this was to be the first aeroplane I would fly.

Unlike today's more sophisticated methods of training, my first pre-flight briefing turned out to be a chat on the way from the Clubhouse to the aeroplane.

'Climb up onto the wing keeping on the black reinforced section and jump into the rear cockpit old chap whilst I prime the engine and make sure the chocks are in place. I'll show you all the external checks next time, but as we are running a bit late, we'll crack on with the lesson,' and that was it.

I wish I had as many pound notes as the times I've heard those unforgivable words since I've been in aviation. But like all beginners, my instructor was God, in my eyes he could do no wrong, and I was keen to obey his every command without question. I suppose if it was going to be just the familiarisation flight, the lack of a full briefing would have been excusable, but as it turned out, that was not the case.

I watched my instructor as he turned the propeller several times by hand. He walked back and switched on the ignition switches outside of both cockpits.

'If it doesn't start when I turn the prop, I will ask you to turn those two switches on the left hand side of the fuselage to the off position, which is down, OK?' he said.

I always thought that switches were on when they were down, so I queried that point with him for safety.

'No it's the opposite way round with aircraft switches, think of it as ladies knickers old boy, when they're down they're off, and when they're up they're on, OK?'

I never forgot the position of aircraft switches from that moment on.

He went on to explain the thumbs up or thumbs down procedure so that I could indicate to him the position of the ignition switches whilst he was turning the prop by hand. Eric set the throttle position in my cockpit and told me to hold the stick hard back and how to close the throttle if the engine started to run too fast. Returning to the propeller, he gave me the thumbs down signal and shouted out 'IGNITION OFF?' I checked the position of my switches and shouted back to him giving the thumbs down sign at the same time. Feeling a little nervous I watched as the prop was set to the correct angle. Eric shouted 'ON' and gave the thumbs up sign. I flicked the ignition switches up and signalled back. I saw the propeller turn, then there was a tremendous roar from the engine as it burst into life, at the same time a gust of wind hit my face taking me completely by surprise. Before I knew it my instructor was leaning into my cockpit and adjusting the throttle so that the engine RPM reduced to a quiet tick-over. Eric jumped into the front cockpit, secured his harness and at the same time shouted down the Gosport Tube asking me if I could hear him. I said that I could, but wondered if it would be more difficult to hear him when the engine was revved up and the wind from the slipstream would be roaring past my head. Eric waved his arms at a young man from the hangar staff that had been standing by our aeroplane waiting to remove the chocks, his head seemed dangerously close to the turning propeller, but he obviously knew exactly what he was doing.

'Put your hands and feet lightly on the controls Ray, and follow me through as we taxi out to the runway.' Eric's voice now took on an air of authority that, as far as I was concerned, demanded the status of "sir" whilst addressing him during a lesson. Prior to getting into the Tiger Moth, I had been told virtually nothing about the controls, so I was glad that I did at least know something about aeroplanes, otherwise I would have been worried about the pedals under my feet which kept moving vigorously from one side to the other. My instructor said something about checking the "Mags" before we taxied out, but I had no idea what was happening, and since he didn't mention it again, I assumed that I was expected to do nothing. At the end of the grass runway we stopped. I heard Eric shouting out something about T.T.M.F.F.G.H.H. So I shouted back down the speaking tube…

'What does all that mean sir?'

'Don't worry about that now old chap, it's all in your Aircraft Check Notes' he informed me. I pulled the checklist from the pocket of my borrowed leather jacket, but it was immediately snatched from my hand by the slipstream of the propeller and whisked off down the airfield like tumbleweed in a desert storm.

We taxied onto the runway quite close to a bright orange windsock that barely moved in the light breeze. 'Off we go'…

Those three words from my instructor made my heart race with excitement. I had waited so long for this moment, and at last it was here. The noise from the de-Havilland engine increased to a roar as we picked up speed and bounced lightly along the freshly mown grass of the runway. The sound of the slipstream increased as the tail of the aeroplane slowly lifted enabling me to see the runway ahead. We remained on the wheels for a few more seconds, then all the bumping and wobbling ceased, and we became airborne, flying smoothly just above the ground.

We picked up speed quickly, just skimming the fence at the airfield boundary. The open cockpit dispelled any smells of petrol or exhaust fumes, only the scent of a fresh Winter's morning alerted my senses, and as I looked down at the beauty of the fields, trees and houses slowly diminishing in size beneath me, I felt for the first time that inexplicable feeling of freedom, a privilege only afforded to those who choose to fly.

I enjoyed my first lesson more than words can express, although most of the time I had little idea of what was happening. I was allowed to hold the controls whilst being told about flying straight, turning, climbing and gliding. Then Eric looped and rolled the aircraft a couple of times whilst I clung desperately to the seat, terrified that I was about to fall out.

All too soon it was over, and we were coming in to land. As we lined up with the runway the engine cut back to a tick-over. I could hear the magic tone of air whistling through the wing struts, a sound that thrills me even to this day. We crossed low over the airfield boundary, floated for a while, then sank gently onto the ground. My first lesson was over.

It is only when I look back now at the initial entries in my very first logbook, that I realise how poor the standards of flying training were in those days. I don't blame the instructors; it was the whole outlook on civil aviation in the late 1940's and early 1950's that lacked proper monitoring and control. I seem to remember that the responsibility for aviation matters passed from one government department to another. The Ministry of Aviation, the Ministry of Transport, the Board of Trade and at one stage even the Ministry of Agriculture and Fisheries was in charge of flying matters. All had a go at looking after the interests of pilot training! A minimum flying time of 30 hours to complete the course was laid down, but there was very little control over the method of teaching.

Flying club instructors were left to make up their own minds about the content of pre-flight briefings and the minimum time spent on each flying lesson. In my case, what should have been a forty-five minute familiarisation flight to see that I was comfortable in the air and if I had any aptitude for flying, turned out to be five lessons all rolled up into one: 1. Flight familiarisation. 2 The effect of the controls on an aircraft in flight, parts one and two. 3. Straight and level. 4. Medium turns, and 5.Climbing and gliding. In addition Eric found time to throw in a couple of aerobatics for good measure. Under today's training standards, each one of those lessons would demand a full pre-flight briefing, and would take between forty-five minutes to one hour to teach each of the five lessons, on average a total of between four and a half, and six hours flying time. My first lesson went through the lot in forty-five minutes with time to spare for my instructor to show me how good he was at loops and slow rolls.

Anyway, I enjoyed every single second of the flight and would have liked to ask my instructor one or two questions when we landed, but unfortunately his flight schedule was running late, so, other than when we were walking back to the clubhouse from the aeroplane, I never had a chance to chat with him at all. As we entered the clubhouse Eric just had time to tell me I had done very well. This had me baffled, because most of the time I didn't really know what was going on.

Nils was waiting for me when we landed, so after making a booking for my second lesson, I gave him a lift back to Oxford. We were both very keen to fly, and it wasn't long before I confided in Nils telling him how I had been a little confused during my first lesson. Nils put my mind at rest assuring me that everyone felt a bit like that after their first lesson.

'I've completed six hours and I'm still covering lessons one to six' he said with a certain amount of pride.

It was only years later when we had both become instructors, that we recalled those early days on the Tiger Moth, and realised how poor the training standards were.

In the beginning I could only afford a couple of flying lessons a month, so progress was naturally rather slow. However, in February my salary was increased by £300 per year, at the same time my company car, an Austin A30, was exchanged for a brand new Morris Cowley, a much larger and more impressive looking car. All in all things were looking up.

One day early in March, I made a routine sales call on the buyer for Clinch's Witney Brewery in Oxfordshire. It was another clear, beautifully crisp morning when I left the offices of the Brewery. As I was about to get into my car I noticed a jet airliner passing overhead. It must have been flying at 35,000 feet or more. The aircraft appeared no more than a silvery dot, whilst the water vapour from its engines formed a thin white cloud like a needle threading cotton through the clear blue sky. I looked at the briefcase and samples lying beside me in the car, and knew that selling was no longer for me. How ever difficult or expensive it was going to be, I had to find a way to qualify for a living in the world of flying.

CHAPTER 6.

Revelation.

It had stopped raining, and the clinking of cups signalled that it was time for a cup of tea for those who were well enough to handle a cup.

Our small four-bedded room was attached to the main casualty ward at the Radcliffe. The occupants of the annex were all considered to be long-term patients deemed for a lengthy stay in hospital.

The four of us occupying the annex at that time were all suffering from major accidents of one kind or another.

Stan, a police sergeant, who occupied the bed opposite to me, had received severe head injuries in a car crash. George, in the next bed to mine was suffering from a dislocated hip and fractured pelvis, the result of a motorcycle accident. The bed in the opposite corner of the room was occupied by Robin Melville, a serving RAF officer who, like myself had been involved in an aeroplane accident. Robin was suffering from spinal injuries and a broken ankle. Because two of the patients in the annex happened to be pilots, the annexe was renamed "The Officers Mess" by the nursing staff, and what a mess it was too.

I was glad to be out of the main part of 'C' ward. Both the OM (Officers Mess) and the main ward shared the same nursing staff of course, but 'C' ward, was also the main casualty reception ward, which meant that throughout the day and night casualties were being admitted to the ward in various states of suffering before being transferred to other wards, or sometimes just dying.

Saturday nights were always the worst. It was not unusual for several cases to be admitted to 'C' ward at night, their screaming, groaning, and vomiting took some getting used to. Several of the patients were admitted for a twenty-four hour observation period because they had banged their head in some way or other, usually after being involved in drunken brawls. Most of them were still very drunk when they arrived in the ward.

I began to dread Saturday nights. The ward became a sort of clearinghouse for almost every male person admitted into the Radcliffe. Emergency cases lay side by side with vomiting drunks who were swearing and cursing at everyone in sight. Seriously ill patients trying to cope with their own suffering and fears were treated to a nightmare performance of foul smells, yelling and shouting from the self inflicted drunks who vomited in their beds, on the floor and in the faces of those trying to help them. My heart went out to the nurses and medical staff who somehow took everything in their stride even with patients who decided to add violence to the evening's nightmare by physically hitting out at the staff.

Things sometimes happened when you least expected them. I remember one such incident that turned out to be a nightmare for me when it happened.

It was Sunday night about eleven-thirty; well after the main lights of the ward had been switched off. Dimly lit orange night-lights at either end of the ward served to make out the individual shapes of the beds and ward furniture. The effect of their warm glow made the ward seem much more peaceful than at other times, although the usual assortment of groans, sighs, coughs, snoring and the occasional fart acted as a constant reminder that the semi peaceful atmosphere could erupt into something more sinister at any second.

Suddenly a patient at the far end of the ward started to scream. Then the fellow in the next bed to him started to shout for help, his voice trembling with shock. I was physically attached to the traction apparatus that held my body in place, and unable to do anything. Then came a very loud hissing noise that sounded like high-pressure air escaping from something. The night sister suddenly entered the ward and ran past my bed, her torchlight flickering from bed to bed in search of the poor soul in trouble. Within seconds screens were hastily drawn around the troubled man's bed; his screams now subsided to whimpering pleas for help. A bright light above the patient's bed had been switched on creating a dramatic shadow-theatre effect of the intense activity that was being carried out behind the green canvas screen surrounding the bed. I watched the shadows of the nurses as they desperately struggled to help their patient. Moments later a doctor arrived and quietly slid behind the screens re-appearing in silhouette on the shadow-theatre screen.

After a while the patient's pathetic whimpers became weaker and finally stopped altogether. An indescribable smell began to fill the ward. One of the nurses lit special candles to facilitate a chemical odour that eventually overcame the awful stench. I was now wide-awake, the severe pain in my legs reminding me that I must be due for another pain killing injection. The motionless patient was taken quietly from behind the screens on a trolley and wheeled out of the ward. We never saw him again.

Shortly after a nurse hurried down the ward and switched on the bedside light of the empty bed next to me.

'Someone coming in?' I asked.

'You should be asleep' she answered.

'Some hopes' I thought. Moments later I heard the sound of a man shouting and cursing as he neared the ward. The rubber doors were pushed open to reveal a large man sitting in a wheelchair pushed by one of the night porters. My heart sank as the chair and its contents were wheeled to the empty bed next to mine. A nurse who had joined the porter was trying to encourage the man to sit on the bed and get undressed. The porter seemed in a hurry to get away, and to my astonishment left the poor nurse to cope with this huge man who was obviously very drunk and seemed likely to become violent.

'There's nothing f…..g wrong with me' the man was shouting.

'Shhh, there are a lot of very sick people in this ward.'

The nurse's efforts to quieten the man down were having little effect. I was horrified to see him stand up and take a swing at the nurse. Fortunately he missed and fell crashing to the floor. Before anyone could shout for help another nurse arrived and joined in the attempt to get the man into bed, which he flatly refused to do. Eventually, to my astonishment, they left him sitting on the edge of the bed facing me, switched off his bed light and left the ward threatening that if he wasn't in bed by the time they returned there would be serious trouble!

He eventually quietened down a little, although still cursing and mumbling to himself. My real fear was the damage he could do if he fell over and tried to save himself by grabbing the contraptions that were holding me together. At that time my left leg was immobilised in a straight-leg plaster, my right leg held in traction with a steel pin through my knee attached to wires and a weight suspended from a pulley, my left arm and shoulder were broken and being supported by a sling attached to a stand. There were also two bottles of liquid on stands drip-feeding via tubes into my arms, a drain leading from a hole in my right thigh, and all the fingers of my left hand were in plaster. All this left me in little doubt that I was in no fit state to take on this huge Scotsman if he decided to have a go at me, which, by the look of him seemed very much on the cards.

'Who the f...k do yous think yous f.....g looking at?'

'No-one.' I hastily replied.

'So yous think I'm f.....g no-one do yous Jimmy?'

He stood up and lurched towards me, swayed a moment, then fell backwards onto his bed. At that moment a doctor appeared and spoke to the Scotsman, telling him to be quiet, he explained that because he had been inflicted with a head injury, he would have to stay under observation for twenty-four hours, then if all was well, he would be allowed to leave. After a considerable amount of fuss he gave the man an injection, smiled at me, and left the ward.

'Did you fetch him, yous bastard?' he was glaring at me again.

I had hoped the injection would have knocked him out, no such luck, he started on me again, so I pretended not to hear him as I lay there in sheer terror. For a while he was very quiet, and I thought he had fallen asleep. I was just beginning to relax a little, when the Scotsman stood up very suddenly. He swayed slightly and leaned towards me! His head had blood stains showing through the bandage and his breath smelt like a distillery.

'Whas happened to yous Jimmy?' he asked.

'I was in an aeroplane crash mate' I said hoping he may become a little friendlier.

'Yous a f.....g liar,' he said.

Our interesting conversation was interrupted by the Night sister arriving to administer my injection. At least this would take away the agonising pain in my body even if it didn't remove the pain in the arse occupying the next bed!

The injection brought relief almost immediately.

'Try and get some sleep if you can now Ray, it will soon be morning' the nurse said as she turned to leave.

'How can I?' I said, 'I can't take my eyes off Jock here, if he falls and grabs this contraption I'm attached to, I've had it.'

Moments later, the nurse returned with a small hand bell.

'There you are dear' she said, 'you can rest now, all you have to do if he gets up is ring the bell, and one of us will come straight away', she hurried off.

I've never been able to work that one out; I stayed awake for the rest of the night, the bell firmly clutched in my serviceable hand, waiting to ring for help if needed. Jock eventually fell asleep and snored loudly for the rest of the night. He was discharged the following evening and left without another word to me.

All that was months ago. Now, in our small annexe (The O.M.), there was no screaming, I had had my pain killing injection, and the ward was at peace. Through the skylight, I could see the hazy halo around the moon; it's pale circle fading as I slipped into blissful sleep.

Grunts, groans, enthusiastic farting and sighs of relief signified that the early morning bedpan round had commenced in fine style. Everyone in his own little screened-off world, concentrating on the job in hand, whilst at the same time being entertained by the sounds of others engrossed in the same task. Such is the close companionship of ward life.

I had long since overcome the initial embarrassment that accompanied the bedpan round. Every poor sod had his own individual problems to cope with according to the extent of his injuries and disabilities, me included. My particular lot was that I had to attend to the wants of nature in a lying position. This meant that I had to be hoisted up by two nurses, and a bedpan slid under my bottom, before being lowered down again to perform my duties! Which, to say the least was extremely difficult, and bloody uncomfortable.

The first ten or maybe twenty efforts for me turned out to be impossible, which in turn led to a severe case of constipation. Laxatives were tried on several occasions without result, followed by two enemas, which also failed. By this time I was beginning to feel sick and extremely uncomfortable. The whole business was very painful, and I can only liken it to what one imagines it would be like trying to give birth to a house brick!

Help came at last in the form of a very young nurse, accompanied by the ward Sister, and a couple of student doctors.

'We're going to carry out a manual extraction Raymond' the Sister announced, 'not pleasant' she added 'neither for you or the nurse. We've picked the nurse with the smallest hands.'

I didn't quite understand the full meaning of "Manual Extraction", if I had done so I wouldn't have been lying back smiling at the Sister!! The screens were drawn around my bed, and the young nurse donned a rubber glove. It was when the gloved hand was immersed into a tin of Vaseline that I began to get the idea.

'She can't be' I thought, but sadly she could, and did.

The recollection of what followed still makes me wince; therefore I will describe the incident briefly. Legs complete with plasters and traction weights were hoisted up by the Sister, assisted by the student doctors. As I slid further down the bed, I soon forgot the excruciating pains from my legs. I must have looked like I was about to give birth, and by the time they finished with me that's exactly what it felt like.

The nurse thrust her gloved hand inside me, with the enthusiasm of extracting the innards of a chicken! It felt to me like the arm of a weight lifter had been inserted up to the elbow! A sharp intake of breath, followed by a pathetically weak scream, was the best I could manage. Sweat trickled down my face. The poor little nurse began to break up the offending "House Brick" inside my bowel. I looked at the student doctors for some kind of sympathy…the bastards were grinning. After what seemed an age it was all over. I felt both relieved and sick. I thanked the young nurse who had carried out the unenviable task so efficiently, and asked the Sister if I had given birth to a boy or a girl! I also carefully noted the faces of the two student doctors in the hope that one day I would be given the opportunity to reap my revenge.

Even in the four-bedded annex we sometimes managed to find questionable entertainment from another chap's misfortune. Today it turned out that dear old George in the next bed to me was destined to entertain the rest of us in the OM.

George, a very good-humoured Yorkshire man, had the privilege of being the only one in our ward entitled to a special bedpan. His "DELUX MODEL" had rubber inflatable sides to help cushion the effect his weight would have on his recently replaced hip.

George frequently kept us entertained with jokes, tales of his numerous girlfriends, and complaining about there not being enough "snap". (His word for food).

Carefully covered bedpans were being collected by the ward daily help girl, and a sigh of ecstasy from behind George's screen signified that he was drawing events to a close. Suddenly there was the sound of a clanking chain, followed by an enormous bang and a blood-curdling scream!

The ward went deathly quiet, save for the sound of nursing staff hurriedly making for George. From behind the screens there followed a mixture of giggling from the nurses, and extremely foul language from George.

Eventually the screens were drawn back, and there sat George in a freshly made bed, with clean linen, and the ward caretaker replacing the chain and handle above his bed. George, although deathly white, managed a half-hearted grin. We were all dying to know what had happened and eventually he told us.

'As you lot may have guessed, I'm suffering a bit from diarrhoea. No problem, pans deep enough, it were this ere bloody chain that started all the trouble,' he said. 'I was hoisting myself up with me left hand so that I could wipe me backside with tuther hand, when bloody chain broke! Down I went, trapping me, which were bad enough, but at that point the rubber ring bust round'th pan, and with support chain gone, I couldn't get up, so there I was covered in shit, with me hand trapped up me arse.'

We collapsed in tears.

'It's not bloody funny mate. You lot er worse than't bloody nurses.'

The ward was being hurriedly tidied up, floors polished, beds made and carefully aligned ready for the consultants ward round. Today I was to meet my new surgeon Mr Morgan for the first time. I awaited the occasion with mixed feelings.

A small group of persons entered the main ward and slowly, bed by bed, made their way towards the annexe. As they grew nearer I could hear the deep and rather gruff voice of the Consultant Orthopaedic Surgeon talking to the patients and the cluster of doctors and nurses gathered round him. Eventually the group entered the annexe, and came straight to my bed.

'This is Raymond ' the Sister said. 'He was involved in an aircraft accident and is suffering from multiple injuries!'

She was addressing a very distinguished looking gentleman, I would say he was in his mid fifties and immaculately dressed in a dark suit. Sister handed him a large folder that contained my x-rays and medical notes. He looked at me for a brief second and nodded, his expression was one of concern.

Whilst he continued to examine my x-rays, I studied him carefully. All my hopes for the future depended on this one man. He was talking to the highly attentive group of medical staff in white coats gathered around him. I remember thinking: Please God encourage this man to try and save my legs.

As I listen to him, the near panic I had been feeling, gradually faded away. My greatest fear was to lose my legs, but somehow, by just looking at this man, I felt that if anything at all could be done to save them, he could do it. I listened to his gruff voice explaining technicalities to his staff. The concern showed on his face as he gazed out from under large bushy eyebrows, first at my x-rays then at his staff. I remember thinking that the slight stoop he had was probably caused by working endless hours bent over an operating table.

Finally, he turned to me and a warm smile spread across his face.

'Hello old chap, you've obviously had a rough time' he said reaching out as if to shake hands, but he just held my hand firmly and went on.

'My name is Mr Morgan, and I'm pretty sure that with a little help from you we can do a lot to put you back together again.'

No doubt he could see the tears of emotion welling up in my eyes. He gripped my hand a little tighter and said…

'I'm just going to take a look at you, don't worry old chap, I won't hurt you.'

He spent quite a time examining various parts of my broken body in great detail. Students were asked various questions, and notes were made. Finally he arranged for more x-rays to be taken. His final words were…

'I think we'll make a start tomorrow, have a good nights sleep and leave the rest to us.'

With that he was gone.

I lay there in a daze with feelings of fear and excitement. Soon after the ward round had been completed, Sister returned to my bedside smiling all over her face.

'You should be pleased that Mr Morgan is taking over your case', she said, 'he's the Senior Orthopaedic Consultant Surgeon in this area, and if anyone can help you, he most certainly can. You will be going down to theatre tomorrow morning at eight o'clock, I'm not sure exactly what he plans to do' she went on, 'but he will take a good look at all your problems. Cheer up, you're a very lucky man.'

Now this business of "being very lucky" does tend to mystify me! OK I can understand that on this occasion I was indeed lucky to have such an eminent surgeon looking after me, but I do have to raise the odd eyebrow when visitors see me laying there with practically every moving part buggered up, and say 'You're lucky.'

After the surgeons left the ward I turned to George wondering what the great man had said to him. He sat up in bed looking quite pleased with himself.

'Got a date with a nurse?' I asked.

'Little I could do about it if I had' was his honest reply.

I continued to wind him up.

'Won the pools then?'

'No', he said, 'I'm going to leave you shortly.' He pointed towards a pair of crutches propped up against the end of his bed.

'When I've got the hang of these little boys, I'm off.'

'Thank God for that', I said.

Two fingers appeared from behind his bed sheets.

I hadn't known George long, but he had become a valued friend and I would miss him greatly when he left.

The day passed slowly. Only after bedsores had been powdered, pillows carefully arranged, wounds dressed, pills taken and another of the regular morphine injections administered, could I fall into blissful pain-free sleep.

That evening a "NIL BY MOUTH" notice was attached to the foot of my bed, announcing to all that I was for the operating table the following day. I lay awake for some time with mixed feelings of optimism and apprehension. Thankfully I had no conception that this was only the beginning of a long and painful process of healing that would take two years to complete.

A strange thing happened that night, usually I would wake up well before my next injection was due, which at that time was every three hours throughout the day and night. On this occasion I woke up to find that the screens had been placed around my bed, the bed light was on, and one of the night nurses was bending over me calling my name. The duty doctor had obviously been called, and was adjusting one of the inauspicious bottles suspended above me. I appeared to be saturated with sweat, and I could hear my heart pounding away in my ears. What happened after that seemed vague, I can only remember the familiar sting of an injection into my bottom again, and the next thing I knew it was morning.

I awoke to the usual sounds of activity in the ward. The screens were still around my bed, and my first thought's were: 'I should be having an operation today, but what was all the fuss about last night?' There was a faint smell of vomit, but my bed clothes were spotless and there were no signs of me having been sick. After a short while a nurse appeared to administer two injections, one was my usual painkiller, and the second was a pre-med injection. Screens were then removed.

Something had obviously happened to me during the night, but I was too frightened to ask. There was also an increase in the burning pain I had in the rear of my right thigh where my broken femur had pierced through the skin. But I didn't want to make a fuss about it, so foolishly I kept quiet.

'Are you OK Ray?' George was looking at me with concern from the next bed.

'I think so', I said, 'I'm not sure what happened last night though.'

'Well as far as I can make out, you must have had a nightmare about your accident',

'Were you awake?'

'Yes, and you screamed the bloody place down…frightened the lot of us fartless!'

It didn't matter what George said, it was always accompanied by a warm smile.

'Sorry mate.'

'You also pulled all your drips out. Some folks will do anything to get the nurses attention!'

CHAPTER 7.

The Big Question.

The head porter at the Radcliffe, Mr Gwyn Jones, was a tall heavily built man who weighed about fifteen stone. He had a bald head, wore heavily rimmed glasses and in my opinion was the absolute image of the famous bandleader, the late Mr Billy Cotton senior. Gwyn had taken me to the operating theatre on two previous occasions during the first few days after my arrival. Once again he arrived at my bedside smiling down at me through the "jam-jar bottom" lenses of his spectacles.

'Time to go on Ops Biggles,' he said laughing at his own joke.

The ward Sister fussed with my blankets for a second.

'There is nothing to worry about Ray, it will all be over and you will be back in the recovery ward in no time.'

With that she hurried off in her usual blustery manner.

George from the next bed waved his hand and wished me luck, with that we were off on our way to the operating theatre.

'How are you feeling?' Gwyn asked, as we proceeded along the seemingly endless corridors to the operating theatre.

'Not too bad, just a little nervous.' In fact I was petrified.

My thoughts ran riot as I watched the lights of the corridor passing overhead: 'Would this be the last few moments of my life?' I have always been terrified by the thought of dying under anaesthetic. I suppose everybody is really.

'You've got the best surgeon around here for a mile or two Ray.'

Gwyn had become a friend ever since the day I was admitted to the Radcliffe. Unfortunately his words of encouragement did little to quell my innermost fears as he wheeled me at considerable speed along those gruesome dark green corridors.

We entered the small anaesthetic room with its all too familiar smells of ether and antiseptic. Gwyn gave me a friendly pat on the head.

'See you later' he said and left me to my fate.

A theatre nurse dressed in dark green overalls with hat to match was grinning down at me.

'Any rings, jewellery, false teeth, or false bits of any kind?' I hardly recognised my own voice as I replied in the negative. Then the anaesthetist who had visited me the previous evening appeared at my side.

'We're ready for you now Raymond.' I always get suspicious when anyone calls me Raymond instead of Ray; it usually meant trouble when my mother used to do it.

During my previous couple of visits to the operating theatre I had been more or less semi-conscious when I arrived, but this time it was different. Everything was crystal clear and I was very much aware of what was going on around me. I tried to act casual, but I'm sure my efforts were not very convincing.

The preliminaries were soon over, the anaesthetist announced…

'This won't hurt' before stabbing me in the arm with a large needle. He then asked me to count backwards slowly from ten to one. I can't remember getting past five. One of the theatre nurses told me sometime later that I had mumbled 'I have control' just before passing out and the anaesthetist apparently commented 'Not this time old friend.' I suppose the dizziness one gets when being anaesthetised must have made my half conscious brain think that I was carrying out a spinning exercise with a student. On such occasions it was sometimes prudent to take over in a hurry if your student froze on the controls and you had any aspirations of living to an old age!

There is one thing that amazes me about anaesthetics, there never seems to be any time lapse between passing out in the theatre and regaining consciousness in the recovery ward. It's instantaneous. For instance, you can go to bed at night, sleep for several hours, and when you wake up you are always aware of the passing of time. But under anaesthetic the time span between counting the numbers and waking up again seems to be instantaneous. I am told that many patients are convinced that they have not been operated on because of this strange illusion of missing time. And so it was on this occasion, I had no sooner started to count, when I heard the distant voice of a nurse telling me to wake up. I was on a trolley moving swiftly along the same green walled corridor. Then the bright lights faded and I drifted into oblivion once more.

I awoke some time later in the recovery ward, the lights were dimmed to night-time intensity. The first thing I could remember was the acute pain in my legs. A nurse was by my bed and I heard myself pleading with her to give me something to take the pain away. The next thing I remembered was Mr Morgan bending over me in the recovery ward and injecting something into my back that brought instant relief and a feeling of deep peace. I had no idea how late at night it was as the consultant surgeon sat by my bed explaining things to me.

'We've made a good start to put things right for you old chap, but I'm afraid there is a long way to go yet. In addition to the fractured Femur which was operated on and put in traction shortly after you arrived, I'm afraid that you have sustained a further twenty-five or so rather complicated fractures to the bones in the lower part of your legs and both ankles. Some of the bones have been badly splintered. Don't worry old chap there is an excellent chance that we can save both your legs, but it will take time. Your left arm is broken in a couple of places and two of your fingers were fractured, so we have lined things up and your arm will be in plaster for a few weeks. The dental surgeon will take a look at your teeth when you are feeling a bit better, but there's nothing serious needs doing. I believe your eye was placed correctly into its socket by the doctor at the scene of the accident and was also attended to by our surgeon when you arrived. The minor hairline fracture to your skull should cause you no problems. I have to say that you are indeed very lucky that your body stood up to the massive shock of all these fractures occurring at the same moment, perhaps just one more fracture would have been too much for your body to take. You're a tough little chap. I'm sure we can, in time, get you out and about again, albeit with crutches or maybe a stick.'

Although not exactly overjoyed by learning the full extent of my injuries, I knew that I was in the very safe hands of this man. For me it was the beginning of a two year struggle that would be fraught with pain and disappointments in what seemed to be a never ending struggle to walk again. As Mr Morgan left the recovery ward, his departing words slowly began to sink into my partially dimmed consciousness. Until that moment I had only been concerned with whether or not my legs could be saved, but now the surgeons words hit me with the full force of reality. I will probably need crutches or a stick for the rest of my life. These words spelt out clearly that my professional flying career was at an end. The probability of this had obviously been on the cards since the day I had been admitted to hospital, but I had been so concerned with the thought of loosing my legs altogether, that I had never really considered my future as a pilot. From now on things were vastly different. A psychological struggle had been added to the physical battle and I wasn't at all sure I could handle that side of things. It came as quite a shock to realise that, for the first time in my life, I had no control over my future.

Worried sick, I asked the recovery ward Sister if it would be possible for me to see Mr Morgan again that night, but he had already left the hospital and would not be returning to the Radcliffe for the next couple of days.

So began the long and agonising wait. I rehearsed a thousand times the words I would use to try and make him understand that I just had to return to flying. The big question was, did he think he could operate on my injuries and, however long it took, bring me back to a sufficiently high standard for me to pass the stringent professional aircrew medical again? Waves of apprehension came over me as I imagined his replies. How could I make him understand that I had no intention of doing any other job? Stick or crutches?... neither if I had anything to do with it.

Suddenly the torturous sick making pain took over my body again. All thoughts of flying were instantly stripped from my mind. I vomited before I had a chance to ring the emergency bell for help and cursed aloud.

Next morning Gwyn collected me from the recovery ward and took me back to 'C' ward annexe. He wheeled my bed slowly along the dismal corridors of dark flaking paint, the regularly spaced lights reflecting in his heavy rimmed glasses. A nurse accompanied us, steadying the drip feed bottles suspended from the traction framework.

Whilst pushing my bed Gwyn leaned forward to speak to me...

'George has gone.'

'How long?' I said.

'He started using his crutches the day they took you to theatre and he was released this morning.'

We rounded the corner and entered the brightly lit ward. Gwyn pushed my bed through the rubber swing doors of the annexe and I saw George's empty bed had been made up ready for the next patient. Although I had only known the chap for a short while, George's good humour and warm-heartedness made him a friend who would prove hard to forget.

Sister Heathfield, Sonia, although no one dared to call her by her christen name, greeted me as we entered the annexe. She was a very attractive, professional person who ran the ward with the strictness and efficiency of a sergeant major. She asked me how I felt, and handed me a small piece of paper. It was a message from George. I unfolded the crumpled note and read it. 'Had to go mate, too many girls can't live without me! Will come and visit, take care, George.' I looked forward to him visiting, but sadly I never saw him again.

That evening Valerie arrived at the ward entrance dead on six p.m. Sadly, after eleven years of marriage, Mary and I had separated. My dear little son Eddy was eight at the time, and although he was living with his mother, Mary and I had remained friends and there was never any problem about me seeing my son at any time.

When Mary and I split up, I had lived in quarters on Oxford Airport. Then I met Valerie who came to work at the Airport. We finally got together and I had been living with Valerie and her daughter Laura for three happy years when the crash occurred.

Valerie had visited me every evening since the accident without fail. She was never late, and invariably the first to enter the ward at visiting time. I literally lived for her visits. Val was employed as a secretary in the Aircraft Sales Department of CSE at the same time as I was employed as Chief Flying Instructor of the Basic Training Wing at Oxford Air Training School.

Although it was seven miles to and from the hospital Valerie visited me every evening without fail and never missed once during the whole two years I was destined to stay there. She also wrote to me daily bringing the letter with her each night so that I had something to read before going to sleep. This evening was no exception; she arrived carrying some flowers looking a little perturbed. Bending down to kiss me, she whispered...

'How are you Darling? the Sister tells me that you are upset about something, what's the matter?'

She drew up the visitor's chair, sat down and laid the flowers on my bedside cabinet. Struggling not to show any emotion I poured out my heartfelt troubles, telling her all that Mr Morgan had said to me. I explained that I was very worried about the possibility of not being able to fly again. Valerie held my hand tightly, almost as if she didn't trust me to let go!

'Is that all, I thought it was something more serious than that.'

Valerie had a special way of dealing with me that never failed. A few well-chosen words from her always seemed to bring any anxieties I may have had, down to size. She fluffed up my pillows and put her arm around my neck.

'It's early days yet; you mustn't get yourself worked up like that. Sister said that she has seen patients, far worse off than you, walk out of here as if nothing had been wrong with them.'

She was probably lying to make me feel better. In fact it did sort me out and I felt annoyed with myself for making such a fuss.

As usual, visiting time passed quickly, and soon it was time for the visitors to leave. Valerie was invariably the last one to leave the ward. I watched her tall slim immaculately dressed figure as she left, turning to wave as she reached the door. I also noticed that she called in the Sisters office on her way out. 'That could mean trouble for me' I thought.

Visitors would arrive and assemble in a room next to the ward. At dead on six o'clock a bell would ring which signified the visitors could enter the ward. Usually the ward was quiet up to that point, but the sound of the visitor's bell usually forecast that all hell would break out at any moment. Saturday evenings were usually the worst. The bell would ring, and all us inmates would glance nervously towards the doors as they burst open to reveal visitors of all shapes, sizes and ages hurtling down the ward towards us. Most were bearing gifts which varied from flowers, chocolates and fruit, to suitcases, bundles of clothes, and once a parrot in a large cage, who just had time to announce that 'Polly is a good boy' before being ejected from the ward by a very irate staff nurse. The invasion of visitors was usually followed by a deluge of noise, laughing, whispering, crying, sneezing, coughing, and screaming. Family members would deposit gifts of cakes, grapes and chocolates etc. on the bedside lockers of the patients, and frequently stayed long enough to devour the lot. After an hour the bell would ring again and our visitors would depart leaving bewildered patients with scraps of silver paper, cake crumbs and a few grape storks. The whole performance could be a nerve shattering experience.

As predicted, Val's visit to Sisters office spelt trouble. Next morning, after ward round, Sister appeared by my bed, hands on hips and looking very superior. I recalled that such a look from my mother when I was a small boy usually forecasted a telling off.

'Your wife tells me that you are getting yourself all worked up about nothing.' Sister spoke with a quiet but concerned voice.

'Valerie is not my wife,' I answered, slightly on the defensive.

'Don't be evasive Ray… if you have any problems, you tell me; don't just lay there worrying yourself sick. You must remember that a positive state of mind helps a lot towards your recovery. Now just what is worrying you?'

'Nothing,' I said, and immediately regretted it.

'That's it, if we're going to play silly games we'll see if some fresh air will do the trick,' She moved closer, almost nose to nose.

'I'm going to put your bed into the staff car park, that should brighten your ideas up a bit, and when you come back, I'll ask you the same question again.'

I couldn't believe that Sister really meant what she said, but I was wrong! Shortly afterwards Gwyn arrived grinning from ear to ear.

'Who's been a naughty boy then? This is a first, I've never had to dump anyone in the car park before.'

To tell the truth I was thrilled to bits, anything to be away from the smells of the hospital would be marvellous. Gwyn positioned my bed onto one of the ambulance parks, chocked up the wheels and left shaking his head in disbelief.

It was a lovely clear day, and the air outside smelt pure and wonderful. After a short time a nurse appeared with a cup of tea, which I had to drink out of what looked like a small teapot, sucking the tea up through the spout whilst remaining in a lying position. I thoroughly enjoyed being outside on the car park, several people came over for a chat, all of them bemused by the story of how I got there. The old Radcliffe Infirmary in fact didn't have any facilities for patients to be outside at all. One thing I will always remember is a very small bird, I think it was a Wren, flew down and perched himself on the upper traction framework of my bed. He chirped away for several seconds before flying off again. The whole experience was wonderful and certainly had the desired effect on my mental attitude.

I returned to the ward refreshed and had a long chat with Sister Heathfield. She was very understanding and went to great lengths to explain the problems that my injuries presented. She spoke highly of my surgeon Mr Morgan, and said he is obviously very interested in your case. Not so much the individual breaks and fractures, but the complications they presented collectively as multiple injuries.

'My best advice to you is to have a chat with Mr Morgan on your own, preferably when he is not on a ward round with his staff. If you like I will let his secretary know that you would like to see him when he can find time to fit it in.'

Two days later Mr Morgan turned up at my bedside quite unexpectedly around five o'clock in the evening. He had none of his usual entourage with him, so it was obvious that he had somehow found time to visit me personally for a chat, no doubt at the request of Sister Heathfield. His expression was warm and friendly with none of the standoffishness that one often associates with highly respected professional people. Nevertheless I was just a little nervous talking to him at first, but he soon put my mind at rest when he asked Sister to "Whistle up" two cups of tea.

I apologised for wasting his time, but the remark passed him by without comment.

'I understand from Sister that you are, quite understandably, worried about what's going to become of you in the future.'

His warm voice had an immediate calming effect on me. I was filling up a bit, so I just nodded... he continued...

'Well old chap, I won't lie to you. The fact is that at this stage we can't be absolutely certain. You have a multitude of problems, but one way or another they can all be dealt with. I'm pretty certain that we can save your legs, although we will have to wait to see how well you mend.'

Sister placed the teacups on my bedside table and slipped away without a word. I took a deep breath and reluctantly asked him the question I had been longing to ask, dreading the answer I was almost certain to receive.

'I know this is a difficult question sir, but what is the best I can expect and how long do you think I will be in hospital?'

Mr Morgan passed my spouted teacup over to me, putting it carefully in my right hand. He stared at me from under his bushy eyebrows for a second or two, obviously summing up how much he thought I could take.

'You must understand that at this stage it is impossible for me to answer those questions with any degree of certainty. Your biggest problem will be the mobility of your ankles. We have plans on how to fix them up, but even if we are totally successful, your longest battle will be with the physiotherapist afterwards. It will take a great deal of courage and determination on your part. However, if all goes well, and we have every hope that it will, you should be able to walk on your own legs, possibly with the aid of a stick.' Before he had a chance to give me an indication of time, I found myself blurting out.

'But what about my job, I must get back to flying as soon as possible otherwise all my licences and qualifications will be time expired.'

I didn't realise until much later how silly my outburst must have sounded. There was a long pause, his eyes seemed to tell me something that his lips refused to say.

'Nothing's impossible old chap, just trust me, stay optimistic, and lets concentrate on one step at a time. I will do all I can surgically, the rest is up to you. Just remember these things cannot be hurried.'

Keen to extract a little more optimism from him I asked...

'But it's not absolutely impossible.... not totally out of the question is it?'

He smiled at me warmly and said...

'My dear old fellow, if it's at all possible, I'm sure you will do it.'

I could have hugged the man, nothing he had said seemed very hopeful as far as flying was concerned, but he hadn't written the idea off completely, and that was all I wanted to know.

From that day onwards we were to have many more conversations. Although he was an extremely busy man, he frequently found time to visit me for a chat, usually late in the evening when he had finished operating for the day. I can never find words to thank Mr Morgan or to explain how much those intimate chats helped me through the two long years of suffering that followed.

My friend Nils Bartleet whom I had known since we first learned to fly together, was in the aircraft with me when we crashed. He too was employed at Oxford Air Training School and was working as one of the instructors on my flight. Nils had been seriously injured in the crash and I hadn't seen him since we were in intensive care together, even then I had only caught a brief glimpse of him through a glass partition. Nils was sitting up in bed with an oxygen mask strapped to his face. He saw me when he was being wheeled into the cubicle next to mine and just managed to raise a hand to me. I can remember little more after that. He was taken to a different ward, and I heard later that he had a tube inserted into his throat, after that he was unable to speak, and communicated by writing messages on a pad. When he gained consciousness after his first operation the words he wrote on his pad were 'Am I dead?' It upsets me to write about it to this day.

At the time I didn't know how desperately ill Nils was. I had asked about him on numerous occasions, and was always told that he was OK. In fact he was far from OK and had very nearly died from the internal injuries he received when we crashed. I had been at the controls, and Nils had asked to come along for the ride. So technically, although I lost control when the main spar of the port wing broke and we hurtled down into the hangar, I had agreed to take him with me and was responsible for the condition he was in now. That thought was devastating.

One afternoon, after we had been in hospital for about six or seven weeks, Sister told me that Nils was well enough to visit me from his ward in a wheelchair, if I felt that I could cope. It was then that she explained why she had asked if I could cope.

'Nils has been very ill but is definitely on the mend now.'

I asked exactly what had happened to him, and she told me that he had suffered a ruptured liver and a torn spleen, as well as a broken ankle.

I obviously wanted to see my old friend, and prepared myself for what I imagined he would look like. Sister once again said…

'You don't have to see him if you're not up to it.'

She was a wonderful woman, and could obviously see the look of apprehension on my face, she knew perfectly well what was going through my mind.

'Yes.. yes of course, I'd love to see him' I said.

'All right, he'll be down sometime this afternoon.'

Later that afternoon, I had been given my usual painkilling injections, and was feeling a little drowsy, when suddenly I was brought to my senses.

'Look who's here to see you Ray.' I opened my eyes, and couldn't believe the sight before me. There sitting in a wheelchair was the figure of a very frail little man, slightly hunched forward, his complexion sallow and yellow. I could hardly believe that this was my old mate Nils.

My first thoughts were: 'Oh God, what on earth have I done.' Nils peered at me through glazed eyes, with a weak smile on his face. The nurse pushed his chair nearer to my bed, and he held out a trembling hand towards me. I caught hold of him; my eyes over-brimmed with tears, and blurted out 'Hello mate.' Nils slowly scribbled something on his pad, and passed it to me, it read. 'That was a bloody awful landing Ray.'

We only stayed together for a few minutes, both of us struggling with our emotions.

'I think we have done very well for one day.'

The voice came from Nils's nurse who had stayed close by him throughout our short meeting. I looked at her to thank her for bringing Nils to see me; she too had tears in her eyes.

'Time to say goodbye for a little while, we'll come and see you again soon.'

I said cheerio as I watched this frail little chap being wheeled away. Prior to the accident he had been a very fit and active man, he was a damn good pilot and flying instructor, and if he hadn't have asked to come with me on that last flight, he wouldn't be in that awful wheelchair looking like that.

I was in a bit of a state after Nils left the ward, and an understanding staff nurse put the screens around my bed for a while.

Nils's words reminded me of the time we spent training together. Looking back it seemed to be only yesterday.

CHAPTER 8.

First Solo.

When I was learning to fly I continued with my job as a salesman, fitting in my flying lessons whenever time and available cash allowed.

My instructor Eric Stowe was an assistant instructor, as such he was not permitted to send students on their first solo flight. This meant that when the time came I would have a solo check with the CFI Mr Cockburn.

Eric had scheduled me for a CFI's check when I had only completed three hours thirty minutes flying training in Tiger Moths, of which just thirty minutes had been spent on circuits and landings. The average time to first solo on a Tiger Moth is about eight to ten hours. Obviously being a very inexperienced student pilot I had no idea that I had been put forward for a first solo check, or how ridiculous this was. It was all a bit hit and miss because my instructor never seemed to know what lesson I was up to when I arrived to fly, and always asked me what I did last time I flew. He never referred to a student's progress sheet, perhaps they didn't have such a thing in those days! Anyway, when I arrived at the airfield I was surprised to be told that I would be flying with the CFI and not my usual instructor Mr Stowe.

Before going out to the aeroplane, Mr Cockburn explained that we would first leave the circuit so that he could run quickly through all the upper air work I had been taught to date, then we would return to the airfield for a few circuits and landings.

The CFI watched me carefully whilst I carried out the external checks on Tiger Moth G-AOEL. I had hoped to fly this aeroplane, as it was the only one of the three Tiger Moths at Oxford that I hadn't flown. The aircraft had recently been purchased by the Club and instead of being red and silver like the other two Tiger Moths, it had been sprayed a beautiful light blue colour and looked magnificent.

I was a bit worried because I had never flown with anyone other than Eric Stowe. Mr Cockburn gave me the impression that he was a very stern and exacting man, whilst Eric was always relaxed and pleasant to fly with. Also I could understand Eric's instructions clearly when he spoke into the Gosport Tube. I was pretty sure Mr Cockburn would be a totally different character.

Whilst the engineer stood by ready to swing the propeller, Cockburn, affectionately known as Coey, but not to his face, climbed into the front cockpit, strapped himself in, and grumbled almost imperceptibly down the Gosport Tube…

'How do you hear me?'

I could just about understand him, and he sounded pissed off before we even started!

'Loud and clear sir' I replied.

The first thing to go wrong was the aircraft refused to start. The ground Engineer shouted to Coey informing him that the impulse on the magneto was sticking. There was a grunt from the front cockpit as the CFI undid his seat belts and climbed out again obviously in a bit of a huff!

I sat there wondering what was going to happen next. The engineer must have seen the worried look on my face and winked at me whilst Mr Cockburn was delving under the engine cover. After a few seconds he climbed back onto the wing, groped around head first in the front cockpit, eventually emerging with the stick (Control column) in his hand. He lowered himself off the wing, stumped round the front of the aeroplane, lifted the engine cover, and gave something a hearty smack with one end of the control column. There was a distinct click from somewhere inside the engine. With that he secured the engine hatch, climbed back into the cockpit, and strapped himself in again without a word to me. Finally the engine started. Apart from being nervous about flying with the boss, the engine noise made it practically impossible for me to understand a word my instructor said.

Coey carried out the magneto checks at eighteen hundred RPM; he then closed the throttle to check the tick-over. As he gave the signal for the engineer to remove the chocks from under the wheels, I saw him lean forward towards the Gosport Tube to say something to me. There followed a grumpy mumbling punctuated by a brief coughing fit. I didn't understand a word he said! Mr Cockburn then waved his hands vigorously above his head. I had never seen Eric hold his hands up like that, but common sense told me that the instruction was for me to take control. Being as nothing else was said until we reached the holding point at the end of the grass strip, I must have made the correct assumption.

We sat there for a while neither of us saying a word. Suddenly my dual control column was being waggled furiously from side to side, and the throttle, which I had set for fast tick-over, was snapped closed. I sat there wondering what the hell was up. Suddenly I heard the CFI shout full volume down his speaking tube.

'WAKE UP BOY.'

Wake up indeed, I've never been more awake in my life. I sat there scared stiff in case I did something wrong. Somehow I knew this wasn't going to be my day. I fumbled through the take-off checks and shouted down the speaking tube, which was connected directly to Coey's ears.

'READY FOR TAKE-OFF SIR.'

Nothing happened, no reply, not a sound from the front cockpit, so I started to turn the Tiger Moth to face the approach and make sure it was clear to line up, when another Tiger Moth just skimmed over our heads and landed a short distance down the airfield. This brought about an even more vigorous display of the CFI's hands, the sort of gesture that generally means... I give up!!

Eventually we got airborne. As we climbed straight ahead through 500 ft. I heard Cockburn's voice mumbling away again, sounding a bit like a poorly tuned foreign radio station, and made just about as much sense as far as I was concerned. This got me really worried because I knew that I was not going to understand anything the man said, which apart from anything else could be very dangerous. I decided to pluck up courage and shout as loud as I could down the Gosport Tube.

'I can't hear a bloody thing you're saying.... SIR.'

Strangely this had no effect at all. I began to feel miserably out of control of the situation. Thoughts of giving up flying altogether passed briefly through my mind, but I dismissed them just as quickly, after all this wasn't entirely my fault. I wondered if other students had had the same problem when flying with the CFI, I had never heard anyone mention it. Perhaps it was just me.

As we passed through 2000 ft. the CFI waggled the control column and again mumbled something quite unintelligible. He had waggled the stick so furiously I assumed that he had taken control. For once I was right. He lowered the nose of the aircraft and closed the throttle. With the engine gently ticking over I could just about understand what Coey was saying...

'I want you to climb to safety height, level out, carry out your checks and do me a spin to the right, I'll tell you when to recover. Do you understand?'

I shouted 'yes sir' down the Gosport Tube, and with that he opened the throttle fully, waggled the stick, then held his hands above his head. 'I think I'm getting the hang of this' I thought.

It was at this point I became seriously concerned. The fact was that although I had been taught how to stall an aeroplane, I had never had a lesson on spinning. The nearest I had ever got to spinning an aeroplane was when Eric Stowe, at the end of a lesson in turning, demonstrated how easy it is to get into trouble by inadvertently applying too much rudder during a turn. He had shown me how the secondary effect of the rudder would cause the aircraft to roll further and also start to descend. He then demonstrated what would happen if opposite aileron was applied to stop the rolling and the stick eased back to stop the descent. The result was that the airspeed decreased rapidly until the aircraft finally stalled and commenced spinning.

So being somewhat naïve, I assumed that the demonstration by Eric had been my spinning lesson, and that this was the manoeuvre Coey wanted me to carry out now!

All the while we were climbing to our safety height of 3000 ft. I tried to remember what Eric had shown me. I had no idea that in fact the CFI wanted me to stall the aeroplane and apply full rudder at the point of stall in order to enter a proper spin, and even if I had known, I had no idea how get out of a it!

I levelled G-AOEL out at 3000 ft. carried out my pre-stall checks, made sure my straps were very tight, and carried out a clearance turn to make sure I wasn't over a built up area and there were no approaching aircraft. I shouted into the speaking tube…

'OK sir, I'm ready to commence, are you strapped in tight?'

Again there was no reply from the great man. So I said to myself: 'Right here goes.'

There was no finesse about it; I slammed the aircraft into a steeply banked turn that Coey obviously wasn't expecting because I saw him make a grab for the padded area of the instrument panel in front of him. As the poor old Tiger Moth creaked under the strain of an over-banked turn, the nose dropped viciously and I hauled back on the stick as hard as I could! I remember involuntary blurting out … 'Oh Christ!' as the aircraft flicked over onto it's back and hung upside-down for a couple of seconds. Then as if determined to get it's own back on me for grossly mishandling her, she flicked back in the opposite direction and started to rotate quite violently towards the ground.

I fully expected an immediate reaction from the front cockpit, but Mr Cockburn remained silent as the little Tiger Moth continued pitching rolling and yawing on it's way down towards mother earth, the wind howling through her wing struts.

I gripped the stick tightly with one hand and held on for grim death to the side of the cockpit with the other, waiting for my instructor to shout recover. It also passed through my mind rather forcibly that I wasn't sure what to do when he did shout!

A panicky glimpse at the instruments showed the altimeter unwinding rapidly. We must have lost about a thousand feet or so when Cockburn's head appeared more prominently from the cockpit in front.

'RECOVER.'

His voice boomed out calmly and clearly through the earpieces of my flying helmet. I seemed to remember Eric had said something about opposite rudder and stick forward when recovering from a spin. But stick FORWARD when plummeting down towards the ground? Surely not!

I had to give it a go and I thanked God for the comforting knowledge that I had a very experienced instructor sitting in the front cockpit. I slammed on full rudder in the opposite direction to the spin and whacked the stick hard forward desperately hoping that this would work.

The rotating stopped alright but now we seemed to be skidding violently sideways, partially upside-down and heading towards the ground at an even more alarming rate.

'I HAVE CONTROL.'

Cockburn's voice was loud and clear.

I let go of the stick with considerable enthusiasm! Something was obviously wrong, how could I be expected to recover from a spin properly when I had never done one before?

I felt Coey straighten the rudder, roll the aircraft level and ease the Tiger Moth out of the dive. Phew!! My instructor hadn't said another word, so I thought that he expected me to take control again and shakily opened the throttle to regain the correct cruising RPM, but it was immediately slammed closed again by Cockburn, trapping my hand between the throttle lever and the mixture control.

As we were gliding quietly down I heard the indistinct mumbling of the CFI's voice. It sounded something like this...

'Blyth.. mumble.. sort you out...mumble...not bloody safe... mumble... kill yourself.'

I understood enough to know that I was in for it when we landed. Mr

Cockburn flew the aeroplane all the way back to the Airfield without another word being spoken, whilst I sat there feeling miserable, my left hand spurting warm blood into the fingers of my flying gloves.

We landed back at Kidlington, taxied to the dispersal area and stopped the engine. Coey got out and stumped back to his office without a word. He was undoubtedly a brilliant pilot with several thousand hours flying experience on Tiger Moths, so I knew that whatever scrape I got myself into in the air, I was perfectly safe whilst he was with me. Nevertheless I was still annoyed because the only type of spinning I had been shown was spinning off a turn, and that had been a demonstration in which I took no part.

When I finally plucked up enough courage to follow Coey into the Club, Sandy was there pouring a much needed mug of tea, which she handed to me.

'How did you get on Ray?' she said...

'Don't ask' I whispered as I sat down quietly to wait for the inevitable bollocking.

At that point I could hear loud voices coming out of the CFI's office. Sandy could see I looked a little upset and said...

'Eric's in there with the boss, don't worry, he'll be out to see you in a moment.'

'Oh God!' was all I could say.

Eric emerged from the CFI's office looking quite upset.

'There's been a bit of a cock-up Ray, that spinning fiasco was definitely not your fault old chap.'

Was I pleased to hear those words?

Determined to get things right, I returned to the airfield the next day for another lesson. The surface wind was within limits for the Tiger Moth. So I was able to have a full hours spinning lesson with Eric plus a couple of circuits and landings. Once I had been shown what spinning was all about, I could certainly understand Cockburn's frustration with me the previous day.

The following afternoon I found myself back at Kidlington Airfield climbing into the rear cockpit of G-AOEL with Mr Cockburn sitting in the front seat ready to check me out again. The sky was scattered with streaks of gloomy grey stratus cloud occasionally allowing a glimpse of a pale wintry sun to shine through, typical conditions for the time of year. Fortunately the surface wind was steady at about eight knots and blowing straight down the runway. Conditions were in fact perfect for circuits and bumps in a Tiger.

I had a full and very detailed briefing from Coey this time, and knew exactly what was expected of me. He also surprised me by apologising for the events that occurred during our previous flight together, and said that under the circumstances I should never have been put up for a pre-solo check. Pre Solo Check? Until that moment I thought it had been a CFI's progress check and had nothing to do with sending me solo.

This time everything went well with the upper air work, and after half an hour we returned to the airfield for a few circuits and landings.

The first landing I thought was quite good, it didn't bounce, although I did have a bit of a problem keeping absolutely straight after the landing. There are no brakes on a Tiger Moth, so after landing the only thing that keeps the aeroplane straight on the ground is the airflow over the rudder. Consequently as the aircraft slows down after landing, the airflow decreases and the rudder becomes less effective, which in turn calls for a more aggressive use of the rudder controls.

We taxied back to the holding point again, and after carrying out the pre-take-off checks I lined G-AOEL up on the runway and took off. All went well until I got to the stage when you round out just above the ground and wait for the aeroplane to start to sink. The idea then is to hold off as long as possible without gaining height until the aircraft stalls and sinks gently onto the runway on all three points. (The two main wheels and the tail skid). If however you start to raise the nose of the aeroplane before she starts to sink, the end result is that you start to gain height again. Sadly on this occasion that's exactly what did happen. We floated over the ground with the throttle closed and I misjudged the rate of sink easing the stick back too early which caused the aeroplane to climb. Now the correct thing for a student to do at this point is open up the throttle and go round the circuit again. Did I do that? No! Instead I tried to be bloody clever and copy something I had seen my instructor do when I had rounded out a bit too high previously. I noticed that he had lowered the nose slightly, given the engine a short burst of power, which corrected the situation and allowed me to continue with a second crack at the landing. So this time when I rounded G-AOEL out too quickly and began to gain height, I decided to show Coey how clever I was.

I opened the throttle giving the engine a good burst of power, but omitted to lower the nose a little. Instead of helping the situation of course, it made things ten times worse! The aeroplane shot up another thirty feet into the air, so when I closed the throttle instead of being just above the ground, the aircraft was about to stall at the height of a two-storey building! It could only have been split seconds before the aeroplane would have thrown itself into the ground when Cockburn shouted...

'I HAVE CONTROL' at the same time applying full power and saving us from a potentially nasty arrival.

It was just about the most stupid thing I could have done, but it taught me a lesson. A lesson that I have passed on to all the flying instructors I have trained since. 'Students will always copy their instructor, so never do anything whilst you are instructing that you don't want your students to copy.'

Coey never lost his cool, he simply pointed out how dangerous it was to mess around with the throttle whilst attempting to land a Tiger Moth.

'I suppose you have seen Stowe doing that sort of thing' he said. 'Just remember that your instructor is far more experienced than you'll ever be, he will occasionally use his skills to avoid an accident, never try to copy him.'

In a funny way the incident and Mr Cockburn's somewhat calm reaction to it made me feel a lot more relaxed about flying with him. From there on the lesson went well. I had completed three or four good landings, and also carried out a practice engine failure after take-off procedure, when Coey asked me to taxi back to the holding point again for another take-off

I had reached the markers and turned the aeroplane crosswind and waited for my instructor to tell me to take-off. But Coey was undoing his safety harness and getting out. He removed the seat and control stick from his cockpit, secured the harness then came back to speak to me.

'I want you to carry out one more circuit and landing, this time on your own. The only difference you will notice is that without my modest weight the aeroplane will lift off earlier than before, and when you round out for the landing, the aeroplane will float for a longer time. If you are in any doubt about the way the landing is going, don't f---- about with the throttle, go round again.'

With that he wished me good luck and started to walk back towards the Club.

As he spoke I could feel my pulse rate quickening. I watched Coey for a moment as he walked away. Suddenly he stopped, put the cushions and stick he had removed from the front cockpit onto the ground, removed his flying helmet and sat down on the grass by the side of the runway.

I systematically ran through the pre-take-off checks... Trimmer set two thirds forwards. Throttle friction nut finger tight. Mixture fully rich. Fuel turned on and sufficient in the tank for the intended flight, I looked up at the fuel tank situated between the upper wings and checked the tiny needle against the tail down graduations of the tubular glass fuel gauge, it was showing about three quarters full, sufficient for over an hours flight. I remember thinking: 'that should be enough Ray boy, it only takes five minutes to fly a circuit!' I continued with the checks. Auto slats unlocked. Free movement of the compass verge ring and apparently serviceable. Altimeter set to zero. Engine oil pressure normal. Hatches secured. Harness correctly fastened and done up tight, and finally, full and free motion of the controls. I looked back at Coey again, he was still sitting on the grass. I turned the aeroplane to make sure the approach was clear, took two or three deep breaths and taxied onto the runway.

Everything I had been taught was running in detailed sequence through my mind…. Line up with the runway and run forward for a few yards to make sure you're correctly lined up and the tail skid is straight. Select a point ahead to keep straight on, then open the throttle smoothly to the full throttle position, keeping straight with rudder.

The engine seemed to snarl back at me louder than usual as we slowly began to move forward. Then things began to happen much more quickly. I eased the stick gently forwards and the tail popped up giving me perfect vision ahead. It seemed strange not to see my instructor's head poking out of the cockpit in front of me, strange but great. I kept the aeroplane running straight down the runway with gradually lessening movements of the rudder, then, with an almost imperceptible backward pressure on the stick, we were airborne souring graciously upwards towards a watery sun… a truly unforgettable and magic moment.

As we passed through 300 ft. I locked the auto-slats and adjusted the trim lever at the same time making sure we were still climbing straight ahead. A small adjustment to the pitch attitude of the aeroplane was necessary to keep the airspeed constant at 55 knots.

I was flying on pure adrenaline, the slipstream beating against my leather helmet and goggles. Since a child I had dreamed of this moment and that one day I would roll and loop my tiny aeroplane high amongst the towering cumulus clouds that stand like mythical castles guarding the crisp clear blueness of the heavens, and now my dreams were beginning to come true.

Keeping a good lookout for other aircraft, at 500 ft. I started a climbing turn to the left rolling out on the crosswind leg and checking that I was tracking at ninety degrees to the runway. Then approaching 1000 ft. I began to level out and throttle back to 1900 RPM. We were in balance, trimmed for level flight and turning down wind. It was all happening so quickly.

Down wind now, landing checks complete. We passed over the cement works chimney, affectionately known as "Smokey Joe", it's pure white smoke curling lazily into the sky. In the distance I could see 'Blenheim Palace', home of Sir Winston Churchill, it's immaculately laid out grounds no more than two miles from the airfield boundary. But no time for all that, now the all-important decision of where to turn on to the base leg and prepare the aircraft for landing had to be made. I remembered my instructor's words. 'When you appear to be one wings width past the threshold end of the duty runway start turning on to the base leg.'

My little blue Tiger Moth responded instantly to the slightest pressure on the controls. It seemed that without an instructor on board both aeroplane and pilot were more alert. Finally we were on the approach to land. Auto-slats unlocked, throttle closed and the engine ticking over beautifully with that magic sound of the sound of the slipstream whistling happily through the wing-struts.

Nicely lined up with the runway, airspeed 55 knots, and trimmed to glide. The windsock still showing a light breeze straight down the runway, perfect. As we passed over the threshold at about 100 ft., I saw Coey standing up now and watching me. 'Dear God... I've got to get this right!' About twenty feet above the ground I commenced a gentle round out, floating level at about two feet above the surface of the grass runway. The noise of the wind whistling through the struts gradually died away, all that could be heard now was the gentle throbbing of the 120 horsepower Gypsy Major engine as it ticked over contentedly.

I remembered Coey's words…

'Don't be caught out, without my weight in the aeroplane it will float for a longer length of time before it starts to sink.'

How right he was, we seemed to float forever. I knew if I started to get the stick back too early we would climb, that's the last thing I wanted, and if I got the stick back too late we would bounce all the way down the runway, and I certainly didn't want that to happen either. As the airspeed slowly decreased I felt her start to sink. I eased the stick back slowly until I felt it hard back against the seat. Then to my delight I felt the wheels rumbling on the grass surface of the runway.

It was all over far too quickly. I can't really explain how I felt at that moment. It was a mixture of wanting to shout out with joy, and bursting into tears. In fact I did neither! I taxied back to dispersal weaving from side to side to ensure the way ahead was clear. As we stopped I saw Tony the engineer walking towards me carrying the wheel chocks. I knew that the

CFI would be watching me although I couldn't actually see him, so I made sure that the shut down procedures were done as per the book. Then Mr Cockburn seemed to appear from nowhere. He checked that I had switched the ignition switches off, straightened the propeller, and then came over to me. I was still sitting in the cockpit grinning from ear to ear and trying to take it all in. Cockburn shook me warmly by the hand and said…

'Congratulations young man, now we can continue with the course and teach you how to fly properly.'

It was some time before I learned that Mr Charles Cockburn had been the Chief Test Pilot at Kidlington during the war, when the airfield was used as a maintenance unit for servicing military aircraft.

CHAPTER 9.

The Covert Feast.

Robin Melville, the young RAF Officer who occupied one of the four beds in the small annex to C ward, met his fate in a flying accident when he was stationed at RAF Little Rissington undergoing a course of instructor training. The aircraft he was flying, a D.H. Chipmunk, crashed on the RAF Airfield at Morton-in-the-Marsh. Robin escaped with serious injuries to his spine, that in all probability would leave him paralysed from the waist downwards for the rest of his life. Sadly the instructor flying with him was killed instantly on impact.

Robin had spent a considerable time in the intensive care unit at the Radcliffe before the doctor's considered he was well enough to be moved to a ward. He had now recovered sufficiently to be transferred to the RAF rehabilitation hospital at Stoke Mandeville. So an unofficial farewell party for Robin had been planned for the four occupants of the annex.

The chap who had taken over George's bed was a very pleasant young man by the name of John Villarnis. John had come to grief on his motorcycle, which left him with a broken femur in his left leg. He was a good looking chap, about eighteen years old, slight of build, with long curly dark brown hair. John was quietly spoken, smiled a lot and never seemed to moan or grumble about anything. When he first arrived he seemed to be more worried about the state of his motorcycle than himself. Shortly after arriving in hospital, someone had given John a small bright red woollen monkey as a get well present, which the nurses had tied to the traction apparatus supporting his leg. Both John and the monkey were very popular with the young nurses.

John turned out to be a keen amateur photographer with great ambitions to travel the world as a professional in this field. Later I will explain how his keenness to take "unusual" photographs with me acting as his assistant, got us both into a spot of bother!

The idea of a farewell party for Robin had been suggested by our friend and favourite porter, Gwyn Jones. This man had a heart of gold and would go out of his way to help anyone, especially long term patients and children. For instance, he once turned up at my bedside carrying a very small boy from the children's ward in his arms. The little fellow was apparently mad about aeroplanes. Gwyn had told him that there were a couple of pilots in 'C' Ward Annex, and the Sister in charge of the children's ward kindly allowed Gwyn to bring him over to see us in the hope that it would cheer him up a bit.

Rupert was a cracking little boy with curly blond hair and very rosy cheeks. We had a long chat and I remember his first question was 'What's it like to fly a plane?' His little face lit up as I told him how great it was to soar up into the clouds and sometimes skim the trees and chimney-pots like a large bird. I told him that one day, if he really wanted to, he would more than likely fly an aeroplane himself. When he left he gave me the sort of hug you would die for, then Gwyn, who seemed equally happy, took him back to the children's ward. From then on Gwyn frequently brought me little pictures that Rupert had drawn depicting crashed aeroplanes with masses of blood drawn in red crayon all over the page!

Gwyn, who was a very kind and generous person, loved children, he also loved horses and frequently spent his hard earned wages in the local bookmakers. As far as I could make out Gwyn didn't win very often, but when he did back a winner it was a safe bet that he would spend the whole of his winnings on little treats for the occupants of the children's ward.

Just before Robin Melville was due to be transferred to the paraplegic hospital at Stoke Mandeville, Gwyn was fortunate enough to have a win on the horses. He came into the annex looking very pleased with himself, announcing, that with Sister's permission, he intended to organise a "clandestine" party for the four occupants of the OM as a sort of farewell party for Robin. We all tried to discourage him from spending his hard earned winnings on us, but Gwyn would have none of it. His idea was to provide us with a nice meal and a glass or two of wine, all to be served in great secrecy to avoid the displeasure of the less fortunate patients in the main part of the ward. The operation, code named "Blow-out" would take place after lights out. Sister was duly approached about the idea, and probably because we were all long-term patients, agreed to turn a blind eye to the proceedings providing we were all restricted to one glass of wine, fortunately the size of the glass was never mentioned. We also had to promise that we didn't disturb the patients in the main section of "C" ward. The covert operation was planned to take place on the evening prior to Robin's departure.

Gwyn set off to purchase four fillet steaks, some vegetables, and a couple of bottles of wine with his winnings. He also mustered up the help of a friend who worked in the hospital kitchens and agreed to stay on late to cook the meal which was to be served immediately after official lights out. The tricky bit was devising a method of getting the cooked meal past the twenty or so patients in the main part of the ward without any of them noticing! We left the problem to Gwyn's ingenuity and waited for the day to arrive with great excitement, desperately hoping that the four of us would remain well enough to make the banquet a success.

The plans for operation "Blow-out" were on schedule and appeared to be going well, although three of us were still receiving strong medication. Fortunately none of us were scheduled for a visit to the operating theatre at the time. Our only concern was Stanley the ex policeman, who was suffering from the severe head injuries he sustained in a car crash. His moods were somewhat unpredictable, he would sometimes go for days without any sign of trouble, then he would suddenly pass out without any warning. Only a few days previously he had frightened everyone when he collapsed headfirst into a bowl of soup. One moment he seemed OK, the next he was face down drowning in a bowl of tomato soup. We watched in horror as he enthusiastically inhaled one of Heinz 57 varieties in through his nose with a noise that resembled water escaping down a partly blocked sink. Then as the bowl almost emptied in one suck, we were all astonished to see Stan blow the lot out again replenishing the bowl almost to the brim, scarcely spilling a drop. In those days we didn't have the luxury of an alarm button for each bed, so we all started shouting as loud as we could for a nurse. Robin, who was in the closest bed to Stan tried to push the soup bowl from under Stan's nose with the aid a crutch he kept by his bed. Unfortunately his enthusiastic thrust missed its mark and the rubber end of the crutch poked poor old Stan in the ear. Robin's efforts did however succeed in forcing Stan to slump over sideways gasping for breath. Fortunately nurses were quickly on the scene.

Although we realised that Stan would not be permitted his one glass of wine during operation "Blow-out", we hoped he would be well enough to enjoy a mouthful or two of fillet steak. Incidentally, because of the tomato soup episode, Stan was hence fourth nicknamed No 57.

Finally the great day arrived. In the morning Sister announced that she had delegated one of the staff nurses to be present throughout the proceedings for obvious safety reasons. We all thought that this was an excellent idea, and asked if we could have one each! Our request was ignored.

Valerie, who knew all about our planned midnight feast, turned up early and spent most of visiting time warning me of the dangers of drinking anything remotely alcoholic whilst on medication. I tried to pacify her with endless promises, crossing my heart etc. and begging her not to cause any trouble with the Sister.

At last the visitors left, the bedtime medicine round had been completed, and individual medical problems had been dealt with. Finally the lights of the ward were dimmed.

I looked across at No 57; he seemed to be alright, although the previous night he had given us yet another ghastly fright. We were all asleep, it must have been around midnight, when Stan suddenly let out the most horrific blood-curdling scream I have ever heard. It was a terrifying sound, the like of which I never want to hear again as long as I live. Unfortunately it didn't end there, the scream was followed by a pathetic plea for mercy, followed by crying and sobbing. We all sat bolt upright in bed feeling very concerned for Stan. Everyone breathed a sigh of relief when the house doctor arrived on the scene, drew the screens around Stan's bed and administered something to make him more comfortable. In the morning dear old Stan quite unnecessarily apologised to us for the disturbance.

'I'm sorry chaps, I'm afraid that I live in terror of going to sleep these days, I would rather be dead than keep having these bloody nightmares.'

His voice quivered as he spoke…

'I will never forget, and I can never forgive those bastards for what they did to us.'

We listened as Stan told us that he had been one of those poor devils that had been captured and tortured by the Japanese during WW2. He never mentioned the grim details of what happened to him, he didn't have to, his screams said it all.

But that was last night, thankfully No 57 seemed to be much better now, and like the rest of us, he was looking forward to the arrival of our late night feast.

We all wondered how a cooked meal could be smuggled past the less fortunate patients in the main ward who would be settled down for the night. We didn't have long to wait.

In the distance the sound of a trolley could be heard approaching the ward.

The rubber doors to the annex swung open and one of our staff nurses appeared grinning from ear to ear. Then to our astonishment Gwyn emerged wearing the full regalia of a surgeon about to operate, pushing a surgical trolley covered with a white linen cloth. I wondered how many patients in the main ward had been fooled by his ingenious scheme, surely the delicious smell of cooked steak and onions emanating from the trolley as it was wheeled past them on its way to the OM had been a bit of a give-away!

Sister, who was now off duty, had thoughtfully left a few candles with the night staff; these were lit and placed on our lockers. When the bedside lamps were switched off, our small four-bedded room took on a warm friendly glow.

A champagne cork popped, and we were on our way.

Most of us had been deprived of alcohol for months. We were all on drugs of one kind or another, so the effect of even the smallest amount of alcohol took immediate effect.

John Villarnis started the ball rolling when, halfway through eating his deliciously cooked steak, he started to sing an unrecognisable song with indecipherable words that gradually faded away as he fell asleep. Stan ate a small piece of steak, had a sip of champagne from Robin's glass when the nurse wasn't looking, then called for a bed pan and fulfilled the task in hand.

The effect of Stan's predicament was immediate. An odorous mixture of steak, onions and crap instantly altered the ambience of the room. But stout-hearted as ever, the occupants of the OM pressed on regardless. I'm afraid that Robin and I both disgraced ourselves that evening. Robin drank several "small helpings" of wine together with one sizeable glass of champagne. He then had to be muffled by the nurse whilst attempting to entertain us with a boisterous rugby type song. He finally fell asleep having first moistened his bed due to a misfortunate inaccurate aiming accident! Finally I was apparently totally plastered after consuming half a glass of champagne, and having enjoyed several mouthfuls of beautifully grilled steak, was saved from falling out of bed by the quick reflex actions of dear old Gwyn whilst demonstrating my aerobatic skills as a pilot with exaggerated hand gestures.

But the evenings entertainment wasn't quite over. I was suddenly afflicted with an acute attack of very noisy hiccups, that, in spite of all the customary methods of cure, just went on and on and on. Finally the duty doctor was called in to give me an injection that knocked me out completely in a flash.

Needless to say the party was deemed to be a great success. The night nurse who courageously looked after us throughout the proceedings, informed us later that Gwyn had refused to leave the ward until he was certain that we were all sound asleep and safely settled for the night. What a very caring and generous man he was.

We were all sorry when Robin left us the following morning to take up the great challenge that awaited him at Stoke Mandeville Hospital. He was a very charismatic chap, the life and soul of the OM. It is always very sad to see a newly made-up bed where an old friend used to be.

The nurse informed us that another long term patient would be joining us in the OM. Robin's bed was removed altogether. A porter returned pushing a large bed that had an impressive array of pipes, wires, tubes and bottles attached to its framework. Our loveable Sister who was in attendance announced...

'This is Claude who has just been released from intensive care, he has come to join you in the annex. I hope YOU LOT are NOT going to give him a hard time.'

The replies came thick and fast.

'Absolutely Not'... 'Good lord never'... 'You know us better than that Sister.'

Claude was encased from head to feet in plaster. His head was just visible at one end and his toes poked out at the other. The poor chap looked as if he had been hit by a train or maybe flattened by a steamroller. He lay there silently on top of his bedclothes with his eyes closed, apparently asleep. John stared at him for a moment then whispered...

'He looks half dead to me!'

A few days passed during which time our new ward-mate said very little. Stan had another of his bad turns, John upset the lot of us by contracting a bad attack of diarrhoea and I became increasingly worried about a continuous burning feeling in the back of my right thigh.

The gaping tear where my fractured femur had penetrated the skin in my right leg had been stitched up at the same time as the leg was put into traction. Since then the other injuries sustained to the Tibia and Fibula of both legs had been operated on, but the bandage around my right thigh had remained untouched. Repeated x-rays had been taken to see how the femur was mending. So, in spite of the stinging pain, I assumed the wound concealed by the bandages was healing satisfactorily.

Late one night the duty nurse came into the annexe accompanied by a doctor that I had not seen before. The room was in darkness except for the dimmed night lighting. As she approached my bed I pretended to be asleep. She shone her torch on me for a brief moment and whispered to the doctor…

'This patient has serious multiple injuries, I'm afraid there is not much more we can do for him.'

She moved on silently to the next bed with no idea that I had overheard her comments. I lay there wide-awake for the rest of the night shocked by the conversation I had overheard. My mind ran riot, I reasoned with myself that there could obviously be more than one way to interpret what she had said, but considering the burning pains in my thigh, I thought the worst.

The following morning the atmosphere in the ward seemed totally different to me. My mind was in turmoil. All I could think about was those fear-provoking words I had overheard during the doctors round the previous night…. '*I'm Afraid there's not much more we can do for him.*' I was convinced there was something seriously wrong with me that, for some reason, they had decided not to tell me about.

Moments later another jab of burning pain in my thigh added conviction to my thoughts of gangrene or tumour. I was desperate to know the truth yet too afraid to ask Sister for fear of what the answer would be.

The days dragged on and on during which time my mental state deteriorated until, in the end, I plucked up enough courage to investigate the matter for myself.

Initially the bandages had been applied tightly to secure the broken femur whilst the leg was in traction, but now the swelling had gone down significantly and the bandages had become reasonably slack.

I tried to convince myself that the pain was probably caused by one or more stitches catching on the bandage. But to make absolutely sure I decided to wriggle my hand gently down between the bandage and the back of my leg. This was quite difficult to do with my leg still in traction. Eventually a sharp pain signified that my fingers were in contact with the wound. There seemed to be no sign of any stitches but the whole area was extremely hot and very sticky. When I withdrew my hand I got the shock of my life. It was completely covered with the foulest smelling bright yellow substance that looked similar to the yokes of several eggs. This horrible sight, coupled with the night nurse's conversation with the doctor, rendered my morbid thoughts into overdrive. I was convinced that things were far worse than I had been told.

God knows why, I stupidly tried to keep the discovery to myself, but later that day the ward help lady that used to make our beds remarked on the unusual smell that persisted even after the bedclothes had been changed. My face must have portrayed my feelings because she asked me what was troubling me?

At that point I could hold back no longer and just blurted out…

'I think I've had it. I'm sure I've got gangrene or maybe something worse, but please don't say anything to Sister, I'm sure she already knows about it and doesn't want me to find out.'

Of course the poor woman went straight to Sister, who was at my bedside within seconds. I told her of my discovery and said that I fully understood why they didn't want me to know I was probably going to die. Sister put her hands on her hips and gave me one of her old fashioned looks.

'That's the first I've heard about it, we'll end all this rubbish once and for all.'

She left my bedside returning moments later with a surgical tray. Having pulled the screens around my bed, she asked…

'How long have you felt this burning pain?'

'About two or three weeks'

I winced as I knew she would go ballistic…

'How many times do I have to tell you that if there is anything, and I mean *ANYTHING* wrong, you tell *ME*.'

Sister was bending over my leg cutting away some of the bandages and removing the packing. Suddenly she stopped, and looked quite concerned at what she saw.

'I would like the doctor to take a look at this, I'll be back in a couple of minutes.'

Sister left and returned with Mr Morgan's Registrar. He examined the wound, and announced that he was damned! Then left the ward taking my records with him.

He returned to my bedside a few minutes later accompanied by Mr Morgan himself.

'For some inexcusable reason the notes concerning the wound in your thigh were not written up old chap. I'm afraid the stitches have pulled out, and the wound has become infected! It will need to be cleaned up properly and re-packed from the inner part of the wound first in order for it to heal properly.'

Sister, having decided to do the job herself, returned with kidney dish, masses of cotton wool, a bottle of antiseptic, rolls of bandages, some scissors and a very long pair of nasty looking tweezers. The next few minutes were not very pleasant for either of us as she removed all the fowl smelling puss from the wound, trimmed off the dead skin and packed the hole with masses of sterilised bandage. She looked at me like a mother sometimes looks at her child when he's been naughty and said…

'Now what's the matter?'

Almost at the point of tears I said…

'Is it cancer?'

She straightened up and pointed a finger at me,

'Ray…'

She paused for a second, then, changing her attitude, said in a much softer voice.

'No dear, it's not cancer! Neither should it have been allowed to get to this dreadful state.'

With tears welling up in my eyes, I told Sister about the conversation I had previously overheard between the nurse and the doctor on their night round, and how I had put two and two together. Sister obviously felt sorry for me, a rare occurrence as far as I was concerned. She smiled stroking my head.

'You poor thing, I can understand how you must have felt. I expect the nurse was referring to the fact that there was little we could do until the injuries to the bones in your legs start to mend. Even so she had no right to say anything like that in front of you, even if she did think you were asleep, I must have a word with her.'

That night I slept well.

During the time I was a patient in the Radcliffe I met, or in some cases heard from a distance, several patients with various musical talents.

One young man, somewhere down the far end of the main ward, used to play his guitar in the evenings after our visitors had left. Usually he played blues music very quietly until just before lights out. Someone else used to sing a bit, and another chap occasionally attempted to play a tune on his mouth organ.

We were talking about this one evening when Claude, who had been feeling much better since his plaster cast had been removed, astonished everybody by announcing that he too was musical.

We always thought of him as a bit of a rough diamond and were surprised to learn that he was apparently a musician. John Villarnis asked him what sort of music he was interested in. His answer was somewhat surprising.

'I only plays one tune.'

Keen to know the extent of his musical prowess, John asked him if it was a classical tune?

'I plays God Save the Queen. Usually limited to the first line I'm afraid, depends on my fitness at the time.'

We were all mystified by Claude's remarks. John, eager to learn more, asked what type of instrument he used to play? The reply was most unexpected.

'I uses my backside matey, I does it by applying various pressures whilst breaking wind.'

'You mean you fart the national anthem?' John asked disbelievingly.

'That's right matey.'

Our hearts sank. We took him at his word, hoping we would never be called upon to judge his skills.

Alas, one quiet evening, after an excellent supper of beans on toast, Claude proudly announced, that whilst there were no visitors around, he would give us a demonstration of his expertise and attempt to entertain us with a rendition of the first line of the National Anthem. We pleaded with him not to exert himself, but sadly he insisted.

Claude pulled himself up in his bed, cocked his bottom over to a forty-five degree angle to ensure we would benefit from the full volume of his instrument, and pulled back the bed-clothes to reveal a large bare bottom.

His face contorted as the first note blasted out with gusto. Stan, being in the closest bed to Claude, slipped deeper under his sheets. The second note echoed across the ward, it was half a tone out, but quickly corrected.

I turned to look at John Villarnis who was sitting bolt upright in his bed with an expression of horror on his face. He glanced nervously at the door, no doubt praying that Claude's performance could not be heard in the main ward. With the speed of sound John's head swivelled back to look at Claude as the third staccato note echoed forth, clear and sharp as the first, but ending in what could only be described as a bit of a splutter, and a few smacking noises, which sounded like a slow round of applause.

'Bloody Hell!'…So that's what they mean by playing by ear' John remarked.

I looked over towards Stan's bed, but he had completely disappeared under his bedclothes.

Claude, fists clenched tight, face bright red, was struggling to produce the fourth note. He took a deep breath and screwed his face up until it was purple. We sat there in breathless (Literally) anticipation, but the end came suddenly. Claude produced a high-pitched squeak followed by a bubbling sound whilst his eyebrows shot up in surprise. There was no question about it; Claude had disgraced himself filling the ward with the most obnoxious smell.

Behind drawn screens, Claude received a severe telling off from a very irritate nurse, whose unenviable task it was to clean him up and change his bedding. Later he tried to explain his failure by the use of technical terms!…

'Them lower notes is the hardest.'

We took his word for it and were relieved that the performance was over, hopefully never to be repeated. Since that day, I have never listened to the National Anthem without thinking of Claude.

Obviously hospital life is not all laughs, quite the reverse. Sometimes the weirdest things occur which are difficult to understand at the time and can be very frightening.

For instance one night I was awakened from a deep sleep by a gentle tap on the shoulder. Warily I opened my eyes, fully expecting to see the nurse with my three hourly top-up injection, but as my eyes gradually focused in the dimly lit ward I saw something that made my blood run cold. I had never taken the existence of alien life seriously, and always said that seeing is believing as far as I was concerned. But there it was, the indisputable authenticity I hoped I would never live to see. The hideous shape of an alien was standing by my bed glaring down at me with soulless eyes! To say I was petrified would be the understatement of all time. A tall completely naked form with several long glistening antennae protruding from its head stooped over me motionless and silent. I froze to the sheets, unable to move or even shout for help.

Apart from his eyes that reflected the dim orange ward lights, his face appeared to be featureless. To my horror he started to move. I reckon there was about twenty or so of these antennae each about twelve inches long, that waved about as the alien creature slowly bent down towards me and tilted his head to one side. He remained completely silent, and as he drew closer I detected a truly wild look in his eyes. When his head was only a few inches from mine he slowly pointed to his lips!

'Good God' I thought, 'the bloody thing wants me to kiss it!' Terrified, and totally incapable of moving, I had no choice but to consider the alien's diabolical request seriously. What would it do to me if I refused?

This may sound funny, but I can assure the reader that this really happened, and being awakened from a deep sleep in the middle of the night by a seemingly shapeless form with antennae protruding from it's skull, and wanting to be kissed, is anything but humorous.

'Here goes' I thought, 'anything to get rid of this thing.'

I closed my eyes and puckered up my lips, waiting for the worst! Suddenly a bright light shone in my face. 'This is it' I thought: 'I'm going to be beamed up and taken to another planet.'

'What on earth do you two think you're doing?'

A sharp, clear female voice echoed through the night. I opened my eyes to see the duty night nurse standing by my bed holding a torch. Then she whispered…

'Come along Jimmy you are a naughty boy.'

She led naughty Jimmy, my terrifying alien, away leaving me feeling like pratt of the month! Ten minutes later the nurse returned to explain that poor old Jimmy was from the neurological ward and had recently had a brain operation that left him temporarily unable to speak. So he had developed a habit of getting up in the night and wandering around his ward cadging cigarettes. This time he had managed to slip out of the neurological ward unnoticed and descended on the annex to C ward where he proceeded to wake me up for a cigarette! Apparently the antennae were the ends of long metal stitches that were holding a part of his skull in place until the wound healed. Thank God I never kissed him!

CHAPTER 10.

Eminent Visitor.

After the first thirteen weeks of hospital life, the good news came through that recent x-rays of the femur in my right leg appeared to show the bone was mending and within the next week or so would probably be taken out of traction and placed in a full length plaster. Having been physically attached to my bed via wires, pulleys and a heavy weight for four months, it would be sheer ecstasy to be able to sleep on my side again.

I would then have both legs encased in full-length plasters from the tip of my toes to the top of my thighs. But unfortunately the breaks in the lower part of my legs and ankles were still mobile and not mending as expected. After such a long period I was beginning to feel a bit depressed.

It was a few days after my latest visit to the x-ray department when my suspicions were proved to be correct and my surgeon Mr Morgan brought me the bad news.

'I'm afraid that the operations I carried out on your left and right Tibia's have not been as successful as I had hoped old chap.'

Removing a bundle of x-rays from the large brown envelope he was carrying, Mr Morgan selected two and held them up to the light so that I could see.

'Due to the end-on impact your legs received, both of your tibia bones received severe pressure fractures that shattered them into dozens of small fragments, and it's proving to be a problem to get them to knit together and mend. So I have decided to take a small section of bone from your Pelvis and graft it into your legs.'

My face must have portrayed that I was not overjoyed by the news, so my surgeon leaned forward to accentuate the point he was about to make.

'Don't be despondent, you're a tough little chap, and between us we'll get you up and going again.'

After many painful weeks in hospital, it was shattering news to be told that I was virtually back to square one again. I clung to Mr Morgan's every word. There was still a good chance that I wouldn't have any amputations.

It was late the same evening, around nine o'clock when Mr Morgan returned to my bedside. He looked very tired and must have spent most of the day in the operating theatre, yet he still found time to make a special effort to come and see me without the formality of a ward round. It was typical of this very caring man.

'I have given your case some thought Raymond, and this time, instead of grafting bone from your hip I intend to use bone from the hospital bone bank, you've had enough problems without me making it worse.'

I was amazed to learn that there was such a thing as a bone bank, and shuddered to think where the bone actually came from.

'I will also be arranging for you to be transferred to the Nuffield Orthopaedic Hospital once your femur comes out of traction in a few weeks time. They have all the specialist equipment for long term orthopaedic patients. You will be very comfortable there.'

As he left my bedside he added...

'Now don't lay there worrying old chap. Leave all that to me.'

There was always encouragement and optimism in his voice.

The idea of leaving the Radcliffe was a bit of a shock. I had been nursed with great care and affection and I would certainly miss all the staff, all with the exception of Matron with whom I had suffered several altercations.

Gwyn, our great friend and head porter, used to spend some of his off duty time playing cards with me, nothing serious, just a few coppers would change hands. He was a truly great guy, and because my left arm and hand were still in plaster, he made a special "Card Holder" out of wood. It stood quite firmly on the bed and held the cards displayed in the way that one normally holds a hand of cards.

On this particular occasion Gwyn had lost every hand we played, and when this sort of thing happened, he always pretended to be upset and annoyed. True to form he accused me of cheating, which of course called for sarcastic and unsympathetic remarks from the rest of the mob in our ward. Unfortunately he was unable to try and win his money back as he was about to go on duty again. To get his own back on me for winning, he pushed my bed into the centre of the ward, jacked it up off its wheels and walked out!

It was just my luck that within minutes of Gwyn leaving me stuck in the middle of the ward, in walked the Matron, arms folded and looking very irritated! All my so-called mates in the ward were giggling and tittering which didn't improve matters.

'What do you think you are doing Mr Blyth?' The Matron's face showed no indication of amusement.

'I'm laying in bed Matron.'

That sounded more arrogant than I had intended and I instantly regretted my poor choice of words.

'That is rather obvious. And how did you get in the middle of my ward?'

Her face was now red with rage. At that moment one of the nurses entered the ward, took one look at my bed in the middle of the annex with matron glaring at me, and shot out again.

I obviously couldn't drop dear old Gwyn in the soup, so I told Matron that I had been asleep and had no idea how I arrived in the middle of the ward.

Sensing the very uncomfortable atmosphere, the three other patients in the annex mysteriously and somewhat suddenly had fallen asleep! Matron looked at them for a few seconds, and then as she turned to leave I believe I detected the resemblance of a smile flicker briefly across her face. Moments later a rather flustered nurse returned and pushed my bed back into its allocated position. Unfortunately this was not the last time I was to invoke Matron's displeasure.

Valerie and her daughter Laura arrived at visiting time, and to everyone's amusement Laura was carrying an enormous Sunflower that wobbled about on the end of an extremely long stalk. John Villarnis in the next bed kindly offered his empty urine bottle to be used as a bedside flowerpot for the unusual gift. The urine bottle had to be jammed upright in my bedside cabinet drawer, and the stalk of the flower leaned against the wall to stop it from toppling over, which left the large yellow flower towering over my head like an old-fashioned streetlamp. All agreed that it was indeed a magnificent sight.

Visiting time passed very quickly and soon all the visitors having had their fill of our grapes, chocolates, sweets etc. finally left the ward and peace returned, but not for long.

I was just snuggling down looking forward to reading Valerie's letter and my bedtime cup of Horlicks, when I suddenly became aware that Matron was standing at the entrance of the annex. I couldn't believe it, we hardly ever saw Matron, and today she had visited the ward twice. The huge Sunflower was now drooping over at a threatening angle just above my head, perhaps Matron wouldn't take any notice, but that was not to be the case.

Matron's eyes focused on the urine bottle poking out from inside my locker drawer. I cringed as she slowly raised her eyes to follow the line of the tall green stalk protruding from the bottle. By the time her eyes reached the huge sunflower her mouth had dropped open....time stood still. I closed my eyes and desperately hoped to wake up from the nightmare. For a moment she just stood there at the end of my bed with her arms folded, a tall slim immaculately dressed woman in her black and white starched uniform, her ghostly white face framed by neatly styled silver hair, glaring at me through gold rimmed spectacles with the severity of a Gestapo Officer.

'Mr Blyth.' she hesitated for a second. 'Do you mind telling me what that is and kindly explain how it got there?'

I swallowed hard.

'It's a Sunflower Matron.'

Before I could answer the second part of her question Matron snapped ....

'Do you try to be offensive, or does it just come naturally Mr Blyth?'

There was no sign of a smile on Matron's face this time. Not wishing to hear another word from me, Matron turned abruptly and strutted out.

Within a microsecond a very red faced Sister appeared by my bed. She removed the Sunflower and returned the urine bottle to its rightful owner. Then, straightening my bed-clothes she said...

'Somehow you have managed to get on the wrong side of Matron twice in one day, an achievement seldom accomplished by patients in my ward. You may consider this to be some kind of record, but I strongly recommend that you don't make a habit of it, and may I suggest that you apologise to Matron when she next visits the ward.'

One thing about being in hospital is that you have more than enough time to think about life and take stock of yourself. Today I was lying in bed wondering what the future held for me if I was unable to fly again, when my thoughts were gradually interrupted by the awareness of a rather unfamiliar sound. It was a sort of weird thump-clang, thump-clang noise that seemed to be approaching the annex from inside the main part of C Ward. The sound stopped just outside the flexible rubber doors of the OM. By this time most of us were intrigued to see who or what was about to enter the ward. There was a sort of confused fumbling on the far side of the doors as if someone was having difficulty opening them. Then swoosh… the doors burst open like they had been hit by a force eight gale.

For a moment I just couldn't believe my eyes, there stood Matron accompanied by a short muscular man, stooping forwards, his legs slightly apart. There was no doubt about it; it was Douglas Bader. (Later to become Sir Douglas Bader)

His keen eyes searched the ward for a second, then he muttered something to Matron who pointed at me!

The great man lurched forward heading towards my bed. I was so shocked that I quite involuntarily blurted out … 'GOOD GOD'…

'Sorry old boy, he's not here, you'll have to make do with me.'

Bader's unmistakable gruff voice sealed my state of shock, and I just sat there with my mouth wide open. He reached my bed and greeted me with a firm handshake.

'How are you old boy?' he said.

He looked me straight in the eyes with a concerned expression on his face. A tricky moment followed when Douglas Bader went to sit on the edge of my bed. Unfortunately the wheels had not been properly locked, so when he leaned against the side of the bed, the whole shooting match started to move sideways across the ward. Bader, who somehow managed to hang on, cursed as the bed slid across the floor and collided with John's bed. The sudden jolt made the traction weights hanging over the end of my bed swing like giant pendulums, causing my leg to move up and down like a village pump handle. The matter was soon rectified by Matron with the help of a nurse.

We only chatted for a short while during which time I told him about my crash and that I was still living in hope that I wouldn't have to have my legs amputated.

Bader spoke with sincerity about the importance of confidence in oneself, and the need for a positive attitude towards recovery. He assured me great advances in surgical techniques and antibiotics had been made since the days when he crashed in 1933.

'Either way, you'll have a bit of a struggle on your hands at first old boy, but stick with it, never give up hope, and you'll come through with flying colours.'

Those inspiring words, coming from a man that I admired so much, gave my confidence that added boost it so desperately needed.

He stood up to leave, paused for a moment, grinned and said…

'Then you can polish up on your formation flying!'

I couldn't believe that he had remembered our miserable efforts when the instructors at Kidlington carried out a formation flypast in his honour five years previously.

'Was it that bad sir?' I said.

He winked, patting me firmly on the shoulder and stumped out of the ward, leaving me lying there wondering if I had dreamt it all.

Bader's unannounced visit to the hospital really had nothing to do with me at all. He had in fact called at the Radcliffe to see a young boy who had had his legs amputated. Gwyn our head porter had been introduced to Bader, and it was he who mentioned that there was a pilot in C ward who had been involved in an aeroplane accident and was suffering with multiple leg injuries. So it was sheer luck that I actually came to meet the great man.

As the unmistakable clank of Bader's footsteps died away, I recalled our efforts at Oxford Air Training School when we practiced formation flying ready for the Douglas Bader fly past he had just referred to.

Oxford Air Training School, was under contract to the Ministry of Defence to train a number of students to fly under the RAF Scholarship Award Scheme. Seven of these students came from King Edward's School Oxford, which was Bader's old school. So it was arranged that these seven students would fly in a formation flypast over the School grounds accompanied by their instructors whilst Bader was attending a sports afternoon at the school. The formation was made up of six Piper Colt aircraft, with a Chipmunk aeroplane in the lead. After the flypast all the students who took part in the formation were privileged to be introduced to Douglas Bader.

The Boss of Oxford Air Training School, Mr Rex Smith selected seven instructors to fly the aircraft in formation accompanied by the seven students from King Edward's School.

The overall CI decided that it would be prudent to have a couple of practice runs before the great day itself, and how right he was!

Individually we had all done quite a lot of formation flying in the past, but none of us had flown in formation with any of the others selected for the fly past. In fact many of the chaps hadn't flown in formation for several years, since their RAF days in fact.

The Piper aeroplanes we were to fly on the day were excellent little training aircraft, but when it came to formation flying it was rather like trying to fly half a dozen umbrellas in formation!

It was a clear Summer's morning when we all piled into the briefing room at Oxford to be briefed for our first practice by our Chief Instructor Capt. Bill Jordan (Ex-RAF V Bomber Capt.).

Bill was to fly with us on the first few practice flights, but on the actual day the lead aircraft would be flown by Peter Corlett, a private pilot who owned a Chipmunk aeroplane and was a lecturer at King Edward's School, the School that our formation was to fly over during Bader's visit. Peter also ran the schools A.T.C. Squadron and it was his squadron's cadets that were training to fly at Oxford Air Training School and would be accompanying us in the aircraft during the fly-past.

The plan was for the seven aircraft to initially form up in line astern formation (One behind the other). Then change to a 'V' formation as we passed over the School's playing fields where Bader would be attending their Annual Sports Day. Not a very ambitious procedure. Simple enough I here you say. We all thought so, but it turned out to be a lot more difficult than any of us had imagined. Basically because very few of us were in current formation flying practice.

We had been briefed to take-off and climb to 1,500 ft., where we would form up initially line astern. My position was number three. When we reached a point one mile from the School, we would change to a tight 'V' formation. Then, after making a couple of orbits of the school, we would change formation back to 'line astern', returning to the airport, complete a low run past the control tower and break formation left for a stream landing. For R/T purposes, the formation was called 'Blue Section.'

As we left the briefing room and headed for our aircraft, most of us were wondering about the skills of their fellow pilots. Bill obviously insisted that the whole thing must look professional for Bader, and therefore we would be required to fly in tight formation. Anyone who has had experience in formation flying will tell you that keeping station in close formation in a light low-powered aeroplane calls for a considerable amount of concentration. We were required to remain within one aircraft's fuselage length longitudinally and half a wing length laterally whilst in the 'V' formation. When you do this type of flying all your concentration is devoted to keeping station with one other aircraft in the display, and except for the times when formation changes are being carried out, you don't take your eyes off the aircraft you are marking. That of course doesn't stop you from worrying about how bloody close the aircraft on your tail is!

Having never previously flown in formation with any of the other six chaps, I was just hoping that they were as competent as they appeared to be on the ground. No doubt they were all having similar thoughts.

So off we went. The Chipmunk was already airborne and climbing away in a shallow turn to the left, as the rest of us lined up in turn and took off. The idea now was for us to follow our allocated lead aircraft as briefed, eventually slotting in behind the Chipmunk in line astern.

That was the idea, but things didn't quite work out as planned. Whilst I was lining up for take-off, I temporarily lost sight of number two who was now airborne. I assumed he was turning left and climbing out to join up with the Chipmunk. As I became airborne I heard number four call 'rolling' and knew that he would shortly be forming up behind me. But where the hell was number two, the aeroplane I should be following? 'This is a bloody good start' I thought. I couldn't see him anywhere, and as we were briefed to maintain radio silence except for standard calls, I refrained from using the radio to find out where he was. I had little choice but to make for the Chipmunk, who I could see high up to my left, and then hang back to allow number two to slot in when he finally joined us…. BUT HE DIDN'T…. he was nowhere to be seen.

Whilst I was in a left turn I allowed myself a quick glance behind and was pleased to see that number four, flown by Johnny Johnson, an ex Lancaster pilot, had slotted in tight behind me. But there was no one else in sight anywhere in the sky other than the Chipmunk. A few more minutes passed, I was close enough to see Bill Jordan glaring at me from the cockpit of the Chipmunk. 'Not pleased' I thought. Suddenly a Colt aeroplane shot past my starboard wing tip missing it by about twenty feet. The pilot who had obviously been making an enthusiastic attempt to catch us up had misjudged our speed and approached us far too fast, the amusing thing was, he tried to slow down by quickly lowering full flap, which shot him up high above us, finally disappearing again somewhere behind me! The radio crackled for a brief second and a couple of very non-standard calls broke the radio silence…

'Is that you Eric?'… followed by…'SHIT! that was close.'

Then Oxford Control, who didn't catch any of that said…

'Aircraft calling Oxford say again your last message!'

That was enough for our leader, who by now was smouldering in his cockpit and obviously getting fed up of flying around in circles waiting for the rest of the formation to appear. His voice boomed out over the radio.

'Blue section return to base and land,' adding, 'and keep to standard R/T procedure.'

It was only when I was turning on to the final approach to land that I saw the other four missing aircraft as they appeared from all directions to rejoin the circuit overhead the airfield: 'What a cock-up' I thought. Bill will be upset when we get down. I was right, Bill was bloody furious.

As we made our way over from dispersal to book in I saw Bill, hands on hips, waiting for us outside the Ops. door.

'If that's the best you lot can do we might as well pack up now before somebody gets killed. What the hell were you guys playing at, prating about all over the sky like a bunch of bleeding fairies?'

He pointed to the briefing room, and we all filed in like a bunch of naughty boys being sent to the headmaster's office.

It turned out that number two in the formation, the one I was supposed to have followed but unfortunately disappeared without trace, had seen a Chipmunk to his right which he had mistaken for Bill and chased after it, only to find, when he did eventually catch up with it, that it was one of the Oxford University Air Squadron Chipmunks from RAF Bicester. By that time he had lost us altogether. The remaining aircraft had followed him for a while, realised the mistake, then failed to find the rest of us.

We all mumbled a few feeble excuses which made no impression whatsoever on our valiant leader. So we just had to sit there through a very painful de-briefing.

Minutes afterwards we were on our way back to the aircraft for a second attempt. This time we had been briefed to take-off all together, lining up on the runway with the Chipmunk in front followed by two sections of Vic three formations. I remember thinking if one of these chaps doesn't keep straight during the take-off run we're going to be front page news in tomorrow's papers!

We were all lined up on the runway when Bill's voice came over the R/T. 'Blue section rolling, rolling go.' Six sweaty hands clutching six sticky throttle levers obeying Bill's command as we moved forwards slowly and trundled down the runway. If it hadn't been so bloody frightening, it would have been funny to watch. In the lead aircraft Bill had lowered one stage of flap and was holding the power back slightly in order to allow the slower Piper aircraft to keep up with him during the take-off. In fact we would have all been a lot better off if he had opened up to full throttle. As number three in the formation I was placed on the extreme left-hand edge of the runway where I worked desperately hard to try and hold my position during the take-off run. But the lead aircraft was definitely NOT going fast enough.

Finally the Chipmunk staggered into the air and climbed away incredibly slowly. But the six little Piper aeroplanes were still hopping up and down like frogs, running out of runway fast. Out of the corner of my eye I saw poor old Johnny Johnson in trouble. He was hunched forward over the controls desperately trying to get airborne without overtaking the Chipmunk. When he did get off the ground his aircraft shot forward and Johnny obviously throttled back to keep station. The Colt flopped back onto the ground, bounced up, and staggered into the air just managing to clear the perimeter fence by inches. Our Air Traffic Controller, Ben, said later that he watched in horror as first one aircraft then another hopped up, waffling for a second, then plummet down again! We must have looked like a bunch of fledgling ducks trying to fly with their mother for the first time.

As the gaggle climbed precariously away, the radio blasted into life again and a terror stricken voice screamed out…

'FOR CHRIST SAKE GET OUT OF THE BLOODY WAY!'

Not knowing which was about to collide with another aircraft, everyone opened up to full power with astounding enthusiasm and seven little aeroplanes scattered in all directions. I hung on for grim death as my aircraft was blown all over the sky by the slipstream from several aircraft waffling around a few yards ahead of me.

Eventually everything calmed down, and somehow we all managed to regain our correct positions in the formation.

'Blue section, line astern, line astern go.' Bill was at it again, oblivious to the fun and games that had gone on behind him.

As per the briefing, Johnny slid his aircraft neatly under the tail of the Chipmunk. I followed behind Johnny, and the Piper on my right, flown by Eric Livett, an ex-RAF Valiant Bomber Pilot, slid in behind me. This in turn was followed by the other   formation of three who were way out to our right. All went reasonably well; at least it wasn't too bad for the first four aircraft, but the tail-enders were in trouble again. I was told later, by a chap who had observed our efforts from the ground that he thought our line astern formation reminded him of a sidewinder snake, and added sarcastically…

'If the formation could have been joined together somehow, rather like a whip, the last aircraft would have undoubtedly made a loud crack!'

You couldn't get a worse insult than that could you?

Our formation practices continued for a couple more days, eventually, with all our problems ironed out, we took off on the 26th July 1963 and carried out the fly-past as planned, our seven aeroplanes apparently looked quite reasonable, and pictures appeared in the local press. It has to be said that all the instructors who took part were in fact professional pilots with thousands of hours flying experience between them. But such is formation flying, whether in large or small aircraft, fast or slow, there is no substitute for regular current practice.

CHAPTER 11.

Saved by the Belt.

Not long after Douglas Bader's visit to the Radcliffe my right leg was taken out of traction and I was informed by the Sister that plans had been made for me to be transferred to the Nuffield Orthopaedic Hospital within a day or two.

I was not overjoyed at the idea of leaving my fellow patients and the wonderful staff at the Radcliffe that had taken care of me for the last few months. Sister told me that I would be taken to Burrows Ward and the person in charge was Sister Finity.

When Sister left I looked at John reading his book in the next bed.

'I'm off to the Nuffield tomorrow' I said, expecting some sign of remorse.

'Thank God,' he said, and continued reading his book without even looking up.

'Charming' I thought, but then he added...

'You will no doubt be extremely delighted to know that I too will be transferred to the Nuffield in a week or two, so you won't be getting rid of me quite so easily mate.'

I made out to be gutted, but was really pleased, and hoped that we would be together in the same ward again.

When Valerie came to see me that evening, she seemed delighted to hear that I was being transferred. Although this meant it would add an extra three miles to her journey each time she visited me, it didn't seem to worry her at all, and when I was having a bit of a moan about leaving the Radcliffe, she quite uncharacteristically snapped at me...

'Where's all this determination to fly again gone? These people are doing all they can to help you, you should be grateful.'

Valerie wagged her finger at me and continued...

'You must look upon this as another vital step towards your goal, and without it there would be no possibility of you ever recovering to the stage when you could pass an aircrew medical again.'

She was right of course, and I had to smile because it was rather like being told off by my mother.

Dear old mum, the thought of her reminded me of when I was a small boy and made my first attempt to fly under my own steam. Valerie sat by my bed whilst I told her the story of my first efforts to get airborne.

It was during the Second World War. My mate Eddy and I were about nine years old at the time. We had already been turned down when we offered our services as "Spitfire Pilots" to the RAF recruiting sergeant, and my attempts to build an aeroplane out of tea chests with a plank as wings and an old gramophone motor as the engine had also failed to get me in the air, even after the refinements of a larger plank for the wings, the addition of paper instruments and pram wheels fitted to replace the wheels drawn on the sides of the tea chests.

My endeavours to fly needed a complete rethink. Finally I came up with a great idea and set about creating my new invention in my dad's workshop. I spent hours hammering away preparing for the momentous day when I would zoom proudly over the chimney pots of our neighbour's houses.

Looking for suitable material, I searched the contents of my mother's linen chest for the much needed fabric to cover the wings. I discovered a couple of brand new sheets that would do the job nicely and surely wouldn't be missed. I cut the sheets into suitable length strips and nailed them to a wooden framework. Just a few more technical refinements and the job was almost finished.

When Eddy saw what I had done to my mother's sheets, he quickly opted out of helping me. This was understandable as he was already in her bad books for bringing Mickey, his pet mouse, into our kitchen. Unfortunately it escaped, which left my mother standing on a chair and screaming hysterically until Mickey was caught and popped back into his box.

Eddy withdrawing his services meant that I had to appoint another undercover agent to assist me with my secret invention.

Brian Canham from next door was the obvious choice. He agreed immediately and after a short initiation ceremony, Brian became my secret agent, although I never actually told him what my plans were until a few minutes before take-off.

I hid my invention from my mother purely for security reasons, my security mainly! The wings being placed in the dried-up dyke at the bottom of our garden and covered over with potato plant tops freshly cut from next door's garden.

The day for my first trial flight arrived. Mother had gone into the town shopping, so the coast was clear, a perfect opportunity for a first solo.

Brian, who had volunteered to assist during the launch, helped me to uncover the wings and bring them into the house shortly after my mother had left.

Excitedly I revealed my plans in detail. I showed Brian a photograph of the famous "BIRDMAN" in my 1939 Boys Annual. I explained that he had strapped wings to his back and jumped out of an aeroplane. In the absence of an aeroplane, I explained that it was my intention to jump out of my bedroom window instead! Brian looked uncomfortable and said he would like to resign from the secret service! but it was too late for all that.

The first task was to get the wings into the bedroom before mum returned from her shopping trip. This proved to be more difficult than I anticipated. They were about seven feet long and had to be juggled around quite a bit to get them up the stairs. During this process a small tear appeared in one of the wings, which was quickly rectified with the aid of a safety pin. Also there was the minor problem of a protruding nail that ripped the wallpaper in my bedroom, but nothing serious.

Soon I was standing on the window-ledge clutching the wings that Brian had passed out to me with some difficulty. Outside the window there was a small ledge just wide enough to stand on whilst I tried to get my head through the hole I made between the two wings. My thoughts were positive, soon I would be gliding over the rooftops and when my mother returns from the shops she will look up at me with great pride!

I was ready for take-off. I must admit not much thought had been given to the problem of landing. Brian suggested that I should have a cushion placed in the garden under the window for emergencies. I told him straight that he was deliberately putting obstacles in the way.

Almost ready to go, I called for Brian to pass me the toy pilot's goggles that I had borrowed from Eddy, but there was no reply. It was impossible to turn round without falling off the ledge. I called again. Not a word from Brian. I had to think quickly: 'It was now or never, I'll go without the goggles.' I started to lean forward in order to glide gracefully off into the wide blue yonder.

Suddenly someone grabbed me by the seat of my trousers and hauled me backwards so violently that I landed on the bedroom floor with my beautifully constructed wings clasped together like praying hands jammed in the window frame.

'What the bloody hell do you think you're doing?'

My mother's ear piercing shriek struck fear into my heart.

'Just wait until your father hears about this…You'll be in for it this time, haven't you got any brains at all?'

I hadn't been at all nervous about jumping out of the bedroom window because the roof of the outside toilet, which I hoped to clear, was only about six or seven feet beneath my bedroom window, but my false confidence left me in a flash when I heard my mother threatening to tell my father. There was little doubt in my mind that corporal punishment was inescapable and my adventure had been ruined.

By the time I had finished telling Valerie the story it was time for the visitors to leave the ward.

This was to be my last night in the Radcliffe. I had just settled down after lights out when Gwyn popped in to say goodnight. He was on night duty, but said he would try to get over and say goodbye before the ambulance arrived to take me to the Nuffield in the morning. He was bound to be tired having been on duty all night, so I told him not to bother. But I knew I was wasting my words, he would be there! I thanked him for all he had done for me, and his generosity to all of us in the OM. I would certainly miss him very much.

The ward seemed strangely calm and peaceful. It was unusual for it to be this quiet. I suppose it was the effect of the pain killing injections that contributed to my feeling of nostalgia, but the thought of leaving the dedicated and caring staff that had looked after me for months was difficult to bear. I knew them all so well, in a way they had become friends, and I wondered how I would cope without them.

Time was passing slowly when the Duty Night Nurse tiptoed up to my bedside and said...

'Not asleep yet?'

'I'm off tomorrow' I whispered.

'I know' she said, fussing around my bed, straightening sheets and puffing up the pillows. 'Would you like a piece of hot buttered toast?'

This had happened many times before, and made it worth while not being able to sleep.

'Yes please' I said.

Next morning after very little sleep, all the chores of early morning life on the ward had been completed. Outside it was a windy, dismal day. The sky was so dark that the ward lights had been turned on again. I lay in bed apprehensively waiting for the transport to arrive that would take me to the Nuffield.

Lots of small talk went on between the four of us, John, Stan and Claude were all doing their best to make me laugh but, try as I may, I found it very difficult to hide my feelings of sadness. Every time the ward door opened, I thought this is it.

Finally I was right. The swing doors burst open and two ambulance men appeared with a stretcher followed by a nurse. Then I recognised the unmistakable figure of Gwyn standing in the doorway. He had been on duty all night, yet still stayed up to come and see me off. He smiled and pointed at me in a way a schoolteacher does when he is about to ask a question, but said nothing.

'This is it chaps,' I said trying to give the impression that I was unconcerned. They lifted me onto the stretcher-trolley and pushed me around the OM so that I could shake hands with my three mates who were sitting up in bed and appeared to be delighted to see me go!

'You needn't look so ruddy pleased' I said.

'Glad to see the back of you' Claude blurted out.

Stan didn't look too well. We were all concerned about the poor chap, and I wondered what would become of him in the future. Finally John Villanis said…

'Try and work it so that we can be together when I get there in a few days time.'

'Not a chance in hell.' I said.

Then everybody wished me the best of luck as I was pushed out of the OM for the last time.

As we passed down the main ward some of the patients who I didn't know gave me a friendly wave. There is a sort of comradeship in hospital rather like service life.

When we reached Sister's Office we stopped, and Sister appeared at the door carrying a large bundle of papers and X-rays, which she gave to one of the ambulance men, instructing him to give them to Sister Finity in Burrows Ward. Then she turned to me and said...

'I've told Sister Finity what an awful bundle of trouble she is taking on! Now try not to distract the nurses from their work too much, and DON'T upset your new Matron!'

She bent down and kissed me on the top of my head, and hurried off before I could say a word.

I struggled not to show any emotion, but failed miserably, and I'm sure I didn't really say anything that made sense.

Then came the moment I had been dreading ever since I had been told of my transfer to the Nuffield. Saying goodbye to the Big Man. Gwyn held both my hands and started to say something, but his words failed and he just stood there. They pushed me up the ramp and hoisted me into the ambulance, as they closed the doors I caught sight of Gwyn removing his jam-jar bottom glasses, and wiping his eyes with the back of his hand as he turned away.

CHAPTER 12.

First steps.

The first flurries of winter snow were falling, making a beautiful sight for us to look at through the large French Windows at the end of Burrows Ward.

I recalled an amusing incident that took place one Winter's morning during my early days of instructing at Kidlington, and how grumpy everyone got when snow caused flying to be cancelled......

November had laid her first timid frost on the hedgerows and rooftops. The days were growing shorter, low overcasts and prolonged mists became monotonously regular. Then, towards the end of the month, rain turned to snowflakes, bringing with it the strangely peaceful atmosphere that takes over when snow falls.

I remember one occasion whilst I was still employed by Bells Distilleries, selling whisky during the weekdays and instructing part time at Kidlington during the weekends. It had been snowing all week. Saturday morning arrived and I drove cautiously through the airfield gates to have a friendly chat with my mates who were employed as full-time instructors at the flying club. The airfield was stark white and our precious Tiger Moths were all tucked away safely in No. 1 Hangar.

As I trudged my way ankle deep in snow from the car park towards the old Nissan Hut, my attention was captured by a strong smell of burnt toast and coffee emanating from one of the partly open windows. Icicles hung like stalactites from the snow capped "Crewroom" signpost. Kicking the clogged snow from my boots I opened the door and stepped inside. The snow swirled in the doorway as I entered and I was warmly greeted by…

'For Christ's sake close the fucking door.'

Inside the hut the heat resembled that of a blast furnace. The mood however was not so hot. Half a dozen decrepit old chairs occupied by half a dozen decrepit old instructors surrounded a brightly burning coke stove.

Trying to lighten the mood I said…

'The airfield looks absolutely beautiful covered in snow chaps.'

My enthusiasm was rewarded with a string of obscenities. I tried again…

'Any chance of a coffee chaps?'

'Two sugars, no milk' Scotty replied without even looking up from his newspaper.

'I suppose a round of toast is out of the question then?'

My request was completely ignored.

'Oh come on you miserable bastards, it's not that bad.'

A cushion hit me on the back of my head with considerable force.

'OK fellers, if you want to be like that I'll forget the Bells Whisky samples I brought in for you, the Ops staff will appreciate them if you don't.'

Immediately I was surrounded by the bunch of sanctimonious hypocrites.

'What's up Ray old mate, can't take a joke eh? Where's your sense of humour old boy?

One thing guaranteed to upset flying types is being grounded by inhospitable weather conditions. But things were different now, flying for me had ceased. I had been in the Nuffield Orthopaedic Hospital for about six weeks. All the staff were wonderful and made me feel at home from the moment I arrived. Sister Finity turned out to be a really kind, motherly person. There were also lots of cracking looking nurses around to brighten a chaps day.

John Villanis had been transferred from the Radcliffe and thankfully was once again in the bed next to mine.

A few days after I arrived at the Nuffield, Mr Morgan operated on my left leg again. I was told the operation had been a success, although further Ops were planned for the months ahead.

The gloomy prospect of spending my first Christmas in hospital was almost a certainty. We were told that relatives would be invited to stay throughout the day, and would be able to get their Christmas Dinner in the Visitors Restaurant, whilst the patients enjoyed the "luxury" of eating their Christmas Dinner in bed.

Fortunately, I was never short of visitors. The Nuffield had no restriction on visiting times, therefore friends and relatives could pop in at any time between 10.30a.m. and 9p.m. seven days a week. Valerie continued to visit me every evening, never missing once. I also received a letter every day from Valerie's daughter, Laura was now twenty-one and worked in London as secretary to the editor of the popular magazine "Tit Bits".

Sister Heathfield and other members of the staff from the Radcliffe kept their word and came to see me whilst I was in the Nuffield, and my dear old friend Gwyn visited me regularly throughout the remainder of my two year stay in hospital.

I also received regular visits from my fellow instructors at Oxford Air Training School, and some of our airline students set up a roster, taking it in turns to visit me. Their regular visits helped to make my lengthy stay in hospital more tolerable.

One afternoon I lay in bed watching the snow falling outside, when a voice behind me said...

'How's it going Ray?'

I recognised the voice immediately and turned round to see Nils Bartleet standing by my bed! I hadn't seen him since that dreadful day when his nurse wheeled him into my ward at the Radcliffe. It was wonderful to see him again. He was using a walking stick at the time, but he looked almost back to normal.

We laughed and spoke of old times when we were both trainee pilots eleven years earlier. Nils told me that he hoped to go for his air-crew medical again in a few weeks time, and all being well he would return to his flying instructor's job at Oxford. This was indeed good news.

Our reveries were interrupted by Sharon, a young nurse much loved for her sense of humour. She stood by my bed with a broad grin on her face.

'Mouth, Armpit or Bum?' I looked at the thermometer she was waving in front of me and considered my options carefully. An over active imagination provided me with a vivid picture of where the thermometer may have been placed for the previous patient. I had no choice.

'Armpit please nurse' I replied.

With the nurse now in attendance, Nils promised to let me know how his aircrew medical turned out, and I wished him all the best as he left the ward.

The nurse's request reminded me of another incident involving a surgical thermometer that took place one Winter's day when I was a small and rather crafty little boy....

Outside the snow had been falling heavily most of the morning. My mother had lit a fire in the bedroom, a luxury always associated with bad colds, illness etc..

In order to avoid being taken to school that day, I had been faking the symptoms of a bad cold, making out that I was very poorly. Unfortunately my performance had been so convincing that my mother sent for the doctor.

I had just been given a mug of hot tea, when there was a knock on the front door. The doctor had arrived.

Doctor Chadwick was an enormous man who must have weighed over twenty stone. He looked like a character straight out of a Dickens novel, bald on top with long grey bushy side-burns that framed a friendly, rosy old face. He was always out of breath, which caused him to talk in short broken sentences giving the impression that he was more abrupt than he possibly meant to be.

After a short chat with my mother, he turned towards me and donned a pair of gold half-rimmed spectacles.

'Now young man, do you feel sick?

'Yes sir.'

'Dizzy?'

'Yes sir, a bit.'

'Sore throat?'

'Yes sir.'

'Hmmm!!....'

He peered at me over his spectacles, and put his hand on my forehead.

'Open wide and say Aaagh.'

I obeyed his instructions, and felt sure he was on to me. I had to do something quick to convince him I was ill enough to be off School.

Producing a stethoscope from his brown leather case, he proceeded to listen to my heart beating, which by now was thumping away with the sheer terror of being caught-out and pronounced SHAMMING!

'Hmmm!....' (The sort of Hmmm...that sounded serious).

Mother looked worried, but she couldn't have been half as worried as I was! Perhaps I could make myself sick by thinking of something absolutely foul. I tried and it didn't work.

But then, just as I was giving up all hope, my opportunity came. Doctor Chadwick fumbled in his top pocket for a moment, and produced a silver tube from which he removed a slender glass thermometer. Leaning forward again, he said...

'Under your tongue young man,' thrusting the thermometer firmly into my mouth.

Mother asked him if he would like a cup of tea, and then slipped downstairs to get it from the freshly brewed pot. Doctor Chadwick had his back to me and was warming his hands by the bedroom fire. In a flash, I removed the thermometer from my mouth and popped it quickly into the half empty mug of hot tea my mother had brought up to me just before the doctor had arrived: 'This should do the trick,' I thought, maybe I could be off school for a couple of weeks with a bit of luck. I left the thermometer in the tea for as long as I dare, then popped it back into my mouth, it felt very warm indeed. At that moment the Doctor turned towards me whilst studying his pocket watch. It was time to remove the thermometer and examine the scale, which would undoubtedly confirm that I should definitely not be at school. He studied the thermometer for a few seconds, moving it closer, then further from his face as if he was having trouble focusing on the scale. His eyebrows shot up suddenly as he spoke.

'Good God!'

Mum came in with a cup of tea for the Doctor.

'Has the boy ever lived abroad?' he asked.

'No' mum replied looking puzzled.

The thermometer, having been shaken down to normal temperature was once more thrust into my mouth.

Doctor was sipping his tea, and explaining to mum that the mercury in the thermometer had reached the top of the scale, and by the same token I should be dead.

Fortunately for me, whilst all this was going on, both my mother and the Doctor had their backs towards me, and I was able to repeat the process all over again. But I soon wished I hadn't as I realised that I could wind up in hospital.

Should I own up?.....never!... mum would kill me. With my mother watching nervously over the doctor's shoulder, he examined the thermometer for a second time. Frowning heavily, he slowly leaned forward and glared at me, it was all I could do not to scream with fright. Finally he straightened up, and with a disapproving grunt, snapped the thermometer in half, passing the remains to my mother for disposal.

'Obviously something's wrong with the thing, it's of no more use to me,' he said. 'Keep Raymond in bed for a couple of days, feed him liquids, and call me if he doesn't get better.'

With that the doctor left. I suddenly realised that my mother was looking at me in a rather "old fashioned" manner.

'You are up to something my boy' she said.

In the interests of my personal safety I swallowed hard and said nothing. Fortunately my mother never did find out what I had been up to.

John Villanis had already been issued with his wheelchair, and made a point of whizzing around the ward most of the day to make me jealous. But not for long.

I was excited to learn that a specially adapted wheelchair to suit my individual requirements had been ordered from the manufactures and hopefully would arrive within a few days. But first my surgeon Mr Morgan wanted me to have a crack at standing up. This would be the first time that I had used my feet and legs for eight months.

The thought of standing after all this time began to worry me. I had been told that I still had several bone fractures in my legs and ankles that had not completely mended. My mind was put to rest at the next surgeons ward round, when it was explained to me that putting weight on correctly aligned fractures whilst they were held firmly in place by plaster casts, sometimes encouraged the flow of callus which would help the fractures to mend more quickly. I was also warned that the process of standing up for the first time would probably be quite painful, which I soon found out was a gross understatement.

After a further trip to the plastering room to have the casts reinforced and bowler irons fitted so that I could stand up without cracking the plasters, I had only a few days to wait before I was wheeled in my bed to the Physio Department for the great event.

Linda, my physiotherapist, was waiting for me all smiles. I thought perhaps a little bluff would help my ego, so I said…

'Come on let's get on with it Linda, I want to be out of here and flying again in a month!'

'It may take a little longer than that' she said.

My bed was being pushed towards two parallel bars that were supported by a line of steel posts firmly secured to the floor of the Physiotherapy Department. Linda adjusted the height of the bars and locked them into position. One of the porters turned my bed so that it was sideways on and just touching one end of the bars.

'Now we have to take this slowly Ray, and don't be upset if it seems impossible to start with.'

Linda's face was no longer smiling; she was obviously very concerned about what was about to take place. She added…

'Remember you haven't used the muscles in your legs and ankles for a long time, more than thirty weeks in fact, so they will be weak. You will gradually get stronger, and don't worry we won't let you fall.'

Two beefy porters were looking at Linda for instructions, and I just wished that my dear friend Gwyn could have been one of them. This was an epic moment for me.

Linda addressed the porters.

'I want you to support the patient one each side whilst I swing his legs over the side of the bed.'

I was sitting on the edge of the bed. My legs, that had been set in full-length plasters with a twenty-degree bend at the knees for support, were pointing straight out towards the parallel bars.

'I am going to lower your legs slowly to the ground and the porters will support you so that you don't fall over. If it hurts too much shout out and we will lift you back onto the bed, OK?'

I nodded nervously. As my legs were slowly lowered to the floor, I began to sweat. It was fear all right, fear of the pain I knew was bound to grip me at any second.

Linda asked if I was alright. Having no intentions of giving up at this stage I nodded for her to continue. I sat on the very edge of the bed with my feet just touching the ground. Linda stood in front of me gently holding both my hands whilst one of the porters adjusted the height of the bed slightly so that it would be easier for me to lean forward and take the full weight of my body on to my legs.

'On the count of three, we are going to start to ease you forward so that you are standing up, OK?'

I heard myself saying Yes, but I wasn't really convinced that I was ready at all.

'One, Two, Three'…

The sudden shock of pain was indescribable. In spite of the fact that the new plasters fitted tightly, I felt my legs being pushed further down as they took the full weight of my body and the broken bones pushed closer together. The agony increased rapidly as my legs started to swell inside their casings.

'Christ' I believe was the only word I managed to say! I wonder if he heard my pathetic call?

Sweat ran down my face and I started to feel dizzy again. Linda, still in front of me guided my hands to the bars and then supported me by my shoulders.

'Are you alright?' she asked.

I managed to blurt out an unconvincing 'yep.'

'You're doing very well.'

The porters were great; they held on to my arms with a grip of iron, at least I knew there was no chance of falling over.

'Can you see if you can support yourself with the parallel bars?' Linda asked.

I reached forward without saying anything and tried to support myself. Immediately I started to twist round. Neither Linda or I had remembered that I had virtually no strength at all in my left hand which had been damaged and only recently been taken out of its final plaster. It was completely useless; in fact I couldn't even tighten my fingers to make a fist. Saved by the Porters I remained upright whilst the left hand parallel bar was raised to the height of my left armpit. By this time my legs had swollen to what seemed bursting point, the pain was excruciating, and sweat dripped from my chin.

I desperately wanted to succeed, but inwardly prayed for it all to end soon.

In the end I managed to get as far as taking my weight with my right hand clutching the bar at waist height and the other bar supporting me under my left armpit with a pillow to cushion the weight. Then, by awkwardly swinging both legs together it must have taken several minutes to awkwardly lurch my way to the end of the parallel bars. I was helped to turn round by the porters and told to wait for a minute whilst Linda re-positioned the bed. But I wasn't going to stop now, and managed a somewhat slower repeat performance arriving at the side of my bed completely exhausted. The agonising pain seemed to spread over the whole of my body, and I began to feel sick.

The porters hoisted me back onto my bed. Linda said I had done extremely well. But I knew that I was kidding myself, I had taken most of my body weight with my right hand and left armpit, and I was keen to have another stab at it.

'We'll try again tomorrow.' She said.

'How about this afternoon?' my remarks were ignored.

I returned to the ward feeling disappointed and down hearted. Then Sister Finity turned up by my bed and said in her Irish brogue…

'Get a grip of yourself Ray! Rome wasn't built in a day to be sure. You ought to be proud of what you have managed to achieve today, and you should also be grateful to Linda, she's determined to get you walking again.'

Later that day a new arrival appeared on the scene and was allocated the vacant bed next to mine. At the time I had no way of knowing that this person would alter my perception of humanity forever.

My first impression of this young man was that he looked extremely fit and strong, the sort of chap you would expect to play Rugby or take up Boxing.

He dumped a small suitcase on the bed and introduced himself as Desmond Harper; he was in for a minor operation on his left knee and expected to be in hospital for a few days.

Des originated from Jamaica and was at present attending a college in Oxford, training to become an accountant.

The next day Desmond had his operation spending the night in the recovery room. Meanwhile I was taken to the Physiotherapy Department again, only to give a repeat performance of the previous days efforts. It didn't seem quite so painful as the previous day, so I left Physio feeling exhausted but much happier.

That evening John Villanis and I had a long chat about his intended career. Keen to become a professional photographer, he had been preparing a portfolio of his photographs prior to his unscheduled arrival in hospital. I suggested that whilst we had the opportunity, we could set about making a series of interesting photographs headed "Life in a Modern Hospital".

'What do you mean, WE ?' John asked.

'Well' I said, 'when I get my wheel chair I could act as your assistant, it would be great fun and something to occupy our minds.'

John was not all that keen about my suggestion. He had taken a couple of photographs of the nurses when he was a patient in the Radcliffe, Matron caught him in the act and all hell broke out.

John gave the matter some thought and eventually agreed to have a shot at it, so we planned to start work on the album just as soon as I took delivery of my wheelchair.

The idea had great potential and needed to be kept secret to avoid interference. Mischievous plans for future "missions" were discussed in detail and hands were shaken on the deal.

Christmas Eve arrived. Desmond returned to Burrows Ward a couple of days earlier and seemed quite pleased with the results of his operation. The Physio Department had supplied him with crutches and he was allowed to go home. He packed his few belongings into a case including a long list of do's and don't's from Linda who had also been looking after Des. He wished John and I a Happy Christmas, then hobbled off awkwardly.

During the evening we were entertained by the hospital choir who sang carols whilst several of our visitors busily consumed the fruit and chocolates they had brought in for us to eat over Christmas.

I looked around the ward at my fellow patients sitting up in their beds listening to the lovely voices of the hospital choir, each no doubt with his own special memories of Christmas's past and wishing they were anywhere but in hospital. But the nurses and staff were marvellous, and went out of their way to make us all feel as happy as circumstances would allow.

Later that evening, just after the main lights in the ward had been dimmed, the choir sang to us again. Their voices created an atmosphere of warmth and peace. It was a very moving experience.

We awoke to a chill Christmas morning. All the windows in our ward were encrusted with frost. After the usual ward routines were over, we each received a peck on the cheek from the night nurses before they went off duty. John tried to enter into a more affectionate clinch with one of the nurses and almost ended up on the floor as the poor girl fought gamely to escape his ardour. When the day staff arrived, we all received another peck on the cheek. John, wishing to avoid all the cheers and boos he got for his previous performance, decided not to push his luck this time and got called chicken instead.

It wasn't long before we were all sitting up in our beds, dressed in paper hats and looking like a bunch of lunatics. Sister Finity gave everyone a small carefully wrapped present. Mine was a book about the skills of 'Basket Making.' A thoughtful gift as I had been assigned to basket making in the OT department as therapy for my left hand.

After a hearty breakfast of Ham and Eggs for those who's diet allowed it, a pretty little nurse, who I had never seen before, entered the ward pushing a decorated trolley loaded with glasses of various coloured milk drinks. She was eagerly assisted by a pale-faced young man dressed in pyjamas and a flashy dressing gown. Although the poor chap walked with the aid of a stick and didn't look at all well, he had obviously volunteered his services to help distribute the drinks to those of us less fortunate patients who couldn't get out of bed. The young man was closely followed by one of our regular daily help ladies sporting a small dustpan and brush. Every few seconds she would stoop down and run round in all directions vigorously sweeping a series of small back balls, about the size of marbles, that rolled around the floor and seemed to appear from nowhere.

I looked at John's puzzled expression, he had also seen what was going on and obviously thought it was some kind of wind-up.

I couldn't take my eyes off the strange spectacle as it advanced slowly along the ward. When the three of them finally got to us, the nurse asked us what flavour of milk shake we would prefer. Being a little suspicious we both went for a plain glass of milk, whereupon it was duly poured out and juggled over to us by the young man in the flashy dressing gown. As he wobbled unsteadily back towards the nurse to collect another glass of milk, I noticed a number of these round black balls roll out from the leg of his pyjamas. The small cluster was instantly chased, swept up and deposited into a large paper bag by the agile daily help lady! Knowing how diplomatic John can be, I cringed when I saw the look of horror on his face....

'Good Lord that isn't crap is it?' he said.

I watched to see yet another collection of small balls roll across the ward floor being chased by the assistant as they disappeared under a bed.

'I think it must be' I said.

'Bloody Hell'... John's final remark tapered off to a whisper as he saw Sister Finity
approaching.

A quiet word with our dear Sister revealed all. The young man had suffered some kind of paralysis, leaving the poor chap with no control over his bowels. He was due to have a further operation, but for the time being, the temporary method of dealing with the problem seemed to be less than efficient. The drugs he had to take caused severe constipation, hence the small black balls.

'He's a lovely boy' Sister said, 'and we don't want to deprive him of taking part in helping out on the wards at Christmas in the same way as all the other patients who are fortunate enough to be able to walk.'

Christmas dinner arrived at midday escorted by our consultant surgeon Mr Morgan dressed in full operating theatre regalia, he was accompanied by Sister Finity similarly dressed. To everybody's amusement he purposely made a complete cock-up of carving the turkey. As the carcass rolled backwards and forwards on the carving dish we all wondered how we had survived his use of a scalpel. Everyone cheered and laughed as Sister pretended to wipe the perspiration from our surgeon's furrowed brow. Most of us sat up in our bed's drooling over the delicious mouth watering odour's that emanated from the "Operating table". Generous portions accompanied by the usual Christmas fare were handed out to those who were not on special diets, and a good time was had by all.

Christmas day past quickly. The nurses took part in various games together with the numerous visitors who had joined us for the day. Valerie and Laura spent the whole afternoon and evening with me. Also Sister Heathfield and Gwyn from the Radcliffe paid a short visit to the ward.

Considering we were bedridden patients, I can safely say we all had a marvellous time, thanks to all the members of the hospital staff who were truly wonderful.

The evening finally at an end, our visitors left and Sister dimmed the ward lights to a mere glimmer. Once again peace and calm returned to Burrows for a while.

From my bed I could clearly see the stars twinkling in the night sky. My mind returned to the days when I observed the night skies from my home built observatory.

CHAPTER 13.

The Night Skies.

My ambition since childhood had always been to become a pilot, but I also had another great interest in the sky. Astronomy had become a serious hobby of mine for many years, ever since I had been given a book on the subject by an old watchmaker friend of my father's. As mentioned in an earlier chapter, having optimistically put our names on the Brackley Town Council's housing list before we were married, Mary and I were very surprised to be allocated a house within a week of sending in our application. The house was brand new. In fact it was still under construction.

In those days living together before marriage was unheard of. So we were thrilled by the premature allocation of a brand new house, and got married as soon as the house was completed in the summer of 1954..

One clear Winter's night a few months after we had moved into our new house, I was standing outside the front door in the pitch dark looking at the stars and trying to memorise the names of some of the constellations. As my eyes adjusted to the darkness I became aware that there was someone standing outside our neighbour's house that appeared to be doing the same thing. It turned out to be Ray Coulton who was our neighbour's son. I had not met the chap previously as he lived in London and attended the Imperial College of Science where he was studying for a Ph.D in Nuclear Physics.

Our common interest in astronomy soon led to a great friendship. We were both members of the British Astronomical Association; with an interest in Selenography, the study of the surface of the Moon.

It was not long before we discovered that there was another member of the BAA by the name of Julian Barbour who lived just a few miles away. He was listed in the BAA handbook as an observing member helping with the detailed mapping of the Moon's surface under the direction of Dr Percy Wilkins.

Having arranged a meeting with Julian, we arrived at his house to discover he lived with his parents in a lovely old mansion set in several acres of garden just outside the village of South Newington. You can imagine our surprise when we discovered that Julian owned a magnificent Astronomical Observatory complete with a rotating dome. The observatory contained a large equatorially mounted, mechanically driven, Newtonian Telescope manufactured by Irvin and Sons, famous scientific instrument makers of London. It's dimensions were twelve inches in diameter and approximately seven feet long. It was an extremely powerful instrument for its day. When observing the Moon using the x360 magnification eyepiece the results were truly breathtaking.

From the very beginning we all got along extremely well with one-another. Ray and I frequently visited Julian's observatory whenever the night skies were clear.

The sky for me was the common denominator of my interests, flying and astronomy, these two subjects fascinated me above all else.

Studying the Moons surface in the early 1950's was very exciting. No-one at that time had set foot on the earth's closest celestial neighbour, and no rocket had orbited or reached its surface. So, although a tremendous amount was already known about the Moon, the serious amateur astronomer still had an important role to play in mapping small areas of the lunar surface in great detail. The three of us were given various projects to work on by Patrick Moore, who had recently succeeded Percy Wilkins as Director of the Lunar Section of the BAA. I remember spending one exciting evening mapping a small area on the surface of 'Clavious', a large crater in the southern hemisphere. We had to measure the various heights of the crater walls, and the depth of some of the smaller inner craters. This was achieved by using a micrometer eyepiece to measure the length of the shadows, and applying our measurements to a special almanac that took into account the angle of the Suns rays on the Moons surface at the particular date and time the observation was made. This could best be done when the "Terminator", the dividing line between the light and dark portions of the moon, was near to the object being studied. The whole subject was most fascinating.

Many months later, when Ray Coulton was home on another long vacation from College, he obtained a part time job working in the laboratories of the Northern Aluminium Company that was based in Banbury. This turned out to be very handy as I planned to build my own telescope and observatory in the back garden of our house, and Ray Coulton kindly volunteered to help.

I had to apply for planning permission and was more than surprised to note that there were no objections from the planning authorities at all. The application was approved without any request for plans. I later found out that the lack of any objections was due to the planning committee mistakenly interpreting my application to build an observatory as an application to build a conservatory!

Much to Mary's consternation I used our spare bedroom as a workshop. Building initially began with the construction of a large wood-framed telescope. Julian Barbour kindly gave me some spare optics he had no use for with his own telescope. The most expensive item however was the twelve inch diameter optically ground mirror, which I had to have professionally made.

My telescope was to be exactly the same size in diameter and focal length as Julian's telescope, this helped a lot with the design as I could crib many ideas from his professionally built instrument.

Ray Coulton's part time employment at the Northern Aluminium Company came in extremely handy as he was able to obtain all the aluminium sheeting used for constructing the observatory dome at cost rate. In no time I had drawn the plans, the concrete foundations were laid, and work had begun in earnest.

It took two years for me to complete the project, during which time my wife gave birth to our dear little son Edward. I think that must have been the happiest day of my life. He was christened Edward after my closest friend who I had known since my first day at school when we were both five years old. During the Second World War we made a childhood pledge to name our first sons after each other if we ever had children of our own. I kept my promise, but sadly there was to be no little Raymond christened after me as my dearest friend was killed when he was just twenty-two years old.

After hours of hard work I finally completed the wooden framed telescope. Now came the time to see if it actually worked.

In order to test the instrument I propped the heavy frame on a couple of chairs so that it pointed out through the bedroom window. First the alignment between the primary and secondary mirrors had to be finely adjusted, then when it had all been set up I turned the light off and looked through the eyepiece for the very first time. It was a very exciting moment.

As the two chairs supporting the telescope were near enough the same height, the telescope was pointing horizontally out of the bedroom window looking across the open countryside to the West. I peered through the x360 eyepiece to see a very bright object totally out of focus. Initially I was puzzled because I couldn't make out exactly what I was looking at. Then gradually, as I turned the brass rack and pinion focusing mechanism, the object came into sharp focus.

I stood there in utter amazement. A large spiral of intense light glowed in the eyepiece. It took several seconds for the object to register in my brain. Then I suddenly realised that I was looking at the element inside the bulb of a large obstruction light on the top of a radio mast on Croughton Airfield at least five miles away. I couldn't believe my eyes. If there had been a fly on the bulb at the time I would have been able to see it clearly.

That evening I proudly treated members of the family to a look through the eyepiece of my homemade telescope and see the detail of a light bulb filament several miles away.

The next morning Ray Coulton and myself were eager to take the telescope out of the bedroom and secure it to the equatorial mount in the observatory.

Then came the hiccup! Well not so much of a hiccup as an outright disaster. I was shattered to discover that there was no way that the telescope would pass through the bedroom door or even out of the bedroom window! After all that sweat and toil there was only one thing for it, I had to take the thing apart. But that wasn't all, the joints of the wooden frame were securely glued, so in the end the major part of the telescope had to be destroyed.

But it's an ill wind etc.. We finally finished up with a beautiful, 12" diameter, aluminium tube. It had been specially rolled and welded at the Aluminium Co. in Banbury where Ray Coulton was employed during his summer vacation from college.

There was great excitement the day we brought the tube back to Brackley with it's end sticking out of the rear window of my car like a huge cannon.

Within no time I had fixed the spider bracket for the secondary mirror into the tube and constructed a new adjustable cell to hold the main mirror. The next job was to paint the inside of the tube matt black to prevent erroneous light reaching the eyepiece. Finally the rack and pinion eyepiece mounting was fitted on to the tube at the focal length position, the small finder telescope was positioned close to the main rack and pinion assembly, and the sliding counterbalance weight securely bolted to the tube at the fulcrum point. Needless to say this time everything was checked to make sure that the telescope would pass through the door when completed.

The new aluminium telescope worked perfectly. Also the homemade equatorial mount, which I had struggled to perfect for months, worked satisfactorily.

It had been twenty-five months since I first decided to build my own telescope. Now I had a perfectly serviceable 12" Newtonian Telescope mounted inside a rather impressive looking observatory with fully rotating dome and sliding shutters.

Needless to say, the neighbours thought I had gone completely mad, guessing that I had built some sort of flying saucer in my back garden. Someone must have informed the town council because the Chief Planning Officer wrote to me saying that I would probably have to pull it down. I invited the planning committee over to take a look at it in action one evening. Fortunately it was a clear night when they arrived and I was able to show them impressive views of the Moon's surface as well as the Andromeda Nebula and the rings of Saturn. They were very impressed and I was not asked to remove the observatory from my garden.

I can recall one funny incident that happened when I was putting the finishing touches to the observatory dome. My dear mother-in-law, who had transferred her religious beliefs from the Salvation Army to the Jehovah's Witnesses, decided to bring a number of her Jehovah's Witness friends to visit the observatory. I had no idea of their planned visit and unfortunately on that particular evening I was painting the inside of the observatory dome with matt black paint.

The uppermost section of the dome was some twelve feet above ground level, so in order for me to reach the top I was standing on an upturned beer crate, which was balanced precariously on a rather springy scaffold plank placed across the walls of the observatory.

Electricity was supplied to the observatory by means of an overhead cable from a cash operated electricity metre in our council house.

Suddenly… 'Plink'… all the lights went out in the observatory. So there I was in total darkness, several feet in the air with paint brush in one hand and a large tin of matt black paint in the other. Not the sort of thing I usually do for fun.

I tried to call out in the darkness for help, but there was no reply, so I assumed that Mary was hunting around trying to find some coins to feed the meter.

I was in a very precarious position and when I heard Mary's footsteps coming up the path from the house I tried to turn slightly in the hope of finding some means of support.

CRASH.... down I went onto the wooden floor of the observatory ripping the arse out of my trousers on the metal telescope stand in the process. The two-litre tin of black paint followed close behind emptying itself all over the observatory, me included.

Needless to say I was in agony, rolling about the floor in the pitch dark. Naturally enough I let go a crescendo of top choice obscenities. But that wasn't the end of it ...... 'Plink'... The light came on again as Mary fed the electricity metre. But if Mary was in the house feeding the metre, who was it that I heard walking up the path? My eyes focused on the doorway, and there to my horror stood my mother-in-law, looking very embarrassed, together with several of her Jehovah's Witness friends.

I never regretted building the observatory. Night after night, whenever weather conditions permitted, I stood for hours at the telescope marvelling at the awe-inspiring sight of the heavens.

CHAPTER 14.

The insufferable request.

To everyone's surprise, a couple or so weeks after our Christmas dinner in the Nuffield, Desmond Harper returned to Burrows Ward. I had expected to see him as an out-patient attending daily for physiotherapy, but he had been admitted to hospital again, and initially occupied a bed at the far end of the ward. I took little notice at the time, thinking he had probably encountered a minor set back with his knee.

On the same day that Desmond returned, my brand new wheelchair arrived from the manufacturers. Unfortunately I soon discovered that all I could do was move round in circles because my injured left hand was unable to grip the thin chromium plated hand wheel properly. The chair was returned to the factory to have small handles fitted, rather like a ships wheel. The idea worked perfectly and, although progress was extremely slow to start with, I was free to move around the ward under my own steam.

The following day, an unusual thing occurred when I returned to the ward from the Physiotherapy Department. Mr Morgan, having completed his ward round came over to me and said…

'Raymond, you have been under my care now for many months, I think we understand and trust each other fairly well?'

I became apprehensive about what he was going to say next, this could be his way of easing me in to some bad news. I nodded in agreement to his statement, but I wasn't prepared for the conversation that followed…

'I wondered, being a long term patient yourself old chap, if you would mind us putting young Desmond Harper in the next bed to you again?'

This seemed to be an odd question. Des had already spent a few days in the next bed to me prior to Christmas and we had enjoyed one another's company.

'Of course I don't mind.' I said.

'Now don't be in too much of a hurry to agree until I tell you the whole story.'

The surgeon's expression said it all, I could tell something was seriously wrong with Desmond...

'He's not going to die is he?' I said.

Mr Morgan sat on my bed and leaned forward so that he could talk to me without being overheard by anyone else.

'I'm afraid that is the case, unfortunately he is going to go through a rough time, and he hasn't very long to live!'

I was absolutely stunned. Mr Morgan looked grave, as if he was wondering whether or not he should have confided in me.

'Sister tells me how Desmond enjoyed talking to you about aeroplanes, playing cards and having a laugh together when he was here previously. I think your friendly attitude will help him a lot, especially later on.'

I was lost for words. I felt privileged that I had been chosen to try and help in some minor way, but my strongest emotion was one of utter fear.

'It's not Cancer is it?' I whispered.

'I'm afraid so. It started some time ago in his leg, but it has spread rapidly in a very short time and I'm afraid there is very little we can do for him.'

This was dreadful, I could hardly speak...

'Does he know?'

'No not yet, neither does he suspect anything. His mother has been told but refuses to believe it.'

Mr Morgan thought for a second or so then continued...

'If he ever tells you that he thinks he may have Cancer, or asks your opinion, you must not tell him anything about our conversation. You should inform Sister Finity, or myself and we will deal with it, do you think you can handle that? I'm sorry to burden you with this old chap, but there really is a good reason...'

I felt very emotional and had to take a deep breath. Could I handle it? a good question. In my mind Desmond now seemed a completely different person. Could I lay in the next bed to poor old Des day after day as if nothing had changed, and listen to him enthusiastically telling me about his plans for the future when I knew he was dying and there was no future for him? I wondered if I would eventually crack up thereby giving the game away?

Mr Morgan's voice interrupted my thoughts...

'If you think it will be too much for you to cope with old chap, you must say so, and I will arrange for him to be placed elsewhere. But before you make your decision, I want you to know that I didn't come to you without first considering things very carefully and having a long chat with Sister. Desmond is a most likeable young man, but as his illness progresses he will change, that is to be expected. I would like the person who is going to be in the next bed to him for the last few weeks of his life to be considerate and understanding. That my dear chap, is a difficult task, but having known you now for many months, I think you are the sort of person I can trust to help Desmond during the last few days of his life. I came to this conclusion having observed the optimistic approach you have adopted towards your own problems. Also, I had to make the difficult decision of whether or not it was ethical for me to tell you about Desmond's illness in the first place.'

My surgeon went on to explain that it would undoubtedly be very difficult towards the end, and a non-caring person, or someone not in the know as to what was happening, could make Desmond's last few days even worse than they need to be.'

The expression on the consultants face spoke volumes, and I realised that it must have been a difficult decision to speak about Desmond to a fellow patient. In a way I felt privileged that he had chosen to confide in me. So, being the type of person who makes up his mind quickly, I said...

'OK sir, I'll do my best.'

'Thank you, I had a feeling that you would understand. Now, if you need help at any time just tell Sister. She will be pleased that you have agreed to help, and remember, you must say nothing to anyone else in the ward about Desmond's illness, you have our trust, and deepest thanks. Good man.'

With that he gave my arm a friendly squeeze, and left the ward.

This had been a terrible shock. I had no idea that some cancer patients were dealt with in Orthopaedic Hospitals. I thought that most of them were sent to the Churchill Hospital for radiotherapy treatment. As far as I know Chemotherapy was not widely used to battle cancer at that time, and even if it was it certainly wasn't used in Desmond's case, which may have been because the illness was too far advanced.

I lay there for some time thinking about Desmond. I dreaded the thought of listening again to his passionate plans to qualify as an accountant, when all the time I knew he was dying. I wanted to be there for him, and I prayed that I would be strong enough not to show any weakness. Even so, I had no idea that witnessing the last six months of Desmond's life would affect me so deeply. I had indeed made the right decision, a decision that I would neither regret nor forget for the rest of my life.

CHAPTER 15.

Operation Blenheim.

A few more weeks in hospital passed by. Desmond, now back in the next bed to me, had not shown any visible signs of deterioration.

I had undergone the fourth operation on my right ankle, which had unfortunately slowed up my progress on the parallel bars.

However I became a "dab hand" with the wheelchair.

Sister James, who was in charge of the female patients in Fielden Ward, asked our Sister if she could arrange for me to attend Occupational Therapy at the same time as one of her patients, a Miss Anne Herbert who had recently been admitted to the Nuffield with both legs badly smashed up.

Understandably Anne was very depressed and worried, not only about whether or not she would be able to walk again, but also about the gross disfigurement of her legs, which must be far more devastating for a young lady than it would be for a man. So it was suggested that I could have my bed positioned next to Anne's as if by chance during our next session in the OT department. It was hoped that Anne would gain some confidence from talking to someone who was recovering from similar injuries, and could perhaps cheer her up a bit. If all went well the arrangement could continue for some time to come. Anne, who turned out to be a very attractive young lady, was quite withdrawn when we were first introduced, but as soon as she realised that my leg injuries were as complicated as her own, she poured out all her worst fears to me. I had been through exactly the same sort of psychological problems that she was experiencing now, and I believe she gained some comfort from talking to someone who understood how she felt from a patients point of view.

Before we parted that afternoon I was able to make her laugh, and it was good to see her waving happily as the porter pushed her back to Fielden Ward.

From then on we met in the OT dept most days. We both experienced set backs of course, but we looked forward to our daily meetings which became a valuable part of both our recoveries.

One day Sister asked me if I would mind writing letters for a young man by the name of Joe. Joe was twenty years old and unfortunately mentally handicapped, he had been admitted to Burrows Ward with a broken arm. Joe had a girlfriend named Wendy that visited him occasionally who was also a resident patient in the same home for mentally handicapped persons, so it became my job to write letters for Joe to his girlfriend. Once a week I would sit by Joe's bed in my wheelchair and write a small love note to Wendy and sign it in Joe's name. Each time I would ask Joe what he would like me to say in the letter, and every time the answer would be the same.

'Say I'm very worried, tell her I don't think I'm ever going to get out of here and come back to the home.'

Obviously I couldn't write a gloomy letter like that to the poor girl, she would have been heart broken.

'Write something nice and mushy!' I told him.

'You write it,' he said.

So once a week I would write the sloppiest love letter I could conjure up for Joe. When I read the letters back to him before they were posted, he would laugh and think they were wonderful.

It backfired of course. One afternoon Sister Finity stumped out of her office and made a bee-line for my bed, she was carrying a piece of pink writing paper which I immediately recognised as one of the letters sent to Wendy.

'Did YOU write this stuff' Sister said, waving the notepaper in front of me.

I took the letter from Sister and began to read it.

'Oh God' were the only words I could muster up. Sister Finity held her head to one
side with her hands on her hips, and said in her Irish brogue.

'It's a disgrace to write such sexy muck, so it is.'

'What's wrong Sister? Joe thought they were great.'

'Great they might be to you Mr Blyth, but one of the young nurses from the home who reads the letters to Wendy, and she writes the replies which you read out to Joe. Now Wendy's nurse has come all the way over here to meet you. She's either thinks you're a pervert or she wants to meet you for a more depraved purpose so she does.'

When Sister called me Mr Blyth, I knew she wasn't joking; she always called me by my Christian name, so I knew that this time she was really upset.

'Should I speak to the nurse and apologise' I asked.

'Not a chance. She's probably half your age, you'll stay well away from her, you've done enough damage' she snapped.

'You're jealous Sister.'

It was meant as a joke of course, but I immediately regretted saying it. Sister turned on her heels, mumbled something I didn't understand and hurried off to her office. That was the last time I wrote a letter for poor old Joe. However, he was discharged from hospital and returned to the home the following week. I also made a point of apologising to Sister Finity, I was truly sorry, and she was the last person I would ever wish to offend.

Desmond and I were engrossed in a game of cards one afternoon when a very friendly voice suddenly said...

'Who's winning?'

He startled us a bit, because he apparently appeared from nowhere, or at least that's how it seemed to us at the time.

'He's winning,' I said pointing to Desmond.

'Allow me to introduce myself, my name is Tom Swift, I keep myself occupied a couple of afternoons a week walking around the wards and having a chat to patients who appear not to have visitors at the time, that's if they want to have a chat of course, not all of them do.' He smiled as he spoke, and added, 'Please tell me to bugger off if I'm interrupting your game of cards.'

He was a middle aged man, rather short, about five feet six at a guess. It's hard to tell when you're in bed. He was very smartly dressed in a dark suit, white shirt, a very colourful tie with brightly coloured flowers all over it, and highly polished black shoes.

Des and I introduced ourselves, and invited him to sit with us and join in our game of cards, which he agreed to do without hesitation.

'We only play for pennies' Des said.

'That's no problem' Tom answered, slapping a handful of loose change on Des's bedside cabinet.

After cleaning us out at cards, Tom was interested to hear all about our various medical problems, our families, jobs, in fact anything that kept us interested and talking. John Villanis also joined in the conversation, and when Tom finally left, we all agreed that he was a very nice person and looked forward to seeing him again when he next visited the hospital. I noticed that he also called in to see Sister in her office before he left the ward.

Tom Swift soon became a regular visitor to our bedsides, and it wasn't long before we looked upon him as an old friend. He did everything he could to make us comfortable, even volunteering to run small errands for us, such as nipping to the shop for Fish and Chips occasionally. He always seemed to brighten up the day whenever he visited. His cheery red face would buckle with laughter when we used to tell him all the latest dirty jokes that were circulating around the ward.

Every Sunday morning there would be a short service conducted in the ward. Sometimes the lesson was read by a member of the hospital staff, or the local Salvation Army, or maybe a Methodist Minister, and so on. On this particular Sunday I remember it was snowing hard. Tom joined us just before the service was due to start, his face was bright red with the cold, and small flakes of snow were still melting into his black curly hair. I asked him if he would be staying to join us for a bit of hearty singing.

'I think I better had,' he said, 'even if it's just to keep you three reprobates in order.' His eyes twinkled as he spoke.

The battered hospital piano was noisily wheeled into the ward just as Sister appeared accompanied by a couple of junior doctors. Des, wishing to give the best performance he could when the singing started, decided to blow his nose. He did it with such gusto that it also made him break wind loudly.

'For Christ's sake don't do that when the ruddy Vicar appears Des,' I said winking at Tom Swift, who was laughing his head off.

Sister started the ball rolling by addressing all the occupants of the ward. 'Today we are more than pleased to welcome to the ward, your friend and mine, THE REVEREND TOM SWIFT who will conduct today's service!!

Tom stood up and removed his overcoat revealing his dog collar. At this point I distinctly heard Des's voice in a whisper.

'Oh Jesus, Tom's a vicar.'

I was so shocked at Tom turning out to be a priest that I spent the whole of the service trying to remember all the non-Christian type jokes and swearing that had gone on in his presence during previous weeks.

Shortly after the service, Tom, now very much the 'Rev. Swift' in our eyes, returned to our bedside smiling. We were very embarrassed and started burbling out apologies for not conveying the respect his position in life demanded. But Tom put our troubled minds at rest making us promise that we would keep him up to date with the latest jokes circulating the hospital, so that he could relay them to his friends in the local pub on Saturday nights.

A Couple of months passed by, during which time John Villarnis and I were making steady medical progress towards recovery. But sadly there was a noticeable deterioration in Desmond's condition. John had no idea that Desmond had cancer, although I'm sure he could see that something was seriously wrong.

Providing I took things easy, Mr Morgan decided that it would be good for my morale if I was allowed to go home for a couple of days. At the time I crashed, Valerie and I were living in a large mobile home situated on Oxford Airport. So there were a couple of conditions to my being allowed home. First I had to have a suitably made lifting chain and handle fitted to my bed in the caravan so that I could pull myself up, and secondly I would need to have a ramp made so that the wheelchair could be wheeled up to the main entrance door. These problems were soon overcome. I made a few rough sketches of what was required, and Val gave them to the engineers at CSE Aviation. The jobs were completed and in situ within a couple of days, together with a little note that read, 'With Compliments from the lads in the Hangar, Get Well Soon.'

It was wonderful to be away from the hospital if only for a short time. It had been forty-seven weeks since the crash, and this was the first time I had slept away from the smells and sounds of hospital life since I was initially admitted.

I was still in two straight leg plasters, although the term straight leg doesn't really describe the casts accurately. In reality my plasters had been set with a slight bend at the knees, about 20 degrees in fact. The Physiotherapy Department had issued me with an underarm crutch for my right arm, and a gutter crutch for my left arm. The net result of all this was, when I was hoisted up out of my wheelchair to try and walk, I looked like a very wobbly and badly constructed table.

The first time I had stood up on my own with all these bits and pieces to aid me, I just swayed around for a few seconds unable to do anything other than stand there.

'Try taking a step,' Linda said.

'How the bloody hell can I?' was my reply. 'How can I lift up my leg to push it forward if I can't bend the knee?' I asked.

Linda suggested that I should lift the leg up from the hip.

'You try it' I snapped rudely.

Eventually I made a desperate attempt to lunge forward and crashed to the ground scattering bits of plaster all over the place.

I frequently flattened Linda when she attempted to prevent me from falling. It was a bloody painful experience for both of us, but we still managed to laugh about it most of the time. In the end I achieved a couple of wobbly steps. Linda who also looked a little shaken, called it a day and I returned to the ward in my wheelchair feeling utterly hacked off.

At this stage it seemed to me that it would be impossible to ever walk with some form of normality again. A feeling which was enhanced still further when I was told the next day, after X-rays had been taken, that both legs were still broken and showed little signs of mending. How long could this go on?

So having had two comfortable days and nights in our mobile home, and having been shagged to a standstill, I was set up for whatever I had coming to me in the operating theatre.

After a few more days and many more crashes to the floor of the Physiotherapy Room, I could just about stump around for a few steps with the minimum amount of assistance from Linda, and the maximum amount of help from God.

Desmond looked ill and was beginning to lose weight. The knowledge of this poor young man's fate was beginning to get me down. Many times I was close to tears when I listened to him telling me about his hopes and plans for the future, knowing full well that such things would never be. The only person I did confide in was Valerie, I had to talk to someone about it and she was the one person I knew I could trust.

I desperately wanted to do something special for Desmond, and then one evening just before lights out I suddenly had a great idea. It would mean bending a few rules, but what the hell, Des was my friend, he didn't know he only had a short time to live, and I did. Besides, if I could get away with it, the surprise I planned for him was just up my street.

A few months before my aircraft accident I had purchased a lovely old 3.8S Jaguar car that had become my pride and joy. On the morning of my second days "leave" from the hospital, I was eager to see how it felt to be sitting in the driving seat again. I waited until Valerie had slipped out for a while to do some shopping, then after a monumental struggle, considerable pain, and a hell of a lot of swearing, I finally managed to get into the driving seat of my Jag; with my wheelchair parked close alongside. I found that I could just sit behind the wheel with the seat pushed back to its maximum position. Unfortunately the car didn't have an automatic gearbox, but I wasn't going to be put off by such trivial matters as a manual gearbox. I practiced for a while dipping the clutch, and depressing the accelerator without the engine running. As I expected, this proved to be quite difficult but it was by no means impossible. After a while I discovered that I could operate both the clutch and the accelerator by twisting my bum from side to side in the seat, which moved my plastered legs backwards and forwards from the hip. Then came the big question. Did I have time to start the car up and attempt a whiz round before Val returned from shopping? If the future plan I had in mind for Des and myself was to succeed, there was no time for second thoughts. So I fastened the old seat belt and the game was on.

At the first press of the button the car started, 'Marvellous', a quick look around to see that there was no-one about. I grabbed hold of my left leg with both hands, and placed it carefully in front of the clutch pedal. The right leg was already in place over the accelerator, and the gutter crutch was swapped over to my right side so that it could be used to stab at the foot brake in emergencies. One huge thrust and the clutch was down, the gear engaged, and with one enormous leap, and a screeching of tyres, we were off hurtling down the road towards the perimeter track of Oxford Airfield.

'Hells Bells, what about the bloody brakes?' I thought. The car accelerated faster and faster. We shot across the perimeter track and onto the grass airfield. Thank God there were no aircraft about. Assisted by the powered steering I swung the car round into a skidding turn back towards the caravan, I saw someone in air traffic control staring at me through binoculars, but I was too busy to wave. My right leg in it's full length plaster case was jammed hard against the accelerator and I couldn't move the blasted thing. I turned off the ignition switch and grabbed the handbrake just clouting the empty wheelchair as we skidded to a halt, followed immediately by a cloud of dust.

'That was absolutely bloody marvellous' I thought.

Valerie, who had unfortunately seen the latter part of the "practice run in the jag", gave forth with a lecture second to none. Then after assuring me that I was totally mad, listened to my plan.

'I intend to sneak Desmond out of hospital and take him for a ride around the grounds of Blenheim Palace in my car…It's a beautiful place, it will do his moral the world of good, I'm sure he'll love it.'

'You can't do that, you'll kill yourself, and more to the point you could kill someone else' she said.

'Not with plenty of practice on the airfield' I argued.

It would take pages to reiterate the lengthy argument that followed before I finally convinced Val that nothing she said would change my mind.

A few days later I was back in the ward. The removable side plate of my wheelchair had been taken to the hospital workshops to be straightened after I had bumped into it with the car, but I never told anyone how it got dented.

Later I spoke to John Villarnis and told him about my plan to drive Desmond around Blenheim Park.

'You'll never get away with it' he said. 'If you actually manage to get out of here with Des, which I doubt, you are bound to come to grief in that car of yours, especially when you try and drive through Oxford City Centre in those straight leg plasters, I suggest we think of something more safely attainable.'

'Not a bit of it John, my mind is made up but I will need your help.'

My request for help seemed to stun John for a moment. His face took on a sincerely worried look. He ran his hands through his curly black hair several times before answering.

'OK, but it depends on what you want me to do Ray.'

We brought our wheelchairs closer together so that we couldn't be overheard.

'Here's the plan'…

I outlined my scheme to John and the part I wished him to play. He stopped looking worried and turned pale instead.

'Bloody hell Ray, where do you get such hair-brained schemes from? It's impossible, and even if we do pull it off we will be thrown out of here for certain.'

'Never mind all that John, are you up for it mate?'

John looked is if he would chicken out, so I added...

'Just think of the fun poor old Des will have, surely he deserves it.'

My final remark seemed to clinch the deal and John indicated that he would be willing to help, but obviously Des had to agree to the plan.

There was no trouble in getting Desmond to agree. He really was a great guy, with lots of spirit, and in spite of the fact that he was in considerable pain; he would still do anything for a laugh. Somehow, under the circumstances, with me being the only person other than the staff to know about Desmond's terminal illness, I felt that I would be forgiven for bending the rules a little in order to give Desmond a bit of excitement. But I had to be sure in my own mind that I could pull this off without us being involved in a serious accident.

Operation "Blenheim" as we called it, was planned to take place the next time I was allowed to go home for a couple of days, which on average turned out to be about once every three or four weeks. In the meantime the three of us had just as much fun planning the operation as we hoped to have on the actual day. Most evenings after our visitors had left, we would huddle round Des's bed and discuss each person's part in great detail, giggling away like three naughty schoolboys.

A week passed, during which time we had managed to get into trouble twice. As I have mentioned before, Desmond loved to talk about anything that concerned flying. So I decided to teach him and John a bit of formation work using our wheelchairs. We soon became very proficient at travelling up and down the ward in Line Astern. And in more spacious surroundings such as the Physiotherapy Hall, I taught them formation changes from 'Line Astern' to section Vic Three, Echelon Port and Starboard.

Having reached a highly proficient standard, a mission was planned to visit the Ladies Ward one evening after the visitors had left. Ann Herbert invited us over for a glass or two of white wine. Having first collided with the doors, we made an impressive entrance into the Ladies Ward in a 'V' formation, greeted by cheers from all the female patients. One elderly lady kept shouting give us a kiss! But we were threatened with immediate ejection by the staff nurse if we didn't behave ourselves. Unfortunately when we returned to our own ward rather late in the evening, and maybe just a little worse for drink, we were greeted with…

'I am not amused' from the duty nurse.

She obviously failed to appreciate the skill in our sweeping line astern entry and skilful night landing after lights out!

On another occasion, Des and I provided close formation escort to John on a photographic detail around the hospital. John, anxious to get photographs for his "Life in Hospital" album, led us down to a small room near to the operating theatre. We sneaked in quickly, John with his camera at the ready. On entering we saw something lying on a table wrapped up in a green coloured sheet, John took a quick flash photograph just before someone shouted from behind us…

'What the hell do you think you are doing?'

This necessitated a high-speed retreat back to the ward. But it didn't end there. We think John had probably photographed a dead body, he was visited by the Matron who threatened to confiscate his camera if he caused any further trouble, and I got the blame for leading him astray.

During the week my Physiotherapist Linda Marklew informed me that it would be OK for me to go home for the weekend, and return to the hospital at nine a.m. the following Monday morning. This was the opportunity we had been waiting for to carry out operation "Blenheim". I just had time for a last minute briefing with John and Desmond before being bungled into a mini ambulance, complete with wheelchair, and taken to my home on the airfield.

I spent most of that evening and well into the night trying to convince Valerie that it would be perfectly safe for me to drive with my legs in plasters. The car was locked up, and Val knew that I had the only set of keys. In the end she said…

'Do what you like, I know that I wouldn't be able to stop you even if I wanted to, but I will have nothing what-so-ever to do with it,' and that was that.

Next morning, back in Burrows Ward, John, who was now able to walk without the aid of crutches, asked Sister Finity if he could push Des around the hospital in his wheelchair for a while. He had done this several times before, so his request was granted without suspicion. Meanwhile, back on the airfield, I had started up the Jag at nine a.m. precisely and proceeded cautiously down the Woodstock Road on my way to the Nuffield Hospital. It was a clear morning and the weather forecast for the day looked promising. I was still wearing my hospital pyjamas and dressing gown. This was mainly for two reasons. First of all I couldn't get normal clothing over the plasters that stretched from the top of my legs to the tip of my toes, and secondly I hoped that, if I was caught, I would be judged more sympathetically!

At ten past nine I had reached the outskirts of Oxford, and was approaching what was obviously going to be the tricky bit, driving through the city centre. Fortunately I didn't encounter any difficulties until I reached the traffic lights in the centre of the city. My heart sank as I watched the bloody things turn RED just before I reached them! I had positioned my left foot over the clutch when I first entered the car, the only way I could move this leg now was by twisting my body around in the seat, and by so doing I was able to depress the clutch, a technique I had perfected in advance on the airfield. But today it all seemed a lot more dramatic with scores of cars and pedestrians milling around, totally different to the solitude and calmness of Oxford Airport's perimeter track.

A quick lurch round in the seat and the clutch pedal was fully depressed, but the engine was screaming away like a Stuka dive-bomber! In a brief moment of sheer panic I had applied the handbrake just a little too enthusiastically which caused the car to skid to a halt at an embarrassing angle a few inches past the traffic lights without hitting anything. I noticed one or two nosey types staring at me as I struggled to lift my right leg off the accelerator. By the time I had succeeded the lights had turned to green, and the chap in the car behind me was using his horn with the enthusiasm of a Boy's Brigade Trumpeter. I twisted sideways in the seat releasing the clutch with a snap, my right leg also shot forward hard on the accelerator, the tyres screeched, and the car bloody nearly took off! Thank God there was no one in front of me.

I had one or two small setbacks of this kind before finally arriving at the Hospital car park at five minutes to ten feeling a little exhausted.

Having parked the car as far away from the main doors as I could, I waited for John to appear with Desmond in his wheelchair as planned. It was a nerve-racking business; I hunched myself down in the car trying not to look conspicuous. Practically every member of the hospital staff that knew me passed through those doors, I felt certain that sooner or later I would be spotted, but fortunately no-one took any notice of me.

I was very relieved when John and Desmond emerged through the main doors. As planned I started up the car and jerked my way towards the door. All we had to do now was bungle Des into the back as quickly as possible without being discovered. John succeeded in getting the removable side of the wheelchair off, but just as he was about to push Des on to the back seat, a porter hurried over to us and asked if he could help! I was convinced the game was up, but strangely enough the porter never looked at me at all, he simply helped Des into the back seat, covered him up with his bed blanket and waved goodbye. I told John to hide the wheelchair as planned, and I would meet him back there at two o'clock sharp. With that, after a couple of false starts, we were on our way to Blenheim Palace.

Having gained a little more confidence, the journey to Blenheim Palace seemed reasonably uneventful; perhaps it was because the morning rush hour traffic had ended.

It was a joy to see Desmond laughing away and thoroughly enjoying himself. I could see him clearly in the rear mirror, which I had adjusted in order to keep a watchful eye on him, and relied on the wing mirrors to keep a lookout for the police. He was well covered by the blanket John had smuggled out with him, but seeing him out of the context of the ward made me realise how really ill he looked. His face was gaunt, his eyes sunken, and the usual colour of his beautiful dark brown skin had become pallor and almost yellowish. But to see him looking so excited was a million dollar bonus as far as I was concerned.

I had been worried about the possible reactions of the gateman at Blenheim Palace when we arrived looking like a couple of escaped patients. So, after lots of persuading, Valerie reluctantly promised to telephone the estates office to explain the purpose of the visit and see if they would agree to allow us into the park free of charge.

As we drove through Woodstock I began to feel a little apprehensive. Mobile telephones hadn't been invented in those days so I had no way of knowing whether or not Valerie had been successful in contacting the Blenheim Estates Manager.

I carefully positioned my gutter crutch on the brake pedal of the car as we drove slowly up to the impressive Gold and Black entrance gates to Blenheim Park. If anything was to go wrong with our plans, this would be the time for it to happen. I wound the window down to speak to a smartly dressed official who approached us with a broad smile on his face. Judging by his pleasant expression, Valerie must have been successful in obtaining permission for us to enter the grounds. He bent down to peer inside the car and his expression instantly changed to one of complete disbelief.

'Blimey, where on earth did you come from?' he said.

I suppose I must have looked a little strange, sitting behind the wheel of a Jaguar outside Blenheim Palace at 10.40 in the morning, dressed in pyjamas and dressing gown.

His mouth dropped open even wider when he caught sight of Desmond stretched out across the rear seats. He had obviously become too hot and discarded the blanket; an oversize hospital nightshirt was now all that covered his frail body.

'May I ask you gentlemen exactly what you are doing here?'

I could understand why the gate attendant was suspicious, he obviously hadn't received any communication from his office about us and probably thought we had escaped from a mental home!

I looked in the mirror at Des, I felt desperately sorry for him, he was clearly in pain and sipping the morphine based medicine from a bottle that he always carried with him.

'Come on Ray,' I thought to myself, 'this is Des's day out, you've got to explain why we are looking like this, and why we obviously need permission to drive round the grounds instead of parking the car and walking.'

The gate attendant stood patiently by the car whilst I tried to explain the situation. But unfortunately I was unable to say anything about Desmond being terminally ill. Also, if he called the police, I would have been in endless trouble.

My only hope was that Valerie had contacted the Blenheim Estates office. I asked the bewildered gate-man if he would mind getting in touch with his office, assuring him that if he did so the matter would be cleared up immediately.

Fingers crossed I watched the attendants face through the small window of his gate office as he spoke to someone in authority on the other end of the telephone. Occasionally he looked towards the car as he spoke, showing no sign of the instructions he was receiving from his employers. Finally he strolled back to the car, and bent down to speak to us…

'Everything's quite in order sir, I suggest you keep to the main roads.'

He paused, then added…

'I hope your friend will enjoy himself sir, have a lovely day.' With that he allowed us through.

We drove around the grounds for a while, stopping for a moment outside the Palace itself so that Desmond could have a good look at this magnificent building.

'I'd like to go in there one day Ray' he said.

'I'll take you mate when you get a bit better' my voice faltered, and I felt terribly guilty for making a promise I knew I would never be able to keep.

Finally we parked by a large lake, and sat there for a while admiring the natural beauty of the palace grounds and eating the sandwiches that Val had packed for us.

Desmond told me of his childhood in Jamaica, and the happy times he had with his father whom he loved so much. Then he cried a little as he described how his dad had tragically died when Des was only twelve years old. He told me how his mother had remarried and of the abhorrence that now existed between himself and his Stepfather.

We were in the grounds of the home of Sir Winston Churchill, so I told Des of the time when I had been one of two instructors who taught the young Winston Churchill, son of Sir Randolph, to fly at Oxford Airport. It made Des laugh when I told him about the boisterous games we used to play in the flying club bar after a days flying. Winston used to smoke the same large cigars as his Grandfather, and we would take it in turns hitting him on the top of his head with a tin tray in order to knock the ash from his cigar! The first to succeed would get a free drink paid for by the other participants.

As we pulled up at the main Blenheim gates to leave, the attendant came out to ask if we had enjoyed ourselves. He gave each of us a postcard showing the inside of the Palace, and a lovely coloured brochure with the compliments of the Blenheim Palace Estate.

Desmond was delighted, and invited the gate-man to Burrows Ward for a cup of tea!

The journey back was not too bad, and we arrived at the hospital a few minutes after two o'clock, unscathed. As planned, I initially parked the car in the staff car park which was right outside the visitors entrance doors of the Nuffield where I saw John was waiting with Desmond's wheelchair. As soon as he saw us, he shot out and opened the rear door of the car. He started to say that no-one had asked where Des was, but cut the sentence short with...

'Oh shit!'

He slammed the car door closed, and hobbled back into the hospital pushing the still empty wheelchair. Straight away I saw the reason for John's hasty retreat. There, right alongside us, Mr Morgan our esteemed surgeon, had drawn up in his car and was getting out. I remember thinking: 'all this way, and we've blown it at the last minute.'

Mr Morgan stood for a moment between the two cars, putting his jacket on; it was like waiting for the death sentence to be pronounced. He looked at me, smiled and began to walk away. Then what he had seen suddenly registered. He stopped abruptly, turned round and headed back towards us. I told Desmond to leave the talking to me, and wound the car window down.

Mr Morgan bent down to speak to me, his rugged face folded and his bushy eyebrows knitted themselves together into a frown as he peered into the car. Although his face was still directed towards me, his eyes were focused firmly on Desmond curled up on the rear seat. Then, just as I was about to burble out some sort of explanation, he spoke to me, his gruff voice no more than a whisper.

'I don't want to know about this Ray... I haven't seen you. Have I?'

'No sir' I replied. As he turned to go, a gentle smile spread slowly across his face. He walked away quickly passing through the swing doors and out of sight.

Somehow, unaccountably, we hadn't been missed by any of the ward staff. Or had we? Nothing was ever said to me about it, so I will never know for certain.

For me it had been a very emotional day. That day has now become one of my most cherished memories.

Weeks passed. Desmond Harper's physical condition was deteriorating rapidly. All the medical staff were doing everything they possibly could to help relieve him of the terrible pain he was obviously suffering, but there was little they could do to help the depressive state that had gradually taken over his mind. He had never asked the hospital staff about the seriousness of his illness. Consequently he still had no idea that his body was rapidly being taken over by cancer.

Late one afternoon I was returning to Burrows Ward from the Occupational Therapy Department in my wheelchair, when I came face to face with Sister Finity. She looked extremely worried and asked if I would mind helping her to persuade Desmond to return to his bed in the ward. He had apparently locked himself in one of the toilet cubicles and was refusing to come out. Sister said that he sounded desperate and knowing that I got along pretty well with Des, she thought that he might see sense and return to the ward if I had a word with him. Otherwise she would have to get a porter to unlock the door from the outside and forcibly move Desmond back to the ward, which was the last thing she wanted to do. I agreed to help if I could although, knowing how stubborn Des had been of late, I doubted if he would listen to me.

Sister took me up to the patient's washroom where all the toilet doors were open with the exception of one.

'Is that you in there Des?' I said.

There was no reply, but I could hear Desmond taking gasps of air, and as far as I could tell, he was obviously in grave trouble. I manoeuvred my wheelchair as close to the door as I could.

'What's up old mate?' I whispered, 'you can talk Des, there's no-one else in here.'

Des didn't answer. I looked back at Sister Finity standing silently by the entrance door. She nodded for me to continue.

'Is there anything I can do for you Des? just tell me what's up mate, you can trust me, you know that.'

I waited for a reply. I heard Des take a deep breath, before he spoke.

'I've had enough,' his voice was weak and faltering. 'I can't take any more, the pain, it's bloody killing me… I'm shitting blood here Ray... I'm frightened, just can't take any more.'

His words gave way to sobs. I felt so desperately helpless. Des obviously needed immediate medical assistance, and Sister didn't want to have him dragged out. I searched my brain for the right words to persuade him to unlock the door, but could think of nothing. For nearly six months I had slept in the next bed to Desmond knowing he was slowly dying, but until this moment I hadn't realised how much of a close friend he had become. The mental stress of all this was now beginning to affect me as well. Rightly or wrongly I also felt angry that they had chosen to tell me that Desmond was dying, when he didn't even know himself. I just sat there in my wheelchair not knowing what to say.

Sister crept up behind me, placed her hands on my shoulders and whispered…

'He MUST come out now Ray, otherwise I will have to get the porter.'

On the spur of the moment, without thinking, I shouted at the top of my voice…

'Come on Des, open the door and stop f.….g about. No-one can possibly help you if you're locked up in the bog feeling sorry for yourself. We all have our bad days you know, now be a good chap and open the bloody door, they'll have you fixed up in no time… come on mate, move yourself.'

Sister let go of my shoulders as if she had received an electric shock. I thought the only hope of getting Des out quickly was to provoke him,

Thankfully it worked. Desmond slammed the door catch back and opened the door. I was shocked to see the distressed condition he was in. He had dragged himself sideways into his wheelchair, and sat there in his nightshirt saturated in dark red blood. He looked at me, his gaunt, pathetic little face and tear-filled eyes made me feel like the cruellest bastard on earth for shouting at him. He just stared at me as if he had seen me for the first time.

'Come on mate, you'll soon feel better when the doctor takes a look at you.' My choice of words sounded totally inadequate.

I backed off quickly as Des propelled his wheelchair straight at me.

'You're not going to take a pop me at me are you Des? It's bad form to thump a cripple mate!'

He swung his wheelchair round sharply and headed for the door at great speed, as he passed me I turned my head away so that he didn't see any sign of the telltale tears streaming down my face.

When I returned to the ward Mr Williamson, one of the older and slightly senile patients in the ward was being told off by the Staff Nurse for flashing his Willie at the visitors as they passed the end of his bed: 'At least there is still a humorous side to hospital life' I thought.

The very next day, all of us who were considered fit enough were taken to the OT department to "enjoy" a general interest lecture given by a very kind gentleman from the Forestry Commission. The subject chosen for our afternoon's entertainment was "Conifer Trees", a lecture that promised to be as exciting as watching paint dry.

About a dozen of us were taken in our beds to the Occupational Therapy Department. The beds were placed so that we faced a large blackboard next to a table supporting a small tree in a plant-pot. Before the lecture started, the Senior Occupational Therapist on duty asked me if I would mind saying a few words of appreciation to the speaker when he finished his lecture. I began to understand the true meaning of "a captive audience".

Unfortunately, although from previous experience one has to say not totally unexpectedly, things started to go wrong at an early stage. About ten minutes into the scheduled one-hour lecture, the sound of gentle snoring emerged from a member of the audience. It was a bit like a cat purring to start with, but gradually rose to a sort of farmyard snorting that ended thankfully with a rasping snap and a short apology.

Everybody looked a little embarrassed but finally we settled down again to learn more about the mysteries of conifer trees. It wasn't long however before our snoring artist decided to give a repeat performance, this time with considerably more gusto. The snoring grew louder and louder, sported a throaty effect that seemed likely to develop into a coughing fit, but didn't. Instead it encouraged a rather elderly lady in the next bed to join in with a rather nasty sounding snarl, and before you could say knife, there were several others at it.

I felt sorry for the speaker, who pressed on regardless, increasing the volume of his voice in an attempt to be heard over the din, which by now had reached ear-shattering proportions.

Ann Herbert, who was in the next bed to me, was trying to conceal her amusement by covering up the lower half of her face with the bedclothes. The final blow, or should I say shock? came when someone decided to add a loud and rather prolonged fart to the proceedings, the like of which reached barrack room standards. I looked round to see if there were any of the OT staff around who could help to rouse some of the half-dead audience, but unfortunately not one member of staff was in sight. After a while our lecturer suddenly stopped talking about trees and asked if those who were still conscious would like him to pack up or continue with his lecture. Of course those of us that were still awake insisted that he should continue. Somehow the poor chap struggled on to the end of his talk. He did ask if anyone had any questions they would like to ask him, but no-one had. At that moment the doors burst open and several porters arrived to take us back to our wards. The sudden bang startled everyone and woke up those that were still asleep!

Having been asked to say a few words of appreciation, I thanked our resolute lecturer for entertaining us with his superior knowledge of conifer trees, adding somewhat embarrassedly that everyone present had enjoyed the lecture immensely. My fellow patients mustered up a weak applause. With that the man from the Forestry Commission mumbled something to the effect that he too had found the afternoon considerably entertaining, picked up his small tree in the plant pot, and left.

Following the surgeon's ward round one morning I was taken to the plaster room to have both of my long leg plasters removed and replaced by much shorter gaiter plasters which stretched from just below my knee to just above my ankle. I was overjoyed, as this was a real positive sign of improvement. But I hadn't realised that it also meant I would now incur more pain in my knees and ankles which had been immobilised for many months by the long leg plasters. Had I known the extent of suffering that was to follow, I would not have been so keen to be making my way to physiotherapy.

I had become reasonably self-sufficient over the weeks and was walking quite well with the aid of crutches. But now, with nothing to support my knees and ankles, it was going to be a completely different ball game. Dignity was also at stake, for without the bowler irons, which were attached to my former full length plasters, I suddenly became six inches shorter. No longer would I tower magnificently over Linda when she assisted me, instead I had become an unquestionable short-arse. I was even an inch or so shorter than I had been before the accident. The reason being Mr Morgan had shortened my left leg so that it would be the same length as my right leg which had lost about an inch during the many operations needed to mend the multiple breaks it had sustained. This prevented me from having a permanent limp for the rest of my life. I was certainly grateful for that, but I was only five feet eight inches tall before the crash, now I was five feet seven, any shorter and I would need wheels on my backside! The whole thing could have been quite distressing.

Linda walked over to me beaming from ear to ear as usual.

'Well this is a great day for you Raymond, isn't it?' she said.

She was holding a pair of my shoes that Valerie had brought in weeks earlier. The shoes had been kept in my bedside locker, waiting for the day when perhaps I would be able to wear them again.

'The Orthopaedic Engineer has taken a look at these Ray, and as your leg plasters held your feet in a down pointing attitude, he will probably have to raise the heels quite a bit to get you going' she said.

'That does it' I thought, apart from being a short-arse 'I'm going to be mincing around in high heeled shoes.'

Linda was undoubtedly preparing me for the tough time that lay ahead. The bandages holding the splints to my legs were removed.

'Not much there.'

Linda was referring to the small angle of bend in my left knee, but, seeing that I was sitting there in the rather floppy short pants the hospital had provided, the double meaning of her remarks caused us both to giggle.

'Your legs have been in and out of plaster for over eighteen months, therefore your muscles have wasted away quite a lot and the joints in your knees and ankles will be very stiff and painful, so don't expect too much at first.'

I listened intently to everything Linda was saying. She was not the sort of person to exaggerate, even so, it was impossible to imagine what it would be like when I tried to stand up without the support of the plasters that had previously held my ankles and knees rigidly in place.

Linda wrapped bandages that had been soaked in a bucket of ice water around my knees. After about twenty minutes she removed the bandages and started to work on the left knee again. Immediately I felt a most distressing pain shoot through my leg. I now realised for the first time how vulnerable to pain I would be when I tried to stand without the support of plaster casts.

'I don't think you will be able to stand up at all Ray until we have built up the muscles in your legs' Linda said.

The problems were all too obvious. My legs were as slim as baby's arms, with huge lumps where my knee joints were. Then, from below the knee they gradually tapered out again to my ankles where the skin was shining like an over inflated balloon.

'How am I going to build up the muscles in my legs if I can't bend them to do any exercises Linda?'

'All in good time' she said.

I felt so frustrated at her reply, what the hell did she mean all in good time? I've already been in hospital for over eighteen months. For a moment my mind snapped and I became irrational.

'But I haven't got any time Linda, I need to get out of this bloody place soon. It's not just the aircrew medical I have to pass, the longer I'm away from flying the more I will have to do to regain my licenses, written examinations, and flight tests! Can't we push things on somehow? Pain injections or something? I'll put up with anything in order to get things cracking.'

I was being totally unreasonable. Linda simply ignored my outburst and took advantage of my sudden eruption to continue working on my left knee, hoping to get another degree or so of movement out of it without me noticing.

'I'm sorry Linda, it's not your fault, I wouldn't be getting on as well as I am if it wasn't for you, but we have to get crack.....Aaaagh, shit that hurt!'

Then followed the most torturous half hour I had spent in the Physiotherapy Department, with plenty more to come.

With the help of porters I tried to stand up between the parallel bars. But I had no strength in my legs at all, they just buckled and I could do nothing about it.

I returned to the ward totally disillusioned. I was beginning to have serious doubts about being able to fly again. But I was determined not to give in.

There was however a good side to my lengthy stay in hospital. My father regularly brought my son Eddy in to see me. He would tell me about his adventures at school and all he mischief he had been up to. Ed could always brighten the dullest days for me, and still does, he's my pride and joy.

Over the next few weeks Linda worked relentlessly on me twice a day, my progress was also being closely monitored by Mr Morgan. Each painful visit to Physio seemed to follow a pattern of carefully planned torture! First the dreaded ice treatment. Linda arrived with a bucket half full of ice cubes topped up with ice cold water. She soaked long lengths of bandage in the ice water, and wrapped the freezing bandage around my knee. Then after the ice had taken its effect, numbing the knee until it felt almost frozen solid, she would begin to gently force the leg to bend a little more. The ice would deaden the agony a little, but by no means completely. Her eyes never left mine, watching for every telltale wince. Then she would measure the angle of bend attained at the end of her efforts, and make the appropriate entry on my notes, always remembering to give me those much appreciated few words of encouragement.

'You've gained half a degree movement with your left leg today Ray, that's very good, you should be pleased.'

Linda repeats the process all over again on my right knee. Then she replenishes the bucket of now melted ice with more ice cubes and applies the same treatment to my ankles. The lateral movement in each ankle is almost non-existent, the pain level bordering on totally unbearable, but gentle hands work smoothly and untiringly, persuading the ankle to give just a fraction more. She dries my feet and wraps them in warm towels and leaves the room for a few moments. When she returns, Linda is carrying a large bowl of hot melted tallow. She carefully lowers my left hand in the bowl up to the wrist. It's very hot. After a few seconds she removes my hand from the tank, the tallow is allowed to dry, then the process is repeated several times until I appear to be wearing a thick white tallow glove, this retains the heat and helps her to exercise my fingers that were still unable to make a fist or grip anything. Linda assures me that in time everything will get back to normal, but it could still take weeks or even months. As she works on my hand manipulating the fingers, the dull aching is mellowed by the warmth of the wax, she watches my every reaction, and I am moved by the tender caring nature of this dedicated young girl.

'Try clenching your fist up as tight as you can Ray' she says.

I try hard, and it feels for all the world that it is clenched tight, but when I look I am disappointed to see I could easily place a table tennis ball in the partly opened hand I thought had become a fist. Linda peels the tallow off like a glove and gently places my hand back on my lap saying…

'We must be patient.'

One more torture before we begin the slog between parallel bars. I am wheeled up to a trolley supporting a small electrical device. The electrodes are first placed on my left hand, the machine is switched on. A sharp electric shock starts to pulsate at regular intervals, the current passing through the muscles of my hand making it move spasmodically with each electric pulse. Linda leaves it to me to control the intensity of the shocks. Eventually I get it to its maximum strength, the chronic pain is causing sweat to run down my face, yet the movement in my fingers is barely perceptible. Finally the electrodes are placed in turn on my left and right ankles, the pulsating shock is once more turned on producing painful convulsive movements in my feet.

At the end of the session, Linda wipes the sweat from my body and prodding my nose with her finger says…

'Remember, WE have no time for thoughts of failure or self pity, and however impossible it seems now, WE are going to win, and don't you forget it.'

I never forgot it, and I will never forget Linda for her continuous and tireless efforts to get me back to full strength.

One morning in the early hours, just as it was beginning to get light, Desmond called out to me. He sounded frightened, although he didn't actually raise his voice.

'What's the matter old mate?' I asked.

'Am I awake or dreaming?'

'You're awake Des' I said, 'can't you see its just beginning to get light?'

Desmond sat up in bed and was very quiet for a few seconds, then to my horror he said…

'I can't see anything Ray.'

I felt myself go cold, I was dreading anything like this happening, and I don't know what made me say it, but I answered him immediately.

'Ha that's those drugs you're on mate, they told me about them, they didn't want to frighten you, but they told me to tell you that it was just the effect of the drugs if you couldn't see, and it should only last for a short while.'

Desmond was strangely quiet; he sat upright in his bed, his head moving from side to side. Then he slowly held his hand out towards me, I caught hold of it, and for a while I sat there holding his hand tightly with tears steaming down my face. Then without another word he lay down again and went to sleep. I buried my face in the pillow and wept silently.

Desmond slept on, and as soon as Sister Finity came on duty, I struggled into my wheelchair and made my way to her office. I told her what had happened and the dreadful lie I had told Desmond, then I sat back and waited for the reprimand I deserved.

Sister questioned me about Desmond's reactions to what I had told him, then after some thought, she said she would inform the nursing staff of what had happened, and we would leave it like that until she was able to speak to Mr Morgan.

Later that day Mr Morgan came to see me whilst I was in OT. I apologised for lying to Desmond, explaining that under the circumstances I felt so sorry for him and really didn't know what to say. Then he gave me a look that I had come to recognise as his 'bad news' look.

His bushy eyebrows half frowning Mr Morgan told me that Desmond probably would not be with us for very much longer.

I had been expecting this news of course, but to have it confirmed was devastating. I had been next to Desmond day and night for over six months knowing that he was dying. Every day we had talked of the future, of our plans together when he qualified as an accountant and I would probably be able to pull a few strings so that he could be employed in our accountants office at Oxford Airport. All this time Desmond knew nothing of his true illness and inevitable destiny. The strain of this relationship was unbearable.

When I returned to the ward from OT my heart sank. The screens had been drawn around Desmond's bed. I could hear the voice of our good friend, The Reverend Tom Swift, talking quietly to Sister from behind the screens. Sister called Desmond's name several times, but I never heard him answer, and without being told I knew my friend had finally slipped deep into the peaceful chasm of death and at last felt no more pain. Although I felt that a great weight had been lifted from my shoulders, I was absolutely heartbroken.

Des was buried in an Oxford churchyard a week later. I attended the funeral with Staff Nurse William's who took me complete with wheelchair to the funeral in her car. The Reverend Tom Swift officiated at the request of Desmond's mother.

Needless to say it was a very sad affair, but the thing that really bugged me was the vast number of people that attended the funeral. There must have been in excess of one hundred mourners and, with the exception of Desmond's mother and Tom Swift not one of them had bothered to visit Desmond during the six months I was in the next bed to him in hospital. I was disgusted with them; to my mind they were nothing but a bunch of hypocrites.

Throughout the church service I couldn't take my eyes off the coffin. It was hard to believe that my friend's frail body was actually in there and that I would never see him or speak to him again. In my mind I could hear Desmond's voice, I could hear him laugh and I could hear him crying. I prayed that God would forgive me for all the lies I had told Desmond to protect him from the dreadful truth. But somehow I have never forgiven myself.

Tom Swift, bless him, broke down during his sermon at the point when he mentioned the great courage Desmond had shown throughout his long and painful illness.

The church service itself was the same as others I had attended, but the burial ceremony by the graveside took me by surprise as it seemed to be more of a celebration than a funeral.

I suppose it was the standard way for funerals to be carried out in Jamaica. Everyone was dressed in the brightest of clothes and seemed to be extremely happy. It got a bit tricky at one stage when Tom came to the ashes to ashes bit. One of the mourners, who had been prancing around the graveside, suddenly shouted hallelujah and gave the vicar a hearty slap on the back which, had it not been for his extreme agility, would have sent him head first into the grave.

As we drove away from the graveyard the sounds of joyful singing gradually faded and I was glad to get away from it all. I felt a mixture of loss, sadness and relief from the strain of knowing what the ultimate outcome of Desmond's illness would be. He was the bravest young person I had ever known, and the last six months had taught me the true values of life and friendship. Even to this day I frequently find myself crying when I think about him.

That night, after the visitors had left the ward and the lights were dimmed, I looked at Desmond's empty bed, and whispered quietly…

'You're at peace now Des old chum.'

Then somehow I felt at peace too. That night, in the silence of the ward, I gazed at the multitude of stars that shone brightly through the large windows opposite our beds and wondered where Des was now. Finally I slipped into a blissful nights sleep.

Having Tom Swift as a friend restored my faith in the church and the clergy. He visited me again shortly after Desmond's funeral and the question of my faith was raised, so I told him of the times when I had felt totally rejected by the church on more than one occasion.

It started when I was about ten years old, my friend Eddy had been a server in a small church in King's Lynn. One day I arranged to meet him after a rehearsal. It was raining quite heavily as I stood outside by the arched gateway listening to the distant sound of the choir singing. To me it seemed a very beautiful but sad sound, and I would have given anything to go inside and listen. I walked down the path from the gate to the main door, rain dripping off my school cap and nose. I sat down on a little bench just inside the porch. Moments later the vicar, dressed in all his robes, appeared at the door.

'And what do you want lad?' he asked.

'Can I come in please?' I asked, feeling a bit like a pauper begging for something!

The vicar looked at me suspiciously.

'Certainly not' he said, 'this is a rehearsal, come back on Sunday with your parents, now off you go.'

That experience of rejection from the church has never left my memory.

The next rebuff happened a few weeks after my aeroplane crash whilst I was recovering in the Radcliffe Hospital.

Heavily dosed up with pain killing drugs, I was feeling sorry for myself at the time and needed to speak to someone from the church.

Late one afternoon Robin Melville, a patient in the ward with me, had a visit from a Catholic Priest. They pulled the screens around his bed, and I could hear the priest talking quietly to Robin. I asked one of the nurses if she would ask the priest if he could spare a few minutes to talk to me before he left. Eventually after the screens were drawn back I saw the nurse ask the priest if he would speak to me. He looked at me, then said something to the nurse, picked up the little briefcase he had brought in with him, and walked out. She came over to my bed and said that unfortunately he was pushed for time and had to rush off.

Once again I felt rejected by the church. Surely the least that priest could have done was walk over to my bed and tell me he was too busy to talk to me right now, but he didn't even consider that I was worth the time of day. Those two incidents made me feel totally rejected by the church. Since then of course my faith had been restored by the love and kindness of The Reverend Tom Swift who had become a true friend.

Also I had experienced another rather unusual incident connected with the church which had not been at all unpleasant.

Before being transferred to the Nuffield, Paul Reed, a fellow flying instructor from Oxford Airport whose ultimate ambition was to become a flying missionary, visited me in the Radcliffe and gave me a small bible that I have treasured to this day. At that time he was neither priest nor preacher of any kind, but he took the trouble of listening to the problems I had with my faith.

A few months later Paul came to see me again and, with Sister's permission, arranged to take me to a church service near Oxford the following Sunday morning.

It was all very exciting; he rolled up at the hospital with a mate of his in a borrowed fifteen-hundredweight builders truck. I was secured to a wheelchair with an aircraft tie-down strap, bundled unceremoniously onto the back of the truck and told to hold on tight. After a hair-raising journey we arrived at a little church on the outskirts of Oxford, where I was unceremoniously hauled from the back of the truck and wheeled into the church. I spent the whole of the service parked in the aisle wearing pyjamas and a dressing gown. The vicar kindly welcomed me, and spoke to me again before I was dumped back into the truck and returned to the Radcliffe.

CHAPTER 16.

Grasping at straws.

Laying in a hospital bed certainly gave one time to think. My mind always used to return to the past.

In the early days of my flying training, way back in 1957, the arrival of our dear son Eddy changed our lives completely. It was a wonderful feeling to be a father and be blessed with the little son I had always wanted. He turned out to be everything I had prayed for. I was so proud of him when he was little, and when he grew up he became the best friend I ever had.

Mary gave up her job when Eddy was born, and paying for flying training was now way down on my list of priorities.

My aim and keen ambition to make aviation my full-time career never wavered, and I tried to fit in at least two or three lessons a month.

By August 1957, my training had progressed to navigation and cross-country exercises. Then, just as everything seemed to be going well, I had my first encounter with fear!

It was a clear, rather cold day with very little surface wind. I was sent off solo in Tiger Moth G-AMEY to practice steep turns, carry out a solo spin and round off the flight with a practice forced landing on the airfield. My logbook tells me I had a total of seven hours fifty minutes solo flying experience at that time.

The fully developed spin was still in the training syllabus in those days and when authorised for solo spinning you were required to carry out the exercise over the airfield so that your instructor could see that you did in fact put the aircraft into a fully developed spin and recover after three complete turns.

Having completed the steep turns, I climbed the aircraft to 3000 ft. over

Kidlington Airfield and carried out my mandatory solo spin, levelling out at 2000 ft. Then, having checked that the area was clear of circuit traffic, I unlocked the auto slats, closed the throttle to simulate engine failure, and commenced the practice force landing.

Gliding down at 55 kts. I was heading towards my selected 1000 ft. area when things started to go wrong. To start with I had concentrated far too long on my emergency checks and allowed the aircraft to drift off my planned descent path. Also we were now down to 800 ft. without having cleared the engine. I hastily opened the throttle to the full power position, to my dismay nothing happened. There was no response from the engine at all, it was as dead as a door-knocker!

It's surprising how quickly you remember things when it's too late... my instructor's words of wisdom soon came rapidly to mind: 'Never lose sight of the selected landing area,' and 'Never open the throttle too quickly as this can cause a rich mixture cut and stop the engine.'

I didn't think I had opened the throttle too quickly, but to be absolutely sure I closed it and opened it again slowly, but there was no response from the engine. I quickly checked that the fuel was still on, there was plenty of petrol in the tank, and the ignition switches were both still in the 'on' position.

By this time I was down to 500 ft., not only that, I had lost sight of the airfield into the bargain! At this point one of three things can happen. You can panic. You can pray. Or you can do your best to stay cool and attempt to work things out. I dismissed the first two alternatives, but at 500 ft. there wasn't much time to work things out! I strained to look back over my shoulder searching for the airfield, but dressed in a thick leather jacket with an enormous fur collar, turning your head to look directly behind you wasn't the easiest thing to do.

From there on things got worse. Whilst I attempted to look behind me I unwittingly allowed the nose of the aeroplane to pitch upwards slightly, resulting in a rapid loss of airspeed. The pressure on the controls began to slacken off and the aeroplane started to buffet slightly. Needless to say this swiftly drew my attention back to the cockpit and a quick glance at the airspeed indicator showed that we were almost on the point of stalling. At the same time the previously wind-milling propeller decided to stop turning altogether and now stood up like a plank in front of me. I quickly pushed the stick forward to increase the airspeed. With the engine stopped everything seemed eerily quiet, just the wind whining through the struts.

I had been taught how to restart a Tiger Moth engine in flight by diving vertically for about a thousand feet, but now at 300 ft. restart was out of the question.

There was only one thing left to do, force land straight ahead, any attempt at making steep turns at this height, with my very limited experience, would surely have been fatal.

A few seconds after passing through 150 ft., I was trying to avoid telegraph poles and trees. There was virtually no wind to help slow down the ground speed. I was desperately trying to remain calm as we skimmed over a couple of garden sheds, hit the ground with the main wheels, and bounced several times, eventually stopping the right way up a few yards short of a wooden fence. Having rejoiced at still being alive, my second thought was that my instructor, Mr Cockburn, wasn't going to be at all pleased with me.

My recollections of what occurred in the next few seconds are not too clear. I remember thinking that strangely it had begun to snow! as large flakes of fluffy white stuff floated gently down around the Tiger Moth. I sat for a moment trying to calm myself down. A second glance revealed that it wasn't snowing, I had apparently arrived unannounced in the middle of a poultry farm!

That may sound funny, but believe me, with my solo flying hours in single figures, it was anything but funny.

Fortunately no one had been hurt and amazingly there was no apparent damage to the aircraft or the farmer's property. Like me however, I expect the hens and turkeys were suffering from shock.

Within seconds I came face to face with a very worried looking farmer. He invited me into his house where we both had a much-needed glass of whisky before making the necessary telephone calls to the police and the aerodrome. The field I had landed in was quite close to Woodstock, so I returned to Kidlington on foot. The greeting I received from Mr Cockburn was far from a hero's welcome…

'What the bloody hell were you playing at Mr Blyth?'

Under the circumstances things could have been a lot worse. There followed a lengthy verbal dissertation from the CFI on the finer points of airmanship and engine handling.

Later that day the wings were removed, from G-AMEY and she unceremoniously returned to Kidlington on the back of a lorry.

Needless to say, when I next returned to the airfield for a flying lesson, Mr Cockburn made sure I was thoroughly checked out before grudgingly allowing me to fly solo again.

The incident in the Tiger Moth was my first flying accident. Throughout my part time flying training I was still employed full time as a representative in the licensed trade, and it would be reasonable to say that I had also experienced more than my fair share of car accidents whilst employed in the angelic profession of selling booze.

Compared with today's traffic there wasn't a fraction of the vehicles on the road in the early 1950s. Drinking and driving wasn't looked upon with anything like the same severity as it is today, and the breathalyser hadn't been invented. Within reasonable limits there was no set limitation to the amount of alcohol you could have in your body whilst driving. If you were unfortunately involved in an accident, the test for being under the influence of alcohol was usually to walk along a straight line without staggering! Its difficult to believe now, but if you were a salesman selling to the licensed trade in the late 50s and early 60s, your employer expected you to entertain your customers by joining them in a drink, it was an accepted part of the job and all expenses were paid. So whilst making pub calls I would offer the licensee a drink, and if he accepted, I would join him with a glass of my company's product as a matter of courtesy. This usually meant drinking half a pint of beer or a short at each of some twenty to thirty calls made between the opening hours of 10am to 2pm and frequently making further calls on clubs during the evening.

I first came to grief one evening whilst on my way to call on a free house just outside Dunstable in Bedfordshire. I was selling "Babycham" at the time, and had already made quite a few calls on public houses belonging to the Luton Brewery during the day. I was staying in a hotel at Dunstable that night and decided to make a few more calls in the evening so that I would be able to finish work earlier the following day and return home for the weekend.

The back seat of my car was loaded with drip mats, samples and a pile of celluloid Babycham models. It was a dark miserable night, cold and drizzling with rain. Driving along a narrow winding road between Dunstable and Whipsnade, I wasn't really feeling on top of the world, probably due to consuming several pints earlier in the day. In front of me I could just make out the rear lights of a car, eventually I lost sight of it as it turned off the road. The next thing I can remember is an almighty bang as I hit a car full belt straight up the rear!

The impact sent the plastic Babycham models, samples and hundreds of drip mats showering down on me, there was a tinkling of broken glass and I could still hear the whirling sound of a hubcap as it spun to a standstill on the road. To my astonishment, almost before the last piece of wreckage fell to the ground, an Officer of the Law was tapping his pencil on the off-side window of my car.

Wiping the blood from my mouth I stared at him wondering how the hell he had appeared on the scene so quickly. He peered into the car, and I could see by the reflected light of his torch that he looked quite pleased with himself. He made a circling motion with one finger, which I took to mean 'wind your window down.' But the handle came off in my hand as I tried to turn it. With some difficulty I managed to open the door. The Officer popped his head inside the car and smiling said…

'Trouble sir?'

It wasn't so much what he said, but the way he said it that made me think: 'This chap really loves his job.'

I have always been guided by the policy of turning a defensive situation into one of attack, so I immediately leapt into verbal action!

'Did you see the way that stupid bastard slammed his brakes on?' I said.

The policeman, who seemed to be even more amused by my outburst, was now removing a notebook from his breast pocket.

'Well sir' he said… I interrupted him, I wasn't going to let him start on me until I'd said my piece…

'He went round that corner like a bloody madman and slammed his brakes on without any warning' I spluttered still bleeding from the mouth.

'Settle down sir.' The Officer licked his pencil and noted the details from the tax disc.

'Never mind about settle down ….why don't you ask that maniac what he's playing at?' I said pointing to the crumpled back of the car in front.

The Policeman's acrimonious attitude never changed. He took a deep breath and said…

'I've got some very bad news for you sir. You may have wondered how I appeared on the scene rather quickly, so to speak?'

He now had a sadistic grin on his face that made me feel very uncomfortable, but even so I wasn't prepared for what he said next...

'The fact is, the car you smacked up the rear end is believed to be a stolen vehicle. It has been parked here for a while and I've been keeping an eye on it from over there' he said pointing to where a police car was partly hidden by bushes on the opposite side of the road; 'We have good reason to believe that the culprit will be returning to collect it later, although it won't be much good to him now sir will it?'

Grasping at straws I said...

'Well it wouldn't have happened if he'd left it there with its lights on would it?'

The Officer tapped his pencil triumphantly on his notepad in readiness for more particulars and said....

'The lights were on sir, but it appears you've knocked em out.'

Well that was that. It cost me an endorsement for driving without due care and attention, plus a fine of £25. (About two weeks salary in the fifties).

My company car was a write-off. Consequently flying training had to be put on hold for a couple of weeks whilst I travelled around by bus and train, lugging a huge suitcase of samples around with me and staying in hotels for days on end. Eventually the company supplied me with another car. But I only had it for a month when disaster sadly struck again.

This time I was rounding a bend on a steep hill near Offley in Bedfordshire, notorious for it's camber being the wrong way and the number of accidents that had occurred there.

Due to working conscientiously all morning, I was caught suddenly by an urgent call of nature. Concentrating more on finding a toilet quickly than my speed, I took the corner slightly too fast, crept unavoidably to the far side of the road "scraping" a car travelling in the opposite direction. Like a clot I panicked and kept going. I'm not at all proud of that, I can only assume that it was the drink that made me do it. However, a short distance down the road I thought better of it and decided to report the matter to the Police. But first I had to think of an excuse for not stopping at the scene.

So I called in at my Area Manager's house just a few miles up the road on the outskirts of Luton. Fortunately for me he was in at the time, although not very pleased to see me under the circumstances. I explained what had happened, and after a cup of very strong black coffee I left his house and headed for the Local Police Station. On the way I called in at a chemist shop to purchase a large bandage, which I wrapped round my head and secured with a safety pin.

Three quarters of an hour after the incident I stood in front of the Station Sergeant reporting the accident.

'Ha, we've been looking for you sir, why didn't you stop at the accident?' he asked.

'Well officer. I cut my head rather badly when I swerved to miss a dog that ran out in front of me, I believe I may have just scraped a car travelling in the opposite direction but he didn't stop.' My voice almost faded into imperceptibility as I realised what a load of unconvincing crap I was saying.

160

The desk Sergeant glared at me for a moment then said…

'It may surprise you to learn that the driver of the other vehicle didn't keep going sir… far from it…in fact he's still there waiting for the garage to collect his car. When, as you say sir, you "scraped" him, you did in fact take his front off side wheel clean orf !'

Fortunately no one had been hurt. Drink was never mentioned. The charge was 'Driving without due consideration for other road users', my licence was duly endorsed again, and I was fined £50.

My employers were, to say the least, not at all impressed with my succession of road accidents and withdrew my company car. I was given the choice of providing my own transport, or leaving the company.

I came to an arrangement with a car hire and sales company in Birmingham who provided me with a brand new Vauxhall Victor at an agreed monthly hire rate, which after twelve months would convert to a hire purchase agreement without me having to find any further cash for a deposit. But having had to pay £75 in fines, and taken on the expense of hiring a car, my flying training activities had to be severely curtailed. So I started looking for a higher paid job.

I'm sure that things are different now, but in the 1950s there was a sort of alcoholic ladder that one had to climb in order to secure a top job selling to the licensed trade. For instance representatives working for company's that sold mineral waters, or fruit juices or maybe cider, were considered to be on the first rung of the well-paid ladder. But the Reps who were employed by nationally known distillers of Gin, Whisky, and Brandy etc. had the highest paid jobs in the industry. Eventually I rose to the top and landed an excellent job with Bells Whisky, but this meant I had to stay away from home most of the time and I was also drinking far too much. All this was causing problems at home that threatened my marriage. I worked for Bells for two years before smashing their car up completely, for which I was awarded the sack! Fortunately by that time I had gained both my pilots license and my assistant flying instructors rating, and was instructing at Kidlington on a part time basis. But part time instructing as an assistant instructor didn't pay enough to take care of all the monthly bills.

An advertisement for a trainee free trade manager for Courage's Brewery appeared in the Daily Telegraph. I applied for the job, and after attending two interviews was miraculously offered the job in spite of owning up to my series of car crashes.

It was a really good job with lots of potential. If I had lasted long enough, I could have trained to become a tied trade manager responsible for the overall control of a number of Courage's Hotels and Public Houses in the South Buckinghamshire area. But sadly I blotted my copybook again.

Initially I was sent to learn all about wines with 'Charles Kinlock Ltd.' the wine and spirit subsidiary of Courage's Brewery. I was supplied with a brand new Vauxhall 101 car and had to commute daily from Brackley in Northamptonshire to Kinlock House in Park Royal, North London. I had my own parking space in the executives car park clearly marked R. McKenzie-Blyth.

For a while I worked in the order department taking orders by telephone for wines and spirits from the Licensees and Managers of Courage's Hotels and Pubs, as well as obtaining orders from the off-licence managers who's wine shops were called "My Cellar's".

It was very interesting to learn about various wines that Kinlock imported from all over the world. Every morning at ten o'clock precisely a bell would ring summoning selected members of staff, of whom I was one, to the cellars for wine tasting. We were each given a number of glass vessels containing wine identified by letters of the alphabet. Then we went through the procedure of visually examining each sample of wine, sniffing the contents of the glass, and finally taking a sip, swilling it round your mouth and spitting it out. Finally we had to write down the vineyard we thought the wine came from together with the year of its manufacture. Afterwards, we would receive a short lecture about the day's selection of wines from the Managing Director who was a Master of Wines.

The next stage would have been to work with the free trade manager for a while in order to learn all about Courage's various beers, and finally join the tied trade department where I would learn about Hotel and Public House Management. But sadly that was not to be. I must admit I'm ashamed at the way I behaved, which quite rightly earned my instant dismissal.

It all happened at a special luncheon laid on at 'Kinlock House' for managers of the company's 'My Cellar' off licenses. At a guess I would say there were about two hundred or so off-licence managers in attendance, together with about thirty trade representatives. On the head table sat the guest of honour, who was a Director of a well known Spanish Vineyard, the local Mayor, several Councillors, and in the Chair the Managing Director of 'Kinlock House.'

I sat at one of the staff management tables with several sales representatives from Kinlock House.

The trouble started when one of the reps sitting at our table started to jibe me about my previous employment as a whisky salesman...

'I believe you used to work for Bell's Distilleries didn't you?'

Having already consumed a couple of large glasses of red wine, I stupidly started to boast about the vast amount of whisky I used to drink during my previous employment.

'I expect this stuff is nothing to you then' he went on.

I fell for it, hook, line and sinker! From then on I set out to show these wine rep types just how an ex-whisky salesman could see them under the table!

The next thing I can remember is waking up. I was lying on the floor in one of the compartments of a passenger train! I struggled to pull myself up onto the seat. The train was packed to the point where passengers were standing in the corridor, yet there was no one else in the compartment with me! God alone knows how objectionable I had been.

I sat there dazed, the passengers peering at me through the corridor window rapidly turned their backs on me when I looked their way.

Feeling like death, I took a look at myself in the small mirror on the wall of the carriage. What a sight, the immaculate black suit I had been wearing for work that day was now in a worse state than a grave digger's overalls, covered in a mixture of dust, cigarette ash, hairs and chewing gum obviously collected from the floor of the train. My tie was missing altogether, and there was no sign of my briefcase.

How I boarded the train in the first place was a complete mystery, neither did I have the slightest inkling of where the train was taking me.

Eventually we pulled into a station and I heard the voice of a porter shouting Aylesbury. I staggered onto the platform, with scowls of disapproval from fellow passengers who left the train with me. When I reached the ticket collector I couldn't find my ticket, indeed I didn't know if I ever had one. He took one look at me and let me through, I'm not sure whether it was pity or disgust that determined his action.

I didn't seem to have any money, so through a massive alcoholic haze I telephoned Mary from the station call box reversing the charges and asked her if she would mind collecting me from Aylesbury railway station. When she arrived and saw the state I was in, she was horrified. I've never felt so ashamed as I did at that moment, but there was far worse to come.

The next morning I apprehensively returned to London by train, looking immaculate and feeling terrible. In the hope that my briefcase had been handed in, I made enquiries at the lost property office and was amazed to find that it had. I had no idea where my car was, and I shuddered to think of being told what had happened at the dinner the previous day.

The attitude of the gateman at Kinlock House, who usually greeted me with a smile and a polite salute, gave me some indication of what was to come. He looked at me as if I had crawled out from under the nearest stone and said…

'Oh, it's you. The General Manager said if you have the gall to turn up, I was to instruct you to go straight to his office.'

I began to feel sick.

I stood outside the GM's office for some time waiting to see him. The door opened and the General Manager stood for a moment glaring in obvious disgust. I immediately started to apologise, but was told to shut up and sit down.

I flopped into the chair in front of his desk and waited for the inevitable.

'Here are your cards, and here is a cheque. You can consider yourself exceedingly lucky to be paid up to the end of the month.'

Obviously I had behaved extremely badly, but I still didn't know what had happened. I didn't want to leave that office until I had found out exactly what I had done and apologised for my behaviour.

The General Manager was in fact an extremely nice chap. He had been my immediate boss for the short time I had worked at Kinlock House, and up to my performance the previous day he had been pleased with my progress.

I apologised profusely and said that I honestly had no recollection of what had happened the previous afternoon.

My boss, or rather ex boss, walked over to the window and said…

'I'm not exactly certain of all the details. But I'll tell you all I know, which I am sure will be enough to satisfy your curiosity. I assume you realise that you had far too much to drink during the early part of the lunch?'

I nodded.

'To start with you became very noisy and disagreeable with the people sitting with you at the table. They tried to calm you down, and by the time it came to the speeches you had already been told to quieten down by myself.'

He cleared his throat, and stood silent for a moment. Then he began again.

'When our Managing Director introduced our guest of honour, saying that his vineyard produced some of the finest wines in the world, you stood up and shouted Rubbish! You continually interrupted his speech, and was eventually asked to leave the room. You then staggered up to the head table and started arguing with our Managing Director, banging the table and inviting him outside promising to deck him. Finally, after being escorted from the dining hall, you went straight up to the Managing Director's office, sat at his desk, and frightened his secretary to death ordering her to fetch the Managing Director immediately. Eventually two of our porters took you to the railway station whereupon you were bundled onto the train and taken to your nearest home station.'

I sat there in silence unable to find suitable words to describe my feelings of total disgust. I just couldn't believe that I had behaved in such a dreadful manner. Obviously I didn't try to excuse my actions. I was fired, and justly so. I asked if I could see the Managing Director so that I could apologise to him personally, but he flatly refused to speak to me.

Some days later I was surprised to receive a letter from his secretary to say that he was prepared to give me a reference on the basis that my actual work with the company had been satisfactory.

I later learned that one of the off licence managers had also been blind drunk at the same luncheon and started a fight, his wife joined in and they both finished up being taken to hospital, and I believe another off licence manager had a heart attack and later died.

At the time I never actually thought of myself as an alcoholic, but obviously I was on the brink of becoming one. Drink was not only destroying my career in the trade, but it was also destroying my marriage.

Having been fired, I returned home from London deeply saddened by my own stupidity, wondering if I would ever find another job that would pay the sort of salary I needed to look after my family. I would have to be a fully qualified QFI before I could afford to change my profession to full time flying. At that time the pay for working as an assistant flying instructor was about five shillings per flying hour.

This is where I believe my Guardian Angel, the one with the weird sense of humour, stepped in. By the most remarkable and absolutely unbelievable coincidence, when I arrived home, there on the doormat was a letter from the Sales Director of Sandemans Port offering me employment as a representative to sell 'Porto Branco' a new white port that they had just introduced to the licensed trade. It seemed like a miracle, I could hardly believe my eyes. I had applied for a job and been interviewed by Sandemans years earlier. At the time I had been told that they had no vacancy to offer me on their sales team, but they would contact me in the future should a suitable vacancy occur. But that was at least two years ago, and I never expected to hear from them again. It was a truly remarkable coincidence that a letter offering me a job should arrive through our letterbox on the very day I lost my job at Kinlock House..

CHAPTER 17.

Dubious predicaments.

I lay in my hospital bed, my thoughts once again returning to my early flying training days.

Nils Bartleet, the chap who started his training on the Tiger Moth about the same time as me, also came up against financial problems which prevented him flying as regularly as he would have liked. Nevertheless he was making good progress flying whenever he could afford to.

I arrived at the airfield early one sunny Sunday morning to find that Nils, who had not gone solo to date, was already airborne with his instructor practising circuits and landings. Tony Marchant, the duty engineer, was sitting on the grass outside the clubhouse waiting to refuel the aircraft when it landed, so I decided to join him and watch Nils being put through his paces.

It was a reasonably calm day with just a light breeze straight down the runway, ideal conditions for circuit training. After a while Ken Scott joined us on the grass. Ken, now a qualified pilot, was building up his flying hours with the intention of embarking on a flying instructor's course.

We watched as the red and silver Tiger Moth taxied back to the holding point ready for another circuit for the umpteenth time that morning, when Ken suddenly remarked…

'It looks as if old Nils is going on his first solo.'

His instructor had climbed out of the aircraft and stood talking to Nils in the rear cockpit.

Before long Nils was lining the Moth up on runway 08 ready to take-off on his first solo flight, his instructor, F/Lt Bunny Austin from RAF Central Flying School, was now slowly making his way back to the clubhouse from the far side of the airfield carrying his flying helmet and the removable seat from the front cockpit.

The sound of the Tiger Moth's engine now at full throttle reached our ears. In no time Nils was airborne. 'Well done mate' I thought.

Bunny stopped and turned to watch as the Tiger Moth sped passed him, then, halfway back to the dispersal area, he decided to sit on the grass and watch his student's first solo landing.

The three of us were chatting away, when Ken Scott brought our attention to the windsock. The earlier breeze was no longer blowing straight down the runway, in fact it had veered off about 45 degrees and was increasing in strength. One minute there was virtually no wind at all, the next it was blowing at about 15 kts. across the runway, not the sort of thing to happen to a chap on his first solo.

The distant drone of the Tiger Moth's engine sounded like a bumblebee as the little aircraft turned onto the downwind leg of the circuit. Nils had obviously failed to notice the wind change, which instead of being behind him was now blowing the aircraft sideways. His instructor had obviously seen what was happening as he had clambered to his feet and stood with his hands on his hips staring at the Tiger Moth as it "crabbed" towards the airfield. By now we were all standing up, our eyes glued to the red and silver dot as it turned onto what should have been the base leg of the circuit. It must have been obvious to Nils that something was radically wrong because his aircraft had reached the extended centre line of the runway without having any base leg on which to lose height. I felt sorry for him, the last thing you need is a sudden change in the surface wind when you are halfway through your first solo flight.

Ken summed up what we were all thinking…

'Surely he's not going to attempt a landing off that approach, he's far too high.'

Nils however had other ideas and started to bank steeply towards the airfield. He was indeed far too high, and drifting sideways across the runway. In one last desperate effort to put things right, he stuffed the nose of the aircraft down sharply which caused the airspeed to increase considerably, and headed straight for his instructor Bunny Austin!

Bunny by this time had adopted the stance of a tennis player waiting to receive a fast serve, legs apart and slightly bent, leaning forward, obviously not too sure which way to run!

The Tiger was descending at such a rate we could actually hear the wind whistling through the wing-struts. Bunny, helmet and cushions from the front seat clutched under one arm, started to walk quickly to his left. Nils, who I'm sure must have been looking out of the opposite side of the cockpit and still hoping by some miracle to land off this approach, had obviously not seen his instructor at all. As Bunny made a last minute dash to the left, Nils turned slightly and headed straight for him again. The three of us watched in stunned silence. Bunny, pursued by the Tiger Moth, was running like a greyhound, at the last second he dropped the items he was carrying, and threw himself flat on the ground as the aircraft skimmed over the top of him. At that point the Moth's engine spluttered into action and the aircraft climbed away from the airfield.

'Bloody hell that was close' I said.

Bunny was now sitting upright on the grass. There was no radio to relay instructions to his student, so Nils had to sort this one out for himself.

A few minutes passed whilst Nils climbed the aircraft back into the circuit to have another stab at landing. We lost sight of him for a while but could still hear the engine, which seemed to be much further away this time.

Bunny, having collected his cushion and to some extent his dignity, donned his flying helmet and started to walk slowly back towards the dispersal area. He had just stopped to tie up a shoelace when, to everyone's horror, the Tiger Moth suddenly re-appeared extremely low, skimming the perimeter fence and heading straight for his instructor again at a hell of a lick.

Because Bunny was now wearing his flying helmet he obviously hadn't heard the Tiger Moth roaring up behind him. We all started to shout, jumping up and down and waving our arms. But it was too late, Nils, who was still trying to attain the world speed record for landing, saw Bunny at the very last second and pulled up narrowly missing the head of his unsuspecting instructor.

Poor old Bunny, having thrown himself to the ground for the second time, dragged himself to his feet and stood watching the aircraft as it climbed away for a third attempt at landing. Nils must have noticed the windsock at this stage and realised what was causing all the trouble. He climbed back up to 1000 feet, and carried out a very wide circuit, finally lining up for an approach into wind, ignoring the marked grass runway altogether. His instructor had run back to the centre of the airfield and was gesticulating vigorously indicating the direction he wanted Nils to attempt his landing.

Finally, to everyone's great relief, Nils crossed over the airfield boundary quite sedately heading into wind. The landing wasn't the best he had ever made, but he was down safely. Bunny, obviously feeling very pissed off, gave his student some colourful advice when the aircraft closed down in dispersal.

Although it seemed amusing at the time, none of us realised how dangerous the situation had become. It was a hell of a thing to happen on a chap's first solo. Considering his limited flying experience, Nils coped extremely well. That evening Bunny Austin, several club members and myself joined Nils in the saloon bar of the Bear Hotel Woodstock to celebrate his hard earned first solo, and of course, the fact that Bunny Austin was still with us.

Over the next seven months I did as much flying as I could afford. Flying mostly at weekends, it had taken me just over eight months to qualify. But not without a couple more altercations with our CFI Mr Cockburn!

I enjoyed flying with Eric Stowe, his one fault was that he was a bit undisciplined as far as the rules were concerned, a fault that unfortunately cost him his job in the end. Usually when he flew with me he would finish each lesson by doing a few aerobatics, which he knew I enjoyed immensely. But as I came to realise later in my career when I became a flying instructor myself, students tend to copy their instructors. I was no exception.

One beautiful July morning I was sent off solo to practice map reading in the local area when the urge came over me to have a go at looping the aeroplane on my own. I had not been given any instruction on aerobatics whatsoever, but I had been in the aircraft enough times when my instructor had looped the Tiger Moth to have a stab at it myself.

To be on the safe side, I climbed my favourite Moth G-AOEL to three thousand feet and carried out my pre-spin and stalling checks, which I had noted when flying with Eric, were the same checks he did prior to aerobatics. With my heart pounding in my ears I lowered the nose of the little blue biplane and throttled back slightly to ensure the engine didn't over rev, but even so the engine seemed to scream loudly as we dived towards the ground. The airspeed soon built up to 110 kts. Then, overcoming a strong urge to "chicken out", I eased gently back on the stick. The nose of the aeroplane shot up so quickly that my head was forced down hard on to my chest. Realising I had pulled back too hard I relaxed the backward pressure slightly, too much in fact because now we were upside-down and I was hanging by my shoulders in the Sutton Harness with the engine spluttering as if it was about to stop. Whether the wings were parallel with the horizon whilst in the inverted attitude, I'm not sure, but there was an extremely good chance that they weren't! Things became a bit quiet, so I eased back on the stick a little and we were soon hurtling towards the ground. I throttled back to prevent the engine from over-speeding, at the same time increasing the backward pressure on the stick slightly to complete the loop.

I had carried out my first solo aerobatic manoeuvre, but my feeling of exhilaration was short lived. My attention was drawn to the glint of silver wings reflecting the sun less than a thousand feet above me. A second look confirmed that it was another Tiger Moth.

I felt sick at the thought of how close I must have been to the other aircraft when we were upside-down at the top of the loop, worse still I wondered who was in the aircraft and whether or not the pilot had seen me. My question was answered immediately after I had landed and taxied into dispersal.

'Mr Cockburn would like to see you in his office.'

Sandy looked serious and obviously had some inkling of what I was in for.

I entered the Chief Flying Instructor's office and stood motionless in front of his desk. For a few moments Mr Cockburn ignored me and carried on writing something on one of the newly adopted student pilot's progress sheets that looked strangely like mine. Suddenly he slammed the pen down on his desk so hard it made me jump! Glaring at me savagely he said…

'Mr Blyth, give me one good reason why I shouldn't throw you off the course?'

He had obviously seen my attempt at a loop or been told about it by someone else who had seen it. Before I could think of anything sensible to say he continued…

'I'm not worried about you, if you want to go and kill yourself that's up to you, but not in one of my aeroplanes young man.'

I felt dreadful. This could mean the end of my dream of a flying career.

I stood there like an airman in front of his CO on a serious charge. Coey hadn't finished with me yet. Before I could even begin to apologise he continued…

'Do you know how close you came to me boy?' adding 'Have you been taught aerobatics?'

'No sir.'

He stared at me in silence for a long time, obviously considering what action to take. I'm sure that if I had been ten years younger I would have pissed my pants.

'I am very disappointed with you, very disappointed indeed. What, if anything at all, have you got to say for yourself?'

I thought for a second, but before I could utter a sound Coey started up again.

'One more chance my lad, just one more, that's all. If I see, or hear of you acting irresponsibly in one of my aeroplanes again, you'll be off this airfield before you know it. Do I make myself clear?'

'Absolutely sir.'

'Right now get out of my office.'

I left the CFI's office feeling very small indeed. Eric, my instructor, approached me as I was leaving the club...

'What on earth made you do that Ray, apparently you passed the CFI's aeroplane upside-down, have you got a bloody death wish or something? When you qualify for your license I'll teach you how to do aerobatics properly lad.'

A few weeks later I had to endure another misadventure with Mr Cockburn. This time it was during my dual qualifying cross-country.

In the 1950's your PPL was issued after passing three written examinations, completing a triangular solo cross country flight which included making two landings at other airfields, and finally passing a flying test with a Royal Aero Club examiner. But before you were allowed off on your qualifying cross-country flight, you had to carry out a fairly long dual cross-country that included landing at another airfield. Unfortunately for me Mr Cockburn decided that he would fly with me on my Dual Cross Country. Our route was to be Oxford to Thruxton and land. Then take-off from Thruxton to over fly Portsmouth and return to Oxford.

After the aerobatic incident I was far from being Mr Cockburn's favourite student, and to make things worse I never could understand a word he said when he spoke to me through the dreaded Gosport Tube.

Having had my flight plan checked by Coey, we set off in Tiger Moth G-ALNA bound for Thruxton Airfield. We climbed to two thousand feet over our airfield, I noted the time on my flight log and set course for Thruxton. We had only been flying for about ten minutes when Coey said something which I took to be 'Is your heading all right?' so I said 'Yes sir', and continued on course looking out for my first check point. In fact what Mr Cockburn had said was 'There's an aircraft on your right.'

The next time he spoke he shouted quite clearly...

'Are you going to turn boy?'

Having not seen the other aircraft and thinking he meant was I going to alter my course I replied...

'No sir!'

With that Cockburn blew a gasket, snatched the controls and put the aeroplane in a screaming turn to the left. At that point I saw the other aircraft, a Chipmunk, pass within a few hundred yards of us and realised that I had not only totally misunderstood the CFI's comments, but also kept a pretty poor lookout.

Coey waggled the control stick and then held his hands above his head in the front cockpit, indicating that I was to take control again. I turned the aircraft back on to its original heading at the same time trying to regain my composure and find out exactly where we were. I could hear Coey mumbling and swearing through the Gosport tube, but I had no idea what he was saying. It was a dreadful start to my dual navigation test.

I was trying to understand what Coey said, and not concentrating sufficiently on my map reading or holding a steady course. Every few minutes he would say something, I would ask him to repeat his message, whereupon he would slam the throttle closed so that I could hear him.

After about twenty minutes I was totally lost and had no idea where we were. Suddenly the throttle slammed closed and an angry voice shouted…

'Where are we now boy?'

I hadn't got a clue, so I stupidly suggested a position that I thought would satisfy him, only to hear him bellow out…

'Rubbish.'

Somehow we miraculously arrived overhead Thruxton. By this time I was twenty minutes late on my ETA, completely demoralised, and to round things off my landing was abominable. I could hear Coey cursing as we bounced all the way down the runway like a Kangaroo.

As soon as I stopped the engine, my irate CFI stood up on his seat in the front cockpit turned round and towering over me shouted angrily…

'Is there something wrong with your blasted compass?'

Before I could reply he climbed out of the aeroplane, lifted the tail up manually with me still inside the cockpit, and staggered around moving the aeroplane through about ninety degrees. He slammed the tail down and shouted…

'What does your compass read now?'

I told him. He peered into the front cockpit to read his compass.

'Your compass is working perfectly Mr Blyth, it reads exactly the same as mine' he was obviously infuriated.

I noticed a couple of bemused pilots from the Thruxton Aeroplane Club looking at me with broad grins on their faces, which didn't improve my ego at all.

A similar fiasco took place on our flight back to Kidlington. I knew I could do it, but whilst I was with Coey it was a combination of nerves and misunderstanding that made things go repeatedly wrong. If I had been on my own I would have hung out of the cockpit and banked the aeroplane over so that I could positively identify my position. But if I did that with Coey on board I knew he would have gone ballistic!

When we finally landed at Kidlington, Coey flung off his harness straps and strutted back into the Club with a face like thunder. As usual I followed him in through the Club door feeling devastated. As we entered the clubroom we were met by Eric my instructor, who asked Coey how I got on with my dual cross-country.

'Cross country?…more like a blasted mystery tour than a navigation exercise.' He said entering his office slamming the door behind him. I wanted to shrivel into oblivion.

Seconds later the CFI's door opened again and Coey beckoned me into his office, at the same time he said to Sandy…

'I think perhaps a cup of tea and a couple of Asprins would go down well.'

I saw Eric turn away to hide a grin as I followed Coey sheepishly into his office.

Coey sat on the corner of his desk, produced a pair of spectacles from his top pocket, and began cleaning them with a less than spotless handkerchief.

'You will have to do some more dual navigation before you set off on your qualifying cross country, and if you don't improve your lookout you will be killed boy.'

The words of my instructor hit hard. It was the second time I had not seen another aircraft where Cockburn had been involved, and I knew I was skating on thin ice if I wanted to get through my flying course successfully. Just before I left his office Coey said…

'I will be on holiday for a couple of weeks Blyth, but a Mr Jones will be coming over to Kidlington to stand in for me as CFI whilst I'm away, I suggest you fly with him.'

A few days later I turned up at the airfield to fly with Mr Jones who was standing in as CFI. Once again there were no detailed notes on my student's flight record. Nothing was mentioned about my fiasco with Mr Cockburn. All it said was dual cross country number three. So I told Mr Jones a fib and said that I had been cleared to carry out my qualifying solo cross-country when the weather was suitable. To my surprise he said…

'No time like the present.'

So at 11 a.m. on the 28th August 1957 I took off in my favourite Tiger Moth G-AOEL bound for Portsmouth, and Thruxton Aerodromes. I took with me the all-important cross country authorisation form that had to be countersigned by the CFI at each of the two airfields I landed at to say that I had made a satisfactory landing and had displayed a good standard of airmanship.

Lucky for me everything went perfectly from start to finish. I had certainly learnt the dangers of not keeping a good lookout for other aircraft whilst flying with Mr Cockburn, and I also made sure that I never lost track of my position at any time during the whole flight.

When I landed back at Kidlington, I got out of the aeroplane beaming from ear to ear, only to receive a strict telling off from Bunny Austin for taxying too fast and staying too long on the ground drinking tea at Portsmouth, which caused me to be overdue on my return to Kidlington.

I had already passed my written examinations before commencing cross-country flying. So all I had to do now was pass my flying test, which I took with Mr Jones the following week in G-AOEL and passed. The first step towards becoming a professional pilot and instructor had been taken, but there was still a hell of a long way to go.

Naturally my first passenger was my wife Mary. After that I waited for a suitably calm day to take my little son Eddy up for his very first flight. On the 19th October 1957, when Eddy was just seven months old, I wrapped him in a warm blanket and sat him on his mother's lap in the front cockpit of a Tiger Moth. We flew for just ten minutes on a low level circuit round the airfield. He wasn't a bit frightened by the engine noise or the slipstream. When we landed Mary took what is now a much treasured photograph of Eddy sitting on my knee by the aeroplane. Mr Cockburn shuffled past and mumbled...

'One for the family album Mr Blyth, one for the album?'

Having attained my PPL my aim was to become a professional pilot and flying instructor, but there was still some considerable way to go. Nils Bartleet, who seemed to be earning far more money than I was at that time, passed his PPL test and immediately paid to be checked out in the de-Havilland Chipmunk. I flew with him over Oxford City and instantly fell in love with the aircraft. It was sheer luxury to fly in a totally enclosed cockpit with radio intercom instead of shouting down a Gosport Tube. The instrument panel was a little more sophisticated and, with the addition of flaps and wheel brakes, the Chipmunk was a far more interesting aeroplane to fly.

I decided there and then that this would be the best aeroplane in which to gain suitable experience before embarking on the Flying Instructors Course.

Essentially the next thing to do was gain as much useful flying experience as possible whilst accumulating the mandatory flying hours required before commencing an instructors course.

At the time I thought it would be immensely helpful financially if I could join the RAFVR and hopefully build my hours up by flying service Chipmunks which were still being flown by part time RAFVR officers in the AEF squadrons.

I applied to the MOD asking if I could be transferred from the Territorial Army to the RAFVR for my remaining reserve commitment as I preferred to fly aeroplanes rather than drive tanks! It took weeks for them to reply, and I had just about given up hope when I received a letter from RAF training command to say my letter had been passed to them for further action. They went on to inform me that the Volunteer Reserve Squadrons had ceased to operate in 1953, and pilots that flew with the Reserve Squadrons who wished to continue flying part time, had been transferred to the RAFVR (T). I was advised that I would be eligible to apply for a commission in the RAFVR(T).

The letter went on to say…

'If you are successful in your application for a commission, and also hold a fully qualified Civil Aviation Authority Flying Instructor's license, you could make further application via Oxford Air Training School to the Royal Air Force Central Flying School for approval to train RAF and CCF candidates to fly under the scholarships award scheme. Assuming you then pass the RAFCFS flying instructors flight test, you could make a further application through your VRT squadron for a wings badge test which would have to be carried out at CFS. If successful you would be posted to fly with one of the AEF squadrons. But no guarantees can be given.'

On paper it seemed a long and complicated list of probabilities, and there was certainly no hope of flying service aircraft for some time to come. But I certainly wasn't going to give up altogether

A further year passed, during which time I struggled financially to build up my flying hours. The minimum experience requirement before one could commence a flying instructor's course was 150 hours in command of an aeroplane, which had to include 30 hours on the type of aircraft to be used for the instructor's course. This meant that in order to pay for the extra flying hours needed, I had to find something in the region of £1500. (The equivalent to about £25,000 in today's money) to pay for the extra flying hours I needed.

At the time there were no Further Education Grants available for pilot training courses so, after considerable thought, I applied to the United Dominions Trust for a loan. After being interviewed by one of the official's of the Trust, the UDT agreed to lend me enough money for the flying instructors course, providing I was appropriately insured to cover the loan. The problem was that I still had to find enough money to pay for the shortfall in hours needed before I could actually start the course.

Back at Kidlington Airfield Mr Cockburn seemed to be getting very disgruntled with everybody and everything.

One Saturday afternoon I arrived at the Flying Club to be greeted by Eric Stowe grinning from ear to ear. He told me a really amusing story that concerned our esteemed CFI.

Apparently there was a young student strapped in the rear cockpit of one of the Tiger Moths. Eric, having swung the prop to start the engine, was about to climb into the front cockpit when Mr Cockburn rushed out from the club to inform him that he was urgently required to speak to someone on the telephone. Cockburn, having just landed with another student, was still in his flying gear so, in order to avoid any delay in the day's flying programme, decided to take over Eric's student.

Eric informed Coey that the student he was about to fly with had reached the stage of circuits and landings, but to date had not gone solo. Mr Cockburn nodded to the student in the rear cockpit and climbed into the front seat.

After an hour of bouncing down the runway making fruitless efforts to land, Coey, true to character, finally lost his rag completely and shouted down the Gosport Tube...

'For God's sake wake up. What the hells up with you? Have you nodded off completely? How many more times do I have to tell you, the aircraft needs to be fully stalled with the stick right back when the wheels touch the ground. Now come on man relax, open your bloody legs so that you can get the ruddy stick fully back.'

After a further couple of circuits resulting in bigger and better bounces,

Coey had had enough; he took over the controls, taxied back to dispersal and shut the engine down. He was then heard by a member of the ground crew to shout hoarsely at his student…

'You must get the stick hard back in your balls, don't you know where your balls are boy?'

Cockburn hoisted himself out of the front cockpit and turned to stare in horror at his student, a red faced young lady who had removed her flying helmet to reveal long blond hair! Coey mumbled something of an apology, and shuffled off back to his office looking extremely embarrassed.

My initial instructor Eric Stowe suddenly parted company with the Oxford Aeroplane Club soon after I had qualified for my PPL. I never found out why he left or what became of him. Shortly after Eric's departure Mr Cockburn resigned his position as CFI and joined Southend Aero Club as their CFI. Rex Smith, an ex RAF wartime pilot and flying instructor who had been instructing part time at Kidlington, then took over as CFI on a full-time basis.

In order to get the best value from my flying whilst building up sufficient hours for the instructor's course, I took some sound advice from Rex Smith…

'A good instructor should be capable of handling his aeroplane competently in any attitude. If I were you I would sign up for an aerobatic course as soon as possible.'

He also advised me that if I wanted to learn aerobatics properly, there was no better aeroplane than the Tiger Moth.

It was a fine clear day with a touch of ground frost when I taxied out with my instructor in G-AOEL. A light breeze that barely nudged the windsock from rest, completed the ideal conditions for my first aerobatic training lesson in the Tiger Moth.

Bunny Austin, my instructor on this flight, said that we had better practice a few more spins before commencing the lesson I had been briefed for which was "Looping".

To start with he asked me to carry out a couple of spins, one to the right and one to the left. Then, shouting down the Gosport Tube, he asked me if I had ever been in an inverted spin. I said that I hadn't, so we climbed to 5,000 feet and levelled out. I had heard one or two horrific tales of what an inverted spin was like, so I thought I was prepared for the next few minutes…. I wasn't!

The Sutton Harness that secures the pilot into his seat in a Tiger Moth consists of four leather belts. Each belt has a series of reinforced holes through which a peg can be passed. The idea is to put the two lap belts over your legs and the two upper belts over your shoulders. The metal peg is placed through the holes of all four belts where they cross over your body at the front. The peg is then secured in position by a locking pin.

It's in the pilots own interest to ensure that these belts are holding him as tight as he can get them otherwise, when the aircraft is inverted, his bottom comes off the seat and he finds himself hanging by his shoulder straps. I had experienced this several times before when Eric Stowe had carried out a few demonstration "slow rolls" during my basic training.

Checks completed, Bunny rolled the Tiger Moth over onto its back and closed the throttle, commencing an inverted glide. That was scary enough, but now Bunny pushed forward on the stick so that we commenced an inverted climb. I thought I had done my harness up as tight as possible, even so, the small amount of inverted 'g' forced me out of my seat completely, and I was hanging upside-down by my shoulders with my backside an inch or so off the seat. Worse was to come.

As the airspeed decreased, Bunny shouted through the Gosport Tube…

'Hang on Ray I'm going to apply full rudder now and we should go into an inverted spin.'

Too bloody right it did! For a moment I couldn't tell what was happening. Then came the worst flying experience I'd encountered to date. The aircraft was rolling pitching and yawing, but instead of being the right way up as in a normal spin, we were upside-down and on the outside of the manoeuvre being forced outwards from the aircraft. I tried to hang on to the seat but it was hopeless. Certain that I was going to die, I closed my eyes, I could hear Bunny shouting something or other but I couldn't tell what he was saying. We didn't carry parachutes and I was just praying that I wasn't going to be forced out of the cockpit. Suddenly we appeared to be spinning the right way up and eventually we had recovered back to straight and level flight. With that we returned to the airfield and landed.

That was the end of my first lesson in aerobatics. I'm pretty certain that Bunny didn't look much better than I was feeling when we walked back into the clubroom.

Fortunately my aerobatic training was being carried out by two very experienced instructors, Rex Smith and Bunny Austin, and apart from the inverted spin, I enjoyed every minute of the course.

Before long I had reached the stage when I was cleared to practice loops, stall turns and barrel rolls solo. I had however been warned by Rex that the Tiger Moth was not the easiest aeroplane to slow roll accurately. How right he was, I must have fallen out of more slow rolls during that course than an habitual drunk falls over in a lifetime.

On occasions I would take a friend up with me to practice aero's. I have to smile now when I look back at my old logbook and see that the first time my mother-in-law flew with me there was still a thin covering of ground frost on Kidlington Airfield. We took off in the little open cockpit Tiger Moth, climbed in an icy cold wind to seven thousand feet, and carried out thirty minutes of aerobatics. When we landed my courageous mother-in-law was almost frozen solid, but to my surprise she said she really enjoyed the flight, bless her.

I still needed to accumulate as much varied flying experience and "In Command" hours as I could get.

Over a period of time the operating companies and general management structure of Kidlington Aerodrome changed several times. CSE Ltd., who were the main Piper Aircraft Distributors in Great Britain and resident on Kidlington Aerodrome, took over the Flying club. Eventually a new company 'Oxford Air Training School' (OATS) was formed with Capt Rex Smith heading up the organisation as Managing Director. OATS was now on its way to becoming the largest Commercial Pilot Training School in the country.

Thanks to Rex Smith I managed to get my hands on a considerable amount of valuable free flying. Valuable, not just for the purpose of gaining hours, but also for the experience I gained by flying many different types of aircraft. For instance, when the "Shackleton Sales Weekend" took place at Kidlington in the Summer of 1958. I was asked if I would like to help collect aeroplanes offered for sale from their base airfields before the event, and in some cases take them back again after the sales weekend was complete. By the time I finally commenced my training as an instructor in March 1961, I had flown 33 different types of aeroplane and visited 42 aerodromes. Not a record I agree, but considering all this flying was free, I considered myself very lucky.

Two very memorable flights took place during that period. The first was when Rex asked me if I would like to fly G-APBZ which was a Druine Turbulent, a very small single seat aeroplane manufactured by the Rollason

Aircraft Company. It had been brought to Oxford on a sales demonstration tour and a few of us were lucky enough to be offered the opportunity of flying it. The aircraft was tiny, it had a wingspan of twenty-one feet, and it was just seventeen feet from the tip of its spinner to the end of its tail. Being a single seat aircraft, it was of course impossible for anyone to be checked out in the air by an instructor before flying it solo, and this was my first experience of such a flight.

I would agree in theory that it is no big deal for an experienced pilot to take up an aircraft type he has never previously flown without some sort of dual check, it happens all the time. But when this flight took place I had not long qualified for my PPL, in fact my logbook tells me that I had only completed a total of 31 hours solo flying. So I considered myself extremely lucky to be given the opportunity of flying this little single seat aeroplane.

Having received a thorough briefing, I sat in the open cockpit being bounced around whilst Rex relentlessly swung the propeller in order to get the engine started. A single ear-splitting bang, a cloud of blue smoke and the engine was running, sounding very much like a two-stroke motorcycle.

After running the engine up to check the magnetos, I waved the chocks away, opened the throttle very carefully and slowly moved off. It was a fresh morning with no cloud and very little surface wind as we wobbled our way through the dew-glistening grass of Kidlington Aerodrome on our way to the holding point of runway 26. I remembered the wise words of advice given to me by Rex just before starting up.

'You will find that the controls are extremely light and sensitive compared to the Tiger Moth, the tendency will be to over-control, especially with the elevators, so be careful and you'll soon get the feel of her.'

Oxford only had a small Air Traffic Control Tower in 1958, rather like a garden shed on stilts, so having completed the very limited take-off checks, I sat at the holding point waiting for Ben, our controller, to flash a steady green light from his Aldis lamp indicating that I was clear to take-off.

At that point the engine stopped... 'Bloody good start' I thought. It had been ticking over perfectly smoothly one minute, then PLOP it suddenly stopped. The silence after the cheerful bubbling noise the little engine made when it was ticking over was quite a contrast. I checked the cockpit for obvious causes of failure but could find nothing wrong.

As there was no electric starter I had no alternative but to sit there like a lemon and wait for someone to come out and swing the prop for me. A few minutes past whilst Ben, armed with his Aldis lamp, flashed numerous greens at me. I was getting quite agitated stuck out there on the other side of the airfield. Surely someone back there realised that the blasted engine had stopped.

Eventually the crash truck crawled slowly out across the airfield and arrived with a grinning Tony Marchant at the wheel.

'Problems?' he asked.

'No just bloody sunbathing mate!' I replied being all keyed up to fly this thing and in no mood for jokes.

After priming the engine Tony swung the prop for me and it started first time. I was now just a little fearful in case it stopped again when we were in flight. Ben flashed his umpteenth green at me and we were off.

As soon as we gained a little ground speed the tail came up easily and with only the slightest back pressure on the stick, the little Turbulent leapt into the air like a Kangaroo with it's arse on fire. We were airborne right enough, but not for long. In spite of Rex's warning, I over corrected the climbing attitude, lowered the nose a fraction too much, and bounced off the ground again. This time I eased the stick back almost imperceptibly and was relieved to feel the Turbulent lift off and climb away smoothly.

I could see why they called this aeroplane a Turbulent, God knows what it was like to fly a Hurricane!

In a clear blue sky I turned the little yellow aeroplane to the Northwest and left the circuit with the slipstream from the tiny propeller tearing at my flying helmet. After twenty minutes flying in the local area I had the feel of her and rejoined the circuit. As we came into land the sensitivity of the elevators became paramount and I had trouble keeping the aircraft level during the hold-off. Eventually, after what seemed an age the wheels gently brushed the grass surface of the runway and we were safely down.

Unfortunately on another occasion when I had the opportunity of a free flight, the outcome was a little more serious, it took place on the 11th September 1958. I was supposed to be selling whisky to public houses in the Headington area that day, and called in at the airport on my way to work.

As I clambered out of the car carrying a few miniature bottles of whisky for the lads, Peter Clifford came over to me and asked if I would like to accompany him on a flight to Limivadi in Northern Ireland in order to deliver a Gemini aeroplane he had sold to a farmer that owned a disused airfield. He said he would be collecting an Auster in part exchange for the Gemini, and offered me the opportunity of flying it back to Kidlington with him.

'The whole thing shouldn't take more than five hours, we'll be back by teatime' he said.

Well, I couldn't possibly refuse an offer like that.

Less than half an hour later we were airborne in Gemini G-AMKZ on our way to Northern Ireland. The journey over the sea seemed to take ages, I was glad that we were in a twin-engine aeroplane, although I fully realised we would be in a single engine aeroplane on the way back.

Peter Clifford could fly anything with wings, as an ex-wartime Test Pilot and Kings Cup Air Race winner he was very well known and highly respected in the world of civil aviation.

Flying with someone as experienced as Peter I felt sure that nothing could possibly go wrong, big mistake!

As we arrived overhead Limivadi Aerodrome I could see that it was a disused military airfield with at least one half-decent tarmac runway. Peter did a low run to examine the surface of the runway, and made his decision where to touch down.

'Check your straps are done up tight Ray, you can't really tell what the surface is going to be like with these pre-war runways.'

Never was a truer word spoken. The undercarriage safely down and locked we turned onto the final approach. As we skimmed over the first section of the runway, I couldn't help noticing the awful state of the surface.

Peter made a smooth landing on the main wheels, but after that things went rapidly wrong. When the tail wheel came down there was one hell of a thump followed by a loud bang and an awful grinding sound. A blast of cold air swept into the cockpit accompanied by clouds of swirling dust. I grabbed the top of the instrument panel as the aircraft tipped up onto its nose. Peter and I lurched forward in our straps as the propellers struck the ground with a crunch. We slid along the rough surface of the runway with sparks flying everywhere, finally coming to a halt and absolute silence.

I looked at Peter who was absolutely covered in dust.

'BUGGER' he said with some considerable feeling!

'What happened?' I asked.

'I'm buggered if I know....Pardon?' was the rather sharp reply.

Peter Clifford's eccentricity of ending all his sentences with "Pardon" didn't leave him even in times of crisis! We were both tilting forwards in our straps, as the aeroplane had come to rest on its nose. Peter unfastened his safety harness and eased himself out of the cockpit whilst I staggered out behind him.

We stared in amazement at the wreckage. The tail section and most of the rear end of the fuselage was hanging off. Bits and pieces of wreckage were strewn all over the runway with some of it still attached to the front half by the control cables.

Normally Peter was immaculate in his appearance, but now he looked as if he had just crawled out of a huge dustbin.

'I haven't got a blasted penny on me, and I've left my cheque book in the office. How about you Ray...Pardon?'

'About a couple of quid I think! But we can't go anywhere looking like this' I said patting clouds of greyish dust off my black business suit and desperately trying not to laugh.

'We can't go any-bloody-where at all without money...Pardon?'...Peter replied.

A farm truck approached us at great speed and screeched to a halt alongside the wreckage.

'I hope you don't think I'm going to accept the aircraft in that state?'

Presumably that was meant to be a joke, but Peter was in no mood for joking and the farmer's remarks didn't go down too well.

'Nobody's been injured, I think we're both perfectly OK Mr O'Leary, how nice of you to ask ... Pardon?'

The farmer apologised immediately for his thoughtless greeting and, after examining the extent of the damage, we all squeezed into the cabin of his truck.

As we drove towards the farmhouse Mr O'Leary explained that the airfield was built during the 1939-1945 war, and the runways had been constructed in tarmac sections. Over the years, many of these segments had partly sunk into the ground, leaving the metal dividing plates protruding between the sections. One possible explanation for what happened when we landed, is that the freely rotating tail wheel may have hit one of the dividing plates side-on as the tail came down which caused it to snap off allowing the tail section to hit the ground hard which in turn snapped the fins off and pulled the arse end out of the aeroplane. Peter's grunt signified he wasn't convinced.

Mr O'Leary took us to a hotel in Port Rush, where the Manager, a personal friend of his, kindly allowed us to clean ourselves up as best we could. As we were short of cash and there were no such things as a bankers card in those days, Mr O'Leary kindly offered to lend Peter enough money to purchase tickets for our return flight to London.

We were met at London Airport by Mrs Clifford. It had been a long day and I finally arrived home around dawn. I'm sure that my wife, who thought I had set off that morning to sell Bells Whisky in Headington, remains unconvinced to this day that we had crash-landed in Northern Ireland.

Needless to say the flight to Ireland could not be counted as first-pilot flying, and I still needed to build up a significant number of solo flying hours in order to be eligible for the flying instructors course.

One way to half the cost of flying was to share flights with another pilot. My friend Nils Bartleet also wanted to take the instructors course, so we used to build up our hours by flying together and sharing the cost. Unfortunately one of the flights we shared came very close to ending in disaster.

**Ray McKenzie-Blyth. Author of
'Only the Maker's Name'**

Top Left. 1931. Me with my mother.
Top Right 1934. Miss Pauline Gower who took me up for my first flight when I was three years old.
Centre Left. 1934. Miss Gower's pleasure flight hut at Hunstanton Airfield.
Centre Right. Me around the time when I volunteered to join the RAF as a fighter Pilot at Kings Lynn recruiting office. (They said I was too young!)
 Bottom left. Me aged ten on Marham Aerodrome during WW2. Whitley Aircraft in background.
Bottom Right. 1960. Me at the time when I was instructing RAF scholarship Cadets on Chipmunks at Oxford.

Top left. My Mother aged twelve when World War One broke out in 1914.
Top Right. My Father when he falsified his age at 16 and joined the army in 1917.
Centre. My father when he was Commander of Civil Defence for East Anglia during the Second Word War.
Bottom. Holcombe Avenue end of World War Two celebrations. Author centre back row with his friend Eddy top left, and his mother forth from the left second row.
Little Flop (Adrian Brown) is in the fourth row, second from the left dressed as a pirate.

187

My Father

Above. L to R. HM The Queen, My father, HM the King, Far right Queen Mary.

Below. My Father, second row centre when he turned professional
playing in goal for Wisbech town football club. 1932.

188

My father (Sitting) when he was a part-time fireman in 1935.

King's Lynn Fire Brigade in the 1930s.

Eddy, just a few weeks old with his father sitting on the wing of a Tiger Moth

Eddy with his mother. Mary.

Eddy now aged 15, in the cockpit of a Cherokee with his father.

Now qualified and an experienced pilot, Eddy is in the cockpit of a Nord.

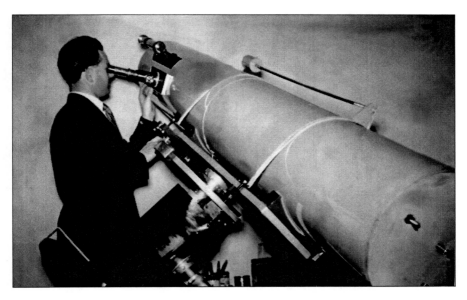

Author with the 12" Newtonian telescope he built in 1956.

This is the observatory he built in the garden of his Council House in 1957, before and after covering the dome.

TOP LEFT The Zlin 526 Trener.   TOP RIGHT. Zlin crash, taken from inside the hanger.
CENTRE. Another view of the crash .
BOTTOM LEFT. They pushed me out onto the car park. BOTTOM RIGHT. In the Nuffield with
Linda my physiotherapist.

CHAPTER 18.

Cumulonimbus.

It was a Sunday morning; the weather was fine, perfect in fact for a cross-country flight in the Tiger Moth. I telephoned Nils and asked him if he would like to share the cost of another flight with me. After a brief chat with Nils I telephoned my father to say that we would like to pop over and see him if there was a suitable field close to his house in Sawbridgworth that we could land a Tiger Moth in. Ten minutes later dad rang back to give me the co-ordinates of a farm belonging to a neighbour of his who agreed to allow us to land in his field. In no time we had worked out the course and were on our way in G-AMEY to have lunch with Dad.

They say that one learns from one's mistakes, and today was destined to be a day of learning!

We found the field easily. Dad, as arranged on the telephone, had pegged a couple of white sheets on the ground in the form of a landing 'T' indicating the direction we were to land.

From the air the field looked more like the size of a postage stamp compared to the large grass area of Kidlington Aerodrome, but we were here now and decided to give it a try anyway.

Before leaving Kidlington Nils and I had tossed a coin to see which leg of the flight we would each fly. Nils won the toss and chose the flight back to Oxford, that left me in the ominous position of attempting to land in the farmer's field. Fortunately the direction of landing into wind was slightly up hill, other than that the field appeared to be as flat as a "witches tit", so the landing was easy and quite respectful.

We climbed out of the Tiger and were surprised to be greeted by a very friendly Policeman, a couple of Boy Scouts and my Dad. The Bobby touched his helmet and announced that my father had asked him if he would mind keeping an eye on the aeroplane whilst we nipped off with him for a quick cup of tea and a bun.

After a very enjoyable lunch dad drove us back to the farmers field. Quite a number of onlookers were gathered around the Tiger Moth and our friendly policeman, who looked most efficient and important, was doing a great job keeping everyone well back from the aircraft.

Large black clouds were building up to the West, which happened to be the direction of our heading back to Oxford. That being the case, we wasted no time in getting started.

It was Nils's turn to fly on the homeward leg, so I primed the engine and swung the prop.

At this point we had to make a very important decision. The surface wind although light, was still blowing down the hill, so we were confronted with the problem of whether to take-off up hill and into wind, or down hill with a slight tail wind component.

Unfortunately we had no way of telling exactly how strong the wind was, or of judging the gradient of the hill we had landed on. I shouted down the Gosport Tube to Nils.

'Your decision mate, you're the Captain.'

Nils replied with a curt …

'Thanks very much!' adding, 'We'll never get airborne trundling up that hill, I think we ought to take-off down hill with a slight tail wind component.'

This was the decision I was hoping he would make, although neither of us were certain if it was the right one or not.

Dad was holding up his handkerchief and pointing at it with his other hand to bring our attention to the wind direction. I nodded and gave him a wave, but my father didn't look too happy.

It was quite a pull to the top of the hill, which convinced me that we had made the correct decision. In fact the correct decision under those circumstances would have been not to attempt a take-off at all.

Nils turned the Tiger Moth to face down hill and gave me the thumbs up sign. I shouted 'OK mate' down the Gosport Tube and we were off.

The aircraft picked up speed pretty rapidly, and before we knew it we were well down the hill with no sign of the tail wheel coming off the ground! I saw dad for a brief second still waving his handkerchief as we flashed past him three quarters of the way down the take-off run. Eventually Nils managed to get the tail up, and I was able to see the somewhat terrifying view ahead of us. First and foremost we were heading straight for our friendly Policeman who had walked away from the rest of the crowd and stood smack in front of us. A few yards further on stood a line of enormous fir-trees quite close together and we were heading straight for the lot.

I knew it was far too late to say anything to Nils, so I just sat there fearing the worst. Nils, trying desperately hard to get airborne started to bounce the aircraft in a succession of hops and leaps. We had obviously misjudged the strength of the tail wind, our ground speed was quite fast, but with the wind behind us our airspeed was considerably slower. At the very last second the Policeman, who was trying to stoop down in a dignified manner, threw himself flat on the ground as we bounced over him. I shut my eyes as the trees loomed up in front of us, and to be honest I don't know to this day how Nils managed to miss them, but somehow he did and we were airborne, literally staggering into the wide blue yonder, both of us considerably shaken by events. But there was worse trouble to come!

It was my turn to navigate on the way back. We set course on the climb levelling out at 2000 ft. After a hair-raising take-off, it was some time before I became relaxed and started to enjoy the flight. Twenty minutes into the flight the cloud ahead seemed darker than ever, and the cloud-base was getting lower, forcing us to reduce height in order to retain forward visibility.

It was not long before it became uncomfortably clear that one hell of a storm was building up ahead of us.

The sky was black and angry when Nils shouted down the speaking tube asking me for a diversionary route to avoid the storm. We took up a new heading and pressed on, but the weather was getting worse by the minute. The sky became black as the storm closed in around us.

Suddenly a blinding flash of lighting followed by the first tell-tale jolt of turbulence rocked the little Tiger Moth, warning us of the severity of the storm ahead.

The next mistake we made could have been fatal. Nils, his voice about two octaves higher than usual, informed me that the fuel was getting low. The fuel tank on a Tiger Moth is situated between the two upper wings. The gauge itself is rather like a steel knitting needle attached to a cork that floats on the top of the petrol, and the needle sits inside a glass tube that protrudes from the top of the petrol tank. Unfortunately the person sitting in the front cockpit (In this case me) is directly under the fuel tank and cannot see the fuel gauge.

'We'll have to go through the storm Ray or we'll run out of fuel.'

Nil's voice sounded very uncertain, more like a question.

I thought carefully before replying. The light forecast winds we had used to calculate our return course were clearly wrong, it was obvious that the wind had veered and we were now battling against a strong headwind. I put my mouth reluctantly against the speaking tube and agreed with Nils to continue on and go straight through the storm. (Inexperience was certainly rearing its ugly head).

Nils turned the Tiger Moth onto its original heading, mumbled something about the one-in-sixty rule, and turned a few more degrees for good luck.

The first large drops of rain began to streak horizontally across the windshield in front of me. I shouted to Nils…

'At least we're still managing to maintain our safety height of 1,500 ft.'

No sooner had the words left my lips than the rain started cascading down in sheets, and forward visibility was rapidly reduced to less than half a mile.

Anyone who knows anything at all about flying will no doubt say that our decision to fly straight through the centre of an active thunderstorm with a light aeroplane was nothing short of potential suicide, and I would be the first to agree. But we were recently qualified private pilots with very limited experience and no doubt very little common sense. We thought we knew it all, Biggles had nothing on us!

The decision we made to penetrate the storm was based purely on the fact that we were low on fuel. At the time I estimated we only had a few miles to fly in order to reach our destination airfield, neither of us had ever been anywhere near a thunderstorm in an aeroplane before.

Without fully realising what was happening we plunged straight into the dark cell of a very active cumulonimbus cloud. Within seconds we had lost all sight of the ground. With uncertainty in his voice Nils announced that he was going to fly on instruments, he hadn't much choice really, we couldn't see a thing.

I think I should explain at this point that flying by sole reference to the instrument panel in a Tiger Moth is considerably different to flying a larger aeroplane with a full flight panel, the reason being that there's an acute shortage of instruments to fly on! Apart from the engine instruments all our aeroplane was equipped with was a turn and slip indicator, airspeed indicator, altimeter, and a P8 compass that was now rendered unreliable by the magnetic effect of the storm.

Both Nils and myself had previously completed the brief one hour "flying on instruments" lesson in the Tiger Moth, which certainly didn't prepare one for flying in anything like the conditions we were experiencing now. Later a more sophisticated instrument course (The IMC Rating) was introduced into the PPL syllabus of training, but that was still some years distant.

We had not been in the storm for more than a few seconds when the real frightening aspects of a thunderstorm took over. We hit the most alarming up draught that forced my head hard down onto my chest. This was followed almost immediately by a vicious downdraught of such ferocity that I felt sure the wings would be ripped off. The bout of turbulence that followed soon after was so vicious that I banged my forehead on the padding at the top of my instrument panel, then instantly left the seat saved from floating out of the aeroplane altogether by my safety harness as the aeroplane seemed to fall out of the sky in the grip of a brutal downdraught. I shouted into the speaking tube to see if Nils was OK but got no reply from him. This had me worried. Fortunately there is a small mirror attached to one of the inner wing-struts on Tiger Moths, rather like the wing mirror of a car, and I could just make out the top of Nils flying helmet bobbing about in the rear cockpit. He appeared to be alright, but I was relieved to see my duplicate controls moving somewhat jerkily, which meant Nils was still in there doing his best to maintain control.

The incessant deluge of rain made it difficult to see anything. In spite of the cockpit visor, water streamed off our goggles and slashed at our faces with the ferocity of a sand storm. One blinding flash of fork lightening ripped and crackled earthwards off the starboard wingtip, so close I could literally taste the acrid electricity in the air. At the same second there was an ear splitting crack of thunder that dwarfed the noise of the engine and roaring slipstream.

Nils struggled desperately to keep the Tiger Moth on an even keel. The airspeed was fluctuating quite a lot and the turn and slip needles were all over the place, as the aeroplane bucked and dived through the storm. Frequently she would flick over to stand almost vertically on her wing tip. Suddenly we hit another cell of violently rising air that forced us up like a rocket. The Tiger Moth gained height at an incredible speed with her nose seemingly pointing steeply downwards. With virtually no outside reference, we were both becoming disorientated.

I noticed that the airspeed indicator needle started to flick excessively back and forth, a quick glance at the pitot head tube confirmed my worst fears…. Ice was forming on the pressure head, which effectively rendered what few instruments we had totally unreliable. I shouted down the Gosport Tube to inform Nils of the ice, but he was far too busy to answer.

The engine started to splutter but fortunately for us it continued running. I began to wonder how much more of this sort of battering our aeroplane could take. From the moment we entered the cloud, I held on to the dual control stick in the front cockpit following Nils's actions as he fought to control the Tiger Moth in this nightmare of a storm.

Slowly the area ahead began to brighten, and we knew we must have been nearing the edge of the thundercloud. We were still being tossed around violently by the turbulence when we began to see intermittent glimpses of clear blue sky ahead. Moments later we were squinting, almost blinded by the sun as we suddenly passed out of the clag and into clear skies. It was like being released from the torments of hell.

For a few moments we just flew straight and level in the warmth of the sun. I heard Nils's exhausted voice through the leather earpieces of my drenched flying helmet...

'We're out of it....thank God for that' .... then...'Christ! Look at the bloody altimeter.'

I quickly glanced at the pitot head, the ice had gone, then I stared down at the altimeter in astonishment, we were flying at seven thousand feet, whilst we had been fighting our way through the thunder storm, the powerful air-currents had taken us up an additional five and a half thousand feet. Most of the time we had been struggling to keep the aeroplane the right way up and with the pitot head iced up neither of us realised exactly what was happening. I'm sure the Tiger was never built for this kind of thing. We were very lucky indeed to be alive. It just goes to show how dangerous it is to think you know it all and fly beyond the bounds of your capabilities.

Nils's voice, now considerably calmer, asked me if I had any idea of where we were. The short answer to that was no! We started to weave around for a couple of minutes trying to identify any recognisable feature on the ground in order to fix our position. Then Nils's voice came over again...

'We're bloody short of fuel Ray, I would say about thirty minutes flying time left at the most. I'll have to find a field to put her down.'

It was a bit late now but I began to wish we had given Dad's invitation to tea a miss.

Then luck was on our side for once, way out in the distance I could just make out a thin trail of white smoke, and realised it must be 'Smokey Joe' the cement works chimney just a couple of miles North of Kidlington Airfield. I shouted to Nils and pointed to the chimney.

We headed towards Smokey Joe, expecting the engine to stop at any second. Minutes later we were touching down on the grass runway at Kidlington.

After landing, Nils taxied straight to the fuel bay and shut down the engine. I breathed a sigh of relief and hauled myself out of the front cockpit. After the violent turbulence of the storm the airfield seemed wonderfully quiet and peaceful. Peering up at the fuel gauge, there was absolutely no sign of the needle at all. When the tanks were refilled, we calculated that there had only been sufficient usable fuel in the tank for a further ten to fifteen minutes flying when we landed. As Nils and I walked away from the aeroplane, the distant rumblings of thunder could still be heard. Yet another unforgettable lesson had been learnt the hard way.

CHAPTER 19.

The First Colt.

My interest in astronomy continued. Often during the winter evenings the red filtered light from my observatory could be seen through the open shutters burning long into the night whilst I peered into the almost frozen brass rimmed eyepiece of my telescope, scrutinising the wonders of the universe. For me astronomy was a very absorbing hobby, I suppose flying and astronomy shared one common denominator, the sky.

Sir Patrick Moore, of "Sky at Night" fame, was Director of the Selenography section of the British Astronomical Association and the person to whom we used to send the results of our nightly observations. I first met him when he came to Oxford to give a lecture at Stow School, and joined him for lunch at the White Hart public house in Whitham. He was indeed a giant of a man, who talked faster than most people could think. I found him to be a most charming person who emanated a contagious enthusiasm about the subject he knew so well. I noticed that Patrick was wearing his RAFVR tie at the time and was interested to discover that he was a Navigator in the RAF during the Second World War. I remember him saying 'I think anything at all to do with the heavens is fascinating.'

My son Eddy was now four years old and already taking an interest in the moon and stars. In order to give him a good start with his education we arranged for him to attend the infant's class of a Private School in Brackley. I remembered Mary and I both had tears in our eyes after we had taken him to school for the first time, looking very smart in his little blue uniform.

I was still working as a sales representative in the licensed trade at that time, and covering a large area of the country necessitated staying away from home quite a lot. In addition to this, all my spare time was spent at the airfield. As a result our marriage began to suffer.

My ultimate aim was, and always had been, to become a professional pilot and make a successful career out of flying. But I would have to qualify as a full flying instructor and gain my commercial pilot's licence before my salary would be sufficient to take on my existing financial commitments.

Now that CSE was our parent company, Oxford Air Training School began to expand rapidly, and it wasn't long before the school started to use Piper aircraft for training purposes.

The first two Piper aeroplanes to be used by the school were Tripacer's G-ARCA, and G-ARGY. Golf Yankee was equipped for basic instrument training. I remember it had a sort of cloth curtain arrangement suspended from a curved rail that obscured the student's external forward and peripheral vision. It also buggered up the instructors vision to a large extent, as he could see virtually nothing at all to the left of the aeroplane! Golf Yankee also carried VOR and ADF navigational aids and was described in the company's new brochure as "A comprehensively equipped aeroplane with radio and navigational equipment, enabling training in instrument flying and radio procedures at an economical rate." And strange as it may seem in this day and age, it really was the "bee's knees" for basic instrument training in the early 1960s.

Following the four-seat Tripacer, Piper Aircraft brought out a two-seater version without wing flaps and named it the 'Piper Colt'. It turned out to be an excellent basic training aeroplane.

The very first Colt to arrive in this country from America was registered G-ARGO. One morning when I popped into the airport on my way to work, Rex called me into his office and asked if I would like to take their brand new Piper Colt on a sales demonstration flight to various flying clubs in the UK. I wouldn't be paid for the job, but CSE would refund any out-of-pocket expenses incurred. I was absolutely delighted to accept this kind offer as I was still trying to build up the mandatory 200 first pilot hours I needed to become eligible for training as an assistant flying instructor.

I arranged to use part of my holiday entitlement from Bells Distillers, and Rex generously agreed for Nils to come with me and share the flying hours as he too intended to take the instructor's course.

Having been duly checked out on the only Piper Colt at present flying in the UK, we were ready for our epic trip around the UK to demonstrate the aircraft to the CFI's and instructors of flying clubs spread over various parts of the country.

G-ARGO was not equipped with navigational aids, in fact it didn't even have a radio transceiver, therefore all the navigation would have to be DR (Dead reckoning), which called for careful planning, especially when flying into airfields close to the London Control Zone.

The met forecast looked good. G-ARGO had been refuelled and parked outside the hangar. At 6.30 am on the 3rd May 1961 Nils and I arrived at the airfield. It was a still, cool morning with a light wispy fog that veiled the airfield. By 8 o'clock the fog had lifted completely, leaving a heavy morning dew sparkling in bright sunlight.

Our initial destination was Edinburgh's Airport based at East Fortune, but as the Colt only had one 15 gallon petrol tank, we planned to punctuate the journey with a couple of re-fuelling stops, one at Netherthorpe, and the second at Newcastle's Woolsington Airport. As the aircraft was not equipped with radio, it was necessary to telephone all our destination aerodromes in advance to gain permission to land without radio and obtain any special instructions concerning their circuit procedures etc.

As things turned out, the flight to Scotland was a little unusual. It started when I dialled the telephone number given in the 'Air Pilot' as Netherthorpe's Air Traffic Control. I was surprised to hear the rural voice at the other end informing me...

'You've come through to the farmhouse, I specs you wants fuel?'

After I had informed him of our ETA (Estimated time of arrival) he surprised me yet again by saying...

'Best buzz the old farmhouse when you gets here and I'll pop over on me bike and herd the cattle to one end of the strip so as you can land!'

By 8.30am we were airborne and on our way. It was a truly beautiful morning with an unlimited visibility at 2000 ft. The journey to Netherthorpe was uneventful, and 65 minutes after take-off we arrived overhead the area where, according to the map, the airfield was located. But we couldn't for the life of us see anything that remotely resembled an airfield.

We circled for a while trying to locate the landing strip, the town of Worksop was clearly visible about two miles to the Northwest, and according to other landmarks we should be directly over Netherthorpe Airfield.

Having descended for a closer look we decided that it must be a rather smallish field with cattle in it, but there was no sign of a windsock!

Nils checked the location several times with his map and being as there was nothing else in the area that remotely resembled an airfield, we decided to make an approach on the only field that appeared to be large enough to land on.

The field had a large clump of trees in one corner. We couldn't see any marked runways, only a few small shed -like buildings and a farmhouse on the extreme Eastern boundary.

As requested by the person I spoke to on the telephone earlier, we made a couple of low passes over the house. During the low runs I was just able to make out a mowed section of grass about 400 yards long and 50 feet wide running in a North Easterly direction from the Southern corner of the field. The cattle strewn all over the runway remained totally unperturbed by our presence. We orbited the field for a few minutes, wondering what to do if nobody turned up to remove the livestock. Eventually a chap on a bicycle arrived and proceeded to drive the cattle towards one end of the field. I was flying the aircraft for the first leg of the journey, so it was down to me to make the landing.

'It looks as though we will have to land whilst the farmer tries to keep those cows clear of the strip.' I said.

Nils tightened his seat belt and never said a word. We had taken off on runway 09 at Oxford, so, in the absence of a windsock, smoke or anything to give us a clue of the surface wind, I decided to land on the grass strip in a North-Easterly direction. This meant we would pass very low over the cattle that had now been herded in an area to the South West corner of the field.

'Let's see if we can get ten out of ten by landing without knocking off the cattle.'

Nils grinned and replied with the customary 'Roger,' he loved anything that was in the remotest way a little tricky.

Attempting a short field approach and landing, we passed between two quite tall bushes, skimmed the boundary fence and passed low over the herd of cows. As the aircraft rumbled onto a rather rough surface, Nils was trying to look back at the cattle, which was not an easy thing to do in the Colt. Eventually he opened the door and leaned out. Barely a split second passed before he slammed the door shut with considerable enthusiasm and shouted…

'There's something that looks strangely like a bloody great bull charging up the runway behind us mate!'

By this time we had reached the boundary fence at the far end of the field, so I decided to swing the aeroplane round to face whatever it was coming at us.

There, sure enough about 150 yards away was an enormous bull trotting and snorting towards us followed by several cows and a very irate looking farmer. I remember thinking what an awful way to end a sales demonstration tour, with the aeroplane and possibly its occupants, smashed to a pulp by a raging bull at the first refuelling stop.

We sat there petrified, the only thing I could do was close the engine down, this would at least prevent the bull from becoming minced beef when he reached the propeller. Nils broke the silence with a rather obvious understatement.

'He looks a bit upset!'

'The bloody farmer doesn't look too pleased either' I said.

The incensed bull stopped just a few feet in front of us snorting loudly and pawing furiously at the ground. One of the cows that had been running up behind the bull stuck its nose firmly up the bulls arse which tended to put him off his stroke for a few seconds, by which time the gasping farmer staggered up and took control of the situation.

After being reprimanded by the exhausted farmer for passing low over his cattle, he announced that he was also the Airport Manager and directed us to a small enclosure which housed the petrol pump. Neither Nils nor I were too keen to get out of the cockpit whilst the bull was still hanging around in the background, but eventually the disgruntled animal wandered off a short distance and we were able to refuel G-ARGO whilst still keeping a very cautious eye on the Bull in case he changed his mind and returned.

Having paid for the petrol we lost no time in getting airborne and away from the irate farmer and his antisocial friend.

Somewhat shattered after the lively start to our flight, we were left wondering how the rest of our "sales demonstration trip" would turn out.

The weather remained perfect for map reading with clear skies and excellent visibility. We arrived over Newcastle Woolsington Airport at 2000 ft. spot on our ETA. Air Traffic Control flashed a steady green light at us indicating that it was OK for us to join the circuit and land.

Within half an hour we had refuelled the Colt, had a nice cup of tea and were airborne on our way to Edinburgh.

When we landed at East Fortune (Edinburgh Airport) we were greeted by the CFI of the local flying club. He had been keeping tabs on our progress by telephoning Netherthorpe and Woolsington to make sure everything was going to plan. Apparently he was amused by the remarks made by the manager at Netherthorpe who said that we had upset his bull and were lucky to get away without being mauled.

After a pleasant meal in the Airport Restaurant, Nils and I took it in turns demonstrating the Piper Colt to instructors and members of the Edinburgh Flying Club.

The sales manager of CSE Aviation had provided us with all the sales literature, which we handed out to those who were interested in our delightful little aeroplane. By the end of the day we had flown in excess of eight hours and were more than ready to sample a glass or two of the local brew.

Nils had already arranged for us to stay at his fiancée's parents house in Edinburgh whilst we were in the area. I made the sad mistake of telling our hosts that I worked as a salesman for 'Bells Distillers'. Thereafter I was treated in a manner that befits someone who represents such a highly reputable Scottish company, and predictably we all got completely sloshed.

The next morning I had difficulty in recalling anything that had taken place during the latter part of the evening. Judging by the terrible hangover I suffered, and the smiles on the faces of the kind family that looked after us, it must have been some party! When we left, our hosts kindly offered to put us up for the night again on our return journey later in the week.

Although the weather at Edinburgh was fine, we were prevented from making the early start we had planned because our destination airport at Aberdeen was in fog.

We didn't want to sit around on Edinburgh Airport all day waiting for the fog to clear at Dyce, so we came up with a cracking idea on how we could make a bob or two on the side.

We parked G-ARGO on the airfield as near as we could to the visitor's car park. There were lots of people sitting around in their cars watching the aeroplanes taking-off and landing, so Nils and I walked around the cars offering short pleasure flights to the occupants. It wasn't long before we had several people interested. We had been exempt from paying landing fees at Edinburgh because we were quests of the Local Flying Club who had paid the airport authorities a block landing fee for us in advance.

I worked out that we could do a quick low-level flight out to sea, around the Bass Rock and back for one pound ten shillings per head, a reasonable sum in 1961. It was a sort of unofficial barnstorming. The flights were booked out on our flight sheet as trial flying lessons....(The one pound ten shilling being temporary membership of the Blyth/Bartleet drinking fund!!) a nice little earner.

By lunchtime the fog to the North had cleared, so we were able to set course for Dyce Airport to refuel there and then fly on up to Dalcross

Airport Inverness to demonstrate the Colt to club members and staff the following day.

We booked in at a small hotel in Inverness for one night, and after a few jars retired to our beds.

When we arrived at Inverness Club House the next morning we were greeted by the smiling face of the CFI who informed us that he had been in contact with Rex Smith at Oxford and arranged to hire our demonstration aircraft for a further seven days. This was a bit of a blow as it meant we would have to return to Oxford by train.

Not in the best of moods, we were taken by taxi to Inverness Railway Station where we waited dismally to catch the overnight train to Oxford.

Rex asked us if we would like to collect the Colt from Inverness on the 13th May and demonstrate the aeroplane to members of the Skegness Flying Club on the return journey. I was delighted to be given the opportunity of completing the sales demo flights, but unfortunately Nils was unable to come with me due to commitments at work.

Seven days later I caught the night train from London to Inverness. After a good nights sleep on the train I awoke to a beautiful sunny morning. Breakfast was served in the dining car which was situated at the rear of the train, so I ate a hearty breakfast whilst enjoying magnificent views of the Scottish Mountains through the huge rear-facing window of the dining car.

When I arrived at the airport to collect G-ARGO the CFI there told me that they were very interested in the Colt and would be placing an order with CSE later in the week.

The meteorological forecast indicated that some patches of low cloud were likely to exist in the area between Inverness and Aberdeen. The worst of the weather appeared to be along the East coast, so I planned to track South and then turn East into Aberdeen for refuelling. With luck I could continue on to Skegness before finally setting course for Oxford in the early evening.

To start with everything went well. The aircraft purred along beautifully, the scenery was magnificent and all worldly troubles seemed to be nonexistent. Surely I was the luckiest chap to be alive... But perhaps not! I was young, enthusiastic, but sadly not very experienced.

Twenty minutes into the flight things didn't look quite so good. I was flying along a valley in the Grampian Mountains. I could see clearly ahead but had failed to notice that the veil of cloud well above me was gradually lowering.

Over enthusiasm combined with lack of experience was progressively leading me into a very dangerous situation. The way ahead appeared to be reasonably clear but unbeknown to me I was considerably West of my intended track. Soon I was flying with precipitous mountain walls on either side of me, blissfully unaware that the cloud above now capped the mountains on either side.

It suddenly occurred to me that I was literally flying down a dangerously narrowing tunnel. My forward vision was deteriorating fast, the rocks on either side were now dangerously close, and the cloud layer above that capped the mountain-tops on both sides was gradually descending, leaving no clear escape from the abyss.

The alternatives were limited, I could risk trying to turn back, but I was certain that I would never be able to turn steep enough to avoid crashing into the huge mountain walls that now appeared grey and hostile on either side. The second alternative seemed even more frightening. I could attempt to climb as steeply as possible straight-ahead through the cloud in the hope that there was no bend in the mountainous corridor I was flying down. Time was fast running out. I tried desperately to overcome the feeling of panic that welled up inside me. I was alone, afraid, and had to make a decision pretty quickly otherwise it would be too late. Then, just to make things worse, there was a sudden marked drop in the RPM.

'Carburettor icing,' I thought: 'that's all I bloody needed!' I pulled out the carburettor heat control. For a few seconds the engine ran roughly then returned to smooth running again.

Aiming for the centre of the misty area ahead, I carefully noted the exact heading on the DGI, opened the throttle fully and started to climb. Within seconds the cockpit darkened and the aircraft began to bounce around as we entered cloud.

Although I tried hard to make a conscious effort to relax, I was beginning to sweat and could feel the tension gripping every muscle in my body. The knowledge that I was flying blindly through a narrow valley between two mountainous walls of rock and in cloud, was stressful enough, but another horrifying thought suddenly entered my head. The turbulence, which was now quite severe, could possibly be causing the directional gyro to precess, which, God forbid, meant that the aeroplane could be wandering off the heading I had selected to steer us between the mountain walls.

The compass needle was swinging around all over the place, making it impossible to synchronise the DI with any accuracy. The experience was nothing short of terrifying, my eyes were glued to the instruments as

I literally waited for the bang that would end it all, it was like playing Russian roulette with God.

The cockpit darkened still further as the cloud thickened. The instruments glared back at me, IAS 85 knots, course steady on 165 degrees, rate of climb 600 fpm, altitude passing through 3000 ft. in balance and the artificial horizon showed that the wings were tipping around but averaging the level attitude. My senses were definitely telling me that the aircraft was rolling and slowly turning to the left, 'the artificial horizon must be wrong.'

Every instrument-trained pilot is aware of the physiological effects of instrument flying. I recalled my instructor's advice…

'Always obey the instruments, never take notice of what your body tells you.'

I knew he was right of course, and I wished he was with me now. The feeling that the aircraft was flying left wing down and turning was so realistic that I had to concentrate very hard to resist an uncontrollable urge to roll the aircraft to the right.

Time ticked on, every second seemed like a lifetime, a lifetime that could end any second. I wondered how close I was to the rocks on either side. The perspex windshield had become opaque. Maybe, there was a mountain face directly in front, a solid wall of rock that would turn the aircraft into twisted wreckage at any second and send me on an untimely journey to the Promised Land. 'Please God, I know I've been a pratt, but please see me through this.' But why should God listen to me now, I only ever speak to him when I need his help. God would have probably replied… 'It's a little late for that my son, I get these sort of requests every second of every minute of every day.'

The turbulence didn't let up. Every violent buffet made my heart miss a beat, my hands ached through gripping the controls tightly and perspiration ran down my face and into my eyes. Everything contributed to a feeling of intense panic.

Slowly the cloud became much lighter. Maybe God did hear my plea after all. Then the most wonderful relief, we were skimming through the tops of fluffy white clouds in bright sunlight with a beautiful clear blue sky above. But the sight of jagged mountain tops on either side of the aircraft made me shiver.

The relief from the tension was indescribable. I thanked God for his protection, then slumped back in my seat and relaxed for a few moments enjoying the warm sun and the beautiful but deadly scenery.

About eight miles ahead the cloud dispersed completely, giving way to clear views of the mountains and streams below. I headed East until I came to the coast, identified my position and eventually landed at Dyce Airport to refuel. It had certainly been a lesson I would never forget.

The flight from Aberdeen to my next refuelling stop at Edinburgh was, by comparison, smooth and straightforward. I stayed overnight with Nils's friends again, this time I made sure that I didn't get sloshed. The following morning I was up and ready to recommence my journey feeling refreshed and sober as a judge.

The flight to Newcastle was very enjoyable. Clear skies and perfect visibility all the way. Having refuelled again, I took off for the two-hour flight to Skegness Aerodrome.

When I landed there I discovered that I only had one person to fly with. The plan had been to return to Kidlington from Skegness, but Rex had left a message asking me to fly to Ipswich and demonstrate the Colt to the Club's Director who was apparently interested in purchasing a Piper Colt.

It was late afternoon when I finally took off from Ipswich and set course. I calculated that it would take one hour fifteen minutes to reach Oxford so, with a bit of luck, I would arrive back at Kidlington before official dark.

Everything seemed to be going well for a while, then I realised that the features on the ground didn't match up with the features on the map! In short, after all that flying around Scotland and Northern England, I had managed to get lost on the last leg home. What a pillock!

I flew around for a bit, but was unable to positively identify anything. Then, as luck would have it, I came across a large grass airfield with an Auster and a Tiger Moth parked outside the control building. After circling the tower a couple of times, the controller flashed a green on his Aldis lamp authorising me to land, but at that moment I saw the letters LT in the signals square and identified the airfield as Luton. (Just a grass airfield in the early 1960s).

A quick glance at the map showed that I was three miles south of track, and with just thirty-five nautical miles to run I decided to ignore the hospitality of Luton and continue on my way to Kidlington.

By this time daylight was fading fast. The sky had a beautiful warmish, orange glow about it, but looking down at the ground it appeared to be early dusk. Lights began to twinkle here and there in the windows of houses, whilst streetlights shone their cones of light on the darkening streets of the tiny villages. I could also see the beams from car headlights winding their way along the narrow country roads. I was enjoying the last stages of the flight home immensely when I was suddenly struck by an intriguing thought: 'I haven't asked Air Traffic to lay a flarepath for me, so if I don't arrive at Kidlington before dark, they will probably assume I have landed en-route and close the airfield down.' Also I had never landed at night.

After the episode in the mountains earlier the previous day, the problem didn't seem so bad. I was still able to navigate quite easily because the lights from the villages and towns stood out clearly and were easily identifiable. With a bit of luck I should just make it into Kidlington before dark.

With no radio I was unable to contact the tower. I had spoken on the telephone earlier to the controller at Kidlington, informing him that I was about to leave Ipswich and estimated I would be arriving at Oxford around 4pm. But it was now almost six o'clock, two hours late on my ETA!

From the air the ground now appeared to be quite dark, but I could clearly see the smoke from "Smoky Joe" the cement works chimney, curling upwards in a long black smudge against the late evening sky. I switched on the navigation lights and increased the intensity of the instrument panel lighting.

Two miles South of the chimney the location of Kidlington Airport was lost completely in the murky darkness. I circled the area where I thought Kidlington should be, but could see nothing that remotely resembled a flarepath. My earlier feeling of confidence about landing in the dark now changed to apprehension. To the South the city lights of Oxford sparkled like diamonds and I could also make out the straggling lights of Kidlington village, but there was no airport to be seen. I still had enough fuel for about ninety minutes flying, so I tried to convince myself there was no need for immediate panic. Then, through the murk, I could see two lines of lights. They were not exactly where I had expected the airport to be, but under the circumstances I was not too far out with my assessment.

Keen to get down and see what sort of a cock-up I could make of a night landing, I hastily completed my landing checks and positioned the aircraft for a straight in approach on the runway which I took to be our North Easterly strip. On the final approach to land I was down to three hundred feet when I saw a ground vehicle coming towards me followed by two more sets of lights.

'Bloody hell, it's a road'! Full power and into a steep climb. God's changed his mind; I'm doomed to die today after all!

I forced myself to keep calm, but things were at a pretty low ebb. As I banked over to starboard I caught a glimpse of a flashing green light. I stared at it for a moment, then realised it was coding OX in Morse. Great, I'd found Kidlington, but where's the flarepath? Having circled the green light at one thousand feet, my eyes focused on one line of very dim flickering lights. Good Lord, they've only put out a single line of flares how the hell am I going to land on that with my non-existent night landing experience? Perhaps another quick chat with God… or perhaps not, I've upset him once today already.

I circled the airfield a couple of times, now flying almost completely on instruments. Finally I plucked up courage and commenced an approach to land, I found it difficult to keep the wings level when looking at the single line of flares, and momentarily lost sight of them after looking at the instruments. Anyway, I managed to cross over the first flare at around one hundred feet at the correct approach speed. I closed the throttle, and eased Golf Oscar down gently, anticipating hitting the ground any second. It felt as though the aircraft was sinking into a huge trench down the centre of the runway as the line of flares seemed to be level with my ears. Amazingly there was only a very small bump, and we were down. What a wonderful feeling!

I thought that was the end of it, but no chance. I turned off the runway misjudging the speed I was travelling. G-ARGO hopped along almost on one wheel and took out one of the gooseneck flares, which toppled over and set fire to the grass.

'Bugger' … after all I'd managed to get through during the day I go and knock a bloody flare over. God was wagging a cautious finger at Raymond.

Eventually I found myself standing at the flying club bar downing the first of several, much needed scoops.

This time I had been lucky. I had certainly learnt some very important lessons over the last twenty-four hours. It is strange how some things work out in life. Some people believe that their path through life is just luck, whilst others prefer to think of it as fate.

My mother used to believe that everyone had a Guardian Angel, and I must say her superstitions were beginning to rub off on me. There had certainly been several occasions when the presence of a Guardian Angel would have explained the narrow escapes from death I had experienced. So I think its fair to say that I believe I have a Guardian Angel who predetermines what happens to me. The only difference is that my Guardian Angel it seems has a very warped sense of humour.

For example, one Winter's evening I was travelling along in my car towards the village of Deddington in Oxfordshire. The weather was atrocious. Heavy rain accompanied by gale force winds made driving very difficult. It was that time of evening when it was neither daylight or fully dark and although the windscreen wipers were working flat out, it was still difficult to see anything clearly more than a few yards ahead.

Having just passed through the village of Anho, I saw the blurred headlights of a car approaching me. Suddenly, in what appeared to be slow motion, an enormous tree came crashing down across the road between me and the approaching car. I slammed on the brakes and skidded a few feet, winding up in a mass of twigs and foliage.

Fortunately for me the tree had fallen from a point behind a high stone wall several yards to my right, otherwise my car would have been crushed by the main trunk, which must have been more than four feet in diameter.

The occupants of the car I had seen approaching were not so lucky. Their car had been struck by the tree at the exact point where the main trunk divided into two enormous branches. Miraculously one branch had flattened the boot of their car completely, whilst the other branch had smashed down on top of the engine. With the front and the back of the car crushed, the roof had split open like the lid of a tin can and I was able to assist the occupants to scramble out from the wreckage, they were somewhat shocked but otherwise unhurt.

But not to be out-done, my dear old Guardian Angel had something more sinister lined up for me in the form of a second, and far more serious, accident when I was returning home later that very same evening.

It was just before midnight when I set off from Deddington to make my way home. The wind had dropped and the skies had cleared; in fact it was a beautiful moonlight night with virtually no one else on the roads.

I was taking a short detour around Anho village as there was a possibility of the road still being partly blocked by the remains of the tree that had fallen earlier.

I remember approaching a bend in the road when suddenly there was a blinding flash......

When I regained consciousness I was in the Intensive Care Unit of the Horton General Hospital in Banbury! It was very frightening at the time because I had no idea where I was or what had happened. My head was swathed in bandages, and I had a blinding headache.

I must have passed out again, because the next thing I remember with any clarity was being told that I had been in a car crash two days previously. I was relieved to see my wife Mary sitting by the bed. She was obviously alright and presumably hadn't been involved in whatever had happened to me. The next thing I remember is the Dental Surgeon taking a look at me and saying he would be able to repair the damage to my teeth as soon as I recovered sufficiently from the hairline fracture to my skull.

To cut a long story short it took a couple of months before I had recovered sufficiently to consider returning to work.

With two large bumps each side of a deep grove in my head and most of my hair removed, my head looked like a freshly smacked arse! I can remember nothing about what happened, so I will have to reiterate events as they were told to me later, and I think the reader will agree that this incredible set of circumstances warrants the belief in a Guardian Angel...

It was past midnight when the accident occurred. A young nurse, who was staying with friends in a remote farmhouse, was fast asleep when she was awakened by the sound of a loud crash. She called the farmer and together they ran to the main road to see what had happened. On arriving at the gates to the farm they found my car wedged underneath a milk-churn stand made of large wooded railway sleepers. One of the sleepers had crashed end-on through the windscreen and passed partly out through the rear window, whilst a second sleeper had also smashed through the windscreen and was protruding out through the roof of the car.

Apparently the top of my head had been split open and was wedged between one of the railway sleepers and the back of the passenger's seat.

The nurse used her dressing gown to suppress the bleeding, whilst the farmer rushed back to the farmhouse to call the emergency services.

The only explanation of how the accident had occurred was that my car had left the road and hit the milk-churn stand end on, knocking the legs from under the stand whilst the base, made of sleepers, smashed through the windscreen. The car was a complete write-off, and God knows how my head remained attached to my body..

One could ask 'Where did my Guardian Angel feature in such an accident?' Well I think the answer is surely the miraculous set of circumstances that saved my life...

If that nurse had not been staying at that remote farmhouse on the night of the accident, or if she hadn't been wakened by the sound of the crash, and if the farmer and the nurse hadn't bothered to investigate the cause of the bang, it's a certainty that I would not be here to tell the tale.

CHAPTER 20.

Flying Instructor's Course.

Rex Smith gave me as much free flying as possible. Whenever an aircraft positioning flight came along, and providing I could get time off from my regular occupation, he kindly allowed me to do the job. He knew that my ambition was to fly for a living and ultimately, if they would have me, work for Oxford Air Training School when I qualified as an instructor. Rex also appreciated that, in order to pay the bills, I had to continue working as a full-time whisky salesman for the time being, and with that in mind he kindly allowed me to complete my flying instructors course on a part time basis.

There were three FIC approved instructors working at Oxford at the time. Richard Dobson who was a South African chap, Frank Sturdy an ex RAF instructor and Bunny Austin a serving Squadron Leader based at RAF Central Flying School Little Rissington who helped out at Oxford part time.

Bunny had worked closely with Rex in the early days of the flying club to standardise their instructional techniques and bring them in line with the RAF Central Flying School's training syllabus. Later, when Oxford Air Training School was formed, the same high standards under the direction of Rex Smith held the company in good stead when they successfully tendered for pilot training contracts with the world's major airlines.

I arranged to carry out my instructor training in the de Havilland Chipmunk. Before starting the course I completed two hours pre-course flying with Richard Dobson, polishing up on everything I had learned to date. I soon realised that I had a lot of hard work to do in order to fly as accurately as the instructor's course demanded. When Richard took over the controls, I made a point of watching how accurately he flew. It was as if the aeroplane was on rails. At the end of my first hours "Brush-up" flying,

I staggered from the cockpit soaked in sweat and feeling pretty hacked off with myself. I was convinced I would never be good enough. But Richard was very encouraging…

'Not bad for the first attempt!' he said 'your real problem is that you are not relaxed enough. Remember once you've got the aeroplane trimmed correctly to the required attitude, you hardly need to touch the controls, just make small adjustments using your finger and thumb.'

Wise words I'm sure, but would I be able to fly within the limits he set for me? I began to have serious doubts.

I lay awake most of the night worrying about the poor show I had put up during my first hour's pre-course flying. They say that problems always seem to be a lot worse in the stillness of the night, well that certainly proved to be the case with me.

I recalled the time when Bunny was teaching me basic aerobatics in the Tiger Moth and I cocked up a slow roll, stalled inverted and fell out of the sky frightening myself to death. Bunny suddenly perked up and said…

'Ray, if you continue to fly like that you would do well to forget the QFI course because you'll never make an instructor whilst you've a hole up your arse!'

Charming. I was furious with myself, but Bunny's remarks made me even more determined to succeed.

The next time I flew with Richard I made a conscious effort to relax in the cockpit. I told myself that my actual thought processes had to be calm and smooth if my body reactions were to follow in the same way. That seemed to work. After a time there was no more tenseness, no more jerky control movements, and I was able to remain within the flight limitations required. The preliminary "accurate flying lessons" were now complete and I was ready to commence the instructor's course proper.

There were four of us on the part time course, Jerry Busby an ex RAF pilot, Bob Timmis a private pilot, Cyril Henson an ex naval fleet air-arm pilot, and myself. We were split into pairs that would work together throughout the course. I teamed up with Jerry Busby and our course instructor was Frank Sturdy.

Frank was a quiet sort of chap, always immaculately dressed, slight in build and sporting a large moustache. He never shouted or lost his temper, and now, after forty years of flying as an instructor myself, I realise that Frank's instructional techniques were second to none.

The flying part of the instructors course worked like this. For each training flight Frank would give us a pre-flight briefing on the blackboard to highlight the sequence of events during the detail we were about to fly. Then he would fly with each of us in turn, teaching us how to present the same lesson in the air. Lesson complete, we would land and a de-briefing would follow. Then after a suitable break, we would fly the lesson again with our allotted course partner, half the flight simulating the student, and the other half simulating the instructor. Finally we would each give our rendering of the blackboard briefing to our course leader. After that we would take it in turns to fly with Frank again, this time he would play the part of a student so that he could assess the progress we had made during our mutual flights.

Throughout the course, this sequence would be repeated for each lesson in the training syllabus. All the blackboard briefings were standardised and had to be learnt off by heart. The course also included many hours of lectures and groundwork.

As far as I was concerned the instructor's course went extremely well. I found Jerry Busby was the ideal person to be paired up with on the course. He was very critical of my flying instructional patter when we flew together, and when our roles were reversed, he didn't object at all when I criticised him in the same way. We both worked very hard to be word perfect with our patter, whilst at the same time endeavouring to fly the aeroplane as accurately as we possibly could. Also whilst playing the role of the student, we purposely made mistakes, which helped us to deal with situations that could occur and were not covered by the standard instructional patter. This showed up favourably during our progress checks with our course instructor.

The Ground School side of things turned out to be far more difficult than I expected, once again proving that I really knew very little about flying before embarking on the instructor's course.

Bunny Austin's lectures on the principles of flight, which included long and more detailed briefings on each of the flying lessons, taught us all a great deal.

The so-called pre-flight briefing, explaining what the student will be doing during his impending flying lesson, is usually quite short, lasting about ten to fifteen minutes. The long briefings are in depth lectures that include far more complicated aerodynamic details, and often take the form of one or two hourly lectures in the classroom. Because these lessons usually finished up with a blackboard full of mathematical theory and dozens of arrows representing the forces acting on an aeroplane in flight, the lectures were frequently referred to as "The Arrows".

Some of the RAF Cat A1 instructors (The real clever boys), could fill a blackboard with mathematical formulae to prove a point, and when you finally grasped the argument they were making, they would chalk up another formulae proving the complete opposite just for the hell of it! Clever stuff, but bloody confusing!.

In all it took Jerry and I one month flying part time to complete the course and be ready for our AFI flight test's with a Panel Examiner.

Not everybody is cut out to be a flying instructor. Unfortunately Bob withdrew from the course on his own account due to the fact that he was not happy spinning the Chipmunk. I felt very sorry for him. He was a really nice chap and several of us tried to persuade him to continue. But he was adamant that instructing was not for him and promptly left. I believe he later took up aerial photography as a profession.

The Chipmunk's reputation of occasionally not recovering from a fully developed spin,

was a frequent topic of discussion. Bunny Austin however told me that RAF Central Flying School carried out exhaustive spin tests on the Chipmunk, and never had one problem with a recovery throughout the tests.

I must say that I personally enjoyed spinning both the Tiger Moth and the Chipmunk, and I was amazed in later years when the fully developed spin was removed from the training syllabus. But not everybody enjoyed spinning. Later when I qualified as an instructor I soon found out that you only had to mention you didn't mind teaching spinning, and you soon found yourself allocated most of the spinning details on the Ops. Board.

My instructors test had been booked for the 6th June 1961 with guild examiner Hector Taylor based at RAF Tollerton Airfield. Jerry Busby was also booked in for his test on the same day, which meant we could make the flight over to Tollerton together and practice our instructional patter on the way.

The day before my instructors test I decided to stay away from the airfield altogether and call on a few of my Bells Whisky customers in Banbury. Having parked my car I was crossing the road to take some advertising material into the Whately Hall Hotel, when I heard the sound of a light aircraft obviously carrying out aerobatics.

When I finally spotted him I could see it was a Chipmunk just West of the town flying at about five or six thousand feet. I watched him for several minutes as he performed a few slow rolls, losing height rapidly as he scooped out of the second half of the roll on every occasion. I wondered if he had an instructor with him, but dismissed the idea because who ever it was flying the aircraft constantly allowed the engine to over rev during his recovery from the rolls.

I continued on my way towards the Whately Hall Hotel but was forced to look up again when I heard the engine of the aircraft literally screaming whilst pulling out from what I assume was another slow roll. By this time I estimate he must have been down to about 1500 ft.

Suddenly he pulled the aircraft up vertically into what I thought was going to be a stall turn, but at the top of the vertical climb the aeroplane flicked over to the left and started to spin. The engine screamed flat out for a few seconds then died out as the aircraft continued to auto-rotate. I watched as the sun glinted on the silver wings of the little Chipmunk fluttering down in silence. There was one short burst from the engine that died away pathetically as the Chipmunk disappeared from view occulated by buildings, then it was obviously too late for a recovery to be affected, and with a sinking feeling in my stomach I knew that the aircraft must have crashed.

I ran back to the car and set off in the direction the aircraft had disappeared from view. As soon as I was clear of the built up area I could see the unmistakable pall of thick black smoke rising up in the distance. Although it was no more than two miles away, it took me quite a while to reach the wreckage as every turn I made eventually led me away from the telltale smoke. Finally I arrived at the open gate to the field where the Chipmunk had crashed.

As I bumped along the rough farm track I was relieved to see that the local fire service had already reached the wreckage. I left the car and hurried towards the smouldering aircraft. One of the firemen came over to speak to me. I explained that I was currently flying Chipmunk aircraft, and offered to help in any way I could. The fireman shook his head...

'You can come and have a word with the Guv, but I'm afraid there's nothing anyone can do for the pilot.'

I should have turned back there and then, but I needed to know if the aircraft was one of our aeroplanes.

I approached the wreckage with considerable apprehension. I could see the aircraft laid perfectly flat on the ground, the wing-tips and tailplane were virtually untouched by fire. The engine was ticking as it cooled and the blackened centre section including the cockpit was unrecognisable. Part of the fuselage bore the red white and blue roundels of the RAF. As far as I could see the only recognisable object in the centre section of the aircraft was the parachute on which the pilot must have been sitting. The remains of the pilot's body had been removed and laid covered over a few yards from the wreckage. As I turned away from the smouldering remains and the awful smell, I could hear the distant sirens of approaching ambulances and police cars. I will never forget those dreadful seconds watching that aeroplane fall from the sky.

The morning of the 6th June arrived. Both Jerry and myself had prayed for good weather and it appeared that our prayers had been answered.

We arrived at Tollerton in Chipmunk G-AOST. It was a fine looking aeroplane that had been sprayed white and silver with a light blue streak down the side of the fuselage. This particular Chipmunk had undergone a Bristol Conversion (Sometimes referred to as a Masefield Conversion), which gave it a dome shaped cockpit hood, not unlike the canopy of a Mk1X Spitfire. When I first saw this aeroplane I was surprised to note that it was not fitted with spinning strakes, a flat surface about thirty inches long added to the top of the fuselage just in front on the fin, its purpose being to aid spin recovery.

Mr Taylor greeted us warmly when we arrived, and after a welcomed cup of hot tea, we were shown into the briefing room where we were asked to carry out a couple of pre-flight briefings on the blackboard. I remember I had to go first and was asked to give a briefing on the primary and secondary effects of the controls part one. Mr Taylor then suggested that we tossed a coin to see who would be the first to take the instructor's flight test.

Having won the toss I walked out apprehensively to the aeroplane and carried out the pre-flight checks, closely monitored by Mr Taylor who followed me round asking pertinent questions about the reasons for several of the checks.

Once we were airborne I felt completely at home, all the nervousness left me and, to the best of my ability, I carried out the various instructional sequences with accuracy and confidence. Finally we did a couple of spins, one to the left and one to the right. I must admit the Chipmunk crash I had witnessed the previous day did come to the forefront of my mind, but fortunately the second we started the exercise, all those thoughts were immediately abandoned.

We landed back at Tollerton exactly one hour and thirty minutes after take-off and my AFI test was complete. To my delight I was informed that I had passed the flying part of the instructor's test. All I had to do now was pass an oral examination and convince my examiner that I was proficient in Meteorology, Aviation Law, and the Principles of Flight etc. I was a little worried about this side of the examination, but in the end managed to pass without making a fool of myself.

Next, Jerry got through his test without any problems, so the flight back to Oxford was punctuated with a few celebratory aerobatics; we were at last Assistant Flying Instructors.

Before we left Tollerton I was able to have a chat with Hector Taylor about my chances of flying with the RAF. AEF. Hector, an ex RAF wartime Pilot, was now serving with the RAFVR (T) as a part time Flt/Lt flying Chipmunks with No. 8 AEF Squadron at weekends and summer camps. He advised me to take exactly the same procedure as the MOD had suggested when I made enquires to them previously. Hector did however offer to help in any way he could when the time came and I had gained sufficient experience to apply.

CHAPTER 21.

My initial "First Solo" Student.

Not long after we had passed our assistant instructors rating, Rex Smith offered Jerry Busby and myself permanent jobs with the Oxford Aeroplane Company. Jerry joined full-time. I decided to take up Rex's alternative offer to instruct on a part time basis until I qualified as a full instructor, my salary would then be on a par with my present earnings working for Bells Whisky, and I could change jobs without any financial loss.

As a part time instructor I was paid at the rate of 10/- (50p) per flying hour. Although this wasn't exactly a highly remunerative job, it gave me the opportunity of gaining the experience I needed. In fact I would have gladly worked part time for nothing to obtain the flying instructional hours required for me to upgrade from AFI to QFI status.

As an assistant instructor with limited experience of training a student from scratch, I was not allowed to send any student on a first solo flight. All trainee pilots had to be checked out for first solo by a QFI (Fully qualified instructor). Sometimes this change of instructor would unnerve the student a little because he had only flown with one particular instructor up to that time.

I wanted to pass my QFI test as soon as possible, so I flew every weekend and every second of my spare time, in fact by the end of 1961 I had accumulated well over 600 hours of instructional flying and passed my full QFI rating. I was now qualified to send my own students on their first solo flights.

Sending a student solo for the first time is quite a responsibility. There is a recognised minimum criteria laid down for the general guidance of instructors, but in the end it depends on the experience, judgement and general gut feeling of the instructor when determining the time is right to send his student on a first solo.

The first person I ever sent solo was a young chap by the name of Haines. He never knew it of course, but I was just as nervous as he was. I remember my feelings throughout the experience.

Before the lesson began I made sure that Haines's Student Pilots Licence and medical documents were all in order and all the mandatory lessons prior to first solo had been written up as satisfactory on his progress sheet. That morning Haines was flying accurate circuits and had made good successive landings, we had also practiced several "engine failure after take-off" procedures. So I decided the time was right to send him on his first solo.

I instructed Haines to taxi back to the holding point of the duty runway and complete his take-off checks one more time, he had no idea I was about to send him solo.

I waited for him to complete his pre-take-off checks, then I explained to him that when he eventually did reach the standard required for first solo, he would notice the aeroplane would take-off much quicker, and climb a little more steeply whilst still maintaining the correct climbing airspeed, the reason being the aircraft was lighter without the weight of an instructor aboard. I also explained that the aircraft would float for a longer period of time after rounding out for the landing, warning him not to be caught out by these three factors.

The reason I let him continue to think he wasn't actually going solo straight away, was I wanted to make sure he listened to those very important points. I remember when I was told I was about to go on my first solo; I was so excited that I hardly heard a word my instructor said after that. So having made sure that he understood everything I had just told him, I informed him that I was going to send him on his first solo there and then. His expression changed completely from a look of confidence to a mixture of surprise and excitement. I told him I wanted him to carry out just one circuit and landing, adding of course that if he did make a cock-up of it he was to overshoot in the prescribed manner and go round again.

With that I advised Air Traffic of an impending first solo, secured my harness to the seat I had vacated, and got out.

I saw the concerned look on his face as he watched me close the canopy of the Chipmunk and climb down from the wing. I gave the fuselage a couple of "off you go" bangs with my hand before walking away trying to look completely unconcerned.

In fact, this being the first time I had ever sent a student on a first solo, I was surprised how confident I did feel about letting him go.

As Haines lined up on the runway, I moved to a position behind the aeroplane so that he couldn't see me watching him. This was also the first time I had ever had to walk back from the far side of the airfield. I remember noting the coolness of the outside air compared to the stuffiness of the cockpit, and the sound of the slipstream swishing over the surface of the tailplane, causing it to rumble as it stood patiently waiting for its pilot to taxi on to the runway.

Having lined up on the runway I watched as my student taxied the Chipmunk forwards slightly to ensure the tail wheel was straight. There was a light breeze straight down the runway, perfect for a first solo. Haines sat there with the engine ticking over for a couple of seconds, then the peace of the early morning was shattered by the roar of the Gypsy Major engine as it snarled to full power.

As the aircraft accelerated away, the sound of the engine dwindled to a smooth hum and I became aware of a skylark singing his little head off in the comparative stillness of a beautiful Summer's morning.

I started to walk slowly towards the dispersal area. In the distance my attention was drawn to the flashing blue light of the crash vehicle as it's crew were called to readiness, standard procedure for a first solo flight. It was at that precise moment the full burden of responsibility hit me and I became acutely aware of the overwhelming trust a student places in the judgement of his instructor.

As the sound of the Chipmunk's engine faded into the distance, my mind recalled the various problems Haines had experienced with his flying during the previous fourteen hours of his training. He had of course successfully overcome all of them, but "What if"… I told myself to calm down, in any case it was obviously too late now for me to do anything about it, he was on his own, and it was up to him.

I watched the silver speck in the sky as it flew steadily round the circuit, listening carefully for the engine note to change when he reduced speed to lower the flaps on base leg. Eventually Haines turned the Chipmunk to line up with the runway for the final approach and landing. I crouched down by the boundary hedge so that my student wouldn't see me watching him. I do things slightly differently now, but this was the first time I had ever sent anyone on a first solo and I was going to make certain that nothing distracted him from making a good landing.

As the aeroplane passed over the fence just a few yards from where I was squatting, the engine backfired a couple of times as Haines closed the throttle. It was like a bloody shotgun and made me jump! Then to my absolute delight, he made a perfect three-point landing. I remember thinking… 'Keep straight lad, it's not over yet.' But I needn't have worried.

When he turned off the runway Haines spotted me and taxied towards me to give me a lift back to dispersal. I don't know who was the happiest out of the two of us. I congratulated him warmly, shaking his sweaty hand and climbed back into the rear cockpit breathing a sigh of relief. This was to be the first of many hundreds of students I was destined to send on their first solo including, many years later, my own son. Every one of them, thank God, landed safely.

Later my boss Rex Smith, who misses nothing, said he had watched my student complete his first solo, and congratulated me on his performance. Those few words from my boss meant a lot to me.

CHAPTER 22.

Flying with the RAFVR.

Having been commissioned to the most humble and lowly rank of Pilot Officer in the Volunteer Reserve, I attended my first camp at RAF Lynton-On-Ouse in 1960.

I was an AFI but so far had not completed 200 instructional flying hours in order to apply for a QFI upgrading test. Also I could not complete my instructor's check with the examining wing of RAF Central Flying School until I became a QFI, which in turn prevented me from applying to fly as a pilot with the RAFVR(T) Squadrons.

However by the time I attended my second VR camp at RAF Waterbeach in 1961, I had passed my QFI flight test with F/Lt Taylor, and my CFS flight test with Squadron leader Jack Curry at RAF Little Rissington, and was now qualified to train potential direct-entry RAF officers under contract to the Ministry of Defence as well as RAF and CCF Cadets under the RAF Scholarship scheme. Finally I applied to join the AEF and was given a further flight check in Chipmunk WK642 by the OC Station Flight, Ft/Lt. Chas Boyack at RAF Waterbeach. The test was a formality really, as I was already training students to fly on Chipmunks at Oxford Air Training School.

So after all that I was authorised to fly service aircraft with the AEF at weekends and annual camps. My friend Nils Bartleet, who had also been commissioned into the RAFVR(T), was checked and authorised in the same way.

Unfortunately I did have a couple of close encounters with the hierarchy during my short stay at RAF Waterbeach. The trouble began when I was introduced to USAF Pilot Captain John Rosenbury, who was an ex Star-Fighter pilot on an exchange visit from the United States Airforce.

I liked old John from the moment I met him. He was a rather tubby chap; red faced with a closely shaved head, and I seldom saw him without a fat cigar in his mouth. I was soon to find out the hard way, that he was blessed with a bazaar sense of humour.

Our flight details were posted up in the crew-room each day. They consisted mainly of short flights taking ATC cadets and their officers on thirty-minute air experience flights in the Chipmunks. Occasionally we were asked to collect spares etc. from other RAF stations, or if we were very lucky we unofficially managed to get our hands on the Jet Provost or the station Meteor V11.

The air experience flights usually took place over a specially designated area a few miles north of Ely City, well outside controlled airspace.

When weather conditions permitted, we used to climb to six thousand feet over a large caravan site that we used as a reference point and, with the cadet's permission, carry out a few gentle aerobatics. Sometimes we would return to the airfield with an over-excited passenger keen to relate his intrepid experiences to his friends, or, on other occasions we would return with a pale faced individual clutching a soggy sick-bag! The process would then be repeated with another eagerly awaiting cadet, and so on throughout the day.

During the week that our AEF squadron was operating at Waterbeach, we were short of pilots. Capt. Rosenbury, who could fly just about anything with wings, was seconded to Station Flight in order to help out with taking ATC and CCF cadets up for their air experience.

In the evenings we usually got together in the mess bar, whereupon John would light up one of his enormous cigars and proceed to tell us about some of the misfortunes he experienced whilst flying Star Fighters for the USAF.

Our camp Adjutant, Tahiti Sam, was a super little chap. We nicknamed him Tahiti Sam because he was engaged to a young lady from Tahiti and spoke of little else.

Sam was a very popular young officer, always joking and always keen to help us out with any problems we may have had. He wasn't a pilot himself, and he made it quite clear that he wasn't too keen on flying. He boasted that the Group Captain was a close relative of his, but he was always pulling our legs over something or other so we took most of what he said with a pinch of salt.

Sam was the proud owner of an assortment of parts roughly assembled in the shape of a bright yellow 1930s Austin Seven. This poorly maintained heap of back-firing junk invariably occupied pride of place on the car park outside the flight office. One could always tell when Sam turned up as his arrival was preceded by a series of loud bangs and a cloud of black smoke from his "Yellow Peril".

The AEF pilots based at Waterbeach during the week I attended were mostly made up of ex World War Two Pilots. A great bunch of lads still keeping their hand in by flying Chipmunks with the RAFVR (T). I may have got the wrong impression, but it seemed to me that the younger regular officers in the mess at that time looked upon us as, "Lower Types", a mischievous bunch of hooligans who tended to frequent their bar in order to wreck the place with monotonous regularity. I can remember the uproar that took place most evenings when the AEF types would disrupt the place with such competitive games as " Who comes knocking at my door?", "The Muffin Man", and "Cardinal Puff," or sometimes enthusiastically playing the more destructive game of in-house rugby whilst many of the regular RAF types attempted to read their newspapers or play a quiet game of snooker.

Misfortune struck one afternoon at the close of the day's flying programme. Capt. John Rosenbury, who frequently flew in close formation with me when we returned to base from the aerobatic area, spotted Sam's bright yellow car on the perimeter track just off the down-wind end of the duty runway. My headphones crackled into action…

'One four to one three, can you see what I see?'

John, who had positioned his aircraft close enough for me to practically see the colour of his eyes, pointed down towards the runway. We had already been cleared by Air Traffic for a low run and break before landing.

'Affirmative, I see him' I replied.

'I guess I'll kinda leave him to you then' said John as he peeled off to go round the circuit again.

It was the ideal opportunity for a beat-up, the barrier was down, I had been cleared for a low run, and there sat dear old Sam close to the end of the runway, a prime target.

Easing up to full throttle I headed straight down the runway at low level towards Sam's bright yellow car…. He was all mine!

I was almost up to him when the doors of the car flew open and two bodies ejected themselves from the car as I skimmed over them. I pulled up turning steeply onto a low downwind position and was about to call 'one three down wind low to land', when a very irate sounding voice blurted out….

'ONE THREE LAND NOW AND REPORT TO THE SATCO's OFFICE IMMEDIATELY.'

I should have expected it, but there was much worse to follow!

John Rosenbury, who had followed me in to land, taxied behind me to the dispersal area. I stopped the engine and climbed out onto the wing as Rosenbury drew up alongside. Sliding back the canopy of his Chipmunk, he sat there grinning from ear to ear...

'Guess you'd better pack the arse of your pants with newspaper mate' he said.

As far as I was concerned his remarks didn't warrant a reply!

I made my way apprehensively up the stairs of the Air Traffic Control building and knocked on the door marked SATCO. A stern voice bade me to enter.

I stood stiffly to attention in front of a savage looking Squadron Leader and said...

'Pilot Officer Blyth, sir, I believe you wanted to see me?'

The SATCO snorted and glared at me for a second, then let rip...

'Apart from being a complete bloody idiot, that beat-up was a dangerous and stupid thing to do, have you any idea at all who was in the car you narrowly missed flattening?'

I began to feel uncomfortable, there were obviously two people in the car, and one of them was bound to have been Sam, but I had no idea who the other chap was?

I swallowed deeply, and before I had a chance to reply, the SATCO, who was now red in the face and looked as if he was about to punch me on the nose, blurted out....

'I'll tell you who it was boy, it was the bloody Group Captain, that's who it was!'

The blood drained from my face and I felt weak at the knees. I couldn't have picked a worse time for a beat-up. But what the hell was a Group Captain doing in Sam's clapped-out car anyway? Then it slowly dawned on me. It must have been Sam's so called close relative that he always claimed he had. One thought was paramount in my mind; 'Christ! I've had it, I'll be on my way home before the day's out.'

I cringed at the sound of my own voice trying to mumble some sort of an apology that ultimately fizzled into silence.

The Squadron Leader stared at me for some moments before he spoke again.

'The Group Captain's with the CO of 25 squadron at the moment. But you can bet your life he'll have something to say about this. You're grounded lad, and you're lucky that I don't have you arrested.

I started to apologise once more and was promptly told to 'shut up.'

Then in a much quieter voice…

'If I hear of just one more incident, no matter how small, that involves you in any way Blyth, you'll be off this airfield and out of the VR quicker than that, do I make myself clear?'

'Yes sir.'

'Get out of my office.'

I saluted, about turned, and left the SATCO's office considerably shaken. When I arrived at the flight office to sign the 700, I was greeted by rousing cheers from a bunch of highly amused pilots, including Captain John Rosenbury.

Tahiti Sam had apparently called in to the flight office briefly asking for me. The Group Captain was indeed Sam's uncle, but I could never understand what he was supposed to be doing close to the end of the duty runway in Sam's clapped-out car.

I asked Rosenbury if he knew that the station commander was in that bloody car, and the bastard couldn't answer for laughing.

'I'm probably going to be chucked out over this, you Pratt…. It's not at all funny.' I said.

The OC Station Flight also gave me a king-sized bollocking, then he told me that I was very lucky because our adjutant, Sam, had put in a good word for me and no further action was to be taken. I was given permission to continue flying until the end of the camp.

Sadly my run of misfortunes didn't stop there. The very same evening I walked into the Officers Mess and was making my way towards the dining room, when somebody crept up behind me and plonked another cap from the hat-stand on my head back to front. At the same split-second the Group Captain appeared accompanied by the Wing Commander. He walked straight up to me and removed the hat from my head and said…

'Mine I believe.'

I stood there paralysed, whilst he carefully flicked the non-existent dust from his cap.

'And your name is?'….

'Blyth sir, Pilot Officer Blyth.' I replied, my voice a couple of octaves higher than normal…

'Ha… You must be the chap who gave us the benefit of your low flying capabilities this afternoon?' he asked.

Before I could answer the Station Commander smiled politely and walked away, closely followed by the Wing Commander who glared at me as he passed. I turned to see Rosenbury tip-toeing off towards the gentlemen's toilet, his hand covering his mouth in an attempt to stifle his laughter. 'I'll kill that bastard' I thought.

Later John and I adjourned to the bar to resolve our differences over a few jars of ale.

During the rest of the week I kept well out of the way of the hierarchy, fully expecting further repercussions about the cap. Fortunately nothing was said. Sam, our well-loved camp adjutant, said that the Station Commander was in fact his uncle, and when I skimmed over Sam's car the Group Captain actually muttered.

'Spirited effort… but I bet he'll get a shock when he finds out I was in your car Sam.'

Then, as he climbed back into the Yellow Peril he apparently asked Sam to….

'Have a quiet word with the pilot of that Chipmunk.'

Nils Bartleet also had a close call during the same week. He was flying in another Chipmunk with the call sign 'One-Two.' I also happened to be in the circuit at the time when I heard Nils call 'finals to land' over the R/T. I saw him turning in towards the runway when a slightly garbled 'Clear to land' from the controller crackled over the radio. Then suddenly, out of the blue, a Javelin from 25 squadron appeared to skim over the top of Nils's aeroplane, its lowered undercarriage only a few feet above the canopy of the Chipmunk. As it descended rapidly in front of Nils's aircraft the slipstream from the Javelin tossed the Chipmunk up in the air and threw it around like a Dandelion Clock in a gale. Miraculously Nils somehow regained control and overshot from the approach. He was most fortunate not to have been killed.

I heard later that the conclusion drawn from the subsequent enquiry was that the Javelin pilot and Nils had both called finals precisely at the same split second, neither of the pilots could hear the others transmission because the Chipmunk was transmitting on VHF, whilst the Javelin transmitted on UHF. The enquiry also assumed that the Controller, who received the transmissions of both frequencies simultaneously, had cleared the Chipmunk to land without noticing the fast jet approaching behind the Chipmunk. It appears that the controller's equipment was able to transmit on both UHF and VHF at the same time and both pilots assumed they had been cleared to land. Nils could not possibly have seen the jet until it was too late to take avoiding action, and I'll never know how the Javelin missed hitting the Chipmunk! Presumably he never even saw it.

Later in the year I received my RAF Form 414a, "Summary of Flying and Assessments" for the annual camp 1961. It read as follows…

"Year commencing 1st February 1961. Annual Camp, SE Aircraft 9.15 hours. Total service flying 365.45. Cat A2 AEF QFI above average. Signed C. Boyack Flt Lt OC Station Flight, RAF Waterbeach".

I can only assume that he must have been suffering from acute amnesia or he was extremely forgiving when he came to sign my assessment! I just couldn't believe he had overlooked my misdemeanours concerning the Group Captain.

CHAPTER 23.

Joining Oxford Air Training School Full-time.

Laying quietly in my hospital bed that evening I recalled the beginning of a chain of events that brought me to a situation close to death, and ultimately left me in the pathetic state I was in at the present time. It all began when I finally achieved my goal of changing my fulltime employment from the world of commerce to aviation ...

Pressed Steel Ltd. had recently purchased a DH. Heron, which they operated from Oxford Airport, and Frank Sturdy, the instructor who did most of my training during my part time instructors course, was sub-contracted to Pressed Steel to fly the Heron together with their Chief Pilot Capt. Otto Altman.

Not long after all these changes had taken place, came the most exciting news. Oxford Air Training School had been awarded a major contract to train Airline Pilots for BOAC and BEA.

In order to meet the high standards required to train professional pilots, impressive new buildings, incorporating ground school facilities and student accommodation were constructed in a remarkably short period of time. A new Air Traffic Control building was built, and CRDF (Direction Finding) equipment was installed. The maintenance section was enlarged, a Flight Simulator Training School was set up and extra controllers were employed to assist our SATCO Ben.

I commenced studying for my Commercial Pilots Licence and Rex allowed me to attend lectures in the ground school whenever I could fit it in between my selling job and part time instructing at Oxford. I hadn't fully realised how much work I was taking on. Trying to fit in all three activities turned out to be a formidable task. I also managed to add a multi-engine rating and night flying training to my instructor's rating during the same period, so that when I eventually joined Oxford on a full-time basis I would be qualified to train commercial pilots.

Having made arrangements with the Central Medical Establishment the next step was to get the dreaded Commercial Pilots Medical out of the way.

I travelled to London by train and made my way to the Central Medical Establishment's offices in High Holborn, arriving, full of apprehension, at the impressive entrance.

I had heard horrendous stories of ambitious young men who considered themselves perfectly fit, ultimately failing their medical because they suffered from frequency deafness, slight colour blindness or any one of a dozen other things. And here was I, hoping to pass a stringent medical still bearing the results of being hit on the skull with a railway sleeper, and sporting a large groove on the top of my head that looked strangely like a misplaced babies arse .

Shortly after arriving, a group of us were directed up several flights of stairs to a small room where we were each handed a glass receptacle and asked to provide a sample of our urine. This caused some amusement when we all lined up in front of a trough and one chap stood there red in the face, grunting and straining but unable to produce a drop. He finally turned to his neighbour who seemed to be doing well, and asked him to be a sport and squirt a drop or two into his bottle as he couldn't perform the necessary task himself! I couldn't help wondering how things would turn out if his generous friend's urine showed signs of the "clap".

We handed in our steaming samples to a medical assistant who for some reason or another held each one up to the light before slotting it into a suitably divided tray. Next we were examined by an orthopaedic specialist who vigorously did his best to dislocate an arm or a leg before handing us over for blood pressure tests, chest X-rays, Audiogram, Cardiogram and eyesight tests.

Then it was time to meet the smiling assassin in a white coat. This "gentleman", better described as a vampire, brandished a sizeable hypodermic syringe and misleading me to believe I would feel no pain, stabbed me viciously in the arm and extracted copious amounts of blood!

Finally we all sat apprehensively waiting to be interviewed by the Air Commodore, a senior physician who would inform us of the results of our medial examination. So much depended on the next few minutes. I looked at the line of chaps sitting there with me; everyone's face portrayed their concern and innermost fears. Whole careers were in the balance and lifetime ambitions could be banished forever.

People were always asking me about the lump on my head, the Air Commodore was no exception. I told him about the car crash and the railway sleeper. He looked quite concerned and said…

'I will need a letter from the hospital you attended, together with details of your head injuries before I make a decision about your aircrew medical.'

I left the medical centre knowing that my future career as a professional pilot was still in the balance. The next day I managed to see the doctor who discharged me from the 'Horton General Hospital' in Banbury. After pouring out my problems to him, he assured me that in his opinion I had nothing to worry about.

'Don't worry, your notes will be in the post tonight young man' he said.

I left it a couple of days, then telephoned CME, asking to speak to the Air Commodore. His secretary advised me that information concerning medical examinations could not be given over the telephone, so I had to wait over two weeks before I finally received a letter marked 'Private and Confidential' with the address of CME on the reverse side.

Feeling quite sick I ripped open the envelope and read the words PASSED MEDICALLY FIT. It was another of those great moments that defy description.

Sadly my marriage to Mary was in a state of turmoil. Although we were still living together, and still loved one another, our lives were gradually drifting apart and had reached the stage where we were going our separate ways socially, a situation that soon proved to be the kiss of death to our relationship. We always seemed to be arguing; both of us trying to hide our disagreements from our little son Eddy.

Things had eventually come to a head when I had to travel to Wales in connection with my work as a salesman.

The company had booked me in to stay in a hotel in Tenby for a week. On arrival I decided to have a wash and brush-up, and opened my suitcase to unpack. I was deeply saddened to find Mary's wedding and engagement ring's tied together by a ribbon inside the lid. Although I knew our marriage was not running smoothly, I was upset to see those rings that had once meant so much to both of us. I tried desperately to telephone home but the phone remained unanswered. I arrived at our house on the Friday, Mary had taken our son and was staying with her mother. I hoped to straighten things out but it was the end of our marriage.

I drove to Oxford Airport in the hope that I would be allowed to stay in one of the newly constructed students study/bedrooms. Rex, who had become a great friend, kindly offered me free accommodation on the airfield for a while.

In the end Mary and I were resolved to separate and Mary agreed that I could see Eddy at any time. I don't think either of us really wanted a divorce. Although we lived apart, we did put on a pretence as much as possible for little Eddy's sake.

I will never forget attending Eddy's school on sports day. It was a warm Summer's day, Mary looked lovely, and all the other mums and dads looked so happy together, it was sad being there with his mother pretending to be cheerful. We stood together watching our little son compete in the sack race and later in the egg and spoon race. I found the whole thing quite heart breaking.

I'd had enough of working in the licensed trade. The time had finally arrived when I could change my full-time career from selling to flying.

I asked Rex Smith if he would take me on as a full-time flying instructor at Oxford before I qualified as a Commercial Pilot. Luckily for me he was pleased to offer me employment. This was the true beginning of a long and successful career in aviation.

I bought myself a second hand Ford Zodiac car and continued to live in the student's quarters on the airfield. I was allocated a number of PPL Students and flew five or six hours every day. I also continued to attended ground school every spare minute I could find, and burnt the midnight oil studying for my commercial pilot exams.

Instructing is a serious business, but it does have its amusing moments. For instance I remember a flying detail that took place one Saturday morning shortly after I had joined Oxford full-time.

I had just completed a spinning detail with a student in one of our Chipmunks, and as I taxied into dispersal, Jerry Busby, who was organising the weekend flying programme, ran out from the Ops. Room signalling me to keep the engine running. After my student climbed out from the front cockpit, Jerry hopped up on the wing and shouted in my ear...

'A chap has just walked into the office claiming he's current on Chipmunks. He's not a member of the Club, so being as you have a gap in your programme perhaps you could check him out. Give him a thorough going over Ray' he said, 'you know what some of these know-it-all PPL types are like.'

I watched as the chap climbed nimbly into the cockpit in front of me. He was already wearing his flying helmet, so I couldn't see his face properly. I waited patiently whilst he took time to strap himself in and plug his headset into the intercom system. There was a click and I could hear his breathing so I started my patter off.

'What's your name lad?'…

'Beadle' was the short sharp reply.

'OK Mr Beadle, I don't know where you've been flying previously, but, with respect, we do things properly here. You may find that I'm not prepared to let you go solo the first time out, that depends on your standard of flying and airmanship' I said confidently. 'Now, so that I can assess your ability I want you to pretend I'm not here and carry out all the drills and procedures you would normally do for a circuit and landing.' Adding, 'Don't be nervous old lad, I'm here to help you if anything goes wrong.' I said pompously.

'Roger' was the rather curt reply.

He then went through the most meticulous cockpit checks informing me in detail of everything he was doing. Finally he pressed his transmit button and spoke to Air Traffic Control.

'Oxford, Golf Alpha Oscar Sierra Tango, request taxi clearance, two on board, dual checkout. Endurance four hours, estimated flight time one hour.'

At once, without the aeroplane moving an inch, I knew by the tone of his voice, and the professional way he spoke to Air Traffic, this was no ordinary PPL.

Having repeated back his Air Traffic clearance, he moved the aircraft forwards a few yards and checked the brakes, he then proceeded to taxi to the holding point whilst carrying out all his instrument checks and explaining to me all that he was doing.

'The Artificial Horizon is taking some time to erect' he said.

'OK you can accept it as it is, or turn back, I'll leave it to you' I said. I heard him mumble something about it being a VFR (Visual Flight Rules) flight as he continued to taxi to the holding point and turned into wind.

His engine checks, run up, and pre take-off checks were perfect. He asked me if I was securely strapped in, and if I was ready for take-off.

I began to feel more like the student than the instructor. 'This bugger's no amateur private pilot' I thought.

The take-off was as smooth as I have ever experienced. He pattered every inch of the way round the circuit. His lookout was thorough and consistent, he even asked me to report any other aeroplanes I may see during the flight, adding two sets of eyes are better than one. Down wind his checks were faultless and included asking me once more if I was securely strapped in. As we turned onto the approach to land, he asked me what type of landing I wanted him to make, so I asked him to make a short field landing, thinking that this usually sorts the men from the boys. He replied with a laconic…

'Roger.'

With full flap selected, he smoothly reduced the airspeed to a few knots above stalling. I must admit the latter part of the approach had my backside biting the buttons off the cushion of my seat. Having crossed low over the airfield boundary we touched down to a perfect three-point landing and rolled to a standstill within fifty yards of the threshold. He pattered every second of the approach and landing.

'Round again?' He asked.

I told him to taxi back to the dispersal area and shut down. I was out of the cockpit in a flash, standing on the wing waiting for him to remove his helmet, which he certainly took his time over. When he did it revealed a man about ten years older than myself with a rather white pinched little face and a wry grin. Within a few seconds I learned that my so-called student happened to be the Chief Flying Instructor and Squadron Commander of the Oxford University Air Squadron based at RAF Bicester. The squadron operated aircraft, and this was their Boss, Squadron Leader Bill Beadle.

I felt quite embarrassed about the whole thing and apologised for appearing to be somewhat condescending in my attitude. I admitted that from the moment he taxied out I was certain that he was an experienced pilot, and by the time he landed I was pretty sure that he was an instructor.

Bill grinned at me from the cockpit and said…

'I wouldn't have expected anything else from such an obviously proficient instructor.'

Little did I know that one day in the future S/Ldr Bill Beadle would become the Flight Standardisation Manager for Oxford Air Training School, and check the training standards of all our instructors on a regular basis!.

Most of my flying was instructing, but occasionally I was asked to deliver new aircraft, or maybe return aircraft to various airfields after they had been to Oxford for maintenance.

One morning Rex asked me to fly Mr Ferrick, our Accountant Director and his Secretary Mrs Patterson, over to Biggin Hill on company business. It was a bit of a boring job because I had to sit around all day waiting to fly them back to Kidlington in the late afternoon.

I had spoken to Valerie Patterson on several occasions, usually when the staff met up in the club bar for a "Quick half" after flying. She was a tall slim, elegant young lady with pretty blond hair. She spoke with a cultured accent, and her general demeanour left one in little doubt that she was very efficient at her job.

Eventually they returned to the airfield and Mr Ferrick asked me if I minded his secretary sitting in the front on their return journey to Oxford.

Valerie and I chatted most of the way back. She told me that she served as an officer in the WRAF during the latter part of the war and later married a service pilot. Their marriage sadly came to an end soon after the war, and Valerie was now living in Woodstock with her nineteen year old daughter Laura.

After we had landed, I acted on a sudden impulse and shouted after her as she walked away from the aeroplane inviting her to have dinner with me in the Bear Hotel Woodstock that evening. She smiled and told me not to be silly. Then as she started to walk away she suddenly turned around and laughingly said…

'OK, if you're serious I'll meet you at eight o'clock in the saloon bar.'

Valerie and I began to see quite a lot of each other, meeting most evenings in the club bar after flying. We shared the same sense of humour, and appreciated the same things in life generally. Over a period of a few weeks we became more than friends. I gave up my living quarters in the accommodation wing on the airfield, and went to live with Valerie and her daughter in their lovely little cottage situated close to the grounds of Blenheim Palace in Woodstock.

Life in general was beginning to brighten up again. I enjoyed instructing full-time at Oxford, and Valerie was a brilliant companion, always laughing and full of fun. But I missed my little son Eddy more than words could possibly express. Fortunately I was still able to see him fairly regularly, and we always had lots of fun on our days out together.

There was still a long way to go as far as my career was concerned. Lots of groundwork and flying instructional experience to be gained before I had all the qualifications I needed for a successful career in aviation. But I could rejoice in the fact that I was already flying most days of the week….

and being paid for it. Also my boss very kindly allowed me a limited amount of free flying in the Chipmunk each week to practice aerobatics so that I could qualify for my instructor's aerobatic rating.

CHAPTER 24.

The Joy of Flight.

When one is confined to hospital life for long periods of time, memories often play an important part of passing the day without dying of absolute boredom. I recalled a flight that, although not anything special, will always remain as an example of what flying meant to me personally…

It was late on a dull autumn afternoon, the sky was almost completely obscured by dark grey clouds. The nostalgic smell of octane and leather brought a smile of satisfaction to my face as I climbed into the cockpit and started the engine of Chipmunk G-AOST.

Within a few minutes we had climbed through the thin layer of cloud and burst out into the clear blue sky above. I was totally alone in another world. A few feet below me a gently waved pattern of snow white stratus formed the basis of an astounding panorama that stretched from horizon to horizon. Here and there tall slender towers of cumulus cloud pushed their way up to several hundred feet above my head, casting long eerie shadows on the rippling cloud below. I allowed the aircraft to descend gently until wisps of luminescent silk sped past the cockpit creating a breathtaking sensation of speed. The sun, now sinking low on the horizon, gradually changed the clouds from dazzling white to soft pink, creating bright golden rims to the magnificent cumulous clouds. The slightest backward pressure on the stick, and we were climbing steeply towards a massive cloud with an inviting cave-like entrance that funnelled its way down into the dark unknown. Then, entering the cave of tiny water droplets with its unpredictable currents of air, I was again treated to an awe-inspiring display of prismatic phenomena second to none. Shafts of light of every colour sparkled in and out of view, sometimes bright and vivid, others just a mere suggestion of a vision as they brushed over the silver wings for a split second and disappeared.

I was at one with the aeroplane that carried me through this breathtaking experience. Ailerons, rudder, and elevators were extensions of my arms and legs. I was in fact living the flight, and seemed to be controlling this wonderful little aeroplane by mere thoughts as we skimmed and looped and rolled in this magic world that is only accessible to he who flies.

Finally, as I throttled back the engine and descended into the dark gloomy pond-like atmosphere below the clouds, I knew that I was one of the luckiest persons to be alive. To be able to fly, and have the privilege of teaching others to fly was surely all that any man could possibly wish for.

It was a very exciting time for all the employees at CSE. The construction of the new school buildings, the Cherwell Block, was completed in record time when Oxford Air Training School was approved for commercial pilot training by the Air Ministry.

The first intake of commercial students from BOAC arrived. Initially twenty-six Flying Instructors and five Ground School Instructors were employed full-time at the school, this number increased considerably over the years as the school expanded.

The flying training was split up into five flights, 'A B & C' flights were responsible for training the BEA and BOAC students and carrying out all the instrument rating training. 'D' Flight looked after the requirements of ex service pilots training for their civil commercial licences, and 'E' Flight was responsible all the PPL training courses which included the RAF Scholarship Contract, Night Ratings, Twin Ratings, and Aerobatic Training. Each flight was controlled by a Flight Commander or Manager who had a staff of five or more instructors.

The company also employed a Flight Standardisation Manager whose job it was to regularly fly with each instructor and flight manager to ensure that high standards of instruction and teaching methods were maintained. I was somewhat shattered when our newly appointed standards manager first arrived, and turned out to be none other than Mr Bill Beadle, the guy I had been allocated to check out in the Chipmunk some months earlier, embarrassingly mistaking him for an inexperienced student!

One morning the telephone rang in the crew-room. One of the instructors answered and shouted across to me...

'What have you been up to Ray? The boss wants to see you in his office.'

'Hells teeth,' I thought: 'it's not often that one gets invited into Rex's office without there being something radically wrong.'

I entered Rex Smith's office uneasily .

'Sit down son, I've got a proposition to put to you about your future with Oxford Air Training School' he said. 'As you know, all our instructors on the Airline Training Flights have to be commercially qualified, and at the moment you have not taken your CPL written exams, so I want to discuss a couple of options with you.'

My heart sank, I had only recently joined the full-time staff at Oxford, and although I was exempt from the CPL flying test, I still had to pass the dreaded written examinations before my CPL could be issued. So I felt sure that my boss had called me in to tell me he was replacing me with an instructor that already held a full CPL licence.

Rex continued….

'First of all, when you finally pass your CPL examinations you can carry on training commercial pilots up to, and including, twin rating standard. Then the company will sponsor you for your Instrument Rating so that you can eventually instruct on the advanced I/R training wing. Your pay would of course be increased accordingly when you pass all the relevant exams.'

I was delighted, my expression obviously showing my relief.

'Hang on a moment Ray; you haven't heard the second proposition I have to put to you. Alternatively, I am prepared to offer you the position of Manager and Chief Flying Instructor of 'E' Flight, the basic training wing, and I must say I think you would fit the bill perfectly.'

I couldn't believe my ears. I had only been employed full-time at OATS for a few weeks, and here I was being offered the prestigious job of Chief Flying Instructor and Manager of the basic training flight.

'I don't know what to say Rex, it's such an unexpected surprise.'

'Well take your time son, there's no immediate hurry, but I would like an answer from you by the end of the week. The job of Chief Flying Instructor will require you to become a Flight Test Examiner, and I am happy to put your name forward to the authorities for approval. The salary will be slightly more than the commercial instructors are getting, and just under the rate for CPL Flight Managers.'

I asked Rex if accepting the position of 'E' Flight Manager would prevent me from attending the CPL ground school prior to me taking the exams.. He told me he would give me every encouragement to continue, adding that he was sure that before long all CFI's will have to have a Commercial Pilots Rating.

He was absolutely right of course, and that's exactly what did happen.

I was thrilled and accepted the job as 'E' Flight Manager there and then.

My new job as a Flight Manager brought with it the distinction of an office of my own, together with a staff of four full-time and three part time instructors.

My initial instructors were Hugh Bain an Australian lad, Tony Smallwood, Jerry Busby an ex RAF pilot and John Williams an ex Royal Navy Pilot. The part time instructors were Bunny Austin who was still a serving Squadron Leader with the RAF, Peter Woodham who was also serving with the RAF as an instructor at CFS, and Curly Wadams, he too was still in the RAF. (Years later Hugh Bain became a Captain with Quantas, John Williams became a Captain with Britannia Airways, and Tony Smallwood became Chief Line Captain with BMA).

Running the basic training wing at Oxford was an extremely interesting and sometimes very challenging job. After the first few weeks in my new job, I had a long chat with my boss about several ideas I had for improving the operation of E flight and basic training in general. My ideas included re-designing the interior layout of the basic training building to include a self-briefing navigation unit, and the design of special gadgets that would assist instructors when briefing students for practice forced landings, together with another much needed device to assist in aerobatic briefings. These units could easily be constructed by our instrument engineers.

Rex was very interested and suggested that I put my ideas on paper together with a few sketches and some idea of the approximate costs etc. This was in fact the beginning of a whole string of ideas that were eventually incorporated into the basic training unit at Kidlington. Several years later, whilst I was in the latter stages of recovering from my crash, Rex asked me to design the interior layout for OATS new flight training centre that was to be set up on Carlisle Airport. I was still a patient in the Nuffield Hospital at the time, and completed the work using a portable drawing board set up on my bed.

The instructors at Oxford were a great bunch of chaps, and we all got on extremely well with one another. But sadly life is such that things cannot be perfect all the time.

One of our FIC instructors, Frank Sturdy, who was the chap that trained me to be an instructor, was now flying regularly as a Captain for the Pressed Steel Company. He retained his desk in our instructor's room and helped out with the instructing whenever he was not flying for Pressed Steel.

Pressed Steel's aircraft, a D.H. Heron, was based at Kidlington so we still saw Frank quite a lot.

One morning I was in the flight operations room when Jerry Busby approached me looking very upset. He took my arm and guided me to one side of the room and said quietly…

'Take a deep breath mate; we have just heard that the Heron crashed at Biggin Hill about fifteen minutes ago. Otto Altman and Frank Sturdy are both on board but I'm afraid there's no further news at the moment.'

John Pooley our Ops. Manager was standing at the Flight Desk with Rex who was talking on the telephone to someone in authority at Biggin Hill Airfield. I took one look at Rex's face as he put the phone down and knew instantly what he was about to say. 'The aircraft apparently burst into flames on impact. I'm afraid that Frank and Otto were both trapped in the wreckage and the fire crew were unable to reach them in time. They're both dead.'

As he walked towards the door, Rex turned to John Pooley and said…

'Try to get Frank's Doctor on the phone please, tell him I'm on my way to inform Frank's wife, and if he could possibly meet me there I would be most grateful.'

It had been a perfect day for flying, no low cloud, no strong crosswinds, and good visibility. But as so often happens, tragedy strikes when least expected. Now dear old Frank was dead, and at the time it seemed that nothing would be the same again.

That evening, after flying and all the aircraft had been put to bed for the night, I wandered over to the instructor's room and was surprised to see several of the chaps still there.

My Australian friend, Hugh Bain, was sitting on the corner of his desk with his feet on a chair listening to his portable tape recorder quietly playing. He loved classical music and frequently had it playing at the end of the day whilst he wound down and wrote up his students progress sheets etc. But this evening there was no writing; he just sat there, his lean figure silhouetted against the window by the glow of the setting sun. Everyone was quiet… each with his own thoughts of what had happened earlier that day. Someone asked about Frank's wife, and I told them Rex had been over to see her. Then, one by one the room emptied, nothing much was said. Finally the Australian and I were the only ones left in the room. Still sitting on his desk, Hugh gazed out at the blood red sunset, his square chin and stubby beard jutting forward. Frank and Hugh had been close friends for a long time. The music on the tape came to an end… Hugh got up

244

and walked to the door, pausing for a second he looked back at me to say something. I saw the unmistakable glint of tears in the man's eyes as he turned away without a word and left the office. I stood for a moment behind Frank's desk, his empty chair turned at the angle he had left it earlier that morning, all his books and papers squared away neatly. There's something morbidly intimate about seeing a dead mans belongings as he last left them. If only he could walk through the door and say... 'Hi Chaps' in his usual inimitable way. Sadly for all of us that would never happen again.

CHAPTER 25.

It doesn't pay to show off.

Although Oxford Air Training School was mainly using Piper Colts as their basic training aeroplanes, they had started to re-equip with a few of the new Piper Cherokee aircraft.

Initially there were two versions of the Cherokee, the PA-28-140 and the PA-28-180. Each of the Training Flights at Oxford retained their own aeroplanes which included at least one of the new Cherokees. The school also continued to use the Chipmunks as they were far more efficient for teaching spin recovery to our students.

I had recently been appointed as one of the Flight Test Examiners at Oxford. At the time there were only 140 examiners in the UK. The appointment meant that I was now authorised to supervise the written examinations and carry out flight tests on students applying for the issue of a UK private pilots licence.

I will never forget the very first PPL flight test I ever carried out as an examiner. The student's name was Cadet Sgt. Dave Wissett, and the aircraft used for the test was Cherokee G-ARVT. As this was my first flight as an examiner, I was determined to carry out the test precisely according to my newly acquired pamphlet *"For The Guidance of PPL Examiners"*. But as it turned out, things started to go wrong before we even got off the ground...

I checked the candidate's record sheets to ensure that he had completed all the mandatory training requirements prior to a flight test. Then, after briefing the candidate, I accompanied him to the aircraft to observe him carrying out his external checks. Wissett was very methodical and covered each item thoroughly. I told him to climb aboard and continue with his cockpit checks.

At that moment I realised that I had forgotten to bring the blank record of test form with me, so I nipped back to the office to collect it.

Feeling pretty important with the examiner's clipboard poised impressively for all to see, I strolled back to the aircraft where my candidate had started to carry out the cockpit checks.

Aware that I was being watched by a number of student pilots who were sitting on the grass outside the Ops room, I wanted to appear as cool as possible and made a point of approaching the aircraft in a nonchalant "examiner like" manner with the intention of leaping up onto the wing and entering the cockpit like a world war two fighter ace! But it never pays to be too cocky, and I cringe to think of what happened next.

Full of self-importance I approached the aircraft with springy steps and leapt imperturbably onto the reinforced area of the wing. Sadly I misjudged the leap and landed clumsily on the starboard flap clearly marked "NO STEP"! Unfortunately for me, my arrival coincided with the exact second my candidate depressed the flap release mechanism to check the movement of the flaps. Bang! down I went like a condemned man on the trapdoor of a hangman's scaffold, landing face down on the starboard wing. I attempted to grab my examiners clipboard that was sliding gently down the wing, but failed. Desperately trying to regain my composure, I ignored the muffled sniggers from the onlookers and limped across the dispersal area in pursuit of the paperwork that had escaped from the clipboard and was now slowly fluttering across the airfield like tumbleweed.

A few seconds later I was safely inside the cockpit trying to make light of the whole thing but desperately needing to rub my painful right shin which felt like it had been hit with a poleaxe. My moment came when the student decided to check the full and free movement of the controls. As he turned his head away from me to look at the left aileron, I seized the opportunity to lean forward and give my aching shin a quick rub, but this too was a bloody disaster. My "efficient" student decided to check the elevators first and hauled the control column fully back with the enthusiasm of a weight lifter, smacking me squarely in the face with the duplicate control column. I must admit the smack in the mouth momentarily made me forget the throbbing pain in my shin!

Wiping the blood from my mouth, I said in a surprisingly controlled voice…

'I appreciate your enthusiasm Wissett, but do you think we could start again without quite so much fervour?'

In the end Cadet Wissett gave a satisfactory performance and passed his test. Since that day I must have carried out hundreds of flight tests, but the name Wissett will always conjure up the painful memory of my first flight as an examiner.

I still had to take my written examinations to qualify for my Commercial Pilot's Licence. In the 1960s it was legal to train PPL students without having a CPL. But when the school commenced training Commercial Pilots all the instructors had to pass the written CPL examinations in London. We were given a few weeks dispensation so that we could continue instructing until we passed the exams. Unfortunately this meant the only time available for the instructional staff to study was early in the mornings and at the cessation of flying, often burning the midnight oil.

Every morning before breakfast at seven thirty, we attended the Morse Classes at our ground school with the other short course commercial students, most of them being ex RAF pilots. It had been many years since I left School, and getting down to studying for exams again proved to be considerably more difficult than I anticipated. For instance I had forgotten all I knew about logarithms, trigonometry, algebra and the like, so I had to buy suitable books to refresh my memory.

Most days I spent four or five hours in the air and frequently took part in the night flying programme as well. Flying, plus studying for my exams well into the early hours, began to take its toll. I had difficulty even understanding many of the questions especially on the mock 'Navigation General' papers. Questions something like…

'In the formula F=32+9c over 5, solve the equation for C when F= 20 degrees.' How the hell was this sort of thing going to make me a better commercial pilot I wondered?

The vagaries of meteorology, and weather forecasting that I enjoyed during my PPL and instructor ratings, now took on a different light. I personally thought the questions were never straight forward, and there were endless weather symbols to be memorised. I never seemed to come up with the correct advanced weather forecast on the practice test papers, and asked myself the question 'If the met-man frequently gets the forecast wrong, how the hell am I expected to get it right?' In the 60s of course there was no weather satellites and forecasting was not as accurate as it is nowadays.

Aircraft Performance examinations gave most candidates a bit of a problem.

The use of calculators during a performance 'A' examination in those days was strictly prohibited. In fact they didn't even exist in the form they do today. During the performance 'A' examination all the calculations were carried out on a set of graphs that were an integral part of the aircraft's performance manual. The examination I took was based on the performance charts for a Bristol Britannia. It was a well-known fact that if your pencil point was not sharp and produced a thick line, the answers one produced from working on an endless procession of graphs would be completely wrong.

Aviation Law for Commercial Pilots although quite simple, was a bit of a slog. You either knew it, or you didn't, so there was no way round it. You just had to sit down and learn reams of the stuff!

I took one week off to attend ground school for a last "cram" prior to the examinations. One particularly hot afternoon we were attending a lecture on the relative bearings of aircraft navigation lights in flight at night. The sort of questions you were likely to be asked were....

"Whilst flying at night, you see the red light of an aircraft at the same level as your aircraft in your two o'clock position with the relative bearing decreasing as the aircraft moves from right to left in front of you. Do you (A) Alter course to the right passing behind the aircraft. (B) Alter course steeply to the left. Or (C) Continue straight ahead at your present height and heading".

The correct answer is in fact (C). But this immediately led to a confrontation between Stan, an ex-RAF Pilot attending the CPL course, and the lecturer. Stan piped up and said...

'It stands to reason if I saw the port navigation light of an aeroplane ahead of me at the same level as me and moving across the front of me, I'd turn pretty bloody sharply and go behind him mate.'

The lecturer, who had heard these clever remarks many times before, explained in careful detail that the aircraft could only be on a collision course if the relative bearing remained constant. Unfortunately this didn't satisfy our ex RAF Pilot. He began to argue...

'That's bloody ridiculous ...' but he was cut short by the instructor who, in the hot muggy atmosphere of the classroom had had just about enough and let rip in his rural Somerset accent ...

'Listen... SONNY, I doesn't give a monkey's f--- what you'd do, I'm here to try and make sure you passes the bloody exam. If you have the same ambition you would well be advised to take my advice and stop bloody arguing matey.'

At that point there was an enormous Bang! All heads turned towards the direction of the bang to see what had happened. A very red faced student was dragging himself up off the floor having fallen asleep. I felt sorry for the tutor, who by now was really hacked off!

'I knows you finds this bloody boring gentlemen' he said, 'but this is what Aviation Law is all about, so if you really wants to be a commercial pilot, I'm afraid you're stuck with it.'

The day the examinations commenced I arrived at London Kings Cross Station and took the underground to the City Centre. In the foyer of the examination hall I met up with thirty or so other worried looking chaps all clutching briefcases waiting to be called in for our first written paper which, we had been told, was 'Meteorology Part One.' In fact it turned out to be paper number one of the Aviation Law exam. No amount of complaining made the slightest difference. The adjudicator simply said it was nothing to do with him, and we either took the exam, or left. Obviously nobody left!

Altogether the exams lasted four days. Most days we had two examinations in the morning and a further exam in the afternoon. We sat twelve written papers (Including the ARB technical papers) covering eight subjects. There was also an oral examination and a practical signals test.

Every morning, and again in the afternoon, we assembled outside the large hall waiting to be invited in five minutes before each exam was due to start. Then we all sat down at separate trestle tables with the inverted examination paper and a blank sheet of paper in front of us.

There is usually an amusing side to these things, and I remember one of the older looking candidates with a huge moustache who had a computer that must have been in use during the 1914-1918 war. He was struggling frantically with his old fashioned instrument during the plotting exam. It had some sort of ratchet attachment on the circular distance/time scale. As the poor chap struggled anxiously to answer all the questions within the allocated time, his old fashioned Navigational Computer rattled and echoed throughout the examination hall like a machinegun.

Later that day during the Performance 'A' examination, pencil sharpeners were in constant use. Occasionally one would hear a sharp crack as a pencil lead snapped, accompanied by a whispered curse from its troubled owner.

On the third day of the examinations we all sat in the tranquil calm of the hall silently struggling with one of our exam papers when suddenly, without the slightest warning, the peace and tranquillity of the hall was completely shattered by an ear-splitting noise that virtually made the place shudder. Several candidates shot up out of their chairs and looked around in horror as the room trembled under the deafening reverberations of church bells, clanging so loudly that I was convinced they were situated in a tower attached to the examination hall.

Thirty faces, some quite pale, some with obvious signs of annoyance and others slightly bemused, glared at the adjudicator for some kind of explanation. As the sound continued to resonate from wall to wall, the adjudicator stood up but it was impossible to hear a word he was saying. As far as we were concerned it was hopeless to try and concentrate on our exam papers, so we all downed pencils and sat there waiting for something to be done.

After about five minutes of ear splitting agony, the bells stopped ringing just as suddenly as they had started. Unbeknown to most of us there was a large church situated at the rear of the examination hall, and apparently the campanologist's had chosen that particular afternoon to practice their bell ringing.

After each of the exams, a mentally painful series of "post-mortems" took place outside the entrance to the hall when pilots compared notes on the answers to the exam questions they had just taken. These discussions always left me in a state of deep depression.

At the end of the week I returned to Oxford convinced that I had failed the exams miserably. Then came the mandatory wait of several weeks before the results were announced. Eventually the dreaded brown envelope turned up on my desk. My mouth went dry, as I clutched the envelope dreading the negative result it could contain. I took a deep breath and ripped it open. Inside was a small insignificant looking piece of paper. It was divided by several lines each bearing the name of a subject in the first column, followed by the marks awarded for that particular exam. The minimum pass mark for each paper was 70%. I skipped the lot in order to read the final line. It simply read, 'The candidate has passed the examination.' I was overcome with excitement. I had convinced myself that I had failed, but there it was in black and white... PASS. I studied the results in detail. As expected, Meteorology carried my worst result 75%. Even that surprised me. My two best papers were Radio Aids, for which I was awarded 98%, followed by Flight Planning at 92%. All the rest were in the eighties. I was so surprised I even wondered if they had mixed my papers up with those of another candidate!

That evening called for a quiet celebratory drink. Even so nostalgia and sadness crept in as I raised my glass to my childhood friend Eddy, who shared the same ambitious dreams with me when we were children. He was dead now, but I will never forget him. 'Cheers Ed.'

CHAPTER 26.

What goes up must come down.

What had once been a childhood dream had finally turned into reality. Although I was now a professional pilot, I had much to learn. The old sayings 'There's no substitute for experience' and 'You never stop learning' could never be truer than in the world of aviation.

At no time during my instructor's course was the subject of human psychology covered or indeed even mentioned. Whether or not this situation has been changed now I do not know, but in my opinion it was a serious omission from the flying instructors training syllabus.

For example, nothing was ever mentioned about the fundamental importance of being able to recognise various types of personality as early as possible when training someone to fly. It may seem obvious, but it can be quite a shock during ones early days as an instructor to find that no two persons react exactly the same when under stress, and however good your standardised instructional patter is, it invariably has to be adapted to suit the person you are flying with at the time. Some individuals have to be coaxed along, whilst others would never learn a thing unless pushed, sometimes quite severely. Everyone is different, and early recognition of your pupil's character, temperament and idiosyncratic mannerisms is essential.

The way a student reacts under pressure is very important. A potential instructor should also be given some idea of how a trainee pilot may react during his first experience of a fully developed spin, and what to do if he freezes on the controls during an attempted recovery.

Obviously none of the above was ever mentioned because it was not on the instructors training syllabus, this seemed to me to be a serious omission. When a newly qualified instructor flies with a real student for the first time it can be quite a shock. Up to that point he has always been flying with another qualified pilot and suddenly he finds himself with someone who had probably never been in an aeroplane before.

During my early days as an instructor, I had several interesting experiences, not all of them concerned directly with instructing, and some of them were far from pleasant, but all of them worthy of a mention.

It was early one Saturday morning when I arrived at the airfield to fly with a couple of our students who always flew with me at weekends. At that time I was only instructing part time at Oxford.

As I entered the airfield gates one of our Chipmunk aircraft took off crossing the Woodstock Road and climbed out to the Northwest. By the time I entered the car park the aircraft had reached a height of about eight hundred feet and was still climbing straight ahead. I left the car and was just about to enter the office doors when the sound of the Chipmunk's engine stopped quite suddenly. I assumed it to be the usual "practice engine failure after take-off" drill, and as it turned out, this was what it was intended to be. I instinctively looked up and saw the nose of the Chipmunk dip down quickly which is the standard procedure adopted to maintain airspeed when an engine fails during take-off. As the aircraft descended, I watched it make a shallow turn and assumed the student was lining up with the field he had selected for his forced landing. Practice EFATO's (Engine failure after take-off) are usually discontinued when the aircraft has descended to a height of 500 feet, so I expected to hear the engine open up to full power any second. Nothing happened; whoever it was up there was either pushing his luck a bit, or had a real engine failure. Then to my horror the aircraft suddenly dipped its left wing and the nose dropped violently to an almost vertical attitude. I watched as the Chipmunk completed about half a turn of a spin before disappearing behind some trees bordering the Woodstock Road.

With a sick feeling in my stomach I waited for the deadly "whomph" followed by a puff of black smoke that invariably follows when an aeroplane has crashed, but I saw and heard nothing. This was the second time I had seen a Chipmunk spin into the ground, the first being the RAF University Air Squadron Pilot from Cambridge I mentioned earlier in this book. This time it was definitely one of the school's aeroplanes, and I was bound to know the chaps on board.

Within seconds the airport crash siren was whaling and the station fire engine sped past. I got back in my car and followed the crash vehicle out of the gate.

As I reached the main road I saw that the fire engine had crossed over the dual carriageway and was bumping at speed over the ploughed field on the opposite side. In the distance I could see the crumpled wreckage of the Chipmunk. It was a pathetic sight with one silver wing stuck vertically upwards from the debris like a slaughtered bird. Then, to my absolute astonishment, I saw two chaps staggering away from the wreckage of the aircraft and recognised one of them as Ken Scott, one of our very experienced instructors, the other person was Peter Bonner-Davis a sponsored airline student.

A short time later, whilst the two lads were in the clubroom enthusiastically downing a glass of brandy before being taken to hospital for a check up, we learned the full story from Ken, who was relating the events to our boss Rex Smith. To the best of my memory this is the way he described what had happened.

'We were climbing out after take-off when I decided to test Peter's reactions by initiating a practice engine failure after take-off. We had practiced several of these previously, and Peter knew the drill very well. So this time I decided not to warn him of the practice in advance so that I could see exactly how quickly he reacted to the situation.

After taking off I could see from my duplicate controls in the rear cockpit, that Peter was moving the elevator trim wheel, therefore I knew his left hand was not on the throttle lever. This gave me the opportunity of closing the throttle without him feeling the lever move.'

Ken stopped talking momentarily to look at Peter who was not feeling too good.

Then he continued...

'What happened next was more my fault than Peter's. I closed the throttle and yelled out *'engine failure'* ... Peter immediately lowered the nose of the aircraft; I was very impressed by his quick reactions. The forced landing area ahead was pretty poor, there was not much of a choice as we were faced with farm buildings and a wooded area with a small ploughed field just beyond. I heard Peter shouting out his engine failure drill as he completed it. Peter slid the cockpit canopy back one notch, and I waited to see if he would turn away from the trees, but when he didn't I took control and opened the throttle raising the nose to climb away, but there was no response from the engine.'

Ken took another swig of his drink and continued...

'By now the airspeed was dangerously low, so I had to lower the nose rapidly to retain flying speed, at the same time I tried to turn to avoid hitting the trees. But it was too late, the airspeed was off the clock, there was a violent pre-stall judder then the aircraft flicked over and started to spin to the left.'

He paused for a moment and another instructor who was listening to Ken's account of what happened remarked that it must have been bad luck for the engine to fail during the few seconds of an EFATO practice. Ken shook his head and said….

'That's not what happened. Unfortunately I didn't make it clear to Peter at any time that this was only a practice engine failure, and that was the problem.'

At this point Peter spoke for the first time, his voice trembled, reflecting the traumatic experience he had just experienced.

'When Ken closed the throttle, I didn't notice my throttle move as my left hand was on the elevator trim wheel. When he shouted, it sounded pretty bloody urgent to me and I was sure the engine had really failed. I was terrified because we were so low and there was no time for questions. I completed my crash checks automatically, which included turning the fuel off to prevent fire. I only realised it was a practice when Ken told me to climb away, by then it was too late as the engine was starved of fuel, and there was not enough height to allow a restart.'

It's an ill wind so they say. After that I never once carried out an EFATO practice with a student in a tandem-seat aircraft without first resting my hand on the duplicate fuel cock to make sure it wasn't turned off.

Things often happen in three's, and unfortunately later the same year we had three successive accidents involving parachutists from the local Skydiving Club. One of them was a very serious and sad affair.

The road from Brackley to Kidlington passed close to Western-on-the-Green Airfield. Occasionally on my way to work I would stop for a moment at Western to watch army parachutists carrying out their practice descents from a tethered balloon. One morning I pulled over to watch the poor buggers jump. It was a beautiful day; all that could be heard was the voices of the airmen operating the balloon truck and the birds chattering in the hedgerows. Now and again the operating mechanism that turned the cable drum could be heard humming away as it allowed the balloon to ascend to its operational height.

I was watching these poor unfortunate chaps being hauled up to eight hundred feet in a basket suspended from an old wartime Barrage Balloon. There wasn't the slightest breeze, so I could just about hear the voices as the instructor gave last minute advice to his students. Then you would see a chap jump out of the basket, and because of the time lag due to the speed of sound, you would hear the instructor shout 'go' immediately after the parachutist had actually jumped, or been pushed as the case may be!

As I watched the silently swaying balloon, an obviously frightened individual suddenly leapt from the basket, his static line trailing after him, followed by the fierce voice of the instructor ordering him to jump. Whilst his parachute was successfully being deployed behind him, his arms and legs were going nineteen to the dozen as he clawed at the air in a desperate and rather pointless attempt to get back into the basket. Then he let out a fearful involuntary scream… 'Muuum!' as his parachute snapped open. I had to laugh but in all honesty there was no way I would have changed places with him. Then as he floated down this poor little man in all his misery, continued to shout "Oh Shit" until he hit the ground where he lay very quietly for a while before scrambling to his feet and gathering up his parachute.

At Kidlington however it was a different tale. We carried out quite a lot of para drops for the local Skydiving Club at weekends. Most of the flying instructors, including myself, had been passed for parachute dropping by a BPA Authorised Examiner.

Frequently, when the weather was suitable, we would take part in parachute training programmes with the DZ located on Kidlington Airfield. Initially we used Piper Tri-Pacer aeroplanes for the job. These aircraft were single engine high wing monoplanes with a fixed undercarriage and four-seats. The method was to remove the rear seats and the door from the right hand side of the aeroplane so that we could carry two parachutists, usually an instructor together with his student. The static line, which pulled the parachute from its pack, was clipped onto a hook situated on the floor of the aeroplane, which also had the pilot's safety harness attached to it. This meant that every time a parachutist leapt from the aircraft, the pilot would receive a sharp tug around his middle.

The drop sequence would begin by the pilot throttling back to decrease the slipstream whilst the poor sod who was about to jump would climb partly out of the cockpit and stand with one foot on the door entrance, and the other on the starboard wheel whilst clutching the wing strut and door frame for dear life. Obviously the wheels had to be locked on after take-off so that the parachutist could stand securely on the rubber tyre without the wheel revolving.

I should explain that the method of applying the parking brake in a

Piper Tri-Pacer involves the use of two levers. First, the pilot would pull back on the handbrake lever, and hold it hard back with his right hand. Then in order to lock the brake into its 'ON' position, he had to pull a small 'T' shaped lever protruding out from the instrument panel with his left hand. Next, for this to work successfully, it was essential to let go of the right hand lever before letting go of the small 'T' shaped lever, otherwise the brakes would be released again. Finally when the pilot let go of the handbrake lever it would spring back to the forward position and the brakes would now be locked on. (i.e. The handbrake lever always rested in the forward position whether the brakes were on or off). The 'T' handle gadget was a fail-safe device to prevent the pilot from inadvertently applying the park brake during his downwind checks and landing with the brakes on.

On this particular occasion I had taken off in Tri-Pacer G-ARGY, the only other person on board was the Chief Parachute Instructor, a very nice chap by the name of Dan Gorman who, like many parachutists, boasted that he would never land in an aeroplane if he could help it.

The idea on this occasion was to climb up to two thousand feet over the dropping zone, and drop a special brightly coloured streamer so that Dan could assess the drift for that mornings parachute drops.

There was no intercom between the pilot and the parachutist, so it was necessary to shout very loud in order to be heard above the noise of the slipstream rushing past the open doorway. Dan had indicated to me that, after dropping the streamer, he would like me to climb the aircraft to six thousand feet so that he could drop out himself and "enjoy" a short free-fall descent. (Rather him than me!)

The streamer went down with no problems, and I got the thumbs up from Dan. As it would take us a further eight minutes to reach six thousand feet, I decided to head out South of the airfield and commence a climbing turn at four thousand feet in order to arrive back over the airfield at the requested height.

Whilst we were climbing I went through the pre-para-drop safety checks that included locking the handbrake so that Dan could stand on the wheel. We still had about six miles to run, when Dan, mad as a hatter, decided to stand outside on the starboard wheel until we arrived overhead the airfield. At the time we were passing over the centre of Oxford city and still climbing at full power.

The drag from his body protruding outside the aeroplane was terrific and caused the aircraft to yaw considerably. I wasn't unduly concerned because Dan was a very experienced instructor and certainly knew what he was doing.

He shouted something to me but I couldn't tell exactly what he was saying, so I throttled back to reduce the noise of the engine and waited for him to shout again....

'ARE THE BRAKES HARD ON?' he said.

For a second I wondered if he was joking, because if the brakes were off, he certainly wouldn't be standing there on the wheel. Anyway, for peace of mind, I thought I had better make sure that they were locked on as hard as possible.

The split second my hand started to pull on the brake lever I realised what I had done, but it was too late. Pulling back the lever whilst the brakes were locked on automatically released the lock. There was a loud bump, the aircraft yawed violently, and Dan was gone!

I banked GY steeply and saw him cart-wheeling down, arms and legs spread out like a rag doll. I was convinced that he had knocked himself out as he was swept back under the tail section.

Although there was obviously nothing I could do to help the poor chap, I instinctively dived GY vertically following him down. Two or three seconds later I could see Dan still struggling to stabilise the vicious spinning motion he was in. I was almost level with Dan when his parachute blossomed out and snapped open and I shot past him at a tremendous rate still heading vertically downwards.

The next second with the airspeed obviously way past the VNE limitation, I was standing on the rudder bar and pulling back on the control column with all my strength in an attempt to pull out before hitting the ground. I regained control at an uncomfortably low altitude, so I decided to climb and fly around for a couple of minutes to regain my equanimity.

Having failed to see where the parachute had landed, I headed straight back to the airfield praying that Dan was alright. I couldn't believe that all this had happened because of a split second's lack of concentration.

Fortunately Dan, being an extremely experienced sky-diver, managed to steer his parachute to land safely on the lawns of Christ Church College, and apart from being a little shaken up he was no worse for wear. He was, however, extremely keen to have a quiet word with me when he arrived back at the airfield in a taxi.

Understandably he let rip at me in no uncertain terms, demanding the refund of his taxi fare back to Kidlington. That evening we got together again and managed to see the humorous side of things over a few beers in the club bar. Apparently Dan didn't hit his head or any part of his body as he left the aeroplane, and I never did find out what had caused the loud thud when he left the aircraft.

The second incident was far more serious. It happened one Sunday morning when we were dropping parachutists from the Skydiving Club onto the drop zone at Kidlington. There were two 'first time' parachute descents to be carried out at the beginning of the days flying.

It was a cool, clear day with very little surface wind. I was airborne carrying a student parachutist together with his instructor. Having levelled out at 1,200 feet, I was number two to another Tri-pacer also carrying an instructor and a young female student who was about to make her first parachute descent, both students were using static lines to deploy their parachutes.

As the lead aircraft approached the airfield I saw the flaps lower ready for the drop. The student climbed out onto the wheel clutching the wing strut. Seconds later she let go and dropped away, the static line pulling her parachute out immediately. We were approaching the drop zone with about a quarter of a mile to run, and as I throttled back to lower the flaps, I was horrified to see that the student who had just jumped out of the aircraft ahead was plummeting down with her unopened chute trailing behind like a streamer.

I will never forget those agonising seconds watching that poor girl fall. Down and down she went until she reached a point when it was obvious nothing could save her. She carried a reserve chute but it hadn't been deployed.

The instructor flying with me had obviously seen the incident and, pointing down in horror at the partly opened chute now motionless on the ground, shouted for me to land as quickly as possible. As we banked over I saw several people running towards the Oxford Agricultural Showground bordering the airfield where the red and yellow coloured blob of the parachute lay close to the airfield boundary fence. A visiting aircraft over-shot the runway whilst a red light flashed from the tower. I descended rapidly obtaining instant clearance to land. We taxied at high speed to the boundary fence and closed the engine down. The instructor with me told his student to remain in the aircraft whilst he and I ran over to the fence where the pathetic crumpled pile of silk was lying a few feet away, the unopened canopy having fluttered down covering the body. Members of our crash crew had reached the scene a few seconds before us, one of them bent over to remove the parachute, he jumped back crying out in horror as the poor girls pulped body made one last involuntary convulsion under the silken shroud. Another man was crying and calling out the girls name as he ran distraught to the fence. Several others stopped short, paused for a moment, and turned away.

The next thing I can remember is hearing the distant siren of an approaching ambulance or police car. The parachute covering the body was gently removed and I too turned away. The poor girl had obviously struck the ground at great speed feet first. I had to turn away from the appalling scene, and returned to dispersal with the student parachutist I was carrying.

Later I learned that at the subsequent inquest ruled that the parachute had not opened properly due to static magnetism. A witness who had observed the incident from the ground with binoculars stated that he saw the girl look up at the parachute streaming out above her, but by the time she went to grab the handle of her reserve chute it was too late. She struck the ground dying instantly.

Personally I was never too keen about parachute jumping, but that very sad incident certainly put the lid on it for me.

After the accident, no parachute activity took place at the airfield until after the enquiry. When the Skydiving Club did resume its activities, the event attracted plenty of advanced publicity which resulted in the airfield being packed with gory onlookers. The National Press were also in attendance, arriving in a privately chartered twin engine Cessna aeroplane.

I was not due to fly at the time, so I was in my office when the event took place. A Tri-pacer, flown by one of our staff pilots carrying the student parachutist and his instructor, took-off and climbed away into the distance, a few minutes later we heard the drone of aircraft engines. I looked out of my office window to see the press aircraft had also taken off again and was now flying in close formation with the Tri-pacer as it approached the airfield for the drop. Obviously I assumed that this had been arranged between the two pilots and the parachute instructor prior to take-off. Even so I couldn't help feeling sorry for the poor chap who was about to make his first para jump. Surely he had enough to contend with without any other distractions.

I continued watching as the two aircraft approached the overhead and saw the student leap from the Tri-pacer. Shielding my eyes from the sun, I could also see that the static line had successfully dragged the parachute from its pack and, breathing a sigh of relief, I was just turning away from the window when suddenly there was a distinctive gasp from members of the crowd. I looked up to see the poor bastard was coming down with two parachutes deployed, neither of them fully opened. I couldn't believe what was happening. Surely there wasn't going to be two fatal accidents in succession!

Apparently the main chute had a thrown line, which means that one of the parachute cords had somehow looped itself over the top of the main canopy preventing it from opening fully. It looked rather like a very small parachute with a large streamer of unopened chute trailing behind. If this happens the drill is, or at least should be, for the main chute to be cut away (Released) *before* attempting to open the reserve parachute. Apparently the student, and who could blame him? thought that two parachutes were better than none, and decided to open his reserve parachute without dispensing with his main chute first.

After that things got worse. The drag from the partly opened main chute was preventing the reserve chute from opening properly. As if that wasn't enough, the idiotic pilot of the press aircraft, hell bent on his journalist passenger getting a "Front Page" photograph, was attempting to spiral around the poor sod as he plummeted towards the ground.

I felt sick as I watched the young man frantically wrenching at the tangled mass of cords above him, desperately fighting for his life. The two parachutes had slowed his descent considerably, but he was still falling at an alarming rate. The whole tangled mess was twirling around like a fairground roundabout, with the main chute only partly opened, and his reserve parachute floating out to the side like a giant writhing snake.

One of the sky-diving club instructors was trying to give the poor lad instructions from the ground by shouting at him through a megaphone. But I doubt if he could hear a thing due to the noise from the engines of the press aircraft that was still trying to fly as close as possible to the poor sod as he fell out of the sky.

I looked away as the parachutist struck the ground to gasps and screams from the on-looking crowd. When I looked back again he was lying face down. Several people started to run across the airfield to assist, but the first to reach him was a little Jack Russell puppy that bounded straight up to him, sniffed him for a second and then piddled on him. It was as if the little chap had been bursting to relieve himself all day.

The ambulance crew in attendance bent over the parachutist for a few minutes. Then there was yet another gasp from the crowd. To everybody's astonishment the chap that I had assumed was dead, suddenly sat up, with the little dog still on the scene and bouncing around him happily. Miraculously the parachutist stood up and, supported by the medics, hobbled over to the ambulance and climbed in together with a young lady and the little dog still wagging his tail.

CHAPTER 27.

Out of the ordinary.

Fortunately I had the opportunity to fly many types of aeroplane whilst working for Oxford Air Training School. Myself and Johnny Johnson, another instructor, carried out most of the initial air test flights on new Piper Aircraft that were shipped in to this country from America. They arrived in huge crates and were assembled, inspected and ground tested by CSE engineers before being handed over to Johnny or myself for flight-testing. In addition to this we also carried out lots of C of A flight tests on privately owned aeroplanes that had been booked in to CSE for their annual checks, engine replacement, or the addition of various types of equipment and avionics etc. It was a great opportunity for me to gain valuable experience flying various types of aircraft that I would otherwise never have had the chance to fly. (I note from my logbooks that by the time I retired from full-time flying I had flown 120 different types of aeroplane).

Sometimes the "excitement" was more than I bargained for. For instance on the afternoon of March 23rd 1961 I was asked to test fly a Tipsy Nipper T66 which had just been released from the maintenance section having had work carried out on its engine.

The Tipsy Nipper is just about one of the smallest aeroplanes a chap can squeeze himself into. Fully aerobatic stressed to +6g and -3g the Nipper has a wingspan of just a little over 19 feet, and its overall length is under 15ft. The Tipsy Nipper has a tricycle undercarriage, and weighs 467 lbs. Its small cockpit is covered by a tidy little perspex dome and, using a hard surface level runway in still air, it will take-off in 300 yards.

As an indication of the smallness of this aeroplane, when climbing into the cockpit the pilot had to lean well forward otherwise the aircraft would tip backwards onto its tailskid with a bump!

I liked flying the Nipper very much, although you had to get used to doing very compact aerobatics. For instance when I first looped the Nipper I found it all too easy to stall as the airspeed drops off rapidly during the first half of the loop. A slow roll also had to be completed quite rapidly by comparison to the Tiger Moth.

On this occasion I was asked to give the engine a good run, and put G-ARDY through its paces. The weather was good with not too much surface wind when I took off and climbed away to the Northwest of Kidlington Airfield.

I levelled off at 5,000 ft. and flew around happily looping and rolling the Nipper. Satisfied that the aeroplane was reacting normally, the next item on the agenda was to see how the aircraft performed during a stalling sequence.

Pre-stall checks completed, I closed the throttle and gently raised the nose of the Tipsy Nipper. There was a slight judder just before the nose dropped at around 33 knots. She stalled cleanly without a wing drop and the recovery was normal. I regained height ready for the next item on the flight test which was spinning. A couple of spins, one to the right, and one to the left proved to be satisfactory. The Nipper had quite a fast rotation, but the recovery was positive taking about one and a half turns after applying full opposite rudder and moving the stick positively forwards. It seemed unnatural to fly in an aeroplane that was so small you had to sit with your elbows actually resting inside the framework of the wing-roots.

Several fatal spinning accidents have occurred over the years, and I suspect many of them could have been avoided if pilots had been taught spin recovery properly.

When I was learning to fly on the Tiger Moth, having completed the dual lesson, I was made to carry out a solo spin over the airfield so that my instructor could see me.

But that's all in the past. For some inexplicable reason the fully developed spin has been removed from the civilian training syllabus altogether, which I consider to be a grave mistake. My argument is how can a pilot be expected to recover from an accidental spin if he has never been shown how to do it?

Anyway, back to the flight test in the Nipper. Having completed two spins I decided to try one hammer-head stall before returning to Kidlington. Another check to see that there were no other aircraft about and we were still over open countryside. I opened the throttle fully and eased the tiny aeroplane up into an almost vertical attitude and waited. The airspeed decreased rapidly and everything became very quiet. As the controls became slack I glanced along the wing tip and realised that I had in fact got the nose up into precisely the vertical attitude, which would more than likely cause the aeroplane to tail-slide before hammer-heading. I knew only too well that this manoeuvre could be very dangerous, causing the aeroplane to momentarily experience the effects of a reverse airflow over the control surfaces as it slides backwards. This can place excessively high loads on the control surfaces, especially the elevators and the rudder. The essential action a pilot must take if he intentionally or, as in this case unintentionally finds himself about to perform a tail-slide, is to centralise the controls and hold them rigidly in place until the aeroplane has stopped sliding backwards, hammer heads, and is diving vertically.

I closed the throttle and checked that the controls were central. Gripping the stick firmly with both hands, I jammed my feet firmly on the rudder and waited, uncertain whether she was going to topple forwards or backwards. We seemed to be hanging there motionless, and then I felt a vicious kick on the stick as we plunged tail first towards the ground. After a couple of seconds the aircraft hammer headed forwards dropping its nose violently and heading for mother earth like a gannet for the sea. The airspeed built up rapidly as I eased the control stick back gently to recover from the dive.

Turning towards the airfield I noticed we were now down to fifteen hundred feet. As there was no radio on board I commenced a climb with the intention of joining overhead the airfield at 2000 ft. for a standard non-radio rejoin. Everything was going along nicely and I was feeling very happy with the world in general when suddenly there was a loud BANG! and the aircraft started to shake violently.

I must have experienced the quickest mood change in history from happy smiles and self-satisfaction, to white faced dry mouthed terror! I snapped the throttle closed, but the vibrations were so severe that I was convinced the engine would shake itself off its mountings if I didn't shut it down completely. Fuel off, ignition off, try to gain a little height…. impossible, airspeed too low. I lowered the nose to attain a safe gliding speed and looked around for somewhere to land. The Tipsy Nipper's gliding angle is steep and the rate of descent in a glide is quite rapid due to the very small amount of lift gained from its stubby little wings.

It was immediately apparent that there was no chance what-so-ever of reaching the airfield. I looked across at the cement works chimney to gain some idea of the surface wind direction from the smoke, and after rapidly searching the area for somewhere to land, I decided that the only chance I had was to attempt a dead-stick landing in the grounds of Blenheim Palace.

I was already quite low and lost more height lowering the nose to make a tight turn bringing the aircraft onto a close crosswind position with the intention of landing on the long, straight driveway heading towards a very tall Monument. The propeller had stopped turning in a horizontal position so I couldn't see it very well from the tiny cockpit to assess the amount of damage. But I did notice that there was something flapping on the leading edge of the starboard aileron.

Heart thumping, I was fully aware that the fuselage of this aeroplane offered little protection to its pilot in the event of a less than reasonable landing. I lined up with the driveway and checked the brakes and fuel were off. Luckily there was no one in sight. A little too high, I side-slipped down the last hundred feet and made a bloody awful landing, luckily without causing any further damage to the aeroplane.

I hopped out pretty smartly and took a look at the front of the aircraft. The first thing I noticed was the propeller had obviously had a good smack from something and was badly damaged, also the spinner was missing altogether. The leading edge of the starboard wing had been scuffed, and what I had taken to be a problem with the fabric on the starboard aileron turned out to be the remains of the spinner that had lost all its texture, wrapped itself around the starboard wing-tip like a piece of cloth, and miraculously stayed there. Everything else appeared to be OK.

I sat on the grass for a moment or two feeling less than happy, when a man appeared running towards me waving his arms frantically. 'Here comes trouble' I thought.

'I'm really dreadfully sorry' he said gasping for breath. 'No one said there was a landing strip here, I hope I haven't caused any problems!'

The poor chap must have been the only tourist in the grounds of Blenheim that day. He was very relieved when I explained to him exactly what had happened and that this wasn't a landing strip at all. He kindly offered me a lift in his car, which he had parked on the grass at the side of the drive.

Joined by his wife, we chatted for a short while before pushing the aeroplane onto the grass verge. As we strolled back to his car I could hear another vehicle approaching at high speed. Someone must have seen me coming down and telephoned the airfield as it turned out to be our crash truck tearing towards us with a cloud of blue smoke trailing from it's exhaust.

The engineer who asked me to test-fly the Nipper was at the wheel, laughing and shaking his head.

'I don't know what we are going to do with you Ray' he said, 'always trying to impress everyone with your forced landing skills, and this time you missed the bloody airfield altogether.'

'I was hoping Mr Churchill would pop out and offer me a large brandy' I said.

'More likely to charge you an entrance fee' he replied.

The engineer had three of the lads from the hangar with him, and after checking the aircraft over, we managed to lift G-ARDY onto the truck and took it back to the airfield with me sitting inside the cockpit looking like a small boy paying aeroplanes.

Our Chief Engineer concluded his report by saying the damage was caused by the spinner detaching itself from the base-plate and striking the propeller blade. The prop was damaged and out of balance. The leading edge of the starboard wing had also been struck by the remains of the spinner. In the end not such a big deal, but enough to cause a few tense moments in the air when the bang occurred and the aircraft started to vibrate. Incidentally, no one from Blenheim Palace ever approached us about the landing.

As it happened, a year later on the 16th August 1962, Peter Clifford won the Kings Cup Air Race in the same aircraft G-ARDY.

Whilst on the subject of mishaps, I was once asked to collect Col. Stewart's Piper Cub from a private strip on his farm which was situated a few miles North of Kidlington, and bring it back to the airport for it's 100 hour maintenance check.

The Piper Cub is well known for its STOL (Short take-off and landing) performance. It seats two persons in tandem and when flown solo, the pilot occupies the front seat. It has a wingspan of just over 35 feet, and the fuselage is a little over 22 feet, so it fits very nicely into a good-sized farm shed, which makes it a very popular aircraft amongst the flying farmers fraternity. As it happened I had never flown a Cub before, so I welcomed the opportunity of adding it to the list of aircraft types flown in my logbook.

Back at Oxford I looked up the aircraft's performance, and noted that the Cub would take-off in a distance of one hundred yards in still air conditions, and with a stiff breeze this distance could almost be halved.

Armed with a set of headphones and a local area map, I set off with one of our engineers who kindly volunteered to drive me over to Col. Stewart's farm in his car.

Arriving at the farm, we entered the rusted gates and trundled down a well-rutted track towards the old farmhouse. The first thing that struck me rather forcibly was that all the fields seemed to be far too small for the operation of an aeroplane however good its take-off performance was. But perhaps the landing strip was situated in a larger field farther up the road. I knocked several times on the farmhouse door, but nobody answered. Assuming the Colonel was probably out on the farm somewhere, we picked our way carefully along a slushy path covered with cow dung to find him. The sound of hammering guided us to a line of tatty looking farm buildings situated at the rear of the house. An old chap, who appeared to be mending a fence, stood with his back towards us quietly having a serious chat with himself. Sensing our presence he turned around and stared at us with his mouth wide open. He had a kind old face with wrinkles that gave me the impression he had laughed a lot during his considerable lifetime.

I apologised for startling him, but whilst I was speaking he cleared his throat, wiped his nose on the back of his shirt sleeve and shouted, quite loudly…

'You must be they gentlemen what's come to take the bosses plane away.'

The small pair of wings on my jacket had obviously given the game away.

'That's right' I said, 'my name's Ray and this is John.'

The old chap thrust out a grubby hand.

'Pleased I'm sure…I'm George the Colonel's Farm Manager.'

His handshake was like a grappling iron that almost brought tears to my eyes.

Trying to hide the bone crushing effect of his greeting, I asked him where I could find the Colonel.

'He ain't ere sir, he's gorn orf for a few days.'

He paused again whilst he had a minor coughing fit, spat on the ground and continued…

'He did say you'd be comin, and I are to show you where tis….If you'd care to follow me sir.'

We followed the old boy to a rickety looking barn, and after a lot of pushing and shoving we eventually managed to dislodge one of the sagging doors from the mud and dragged it open.

'Have't shift a couple of these eer tractors fust' he said.

I could just make out the lines of an aeroplane in the darkness at the rear of the barn. John, the mechanic who had brought me over whispered…

'Better see if there is any damage to the fabric before you go Ray, looks to me as if there could be a few mice or rats in here!'

The day was obviously off to a bad start. I'm not too partial to mice at the best of times, but rats I positively hate.

After several minutes of vigorous cranking the old boy managed to get the tractor's started and removed them from the barn. Next we had the choice of either manoeuvring the Cub round a few bales of straw, or moving the straw out of the way altogether. The farm manager decided the matter for us.....

'Best get em out....cos we gave the wing a bit of a thump pushing her out last time.'

'Great' I thought, we could probably have an aeroplane that's bent, infested with rats and we still haven't seen what state the cockpit is in yet.

After a considerable amount of humping bales of straw and struggling to get the second barn door open, we managed to get the Cub chocked up outside the barn. To my amazement it looked in reasonable shape although the tyres looked a bit flat. Whilst our engineer was taking a good look at the engine, I asked George if he had a pump we could use to put a little more air in the tyres.

'They always looks like that, that's how they supposed to be sir!' There was a pause, then he said...

'She ain't got much petrol in er, she's almost empty.' He pushed his cap back and stood scratching the few remaining hairs on his head, and went on....

'Now which a these ere cans did the boss say wus fer the plane?'

The odds of flying this aeroplane safely back to Oxford were beginning to stack up against me. So rather than take any more risks I said we would nip back to Kidlington in the car and collect a can of aviation fuel.

'No need for that, governor, it'll come to me in a minute.'

I could see that John was quite amused by all this, so I asked him if he would like to leave his car at the farm and fly with me back to Kidlington in the Cub when the time came, suggesting that one of the ground staff would take him back to collect his car later. The amused look on John's face disappeared immediately and he declined my offer with two antisocial words.

Eventually our tireless farm manager produced a rusty five-gallon drum with "AVIATION FUEL" roughly painted in large white runny letters on the side.

'I am definitely not risking my neck putting that bloody stuff in the tank,' I exploded, 'Somebody could have pissed in there, for all I know.'

The old man looked a bit hurt, but as it turned out I didn't have to argue with him as the can was empty.

After a hurried car journey back to Oxford, we returned to the farm with a five gallon drum of aviation spirit, and after spending a further half hour searching around for a suitable step ladder, we emptied the contents into the fuel tank of the Piper Cub.

I spent a considerable time carrying out a pre-flight inspection of the aeroplane, and everything appeared to be in order.

John, who was a first class engineer, had looked at the engine and bet me a pound that it would start at the first press of the starter button. I didn't take him on, but I wished I had because the battery turned out to be as flat as a pancake.

'Hang on Governor, we've got one of them battery chargers somewhere if I can just bring to mind where t'is.' This guy was obviously trying to do his best to help us.

'Don't bother mate' I said, 'John here will swing the prop for me.'

When I was ready to go I asked George how to get to the landing strip. The old chap's face wrinkled up into a smile.

'You be standing in it sir' he said. 'The boss always goes down hill and between them two trees.'

My heart sank. There was little or no wind, the grass was quite long which would obviously provide plenty of drag, and the take-off run to the gap in the trees was about seventy-five yards at best. I thanked our friendly farm manager, patting him on the shoulder to avoid another painful handshake, and reluctantly climbed into the cockpit.

John swung the prop a couple of times, then gave me the thumbs-up. Ignition on, throttle set.

'Contact' one more flick of the prop, the engine coughed and started.

I sat there engulfed in a cloud of blue smoke whilst the engine, sounding rather like a tree saw attempting to saw through a six inch nail, gradually warmed up.

John shouted a hurried 'cheerio' through the cockpit hatch and was about to head for his car.

'You hang on here old chum until I've got this thing into the air. I don't fancy crashing into the far fence and being trapped in a flaming wreck whilst George tries to remember where he last saw a bucket of water!'

I taxied the Cub to the furthest corner of the field and turned to face the gap in the trees at the far end praying that this little aeroplane's short take-off performance was as good as I had been led to believe. I gave the engine a good run-up, tested each magneto again and completed the take-off checks.

The trees at the furthest point of the field looked bloody close to me: 'No use hanging about' I told myself. With my feet hard down on the brakes, stick fully back, I ran up the engine to full power, paused for a few seconds to allow the revs to build up, then released the brakes. As she started to roll I eased the stick gently forward and the tail came up almost immediately. I noticed there was a wire fence about three feet high that stretched across the gap between the trees. If I could keep straight and clear the fence I had it made, but I was finding it difficult to keep the aircraft straight once the tail came up. Bouncing along we were soon past the point of no return. If I tried to abort now the Cub would certainly hit the fence and summersault onto its back. With a clearance of about twelve feet on either side there was adequate room between the trees for the aircraft to pass safely, but we were airborne and heading towards the extreme right of the gap. It was impossible to hold her straight with the rudder. The Piper Cub now started to bank and turn more to the right, I almost stood up on the left rudder pedal, but it wouldn't budge. I used left aileron to prevent the aircraft rolling over whilst the Cub continued to yaw sideways totally out of balance and sliding sideways towards the trees. I didn't have time to look at the ASI, but I assumed the airspeed was only a few knots above stalling speed, so I couldn't pull up to clear the top of the trees without risking a stall. With almost full left aileron I eased the stick back a little and grimaced as we went straight into the trees about a foot or two from the tops, bursting out the other side in a shower of twigs and leaves.

Miraculously the aircraft kept going although we were skidding hideously sideways, I had checked full and free movement of all the controls before taking off, what could have gone wrong? After gaining a few hundred feet still skidding and turning, I lifted my feet from the rudder bar for a second and was surprised to see that the aircraft started to roll rapidly to the left. I neutralised the ailerons and the aircraft immediately flew in balance without any rudder input. At a reasonably safe altitude, I undid my safety harness, and leaned over to peer under the instrument panel. Immediately I saw the cause of the problem. There on the floor, adjacent to the left rudder pedal, was what appeared to be a piece of aluminium that looked very much like a metal foot-rest securely bolted to the cockpit floor. I just couldn't believe it. I'll never know how a thing like that was ever allowed to pass a flight safety inspection. I had obviously taken off with my right foot on the rudder bar and my left foot on the protruding piece of metal next to the left rudder, mistakenly thinking the rudder had jammed.

Apart from the traumatic take-off the Cub handled beautifully, and I had learned yet another lesson, from that day onwards I always checked the floor of the cockpit carefully before starting up.

There was a small amount of damage to the fabric that occurred when I passed through the tops of the trees. John, who I expected would be laughing his head off when I arrived back at the airfield, was keen to know what had gone wrong. He did however manage to muster a wry grin when I told him what I had done. I never actually met Col. Stewart, but I learned sometime later that the gentleman had a false left leg. Maybe the addition of a metal footplate had something to do with resting his metal leg once the aircraft was trimmed out.

CHAPTER 28.

Extraordinary circumstances.

Oxford Air Training School soon became the most important privately operated commercial pilot training school in the world. The company had secured contracts for pilot training from most of the worlds major airlines. The school's flying and ground instructional staff were mostly ex-RAF CFS instructors who had gained the appropriate civilian pilot and instructor ratings when leaving the services.

Rex Smith became the Chairman of Oxford Air Training School. Capt Bill Jordan was appointed Chief Instructor taking overall charge of the flying instructors and ground instructional staff. I continued as the CFI of the Basic Training Flight.

I first met my new boss, Bill Jordan, in 1961. At the time he was a F/Lt in the 'V' force flying Vickers Valiant bombers with 138 squadron based at RAF Gaydon. During the same period I was serving as a part time officer in the RAFVR(T) attached to No 6 AEF Squadron, flying Chipmunks at weekends and annual camps.

A few weeks before Bill was due to retire from the RAF he came over to Oxford to attend an interview with Rex Smith for the job of Chief Instructor for OATS. Later the same day I was introduced to him as my future boss and during the conversation that followed it was mentioned that I was flying part time with the AEF. So Bill, who was still actively flying with the RAF, kindly offered to arrange a flight for me in a Valiant Bomber, an offer I couldn't possibly refuse.

'Stick your uniform on and come over on Tuesday next week at 5.30 am, I'll get you in for breakfast and you can attend the flight briefing before we fly' he said.

On Tuesday the 17th July 1961 I pulled up outside the guardroom of RAF Gaydon at precisely 5.25am and was directed to Flight Ops. where I found Bill waiting for me.

'Just in time for bacon and eggs' he said.

On the way to the mess Bill explained that the sortie laid on for today was to check out Squadron Leader Harry Clearbow as an authorised Captain on the Vickers Valiant.

After breakfast I was invited to attend the briefing and introduced to the rest of the crew. There was a short delay whilst a problem with one of the fuel tanks was rectified, then we were off.

We all piled into the crew bus and set off for the aircraft dispersal point. It was the first time I had been anywhere near a V Bomber, and there it stood, WZ248, a beautiful all white Vickers Valiant. It was difficult to appreciate what gruesome destruction this lovely looking aeroplane, with its deadly cargo, was capable of.

After a lengthy external check we entered the aircraft. I was very surprised how little room there was inside the crew compartment. I had been fitted up with a parachute and shown how to get out of the side door in the event of an emergency. I was then secured into one of the three rearward facing seats behind the two forward facing pilot's ejector seats. From that moment on, I enjoyed a most marvellous days flying that took us out over the North Pole. For a short while I was allowed to stand behind the two pilots looking out over a solid carpet of beautiful cumulous cloud, their anvil tops well below us as we streaked through the sky at 40,000 ft.

Returning to the circuit at Gaydon, I watched poor old Harry Clearbow physically struggling to land the aircraft after Bill had switched off the power assisted controls.

Sometime later I learned that Bill Jordon had been shot down over Germany during the Second World War whilst flying a Wellington aircraft on a night bombing mission. He and his crew survived the crash, but were badly beaten up by civilians who had just suffered fatalities from the raid. Bill was taken to a German hospital with severe head wounds, and later had a metal plate fitted to his skull.

Being an officer in the RAFVR in addition to being a civilian instructor at Oxford certainly had its good points, and six years later this combination of jobs gave me an opportunity I could never have dreamed of.

The year was 1967. Summer passed quickly, and before long October had spread out her icy fingertips, leaving early morning frosts that made the hedgerows sparkle like diamonds. It was one such morning when the telephone in my office rang. It was F/Lt. Peter Woodham telephoning from RAF Little Rissington.

'Hello Ray boy, I've got some exciting news for you mate. How do you feel about giving the Red Arrows their PPL Tests?'

My first reactions were: 'this guy is obviously taking the piss,' so I told him to pull the other one.

'I'm telling you Ray, none of the Red Arrow pilots have got PPLs, and the MOD, in their infinite wisdom, have ruled that they must pass a test with a CAA appointed examiner before they can be issued with a civil licence.'

I still couldn't believe what Peter was saying.

'Come on Peter, surely the most famous aerobatic pilots in the world don't have to have a PPL test, it's bloody ridiculous, and why would they select me to do the test anyway?'

Peter explained…

'It's a combination of you still being a part time pilot with the RAFVR, and also being a Civil Flight Test Examiner. The boss of the Red Arrows, Sqdn Ldr Ray Hanna, asked me if I knew anyone that would fit the bill, so with you in mind I said I knew just the chap for the job.'

The next day Sqdn Ldr Hanna telephoned to thank me for agreeing to do the tests. To my great relief he said it's only the written aviation law paper that we have to take, no flying would be involved. Then, and this was the really exciting bit, he suggested that I flew over to RAF Kemble wearing my RAF uniform so that he could legally take me flying on a practice sortie with the Red Arrows later the same day.

A provisional date was set for the 23rd October. Peter telephoned me on the 22nd to say that everything was on and asked me to call in at RAF Little Rissington first so that we could proceed from there to Kemble in a Jet Provost.

I arrived at the Officers Mess Little Rissington at 09.30am and by 10.30 Peter and I were airborne in Jet Provost XS212 winging our way to RAF Kemble. We did however make one slight diversion so that we could carry out a fast low run over Oxford Airport and "wake em up" as Peter put it.

We landed at Kemble, taxied in, and were met on the flight-line by F/Lt Ian Dick, who had recently been posted to the team. (Some time later Ian became the next Leader of the Red Arrows). We made our way over to the crew-room, me clutching a briefcase with seven copies of the CAA aviation law exam. I was greeted by Sqdn Ldr Ray Hanna, AFC, who introduced me to the members of his team. After a cup of tea we all sat down at a table and I handed out the test papers. Fifteen minutes later it was all over, everyone attaining maximum marks. (What else!)

Shortly afterwards I was invited to attended a pre-flight briefing concerning the aerobatic sequences they were about to perform with me on board. A black and white negative film of their last practice detail was also shown whilst the boss made pertinent comments about the various manoeuvres. The film was shot by the tail chase aircraft used during the Red Arrows training flights.

The briefing complete, I was kitted out with flying suit and bone-dome. Peter had brought a cine-camera with him to film the sequence from the ground. I asked him if he would film me climbing aboard and taking off in a Red Arrows aircraft because I was sure that no one would ever believe me.

Then the moment I had been waiting for finally arrived. We were taken out to the dispersal area where a line of seven immaculate bright-red Hawker Siddeley Folland Gnats awaited, their canopies open and their ground crews in attendance. What a sight!

By 13.25, I was strapped in, plugged in, ejector seat safety pins removed, engines running, and ready to move out. My pilot was F/Lt Ian Dick.

13.30, brakes off and we were accelerating down the runway like a rocket in Gnat XS111 with six other Gnats in close formation. The experience from then on defies description. Short clipped instructions from the leader's voice, a combination of graceful aerial formation dancing, coupled with moments of neck braking G Force, rapid aileron rolls, and incredible closing speeds as we passed terrifyingly close to a Gnat on a reciprocal heading whilst still rolling. I experienced blackouts, red-outs, I banged my bone-dome on the side of the canopy numerous times during the flight and loved every second of it. The Gnat could roll through 360degrees in a split second; it had a 20,000 fpm rate of climb and max airspeed of 690 mph.

All too soon it was over. Wheels down and locked, and we were landing in close formation.

After an enjoyable lunch I was taken up again for a spot of low flying, this time my Pilot was the leader himself, Ray Hanna. Low flying at treetop height at speeds of 250mph was very impressive. Then, to my surprise, I was given the opportunity to have a stab at flying the Gnat followed by a couple of circuits and landings. I was surprised how light the controls were, the rate of roll was so sensitive that I constantly over-controlled. Later I was informed that the actual rate of roll in a Red Arrow's Gnat which had the aileron stops removed, was an incredible 180 degrees in point eight of a second.

That evening I flew back to Rissington in the Provost, said Goodbye to Peter, and drove back to Oxford. I entered the gates of Kidlington Aerodrome as dusk settled. The whole day had been unbelievable. To be given the opportunity of flying with the Red Arrows was indeed a great privilege. A few days later I received a letter from Sqdn Ldr Ray Hanna thanking me for the tests and offering me the opportunity of flying with them again. This letter is now proudly stapled to the appropriate page in my pilot's logbook.

CHAPTER 29.

Being a Flying Instructor.

The instructor's workload increased considerably, Oxford Air Training School was now training hundreds of pilots for most of the world's major airlines. By 1967 my flight alone needed a flying staff of five full-time flying instructors and a further three part time instructors. We were all spending six, seven and sometimes eight hours a day in the air, which is a lot considering that there were pre-flight and post-flight briefings to be carried out in addition to the flying.

Many people tend to think that a flying instructor's job is subject to a considerable amount of stress. On the contrary, most of us look upon our jobs as a most interesting and rewarding profession. In the first place we are being paid to do the one thing we enjoy doing most. Secondly we have the privilege of passing on these skills to others so that they may become professional pilots or instructors, or simply fly for pleasure. One thing is certain, whatever else they did in life, students never forget the instructor who sent them on their first solo flight and gave them the freedom of the skies. Having said all that, sometimes there are frightening moments that we could well do without.

I remember my first nerve-racking experience as a flying instructor. It happened on a lovely midsummer's day back in 1962. Mr Richard Harris, my student was already a qualified private pilot with about two or three hundred hours in command. He was considering the idea of signing up for a flying instructor's course, and was taking a few brush-up lessons before applying for the AFI entrance test.

Richard had telephoned to book an hours flying with me and arrived half an hour before our scheduled take-off, this gave me adequate time to brief him fully on the stall turn exercise I had planned for him.

After the briefing we signed the aircraft acceptance.sheet and stepped out into a warm sunlit afternoon. Clear skies and a well-defined horizon made it an ideal day for aerobatic training.

As we strolled across the grass towards the white and silver Chipmunk that was parked on the dispersal area being refuelled, I asked Richard how serious he was about training to become an instructor.

'It's the one thing I really want to do Ray, I love flying as you know, but it's taking every spare penny I have. The answer for me is to take up flying as a career, then I can earn my living and fly at the same time.'

Richard's enthusiasm was more than obvious as he continued to question me about the Assistant Flying Instructor's Course. Finally I said….

'I'll tell you what we will do Richard, at the end of our aerobatic session today; I will demonstrate the instructor's patter for spinning in the Chipmunk. Then we will climb back to a safe height and you can demonstrate a spin to me, at the same time just telling me what you are doing with the controls. You don't have to try and copy everything I said, just talk me through what you are doing when you enter and recover from the spin. At least this will give you some idea of what instructing is all about.'

The petrol bowser moved off to refuel the next aircraft, leaving Richard to carry out the external checks in peace. I asked Richard to explain in detail exactly what he was doing during his pre-flight checks, and as usual he carried them out without missing a thing. After that he climbed into the front cockpit whilst I removed the chocks and strapped myself into the cockpit behind him.

Within no time we were airborne climbing into a clear blue sky, heading for the aerobatic area West of Kidlington.

Forty-five minutes had passed; we were flying at an altitude of five thousand feet and nearing the completion of the lesson in stall turns. Throughout the lesson we had been using a stretch of railway line as our ground reference feature to judge the accuracy of our stall turns.

'You are not getting the aircraft up into the vertical attitude Richard.'

This is a fault that everyone seems to have when they are learning to stall turn. The correct method is to raise the nose of the aircraft until it's pointing vertically upwards with the engine at full power. When the airspeed falls to just above stalling speed, full rudder is applied in the required direction; the aeroplane cartwheels sideways, the throttle is closed as the nose passes through the horizon and we wind up pointing vertically downwards. Usually a little aileron has to be applied to prevent the further effect of rudder. Thus when it recovers from the ensuing dive, the aircraft should be on a reciprocal heading. Any cruising speed can be used for this manoeuvre, but of course a high starting speed gives you a little more time, and makes the turn easier to practice. A common fault with most students is they think they are travelling vertically upwards when they still have about another twenty or more degrees to go. In fact of course, the fuselage should not be exactly at ninety degrees to the horizon in order to allow for the angle of incidence. But for all practical purposes in the early stages of learning how to do a stall turn, the student thinks he is really travelling vertically upwards when he's nowhere near that angle.

'Not bad Richard, try again, this time I'll tell you when you are at the correct vertical attitude, and don't forget to look at the wing tips as we pass through about seventy degrees and check they are both in the same position relative to the horizon. One last thing, you need to check the further effect of the rudder, which is making the aircraft roll… apply a little opposite aileron at the same time as you apply the rudder …OK?'

'OK Boss.'

This was our umpteenth attempt, and I began to feel we would gain more now from calling it a day and having a chat about our progress over a nice cup of tea.

Richard's final stall turn was much better, although he forgot to close the throttle as the nose of the aircraft passed through the horizon, resulting in me closing it for him to prevent over-revving the engine.

As usual I complemented my student on his efforts, and as promised, we climbed to a safe height so that I could demonstrate a spin concentrating on the instructor's patter. Richard could then carry out a spin himself, something he had done several times before, but this time he would attempt to talk me through his actions. I hoped that this would give him some idea of how important it is for an instructor to co-ordinate his actions with his patter.

We levelled out at six thousand feet over the Oxford designated aerobatic area and carried out the full pre-aerobatic checks.

'OK Richard, I have control, just follow me through.'

'Roger, you have control.'

Richard's reply came through loud and clear.

I made one final area check, no aircraft approaching all round above or below us. We were over open countryside in non-restricted airspace, and I could use the cement works chimney in the distance as a good reference point. I started my patter….

'I am going to carry out a demonstration spin to the left, I shall commence recovery after three complete turns, is that clear?'

'Yes sir.'

'OK here we go.'

'We are flying straight and level at 6,000 ft. which gives us plenty of height to recover by 3,000 ft. Our airspeed is 90 kts. I am applying the carburettor heat and closing the throttle smoothly preventing any yaw with rudder. As the airspeed decreases the aircraft starts to descend, so I am trying to maintain height by applying a steady backward pressure on the control column. Note that the airspeed is now reducing quite rapidly and the nose of our aeroplane is gradually becoming higher. I am trying to maintain height with a continuing backward movement of the control column. The initial indication that we are approaching a stall is that the elevators, ailerons, and rudder are all becoming very sloppy. I will demonstrate this to you so that you can see large movements of the controls have very little effect on the aircraft's attitude. Finally the aeroplane is beginning to judder as the airflow over the wing surfaces begins to break down, can you feel it?'

'Yes sir'

'Good, note the airspeed is just above the stall ... keeping the ailerons neutral I'm bringing the control column fully back and applying FULL left rudder at the same time.'

The aircraft pitched up and slowly rolled left, then the left wing dropped more violently, the nose pitched down below the horizon and the Chipmunk began to rotate, pitching, rolling and yawing quite fast.

I began my patter again, this time speaking a little faster to get the points home during the first three turns of the spin.

'Here we are in the spin. Note the relatively low airspeed, about 54 kts. and the high rate of descent... one turn. two turns... three turns.'

Sierra Tango seemed to me to be winding-up much faster than she usually did. I carried on with the patter.

'Recovering now, check the throttle is closed and apply FULL OPPOSITE RUDDER to the direction of rotation... pause... then we move the CONTROL COLUMN SLOWLY FORWARDS until the spinning stops.'

I moved the control column forwards as I spoke and waited for the spinning to stop. Usually it takes about one and a half turns before the spinning actually stops, but this time NOTHING HAPPENED. The rotation of the spin was gathering speed rapidly. Sierra Tango was not showing any signs of recovering. I checked to see if the control column was fully forward, it was hard on to the compass box in front of it, as far as it could go. My next thought was to double check that the handbrake had not been partly applied as that automatically restricts the full rudder movement.... The brakes were off!

By now we were losing height rapidly, about 300 feet per revolution of the spin. I shouted to Richard to take his hands and feet off the controls, his voice, several octaves higher screeched back through my headset,

'For gods sake Ray, whatever's happening?'

I decided rapidly to start the recovery sequence again from scratch. I carried out the procedure as positive and deliberately as I could. HARD RIGHT RUDDER, STICK SLOWLY FORWARD... I slammed it hard against the compass box, virtually standing up on the rudder. Nothing happened. I began to feel the nauseating gut twisting pangs of panic taking over.

At that moment I had a split second flashback to the Chipmunk I witnessed burning in a field, the remains of the young pilot's body still smouldering when I arrived on the scene. I knew if I lost it now we would be destined for the same ending.

A quick glance at the altimeter told me we were passing through 2,600 ft. The spin was winding up even faster. If we'd been wearing parachutes I would have ordered Richard to bail out and gone with him at this point, but we had no parachutes. I decided to try stick forward plus full power for a couple of seconds followed by stick hard back and throttle fully closed. I knew this was supposed to help recovery from a flat spin, and although this was anything but a flat spin, it was worth a try as nothing else seemed to work. Unfortunately the effect of power and elevator didn't work either.

The figure of 1,800 ft. is impressed clearly on my mind, so I must have looked at the altimeter at that stage. In one last desperate attempt, I slammed down the flaps and applied left aileron. As far as can I remember I still had full right rudder with the control column fully forward. The aircraft, still spinning at a high rate of rotation, began to shudder violently as if it were intent on shaking itself to bits. Convinced we were about to be killed, I started to carry out the crash drill. I shouted to Richard to hold his head up, but he was slumped forward in the front cockpit and made no reply. Reaching up I forced the canopy open. The noise was like the entrance to hell itself. Suddenly, before I had time to turn the fuel off, Sierra Tango flicked upside-down completing what felt like a couple of flick rolls and the spinning stopped. We were in an almost vertical dive. Centralising the controls, and mindful of the possibility of a high-speed stall I pulled the aircraft out of the steep dive.

Straight and level at 600 feet, with sweat running down my face; I asked

Richard if he was OK. There was no reply. I could see from the rear cockpit that his head was tilted forwards and not moving. Obviously something was seriously wrong. I informed Air Traffic Control that we had had a problem with the aircraft and that my student appeared to be in trouble. The airport crash crew came alongside as we landed, and after taking a brief look at Richard, who appeared to be unconscious and breathing erratically, one of them radioed air traffic and asked them to call an ambulance.

One of the ground crew asked me what had happened.

'I'm not absolutely sure,' I said 'but they'll be playing snowballs in the desert before I spin this bloody aircraft again.'

I kept talking to Richard whilst someone released his harness. He looked deadly white and never answered. Two firemen lifted him from the cockpit, and laid him in the recovery position on the grass beside the aeroplane. He was semiconscious when the ambulance arrived.

The ambulance hurried away, it's blue light flashing. I stood there for a moment looking at Sierra Tango, its serene white and silver fuselage sparkling in the sunlight. I placed the chocks under the wheels of the aircraft and murmured.

'What the hell's up with you?'

I reported the incident in detail to my boss who was anything but happy about it and indicated that what happened must have been my fault.

'You probably made a cock-up of the recovery procedure somewhere along the line Ray.'

I explained in detail exactly what had happened, but Rex still wasn't convinced. I checked my logbook which revealed I had spun G-AOST on no less than sixteen previous instructional spinning details. At no time did I have any problems at all with recovery from any of the spins. The lessons included spins from the straight stall, spinning off steep turns, spinning from full powered climbs, spinning off a gliding turn, and advanced spinning, all in G-AOST, and all without problems. But Rex, still not convinced, decided to send me up with Ken Scott, a fellow instructor, to check if I had developed any problems with my spin recovery technique.

I signed the aircraft out and walked over to the dispersal area to carry out a pre-flight check on G-AOST. A few minutes later Ken shouted from the Ops. window…

'Not that one Ray, we're flying in the other Chipmunk, G-AOFF.'

'That's not the one I had trouble with' I shouted back.

'I know that mate, but I'm not going to spin Oscar Tango until the problem has been sorted,' he said.

I spent about thirty minutes flying with Ken, who reported to Rex that he could find no fault with my spin recoveries, or my instructional technique. But Rex was still not happy.

A few days later, considerable light was shed on the matter when F/Lt Bunny Austin called in to see Rex. There wasn't much Bunny didn't know about flying Chipmunks. Stationed at the Central Flying School, RAF Little Rissington, Bunny had accumulated hundreds of hours training RAF instructors in service Chipmunks. Also he had taken part in a Chipmunk assessment programme at the time when the DHC/1: had come under scrutiny by the RAF due to the number of spinning accidents that had occurred.

The three of us sat in Rex Smith's office. First of all Bunny told us that the assessment team could find nothing at all wrong with any of the Chipmunk spin tests they had carried out at CFS. The reason for most of the crashes had been put down to pilot error. Disorientation, incorrect use of controls during the spin, incorrect identification of the spin as opposed to a spiral dive, and sheer panic, were some of the causes attributed to the crashes which occurred whilst spinning RAF Chipmunks. And sadly there had been quite a few.

Bunny, who had taken part in my instructor course training a few years previously, was keen to hear my version of events. So I told him exactly what had happened during my flight with Mr Harris. He questioned me about the position of the handbrake, which serves to limit rudder movement when applied. He also asked about the speed and attitude of the aeroplane during the entry into the spin. We sat there for some time whilst Bunny explained in great detail that aerodynamically spins are affected by the aircraft's attitude at entry, speed, weight distribution, even air temperature and density. But these variants should not affect the standard method of spin recovery.

'As far as the pilot is concerned' he said 'the recovery is exactly the same for all these varying conditions, but there could be certain modifications that would make recovery from a spin difficult. I'd like to take a look at the Chipmunk in question, Sierra Tango.'

As a matter of interest I had noted from the aircraft's flight sheets that it had not been flown on a spinning detail by any of the twenty-five flying instructors since my last flight in her!

The three of us walked over to the hangar where ST was undergoing a maintenance check. As we approached the aircraft Bunny took one look at ST and said...

'Bloody hell Rex, there's your answer. I wouldn't spin that aeroplane if you paid me in gold bars.'

Bunny walked slowly round the Chipmunk.

'Three individual things, any one of which would make me reluctant to spin that aeroplane, all three together and it's a definite NO.'

He pointed to the tail end of the fuselage.

'First of all, the aircraft is not fitted with spinning strakes. Spinning strakes were introduced to this type of aircraft in order to assist during its recovery from the spin. If they are not fitted, a "**THIS AIRCRAFT SHOULD NOT BE SPUN**" notice should be displayed in the cockpit.'

There was no such notice in that aeroplane when it first arrived on the OAC fleet.

Bunny continued…

'Secondly, the aircraft has a short cord rudder, and short cord rudders are not conducive to positive spin recovery.'

He patted the large Spitfire-like bubble canopy, and said…

'This is your main problem. The aircraft has undergone a Masefield Conversion.'

I asked Bunny why the conversion was such an important factor to the spin recovery?

'There's no doubt in my mind that this canopy could be the predominant cause of the trouble you had recovering from a spin. It's much bigger and wider than the standard Chipmunk canopy, and would obviously blank off some of the airflow over the rudder when initiating spin recovery. This combined with a short cord rudder and no spinning strakes could make this aircraft lethal in a spin.'

I asked Bunny why several instructors, myself included, had not experienced this trouble previously whilst spinning Sierra Tango.

'It was probably a combination of the prevailing meteorological conditions, the speed and angle of the entry into the spin, and the design features of this particular aeroplane that together, aerodynamically, produced a spin from which it was almost impossible to recover. Opening the hood, which would have disturbed the intrinsic airflow during that spin, is probably what saved your lives.'

Subsequently a "THIS AIRCRAFT MUST NOT BE SPUN" notice was placed in both cockpits of G-AOST, and I was let off the hook. If we had crashed there's little doubt that the incident would have been put down to pilot error, and no one would have been any the wiser.

I never saw Richard Harris again. I was told later that he had been diagnosed with a serious heart problem, a condition that was obviously not helped by the situation we found ourselves in. Fortunately he had undergone surgery and made a full recovery.

Late one Sunday afternoon in June, my boss asked me if I would like to return Tiger Moth G-AODX to the services flying club at RAF Little Rissington. DX had been lent to Oxford Air Training School by the RAF whilst one of our Tiger Moths was undergoing its C of A. maintenance check. Rex mentioned that John Paul, one of our commercial pilot students, had kindly volunteered to collect me from Rissington in his car and bring me back to Oxford.

John, who answered to the nickname "Froggy", was a Frenchman. He was a tall, very good looking young man with a following of equally good looking young ladies. The fact that he was also exceedingly wealthy probably contributed to his popularity in the club bar.

At 5.30 p.m. I was sitting in DX with the engine running and about to wave the chocks away, when I saw John Paul running towards me frantically waving his arms.

'My instructor Jerry Busby has agreed to drive my car over to Rissington if you would let me come with you in the Tiger?'

I gave him the thumbs up and in no time at all our duty engineer, who had just swung the prop for me, was helping Froggy into the front cockpit. It took a bit of time because being an RAF aeroplane, it carried parachutes that also acted as cushions in each of the bucket seats. I watched John fasten his seat belt in the front cockpit whilst the engineer removed the spare flying helmet and goggles from the aircraft's locker and passed them to him. This particular Tiger Moth had the luxury of being equipped with electric intercom instead of the usual cumbersome Gosport Tubes that we used in our own Tiger Moths.

Finally I waved the chocks away, and within minutes we were airborne steadily climbing out on a Westerly heading over the Oxfordshire countryside.

'Been in a Tiger before Froggy ?'

'No sir eet ees the first time I ave been in an open cockpeeet.'

It only took a few minutes airborne time to reach Little Rissington, and Froggy seemed to be enjoying every moment of it. Being a Sunday evening the RAF were not active, so I asked him if he would like to do a few aerobatics whilst we're up here.

Froggy was silent for a few seconds before answering rather cautiously …

'OK…. sir'

My passenger didn't sound too keen, so I said…

'If you like I'll just do one quick loop overhead the airfield to let them know we're here Froggy…OK?"

Froggy gave me the thumbs-up.

The RAF Control Tower was closed for the evening, but I could see another light aeroplane taxying back to the building they used as a Clubhouse. There were no problems about landing as our flight had been cleared by telephone prior to leaving Oxford.

As we approached the overhead at three thousand feet, I completed my pre-aerobatic checks and double-checked that the area was clear of other aircraft.

'Strapped in OK Froggy?'…

'Yep'….

Down we went into a steady dive. Engine RPM throttled back slightly to prevent over speeding the engine, and checking the slight yaw with rudder, I eased back the stick applying full power as the nose of the aircraft passed through the horizon finally completed a straight forward loop.

Letting down on the dead side of the runway we joined the circuit, landed and taxied to the dispersal area where Bunny Austin came out to meet us.

'A bit subdued for you wasn't it?' he said.

'Well old Froggy here wasn't too keen as it was his first flight in an open cockpit and I didn't want to put him off.'

I climbed out of the rear cockpit and stood on the wing to help Froggy undo his harness.

What I saw made a cold shiver run down my spine. Poor old Froggy had not been strapped into his seat at all! For a moment I couldn't make out what had gone wrong, but it soon became obvious. Froggy, having never been in a Tiger Moth before, and not being used to sitting on a parachute, had climbed into the cockpit, sat down on the parachute and strapped himself in mistaking the parachute harness for the aircraft's seat belts. He was in fact sitting on the safety belts that our engineer had undone for him just before he entered the cockpit, which meant that he had merely donned the parachute and not strapped himself into the aeroplane.

When he realised what had happened poor old John Paul turned deathly white. He tried to force a smile but he was completely traumatized. I must admit that I didn't feel too happy either. If our airspeed had been slightly slower over the top of the loop Froggy would have fallen out. He didn't even realise he was sitting on a parachute. Another lesson learned that could easily have turned into a catastrophe.

Later that evening in the club bar at Oxford, I turned to John Paul who was enthusiastically supping his umpteenth large whisky and said laughingly...

'If I had made one of my frequent cock-ups of that loop Froggy, you could have been a past member of the Skydiving Club by now old chum.'

Froggy grinned sheepishly and consumed the contents of his glass in one gulp.

Over the last several weeks I had spent most of my free time trying to fly the holding patterns given to me by our Link Trainer Instructor Johnny Brakes. I emerged from the wingless black box covered in perspiration and stared at the wobbly black line scribed on the chart table by the auto-crab.

'Did I do that?'

'You sure did old boy, in fact you made a complete balls up of just about everything, not your day eh?'

Hacked off, miserable and convinced that I would never pass the dreaded commercial IR test; I made a booking to spend yet another hour in the godforsaken sweatbox that evening. The date for the actual instrument rating test with a CAFU examiner was looming up fast, and I began to think I was wasting my time.

The I/R Flight Test, renowned as the toughest test to pass in the Commercial Pilot's curriculum, was divided into three parts: 1. Pre-flight action, take-off and climb. 2. Asymmetric flight. 3 (a) Airways procedure, (b) ILS, and (c) A choice of ADF, VDF, or VOR let-down. Looks simple enough but therein lies the depths of hell.

At Oxford we used the Piper Twin Comanche for our instrument rating flight tests. It was a great aeroplane to fly but it proved to be a very unstable platform for accurate instrument flying. (Later, but unfortunately well after my I/F training, the Company reverted to the Piper Aztec, a much more stable aeroplane to fly).

On the day of my IR test a CAA Examiner arrived from the Civil Aviation Flying Unit at Stansted Airport. After a thorough briefing on the route I was to follow during the test, he left me to complete my IFR flight plan. There were several well-known and practiced routes, and certain examiners had their preferences for one or the other. My Examiner was Captain John Belson, socially a very nice chap, but as an examiner his name struck terror into the hearts of all his candidates. John had a reputation for being the toughest examiner of the lot. Although it was not put to me in those exact terms!

Captain Belson informed me of the amount of assistance he was prepared to give me whilst acting as my "First Officer" throughout the test. He also mentioned that he may not be a very good first officer, and as acting Captain it was my responsibility to check that anything I asked him to do, i.e. selecting various radio aid frequencies, altimeter settings etc., was in fact carried out correctly.

We strolled out to the dispersal area where Twin Comanche G-ASLE stood refuelled and ready to go. Capt. Belson followed me every inch of the way as I completed the pre-flight inspection, meticulously taking notes on the fluttering pages of his notepad without uttering a word. In fact he said very little throughout the whole test, with the exception of answering the questions I occasionally put to him as my acting First Officer.

One of the greatest nightmares during the IR test is not making the correct assessment of the wind direction and speed at various altitudes and flight levels throughout the flight. We all prayed for calm weather on the day. As usual in my case, Sod's law took a jovial hand, and half a bloody gale was blowing by the time we were taxying out to the holding point.

After meticulously carrying out all the checks and setting up the instruments prior to take-off, we were finally airborne with me under the I/F screen. Seconds later I was desperately trying to note down a never-ending flow of clearances from Air Traffic Control. I scribbled their instructions on my flight pad and read them back to the controller, at the same time attempting to fly LE within the stringent tolerances allowed.

Non-flying types reading this may not be aware that wind velocity changes with altitude. For example the surface wind on the airfield could be something like 125 degrees at 15 kts. whilst over the same spot at 3000 ft. it could be 150 degrees at 28 kts., and at seven thousand feet it may well be 180 degrees at 45 kts. So you can appreciate the mental calculations that have to be made in order to retain a steady course whilst climbing and descending through the various levels required.

During the second part of the test, having left controlled airspace, we were still being thrown around by severe turbulence when Capt Belson asked me to divert to a NDB and enter a holding pattern.

The forecast winds were way out, which made calculating the new heading and ETA quite tricky. Since take-off I had been flying under the hood on instruments struggling to remain within the stringent flight limitations laid down for the IR test. Although being a flying instructor helps as far as accurate flying is concerned, stress levels under test conditions are always high. Assessing the wind velocity, correcting for drift and flying an accurate holding pattern on a NDB whilst passing amended flight details to a "sometimes impatient" controller calls for a high level of concentration. I was also aware that my examiner was making copious notes about my performance during the test, not a good sign!

After being knocked about by the turbulence for over three hours, we finally landed back at Oxford Airport. I sat in the cabin of LE whilst my expressionless examiner gathered his notes together and put them carefully into his flight case.

'Right, let's get ourselves a cup of tea' he said.

I poured myself out of the cockpit, slithering down the wing onto the tarmac like a bundle of sweat-soaked rags. Capt. John Belson was notorious amongst the examiners for being tough, but he also had the reputation of being reasonably humane and putting his candidates out of their agony by giving them the results of their test immediately on landing. But not in my case! I went into the dispersal hut, telephoned for the fuel bowser to refill LE, then proceeded to flight Ops to sign the aircraft maintenance log. All this time John stood outside trying to light his pipe.

When I emerged from Ops I could wait no longer, convinced that I had failed, I said…

'Not good eh?' John shook his head,

'Terrible, never had worse.'

The bastard could have put it in slightly kinder terms, surely I wasn't that bad.

Most IR students subconsciously prepare themselves for failure on the first attempt, or perhaps hope to get a partial pass. By the same token everyone hopes to pass, and many chaps do in fact pass on their first attempt. But being an instructor at Oxford, I felt it was my duty to pass first time, I suppose it was a matter of pride.

John spoke again, his words hardly penetrating my misery as we entered the airport restaurant.

'I've seldom known such bloody awful weather for a test Ray, you could have opted out, I gave you the choice before we left.'

His words slowly registered, he may have been talking about the weather when he said 'terrible,' On the other hand he had also mentioned my decision to continue with the test in bad weather which probably meant he failed me for flying in adverse conditions.

'Tea or Coffee Ray?'

'Tea please John.'

I began to feel sick. I wish he'd put me out of my misery. We sat down. Captain Belson placed his hat on the table like an orderly officer taking a defaulters parade. He removed the notepad from his flight case and went into a long and very detailed debriefing covering every aspect of the flight, emphasising the fact that I had not changed the altimeter setting from QFE to QNH quick enough at one stage during an overshoot procedure.

'I thought you had forgotten because you took far too long Ray.' The smiling assassin was verbally ripping me apart!

There was a long pause, it almost seemed as if he was trying to make up his mind whether to have me shot or recommend clemency. But I knew him far too well for that. Captain John Belson would have made that decision the second we closed down the engine in dispersal, if not long before.

Returning his notes to his flight case he continued...

'Anyway, taking into account the difficulties facing you whilst flying in those very rough conditions I must say you coped well, and I have no hesitation in passing you on your IR test. Congratulations.'

'Well I'll be buggered.' was all I could come out with.

During the early days of Oxford Air Training School's commercial venture, my flight had the responsibility of flying with quite a number of our foreign students for their first 30 hours training. This was quite a daunting task considering many of them could only speak one or two words of English when they arrived at the school.

Having trained a number of these young men, I must admit that on more than one occasion it occurred to me that a flying instructor's job was not exactly the safest and least demanding job in the world. I sometimes wonder if there is a sort of heavenly grading system unbeknown to me, probably headed up by my Guardian Angel, who carefully selects the most awkward students and allocates them to me personally for training.

I don't think my Guardian Angel likes me very much. Either that or the heavenly spirit to whom I am allocated has a weird sense of humour.

We had an even more worrying problem with some of the students as they were sent to us from countries that were on the verge of war with each other. All instructional staff at Oxford were warned that although these students would be segregated as far as possible in the students Hall of Residence, we would have to be very diplomatic in the handling of these chaps when they came together for ground school and flight training purposes.

At one stage Kidlington became a sort of United Nations clearing house for airline pilots, with students from China, Syria, Iraq, Saudi Arabia, Iceland, Libya and Pakistan, all rubbing shoulders in the flight training centre. We also had Aer Lingus students from Ireland, as well as our own BOAC and BEA students.

Some students remain imprinted on my memory more clearly than others. For instance reading through one of my old frayed log book's, the names of Kwong-Yo, O'Kolo, Zoughhaib, Delifer, Al-Jiran, Quasnick, Seguttson, Atabani, Sanquinett and Vanveen reminded me of the problems I encountered simply trying to make myself understood. Nevertheless, I must admit that most of our overseas students could speak excellent English, but there were one or two lads that had great difficulty understanding anything that was the slightest bit technical.

At the beginning of each residential course, all the new students would assemble in the main lecture room to be formally welcomed to the school by the CFI. Details of the training syllabus would then be explained to them, after which each student would be allocated to an instructor who would take over their training from that point. I remember at one of these initial briefings it became clear that we were in for a tough time.

The students were noisily chatting away as I entered the briefing room with my instructors. Gradually the room grew quiet and everyone respectfully stood up.

'Sit down gentlemen' I said turning to pin the student/instructor allocation list to the notice board.

When I looked back at the class they were still standing. Gesturing with my hands to avoid further confusion, I repeated my request for them to sit down.

Every member of the course was wearing a name badge that had been issued to him by the Bursar when he arrived. One of the students, Mr Kwong-Yo, an immaculately dressed young man, suddenly sat down with regimental briskness, the rest of the class followed suit hesitantly. I continued...

'My name is Ray Blyth, I'm the CFI of the basic training flight and I would like to welcome you all to Oxford Air Training School.'

Before I could say another word one of the students, whose badge bore the name of Atabani, jumped up from his chair and said, in reasonable English...

'I would like to say from all of us others, it is a great honour for you to be here sir, and we will all try properly to fly good.'

A sideways glance at the grinning faces of my instructors standing at the back of the classroom said it all, they were obviously fated to spend endless hours explaining technical details to totally blank faces.

Many, especially the lads from Hong Kong, spoke excellent English, and were most polite at all times. The other side of the coin were the guys who had only taken the trouble to learn two words, 'YES SIR,' which they probably thought would see them through the course. Do you understand? 'YES SIR.' Are you well or do you feel sick? 'YES SIR.' What do we always do before commencing a turn? 'YES SIR.' What are the checks we carry out before stalling?... 'YES SIR.'

Late one very hot and stuffy Summer's afternoon, having spent a miserable hour trying to encourage my student to turn the elevator trim wheel in the correct direction just once in his career. I looked at him sitting there with a fixed grin on his face, having said yes sir to everything and got precisely everything wrong. I'd had enough and quite unforgivably snapped at him...

'OK you gormless twit, we've finished for today, I think it would be a splendid idea if we stuffed the bloody nose down, crashed and burst into flames don't you?'

He smiled, and although the additional verb gave me some hope, his answer was as predicted...

'Yes Sir, PLEASE.'

I agree that it must have been very difficult for these poor chaps to learn to fly without speaking the language. But whose fault is that? The training contract's signed by the sponsoring airlines clearly stated that all students sent to Oxford Air Training School to be trained as pilots, will have a sound working knowledge of the English language. Yet some of them couldn't understand a word of the English. Teaching a student to fly who doesn't know up from down, or right from left is bad enough, but when it comes to teaching him how to recover from a spin, the situation could become seriously dangerous.

In the end nothing surprised me, and I became used to the weird happenings performed in the cockpit. One afternoon my student Mr Delifer was practising instrument flying using the full panel. I put him under the I/F hood. (A device to restrict a pilot's vision to the instrument panel and prevent him from making outside reference to the horizon.) It was a calm day so he had no added stress from air turbulence. After a while Delifer became very quiet. His concentration was certainly not on the instruments because the aircraft had started to wander slowly from its selected heading and height. I refrained from correcting him at this stage so that I could see how long it would take him to identify his mistakes. I could not actually see his face as it was obscured by the instrument hood. However I did notice that he put his hand up to his face and held it there for some time whilst the aircraft rolled still further off course and started to head downwards at an ever increasing speed. Finally curiosity overcame me, and I leaned forwards to peep at him under the I/F hood. What I saw was unbelievable, I remember thinking 'Bless my soul, is this man really going to fly an airliner one day?' I gazed at him in amazement as he struggled to remove some extraneous matter from the eye-watering depths of his left nostril, oblivious of anything the aeroplane may have been doing.

'If you put as much enthusiasm into your instrument flying as you obviously do in picking your bloody nose Mr Delifer, it will probably save you from the misfortune of being splattered all over the countryside!'

That evening I was having a quiet drink with dear old Bill Beadle, telling him about the wonders of the day, when the door of the Club Bar burst open and in rushed a man dressed in Arab head-dress who I vaguely recognised as Mr El-Farta, one of our students. He landed at my feet, on his knees, hands clasped as in prayer, begging me to accompany him outside as quickly as possible. Bill and I looked at each other in astonishment.

'What on earth's wrong lad?'

'Quick, oh quick sir, there will be murder please come.'

Bill and I hurriedly followed the distraught chap out into the darkness of the night, slightly apprehensive as to what may be waiting for us around the corner of the Club building.

It was a moonless night as far as I can remember. But in the shadows, partly illuminated by the lights from the bar window, I could see another chap in Arab type clothing who turned out to be Mr Swhaak, apparently being held in an arm lock, with a long vicious looking knife pressed against his throat. Not wishing to die that early in the evening Bill and I refrained from getting too close to the man with a knife, who I now recognised as my student Mr Atabani. Trying to remain calm, I asked him what on earth was going on, or words to that effect. The chap who had fetched us from the bar was acting rather strangely, running around in a sort of crouched position making a peculiar sound, a sort of whimpering noise. Atabani spoke in a very slow low pitched voice that sent shivers down my back.

'This man insults you, says you not as good as his instructor, you are my instructor, he apologise or I will kieeel him.'

Bill murmured something unprintable, and I had a job not to smile. The chap at knife- point said nothing. So, trying to deflate the situation I said…

'Don't be bloody silly man, he didn't mean it, for God's sake let him go.'

'He insult you, you my boss, I must kieeel him.'

El-Farta, the chap who had been scurrying around like Quasi Modo, started to sob and began jabbering away at Atabani in his own language. There was a great possibility that I was about to witness Swhaak having his throat cut, I was not amused.

'This is your last warning, if you don't let him go I will make sure you are both taken off the course and on a plane back to your country first thing in the morning.'

I was a little surprised by my own authoritative voice, and even more surprised when Atabani released his grip on the unfortunate Mr Swhaak pushing him away violently. But it wasn't over, the man swung round and tried to take a swipe at Atabani, which ended up in a blood bath as Atabani defended himself with the hand that held the knife.

'That settles it' I said 'you to the sick bay, and you stay with me. Both of you in my office at 08.30 sharp tomorrow morning.'

By now several people were gathered outside, and fortunately for Atabani no one had called the police. After I had made a telephone call to the Student's Hall of Residence, Mr Willmore, the School Bursar and an ex. RSM in the Coldstream Guards, turned up and escorted Atabani back to the students quarters whilst his wife, who was a qualified nurse, dealt with Swhaak's cut hand.

Next morning I turned the two students over to my immediate boss Bill Jordon. They were extremely lucky to get away with a severe warning and not get thrown off the course there and then. We didn't have any more trouble with those two individuals. Others were not so lucky.

An unsavoury incident that took place some weeks later, began when a group of students who had been watching a boxing match on the television in the club bar, saw Mohammed Ali win his world championship fight. After the fight, a number of our East African Airways students started to drink heavily and became very aggressive. They were apparently causing quite a disturbance in the bar, and later continued making trouble in the resident's quarters.

After charging around like Zulu Warriors, two of them were seen carrying long knives and overheard by an English student, who fortunately could speak fluent Swahili, to be making plans to execute one of our flying instructors. They were never given the opportunity of explaining their actions. The police were called and the two students were invited to spend the night in a police cell. Next day they were released pending further enquires and allowed to return to the airfield where they were hauled up in front of Bill Jordon, our C/I .

They apologised profusely and begged to be allowed to complete their training course. But Bill wasn't taking any chances. Their agency in London was contacted and arrangements were made for them to be sent back to their country of origin in disgrace.

The same year, a bunch of African students, having celebrated the successful end of their training by drinking large amounts of whisky in the students club bar, dragged the piano onto the airfield and trundled it up to the hard standing just outside my caravan. They then sang their national anthem, primed the piano with petrol, and set fire to it. I was asleep inside the caravan at the time, but bloody soon woke up when I heard the commotion and saw huge flames reflecting on the windows of my bedroom. Fortunately for them they had already successfully completed their CPL training, so they paid for a replacement piano, and nothing more was said.

The boss sent for me one morning and greeted me in his usual manner.

'Come in Son and sit down.'

I sat down wondering what was coming next. One usually gets invited into the MD's office when something has gone radically wrong.

'I need to talk to you about your future with Oxford Air Training School, which at this period in time rather depends on you.'

Rex asked me now that I had my CPL and instrument rating if I had decided which career road I wanted to go down. i.e. The private training side or the commercial side of the operation.

The same question had arisen sometime previously when I was offered the job of CFI of Basic Training. This time Rex asked me what ultimate goal I had in mind.

I said I would like to think there would be an opportunity of getting to the top, maybe even becoming the Director of Flight Training at some point in the distant future.

Rex pointed out that long-term prospects with any business are difficult to predict. But as far as CSE was concerned he felt he could assure me of a reasonably secure future, the rest would be up to me. The fact that I was CFI of the basic training flight at Oxford Air Training School was a good start. But clearly there was much more to running an aviation business than teaching people to fly aeroplanes. There was a lot to learn and more experience to be gained before I would be in a position to be considered for further promotion of any kind.

I left the MDs office feeling more than pleased. All I needed was the knowledge that further promotion within CSE was not completely out of the question. The ball was firmly in my court as to how far up the ladder I could go. In the meantime I assured Rex that I was happy with my job, loved flying, and I didn't mind working seven days a week when the job called for it.

Training commercial students was much easier to organise than training flying club members. With commercial courses you flew with the same students consistently on a daily basis over a set period of months. Continuity, which is essential in flying training, was one thing you didn't have to worry about with residential courses. On the other hand training club members to fly often meant that long breaks were experienced between lessons, sometimes as long as several weeks and the advantage of continuity is lost.

As mentioned earlier, my flight dealt with all the private students as well as sometimes helping out with the commercial lads. The variety certainly made things interesting. One morning I received a telephone call from the C.I. to say that a rather distinguished gentleman had been in touch with him who was keen to commence flying training at Oxford. I was asked to fit him into the programme and told that the boss would appreciate it if I looked after him personally. I was always a bit suspicious about this "priority" stuff, but reading between the lines of the conversation I had with Bill, I assumed there was something rather different about this individual, but Bill wouldn't be more specific than that. As it happened my suspicions couldn't have been more justified, as "different" he most certainly was!

I will give the gentleman his correct title, but for obvious reasons I will have to furnish him with a totally fictitious name. I will call him, The Honourable Sir Angus Wilkinson. A booking was made for me to fly with Sir Angus the following Saturday morning.

On the day, the weather turned out to be satisfactory for a trial flying lesson, so anticipating the arrival of my mysterious student, I stood in the reception office and peered out of the window that overlooked the car park.

Suddenly my attention was drawn to a large, fully camouflaged, Daimler Armoured Car that sped onto the car park and screeched to a halt just outside the main entrance doors. A hatch in the turret slowly opened and a scowling red-faced gentleman wearing a military type crash helmet popped up. At first I thought the military had paid us a visit for some reason or another. But I realised that this couldn't be the case when the rest of the man's body appeared. He was an enormous chap, about six feet two or three inches tall, and at a guess he must have weighed well over twenty stones. He stood by his vehicle for a moment studying the airport direction signs, then headed for the door marked enquires.

The man had the most enormous tummy that hung in a large fold over the top of his belted trousers. He was wearing a beautifully tailored black blazer with brass buttons and a magnificent gold and silver badge sewn to the breast pocket that looked like a family crest of some kind. He also sported an impressive looking school-type tie.

Towering over our Ops clerk he announced…

' Angus Wilkinson, booked to fly with McKenzie-Blyth, tell him I'm here will you?'

He had a very loud, cultured voice, and blurted his words out in short breathless blasts, a problem obviously related to being considerably over weight.

I was standing behind him, so I tapped him on the shoulder, he spun round and scowled at me, but when I introduced myself to him his attitude immediately became more friendly. His hand shake was rather limp and clammy, and his first words were…

'I would like to become a wizard pilot old boy.'

I smiled as I thought the man was joking, but his face remained serious. I listened to him puffing and panting whilst he insisted that he only flew with the most experienced instructor we had.

All the while he was talking I couldn't take my eyes off his blazer and tie. They were splattered with what appeared to be the aftermath of meals lavishly consumed at some time in the past.

I explained that I was by no means the most experienced instructor at Oxford, but he was lumbered with me whether he liked it or not. He seemed to overlook my remarks altogether, and I wondered if I was being set up. I asked him…

'Have you ever flown before?'

'Only in the big jobs Tiger.'

TIGER? Who the hell's Tiger I wondered , then I suddenly realised it was the name he had decided to call me! I already guessed the answer to my next question...

'Have you passed a CAA pilot's medical yet?'

My assumption was correct, he hadn't.

I explained to the Rt. Hon. that the purpose of today's lesson was for him to get familiarised with the sensation of flying in a light aeroplane. But he didn't appear to be very interested in listening to me. All he wanted to do was tell me about some American war films he had been watching, and would it be possible for me to teach him how to "DOG FIGHT" later? I thought he was joking…But unfortunately he wasn't!

Well, this was a first and no mistake. My warped sensed Guardian Angel was at work again. I began to wonder how dangerous this guy was going to be when he got behind the controls of an aeroplane, assuming that he could squeeze himself into the cockpit in the first place.

After a short briefing, I asked the Hon. to fill in a temporary membership form.

'Ah, this must be the legendary blood sheet Tiger' he said.

There was no way that I was going to fly with this chap in a tandem seat aeroplane, he seemed to be an unpredictable character, and I needed to see exactly what he got up to in the cockpit.

I checked the aircraft serviceability record of G-ARJD, and signed out in the Piper Colt.

Sir Angus followed me around the outside of the aircraft whilst I carried out the external checks. I explained the purpose of the inspection to the big man, or at least I tried to, but he showed little interest. All he kept doing was rubbing his tubby hands together excitedly and occasionally laughing out loud for no apparent reason.

Getting the Hon. into the tiny cockpit of the Colt proved to be as difficult as I thought it would be, in fact it was almost impossible to secure the safety harness around the tummy of this enormous man. I also had great difficulty in climbing into the cabin as my student's backside spread partly over on to my seat.

After encountering difficulty in closing the cabin door, I looked with concern at the large belly pressed against the control column in front of my student. Even with his seat adjusted to the fully rear position, there was only a small amount of room to operate the elevators. I sat crammed up against the side of the cockpit trying to force my arm between the two of us so that I could operate the throttle, and seriously considered cancelling the flight altogether, but Angus was just like an excited little boy, and in a way I felt sorry for the guy and didn't want to disappoint him. Anyway, after lots of wriggling and shoving in the cockpit, we eventually reached a stage when we were a little more comfortable and I considered it safe to continue.

Having arrived at the holding point of runway 27 I started to prepare the aircraft for take-off. It was at this point that poor old Sir Angus decided to break wind, and boy, did he ever break wind! Ventilation in the small cabin of a Piper Colt is not very efficient at the best of times, and this certainly wasn't the best of times.

Wondering if I would ever get off the ground without passing out, I called for take-off and was given immediate clearance by Air Traffic Control. Once we were airborne, nature took over again and Sir Angus's backside began to ventilate with the efficiency of the capsulated system in a Climb and Descent indicator, causing the cabin to fill with an obnoxious smell whilst the high pressure in Angus's tummy attempted to equalise with the lower pressure of the cockpit.

By the time we levelled out at two thousand feet, Angus had dispelled all the surplus air in his tummy, at the same time I was desperately trying to get what remained of the dreadful smell out of the cockpit by opening every available vent and hatch.

My student continued to refer to me as "Tiger", which, amongst other things, began to get up my nose. Later in the proceedings it got even worse when he decided that I should more appropriately answer to the name of "ACE".

'Call me Ray' I said.

'OK Ace' he replied.

We flew around for a few minutes whilst I talked about local landmarks, the height we were flying, and the airspeed etc. Suddenly I became aware of strange noises emanating through my headphones. Yeeeow... brrur...dagger...dagger...dagger...brrur...yeeeow. I looked in horror at the eccentric individual sitting next to me who had now moved out of the realms of reality altogether, and was making so-called aeroplane engine and machine gun noises rather like a five year old child...

'Come on Ace lets shoot the buggers down' he said, his shiny red face saturated in perspiration.

A few hurried minutes later we were landing back at Oxford, the profuse sweating of my student having steamed up the cabin windows almost to IMC proportions!

As we taxied in I held the cockpit door open, and took a few wonderful breaths of fresh air. The worrying thoughts running through my mind were... from that little fiasco I was supposed to make an initial assessment of this student's in-flight temperament and, as the book says, decide on a tentative approach for his subsequent flight training.

We reached the Ops. Room, where, to my great embarrassment, and the Ops. staff's amusement, Sir Angus insisted on telling everyone in sight I was an Ace! and that he intended flying with this "Hotshot" again.

Over a period of a month or two, The Hon. Sir Angus attended for several flying lessons at Oxford. He always insisted on flying with his ace instructor, "Tiger". On every occasion he was like a very excitable little boy, entering a world of fantasy and make-believe. I tried hard to get him to concentrate on the lesson in hand to little avail. Each time we never got further than lesson one…. I warned him that he was wasting his money, but my warnings always fell on deaf ears.

'Come on Tiger…we'll get there in the end' he would say.

Going through the mail one morning I found a letter addressed to me and marked 'Private and Confidential.' It was from the medical branch of the CAA. They had been approached by Sir Angus's board of Trustees, who wanted to know in strict confidence if I would report on The Honourable Sir Angus Wilkinson's flying training progress, and asked whether or not I considered he would ever reach a stage in his training where he would be safe to fly solo. I had to be honest, and sadly that was the last I saw of him.

In a way I was sorry because I had grown to like him. He was a most unusual chap and I was amazed that he had ever passed a driving test, but he obviously did and seemed to drive his armoured car quite normally and safely. But flying an aeroplane solo, as far as I was concerned, was definitely out of the question altogether.

CHAPTER 30.

Melancholy thoughts.

I still had a great affection for Mary. She was the mother of my son and it was very difficult to accept that we had split up after eleven years of marriage. But to continue our lives together as they were, would have been torturous for both of us. Words could never express how much I missed my little son Eddy. Lying in hospital with memories of our past days together was very saddening, even to this day it upsets me to think about it.

My new life with Valerie had been vibrant and blissful. She was able to understood the emotional problems I faced after leaving home as she had also experienced the unhappiness of a broken marriage herself. Towards the end of the Second World War Valerie had served as an officer in the WAAF. During that time she fell in love with a Sergeant Pilot, they married, and a year or so later Valerie gave birth to a baby girl. Unfortunately, like so many wartime marriages, their relationship broke down, they parted and were eventually divorced.

Valerie's daughter Laura was nineteen years old when I first met her, luckily she accepted me as a friend and the three of us got along happily together.

We lived in a pretty little cottage on the outskirts of Woodstock just a few yards from the entrance gates to Blenheim Palace. The grounds of the Estate were open to the public at certain times, and the residents of Woodstock were given free entrance to the park.

Woodstock is a very attractive little town situated on the edge of the Cotswolds, dating back to the early seventeen hundreds. In 1874 Sir Winston Churchill was born in Blenheim Palace, and the town is also renowned as the birthplace of the Black Prince.

I loved Woodstock for its old-fashioned street lighting, warm atmosphere and cosy looking stone buildings. We lived in Woodstock for three very happy years, but unfortunately had to leave when Valerie's short term rental agreement expired and was not made available for renewal. Several options were open to us including the purchase of a very nice static caravan. Rex Smith kindly offered to provide us with a suitable site on the airfield if we bought a mobile home, and said he allow us to reside there without paying ground rent. At first Valerie was understandably reluctant about living in a caravan, but after looking at the luxurious residential models available, she agreed to take up Rex's generous offer.

Before long, we were established in a very comfortable mobile home. It had two good sized bedrooms, a modern kitchen, a very cosy lounge/diner with freestanding furniture, and a bathroom with a full sized bath. The van was also fitted with a wood burning stove and full central heating. The site was conveniently situated a couple of minutes walk from the aircraft hangars and our respective offices. We had a small area of ground suitable for a garden, and were given the use of a garage that just managed to house Val's Mini Minor and my second hand Jaguar. Valerie, being eminently "green fingered", soon had our garden in excellent shape with a beautifully smooth turf lawn surrounded by pretty flowerbeds.

As far as I'm concerned there is nowhere quite like an airfield in the early morning, when the mists are rising from the ground and the birds commence their early morning song. Or a summer evening when the sun is setting red against the distant horizon and the aircraft, settled quietly for the night, are silhouetted black against a multi-coloured evening sky. Our little home became a place of laughter and contentment. But now I laid disabled in hospital, and had no idea what the future held.

CHAPTER 31.

Return to past Memories.

At one stage E flight became one of the busiest flights at Oxford. In addition to training our regular PPL students, we had an intake of sixty RAF scholarship students to train under contract to the MOD, and forty Air Traffic Control Officers under contract to the CAA.

As a result Kidlington became very busy, sometimes with as many as ten or more aircraft carrying out circuit training at one time. Therefore to lessen the traffic, arrangements were made for E flight to operate from Staverton Airfield in Gloucestershire. Every morning my instructors and I would each take an aeroplane loaded with students and fly to Staverton and carry out our training programme from a small hut situated on the North East corner of the airfield..

Also my flight was occasionally called upon to help out with the "Awkward Squad". Airline students from A, B, and C flights that had difficulties with their basic flying lessons were sent to 'E' Flight to be sorted out. At one stage the prime candidate for concern in this ominous bunch of gentlemen was one of our African students, a very nice young man by the name of O'Kolo.

Although he actually said very little, Mr O'Kolo appeared to eye me with great suspicion from the time when he first arrived on my flight for continuation training, and having flown with him a few times, there was no doubt in my mind that Mr O'Kolo unfortunately had little, if any, aptitude for flying aeroplanes.

We contacted the sponsoring airline, informing them that we considered O'Kolo to be incapable of reaching the standard of training required to pass his CPL and IR flight tests within the timescale normally accepted as reasonable, adding that it was also doubtful if O'Kolo would ever be safe enough to send solo. Surprisingly the sponsoring airline had no contentions about spending as much money as it would take to get Mr O'Kolo through the course, and issued implicit instructions to continue with his flying training.

O'Kolo was in fact a very polite young man. Although nothing was ever said, I got the distinct impression that he was connected in some way to the hierarchy of his country, and was much more than just a sponsored airline student.

After seven hours of circuit training, during which time little progress was made, I continued to fly two, one hour sessions with O'Kolo every day. Some days he would have completely forgotten the basics of earlier lessons and had to be taken off the circuit for revision. By now I had serious doubts about this young man ever being safe enough to send solo.

Nevertheless, over a period of several weeks, I continued to bash away relentlessly hour after hour on the circuit with O'Kolo. I felt sorry for him, heaven knows he was trying hard enough, but unfortunately getting nowhere. Finally, as is usual with very difficult cases of this kind, I decided to hand him to another instructor, and asked my Australian friend Hugh Bain to fly with him in the hope that a change of instructor would do the trick.

After a few days Hugh begged me to take O'Kolo back, saying...

'This guy's bloody dangerous mate, I think he should be taken off flying altogether before he kills himself and probably take some poor bugger with him!'

After a long chat with Hugh I asked my boss Bill Jordon to contact the sponsoring airline again and recommend that Mr O'Kolo should be withdrawn from the course altogether for his own safety.

The following morning I was saddened by the news that O'Kolo's employers would have none of it. They informed us that he had achieved a high pass mark on the airline's entrance examination papers, and insisted that we continued with his training as they were absolutely certain he would eventually make the grade.

The situation was becoming ridiculous. This student was taking up valuable instruction time on my flight that could well be spent on other students. But I was told to press on with O'Kolo's training in the hope that he would eventually see the light and make good. Not only did he make no progress at all with his landings, his basic flying was also beginning to deteriorate. I was not surprised as this sometimes happens with students when they become frustrated with their own efforts.

There is a very delicate balance between the correct time and the incorrect time to send a chap on his first solo flight. If you hold back too long, he will pass his peak, and his standard of flying will begin to deteriorate. Send him too early and it could very well be the student's last flight.

The basic criteria used to justify sending a trainee pilot on a first solo, is that the student must have completed a minimum of three consecutive landings without any comment or assistance from the instructor, and also carried out a satisfactory practice power failure after take-off. But that had to be the minima. Instructors soon acquire a gut feeling about a student, and this is the all-important factor that has to be added to the equation.

Obviously all students do make mistakes during there circuit training, unfortunately O'Kolo seemed to do little else, and the problem was he never made an attempt to correct any of them. I would sit beside this young man and watch him stare hypnotically into oblivion, gripping the control column so tight that his knuckles showed white under the strain. On occasions his circuit's of the airfield would develop into a mystery tour of the local area! He and seemed to be unaware of what was happening and ignored anything I said to him...

'There is another aircraft to your right O'Kolo, he's on a converging course with us, what are you going to do about it?'

His eyes would widen as he gave the other aircraft a furtive glance, but that was it, he would take no avoiding action and say nothing.

After many hours of circuit training his procedure never changed. I could talk the man through a circuit and landing which he would carry out almost perfectly. Then, having told him to do the same thing again without any help from me, he would proceed to cavort around the circuit and end up doing his best to kill us both.

My student was blind flying through eternity, his insidious attitude remaining static. Left to make his own decisions, the circuit would turn into a near fatality, he never looked anywhere but straight ahead. When he did finally spot the runway he would fly straight at it, diving down without making any attempt at rounding out! At this stage he had completed over 47 hours flying training without going solo, and I swore that another hour on the circuit with this chap, and I would be ready to give up instructing and become a monk.

At the end of each day's flying, the poor fellow would be close to tears, (me too!), I spent many hours on the ground trying to encourage him whilst briefing him in detail on what he was doing wrong. Always he had excuses, worries about home, feeling sick, had a sleepless night and was feeling tired.

Always assuring me he would be better next time and literally begging me for just one more chance. In the air, he said nothing … not a word.

In all other respects he gave the impression of being a very intelligent man. The problem was really a simple one; he just didn't have the aptitude to become a pilot. I'm sure he was terrified in the air but would never admit to it. As soon as he took control his brain seemed to seize up. I tried to help him as much as possible outside the normal training programme. Always when we returned to Oxford after a days flying at Staverton, I would let O'Kolo sit next to me and fly the aeroplane so that he would have the benefit of the extra flying without it counting against his course training.

Then the unbelievable happened…There was one very ominous flash in the pan when I thought O'Kolo had finally cracked it. The average time to reach first solo standard in a basic nose wheel aeroplane is between ten to fifteen total hours flying. Having completed around fifty hours dual flying training, Mr O'Kolo surprised me by making three unprompted safe circuits and landings. So it was now or never. I was faced with an unenviable decision. Was he safe to send solo or not? Earlier we had carried out the mandatory EFATO practice. So technically there was no reason why he should not go off on his own.

I sat in the cockpit beside him, briefing him fully about the difference in the aircraft's behaviour without the extra weight of myself on board. Finally I said…

'I want you to complete one circuit and landing on your own.'

I could see excitement, or was it terror on O'Kolo's face. I also had difficulty in making sure that he was still concentrating on the important things I was trying to tell him.

'If you are not happy with the approach, or if you bounce on touchdown, open up, and go round the circuit again. Do you understand?'

My black friend had no questions, and I prayed to God that he had taken in everything I said to him. I informed Air Traffic Control that this was a first solo, climbed out of Cherokee G-ATJF, secured the safety catch from the outside, and gave O'Kolo the thumbs up.

Over the years I had sent hundreds of students on their first solo flight and never been wrong in my assessment of their ability. I sincerely hoped that my judgement was correct this time. I watched O'Kolo whilst he meticulously carried out his pre-take-off checks before lining up on the runway. Then, with a roar from the 140hp Lycoming engine, my long-suffering friend was on his way.

It was always my practice to make sure I was out of sight by the time my student was on his final approach to land. The fewer distractions he has at this stage, the better. I walked over to the Flight Hut and sat down to listen to O'Kolo's R/T procedure and was joined by a couple of my instructors who expressed their amazement that O'Kolo had been sent solo. We listened to the small radio monitor we had in the flight hut…

'He should be down wind by now, but he hasn't called.' I said.

I stepped outside the hut scanning the circuit for JF, but it just wasn't anywhere to be seen. Neither could I hear any sound from its engine!

'Where the hell is he?' I said.

All the lads stood outside straining their eyes for some sign of the little blue and white Cherokee.

'I reckon that's the last you'll see of him.' Hugh Bain mumbled tapping his pipe out on the side of the hut.

'I bloody hope not.'

We had a direct telephone link to Air Traffic Control, so I got straight through to the Controller and asked him where G-ATJF was.

'I was just about to ring you Ray. Juliet Fox took off without a word, he continued flying straight ahead until he was out of sight, I have been trying to contact him, but nothing heard.'

There was only one of our aeroplanes in dispersal at the time in which Nils Bartleet was about fly with his student.

'I'll have to hold you up Nils, I need your aeroplane to go and look for JF, he is supposed to be on his first solo, and he's buggered off.'

'Not O'Kolo.'

'Afraid so mate.'

'I'll come with you Ray.'

As I was about to climb into the cockpit, I caught the faint sound of an aeroplane engine way in the distance. Hugh Bain already had the binoculars on him.

'It's Juliet Foxtrot all right mate, looks as if he is coming straight over the top at about a thousand feet, what on earth is the pratt playing at?'

I couldn't believe it. O'Kolo banked the aeroplane this way and that, obviously looking for the airfield.

We all watched speechless as O'Kolo took several minutes to sort out his version of a circuit. Finally, he commenced a steep diving turn lining up with the runway about two and a half miles out and far too low! I was on the tie line to air traffic control in a flash.

'Tell that bloody idiot to overshoot and go round again Mike before he hits something.'

'OK Ray, he's just called finals to land, I reckon he's down to about 200 ft'

Through the telephone I could hear the controller's voice instructing Juliet Foxtrot to overshoot from the approach and go round again, but I didn't hear any acknowledgement from the aircraft. The Controller called JF again but there was no response.

I watched horrified as O'Kolo lowered full flap and slowly disappeared from my sight.

Suddenly there was a roar from the Cherokee's engine and JF reappeared in a steep staggering climb still with full flaps lowered! The aircraft must have been very close to stalling when O'Kolo levelled off at about 500 ft.

After an alarming swish-back approach, JF crossed over the airfield boundary, almost taking the fence with him.

'Shit, that *was* close.'

JF hopped down the runway in a series of spectacular bounces, eventually coming to a standstill with a screech and a puff of blue smoke from the tyres.

Unfortunately it didn't end there. O'Kolo, no doubt ecstatic at still being alive, decided not to backtrack and turned off the runway onto the grass, straight into the middle of a bunch of yellow danger flags marking a large patch of soft mud.

'Well done,' another of Hugh's sarcastic remarks.

I was sure O'Kolo would realise he was stuck in the mud and shutdown the engine, but I should have known better, my infamous student was oblivious to the problem and decided he was going to be a "Press-on regardless" type. Opening the throttle to full power he foolishly attempted to taxi JF out of the mud bowl. Instructors and students all started out across the airfield at great pace, waving their arms and shouting in an effort to stop O'Kolo from damaging the aircraft.

I was almost up to JF, it's engine roaring away flat out, when I stopped short in my tracks. My heart sank as I saw the aircraft slowly disappearing in a misty fountain of muddy water, gradually changing its colour from white and blue to sludge brown.

Helped by all the lads on the ground at the time, we eventually dragged JF out of the mud and pushed it back to dispersal with my student still inside the cockpit.

Inwardly exploding I was ready to deal severely with O'Kolo on the spot. Then, to my surprise, he jumped from the mud stained cockpit and ran up to me, flung his arms around my neck and, to my astonishment, started kissing me on the cheek!

'I told you I could do it sir, I told you, … thank you sir, thank you very much'… and so it went on!

A sideways glance at my lot whilst all this was going on said it all.

Hugh Bain had to put his oar in.

'Bloody touching that.' He muttered sucking deeply on his pipe.

The rather sad, although predictable ending to all this was O'Kolo was never sent solo again. I spent several more hours on the circuit with him, but the poor chap just wasn't up to it. He was I'm sure quite a brilliant lad academically, he just wasn't cut out to fly aeroplanes. On the one day he did go solo he met every requirement for me to send him off. I had hoped, like so many students, his first solo would be the turning point from which he would never look back. But this was not to be. Within two weeks he was packed, and on his way home to South Africa. He shook hands with me and left the airfield in tears, a very sad and disappointed young man, and although there was nothing more I could do, I felt in some way that I had let him down.

Flying was pretty routine for a bit, then on the 9th August 1963, I was asked to fly over a farm in Buckinghamshire to take some aerial photographs carrying a photographer from one of the national newspapers.

It was about 9am in the morning when the message came through from Ops. They also informed me that it was quite an urgent flight, so could I be ready to take-off in thirty minutes. I decided to take the Cherokee Six G-ATES for the job as it had a stretched fuselage that was capable of carrying six passengers, also the rear door could be removed easily for filming purposes.

Soon after 9.30am a chap arrived from the national press. Whilst I was helping him to load his equipment into the aircraft, John Pooley our Flight Ops. Manager, came running out to the aircraft to ask if we could take a film crew with us consisting of two men plus their equipment. The newspaper guy didn't seem too keen at first, but the thought of sharing the cost of the flight softened his displeasure considerably. The film crew, who turned out to be from BBC TV News, must have already been in the operations room because they joined us within minutes.

I was bursting to know what all the fuss was about. The newspaper photographer handed me a map with the precise location and name of a farm clearly circled in red ink. It read "Leatherslade Farm".

I was informed that an armed robbery had taken place and over two and a half million pounds in used notes had been taken from a train. Initially the robber's had taken the money to Leatherslade Farm where they hid out for a short while.

That was one hell of a lot of money in those days, probably equivalent to more than ten million pounds today.

We arrived over Leatherslade Farm at fifteen hundred feet, the place appeared to be buzzing with police cars. Flashing blue lights also marked where the approach roads had been blocked off by other police vehicles. I also noticed that there was a fire engine and ambulance in attendance. The BBC cameraman told me that there had been a fire at the farm, but from the air there was no obvious sign of damage. The photographer took his pictures, and the film crew asked me to make several runs over the site. In no time we were on our way back to the airport, the lads on board anxious to meet their deadlines.

Soon after the flight, several of us crammed ourselves into the Chief Engineers office to hear the news on his portable radio. We listened with great interest to the details of an armed robbery that had taken place on the Glasgow to London Royal Mail Train at a place called Bridego Bridge, North London. Afterwards Land Rovers transported the money, all two and a half million pounds of it, in 121 mailbags to the gang's hideout at Leatherslade Farm, which happened to be just a few miles from our airfield.

One thing that made my ears prick up was some lucky chap had found a suitcase stuffed full of pound notes in a telephone kiosk near to Leatherslade Farm. The remarks made by some of the instructors when the news reader went on to say that the finder of the suitcase had handed it over to the local police station, were quite unprintable.

Having marked the farm on my map, I noted that the area around Leatherslade Farm was very interesting. In my opinion offering many good places to hide further quantities of money from the robbery!

That evening, after the cessation of flying, myself and John Mercer, a fellow instructor and a great friend of mine, set off towards Leatherslade Farm in my car. It was still daylight when we parked near to the area that I had marked on my map as an excellent place for the robber's to have hidden some of the stolen cash. There was a security zone fenced off in day-glow tape near, but that didn't trouble us, I was convinced there would be "hidden treasure" in a large refuse dump surrounded by trees quite close to the Farm. John and I slipped quietly through the trees, climbed a small fence and approached the rubbish dump. The waste disposal site was much larger than it appeared to be from the air. It looked, and certainly smelt like it was still in regular use.

We rummaged around furtively for a while keeping our voices down to a minimum in case police guards were still in the area. There were stacks of the usual day-to-day rubbish on the outskirts of the pit, but nothing much of interest to us. Then my eyes focused on a newish looking suitcase smack bang in the middle of the dump half hidden by what appeared to be an old tarpaulin. There was no doubt in our minds that this was it and, working on the basis of finder's keepers, we would soon be rich!

I slithered down the filthy side of the very smelly pit, finally clambering over all sorts of obnoxious objects in order to make directly for the case. John stayed on the edge of the pit keeping an eye out for anyone approaching. When I finally reached the case I found it was locked, and very heavy to lift. I could feel my heart pumping in my ears with excitement as I stumbled back up the sides of the pit towards John, dragging the case with me.

I thought I detected a look of disgust on John's face as I sat down next to him smelling a little pungent. But I was more interested in the case and its contents. We had to make up our minds what to do next, i.e. whether to force open the case there and then, or alternatively try to get it back to the car without being spotted. We decided on the former. Breaking into the case whilst trying to make as little noise as possible proved to be more difficult than anticipated. However, after searching around in the stinking pit again, I came across an old bed rail. It was far too long and clumsy, but under the circumstances it had to do as a lever. After a struggle, one of the locks broke open with a clonk. We looked around to make sure we were not being observed, both feeling somewhat guilty, although at that stage it was true to say that we had done nothing wrong. John, under the prevailing circumstances, decided to keep as far away from me as practicable. I levered the lid up as far as I could without breaking the second lock. John peered inside.

We must have looked funny, secretly peering into the suitcase packed full of old newspapers, women's magazines and innumerable creepy crawlies. We were so hacked off, that we didn't bother to look any further in the dump. I crawled out smelling very nasty indeed. In fact I smelt so badly that John could hardly bring himself to speak to me at all, he just sat there with his head stuck out of the car window taking deep breaths. I was a bit hurt about that; after all it was me that had to do the slithering around in all that muck and squalor whilst he just sat there keeping watch and smelling like a primrose!

What would we have done if we had really found thousands of pounds tucked away in that suitcase? To be honest I don't know. But it would have been bloody exciting to find out.

CHAPTER 32

Red Flare.

Every now again something would happen slightly out of the ordinary. In fact life was never dull at Kidlington Airfield. First solos were frequently celebrated at the bar after flying. Parties were organised for the most outlandish of reasons. Then there were the odd happenings that were not exactly celebratory, just amusing.

For instance I remember back in my early days of instructing, an incident that took place on the airfield that involved Ben, our much loved Chief Air Traffic Controller.

Ben, an excellent Controller, who was now approaching retirement age, had been our air traffic control officer for many years, dating back to the days when only the club's Tiger Moths graced the circuit at Kidlington. Instructions in those days were relayed to aircraft by reading the Signals Square, flashing Aldis Lamp signals, or flares from the controller's pistol. Later, when a radio equipment was installed at the airfield, Ben's dulcet tones over the R/T brought comfort to pilots requiring a QDM or QGH let down whilst returning to Oxford in inclement weather.

One late autumn afternoon, Ben was the instigator of one of those instances that didn't seem all that funny at the time, but looking back on what happened always brings a smile to my face.

Some of the training at Kidlington was now being carried out in fully radioed Piper aircraft, although we still operated three Tiger Moths, two of which had so far not been equipped with radio transceivers. Anyway, on this particular occasion I was flying with my student in Tiger Moth G-ALNA. This aeroplane had not been fitted with radio so we were using the Gosport Tube for relaying messages between student and instructor and observing ground signals displayed in the signals square near to the control tower.

Returning from a cross country flight we were flying at two thousand feet and positioning ourselves overhead the airfield in order to read the signals square and ascertain the runway in use. I shouted down the Gosport Tube to my student Tim Olveson, informing him that it appeared to be a left-hand circuit on runway zero three.

We let-down on the dead side of the runway and continued round the circuit without incident until we were three quarters of the way down the final approach to land. Suddenly I spotted another Tiger Moth approaching to land head-on from the opposite direction. I immediately instructed Tim to overshoot from the approach. As we did so, the pilot of the other Tiger Moth had obviously seen us heading for him and also decided to overshoot from his approach. As we climbed steeply to the right I peered down at our Air Traffic building and was astonished to see that the inside of the tower was apparently on fire, glowing bright red with clouds of white smoke billowing from an open window! I was somewhat bewildered by all this until my perceptive student in the rear cockpit yelled out that he thought we were the ones that were landing in the wrong direction, basing his judgment on the direction the smoke was drifting from the fire in the tower. I looked down at the windsock that hung limply with insufficient wind to lift it, and also noted that tee in the signals square was definitely in our favour. But to be safe I followed the other Tiger who was already on the approach to land again. By this time the Station Fire Engine was doing its stuff extinguishing the fire in the control tower.

Running across to Flight Ops. I caught up with Frank Thomas who was the instructor in the other Tiger Moth.

'What's going on Frank?' I asked.

'You may well ask mate. I was landing on runway two-one as instructed by Ben, when I saw you approaching in the opposite direction on zero three.'

As Frank spoke I realised that his Tiger Moth had recently been fitted with radio, and that he had obviously been instructed to land on runway two-one, whilst we, without radio, were obeying the signals area which indicated that runway zero-three was in use. I told Frank and he said...

'I gathered that something like that must have happened Ray, but what the hell went wrong in the Tower, it appeared to blow up!'

All was made clear when we walked into the operations room and saw our Controller Ben Boult sitting in a chair, his face blackened by smoke, and obviously suffering from shock.

'Whatever happened Ben?'

'I'm sorry Old Pal,' he said spluttering and coughing, 'I cleared Frank to land into wind on runway 21, and was about to pop downstairs to change the signals tee when I suddenly saw you half way down the final approach of runway 03. I honestly didn't see you until the last minute.'

'I thought that was probably the case Ben, but what happened inside the tower?' I asked.

'I went to fire a red Very-light to warn you Ray, but missed the open window and hit the frame instead. It flew around the inside of the Control Room like a blinking fireball, setting light to everything in it's path, it's lucky that no-one was hurt.'

Frank wasn't amused and commented that it could have been fatal if two solo students had been on the circuit instead of instructors. It certainly wasn't funny at the time, but I must admit recalling the incident now does make me smile.

Ben Boult was a lovely person and a good controller. He did his part in World War Two serving as a navigator on Sunderland Flying Boats. He was also a great pianist, and loved playing the old wartime tunes whenever we got together for a jar or two in the Club Bar.

Sadly, not long after the above incident took place, dear old Ben was taken ill and died. I will always remember him as one of the nicest chaps I ever had the privilege of knowing.

CHAPTER 33.

Christmas Past.

There is always plenty of time in hospital to reminisce about past experiences, especially for those of us who were unfortunately destined to spend many months or years recovering. Occasionally something would happen that triggers off a memory of some kind, and in this instance it was the sight of snow falling outside the window of 'C' ward that reminded me of December 1965, the worst Christmas I had ever spent.

The shuddering depths of a severe Winter gripped the airfield. A biting wind swept across the runways bringing with it the first sprinkling of snow. Everyone was looking forward to the staff party that was being organised this year by the engineering lads and planned to take place a couple of days before Christmas Eve in number two hangar. Most of our students were preparing to go home for Christmas, leaving a few Scotsmen and our overseas students still resident on the airfield.

We had all been saddened by the news that our senior instructor Bill Jordon would be leaving Oxford after the Christmas holidays to take up a new post as Head of the Aviation Division for British Steel. He was to be replaced by Eddy Claxton, one of our flight managers who was an ex RAF Transport Command Pilot before joining the flying staff at Oxford.

I was destined to be on duty for the whole of the Christmas period. A notice had appeared on the crew-room notice board asking for a volunteer to act as duty instructor over the Christmas holidays. Things weren't going to be the same for me this year anyway. My little Son was going to spend Christmas with his mother at her parent's house in Brackley. Also Valerie was going to Lincolnshire to visit her parents, and would not be back until after New Years day. So I was quite happy to stay on at the airfield as duty instructor, after all I did actually live on the airport, so it was really no big deal. There would be no flying for five days and the airport was officially closed. My job would be purely to make sure that nothing untoward took place on the airfield during the holiday period. There would of course still be security staff on duty who would be accountable to me in the event of any problems arising.

The plan was that on Christmas Eve I would have an evening meal with the Bursar and his wife, and later join the students for a few drinks in the Clubhouse. Then I would spend a cosy Christmas Day on my own in the caravan, nice and warm watching television and enjoying a glass or two of sherry. I had a cooked chicken ready for warming up in the electric oven, plus tinned peas, tinned carrots, tinned potatoes, and a tinned Christmas Pudding stored away in the caravan, together with stacks of mince pies and a fine Christmas Cake that Valerie had made for me, so all in all it promised to be an unusual, but rather pleasant "bachelor type" Christmas Day. Unfortunately it was anything but!

The hangar party turned out to be a great success. The engineering lads had painstakingly decorated the hangar with thousands of fairy lights. An enormous Christmas tree stood next to an old fashioned type bar with a thatched canopy that the boys had constructed in one corner of the hangar. One of our Chipmunk aeroplanes had been hoisted onto a specially built platform, and lit by spot lights forming a wonderful centrepiece to the dancing area. A local dance band played wartime favourites until the early hours, and a heartfelt speech by Tony Marchant, one of the engineers, wishing all the flying staff happy landings in the New Year, rounded off a wonderful evening.

I awoke to a cold Christmas Eve. Scraping the frost from inside my bedroom window I could see the snow that had fallen the previous day, now appeared as sheet ice. I stoked up the little stove and before long the caravan was as warm as toast. At lunchtime I slithered my way along the slippery roads in the old Jag to visit our local hostelry 'The Bunch of Grapes' a pleasant little Inn about a mile or so from the airfield. The bar was packed with customers heartily singing Christmas Carols and swilling down generous quantities of hot punch served up by the landlord's wife. Pine logs crackled and burned in the old inglenook fireplace, and the expensive smell of cigar smoke completed a joyous festive atmosphere.

I stayed there until closing time. The journey back was quite tricky. Even the few paces from the Pub door to the car were difficult to negotiate on the black ice that had formed on the sloping pavement. I was deeply grateful that I only had a short distance to drive back to the airfield. Even so, the car skidded across the road a couple of times bouncing off the grass verges and sliding gracefully sideways down the road for a few yards. Fortunately there was very little other traffic and I managed to get back to the caravan without causing any serious damage. I sobered up with a strong cup of hot tea and a couple of whisky chasers, finally snuggling up in my favourite chair to enjoy forty winks.

I awoke to a frightful gale that raged furiously causing the caravan to shudder on its jacks. Outside the storm howled angrily round nearby hangars causing them to creek and groan in protest. Before long the lights in the caravan began flickering, but the wood burning stove was doing its stuff, with the electric water pump circulating the almost boiling water keeping the radiators nice and hot. I just had time to shave and smarten up before joining the Bursar and his wife for an evening meal.

The black ice coupled with a gale force wind made the short walk from my caravan to the resident's hall a severe test of ones agility.

After an excellent meal with Barry and his wife Jean, the three of us set off for the Students Bar to join some of the resident lads for a jar or two. One of the chaps who was observing a game of darts in the bar finished up in the care of the Bursar's wife who fortunately was a trained nurse. Apparently, amidst shouts of 'bulls-eye' from the rest of the students, a dart bounced off the board and pierced the poor sod in his starboard testicle!

For me, memories of the final part of the evening seem to have faded into a pleasurable alcoholic mist, but I do remember waking up on Christmas morning shivering with cold and feeling like death itself. Outside the wind was howling around the caravan and there was a metallic clattering sound that seemed to be coming from something on top of the caravan roof. The central heating pump was still switched on but I couldn't hear it running. The radiators were stone cold and ice had formed on the inside of the window panes. Fearing the worst I tried the light switches, and they didn't work either. I shot into the kitchen to investigate the situation inside the fuse box, hoping to see that the wind had caused the main circuit breaker to pop out, but the main fuse and all the other fuses were in place. Obviously the electricity cable serving the caravan must have been severed by the storm. With no electricity to operate the central heating pump, the only heat was from the small wood-burning stove that was unfortunately situated in the entrance area by the door. To add to my misery the water supply to the caravan was frozen solid, and our one and only kettle was electric. Hopefully the contents of the small refrigerator should be OK as the temperature in the caravan wasn't much higher than inside the fridge.

With no electricity I searched around miserably in the grim atmosphere to find out if we had any candles to cheer the place up a bit. 'Merry bloody Christmas Ray' I mumbled to myself.

I had a painful shave in what was left of a bowl of washing-up water left from the evening before and warmed up in a small saucepan balanced on the top of the circular stove. Breakfast consisted of a slice of tinned ham between two slices of bread and very lumpy butter, all washed down with a glass of soda water and a couple of much needed Asprins.

Wrapped up and looking rather like a poor excuse for an Eskimo, I stepped out into the icy blizzard to collect a few logs from the wood box. Even that was a problem as the lid of the box was frozen down solid. In due course I managed to lever the lid open using the flat edge of a garden spade.

Later in the morning I made my way over to the Residential Wing only to find that they too had no electricity and were in a very similar predicament.

I resigned myself to the inevitable, returning to the caravan, cold, fed-up and bloody miserable. Fortunately I kept the stove going and managed to heat up a tin mug full of snow to make a warm cup of tea. It took ages because the top of the central heating stove was sloping and I had to hold the mug upright with one edge resting on the top. The only warmth in the caravan was limited to the small porch area where the stove was situated. Apart from the dim glow of the stove in the porch, and one flickering candle cut down to wedge in the top of an empty beer bottle, the atmosphere in the caravan was cold, gloomy and dismal. In the end I decided to spend the rest of Christmas day in bed. I was so cold; I just lay there shivering unable to sleep. Then I remembered the bottle that cheers, and consumed a teacup or two of Whisky, and slept reasonable well for a while.

I woke up around ten o'clock at night absolutely frozen to the bone. The wind had calmed down and it was pitch dark. I fumbled around hoping to find another candle, but I was out of luck. Then I remembered there was a torch in the glove box of my car.

With the garage doors wide open I sat in the back of the Jag with the car rug wrapped around me, the engine running and the heater on full blast whilst listening to Carols on the car radio and sipping whisky from the bottle. I wondered what my little son Eddy was doing; this was the first Christmas he had spent without seeing his Daddy. I don't think I have ever felt so miserable in my life.

Boxing Day saw the electricity restored to the buildings on the airfield with the exception of my caravan. It turned out that the noise I had heard banging on the roof on Christmas morning was a severed electricity cable swinging about in the wind. I promised myself that I would never volunteer for Christmas duty again.

CHAPTER 34.

Sheila Scott.

During the last year of my time in hospital, I decided to make a few notes about some of my more interesting experiences as an instructor. Later, when I decided to write this book, I was able to tie up these notes with the actual times, dates and aircraft recorded in my log books.

Our newly appointed C/I, Captain Ed Claxton, Known to all as "big-ed"! was on the telephone....

'I would like you to make arrangements to take one of your instructors with you and fly over to Brussels to collect a Cherokee 140. It has been purchased on behalf of "Wills Tobacco Company" It's waiting to be picked up from Gosselies Airport and brought to CSE for its C of A check. I would like it back here as soon as possible Ray.'

The weather forecast for the next few days was reasonable, so I decided to take Tony Smallwood, now known to all as "Splinters", with me and leave for Belgium early the following morning. Tony was a very keen young man. His ambition was to become an airline pilot, so he had taken up instructing as a means of gaining experience and at the same time earn some money to help towards paying for his CPL training later. The trip to Belgium would also be good experience for him. Tony was already proving to be an excellent instructor. I had flown with several of his students, flight-testing them for the issue of their pilots licence at the end of their training and, without exception, I was impressed by the high standard of airmanship all Tony's students had attained. (As it happened, many years later, Tony eventually became Chief Line Captain for British Midland Airways).

On the morning of the 20th of September 1966, having collected some Belgium franks for expenses from the accounts office, we took off from

Kidlington at 10am and climbed out over Oxfordshire in cloudless skies and excellent visibility. We were flying in Cherokee G-ATTK heading for Gatwick Airport in order to clear customs. The aeroplane we were about to collect was not equipped with radio, so we carried the company's portable VHF set with us for use in the aircraft we were collecting.

We cleared customs at Gatwick, made our sea crossing, and were in the circuit at Gosselies Airport by 13.30 hrs. As we were landing I noticed an enormous crater surrounded by bright red flags just off the threshold of the duty runway. Later we were told that an American Star Fighter had taken off, pulled up immediately into a loop and crashed vertically at the end of the runway. A runaway tail-plane was thought to have been the cause of the accident. Unfortunately the pilot was unable to eject and was killed instantly.

A Belgium Customs Officer dressed rather like a 1950s AA motorcyclist, in dark grey uniform and peaked cap, staggered towards us as we taxied into the dispersal area. I didn't understand a word he said, but I did notice the distinct, and very strong smell of alcohol on his breath. I also noticed that he carried a pistol in a holster attached to his belt. He started to get a bit hot under the collar with me because I was apparently not doing whatever it was he wanted me to do. Fortunately at that moment a young man came over and addressed us in perfect English…

'You must be the pilots that have flown over from England to collect Romeo Tango and fly it back to Oxford?

We shook hands and he told us that he had been instructed to look after us during our stay.

Our host then attempted to deal with the inebriated Customs Officer.

'He wants to see your papers, and asks if you are carrying any cargo in your aircraft?'

Our papers were in order, but there seemed to be a problem with the portable radio we had brought over to use in the aircraft we were collecting. The Customs Officer said we did not have the necessary paperwork for the radio to enter Belgium, as it was in effect cargo. This also meant that we could not take it out of the country with us when we left unless the appropriate documents were produced. With the help of the gentleman that met us and was now acting as our interpreter, we tried to explain to the customs man that the radio was purely part of our standard equipment. Unfortunately "Staggering Stanley"(SS) as we named him, would have none of it. He insisted that the radio must not be taken out of the airport without the necessary paperwork. How the hell do we do that I asked. Our host, having spoken to the customs officer, called me to one side and said...

'You are permitted to leave the radio locked in your aircraft overnight, but you cannot take-off with it on board tomorrow without producing the necessary documentation.'

I nodded in agreement to the SS chap and walked over to the car that had been sent to take us to a hotel. On the way our host came up with a suggestion that I was convinced would never work...

'Wait until after ten o'clock tomorrow morning before arriving at the airport, by that time the Customs Officer will be in the pub just across the road. It's a well known fact that he always gets a few pints down him every morning. If you are quick you can submit your flight plan and take-off before he gets back and realises you are on your way!'

'Supposing he gets back before we obtain taxi clearance and takes a pot shot at us with that pistol he was carrying' I said more as a joke than anything.

Our colleague advised us that he would hardly be likely to do that; it just meant that we would have the radio confiscated until they sorted things out with Oxford. In the end I agreed to give it a try although I didn't think we had a cat in hells chance of getting away with it.

When we arrived at the hotel, our host asked if we would like him to pick us up later that evening and take us to a local night club. This seemed to be an excellent idea at the time.

I think it best not to go into detail about what happened that night. I must admit I have very little recollection of what exactly did take place. I have blurred images of dancing with partly dressed young ladies and drinking large amounts of various beverages in highly decorated glasses. I also have vague memories of trying to encourage Tony to get out of the lift when we returned to the hotel, all he wanted to do was travel up and down the various floors singing unprintable ditties at the top of his voice.

The next morning Tony and I sat at breakfast feeling grim and wondering if we would get away with dodging the customs man back at the airport. Searching our pockets thoroughly, we just managed to scrape up sufficient Belgium Francs between us to pay our hotel bill.

A car arrived to take us back to the airport. On arrival we hastily thanked the driver and, still suffering from the effects of the previous evening's entertainment, headed at speed for the airport toilets.

An elderly woman sat on a chair just inside the entrance to the men's toilet demanding to be paid before allowing us to proceed. Feeling rather desperate, I left Tony fumbling for small change and ran through the open toilet door closely followed by the female attendant who, jabbering away furiously, entered the cubicle with me and continued to tap me on the shoulder whilst I was trying to relieve myself.

'For Christ's sake give the woman some money Tony before I burst!'

Having downed a mug of strong coffee in the airport lounge we walked over to Air Traffic to file a joint VFR flight plan. From the tower I could see that G-ATRT, the Cherokee I was to fly back to Oxford, had been conveniently positioned next to G-ATTK, so transferring the portable radio shouldn't take many seconds. It was almost ten o'clock, and there was no sign of the customs officer. Our escort from the previous evening's entertainment arrived on the scene looking like walking death. He forced a rather painful smile, and informed me that both aircraft had been refuelled. Handing me the documents for Romeo Tango, he wished us both good luck and left in a hurry.

I could see the Inn on the far side of the main road quite clearly from the dispersal area and on the stroke of ten, as if by magic, the man from customs suddenly appeared from the terminal, hurried out through the main gates and entered the pub. A winked at Tony…

'Come on old chap, we're off.'

We transferred the radio in seconds and climbed aboard our respective aeroplanes.

I gave Tony the thumbs up sign and both our aircraft's engines started without trouble.

As previously arranged, we checked out with ground control and moved out of the dispersal area straight away, hoping that our friend from Customs was still enjoying his pint, and not looking out of the pub window.

Within minutes we took off in formation, Tony leading in Tango Kilo. His aeroplane had ADF and VOR Radio Navigational Aids, so it was arranged that I would carry out the radio procedures on the portable set whilst still on the Gosselies frequency, after that Tony would take over the transmissions in TK until we called Gatwick on their approach frequency.

As soon as we had cleared the Gosselies circuit, I informed the Controller that we were changing to an onward radio frequency; purposely without specifying which frequency we intended to use. The reason for this, although very naughty and by no means the correct procedure, was to make sure we could not be recalled to the airport.

Flying in close formation with Tony, I saw him look back at me for the pre-arranged signal to change frequency to London Information. But I purposely held back for a few minutes to continue listening out on Gosselie Approach. Sure enough, as predicted, the radio crackled into life....

'Golf Alpha Tango Tango Kilo, this is Gosselie Approach, do you read me, over?'

Tony looked back at me through the perspex screen of his small cockpit. I shook my head holding a finger to my mouth; Tony nodded whilst we both maintained radio silence.

'Tango Kilo... if you read me, please return to the airfield, Customs wish to speak to you.'

There were no further calls from the Gosselie and the rest of the flight was without incident. We landed at Gatwick, cleared customs, downed a quick cup of coffee, and flew on to Oxford, landing back at Kidlington at 14.10 hrs.

All was well, or so I thought, until the following morning, when the phone rang and I was summoned to Rex Smith's office. On my way over to the main office block, I reasoned that the purpose for Rex wishing to see me was possibly to thank us for getting the job done quickly, or maybe there had been some repercussions over the portable radio, and the Belgium Customs were out for my blood.

Walking into his office, I greeted my boss...

'Good Morning Rex.'

'Good Morning my arse' was the laconic reply.

Under the circumstances I considered it prudent to remain standing.

'If it's about the radio Rex, I can explain.'

'Radio, what Radio?'

I started to reply, but Rex cut in...

'It's nothing to do with a radio my son, it's these bloody expenses.'

'What expenses?' I replied pathetically.

'Where did you stay, the Belgium equivalent to Buckingham Palace?'

'Why, what's wrong?'

'WHAT'S WRONG?' Rex exploded.

He pushed a piece of paper towards me on his desk.

'THAT'S WHAT'S BLOODY WRONG.'

It was a note from Gerry Ferric our Accountant Director, which briefly stated the amount of Belgium francs we had taken with us, and the amount we had handed back on our return.

Tapping a pencil impatiently on his desk, Rex listened whilst I feebly explained that we had been taken to a Night Club. I had to admit that neither Tony nor I had any idea of the exact exchange rate at the time. Trying desperately to break down the icy atmosphere, I smiled saying...

'After a couple of drinks Rex, it didn't seem to matter very much about the exchange rates.'

But the look on Rex Smith's face made it quite clear that if it didn't matter at the time it certainly mattered now. I dispelled any ideas that I may have had about passing the matter off lightly with a few jokes, especially when I learned that we had spent over £300 in one evening on entertainment.

'My guess is that you two buggers were paying about ten to fifteen pounds for a pint of …God knows what it was, or even as much as twenty quid for a bloody whisky. If there had been any women involved, I expect Oxford Air Training School would be in the hands of the official receiver by now!'

At that stage I decided the best course of action was to keep quiet.

'I blame you Ray, young Smallwood is a member of your flight, and you are responsible for what happened. I'm stopping this money out of both your salaries; I will leave it to you to explain the situation to Smallwood.

I apologised to Rex… Did I detect the merest impression of a smile on the boss's face as I left his office?…NOT ON YOUR LIFE.

Smoking is totally repellent to me. I just hate the awful smell cigarettes produce. Therefore under these circumstances it is almost impossible to believe that I appeared on thousands of advertisements for Wills Cigarettes. Large, full colour advertising placards were distributed to practically every Public House, Hotel, Tobacconist Shop and General Stores in the country with my face on it. This is how it came about…

W.D. & H.O. Wills Ltd; the internationally known tobacco company, decided to run a competition as part of a national advertising campaign for Wills cigarettes. The contest was open to anyone over the age of eighteen; the outright winner would not only receive a full course of flying lessons, but also win a brand new Piper Cherokee 140 aeroplane.

The competition, probably one of the most impressive advertising campaigns ever launched in the tobacco industry, ran for a number of weeks. A shortlist of qualifying competitors was prepared and those selected were invited to take a flying aptitude test. The outright winner selected from the tests was then awarded a full course of flying training. Having completed the course and qualified for the issue of a private pilot's licence, the winner finally became the proud owner of a brand new Piper Cherokee. The award ceremony was to be held at Oxford Airport, and the actual aircraft to be won turned out to be G–ATRT, the Cherokee I collected from Belgium.

Whilst the competition was in progress, the prize aircraft was completely serviced for the issue of a British C of A. Radio equipment was installed, and the aircraft was re-sprayed in the Wills Tobacco Ltd. colours with their company crest displayed on both sides of the tail fin.

I carried out the C of A air test on G-ATRT, and shortly after the aircraft was rolled out in its new 'Wills' colours, I was asked to fly the aeroplane again whilst air-to-air photographs were taken by Aviation Photographer Peter Hewitt.

The photographs were taken in bright sunshine above a snowy-white layer of stratus cloud. The actual photograph selected for the advertisement was so distinct that I was easily recognisable as the pilot grinning away in the cockpit. Tens of thousands of posters and placards were produced and distributed to outlets throughout the UK. Ironic that the person appearing on the advertisement for Wills Cigarettes absolutely detested smoking.

In total contrast on the 22nd October 1966, I was asked to fly a reporter and cameraman over a small mining village near Merthyr Tydfil in South Wales. We had to film the awful Aberfan disaster after a huge waste tip slid down the side of a mountain destroying a farm cottage and crushing Pantglas Junior School. A total of 144 people died in the incident, 116 of them were young children. It was a dreadful sight that will remain in my memory forever.

The day to day work of the basic training wing was usually intense. Getting our short course students out on time was sometimes quite a problem. For instance ATC and CCF scholarship students were only given twenty-eight days to complete a thirty hour course. New intakes would arrive every fortnight, which meant that we always had two courses running at the same time. One intake would be half way through the course, when the next intake arrived to start training. The trouble would start if there was a spate of bad weather and the aircraft were grounded. Cadet contracts had to be completed during the Summer months, so our only chance to catch up if we experienced a spell of bad weather, was to continue our flying until sunset when the weather was OK. The job had to be done, so very often this meant flying until ten o'clock in the evening. Fortunately for us my section was occasionally allocated other types of flying, which helped ease the pressure of continuous basic training. These jobs were sometimes very interesting, and often quite amusing.

For example, I was occasionally called upon to fly with Miss Sheila Scott, famous for her record breaking flights during the 1960s.

Miss Scott, flying one or other of her two very fast Piper Comanche aeroplanes, broke many of the flying records set up in the 1930's by spirited young ladies who flew mainly in open cockpit biplanes with no radio and nothing but a map and compass to help them navigate over land and sea, sometimes encountering the most atrocious weather conditions.

Records are there to be broken however, and Sheila, flying the same routes achieved considerably faster times, consequently breaking the records set by the young lady pioneers in the distant past. But that of course is the way records are broken in practically all professions. As time goes on machines become technically more proficient, human beings become fitter and live longer and so on. So all the records of yesteryear are bound to be broken in almost every sporting profession. Even so I have to say my heart and admiration goes out to those pioneers who set up the first records in machines vastly inferior to those of today. My personal opinion, though others may well disagree, is that record-breaking flights achieved whilst seated in the comfort of a heated cabin, flying a modern-day aeroplane equipped with the latest high-tech radio navigational aids, and capable of top speeds in excess of 200mph, can hardly be compared to the achievements of those courageous young ladies flying in the open cockpit "string-bags" capable of speeds up to 70 or 80 mph in the 1920's and 1930's.

I first met Sheila Scott in 1965 when she arrived at Oxford Air Training School with the intention of taking a flying instructors course. Her instructor at the time was a great friend of mine by the name of John Bennett, an ex RAF QFI. After a while Miss Scott decided to discontinue with the course as, in her own words, "I don't think I am cut out to be an instructor, I have totally the wrong temperament for the job.".

During her flying career Sheila flew solo round the world, and in 1971 she was the first lady pilot to fly over the North Pole in a single-engine aeroplane.

I flew with Sheila on several occasions, usually in my capacity as a flying instructor carrying out radio navigational training in her Piper Comanche 206, and also her very fast Comanche 400. The paintwork on "Myth Two", Sheila's Piper Comanche 206, was interesting. Part of the fuselage and the tops of both wings were inscribed with messages of goodwill from well-wishers worldwide, the customs of various countries being reflected in their messages. One rather antisocial message read, *"I hope you crash"* which I am told is a metaphor for wishing her good luck, although I didn't feel too happy flying around with that message scrawled across the wings.

The procedure Sheila adopted whilst preparing for some of her earlier record breaking attempts, was to fly the route initially accompanied by an instructor who would point out various navigational aids and procedures to be used, then at a later date, she would fly the same route again solo on an official record breaking attempt. If she completed the flight in a shorter time than her 1930's predecessor, Sheila rightfully claimed the record!

On one unforgettable occasion I was destined to be the person accompanying Sheila on the practise flight for one of her shorter record-breaking attempts. She had to take-off from Ronaldsway Airport in the Isle of Man and fly a course that took her over Dublin and several other locations in Ireland, then cross the Irish sea and over fly designated turning points along the West coast of England, finally returning to land on the Isle of Man at Ronaldsway Airport.

In this instance a soft drinks company sponsored the event, and an appropriate call-sign, "SUNPIP", was allocated to identify the aircraft during the practise run and later during the actual record breaking attempt.

On the morning of the 14th May 1965, I flew her Comanche 400 G-ATDV from Oxford to meet Miss Scott at RAF Northolt London, where a press conference was being held prior to the event.

Having landed I was greeted by the Station Commander.

'Are you anything to do with Miss Scott's flight?' he asked.

I told him I was the instructor designated to fly with her during today's practice flight. He gave out a hearty laugh and said...

'Wait until you meet her manager, he really is something else, rather you than me old lad!'

I was directed to a large room that was being used for a press briefing. On entering I saw Sheila Scott surrounded by reporters, photographers, and a TV crew. A very smartly dressed young man strode up to me and having announced himself to be Miss Scott's Flight Manager, he said...

'Are you the bloke that delivered Miss Scott's aeroplane? I hope the aircraft is spotlessly clean'

His tone of voice annoyed me, so I replied rather abruptly.

'No, I'm Miss Scott's flying instructor.'

He looked at me in disbelief, I'm sure he thought that Sheila was born with wings, and simply zoomed out from her mother's womb with the grace of a Swallow.

He handed me a piece of paper and said...

'This is the route Miss Scott is required to fly on her record breaking attempt tomorrow, she will carry out a practice run today.'

He strutted off only to return moments later looking even more self-important, blurting out in a voice loud enough for everyone in the room to hear…

'You will fly from here with Miss Scott, and over-fly the Isle of Man which will be the official starting point for tomorrows flight, complete the course with her and return to Northolt and land. Miss Scott will then fly back to Ronaldsway on her own later this evening, and subject to good weather she will make her record attempt tomorrow, her takeoff time will be thirteen hundred hours, that is one o'clock to you. I hope that is quite clear?'

I held back the urge to smack him in the teeth. How on earth Sheila had been persuaded to take on the services of this pompous little prick I'll never know.

Looking across the room to where the media were crowding round Miss Scott and her entourage, my thoughts went back to those far off days when courageous young aviators like Amy Johnson, Amelia Earhart, Jacqueline Batten and Harriet Quimby, first set up these records in the 1930's, flying aeroplanes that were literally held together with wood, and fabric. My God, how things have changed.

I approached the obnoxious Flight Manager and laughingly asked him if he had any ideas of how I was expected to get back to Oxford Airport if Miss Scott was to return solo to Ronaldsway having dropped me off at Northolt?

Not surprisingly he missed the point and arrogantly explained the whole thing again, this time pronouncing each word slowly and precisely, finishing up by asking me if I could understand what he said '*this time.*'

By normal standards my nose is reasonably small, but this nasty little bugger was managing to get right up it. As he strutted off again I had great difficulty preventing myself from kicking him up the arse! Obviously he was a well educated chap, I'll give him that, but his mannerisms and character were totally unsuited to any form of public relations work, and he certainly had a greater opinion of himself than the three wise men had of Jesus.

Time was ticking away. I looked at the crowd surrounding Sheila and decided to edge my way through in order to see if she had prepared a flight plan. After much pushing and shoving I eventually managed to get through to her.

Sheila was clutching a large bouquet of flowers, and curls of blue smoke arose from the cigarette suspended at the end of her long cigarette holder which waggled up and down as she spoke to the reporters.

When I finally caught her eye, she stopped talking to the reporters and seemed pleased to see me. I asked her if she had completed her flight plan, and Hey-Presto, before she had time to answer, her bloody manager appeared from out of the ether and said...

'No need to trouble Miss Scott, pilot. I have prepared the flight plan, which you will have to submit to the control tower when Miss Scott is ready.'

I glanced at Sheila out of the corner of my eye. She knew me well enough to know what was coming. I had to get this pretentious little shit on his own.

'Come with me *Sonny*.' My words were delivered as an abrupt order, not as a request.

The Flight Manager looked a little shocked by my tone of voice, but wisely followed me to the adjoining flight planning room. I closed the door behind and as I turned to face the young man he started to say something, but I cut in sharply...

'Shut your trap for a moment and listen to me. You appear to be misinformed, so allow me to put you straight once and for all. I am here to accompany Miss Scott on this flight in an advisory capacity as her flying instructor, as such I monitor her flying, advise her on any navigational matters appropriate to the flight. I attend to any special clearances we have to obtain for her to complete this flight with the minimum of interference, and she makes out her own flight plan which I will check. YOU my son, will keep out of my way from now on, is that clear?'

I took the flight plan from his hand, and tossed it into a waste bin under the map table, and left the cretin standing there speechless.

After an abundance of photographs had been taken, which thankfully excluded me, Miss Scott made out her flight plan, submitted it to control and we finally took off.

To start with the flight went well. Sheila, a former actress by profession, was a very capable pilot, but anyone who flew with her soon became aware of her neurotic nature. She was a very heavy smoker and frequently lit up whilst flying. I was not keen on this and managed to prevent her from doing so whilst she was flying with me.

With good luck Dolls, strewn over the back seat of the cockpit and a champagne cork swinging away merrily from the compass bracket, we set course to over fly Ronaldsway. A few minutes into the flight Sheila suddenly turned to look behind her and said...

'We're off darling, now be a good boy!'

I was quite surprised, and when I asked her who she was talking to, she pointed to the large toy rabbit sitting upright on the rear seat, and laughingly said...

'Bucktooth, he loves flying , he goes with me everywhere.'

I had to laugh, old Bucktooth was obviously enjoying himself as he had a permanent smile on his face!

In excellent weather we climbed to 2000 ft. and levelled off. Our identification call-sign 'SUNPIP' was supposed to allow us limited privileges during the record breaking attempt planned for the following day, and was also to be used throughout the practice run today.

Our first en-route radio checkpoint was Mersey Radar. So I expected Sheila, who is usually very good with her radio procedures, to say something like … "Mersey Radar this is Golf Alpha Tango Delta Victor, we are a Piper Comanche 400 on a training flight and our identifying call-sign is Sunpip... over." Unfortunately she didn't say that at all. This is my recollection of the radio transmissions that followed. Sheila selected Mersey Radar's frequency and pressing the transmit button she blurted out three words...

'MERSEY RADAR SUNPIP'

There followed a brief silence during which time I imagine the radar controllers looked at each other and said 'What the hell was that?' They then made the following call...

'Aircraft calling Mersey Radar say again your call-sign.'

Sheila speaks again, this time shouting just the one word, very loudly...

'SUNPIP'....

I wished I could have seen the faces of the controllers looking at each other in wonderment, and probably saying, 'Who the F...is SUNPIP?'

Before Mersey Radar had a chance to answer, Sheila burst into a rage and shouted...

'Mersey this is SUNPIP, I'm SHEILA SCOTT, this is a practice world record breaking attempt, you should have been informed about this, and given me my position, wake up for god's sake!'

I winced, and asked Sheila to calm down advising her to use the aircraft's full call sign, but Sheila Scott being Sheila Scott would have none of it. The next message from Mersey Radar was predictable.

'SUNPIP, please use standard R/T procedures and say your full call-sign.'

Sheila, now red in the face, burst into tears. Things had gone far enough so I transmitted our aircraft's call sign and explained the situation to

Mersey Radar, who in fact should have been informed of our flight and call sign. I don't know what they must have thought, as my transmission was punctuated by Sheila sobbing into her microphone. The Controller said that he had not personally been informed of any such call-sign, apologised, and passed our onward clearance.

After that fiasco, Sheila settled down again and the rest of the flight was, by comparison, reasonably uneventful.

When we had completed the course and landed back at Northolt, I was saddened to see Miss Scott's "Flight Manager" running out to the aeroplane. Ignoring me completely, he informed Sheila that the original plans for her to fly back to Ronaldsway straight away had been cancelled. Miss Scott was to stay in London overnight and attend a presentation ceremony, and a charter plane had been laid on to fly her from London Airport to the Isle of Man the following morning. I was to use Sheila's aeroplane to return to Oxford straight away that evening, and reposition the aircraft at Ronaldsway Isle of Man by 10am the following morning. What a cock-up.

So me and old Bucktooth returned to Oxford. The following morning I was told by our controller that the record breaking attempt had been cancelled yet again, this time because of a bad weather forecast, but I was to deliver her aeroplane to Ronaldsway anyway and return by a scheduled flight to Birmingham where I would be met and brought back to Oxford Airport.

I was just about to walk out to the aircraft when Ben, our air traffic controller, telephoned me in my office.

'The authorities at Ronaldsway are on the telephone and want to know your ETA.'

I thought this was a bit unusual, and assumed that Ben was referring to the Isle of Man approach controller. So I told Ben that I would be landing at 10am, and to ask them if they would kindly arrange for the aircraft to be refuelled on arrival...

'I'll pass that on Ray, they sounded a bit concerned mate.'

Seconds later Ben was back on the telephone...

'I passed your ETA Ray, but they said refuelling was nothing to do with them and you'll have to make your own arrangements when you get there.'

'OK Ben, I expect Sheila's Flight Manager has put his spanner in the works!'

I took off in G-ATDV at my scheduled time accompanied by my stuffed friend Bucktooth who was still grinning from ear to ear, and landed at the Isle of Man spot on 10 o'clock.

It was just beginning to rain as I taxied in towards the terminal building at Ronaldsway Airport. The Ground Controller instructed me to look for the marshaller who would direct me to my allotted dispersal pad. The marshaller was in fact on the perimeter track in front of me, beckoning me to taxi straight ahead. As I approached him he suddenly indicated that I should turn sharp left towards a large crowd of people standing alongside a dispersal area. I was now taxying towards a long bright-red carpet rolled out on the tarmac a few yards ahead of me, and this marshaller guy was directing me to continue straight up to it.

Gradually it dawned on me what was happening. The marshaller crossed his bats then gave me the close down signal. As the engine noise died away I could hear the sound of a brass band playing with considerable gusto.

Too embarrassed to look directly at the crowd, I pretending to adjust my headset, and with my hand over my face I squinted between my fingers to see a very distinguished looking man with receding hair wearing the Mayoral Chain of Office, sheltering under a large umbrella accompanied by several dignitaries. At the far end of the long red carpet leading up to my aeroplane was a young lady holding an enormous bunch of flowers. The brass band, in immaculate uniforms with highly polished instruments, was playing 'For she's a jolly good fellow' flat out at the rear of the assembled reception committee. Obviously they had not been informed of the temporary cancellation of Miss Scott's record-breaking attempt. I began to feel sick!

Aiming to get this over as quickly as possible, and hoping I wouldn't actually be mistaken for Sheila Scott in drag, I climbed briskly out of the cockpit to the sound of three cheers. Feeling considerably embarrassed and purposely keeping off the red carpet, I started to walk hurriedly towards the Mayor who, by this time, was looking a little puzzled. Before I reached him the Brass Band had fizzled out in stages until silence reigned. All I could hear was the rain beating down on the Mayor's umbrella.

Fortunately his Worship turned out to be an absolute gentleman. He looked a little annoyed at first, but after I had explained the change of plans, he laughed out loud and said...

'Make the best of it young man, you may never get a personal reception like this again.' He was right.

CHAPTER 35.

My Dad.

Obviously, days and months would pass with nothing out of the ordinary happening. Routine day to day instructing and testing student pilots was always interesting, and as far as I was concerned, never boring.

Sometimes light relief was brought about by an amusing incident on the airfield. Such an event took place on Kidlington Aerodrome one Saturday morning.

I was carrying out circuit training in a Piper Colt with a young RAF cadet. We were using grass runway 03 left hand, and there were no other aircraft in the circuit at that time.

As we were descending along the base leg and about to turn onto the final approach, I spotted someone smack in the middle of the duty runway who appeared to be picking mushrooms.

I was annoyed that Air Traffic had not warned us of an obstruction on the runway, so I brought the matter to their attention…

'Juliet Delta turning finals to land, if you care to look out of your window you will no doubt see that there is some Pratt mushrooming on the duty runway.'

A prompt reply came from our SATCO Ben.

'Roger Juliet Delta, continue but be prepared for an overshoot. Incidentally the Pratt on the runway happens to be your father, we are sending the crash truck out to collect him.'

I looked at the grinning face of my student and snapped at him for flying out of balance!

After landing I saw dad talking to our MD Rex Smith. Before I could say a word, Rex spoke up in defence of my father who I must say was looking pretty embarrassed …

'Don't blame your father Ray, it was my fault, I told him there were plenty of mushrooms on the field and it was OK for him to collect a few. I meant the field at the back of the hangar where the lads usually collect mushrooms, but your dad thought I meant the airfield.'

I felt sorry for Pop, he had recently told me that he would love to learn to fly, and I'm sure he had no idea that he was on the duty runway.

My father was the Assistant Sales Manager for 'Britvic Fruit Juices', and at the age of 62, he decided he would start taking flying lessons at the North London Flying Club based at Panshangar, which was the nearest airfield to Sawbridgeworth where my father lived. The Club operated Tiger Moth and Taylorcraft aeroplanes. Their CFI, Derek Desargny, was an ex RAF instructor. Interestingly Derek's father was decorated for shooting down a Zeppelin Airship during the 1914-1918 war.

My father started his flying training on the Tiger Moth, soloing after twelve hours thirty minutes, which was a very respectable time on Tiger Moths, even better for a man who was in his sixties. He made good progress throughout his course, but there was one small hick-up during the final stages of Pop's training that he never lived down.

It occurred when he was sent off to complete his solo qualifying cross-country flight. I happened to be staying with my dad that weekend, and on the Sunday morning the weather looked fine, so we decided to drive to Panshangar Airfield. When we arrived, Derek met us in the car park and asked my father if he would like to do his qualifying cross-country as it was such a glorious morning. Pop was a little surprised, as he wasn't expecting to fly at all that day. But being a typical "press on type", he immediately agreed.

He was told to make a flight plan out to fly from Panshangar to Stapleford airfield and land there to get his flight-plan signed by an instructor to certify that his landing and airmanship was satisfactory. Then he had to fly on to Ipswich Airport and do the same thing there, finally returning to Panshangar.

I was amazed that dad was ready for his solo qualifying cross country because, although he had never shown me his pilot's logbook, as far as I could make out from our previous conversations, he seemed to have done very little dual or solo cross-country flying.

Another thing I wasn't too happy about was when dad started his map reading and navigational training, had been advised to transfer his training from the Tiger Moth to a Taylorcraft, which is a two-seat high wing cabin aeroplane. I personally think it is wrong to make a student transfer to another type of aircraft halfway through his PPL training. But I wasn't instructing for the North London Flying Club so I didn't interfere. I wished later that I had.

Within no time Pop had completed his flight plan, and asked me to look at it before he showed it to his CFI. I could see straight away that his calculations were incorrect. It's not uncommon for students to make silly mistakes under pressure, but he was my dad and I was worried, mainly because I had no jurisdiction over his flying training at Panshangar. So we went through the whole of his flight plan together in detail. Pop corrected everything and took it to his CFI to be checked.

Within an hour of our arrival at the airfield, my dad was strapping himself into the little monoplane G-AFZI. He started up, and moved out on his way to the runway threshold. I can see him now bless him, sitting there wearing his bright yellow pullover, smiling away, waving frantically and giving numerous thumps up signs to everyone as he taxied out. A lump came to my throat....Is dad really ready for this?

At 10.15am precisely, the Taylorcraft took off with Pop at the controls on what turned out to be a bit of an epic qualifying cross country flight.

As the sound of Dad's aeroplane faded into the distance, I walked back into Panshangar Aero Club for a cup of tea, feeling very concerned for my father's safety.

I calculated that allowing for ground stops, Dad's ETA back at Panshangar would not be much before 13.30. Whilst I sat in the Clubhouse waiting for news of ZI, my thoughts turned to dear old Pop, and his irrefutable ability to drop himself in it, especially when he was chatting to flying types....

A few weeks earlier when dad was sitting in the clubhouse waiting for another flying lesson with Derek, a rather pale-faced young man walked in, ordered a cup of coffee, and sat at a table on his own. Apparently dad thought the chap looked a bit lost, so he went over and introduced himself and asked him if he could be of any assistance. The young man said he was waiting to see the Chief Flying Instructor who happened to be flying at the time. I watched the two of them as they chatted away, Pop in his immaculate black blazer with shiny gold buttons sporting the North London Aero Club badge, and the pale faced young man dressed in an open neck shirt and denim trousers. Dad was expounding on the difficulties of landing a Tiger Moth and reminiscing about his many experiences, (Which happened to be all of ten hours flying at the time). The pair were sitting at a table well within earshot of where I stood. Dad was really keen about flying, and I watched him as he drew deeply on his cigarette, blew the smoke into the air and with a knowing shake of his dear old head said...

'This is the life old lad.'

During his conversation with the young man I heard my name mentioned, so I walked over to be introduced.

'This is my son Ray. He's an instructor at Kidlington Airport you know, that's where they train the airline pilots.'

I began to feel a bit uncomfortable.

'This is John, he's hoping to become a member of Panshangar Flying Club… I think he's a little nervous about flying old son, perhaps you can have a word with him and give him a bit of confidence.'

I didn't like the way this was going. I had nothing whatsoever to do with the N.L.F.C.   I saw the smirk on this fellow John's face, and shook hands with him. Then, before I could say a word to the chap, dad started up again…

'No need to be nervous about flying John, I remember feeling just the same when I started, have you ever been in an aeroplane old lad?'

It was crunch time, and somehow I almost knew what was coming. I watched my father's expression change from smug superiority to embarrassed humility in a split second as the young man explained that he had indeed flown before. In fact he had over 700 hours in his logbook having been trained at AST Perth for his commercial pilots licence. He was now employed by BOAC as a first officer flying Comets.

It turned out that John simply wanted to join the Club so that he could hire an aeroplane to take his girlfriend flying later.

Dad's singular remark was…

'Oh blast!'

Back to dads cross country. I glanced at my watch, it was approaching 13.30 and there had been no word from Pop. The CFI Derek Desargny had telephoned Stapleford and was told that my father had landed at 10.55 and taken off again for Ipswich at 11.20 hrs. Those times fitted in with Pop's flight plan. Derek decided to telephone Ipswich Airport to get Dad's take-off time and his ETA for Panshangar. He was informed that G-AFZI had landed there earlier and taken off for Panshangar at 12.30, so by our calculations that meant Pop should have been back with us at around 13.10. He was therefore approximately twenty minutes overdue.

Derek didn't seem over concerned.

'Don't worry Ray, I have every faith in Len, he will be alright, he's probably flying around looking at something or other on the way back.'

I was not convinced; in my opinion dad would have been keen to complete the flight as quickly and efficiently as possible.

Twenty minutes grew to half an hour. By this time Derek and myself were standing outside straining our ears for the sounds of an approaching aircraft, but nothing was heard. I asked Derek if I could take the Tiger Moth and go to look for Pop. But he said it was better for us to wait for news before determining what action to take.

After a further half hour had passed, I was standing anxiously by the telephone in Desargny's office when it suddenly rang. I snatched it up...

'North London Flying Club.'

There was a long pause, then a very rural sounding male voice said...

'Is that the Flying Club at Panshangar?'

I informed the caller that it was. The voice went on to say...

'Do you have an aeroplane with the letters AFZI painted on the side?'

By this time I began to feel slightly panicky.

Derek entered the office, took one look at the expression on my face and moved near so that he too could listen to the voice at the other end.

'Well her's crashed in one of my fields.'

At that point Derek took over the telephone, whilst I flopped down in a chair expecting the worst.

Derek put the phone down and patting me on my shoulder, said...

'It's OK Ray, Len is not hurt, it seems that he attempted to land in this farmers field, hopped over some cows and plopped down into a ditch. I know exactly where he has come down, so we will take the Messenger and one of our engineers over with another propeller just in case there's a chance of flying her out.'

Within an hour we were circling the field in Derek's trusty old Messenger G-AKKC. From the air I could see a crowd of people in one corner of the field, together with a fire engine and ambulance. In the centre of the assembly was Dad's aeroplane. Derek did a tight circuit of the field and decided it was safe to make a landing. I was extremely worried because there was no sign of my father, he would have been easily identifiable by the bright yellow pullover he was wearing, but there was no sign of him in the crowd around his aeroplane. We made our approach to land into wind with the crashed aircraft at the far end of the field. As we passed low over the up-wind boundary I spotted a solitary figure by the fence in a bright yellow pullover giving us the thumbs up and waving like mad. My eyes filled with tears, relieved to see that dad was safe and in good form. Derek aided by his mechanic and several firemen dragged the little Taylorcraft from the ditch, and in no time the damaged propeller had been replaced with the spare prop we had brought with us. The aircraft was inspected for further damage by the engineer, who gave it a clear bill of health. Whilst all this was going on I was able to have a chat with dad who was not a bit shaken by his experience. It turned out that he had got himself completely lost, and decided to land in a field to ascertain his whereabouts. He selected what he considered to be a good-sized field but failed to notice some cattle grazing in the shadows. As he was about to touch down a cow started to cross in front of the aeroplane, so Pop gave a quick blast on the throttle, eased the stick back, hopped over the beast and plopped down into a ditch. My father expressed his appreciation to the emergency services and his surprise at the short time it took them to arrive on the scene.

'They arrived within minutes old son' he told me. It was at this point in our conversation I had to explain to my Dad the embarrassing truth of the matter. The field he had selected to land in actually boarded on Henlow Aerodrome! All the RAF crash services had to do was drive through the gates of the airfield into the adjoining farmer's field to reach Dad's aeroplane. Poor old Pop just couldn't believe he had landed in such a small field when there was a serviceable airfield literarily on the other side of the fence. Pop almost imperceptible remarks....

'Oh blast!'

Derek tested the engine at full power in the farmer's field. Everything was satisfactory so Pop proudly flew it out and we followed him back to Panshangar. The event made the headlines of all the local newspapers.

About a year after my father qualified for his private pilot's licence at Panshangar, John Pooley, our Ops Manager surprised me one morning when he informed me that my dad had telephoned to arrange a type conversion on to the Piper Colt, and a booking had been made for me to fly with him the following Saturday morning. I was amazed that my father had specifically asked for me to be his instructor, because we never had the sort of relationship that would stand up to me teaching my father anything.

Dad was a very intelligent and gifted man, but throughout my childhood he had always been a strict disciplinarian and a stern advocate of the Victorian era he was brought up in. He administered the same kind of corporal punishment that he must have suffered himself as a child. Obviously I had great respect for him and loved him dearly, but I was terrified of his vicious temper. I could never confide in or have a heart to heart conversation with Dad; neither can I remember him ever playing with me when I was a little boy. The saddest thing of all is that I never saw my father kiss or even put his arms around my mother.

Dad's attitude to life mellowed considerably with the passing of time, and now it seemed he was to become my student, a reversal in status that I feared would present problems, but I need not have worried, my father turned out to be a textbook student with no trace of any previous father and son hang-ups.

Pop had always flown traditional type aircraft, and the Piper Colt was the first aeroplane with a tricycle undercarriage that he had flown. I sent him solo on type after two hours conversion training and observed that his first solo landing in the Colt was perfect.

Looking back now, that experience with my father and many years later sending my own son on his first solo, were two of the most cherished memories of my flying career.

Some instructors prefer not to teach members of their own family to fly. One of our instructors, whose name it would be prudent to exclude, asked me if I would teach his son to fly when he arrived at Kidlington having won a flying scholarship with the Air Training Corps. The young man passed his training with flying colours and it was a great pleasure flying with him. I also have to say that it was also a great pleasure giving his mother one from time to time! She was a very elegant and attractive lady in her mid thirties. I first met her during one of our instructor's parties on the Kidlington Airfield and our friendship quickly developed into a more serious affair. But that's another story.

Back to Dad...

Eventually my father bought a Miles Hawk Major G-ADWT. It was a beautiful little aeroplane with a pillar-box red fuselage, and silver wings. The Hawk was a low wing monoplane with two single fore and aft open cockpits, very similar to the RAF's Magister. It really was delightful to fly and great for aerobatics, although it did have a large notice in both cockpits informing pilots that the aircraft was not cleared for spinning. There was no mention of spinning in the pilot's handling notes and nobody could give me any explanation as to why the notices were there. It worried my father a great deal. Panshangar's CFI, Derek Desargny, suggested there was only one way to put Dad's mind at rest, and offered to flight test the aircraft. I said that as it was my father's aeroplane I would take whatever risk there was and test it myself. Having convinced my father that there was nothing to worry about, I strapped myself into G-ADWT complete with a parachute loaned to me by Derek, and took off. Climbing to six thousand feet over the airfield, I completed the mandatory safety checks and carried out a series of spins in both directions. The Hawk Major entered the spin in a similar manner to the Chipmunk, and recovered instantly when full opposite rudder and stick forward was applied. Although dad had no intention of purposely spinning the aeroplane, I'm sure it put his mind at rest.

Unfortunately my father made the mistake of allowing certain members of the flying club at Panshangar to fly his aeroplane purely for the cost of the fuel and a promise to share the maintenance costs. He had no official agreement with them, and when it came to paying for maintenance they refused to pay. In the end it was costing my father more money in servicing bills than he could afford, so the aircraft was sold.

Not long after he sold the Miles Hawk he bought the plans, together with Board of Trade approved materials, and built himself a "Luton Major" aeroplane. He made a beautiful job of it and it was finally registered as G-APUG.

When my father retired as Sales Manager of BritviC at the age of 65, he sold his aeroplane, bought the steel hull of an old lifeboat, and built himself a beautiful 35ft cabin cruiser with centre wheelhouse. He moored his boat on the river at Burnham-on-Crouch, and registered the vessel "Lady Jane".

I never knew very much about my fathers younger days. Mother told me that he made out he was eighteen and volunteered for the army during the First World War when he was really only sixteen years old. He was accepted and joined a cavalry regiment. I have a photograph of him in uniform with his much loved horse "Jess".

Dad was a keen footballer, he turned semi-professional in 1927 playing in goal for King's Lynn football club. Later he turned professional and was selected to play in goal for Wisbech.

During the slump of the 1930s, my father managed to get a job at Leaks Oil Mill in Lynn. Initially he trained as a Cooper and eventually became a very skilled carpenter. He made most of the furniture for our house in Wellington Street. During the same period my father was a part time fireman with the King's Lynn Fire Brigade. I think I was about five years old when he attended two horrendous fires in Lynn, one was when the Majestic Cinema burned down, and the other was a huge fire in the warehouses at Lynn Docks, the latter lasted for several days. I have a treasured photograph of my father driving the Lynn fire engine with its solid rubber tyres and huge brass bell. All the firemen are wearing those beautifully made brass helmets. I believe these have now become valuable collectors items.

As far as World War Two was concerned, I made brief mention in chapter three of this book, to the rather covert work he did in connection with the Royal Family at Sandringham, and his position as Civil Defence Controller in East Anglia and Bedfordshire. All in all he was a father to be very proud of.

CHAPTER 36.

Low Flying.

The pilot's crew-room was buzzing with excitement. The news on the grapevine was that CSE had ordered a Zlin Trener aeroplane from Clifford Aviation Ltd. for the purposes of aerobatic training. The authorities had recently ruled that five hours aerobatic instruction was to be included in the training syllabus for airline students.

The British Aerobatic Team led by Neil Williams, had lost their Zlin aircraft in a very unfortunate accident. Luckily the pilot, James Black, had not been killed, but he did suffer multiple injuries that would put him out of the flying scene for some months. This left the British team temporarily without an aeroplane. An agreement was arranged for the team to use the school's Zlin, mainly at weekends, to practice their aerobatic sequences.

Surprisingly there were only a few of our instructors that were keen to teach aerobatics. As I had a full aerobatic endorsement on my professional instructors rating, I kept hounding my boss to let me teach aerobatics to some of the CPL students allocated to flights other than my own, Rex finally agreed.

I note from my early logbooks, that at one stage I seemed to do most of the spin recovery lessons using the Chipmunk. Now that we had a Zlin to play with, those of us that enjoyed teaching spinning and aerobatics would be able to teach inverted flying and negative 'G' manoeuvres.

The Zlin in some ways resembled the Chipmunk, but it was far better suited to aerobatics. The engine was a Walter Minor 6-111 160hp fitted with a constant speed propeller, the undercarriage was retractable and it also had a fuel system that allowed the aircraft to be flown inverted for a limited period of time. The Zlin was cleared for positive and negative 'G' manoeuvres.

When Zlin Trener G-AVPZ arrived at Oxford I couldn't wait to get my hands on it. but I would never have dreamed that this aeroplane was destined to change my life forever.

Our C.I., Eddy Claxton, checked me out in the Zlin with a thirty-minute dual flight on the circuit. Immediately afterwards I took it up again, levelled out at 2000 ft. and turned it arse upwards to see how well the inverted fuel system worked. It was great, just a few staccato bangs from the engine during the final stages of a half roll, then the inverted fuel system kicked in and the engine was restored to normal power during inverted flight.

World Aerobatic Champion Neil Williams arrived on the scene shortly after our Zlin was delivered and flew the aeroplane regularly. I admired the precision with which this man flew his aerobatic sequences; even in strong winds he kept his display perfectly executed and squarely in the box throughout all the complicated manoeuvres he performed.

Keen to fine-tune my own instructional techniques, I constantly badgered Neil about the finer points of teaching student pilots basic aerobatics. In the end we became good friends. He took me up with him on several occasions and taught me how to execute some of the complicated aerobatic manoeuvres I had watched him perform from the ground. And whenever circumstances allowed I took the Zlin up to practice short aerobatic sequences of my own which I hoped to carry out at the next airfield open day and various sales weekends at Oxford. The sequence I put together was fairly basic, but it looked quite good from the point of view of the general public.

Long before the Zlin arrived on the scene, one of the hardest basic aerobatics I ever had to learn was to complete a really accurate slow roll in a Tiger Moth. It took hours of concentrated practice to perfect, even so I paid for my efforts with the engine stopping on a couple of occasions when I was half way round the roll in the inverted position. When this happened the only way to re-start the engine was to dive vertically almost up to VNE speed, at which point the propeller would start to turn during the pullout and if you were lucky the engine would start. (Fortunately it always did for me).

When the Zlin first arrived at Oxford, I started to teach myself inverted flying. Starting with inverted straight and level flight, then inverted climbing and descending, followed by inverted medium turns, and then inverted climbing and descending turns. I found inverted turning a little strange to begin with, as the controls all seemed to be applied in the wrong directions. Eventually after a lot of practice I really enjoyed flying around upside-down.

Occasionally on late summer evenings, Neil would be kind enough to watch my painful efforts from the ground, greeting me when I landed with a broad smile and saying 'What the hell was that all about Ray?' But he always gave me a thorough de-briefing, and for a World Champion to take that amount of interest in the likes of me, I felt very honoured.

I began practising some of the more advanced "outside" aerobatic manoeuvres. Sometimes I was privileged to have the company of Neil Williams, but mostly I practiced on my own. It took a considerable time for me to get used to the negative 'G' forces, which, due to mistakes, were sometimes far more than I intended them to be. Occasionally, at the end of a practice session, I would land with bloodshot eyes, feeling completely knackered.

A lot of the flying undertaken by my section during the summer months included training RAF and CCF cadets. Most of these young men were very keen to learn to fly. Occasionally one or two were a little apprehensive but every now and again we would get a first class student that stood out from the others.

Cadets Bingham and McKinley were above average students. At the end of his course with us Cadet Bingham joined the Royal Air Force. Many years later I heard that he had achieved the rank of Wing Commander, and was flying VC 10's.

Air Vice Marshal McKinley was still a serving officer in the RAF when his son was sent to Oxford Air Training School to complete his flying scholarship.

I taught young McKinley to fly on the Chipmunk. He had a natural aptitude to fly and completed his first solo in record time. McKinley also scored highly on his written exams. But he could be a bit of a handful!, every once in a while he would bend the rules with a sudden display of over exuberance, one such incident almost got him thrown off the course.

Having completed his first solo, the next stage of his training was to carry out a total of three hours solo consolidation flying on the circuit. He had already completed two of the three hours when I checked him out and sent him solo for his third and final hour of circuit training. He was briefed to remain on the circuit and practice alternate short field landings and glide approaches. I informed air traffic that Chipmunk G-AOST would be flying solo on the circuit and, having watched McKinley take-off, I wandered back to the crew-room. A few minutes later our direct telephone line to air traffic rang, it was the SATCO asking for me.

'Air Traffic here Ray, could you come up to the tower please?'

An invitation to visit the tower usually spelt trouble. So I rapidly made my way up the stairs to the control room where Ben, looking concerned, greeted me with…

'I thought you said the Chipmunk was remaining in the circuit?'

'Yes, that's right, what's happened?'

'He called down wind, and then suddenly peeled off to the right and shot off out of the circuit without a word, I've consistently tried to raise him on the RT but he's not replying!'

I was talking to Ben whilst Mike East, our Assistant Controller, continued to call McKinley without result. Our conversation was suddenly interrupted by the external telephone. Ben answered, I listened to our controllers words trying to interpret what the call was all about…

'Air Traffic Oxford….Yes that is one of our aircraft…Really? ….Oh dear' Ben looked at me, nodded, and continued speaking to the caller…

'Yes I see… right sir, I quite understand…I'd rather you didn't sir… you can leave the matter with us and we'll deal with it from this end. Thank you very much for contacting us sir.'

Ben put the phone down and said…

'You'll never believe it, guess what?'

I was in no mood for guessing games so snapped rather impatiently at poor old Ben.

'Come on for God's sake, what the hell's happened?'

'It's McKinley, he's over Oxford beating up King Edwards School in the Chipmunk, that was the Head on the phone asking if we had an aeroplane bearing the registration letters G-AOST, he's bloody furious, and was thinking about reporting the matter to the police!'

Having vowed to kill the little bastard, I waited anxiously in the tower for McKinley to return to the circuit. A few minutes later G-AOST reappeared and innocently called down wind. Ben instructed him to land immediately and report to the CFI.

Cadet McKinley stood stiffly to attention in my office whilst my wrath rained down on him unmercifully from a great height. I told him that as well as the Head of King Edwards School, the Oxford Police had also been on the telephone investigating a complaint of low flying over the City. McKinley remained silent looking very upset. I warned him that he would almost certainly be thrown off the course.

The bit about the police telephoning was a bit of a "porky" actually, but I needed to scare the wits out of this lad in a manner he would never forget.

Fortunately we were dealing with a problem that had been contained solely between Oxford Air Training School and King Edward's School, so I popped over to Rex Smith's office to tell him what had happened. McKinley, being the son of a serving Air Vice-Marshal, was not just anybody, although it goes without saying his father's rank held no favours in this matter.

It turned out that McKinley had been a member of King Edward's School. The same School that Douglas Bader had attended in his youth and still has a keen interest in. I told Rex that I had succeeded in frightening McKinley into thinking he was for the chop. But went on to say that he was an extremely spirited young man with above average ability as a student pilot. Rex decided that we should let the lad stew for a couple of days, then tell him he was off the hook this time. He was exceedingly lucky not to have been scrubbed off the course. As I left the office a grin spread across Rex's face. I stopped in the doorway and said...

'What'?

'It's a bit like the kettle calling the pot black. If my memory serves me correctly, it was not so many years ago when you were a student and stood in front of me for exactly the same thing, except you caused a panic by flying round Brackley Town Hall in a Tiger Moth, followed by a swift flattening of someone who was innocently digging in his allotment on the outskirts of the town.'

He was right of course; Rex had verbally torn me to bits for low flying all those years ago. I cringed at the thought, and gently closed the office door feeling a bit of a hypocrite. As I walked back to the flight office to deal with young McKinley, I recalled with a feeling of guilt the incident that Rex had just referred to concerning my own questionable flying as a student...It happened like this...

Shortly after I had completed my three hours solo circuit training, and with the CFI Mr Cockburn safely out of the way on holiday, I set off in Tiger Moth G-ALNA on a solo flight with the stupid idea of displaying my limited flying skills and terrorising the inhabitants of Brackley. I had been authorised to fly solo in the local area by Rex Smith, who was instructing part time at Kidlington and acting as CFI in Mr Cockburn's absence.

On reaching Brackley, I descended to the height of the town hall clock tower and flew round it a couple of times. As I was climbing to return to Kidlington, I spotted my brother-in-law Tony diligently working on his allotment. I dived down almost to ground level, skimmed the hedged boundary of the allotments and flattened him together with one or two other guys before climbing away swiftly to return to Kidlington and land.

As I taxied in towards dispersal, I noticed Rex Smith and F/Lt Bunny Austin standing outside the CFI's office. I parked the Tiger Moth into wind and shut down, I climbed down from the cockpit, collected the chocks from the edge of the perimeter track and secured them under the wheels. As I was leaning into the cockpit to lash the control column back with the Sutton Harness, I felt a firm couple of taps on my shoulder.

'Hi Rex... Bunny... How are things?' I said cheerily.

My joyous attitude faded quicker than a snowball in boiling water when I saw the look on Rex Smith's face. I was pretty certain I knew what was coming next.

'Have you been flying over Brackley Ray?'

The game was up, I tried to look innocent but failed miserably. Before I could answer, Rex spoke again.

'I'll see you in my office when you have booked in.'

I signed in and hurried towards Rex's office. Before I reached the door my mate Nils Bartleet came running over.

'You're in the shit and no mistake mate, there's been all hell let loose here since you took off Ray.'

I entered the CFI's office. Rex was sitting behind his desk looking like thunder. Bunny was standing in the far corner of the room with his back to me, looking out of the window.

'This is a very serious matter young Ray, and I doubt if I can do anything to help you. The whole thing is out of my hands now. Your despicable antics over Brackley were reported to the police who have informed me that they intend to take the matter up with the Aviation Authorities.'

I felt weak at the knees and swallowed hard. Rex continued...

'I understand that you flew at rooftop height around the Town Hall clock tower several times before flattening some poor sods who were innocently digging on their allotments just to the West of the town. One of the persons that complained read out your registration letters to me on the telephone as you passed by his bloody window. What ever possessed you to do such a stupid thing?'

I felt the blood drain from my face; it was like being back at School only ten times worse. All I could think of to say was a pitiful 'I'm sorry.'

'SORRY,' Rex blurted ...'Not good enough son.'

Bunny Austin remained standing at the window with his back to me. This was dreadful. Two of the people who were teaching me to fly, who I deeply respected and admired, were as good as telling me that I'd blown it. Any idea I may have had about flying for a career was now obviously out of the window. Unbelievably I heard myself saying...

'I realise what I've done is wrong Rex, I am extremely sorry and I will of course resign as a member of the Oxford Flying Club.'

The look on Rex Smith's face softened a little.

'I authorised you to fly in the local area practising general handling and circuit rejoining. What the hell made you fly thirty miles north and beat the shit out of Brackley for Christ's sake? Up to now Ray you have done well with your flying, and you spoil it by doing something really stupid and extremely dangerous.'

I stood there like a lemon as Rex rendered a final blow.

'The buggers even said they recognised it was you in the cockpit for Christ's sake.'

I felt like a small boy, wishing the ground would open up and consume me forever.

'I want a written report...the truth mind... no bullshit about engine trouble, no-one is going to swallow that one, and I'll have a word with the Aviation Authorities, not that it will do much good I'm afraid... By the way how many hours solo have you completed to date?'

'Around four hours twenty-five minutes with this flight sir' I replied, my voice almost a whisper.

Rex looked at me like a judge about to pronounce the death sentence...

'FOUR HOURS, TWENTY-FIVE BLOODY MINUTES..... JESUS CHRIST.'

I apologised again and crept out of the office. For me the world had come to an end. Everything I dreamed about since I was a little boy had been blown away by a few minutes of high spirited stupidity.

I collected all my flying gear and as I was walking out to my car with tears in my eyes, Bunny Austin caught up with me.

'Don't take it too much to heart Ray, believe me, we've all done it...my advice is to accept the telling off and don't do it again. Hopefully Rex will smooth things out for you.'

Bunny's words made me feel a little better, but I was worried for days waiting to be summoned by the authorities for low flying.

Months later I learned there had only been one telephone complaint from a local inhabitant of Brackley who somehow guessed it was me and was quite upset as he had thrown himself flat as I passed overhead whilst carrying a box of eggs from his hen-house.

I paid for my over exuberance as Rex Smith had certainly frightened me, and I never actually "*got caught*" flying low again.

I have to admit that I have always been attracted to low flying, rather like a moth to a candle flame, both of which could end up with the same fatal result. Now, as CFI of the basic training flight, it was my job to admonish a young student pilot who, in truth, had taken it upon himself to perform exactly the same sort of spirited high jinks as I had been guilty of all those years ago. But this potentially lethal form of flying was against the law of the land, and if possible it was better dealt with by me than a court of law. So, "tongue in cheek" I read the riot act to young McKinley, and, for a short while I let him think that he would probably be thrown off the course, not a good thing to happen to a young student pilot whose father was an Air Vice Marshal.

Unfortunately there are no authorised low flying areas available for civil pilot training in this country. If you fly at any height below five hundred feet without special CAA dispensation, you could wind up in court at the drop of a hat. The same rule applied in the late forties of course, but the law enforcement was not quite so stringent as it is today.

It is however very important for a pilot to be capable of controlling his aeroplane in any flight attitude, and the best training for this is a short course in basic aerobatics.

Occasionally when a young pilot shows a bit of spirit in his flying, he attracts sly remarks from the "white-knuckled control-gripping" brigade of cretins, who call themselves pilots when they have never presented their arseholes to the sun in a lifetime of flying. Who are they kidding? My answer to this bunch of judgmental charlatans is simple. If you have never thrilled to the excitement of looping and rolling high above the clouds in an open cockpit aeroplane, with the hum of a well tuned engine singing in your ears and the slipstream tearing at your face, then you are in no-way qualified to criticise others, so button it.

Back to Cadet McKinley. After a few days I began to get worried about McKinley's attitude. He seemed to have lost the spark, the twinkle in his eye, call it what you will. It was as if the stuffing had been knocked out of him, so I decided to have a fatherly chat with him about the brilliant future he could have. Then, to cheer him up a bit I told him my own story of the Tiger Moth and Brackley Town Hall. After that he brightened up considerably and soon returned to his old self. McKinley completed his flying course in some style. Sadly I do not know what became of him when he left us. There were rumours that he had joined the Army Air Corps. Whatever decision he made about his future I wish him every success.

Instructing is not always the least demanding or safest of occupations, especially if you are training foreign students that speak very little English. One such student that I was blessed with when he was on his commercial pilots, course was a chap by the name of Mr Rand. His flights with me are indelibly fixed in my mind, filed under the heading of "Terrifying".

Mr Rand was one of our first foreign students who's country of origin I consider prudent to omit. He was a pleasant enough chap who presented himself as an immaculately dressed student with no brains and a mind permanently jammed in neutral. I soon learned that Rand had in-built suicidal tendencies that to all intents and purposes included me. His reflex actions, best measured in months rather than split seconds, left much to be desired when it came to such lessons as spin recovery, landings etc. At such times the fact of whether or not we continued to exist depended solely on my quick reactions and strong love of life!

Rand had, with considerable difficulty, completed his single engine training and was now converting to flying twin-engine aeroplanes. He had completed, at length, all the upper air work and had for some time been making miserable attempts to fly round the circuit and land.

One sunny, and deceptively happy, morning I was flying with Rand in a twin Comanche. The surface wind was straight down the runway, perfect for circuit training. But all was not well with Mr Rand. Instead of flying straight and level at one thousand feet in the circuit, I found myself on a mystery tour, careering up and down like a fairground Roller Coaster. Having reached an altitude of fifteen hundred feet on the downwind leg, Rand failed to notice that anything was wrong. I hinted for the umpteenth time that it might be a splendid idea to try and maintain the regulation circuit height of one thousand feet, but Rand glared at me as if I had suggested something indecent. He tightened up his safety harness and adjusted the internal rear view mirror so that he could see himself, and fondled his black curly hair. I sarcastically pointed to the altimeter in an attempt to bring his attention to the aircraft's incorrect height. To my astonishment Rand merely adjusted the subscale of the instrument until it read one thousand feet, and continued to fly on! I seriously began to think that this young chap was purposely taking the piss. I re-adjusted the subscale back to the correct

QFE setting and pointed again to the fact that we were flying five hundred feet too high. Rand did nothing for a few seconds, then he suddenly stuffed the nose of the aircraft straight down like a Stuka Dive Bomber. With my stomach somewhere in the air behind us I was about to take control when Rand hauled the stick back at one thousand feet so hard that I thought I had broken my neck.

The lesson had obviously gotten off to a bad start. But there was more excitement to follow. Due to our spectacular dive, our airspeed was now almost off the clock, so I waited for Rand to throttle back and adjust the airspeed as he had in fact done many times previously. But not today, my illustrious friend decided that it would be a good idea to slow down by lowering the flaps whilst the aircraft was flying well over the max flap lowering speed. Fortunately I just managed to tear his hand away from the flap control in time to prevent the flaps being torn off completely.

Eventually we arrived on the final approach to land for the umpteenth time. The wheels were locked down and half flap had been selected. Thinking my unpredictable student had finally settled down, I brought his attention to the fact that we were approaching far too fast and a little too high. I expected, or rather hoped he would throttle back and adjust the attitude of the aircraft to reduce the speed so that he could apply full flap. But no such luck! He simply stuffed the nose down again and mistakenly raised the wheels instead! By now I was close to becoming a murderer, I took control and called an end to the lesson whilst we were both miraculously still alive. Of course this sort of thing can happen when flying with students from any country. The type of incident described above is in fact very rare. But it can take you by surprise and one needs to be ready for practically anything to happen in this game.

CHAPTER 37.

Tales of the Unexpected.

It was Christmas Eve 1963, when I was asked to deliver Tipsy Nipper G-ARDY to East Midlands Airport at Castle Donington for specialised maintenance work to be carried out on the engine. It was arranged that one of our instructors, Brian Murphy, would fly over in a two seat Piper Colt in order to bring me back to Kidlington. During the latter part of the Second World War Brian flew Boulton Paul Defiant aircraft in the RAF. He was also a highly qualified musician and taught music at one of the Oxbridge Colleges for several years after that war. Eventually Brian felt the urge to return to flying and in due course joined Oxford Air Training School as a flying instructor. I think the best way to describe Brian is to say that he was an educated lunatic, with a rather warped sense of humour.

On the way back from Castle Donington we were having a chat about aerobatics when clean out of the blue Brian asked me if I had ever looped the Colt. Being as the Colt was strictly a non-aerobatic aeroplane, I admitted that the thought had never crossed my mind. Looping a non-aerobatic aeroplane is not such a big deal, as a perfectly executed loop is little more than a steep turn tipped on end as far as wing loading is concerned, but you would need to get it right. If you entered the manoeuvre too slow and stalled at the top of the loop in the inverted attitude, the chances of falling out of the seat would be quite high as the only thing holding you in is a lap strap. Alternatively, entering the manoeuvre too fast, and exceeding the maximum permitted G, would overstress the aircraft and possibly result in pulling the wings off.

The question of whether or not we could loop the Colt safely had to be answered. We tightened up our belts, carried out the necessary safety checks, and from a height of 3000 ft. headed for the ground in a shallow dive. Murphy was flying the aircraft, and I honestly thought he was pulling my leg and would opt out at the last moment. I was wrong. As the aircraft was approaching its VNE speed, Brian eased back gently on the control column and completed a perfect loop in one very smooth movement. Then, to my surprise, he continued into a second loop and just as we came over into the inverted attitude he calmly said…

'You have control dear boy.' and let go of the controls.

Fortunately I was following him through on the controls and was able to complete the loop with little trouble. After that we carried out a series of loops, barrel rolls and stall turns on our way back to Oxford. Unfortunately for me that wasn't the end of it. We were heading for the airfield at 2000 ft. with about ten miles to run. I was flying the aircraft at the time, when Brain suddenly said...

'What would you do if I pulled the mixture control, stopped the engine and threw the ignition key into the back?' (The ignition key of course controlled the magnetos and the starter).

I was looking out over the port wing at the time and laughingly said…

'That's a bit much, even for you Murphy.'

At that point the engine cut out dead, I turned round to see my maniac of a friend dangling the key in front of me.

'OK mate you've had your joke, now lets stop F…..g about and get back to the airfield safely.'

I reached over to take the keys from Brian's hand when, to my disbelief, he tossed them over his shoulder sending them clanging down onto the metal floor of the luggage compartment behind us.

'You stupid bugger.' I said 'What on earth made you do that?'

I just couldn't believe he'd really done such a bloody stupid thing. What the hell happens now, we were too far away to reach the airfield so, swearing profusely, I began looking around for a suitable field to land in. None of them appeared to be large enough. It was too late to argue about what Brian had done. I just shouted at him…

'You have control, you Pratt.'

I undid my harness and clambered over the back of my seat head first into the tiny luggage compartment to look for the ignition key.

'Can't you find them Raymond?' The stupid clot even had a chuckle in his voice.

Panicking slightly I shouted back...

'I can't see them anywhere, I bet they've gone down through one of these chinks in the floor and into the underside of the fuselage, how high are we now?'

'Five hundred feet Raymond' came the calm reply. I shot up banging my head on the elevator trim handle as I scrambled around trying unsuccessfully to get back into my seat. Convinced I'd never make it in time, I flopped back into the luggage bin and crouched down.

'Hold tight Raymond' Brian said with the calmness of a psychiatric nurse, heaven knows he needed to see one.

'If this crash doesn't kill you Murphy, I swear I will' I shouted.

Suddenly the engine gave a few staccato spits and a couple of bangs then burst into life. I tried to scramble up to see what the hell was going on, but Brian applied full power and pulled the aircraft violently up into a steep climb, sending me back into the luggage bin.

Cursing I peered over Murphy's shoulder at the keys firmly inserted into the ignition switch on the instrument panel. Some bloody joke!

There was a penance to pay for Murphy. He spent the rest of the day looking for his car keys in the back of the Colt, with no help from me. After removing a floor panel they were eventually found dangling on one of the elevator cables.

As for me Christmas Eve was far from over. There had been reports on the previous evening's news that a pleasure cruiser out in the Atlantic was on fire and sinking. Apparently the catastrophe had been filmed from the air by a USAF transport aircraft on its way over to this country from America. The film was due to arrive at RAF Upper Heyford later in the afternoon. Our company had been contracted to collect the film from Upper Heyford and deliver it to Heathrow ASAP so that it could be shown on BBC Television News that evening. Being Christmas Eve the charter side of our operation at Kidlington was very busy; so I volunteered to do the job myself in order to gain further experience. The landing at London Airport would obviously be well after dark so, having never even seen Heathrow from the air, I was a little apprehensive. Fortunately for me Johnny Johnson kindly offered to come with me and see me through my first approach and landing at Heathrow, which I gladly accepted.

I had flown with Johnny on a charter flight earlier that month when we had to take a couple of Irishmen on an unforgettable flight to Shoreham in a twin engine Piper PA30. Unfortunately we didn't realise how much they had been drinking before boarding the aircraft. It turned out to be quite an interesting flight. One of the men kept thrusting a spit-ridden half-empty bottle of whisky under our noses, insisting on us taking a swig. In the end we had to pretend to have a slug in order to pacify the man who was becoming very unpleasant about us refusing his hospitality. The final straw came when the other fellow, who had been smoking a large cigar, tried to stub it out on the circular fuel tank selector gear situated on the floor between the two pilot's seats, obviously mistaking it for an ashtray.

But that was months ago, this time our flight to London was to be in a single engine Piper Tri-Pace, G-ARGY. The aeroplane was normally used for PPL instrument rating training and was quite well equipped for its day, with twin VHF Radios, twin VOR and an ADF.

At about four thirty in the afternoon a message came through from Flight Ops to say that the package had arrived at Upper Heyford and was ready for collection. Outside the sun was setting on a bitterly cold airfield, the goosenecks were already lighting the runway for another of our instructors, Ken Scott, who had just taken off on a charter to Birmingham Airport.

We took off into a dark late evening sky to collect the film waiting for us at the American Base. When we landed at Heyford I was told by control to follow the truck that was coming out to meet us on the runway. It turned out to be quite an impressive vehicle with large illuminated letters that spelt out 'FOLLOW ME' on the rear of the truck. I had difficulty in keeping up with the vehicle; it went so fast that we almost became airborne in order to stay with it.

Having collected the drum of film we took off for Heathrow. Our flight to London Airport was far less complicated than I had anticipated. The Controller's at Heathrow took care of us from the time we first called them twenty miles North West of their control zone to the time we stopped our engines in dispersal at the Northern Terminal. I had been very concerned about the possibility of getting lost on the ground at this exceptionally busy airport at night. But all we had to do was follow the various coloured lights on the edge of the taxiways as instructed by Ground Control.

Finally we arrived at the Northern Terminal where a man with illuminated batons marshalled us in to our allocated dispersal area. I closed down with a sigh of relief, but there was more to come. Our short time at Heathrow was destined to end up in a most unusual and amusing incident; the odds against it ever happening again are incalculable.

The Marshaller, who had seen us into our allocated dispersal area, informed Johnny that the film we were carrying was to be delivered immediately to a courier who was waiting for it at the main terminal on the opposite side of the airport. London Airport at night is just a sea of buildings and moving lights. Neither Johnny nor I had the faintest idea where to go or even how to get to the main terminal. So the marshaller very kindly volunteered to take Johnny in his official car. But we would have to wait as there was another light aircraft that had landed and was on its way to the northern terminal, so the marshaller had to guide it into the bay next to ours before he could leave.

I laughingly volunteered to marshal the other aircraft into the bay myself if he would take Johnny to the main terminal straight away. He looked a bit concerned at first, then, to my surprise he agreed.

It had just started to snow, so the marshaller kindly lent me his day-glow coat and handed over the illuminated bats before driving off with Johnny.

I couldn't believe it at first. There I was, standing on the dispersal area near to the northern terminal of London Heathrow Airport, holding a couple of illuminated batons, waiting to marshal another aircraft into a dispersal area.

After a few minutes I could see amongst the hundreds of lights all moving around the airport, that there was a set of red and green navigation lights heading down the taxi-way straight towards me. The lights twinkled and sparkled as little flurries of snow drifted in front of the aircraft forming a mantle of fine snow on the taxiway. I swallowed hard as the noise of the approaching aircraft's engines grew louder. The pilot switched on his main landing light as he drew closer and I set about marshalling the aeroplane neatly into its allocated dispersal area.

I crossed the batons over my head and the visiting aircraft's lights dipped gently as the brakes were applied and the engines cut out.

For a while I stood there in the snow illuminated at regular intervals by the white flash of the still functioning rotating beacon high up on the aircraft's tail. Eventually all the aircraft's lights were extinguished and I stood shivering in total darkness huddled up in the marshaller's coat, which was several sizes too big. After a few seconds, my eyes adjusted to the dark and I could just make out the silhouette of the Piper Aztec in front of me. I heard the door of the cockpit open and the pilot scrambled out onto the wing.

'What a ghastly night' he said.

He switched on his torch and shone it towards me. There was a few seconds silence then.

'Bugger me... it can't be...is that you mate? How the hell did you get to be out here on London Airport marshalling bloody aircraft Ray? I don't believe it.'

It was Ken Scott, our pilot who had taken off from Oxford before us earlier that afternoon. He had dropped his passengers off at Birmingham

Airport and collected two business men to be dropped off at Heathrow. Having dropped his passengers at the main terminal, Ken had been directed to the Northern Terminal area for re-fuelling.

When Johnny and I arrived back at Kidlington late that evening, Ken was already in the bar, no one believed him when he told them the story of the "marshaller" at London Airport. That was just about the most amazing Christmas Eve that I had ever experienced. Ken and I dined out on that little escapade for some time. I'm convinced that such a thing had never happened at LAP before, and it most definitely could not happen these days.

Another interesting flight followed early in the New Year when I was taken to Gatwick to collect a crop spraying aircraft. This time my friend the Australian instructor Hugh Bain flew me over to Gatwick in a Chipmunk. The Piper Pawnee N4634Y I was to collect had no radio equipment, and I have no idea how the aircraft came to be on the ground at Gatwick. All I knew was that it had been arranged for me to fly it out in company with our Chipmunk, with Hugh making the Radio calls for both aircraft.

Everything went quite smoothly and the Pawnee was flown to Kidlington for it's C of A maintenance check.

February arrived and the Piper Pawnee, having had its C of A maintenance check, was wheeled out of the hangar now bearing a British registration. I was asked by my boss to carry out a full C of A air test so that the aircraft could be released for service.

External and internal checks being satisfactory, I took off with the chemical spray-tanks empty to complete the upper-air part of the test first. All the standard manoeuvres were performed satisfactorily within the safety limits of the aircraft, including normal, short field and balk landings. The second part of the test schedule had to be flown at max all-up weight with the hopper tank full, in this case we filled the tank with water.

After carrying out the various full load tests, I completed a couple of low level runs across the airfield to check the spray unit discharged correctly.

Following the spray runs I had to check the emergency quick-dump mechanism, which should release the remaining contents of the hopper in one go.

It was great fun flying this aircraft as it was one of the earliest editions of the Piper PA25s. I was particularly impressed by the short field take-off and landing performance of this nifty little aeroplane, although I thought it was the nearest thing possible to flying a Ferguson Tractor. The pilot is strapped into a primitive looking bucket seat situated in a sparsely equipped cockpit with the bare necessities needed to fly an aeroplane. Fortunately the aircraft now had a small VHF transceiver that had been installed by our radio engineers.

Nearing the end of the test, I asked control if I could check the emergency quick release mechanism by dumping the water onto the airfield. The duty Controller Mike East came back with….

'Roger, you're clear for a low run' adding, 'I'll take a photograph Ray, so keep it close and make it impressive.'

I wondered what he meant by impressive. All one could do was fly low over the field, pull the quick release lever, and be ready for a sudden trim change.

As I turned in low over the perimeter fence, I saw the two lads from Air Traffic standing on the control tower balcony, cameras poised, waiting to take their *"impressive"* photograph. At that point an idea came to me that would make it a bit more exciting for them!

I opened up the 235hp Lycoming engine to full power and flew low down runway 03, our main runway. Just before the aircraft was adjacent to the signals area, I banked to the right and headed towards the tower at approximately 80 mph. Judging by the stance of the chaps on the balcony they weren't too sure whether to make a run for it or stay put. In any event they only had a split second to decide, then it was too late. I pulled the quick release lever and dumped the remaining contents of the hopper (About 100 gallons) in one go. Sadly inertia carried the water slightly beyond the targeted grass area, bounced off the concrete perimeter track in front of the tower, and saturated the two controllers standing on the balcony.

As I turned in to land I heard a very irate voice yelling at me on the R/T. Under the circumstances I avoided parking outside the control tower, and taxied straight down to the hangar.

Once again, and quite deservedly, I found myself standing on the all too familiar carpet listening to the irate tones of the C/I .

'What the hell came over you Ray?'

Before I could answer I was informed in no uncertain terms that not only had I been responsible for drenching two controllers, but I had caused minor damage to one of the air traffic control building's window, for which the cost of the repairs would be deducted from my salary. As I left the office I heard my boss mumble… 'they were hoping for a descent photograph…. not get bloody drowned.'

Later in the club bar I was called upon to buy copious amounts of alcohol for Ben and Mike, two very damp air traffic officers!

TOP Oxford flying club, Kidlington. 1957
SECOND ROW. Oxford Air Training School, Kidlington. 1968.
THIRD ROW LEFT. Halfpenny Green Aerodrome. **RIGHT.** British School of Flying. Ipswich
BOTTOM. Our caravan on Oxford Airport 1967. (Sammy in foreground)

<u>Some of the pilot's that worked at Kidlington referred to in this book.</u> (L to R)

Top Row.	The Author.	Rex Smith.	Hugh Bain.
Second Row.	Bill Jordon.	Johnnie Johnson.	Fred Mercer.
Bottom Row.	Peter Clifford.	Brian Murphy.	Frank Thomas.

Ken Scott with Author in the cockpit of a Chipmunk. **F/Lt. Peter Woodham with Bill Beadle.**

Ben Boult SATCO Oxford. **Mike East ATC Oxford.** **Bob Pascoe. Chairman of BSF.**

After flying the Rapide to Caernarfon **Author at RAF Waterbeach 1962**

Harvard

S A 300 Starduster

C.45

Pitts

Lake Buccaneer

Spitfire Mk 1X

DC3 Dakota

A few of the interesting types of aircraft I had the pleasure of flying

TOP LEFT. Author in his D.H. Rapide. **TOP RIGHT**. The Rapide Cockpit.
SECOND ROW LEFT. Author in Spitfir Mk 1X . **RIGHT.** C45. with the Harvard
THIRD ROW. Author leaving the RAF C30 after an unexpected flight.
BOTTOM ROW. LEFT. After air testing the Argus. **RIGHT.** Leading two of the Toyoto Team.

<u>Three generations of the Blyth family</u>

Top left. Ray with the Mk1X Spitfire. **Top right.** Ray's son Eddy with his C172
Lower centre. Ray's father Len, in Oxford's Chipmunk G-AOST.

Author, right hand seat as TRE Captain checking out the pilot in a C 45

Author instructing in the Varsity Simulator.

Aerobatic Champion Nigel Lamb eight-times British Aerobatic Champion, with the author.

Mike Edwards, Instructor, ex battle of Britain Spitfire pilot and a great friend of the author.

Tony Marchant   **Rex Smith**   **Ray Blyth.(Author)**
i/c Avionics at CSE.   **MD. CSE.**   **MD. Air Caernarfon.**

Top.   Belan with Caernarfon Town in the background
Bottom. Aerial view of Belan Fort and its dock.

CHAPTER 38.

St. Elmo's Fire.

The distant sound of music punctuated with occasional laughter drifted across the airfield from the students bar. It was a brisk clear moonlight night. The Met forecast predicted a deterioration in the weather due to reach us around midnight, which gave us an approximate four hour window of reasonable weather to complete our night flying programme.

Night Flying had now become a very important aspect of the school's training curriculum. It brought with it a sense of excitement, incorporating an almost military discipline. As far as the students were concerned, night flying was one of the highlights of their training. The atmosphere on an active airfield at night always seemed a little more electric than during normal daytime flying. Night flying calls for a high degree of mental concentration, especially when navigating solely by instruments on a dark moonless night.

I walked along the line of five Twin Comanche and four Cherokee aircraft that were to be used that evening, checking that they had all been fuelled up and were ready to fly.

Personally I loved instructing at night, although for obvious reasons, it carried with it a great deal of responsibility and, from time to time, a considerable amount of torturous anxiety, especially when waiting for students to return from solo night cross country flights. But unbeknown to me at the time, tonight was going to be a night flying session that I would not forget in a hurry.

Briefing was due to take place in five minutes, and the ground crew were already lighting the goosenecks placed along each side of the duty runway. I looked up at the vastness of the moonlit sky, an empty silent eternity, sometimes a very lonely place, but at this moment, positively beautiful.

The surface wind had increased slightly, bringing with it the typical chill of a Winter's evening.

As I made my way back to the briefing room I caught the distinct smell of paraffin from the gooseneck flares as they burned away pouring their black smoke into the night, and casting a weird orange glow over the grass runway.

In the dimly lit tower, I could see the unmistakable bald head of "Curly" Wadams, duty instructor for the evening. Curly, a short rather tubby man had joined my flight soon after leaving the Royal Air Force where he had been a Cat A2 flying instructor. He was talking to one of the controllers whilst our newly appointed SATCO John Day, stood motionless in the window scrutinising the ground crew who were now returning from laying the flarepath.

Pilots due to take part in the evenings programme assembled in the briefing room with their instructors. The duty instructor arrived and duly read out the details for each flight, at the same time confirming the aircraft allocated on the Ops board were all serviceable and fuelled up. He read out the predicted weather forecast for the period up to midnight and stated that the scattered thunderstorms mentioned on the regional met forecast posted up in Ops, were not expected to reach our region until well after midnight, and with no delays all our flying details should be complete by 22.00 hrs local time. The zero degree isotherm was given as 5000 ft.

Next the SATCO began his briefing with the aid of a large plan of the airfield. He explained the lighting layout and taxying procedures for the evenings flying using runway 21, right hand circuits. Pilots were informed that RAF Little Rissington and the USAF base at Upper Heyford were both non-active for the evening. Radio procedures and the positioning of aircraft in the movement area were explained in detail, and pilots operating in the local area were advised to maintain a listening watch on Oxford Airport's approach frequency. The local QNH and QFE settings for the next hour were read out. With that the SATCO handed over to the Chief Fire Officer who informed pilots of the procedures to be adopted in the event of an obstruction on the runway. Pilots were asked if they had any questions. Individual instructors then proceeded to brief their own students. A final word from the duty instructor reminded pilots to flash their navigation lights a few times just before starting up their engines.

During the briefing I watched the faces of our students as they made copious notes, their expressions reflecting their enthusiasm and keenness to do well in whatever task they were expected to perform that evening.

The flight programme for the evening indicated that three of the Cherokees would be remaining on the circuit for night circuit training; the fourth would be flying in the local area. The Twin Comanche's were on dual short night navigation exercises.

John Mercer, who in my opinion was a very meticulous and caring instructor, had also turned up at the briefing, but neither he nor I were officially on duty that evening.

When all our aircraft were safely on their way, John and I strolled over to the maintenance hangar in the hope of scrounging a mug of tea. On the way we came across two students, Jimmy French a PPL student, and Harib Sanquinett a resident commercial student. They had both turned up to watch the night flying.

The four of us entered the well-lit hangar and made our way over to the small crew-room where, as always, a battered old kettle steamed and plopped away gently on the coke stove.

'I suppose you types are on the scrounge again' was the greeting we received from the duty engineer.

We sipped our tea and chatted away. All the while I was staring through the internal office window at the two Chipmunks parked at the far end of the hangar. They looked magnificent, their highly polished white fuselages and perspex hoods gleaming in the brilliance of the massive overhead hangar lighting. John, who spotted me staring at the Chipmunks grudgingly mentioned that it was a shame we were not flying those little beauties on such a lovely night, whereupon Harib commented that he would be quite happy to pay for a night flight if that were possible. Jim immediately piped in and said he too would be more than willing to do the same. Both lads happened to be my students, but unfortunately neither of them had sufficient flying experience to commence night training. I looked at my watch, by the time we could get airborne it would be approaching 21.00hrs, there was just time for a quick flip.

It didn't take long before both Chipmunk's were wheeled out of the hangar and refuelled. I popped over to Ops. to authorise the flights and sign out, whilst John did the pre-flight external checks on both Chipmunks. I was to take Jimmy as a passenger in G-AOST and John would take Harib in G-AOFF. As this was one of those rare occasions when we were flying totally for pleasure, John didn't take much persuading when I suggested that we climb out to the South and have a bit of a tail chase in the moonlight.

We taxied the two Chipmunks along the perimeter track following the blue marker lights to the holding point of runway 21. I suddenly noticed, with some disappointment, that the sky was now partly obscured by cloud. I called Air Traffic for a local met update and they informed me that one of our aircraft had reported the cloud base to be 1,500 ft. and they were clear of cloud at 4,000 ft.

We were side by side at the holding point; I could see John's face reflected in the dull green lights of his instrument panel. He looked across at me and gave the thumbs up sign.

John took off climbing straight ahead. We were delayed for a couple of minutes whilst an aircraft on final approach came in to land. By the time we had lined up and were rolling down the runway, the tail light of FF had already faded into the cloud. It wasn't long before we too were immersed in the damp swirling haze, our navigation lights reflecting misty green and red glows at the ends of our wingtips. After a couple of minutes I called John on an agreed frequency to get some idea of his heading and height. He knew I was planning to get on his tail so the cunning old devil merely said he was on top of cloud in clear skies, adding what a beautiful moonlit night it was.

'The crafty bastard's sitting around up there waiting for us to pop up out of the cloud so that he can bounce on us before I get a chance to see him.'

As we passed through 4,000 feet, the swirling mist above the cockpit brightened and we were able to see occasional glimpses of the night sky. The radio was quiet, not so much as a peep from John. I thought for a second or two, then I briefly went over to Upper Heyford's Radar frequency. Fortunately they were standing by and after a short transmission they fixed my position as twelve nautical miles South of Oxford, warning me that another unidentified aircraft was two miles North of me, height unknown. So that's where he is.

Remaining just in the tops of the cloud I thanked Heyford for their help and banked steeply onto a Northerly heading changing back to our agreed radio frequency. The clouds gradually turned into wisps of cotton wool and moonlight streamed into the cockpit. I told Jimmy to keep a good lookout for FF, then easing gently back on the control column, I allowed ST to drift in and out of the cloud tops whilst we cautiously had a good look around for FF. For a second I was stunned by the fantastic scene as we floated across a dazzling sea of moonlit stratus cloud with great twisting towers of cumulus billowing like mountains of crystal on either side. I allowed ST to sink down a little so that wisps of cloud swirled around the cockpit. Suddenly I caught sight of FF, its beautiful white wings skimming and weaving around the cloud formations just half a mile ahead of us at about the same height.

I let ST sink a little lower into the grey surging mist and opened the throttle fully to close in on John. The cloud totally enveloped us for a few seconds then, as I eased up again...

'The bastard's gone!'...

I turned ST to the left and right, John surely couldn't be far away... perhaps he'd gone down to return to the airfield. Both Jim and I strained our eyes for a glimpse of the illusive Chipmunk. Then... there he was again, just skimming through the tops of the stratus cloud, the vortex from his wingtips causing the frothy cloud to swirl around like tiny Catherine Wheels behind him as he dodged between huge moonlit crests of cumulus. John, an ex-wartime pilot, was no fool, he knew his stuff alright, and was obviously enjoying every second. 'Time to put a stop to that' I thought.

By now I was about 300 yards behind him and so far he hadn't clocked me. As John manoeuvred his Chipmunk round great columns of cloud, the effect of the moonlight made them appear as jagged pillars of ice casting long craggy shadows over a smooth sea of white stratus. We had closed to about 100 yards and I was just about to tell John that it was goodnight as far as he was concerned, when he called up and asked me where I was.

'Right up your backside chum.'

I was close enough to see both John and Harib jerk their heads round to look behind them as their aircraft peeled off sharply and disappeared into cloud. Seconds later he shot out of the cloud climbing almost vertically, but I was still behind him albeit some distance away.

John continued to wheel FF over into a very steep turn, but as far as I was concerned I'd got him and it was all over.

'That will be a pint I believe.'

Neither aircraft were equipped with radio navigation aids, other than a basic VHF radio, so we both changed back to Oxford approach and John called for a QDM (Magnetic bearing to reach base). Back came the reply very quickly.

'Steer 020 degrees....we have been trying to call you, there is torrential rain over the airfield at the moment, and visibility estimated at less than a mile.'

That was a bit unexpected. We were still on top of cloud as I rolled ST out on the heading for home. Suddenly the whole of a gigantic cumulus cloud about ten miles to our right lit up like a mountain of pink fire. For a few seconds I was completely blinded by the flash. John called up immediately and said...

'That's a bloody great thunderstorm Ray, I suggest we get back ASAP, I'm going to start my descent holding 020.'

I acknowledged, and decided to follow orbiting first to give us a reasonable separation.

I watched FF disappear into cloud ahead of us, following on about a couple of miles behind.

As we entered cloud the static electricity caused by the storm crackled incessantly in our headphones, making conversation between Jim and myself almost impossible. We were being thrown about severely by turbulence when the gyro in the artificial horizon toppled leaving the horizon bar to take refuge in the top right-hand corner of the instrument. This left me flying on a partially limited panel. Great when you're practicing, not so great in reality at night in a thunderstorm.

Descending through 3,000 feet we were treated to another terrifying flash of blinding lightening. I had been using the method of keeping one eye closed whilst in a thunderstorm, so that alternative eyes could be used to see the instruments if blinded by lightening. But I had been caught out and was struggling to see anything. Suddenly Jim shouted out.

'Bloody Hell! What's that?'

I looked up from the instruments, and there in front of me shimmering blue lights danced and sparkled around the tip of the propeller. I had heard of "St. Elmo's Fire", but never actually seen it. I believe the phenomena is supposed to be harmless, even so I found the sudden appearance of an icy bright blue light arcing around the propeller very disconcerting. After a few seconds it hopped momentarily from the prop onto the leading edge of the port wing where it twinkled away for a few seconds, then, to my immense relief, promptly disappeared.

After an extremely turbulent descent we emerged from the cloud base at 1,200 ft. and I could just make out the bright lights of Oxford City through the torrential rainstorm.

Jim had gone very quiet back in the rear cockpit so I pressed the I/C switch on the control stick and said encouragingly…

'Not long now mate, we're nearly there'….

I had hardly got the words out of my mouth when the engine started to sputter and bang. At first I thought the cause was bound to be carburettor icing, although the carburettor heater had been on all the while during our descent through cloud. Jim came up on the intercom immediately,

'What the hells up now Ray?'

There was little time for conversation; the aircraft was no longer developing sufficient power to sustain height. I checked that the carburettor heater was in fact on, the fuel gauges are on the top of the wings close to the filler caps and I was unable to read the contents, but I knew they were topped up just before start-up less than an hour earlier.

I made a quick distress call over the R/T and, as per the book, headed for a large area of total darkness on the outskirts of the city.

We were now down to 900 ft. with no obvious safe landing area in sight. Checking the magnetos I got a dead cut on the left mag and rough running on the other. Returning to both mags the engine suddenly picked up sufficiently for me to attempt climbing, but we had only gained an extra 200ft or so when the engine started to run rough again. I checked the primer mechanism was securely locked as that can cause similar problems. Actuating the throttle vigorously seemed to help, but as soon as I stopped pumping the engine began to backfire badly.

Oxford Control were calling me. I told them that I was unable to maintain height but by pumping the throttle I could probably reduce our rate of descent and hopefully reach the airfield. They acknowledged and asked for my approximate position. I estimated that we were five to six nautical miles south of Kidlington, but at the moment I was unable to see the airfield ident beacon. Control informed me that FF had landed and cleared the runway.

Rain streaked horizontally across the cockpit canopy, forward visibility must have been down to about half a mile. I transmitted for a QDM (Magnetic bearing to steer to the airfield) Control replied…

'Sierra Tango, your QDM is 025 degrees. What's your height and approximate range?'….

I said I was down to 400 feet but I was not sure of the range, probably about two miles. Another voice that I instantly recognised came on the R/T.

'OK Ray you obviously won't be able to complete a circuit and land on runway 21, so you are cleared for a straight in on runway 03, you will have a down wind component of about 12kts, the surface wind is 220 degrees at 10kts with occasional gusts to 15kts, all our other aircraft have been recovered and the circuit is clear. Have you got your landing light on?'

It was the friendly voice of Johnny Johnson, one of our most experienced instructors.

I switched on the landing light, and turned it off immediately as the light reflected against the rain making visibility even worse.

Seconds later Johnny's voice came up on the RT again.

'Sierra Tango, we've got two cars one on each side of the flarepath, they are facing south with their headlights on, they're flashing them now, can you see them, over?'

The engine was surging badly as I strained my eyes to look for the headlights. I could just make them out at the limit of our forward visibility, surprisingly they were much closer than I expected. I confirmed this with air traffic and told them we were now down to 200 feet. I continued pumping the throttle vigorously trying to maintain what little height we had, every inch counted now. I shouted to poor old Jim telling him to make sure his harness was as tight as possible and warned him that I was about to slide the canopy partly open.

The two cars on the airfield switched their headlights off so as not to blind me. I could now see the wildly flickering flames of the flarepath several yards ahead…. I didn't think we'd make it!

Our airspeed was dangerously low but being down wind our ground speed seemed very fast. My bum tightened as we brushed through the top of the hedge that separated Langford Lane from the airfield boundary. I hauled the stick fully back and the nose of the aircraft pitched up slightly, shuddered and the left wing started to dip, there was a tremendous thump as we hit the ground and stopped a short distance from the first goosenecks at the end of the runway. Suddenly our aircraft was illuminated by the headlights of the crash truck as it came rapidly towards us.

That was probably the worst landing I had ever made, but as far as Jim and myself were concerned we were down safely, and at that moment nothing else mattered. The engine had stopped of it's own accord when we hit the ground. Jim instantly pulled back the cockpit canopy to its full extent and jumped out disappearing at great speed into the darkness of the night without a word. I switched the ignition switches and master switch off. Then, removing my flying helmet, I sat in silence for a few seconds, the rain beating down into the open cockpit and trickling down my neck, a distant rumble of thunder completing the ambience of the moment.

Several of the lads from the crash truck were shouting and milling around the aeroplane with torches, when someone climbed up on the wing and slapped me on the back.

'Am I glad to see you in one piece my ole'… 'I tried to call you several times when we were descending through cloud, but couldn't hear anything because of the terrific static.'

John Mercer had jumped in his car and followed the fire truck out onto the airfield to bring me back.

As we bumped across the rain soaked airfield, John told me that St.

Elmo had also visited him as he descended through cloud. In his case the blue lights had danced around inside the cockpit of FF and frightened him and his passenger to death.

By the time we reached the Club Bar, Jimmy French had lined up a couple of pints for us and apparently downed a large whisky himself. He sat at the end of the bar gently steaming having run all the way back across the airfield in the pouring rain. He looked at me and murmured…

'Whose bloody silly idea was it to go flying this evening?'

Sometimes events occur with a more satisfying result. For instance I remember one night after briefing had taken place and we sat in our cockpit's waiting for the signal from air traffic control to start up.

The crescent moon, that hung like a large Chinese lantern in the sky, slowly slipped behind a cloud and the warm air, scented with autumn freshness, began to stir. Moment's later the night was blackened by a storm and the first huge droplets of water splashed down noisily on our canopies, surely the night flying programme would be cancelled. I looked up at the control tower and could just make out the duty instructor silhouetted by the dim lights of the control room, his face illuminated briefly as he sucked the flame from a match into the bowl of his pipe. It was make your mind up time, the night's flying programme rested entirely on his decision. We waited for a further ten minutes as the storm passed, then to my surprise the signal to start-up engines was displayed from the tower. We carried out our checks and taxied in line to the holding point of the duty runway. All our aircraft got safely airborne and the evening's flying programme was a great success. Who would have thought it after such a dismal start.

It had now been eleven years since I first started flying at Kidlington. At that time there was just two instructors employed at the club. The fleet consisted of two Tiger Moths and one Chipmunk aircraft. All three aircraft belonged to the Oxford Aeroplane Club. Now, under the auspices of CSE, Oxford Air Training School, had become the largest privately operated flying school in Europe, training pilots for no less than 20 of the world's major airlines. At one stage Kidlington Aerodrome recorded just over 220,000 aircraft movements throughout a twelve month period, just slightly less than London Heathrow recorded during the same period. All of this was achieved under the leadership of Mr Rex Smith. Everyone that worked for the company were thrilled when it was announced on the Queen's Birthday

Honours List, that our highly respected and much-loved boss was to be awarded the OBE. It was the third honour that Rex had received in twelve months. He had been presented with a silver salver by the British Light Aviation Centre, and awarded the Pike Trophy by the Guild of Air Pilots and Air Navigators for his excellent work in the field of flying training.

Personally I couldn't have been happier working at Oxford Airport. The flight testing aspect of my job enabled me to fly several rare types of aeroplane such as the Brunswick Zaunkoenig, registered in this Country as G-ALUA. It was a very small high wing monoplane with a single seat and open cockpit. The wings gave the impression that they were positioned far too high above the fuselage, and the tail-plane was situated across the top of the fin and rudder. It had a 51 hp Zundaoo Z9-92 engine, and was capable of taking off at little more than a fast running pace. I only flew the aeroplane once after it had had some work done on the engine, it seemed to have a very flimsy feel to it, rather like trying to control a feather in a gentle breeze. The Zaunkoenig was easy to land and had an impressive STOL performance.

At the other end of the scale, the company had purchased a Beagle Airdale which in my opinion was grossly under powered, with a comparatively poor performance to match. The Airdale we had was eventually sold to a young pilot who paid by cheque. A few days later the aircraft was repossessed because the cheque bounced and the poor chap apparently had no money at all! There was a court case, which ended up with the purchaser pleading that he had had a brainstorm, and he got away with it. Anyway, good for him because the same young man years later qualified as a commercial pilot, and eventually flew as first officer with a well known British airline.

Another aircraft that I had the pleasure of flying was the Miles M11 Witney Straight. In a way this aeroplane reminded me of a 1930's motorcar, with its old fashioned, and rather sparse instrument panel. I loved the combined smell of octane and real leather that you always got when you entered the cockpit of these old aircraft types. I flew the Witney Straight from Oxford to the Coventry Air Show and back.

Another aeroplane I managed to get my hands on was Sheila Scott's first aeroplane, a Thruxton Jackaroo that she named 'Myth One.' The Jackaroo G-APAM was a bastardised Tiger Moth really. The fuselage had been widened to take extra staggered seating, and it had a single cabin instead of two open cockpits. It was great fun to fly. Sheila Scott kindly loaned the aircraft to me and Brian Murphy on a one occasion so that we could fly down to the Isle of White on our day off.

Out of the 120 aircraft types I flew during my career as a pilot, the following are some of the more interesting aeroplanes I managed to get my hands on.:-

Cessna 337C push-pull Super Skymaster, Cessna Skywagon, Piper PA17 Vagabond, Piper Cardinal, Miles Messenger, M17 Miles Monarch, Miles Gemini, Percival Prentice, Percival Provost, Zaunkoenig, Beagle 206, Beagle Pup, Beagle Airdale, Nord, Tiger Moths, Chipmunks, Fairchild Argus, Condor, L40 Metasokol, Miles Hawk Major, Two Dragon Rapide's, Druine Turbulent, Tipsy Nipper, Air Coupe, D H Dove, a Jodel, several types of Auster, Percival Proctor, Lake Buccaneer, Shorts Skyvan, Harvard, a world war two C45, Max Holste Brousard 1521, S 300 Starduster, Thruxton Jackaroo, a very interesting Swedish Pilatus PC6 that weighed over two tons and took off in just fifty feet, and a Mk1X Spitfire.

The 337C was a particularly interesting aeroplane because you had to have a twin rating to fly it, but you were not allowed to take a twin-rating test in it because the 'Push-Pull' engines were in-line, therefore it was impossible to test a pilot's ability to fly with asymmetric thrust in the event of an engine failure.

Occasionally there are sad outcomes to aircraft that one has flown. I tested a Percival Proctor for the issue of it's Certificate of Airworthiness, it was later sold to a couple of keen private pilots who were members of the Oxford Aeroplane Club. Although the Proctor was a basic aeroplane, it could be quite a handful, and if you mishandled her she would certainly bite. For instance the Proctor was quite capable of a very vicious wing drop if you allowed the speed to drop too low when on the approach to land. A couple of months after I flew this particular aeroplane, I learned that it had failed to recover from what appeared to be an unintentional spin. The aircraft crashed onto a disused airfield at Culham, quite near the city of Oxford. The two occupants died on impact. One of the persons killed in that accident was the father of a little boy who attended the same infants school, and was in the same class as my son Eddy. I was told the heart breaking story that at the end of each week the boys in Eddy's class had to draw a picture depicting something of interest that happened to them. This little chap drew a picture of a crashed aeroplane and I believe he wrote… "Yesterday my Daddy crashed and went to heaven." When Eddy told me this sad story it really upset me, in fact it still brings tears to my eyes when I think about it.

There was another serious incident when a commercial student was lucky to get away with his life.

It was October 1966 when one of our Aer Lingus students from 'A' Flight was given permission by the boss to hire a Cherokee 140 and fly home to Ireland for a couple of days. The young man already held a private pilot's licence and was sponsored by Aer Lingus to train at Oxford for his commercial pilot's licence and instrument rating.

I was writing up student's progress sheets in my office when Rex Smith came in looking very concerned.

'I have just received a message from Police Headquarters Liverpool to say that our aircraft has crashed ten miles West of Wrexham. O'Leary apparently has been taken to Liverpool General Hospital. I have spoken to the Ward Sister and he is cut about a bit, badly bruised and suffering from shock, other than that, thank God, he's OK. I want you to fly over to Liverpool now Ray, and see if you can speak to him. If possible I would like you to collect the aircraft documents which I am told he has with him in the ward. If he's up to it, get him to fill in an accident report form, perhaps you could write it for him but make sure he signs it. We will inform AIB and Aer Lingus and take care of the official side from here. Oh, just one more thing, it's OK for you to use Sheila Scott's Comanche 400, so it should only take about 50 minutes flight time. Leave as soon as possible Ray, and give me a bell when you get there.'

Before I had a chance to say a word, Rex had gone. I didn't even get a chance to ask why "A" Flight Manager was not going to visit his student instead of me.

I took Tony Smallwood with me so that he could have a chance to fly in the 400. My logbook tells me it was Monday 17th October at 14.55 when we took off in G-ATDV bound for Liverpool Airport and onwards by taxi to Liverpool General Hospital. Travelling at just over 200 knots the flight from Oxford took 36 minutes. There were a few isolated storms reported, but generally speaking the weather was reasonable, the cloud base was above 2000 ft. and visibility was excellent. It had taken just over an hour from the time Rex left my office to the time we arrived at the Hospital.

We entered the Casualty Ward and were taken over to John O'Leary who was sitting up in bed looking very pale and sorry for himself with a large bandage around his head. The Ward Sister told me that it would be at least twenty-four hours before they could release him as he had banged his head and they needed to keep him under surveillance.

I felt sorry for John; he was understandably in a very emotional state. When he handed the aircraft's documents over to me he couldn't stop apologising for bending one of the School's aeroplanes, which in fact turned out to be a complete write-off. He asked me if I thought he would be taken off the course by his sponsors. I tried to comfort him a little by telling him that our main concern was his physical condition and that he had not been killed or badly injured. I also told him not to worry himself about contacting Aer Lingus as Rex was seeing to all that. After a while John calmed down considerably, and readily made a full statement concerning the incident. I wrote the report on John's behalf, which he read through and signed. The following is a résumés of what he said, and shows how lucky he was not to be killed.

'My routing was Oxford to Belfast via Liverpool and the Isle of Man. I had been map reading to begin with, but after about 50 minutes flying time the visibility started to deteriorate and I became uncertain of my position. I tried to tune the ADF to Liverpool's NDB but was unable to attain a positive bearing. I decided to climb to 4000 ft. during which time the aircraft entered cloud. I levelled out at 4000 ft. still in very thick cloud and noticed that the DGI was not synchronised with the compass, so I made the necessary correction. The ADF needle now pulled round giving me a positive relative bearing to Liverpool's NDB, which seemed to convey that I was considerably off track. I called Liverpool Radar, but at the time they were unable to give me an accurate position because of severe clutter caused by heavy rain and thunderstorms in the area. They did however warn me that I could be over high ground. I began to panic a bit, realising that the ADF needle could be pointing at the electric storm. Also the DGI had again wandered several degrees off the compass heading. At that point I decided to descend below cloud and take a look.'

Surprised by what he was telling me, I asked him…

'What on earth possessed you to do such a bloody stupid thing John? How many times have you had it drummed into you by your instructor that you NEVER descend through cloud if there is the slightest possibility of high ground anywhere near your intended course, unless you are positively identified on radar and given a control assisted descent?'

John shook his head negatively and continued with his statement…

'I realised it would be silly to descend through cloud but I didn't think I was anywhere near high ground. When the aircraft passed through fifteen hundred feet and was still in cloud, I panicked a bit and decided to open the throttle and climb back up again. I remember seeing large boulders appearing out of the mist in front of me, then nothing until I came round inside the cockpit with heavy mist swirling around the wreckage. The No

1 comms radio was still working so I remained in the aeroplane and radioed for help. I was lucky that the aircraft did not burst into flames on impact. I continued to transmit mayday calls until I was found and brought down by the local mountain rescue team.' John signed the statement with tears welling up in his eyes and once again said he was very sorry.

We landed back at Oxford at 18.15hrs with O'Leary's statement and the aircraft documents that he had thoughtfully removed from the aircraft before he was taken to hospital.

Weeks later we learned from the AIB report that the aircraft had struck the side of a mountain at 1,650 ft. 23 nautical miles Southwest of Liverpool. Luckily the angle of the ground at the point of impact roughly coincided with the angle at which the aircraft was climbing. The engine was torn out from the airframe and the starboard wing had been ripped off.

As expected Air Lingus withdrew John O'Leary's sponsorship. It was bound to happen; even so I think they lost a good potential first officer, especially as he had already completed more than two thirds of his CPL training. He had certainly learnt his lesson the hard way and was unlikely to make that mistake again. But all credit to the lad he later managed to scrape enough money together and complete his training at Oxford. I believe he initially became a charter pilot for a private operator, and then went on to join an airline.

Sometimes there were unpleasant aspects to my job concerning the personal lives of instructors that worked for me.

One morning I received a telephone call from Nils Bartleet's sister to say that their father had passed away. Nils was flying at the time, so I volunteered to pass on the sad news to him myself. I had known Nils from the first day we both started our flying training over eleven years ago. We enjoyed each other's company immensely. Nils also became Adjutant of the RAFVRT Squadron when I took over as CO in 1960. Together we had enjoyed many hours flying RAF cadets around the skies in AEF Chipmunks at weekends and summer camps.

I always kept a bottle of Scotch in the drawer of my filing cabinet at work for special occasions, and poured out a generous helping for my friend as he sat hunched and understandably shattered by the sad news I had just passed to him. Nils's father lived in Norway and he had not seen him since his parents divorced many years ago. After a comforting chat, Nils left to take a few days leave in order to sort out his father's affairs and attend to the funeral. Some time later Nils and I were destined to spend many months, in my case years, in hospital after a tragic crash that nearly killed both of us.

In spite of endless days of routine flying and instructing, most of us still managed to clock in an amusing flight every now and again...

It was late evening when I was returning to Kidlington at 1,500 ft. just skimming the cloud tops. The setting sun put on a magnificent display gradually changing from golden amber to dark red as it slid behind the fluffy Stratus clouds on the horizon. In contrast, at ground level the sun had already set and our ground crew were busy laying the goosenecks ready for the night flying programme which was due to take place later that evening. I was flying Twin Comanche G-ASLD having dropped off a couple of our engineering staff at Stanstead Airport. In the dark red glow ahead of me, where seconds earlier the direct rays of the sun had disappeared, my eyes focused on a weird black blob. After a few seconds it became clear that the blob I was approaching at speed, was one of the balloons used at Weston-on-the-Green for parachute training. There was a small basket hanging beneath the balloon, and as I drew nearer I could see that the chap inside the basket was looking straight at me with his binoculars. Although there was an exclusion zone around Weston-on-the-Green for the hours of sunrise to sunset, I knew they were not supposed to allow their balloon to penetrate cloud, or in fact be up at all after sunset without prior warning. It was the ideal set-up for a bit of mischief.

I continued heading straight at the balloon as if I hadn't seen it. The chap in the basket had certainly seen me alright as he was frantically waving his arms in a desperate attempt to attract my attention. I closed in to a range of 1000 yards, then allowed LD to sink rapidly into the cloud apparently heading straight for the balloon's cable. The poor chap in the basket must have thought I would hit the cable and send him on a one-way journey to the "Promised Land." The second I was obscured by cloud I stood the aircraft on its wingtip and turned hard to the right. A couple of seconds later I pulled steeply up and burst through the thin layer of stratus just in time to see the top of the balloon disappearing at speed into the cloud, obviously being wound down as quickly as the winch could operate. I wasn't too worried about being reported, because I was heading straight at him when he saw me and he would not have been able to read the registration letters on my aeroplane. Also the balloon had no right to be up there after official sunset. I assume the chap in the basket had just popped up to take a quick peek at the sunset above cloud, and seeing me heading straight for him, he probably screamed down the telephone link for the man on the winch to wind him down in a hurry. I crept back to Oxford, landed, and said nothing.

On occasions I have seen an instructor rush to the bar at the end of the day and down a rapid pint in order to regain some form of sanity.

In my case, after a miserable week of arse busting, back breaking, and soul destroying circuit training trying to get at least some resemblance of a landing out of my three South African Airways students, I crawled, completely knackered, into Bill Beadle's office and flopped into a chair for a chat.

'Everyone of my bloody students seems hell bent on committing suicide and taking me with them' I said.

Bill took one look at me and burst out laughing.

'Nothing to laugh at mate, you take the buggers up and see what you think…I've been hurled into the ground eight or ten times an hour, day after day, for the whole bloody week, I'm suffering from premature shortening of the spine and a rapidly failing sense of humour.'

It was the end of "one of those days". Everyone gets days like that when absolutely nothing goes right, and the one certain way for me to pull myself out of it, was to let off steam in Bill's office. It always made my old friend laugh, and we invariably ended up in the bar for a couple of swift halves and a game of spoof before retiring for an early night and a fresh start the following morning.

Bill certainly had his moments as well, especially during standardisation meetings, when perhaps two or more instructors would disagree and start a heated argument about some procedure or another that Bill, as Standards Manager, was trying to iron out. Bill never left anyone in any doubt that he was boss. He always made the final decision, which sometimes made him a little unpopular with some of the instructors that disagreed with him.

Bill and I seemed to get on very well together, so we decided to get away from it all and hire a boat on the Norfolk Broads for a couple of weeks in late May. We agreed not to talk about flying throughout the holiday, and predictably in the end spoke of little else. Bill's dear wife June and their two lovely children joined Val and myself on the 'Glimmer of Light' a 36 ft cruiser that we hired from Herbert Wood's boatyard in Potter Heigham. We had lots of fun, and it was a much needed break from the high pressure demands instructing..

Talking of humorous moments, there was another totally unrelated incident that was intended to be funny but came bloody close to giving me a heart attack!

One of our PPL Club Members who flew regularly at weekends, apparently had a rather unusual hobby which I was unaware of at the time. His name was John Wilcox, a very pleasant young man about nineteen years old, well built, perhaps a little on the tubby side, and obviously not short of a bob or two.

John Wilcox, a part time PPL student, had been authorised to go solo by the duty instructor Brian Murphy. You may remember that Murphy was the chap that frightened me to death by throwing the aircraft's ignition keys out of the cockpit when we were at 2000 ft. returning to Oxford from Castle Donington. Anyway, on this occasion Murphy entered the crew-room and said that whilst I had been flying with another student Wilcox had arrived and left a small gift for me on the back seat of his car, and would I collect it now in case we missed one-another later. It was not unusual for the occasional student to bring in a bottle from time to time, so I thought that John had probably done just that. I should have known better! All the other instructors seemed very keen that I should collect the gift without delay. Like a fool, I thought their persistence meant that John had left me something rather special. Having pointed out which car belonged to Mr Wilcox, Murphy returned, rather hastily I thought, to the crew-room.

Young Wilcox's rather expensive looking shooting brake was parked outside the crew-room window. As I approached the car I could see a folded car-rug on the back seat, but didn't bother to look on the floor of the vehicle. Eager to ascertain the nature of my gift, I caught hold of the car door handle …

There was a petrifying roar, and I jumped about a foot into the air as a bloody great Black Panther leapt up at me from inside the car, obviously intent on ripping my head off. I let out a short involuntary scream and staggered backwards whilst the nasty tempered beast spat and clawed at the window. Almost dying of shock, I stood in the car park for a few moments trying to regain my composure when I suddenly became aware of roars of laughter echoing from the open window of the crew-room window. I couldn't help wondering what would have happened to me if the car door had been unlocked.

It turned out that John Wilcox was the owner of a small private zoo near to the town of Tring. He brought his so-called "Friendly Panther" in to show the lads. I didn't have to guess twice whose idea it was to frighten the shit out of me…Moments later I had Murphy by the throat threatening to kill him! The joke was at my expense, but later in the bar, a large whisky paid for by Murphy evened things up a bit.

On rare occasions the odd incident occurs that, although serious at the time, brings a smile to ones face later when recalling the sequence of events to others. One such happening took place on Panshangar airfield many years ago. At the time Luton Airport was just a small grass aerodrome and home to a very nice little flying club that operated Auster and Tiger Moth aircraft.

My father and I were spending the day at South London Aero Club on Panshangar Airfield where my dad had recently learned to fly. The CFI Derek Desargny had joined us for a cup of tea and we were chatting away when he was called to the telephone. Moments later he returned and said …

'Luton have just been on the blower, one of their club members is on his qualifying cross country in a Tiger Moth and was due to land here half an hour ago, his instructor is particularly concerned about this chap because he's apparently a bit scatterbrained!'

We strolled outside to see if there was any sign of the missing Tiger Moth. Sure enough we could hear the distant sound of an aircraft approaching from the Southeast.

'Surely that's not him' Derek commented, 'If it is, he is extremely high for a normal cross-country flight.'

Eventually the small speck of a biplane appeared and passed directly overhead the airfield. We could just make out that it was indeed a Tiger Moth; it's silver wings and yellow fuselage glistening in the brilliant sunlight. He must have been freezing in an open cockpit, in spite of the bright sunlight it was quite cool at ground level, and he appeared to be at least four or five thousand feet above us.

Derek hurried back to the clubhouse to contact Luton and let them know that their Tiger Moth had arrived overhead. Returning to the group of observers he said…

'I've telephoned Luton, it's their aeroplane alright, same colours, they're delighted that he's arrived, and want the Pilot to Telepho….WHERE'S HE GONE?'

Derek searched the sky for the missing Tiger Moth whilst I explained that the aircraft had passed directly over the centre of the airfield and continued on its way still heading Northwest. Derek cursed and ran back into the clubhouse to phone Luton and tell them that their aircraft had passed overhead without landing. Minutes later, when Derek rejoined the small group of club members that had formed outside, the far off sounds of the Tiger's Gypsy engine could be heard once again approaching the airfield. Loud cynical cheers broke out from those standing outside the clubhouse. The Moth, now on a reciprocal heading, appeared to be at the same altitude. The whole thing was a bit like watching one of those old Keystone Cops films!

We could hardly believe our eyes when the aircraft passed directly overhead for the second time without the slightest attempt at changing its height or heading. Someone made the comment that 'the pilot must be blind', which started up an argument with another chap who said anyone who could fly would realise that sometimes airfields are difficult to spot. In fact it can be very easy to miss a landmark if you are inexperienced and fly directly over the top at altitude, the reason being that the wing area can obscure several square miles of the land features beneath. I have been with students many times when they have in fact done just that.

The little yellow aeroplane disappeared over the horizon once again, this time in a South-easterly direction, and poor old Derek wandered off despondently to telephone Luton for the third time to inform them what had happened.

Emerging from his office a few minutes later Derek told me that the CFI at Luton Flying Club was very concerned, as his student must be short of fuel by now.

We were discussing whether or not to send an aircraft up to try and catch the Tiger Moth up and guide the pilot back to the airfield, when suddenly we were startled by the scream of a Gypsy Major engine as the aircraft reappeared at tree-top height and streaked flat-out across the airfield like a demented wasp! The unexpected noise brought the remaining occupants of the club rushing out onto the airfield to see what was going on.

We all stood in amazement staring at the Tiger Moth as it banked steeply over the airfield perimeter only feet from the treetops. Recovering from a wobbly turn it headed straight for the small crowd standing outside the clubhouse, wallowing up and down slightly as the pilot over-corrected on the controls. We all ducked down as it roared over our heads and miraculously avoided colliding with the clubhouse roof.

Everybody was gobsmacked. I wondered if the guy was really a student pilot and thought that maybe it was some kind of a leg-pull? But Derek assured me that Luton definitely said he was a student pilot on his qualifying cross-country. I thought: Never mind about qualifying, he'll be lucky to survive at this rate.

By the time we had regained our composure, the Tiger Moth was turning back towards the airfield in what appeared to be an attempt to land. It was obvious to everyone that he was far too low. I held my breath, convinced the aircraft would fall short of the airfield and clout the fence. A sudden burst of power took the Tiger Moth staggering over the boundary fence in a very ungainly nose-up attitude. The engine cut as the pilot slammed the throttle closed and pointed the aircraft towards the ground in an attempt to land. There was a horrible thud as the Tiger Moth hit the ground, bounced up and became airborne again. It was a truly frightening sight to see it hovering nose up several feet from the ground. All that could be heard was the throb of the engine as it ticked over and the swishing of air as it whistled through the wing struts. It seemed to hang in the sky about 30 feet from the ground. We all winced, waiting for the inevitable to happen. Surely the pilot would recognise his drastic error of judgement open up and go round again. But the guy at the controls was either paralysed with fear or completely oblivious to the situation, either way he had no intention whatsoever of doing anything. The poor old Tiger Moth seemed to grasp desperately at the air for a second, waffling from side to side, then it gave up and hurled itself into the ground. Amazingly it struck the ground tail first. There was a sickening thud accompanied by a loud splitting noise that sounded a bit like the crackle of wood on a freshly lit bonfire. Luckily the aeroplane stayed the right way up. Stopping exactly where it landed with virtually no forward movement at all. Somebody shouted 'F.... me' quite loudly, but no-one obliged. A couple of engineers started to run out to the aeroplane, but stopped and made a quick about turn as the Tiger, engine now flat out, suddenly swung round and headed straight towards them. This chap was obviously a complete maniac. There were a few sharp staccato bangs from the exhaust stubs as the engine complained bitterly at the gross mishandling of the throttle. As I watched the aircraft heading towards us, I could hardly believe my eyes, surely it was my imagination, but no, the upper wings were definitely drooping down, the stress wires were hanging slack and something was dragging along behind the trailing edge of the starboard wing.

The poor bedraggled Tiger Moth staggered gamely towards us, dutifully being swung from side to side by its pilot so that he could see the way ahead was clear. As he drew closer, I observed the helmeted face of the pilot. His goggles were lopsided and there was blood trickling from the side of his mouth. I wondered if the unfortunate chap had lost any teeth during his spectacular arrival. Derek ran towards him signalling desperately with his hands to try and stop the chap from taxying any closer to the refuelling area. Eventually the aeroplane came to a standstill, there was one final splutter from the engine as it cut out and the propeller, which remarkably was still in one piece, stopped turning. All was peacefully silent.

But the performance was not over yet. Looking more than a little haunted, the middle aged student pilot removed his flying helmet, wiped the blood from his mouth and, waving a piece of paper, shouted to the rather pale faced engineer who had just escaped with his life…

'Must hurry old boy, running a bit late. Need to get this signed by an instructor, and could you send someone out to top her up?… bit short on fuel?'

The engineer looked at him in amazement and said…

'I don't think so Biggles, our CFI wants a word with you.'

The pilot appeared to be completely oblivious to the damage his aircraft had suffered; perhaps he was suffering from some form of concussion! The piece of paper he was desperately waving around turned out to be his official Cross Country Certificate that needed to be signed by an instructor at each of the destination airfields to confirm the aircraft had arrived safely, the pilot made a good landing and displayed good airmanship!

The unbelievable optimism of this "press-on regardless" type was shattered when Derek, red faced, had a few words with the man …

'I'm afraid this aircraft isn't going anywhere, neither is anyone going to commit perjury by signing that certificate of yours. They will have to send someone out from Luton to assess the damage and take you back. In the meantime we had better take a look at you and see if you need to see a doctor. What on earth made you career over the airfield like a bloody maniac?'

'I came down to look at the club's name to make sure I'd got the right airfield' he replied meekly.

The poor chap finally realised the seriousness of the situation when he tried to climb out of the cockpit and the lower port wing gave a masterful impression of a swing bridge. I'm sure only those who actually witnessed this spectacular event would ever believe that it really happened. But I can assure the reader it most certainly did. In my opinion the pilot of that Tiger Moth was nowhere near safe enough to be sent solo.

CHAPTER 39.

Mayday.

Human nature dictates that we all make mistakes from time to time. But as in the case of doctors or surgeons and many other professions, a mistake made by a flying instructor could prove to be fatal.

This particular event was recorded on Oxford Airport's approach tapes, and later used by GASCO (The General Aviation Safety Committee) as a clear example of negligence on the part of an authorised instructor who, in this case, happened to be working for one of the clubs based on Staverton Airport in the 1960s.

The incident took place on a weekend. The weather at Oxford was grim to say the least. The cloud base recorded as eight oktas at 800 ft. with smaller amounts of stratus cloud floating around at 600 ft. The horizontal visibility was no more than a couple of miles, and there was slight drizzle. In all, no day for student pilots to be flying solo.

For the non-flying types perhaps I should explain something about the rules concerning pilots flying in various weather conditions. Student pilots can only fly in what is known as VMC weather. (Visual Meteorological Conditions). The rules laid down that govern his flying are referred to as VFR (Visual Flight Rules). Without going into a lot of boring detail about the exact weather criteria governing VMC, suffice to say it requires good visibility, insight of the surface and safe clearance from cloud. Weather conditions that are below this criteria is referred to as IMC (Instrument Meteorological Conditions). The rules appertaining to flight in these conditions are referred to as IFR (Instrument Flying Rules). A student pilot may never fly solo in IMC conditions, and a private pilot must have passed his IMC Rating test before he is allowed to fly solo in IMC situations.

So the reader should bear in mind that the weather at Kidlington on the day this incident took place was only suitable for qualified instrument rated pilots, or student pilots training to fly on instruments in actual conditions accompanied by their instructor.

Just 32 nautical miles due west of Oxford however, the weather at Staverton Airport was totally different. The cloud base there was 2000 ft., the horizontal visibility was given as twenty nautical miles and the surface wind was from the East at 10 to 15 kts. In other words good VMC conditions prevailed.

I cannot remember the exact time, but I think it must have been around mid morning when the drama first started to unfold. I was the duty instructor at Oxford that weekend, but due to the weather most of the Schools flying programme for Saturday had been cancelled. I arranged with the Duty Controller, Mike East, to practice QGH letdown procedures with one of my instrument rating students Mr Sanqunett.

The letters QGH are part of what is known as the "Q" code. This particular group of letters denotes a homing procedure, which is interpreted solely by the Air Traffic Controller using his CRDF (Cathode Ray Direction Finding) equipment to guide aircraft to the airfield in order for them to make a safe approach and land, usually in very bad weather.

The procedure starts with "The Homing". The Controller takes bearings obtained from transmissions made by the pilot, and gives him a series of headings to steer that will eventually bring his aircraft overhead the airfield at a given safe altitude. (The CRDF equipment can only obtain bearings, and no distance information can be given).

Once overhead the airfield the Controller guides the aircraft on to a timed procedure. This consists of an "Outbound Leg", a "Base Turn", and the "Final Approach", bringing the aircraft towards the runway under a controlled descent. The approach is terminated when the pilot becomes visual with the runway, or when the aircraft has reached the company OCL (Obstacle Clearance Limit), whichever occurs first.

Today the weather was perfect for demonstrating and practising QGH letdown procedures at Kidlington. Having thoroughly briefed Sanqunett, who was one of our BOAC students, we hurried out from the Ops building across the wet grass and on to the tarmac where our aircraft G-ATTK waited in the dismal drizzle of a thoroughly miserable morning.

Meanwhile at Staverton Airport, a young student pilot had been briefed by his instructor for a solo cross-country flight from Staverton to Kidlington and return. Later we found out that the instructor concerned had checked the students flight-plan and authorised the flight allowing him to take-off without first checking the actual weather conditions at his destination airfield, i.e. Kidlington.

Our controller's, in this case Mike East, are always pleased to have the opportunity of keeping their hand in with a practice QGH let-down. The CRDF equipment at Kidlington in the 1960s was, by today's standards, very antiquated, although it was the best for its day, but it called for considerable skill and concentration on the part of its operator. Mike however was an excellent controller. In fact I probably owe my life to him when he talked me down safely returning to Kidlington in a most atrocious snowstorm at night.

The following record of the radio transmissions that took place during that Saturday morning is taken verbatim from my copy of the recording tapes in Air Traffic Control at Oxford. I have added my explanatory notes between some of the transmissions. Also it should be understood that there were sometimes gaps of several minutes between many of the transmissions. The transcript from the tape starts at a point where I had been airborne with my student for about thirty minutes. We had passed overhead the airfield and were about to be directed by the Controller on to the outbound stage of the QGH procedure. Our aircraft was Cherokee G-ATTK; the visiting aircraft from Staverton was a Cessna 150 G-ATJU,.

<u>Transcript from the Air Traffic Control tape at Kidlington now held by GASCO.</u>

Tower. 'Tango Kilo turn on to zero five zero, call steady on your new heading.'

TK. 'Oxford Tango Kilo, Zero Five Zero, Wilco.'

JU. 'Oxford this is Golf Alpha Tango Juliet Uniform, VFR from Staverton, hat is the weather with you, it's rather misty here?'
(*The above was the visiting student pilot's first transmission*).

Tower. 'Juliet Uniform this is Oxford, receiving you strength four. The weather here is two and a half kilometres in haze, cloud base is eight oktas reported at eight hundred feet, the surface wind this time is 130 degrees at ten knots with occasional gusts to fifteen knots.'
(NB. *Our Controller had received no previous notification of the flight so had no idea that JU was being flown by a student pilot, and assumed that after passing the Kidlington weather,*

392

the pilot would revert to IFR when he encountered the bad weather ahead of him).

JU.   'Juliet Uniform . Roger.'

TK.   'Oxford Tango Kilo is steady on zero five zero, level at three Zero.'

Tower.   'Tango Kilo Roger, continue turning on to two six zero degrees, call steady.'

TK.   'Tango Kilo two six zero, wilco.'

ON.   'Oscar November, turning finals, contact one lining up.' (*This was another of Oxford's aircraft operating in the circuit).*

Tower   Oscar November land after.

TK.   'Oxford, Tango Kilo just rolling out on two six zero, still at flight level three zero.'

JU   'Oxford this is Juliet Uniform, could I have a QDM please?'
           It is worth mentioning that the words 'please' and 'thank you' are seldom used in standard R/T practice, but bear in mind this was a young student pilot. The QDM he is requesting is a course to steer in order to reach Oxford Airport)

Tower.   'Juliet Uniform this is Oxford. Steer one two three degrees.'

JU.   'One two three. Juliet Uniform.'

Tower.   'Tango Kilo check.'

TK.   'Oxford, Tango Kilo still steady on two six zero, maintaining flight level three zero, over.'

Tower.   'Tango Kilo turn on to two four zero commence descent to one six five zero feet on fox echo one zero four.'

TK.   'Tango Kilo understand turn on to two four zero and descend to 1650 feet on QFE 1014.'
         (The Controller was instructing me to commence my descent on the outbound leg of the procedure. The QFE setting he mentioned is the altimeter millibar setting that will give me my precise height above the airfield. Throughout the whole procedure TK had been flying totally on instruments in thick cloud. Beneath us there were other Oxford aircraft making low level circuits just below cloud. JU, the visiting aircraft was somewhere out to the South West, being flown by a student pilot who was lost.
         UNBEKNOWN TO ANY OF US, JULIET UNIFORM HAD ENTERED CLOUD AND WAS TRYING TO FLY WITH LITTLE OR NO EXPERIENCE OF INSTRUMENT FLYING.

JU.   'Oxford Juliet Uniform check QDM please.'

Tower.   'Juliet Uniform Delta Mike one two zero.'

JU.   'One two zero, Juliet Uniform.

Tower.   'Tango Kilo check.'

TK.   'Tango Kilo just levelling out at one six five zero feet, steady on two four zero, over.'

Tower.   'Tango Kilo turn right on to zero five zero degrees, continue descending to OCL six five zero feet call passing 1200 feet, call base turn complete over.'
         (I read back the instructions the Controller had given me. At this point we were turning in towards the airfield and had been cleared down to the company obstacle clearance limit of six hundred and fifty feet).

TK.   'Tango Kilo is passing through 1200 feet descending on a heading of one zero five degrees, still IMC, over.'
         (IMC in this case signified that we were still in cloud).

JU.   'MAYDAY MAYDAY MAYDAY JULIET UNIFORM

OUT OF CONTROL, I CAN'T DO A DAMN THING...
..I'M DIVING AT A TREMENDOUS RATE....MAYDAY
MAYDAY MAYDAY.'

(We were all flying in atrocious weather. Everyone was concentrating hard on various instructions given to us by Air Traffic. When the Mayday call suddenly blurted out very loud over the R/T it was a shock to all who heard it).

(At this point I need to explain to those reading this who are not familiar with aircraft radio procedures, that when a "Mayday" call is made, ALL other aircraft using the same radio frequency have to cease making any transmissions until the Mayday is officially cancelled. So at the time of the Mayday, we had three aircraft in the circuit in bad weather conditions, that were unable to transmit their positions. My aircraft TK was approaching the airfield at low level still in cloud with an aircraft out of control probably in the same vicinity as myself. None of us flying at the time had any idea of its range. As duty instructor I needed to get down as quickly as possible and try to help).

The next twelve transmissions took place whilst we were all struggling to get back to the airfield.

Tower. 'Juliet Uniform, Roger Mayday.'

Tower. 'Juliet Uniform have you any idea of your estimated position?'
(There was a considerable pause before JU attempted to make a reply, then...)

JU. 'MAYDAY MAYDAY MAYDAY Now down to three thousand feet....... Mayday.'
(Another long pause, the student was obviously still gripping the transmit button on his control column because in our headphones we clearly heard the slipstream as the aircraft gyrated, I also noted the clang of the gyro instruments as they toppled and smashed against their stops. I could barely imagine the sheer terror that poor student was experiencing... or the feeling of hopelessness our controller must have been feeling at the same time).

Tower.   'Juliet Uniform, have you regained control?'

JU.   'I have gained partial control, my artificial horizon has settled down, speed 90 mph, I'm at 2,100 ft. and climbing.'

Tower.   'Juliet Uniform, steer 120 degrees.'

JU.   'My VSI {*vertical speed indicator*) says that I'm climbing rapidly, but I'm maintaining 3,950 ft.'

Tower.   'Juliet Uniform maintain your height. Do not climb anymore, steer 120 degrees.'

JU.   'One two zero……I'll try.'
          (*During his last transmission the young man's voice began to brake-up, he was in desperate trouble and deeply distressed).*
          break

Tower.   'Juliet Uniform what is your height now?'

JU.   (*Student breathing very heavily)* 'I am at 2500 feet….climbing rapidly.'

Tower.   'Juliet Uniform, try to regain as much height as possible.'

          (*Unfortunately this was a great mistake. But the controller cannot be blamed because he himself was not a flying instructor or indeed a pilot, he obviously assumed the pilot of JU was a fully qualified PPL with an IMC Rating. But in effect what he had done by telling the pilot of JU to gain height, was to send him straight back up into cloud again, and the poor lad had no idea how to fly on instruments).*

JU.   *'I'M OUT OF CONTROL,   CONTROLS HAVE ALL GONE LOSE.'*
          (*The wheels of my aircraft were just touching down at Oxford when I heard that desperate transmission from JU. From what the lad had just said it was obvious to me that the aircraft had stalled, it could have been in a spin. I needed to get into the Tower as quickly as possible. I climbed the stairs to Air Traffic*

two at a time, bursting into the Control Room exhausted and breathless. Mike was as white as a ghost. 'Am I glad to see you Ray'... 'Juliet Uniform keeps losing and regaining control, he's in a terrible state, I'm sure if he speaks to an instructor it may help.' Apparently whilst I was running in from dispersal, JU had reported that he had gained control, he said he was at two thousand feet, and Mike said he told him to gain as much height as possible. I said 'Bloody hell Mike, I'm sure he's a student pilot, and you've probably sent him straight back into cloud again.' I asked Mike if he minded if I took over for a while and he passed me the microphone gladly.Somehow I had to give this young man confidence. I decided to do away with formal R/T and just speak to the lad and try to calm him down. I pressed the transmit button)

Tower.   'Juliet Uniform, this is an instructor, everything's going to be OK lad, just tell me if you have control of the aeroplane now.'

(The reply came back immediately, his voice very unsteady and trembling)

JU.   'Oxford, I can hear you, yes I think so, go ahead.'

Tower   'Are you VMC...Can you see anything of the ground old chap?'

JU   'Negative, I have no visibility at all.'

Tower   'Roger, what is your present height?'

JU   'I...er'.....*(there was a long pause...then)*   'I'm at three thousand five hundred feet.'
(The problem that faced me now was that I was not sure how much instrument flying this young man had done, if any. I also had to assume that at some stage his artificial horizon instrument had toppled. If so it may have partially erected, and an untrained pilot could easily assume it was reading correctly when in fact it wasn't. I had to risk it and try to get him to descend gently until he could see the ground without relying too much on his instruments, which he may, or may not understand).

Tower   'Juliet Uniform, hold the controls gently, don't grip them, you'll be able to feel what the aeroplane is doing better. I want you to throttle back to 1800 rpm and allow the aircraft to make a gentle descent until you become VMC. I repeat a GENTLE descent, until you get glimpses of the ground, and check your direction indicator is synchronised with your compass. Keep me informed of your height, over.'

(The student read back my instructions and said he would try to carry out all I had asked him to do. It was noticeable that his voice sounded very much calmer now. I could see from his transmissions that he was out to the North East of Kidlington. The highest ground in that area was 1000 feet, but his QDM showed him to be south of the high ground and I needed this chap to be able to see the ground).

Tower   'Check your DI is still synchronised with your compass. And tell me your heading and the height you are passing through.

JU   Passing through 2750 feet, I am heading 090 degrees.

JU   'I have occasional glimpses of the ground now.'

Tower   'Well done, steer 120 degrees and tell me what your altitude is now?'

JU   'Steer 120 degrees, altitude 2500 feet.'

Tower   'OK continue your descent nice and gently, DO NOT descend below 1500 feet, set your altimeter subscale to our QFE 1014 millibars.'

(JU read back my instructions. His voice had dropped a couple of octaves and he sounded much calmer. Every time he transmitted, Mike checked his bearing on our Direction Finding Equipment, and told me what heading to give him in order to allow for drift. Within a short time the pilot reported a disused airfield on his port wing. We assumed this to be Morton-in-the-Marsh and instructed him to correct his heading to 100 degrees, and once again to check his direction indicator with the compass. Whilst all this was going on one by one the other

three aircraft that had been on the circuit when the mayday commenced, appeared out of the murk, landed and taxied in. Eventually after a number of minor course corrections we brought Juliet Uniform down to 750ft and overhead the airfield).

JU   'I can see the airfield now dead ahead. Thank you very much sir.

Tower   'Well done old chap, join straight in on runway one three.'

(Mike and I looked at one-another with great relief! We had done our bit, but it was undoubtedly the steady nerve and self control of the young student pilot that had saved his life).

When the lad finally stopped the engine of his little Cessna in dispersal, I went out to meet him. As I walked across the tarmac it was still raining. You could barely see across the airfield. The young lad lowered himself shakily from the cockpit and made his way towards me. I introduced myself to him; his hands were sticky with sweat. He started to thank me and at that point he broke down.

Over a nice cup of hot tea we discussed what had happened. From his description of the flight I assumed `that at one stage his aeroplane became fully stalled, and then went into a violent almost vertical spiral dive. Fortunately for him, the aircraft didn't enter into a spin. I deduced this by the fact that his airspeed apparently went off the clock during the dive, and in any case I doubt if he would have recovered from a fully developed spin in cloud with apparently only one hours dual instrument flying practice. He was indeed lucky to be alive, and although he should certainly have turned back to Staverton when he ran into bad weather, with a little help from Mike and myself he did exceptionally well to get his aeroplane on the ground at Kidlington in one piece.

The Club at Staverton were informed by telephone. Their CFI went berserk, and said he would send the instructor that authorised the flight, over to Kidlington and bring the lad back. It was agreed that the Cessna JU would remain at Oxford to undergo engine and airframe stress checks before being aloud to fly back to Staverton again.

The instructor flew over later in the day when the weather improved to collect his student. I was in the Control Tower at the time, and watched the man as he strutted haughtily into our Ops room to book in. He was a tall, well built man, who at a guess I would say was around thirty-five years old. He was dressed in a flying suit covered in badges, which, on closer inspection meant little other than he belonged to a club or two and had a fine set of PPL wings. I was very keen to have a few words with this gentleman and hurried down to catch him before he left. As I entered flight Ops I was enraged to hear the guy shouting at his student in full view of our staff.

'I told you if you ran into bad weather, you had to return to Staverton, how bloody stupid can you get? as far as I am concerned you're grounded and off the course.'

His student never said a word, he just stood there obviously very upset, but the disgusting behaviour of his instructor triggered me off... Although he was not one of my instructor's and not employed by Oxford Air Training School, I technically had no right to say anything to him. But I just couldn't hold back...

'Don't you think he's had enough for one day without being bellowed at by you?'

The instructor swung round to face me looking a bit shocked at being spoken to in that manner.

'Who the hell are you?' he demanded.

I ignored his question and asked him if he was a QFI or an assistant instructor? which upset him even more.

'Only fully qualified instructors are allowed to authorise students on their qualifying cross-countries' he blurted at me with a sardonic tone to his voice.

I invited him into my office. He obviously knew that Oxford was a Commercial School with a considerable reputation in the world of flying training, and he noticeably changed his attitude when he saw the words Chief Flying Instructor on my door.

I mentioned formally who I was without shaking his hand. Then I went on to explain what had happened in detail. He constantly tried to talk over me, but I continued as if he wasn't there. Then I asked...

'How do you explain authorising your student on a cross-country flight without first checking the actual weather conditions at the destination airfield?'

He looked embarrassed and started to shout...

'You're the CFI here and should bloody-well know that it is the student's job to check the weather for himself before he takes off, and I thought he had done just that.'

It was difficult to keep my hands off this moron. I continued…

'I agree, now you tell me whose responsibility you think it is to check the student has in fact obtained the actual weather of his destination airport before authorising the flight?'

He stood there speechless for a moment. Then he said that I was not his CFI, and it was no concern of mine. I told him I was going to report this incident to his CFI as well as the appropriate authorities, and let them take whatever action they may consider necessary, adding…

'You owe that young student of yours an apology.'

He looked at me as if he would like to take a swipe at me.

'Huh, that's not one of my students thank god, he's being trained by one of our part time assistant instructors.'

That last remark of his had left him wide open for one final cutting observation from me…

'Ah' I said 'that explains it. Your assistant instructor is to be congratulated, a lesser trained student finding himself in this situation would almost certainly have panicked and probably been killed. Under the circumstances perhaps it's all to the good that he is not one of your students.'

He stormed out of my office and slammed the door. Infuriated by his supercilious attitude and the fact that he denied any responsibility for authorising a student to fly on a cross country flight without checking the weather at the destination airfield, led me, perhaps a little too hastily, to telephone the Chairman of the General Aviation Safety Committee. He was certainly not impressed.

The following day he turned up in person at Kidlington Aerodrome and asked for a copy of the approach tape that had recorded all the radio calls made throughout the incident.

Ultimately duplicate copies were made available to flying schools throughout the country and used as a teaching aid to demonstrate the dangers of authorising students to fly in predicted adverse weather conditions without the mandatory experience and qualifications.

Following his visit to Oxford, the official from GASCO called at Staverton Airport to interview the instructor responsible for this inexcusable fiasco. We all make mistakes, but this was a situation where a young student pilot could have been killed due to the irresponsibility of a flying instructor.

CHAPTER 40.

Shady Deal.

Christmas 1967 brought with it the sad news that Howard Greenaway, one of our early commercial students, had been killed on Christmas Eve whilst landing in an Aer Lingus Viscount in thick fog. We were told that he was undergoing conversion training at the time and was on the flight deck purely as an observer when the crash occurred.

Working at Oxford Air Training School was never dull. As instructors we worked to strict professional standards. Our method of air and ground instruction was constantly monitored by our Standardisation Manager, Captain Bill Beadle.

Bill, an ex RAF instructor and current CAA panel examiner, would test each of the school's flying staff twice a year. None of us really liked being checked, but it kept us on our toes and was a fundamental element in maintaining high standards of instruction at the school. The check would usually last a full day and consisted of a few pre-flight briefings followed by a couple of hours in the air. There would be a short break for lunch followed by an afternoon sweating it out in front of the blackboard whilst being grilled on all associated ground subjects with special emphasis on the principles of flight and aerodynamics. One's efforts were then recorded in great detail for our boss Rex Smith to scrutinize.

As 'E' Flight manager I met hundreds of interesting people from all over the world. Some famous, others not so famous were passed to 'E' Flight for various types of flying training or flight tests. For instance during the proceeding ten years I had flown with young Winston Churchill, (Sir Winston Churchill's nephew) Jimmy Edwards, Hughie Green, Dick Emery, and many BBC TV personalities. We also trained several Lords, stacks of Sirs, and the odd Honourable or two.

Mary Francis, the wife of Dick Francis the writer and Queens Jockey, came to Oxford to learn to fly during the nineteen sixties. Mary, having fought a long battle to overcome polio in her earlier years, successfully passed her private pilot's medical and took up flying as a challenge. She was a very quiet, gentle lady, her great determination made a huge impression on all of us that flew with her. My good friend John Mercer carried out most of her flying training, and I had the pleasure of flying with Mary when she took her PPL flight test.

Another elegant lady, I will call her Mrs Harrison, came to see me in my office one Sunday morning and said she would like to learn to fly. She was a tall very slim lady, immaculately dressed with slightly greying shoulder length hair. I asked her, as I did with all potential students, if she had any particular reason for wanting to learn to fly. I detected sadness in her eyes, but would never have guessed what she was about to tell me. Two years earlier her ten-year-old daughter had run across the road outside their house to greet her father and was knocked down by a passing car. She died on her way to hospital. The tragedy resulted in the break up of their marriage, and now, in a desperate effort to find something to occupy her mind, she decided to take flying lessons.

She joined the flying club at Oxford, and after about fourteen hours flying training I sent her on her first solo. She was very excited and booked her next lesson for the following week. The strange thing was that I never set eyes on her again from that day to this.

All this brings me to the point of this chapter which concerns the most unusual students that I ever had the misfortune to get mixed up with. They arrived at the airport one rainy afternoon in two enormous flashy American cars looking like a couple of gangsters from the 1920's. Bob, a short fattish chap dressed in a dark suit with a flashy tie, and Sid, a tall slim man who wore a trilby hat and raincoat with the collar turned up! Both gentlemen sported dark sunglasses.

I was intrigued by these two guys, and instead of allocating them to another instructor on my flight, I decided to take them on myself.

They never said what they actually did for a living, so I just assumed from their appearance that they were in some sort of selling business. During the course of one of our conversations I mentioned that I too had once been a salesman in the licensed trade before I became a full-time flying instructor, but they still never offered any explanation as to what they did for a living.

Judging by their expensive cars and some of the comments they made, it was obvious that they were quite wealthy. As far as I was concerned their standard of flying was about average, and I quite enjoyed flying with the lads.

One day, about a month after they had started their flying training, I was carrying out a ground briefing with both Bob and Sid, when, clean out of the blue, Bob asked me how much money I was being paid to instruct at Oxford. Naturally I was a little taken aback by his forthright question, and certainly had no intention of discussing my private affairs with either of them, so I hedged around the subject. Then, to my utter surprise, Bob said…

'You obviously don't want to answer my question, so I'll just say this. Whatever salary you are being paid to fly with Oxford Air Training School, we will double it if you come to work for us in the capacity of Sales Manager and Company Pilot.'

I didn't take his suggestion seriously, but before I could utter a word, Sid had his say…

'The company will supply you with an American car exactly the same as ours. You can use one of our buildings in Banbury as your office, and you can fly us around when we need to go abroad from time to time. What do you say?'

The whole thing seemed so ridiculous that I started to laugh. But these guys soon made it quite clear that they were serious.

I certainly had no intention of leaving my job at Oxford Airport, but naturally I was interested to know a bit more about these chaps and asked them what line of business they were in. Sid tapped the side of his nose and said…

'All in good time my son.'

Naturally this made me even more inquisitive, so I continued to press them further.

'Surely you can't expect me to make up my mind about working for you without knowing exactly what your business is.

They looked at one another for a second, then Bob said…

'Top of the range sewing and embroidery machines with a further interest in the wholesale distribution of Matchbox Toys and other novelty goods.'

I told them that although their offer was interesting, I would never dream of leaving OATS or give up working as a flying instructor. Bob turned his eyes to the sky in a manner that suggested he thought I must be mad…

'What about trying it out part time on your days off. Think it over Ray?'

We left it like that for a few days. During the summer months I didn't get many days off from flying, but I was tempted by the thought of earning a considerable amount of extra cash on a part time basis.

The next time these two characters turned up for their flying lessons I told them that I would agree to their second offer of working for them on a part time basis on my occasional days off and maybe a couple of evenings a week if that would be of any use to them.

Sid explained that they were importing top of the range sewing and embroidery machines from overseas manufacturers, and they were able to cut out the distributor by employing a number of salesmen to sell the machines door to door on a commission only basis. My part time job would be to collect a number of machines from their warehouse two evenings a week and arrange to meet the salesmen in order to relieve them of the cash they had taken and replenish their stocks for another week. I would be supplied with a car when I reverted to full time employment and be paid a small fortune for my services. They would also supply me with the keys to a small office they owned in Banbury.

I thought it all seemed to be a bit too good to be true, and my suspicions were even more aroused when I drove over to their offices in Northampton one evening to meet the sales staff.

I finally found the address they had given me down a narrow back street in the suburbs of Northampton. After a long search I located their office at the top of a flight of creaky wooden steps in what could only be described as a decrepit, and probably condemned, building.

I opened the door to a small, smoke-filled room, and was confronted by a group of disreputable looking guys that looked more like a bunch of murderers than salesmen.

Bob introduced me to his "Sales Staff" as their newly appointed Sales Manager. Convinced that there was more in this set-up than met the eye, I decided to go along with them and find out more, after all it was only a part time job and the money was incredible. It was rather embarrassing because the salesmen obviously knew more about the job than I did. So after a short inquisitive chat with them, I arranged to meet Bob and Sid at eight thirty a couple of evenings later to collect my first load of "Seamstress Sewing Machines".

It was 8pm on a dismal, drizzly night. As I approached their so-called office I suddenly noticed the flickering of a blue light being reflected of on the walls of a building at the end of the street. Something was obviously wrong. I continued straight ahead without slowing down, passing several police cars parked outside the entrance to Bob and Sid's office. Under the circumstances I decided to forget about the meeting, and went home.

Neither Bob nor Sid turned up for flying lessons again. Eventually I found out that Bob was on a two year holiday in one of Her Majesty's prisons, and Sid had done a runner. I never saw either of them again.

What these two rogues had avoided telling me, was that they obtained their supply of beautiful sewing machines from the tailboards of dodgy lorries on a regular basis.

CHAPTER 41

Crash.

The day started like any other day. It was Sunday the 5th of May 1968 (A date that will remain imprinted in my mind forever). I was duty instructor, which was the norm for me at weekends. Valerie and I were still living in our caravan home on Kidlington Airfield. Our family had increased slightly as we now had Sammy and Fiona, two lovely Labrador puppies living with us. We only intended to have one dog, but it was the old story of taking pity on the one that was going to be left behind. Sammy was the more boisterous of the two and became very unpopular on the journey home when he was sick in Valerie's handbag that she had left open on the floor of the car.

My father had driven over from Sawbridgeworth to join us for Sunday lunch and Valerie's daughter Laura, who was now twenty-one and working in London, had come home for the weekend. So all in all, our little caravan was bursting at the seams.

During the morning I had been flying with Mr Krouk who was one of our airline students. The weather was fine with clear blue skies, very little surface wind, and excellent visibility.

We had a cracking Sunday lunch of Roast Beef and Yorkshire Pudding, followed by my favourite, Sherry Trifle.

Whilst chatting with Dad, the subject of aerobatics came into the conversation. I was still doing a high proportion of the mandatory aerobatic instruction with our students as well as practising a more ambitious sequence that I hoped to perform in the Zlin at the next aerobatic competition. Dad, although not a great lover of aerobatics himself, was always interested in everything I did, and asked me about the sequence I was practising. As I was free towards the end of the afternoon, I planned to go through the sequence again and told dad to keep a lookout for the Zlin at about 4.30pm.

Val shouted after me as I left the caravan …

'Be careful, don't take any risks.'

I jokingly replied…

'Don't worry about me, I'm fireproof.' Immediately I thought to myself: 'If that isn't tempting fate nothing is!' It was the first, and certainly the last time I would ever say such a bloody stupid thing.

I flew with Mr Krouk again early in the afternoon completing my instructional details by 15.15 hrs. Permission had previously been obtained for me to use the Zlin for continuation training work, providing there were no other bookings on the aeroplane, and of course that I didn't overdo the privilege.

My friend Nils Bartleet was also on duty with me that weekend, I mentioned to him that I was going to fly the Zlin later in the afternoon to practice my five-minute aerobatic sequence. We must have flown together for more many hours over the previous ten years, and Nils had frequently flown with me in the past when I was practising aerobatics, so when he asked if he could come along, I agreed to take him with me.

At about 16.20 hrs. Nils and I walked out to the dispersal area where Zlin 526 G-AVPZ. was parked. Normally the Zlin is flown solo from the rear cockpit, but on this occasion I asked Nils if he would like to fly in the back as I was used to instructing from the front cockpit. He agreed, and together we carried out the external pre-flight checks and climbed into the aeroplane. I noted that the flap lever had been removed from the front cockpit for some reason which had not been entered on to the aircraft's minor defects sheet. I mentioned this to Nils who agreed to operate the flaps for me from the rear cockpit.

By 16.30 hrs. we were airborne and climbing up over the airfield. Nils had raised the flaps and I obtained clearance from Air Traffic to begin a short aerobatic sequence overhead. After carrying out the pre-aerobatic checks I confirmed with Nils that he was safely strapped in.

There has been a lot written and much conjecture about what happened next. The following, to the best of my recollection, is exactly what happened during that flight.

Approaching the overhead at 2,000 ft. the sequence began with a half-roll into the inverted attitude. After about forty-five seconds inverted flying, during which time we carried out inverted turns to bring us back over the airfield, we entered a shallow inverted dive to increase the airspeed, then

I pushed the stick firmly forward from the inverted position into a vertical climb and completed a stall turn to the right. This time recovering back to the normal flight attitude. Continuing with the sequence, I pulled the aircraft up into another vertical climb in order to carry out a tail slide and hammerhead stall. Papa Zulu stood up vertically on her tail, the airspeed decayed quickly until "Only the Makers Name" showed on the airspeed indicator. Holding the controls firmly to avoid tail damage, I felt the stick kick back as the aircraft slid backwards in a short tail slide finally toppling viciously into a hammerhead stall. Recovering from the ensuing dive, I pulled PZ up into a loop with a half roll off the top to regain altitude. After a couple of safety turns to check the area was still clear I put Papa Zulu into a left hand spin, recovering after one and a half turns and pulling up to complete a horizontal figure of eight. By this time we were down to about 1500 ft. Then, after completing a left handed four point roll, we rejoined the circuit from the dead side of duty runway.

As the flap lever had been removed from the front cockpit I asked Nils to lower the flaps as I turned in to land on runway 26. I saw my father, Valerie and Laura standing by the caravan so I decided to carry out a low overshoot with an upward roll before landing. I asked Nils to raise the flaps and informed Air Traffic that I would break left and rejoin low level. Lowering the nose of Papa Zulu to increase the airspeed as we passed over the runway threshold at 50 feet. I eased the aircraft up into a shallow climb and commenced a slow roll to the right. Everything went smoothly until were about three quarters of the way round the roll, then the aircraft gave a sudden lurch. From that point things went wrong very quickly. The rate of roll decreased and the ailerons didn't feel right. With the stick still hard over to the right PZ stopped rolling for a second and then inexplicably commenced rolling in the opposite direction at the same time turning slowly to the left. I ensured that the aircraft was flying at full throttle and a quick glance at the ASI confirmed our speed was 115 kts. We were losing height rapidly. Something was seriously wrong. In the few seconds left before impact I tried everything in the book to stop the aircraft rolling and descending to the left. With full right aileron and full power still applied I slammed on full right rudder in an attempt to use the further effect and yaw the aircraft to lift the left wing. I shouted to Nils to lower the first stage of flap in a desperate last second hope of gaining extra lift. In the past I had flown with many students when they inadvertently stalled whilst trying to carry out a slow roll, but this was totally different. I could tell that something was radically wrong by the feel of the controls. The airspeed was still over 110 kts. (126mph)., well within normal manoeuvring speed, and there had been no pre-stall warnings of any kind.

My recollection of the last few seconds is rather blurred…We were still partially inverted as the nose pitched down towards the ground and the airspeed built up rapidly. We had turned through approximately 120 degrees to the left of our original heading and were still rolling slowly in the opposite direction to the applied aileron. We were almost inverted and my last memory was seeing this enormous area of jet black hangar roof rushing up to meet us, then nothing.

It could have only been a few seconds from the beginning of the problem to the point of impact, but at some stage during those terrifying moments I remember a thought flashing through my mind about something being wrong with the left wing, but I couldn't be sure.

When I first regained consciousness, I was hanging upside-down in a jungle of twisted wreckage embedded in the top of a hangar saturated in petrol and blood. I have no recollection of pain at the time, and up to that point no one had reached us. I called out to Nils and asked him if he was OK. He answered in a very weak voice that seemed to be miles away, and said he thought he was alright. Little did either of us know the true seriousness of our injuries.

The next thing I can remember is someone calling Nils's name. It turned out to be one of our commercial course students who was the first person to clamber up to the wreckage. He was trying to help Nils in the rear cockpit and his voice seemed a million miles away. Hanging partly upside-down in my harness, with twisted wreckage all around me. I had no idea of how badly I was injured although my knee appeared to be oddly close to my shoulder. I think the rest of my lower limbs must have been mixed up in the wreckage of the engine somewhere out of sight. Strangely it didn't seem to matter very much at the time.

I must have drifted in and out of consciousness for a while because the next thing I remember was other voices gradually getting nearer, and I started to feel a burning pain in my right leg. I could see something protruding from the area of my thigh where I felt the pain. The only part of my body that I was able to move at all was my right arm, so I deliriously tried to remove the object stuck in my thigh by pulling at it with my right hand. I soon stopped when I saw my knee moving and realised that I was tugging away at the broken end of my femur bone which was protruding through the side of my blood soaked flying suit!

I can remember hearing the sirens of the emergency services as they approached the airfield, and at sometime during all this I began to feel warm and comfortable. I seemed to be drifting around peacefully watching everyone attending to Nils. It's peculiar how the brain reacts to extreme stress, because I thought I was actually looking down at myself in the midst of the wreckage.

A sudden pitiable scream from the rear cockpit brought me back to reality. Nils was probably being extracted from the rear cockpit.

Then a voice said…

'Stay with us Ray, you'll be alright mate, the doctors have arrived.'

For a short while I was in the most excruciating pain, which gradually became less and faded away again. Then a chap with some kind of saw leaned into the mangled wreckage that surrounded me, and whilst he was sawing away I felt his face brush against mine, and of all the stupid things to remember is that I thought: 'this chap hasn't shaved this morning, that's not on!'

One of my eyes started to hurt badly and sometime later one of the nurses told me that my right eye was displaced from its socket when I arrived in casualty.

I have vague memories of being connected to a bottle of something that was held above my head whilst ropes were being tied around my body to stop me from dropping to the hangar floor when they cut through my harness.

My father, Valerie and Laura had been within fifty yards of the crash when it occurred; and were extremely lucky to have escaped injury themselves, it must have been terrible for them. Later I learned how utterly frustrated and helpless my poor father had felt, unable to reach us high up in the hangar roof. Also our two dogs, Sam and Fiona must have sensed the accident because they went completely berserk, ripping the curtains and cushions to pieces and generally wrecking the interior of the caravan.

Lots of people who had observed the crash from the main road poured into the airfield for a better view of the gory crash site. I was told later by my father that one stupid clot came into the hangar smoking a cigarette whilst we were still trapped in the wreckage above him. Peter Hewitt, who was one of the first on the scene, screamed at him to get away from the area as there was a pool of petrol on the floor of the hangar. The man threw his cigarette down and stamped on it without thinking, so it was a miracle that the hangar didn't go up in flames there and then. Peter was so incensed by the man's actions that he knocked him to the ground and dragged him from the crash area assisted by my father.

I also remember being in the ambulance with Valerie, a doctor and an ambulance man by my side. Whilst they were cutting my clothes off I was very keen to know if anything was missing in the region of my private parts! and was considerably gladdened to learn that everything remained intact.

Fortunately they had managed to release Nils from the wreckage first. He was very ill suffering from severe shock, a torn spleen, and ruptured liver. They rushed him off to the Radcliffe Infirmary Oxford straight away in an ambulance with a police escort.

I remained trapped in the wreckage for a further hour or so before they were able to separate me from the tangled web of metal that pinned me to what was left of the cockpit. I never realised that it was possible to be given blood without first being cross-matched, But I was told that they had to set up a form of blood transfusion for me whilst I was still up in the hangar roof.

When I arrived at the hospital, I was taken to the emergency unit where I remember seeing Nils through some sort of glass panel. He looked at me and managed to raise a hand. The sight of him in that condition upset me terribly and I desperately wanted to speak to him, but this was obviously impossible.

Prior to going to the operating theatre, I had to have my stomach pumped out, so I saw Valerie's lovely Sherry Trifle for the second time that day! Somehow none of this seemed real.

When one has been drifting in and out of consciousness, it is difficult to differentiate between actual memories and things that you were told happened. I have a vague recollection of being taken down dark green corridors to the anaesthetic room, then nothing. My first memories after that must have been a few days later when I was crying out in agony and a nurse was wiping away the sweat from my face. Little did I know that this was the beginning of two long years in hospital.

Pain, the severity of which is impossible to describe, descended on me like the wrath of God, and from that instant, faces, voices, the awareness of day or night and the passing of time, became inconsequential. All that mattered, all I craved for was the sharp sting from the merciful hypodermic needle injecting morphine into my body every three or four hours, bringing temporary relief from the excruciating torment of unbearable pain .

CHAPTER 42.

The history of the Zlin crashes.

So that was it. I had been lying in a hospital bed trying to recall all the events of my past life, from my childhood dream of flying, to the crash that took seconds to eradicate all that I had accomplished. At the time of the crash I had completed a total of 3,170 hours instructing, including 311hours in the Zlin.

With final reference to my crash in 1968, I should point out to the reader that any aerobatic procedures flown by pilots in this country must have advanced permission from the CAA if they are to be carried out at low level. I did not have this authority at the time of the accident.

Many weeks after the crash I was interviewed in hospital by a member of the Accident Investigation Branch (AIB). The technical description I gave to the investigating officer was precisely the same in content to that described in the previous chapter. Later whilst still in hospital I was relieved to receive a letter from Mr R.A.Webb, Head of Aviation Safety (Licensing 1.) to say that a decision had been made not to take any action against me concerning the accident. However, I was disappointed to see that the cause of the accident was described as "Pilot Error" in the report, which seems to be an opprobrious label that is slapped on any pilot, dead or alive, when the actual cause of a crash remains unexplained.

In June 1970, the Zlin aircraft that replaced Papa Zulu also crashed whilst being flown by world aerobatic champion Neil Williams. Neil's description of the aircraft's behaviour leading up to the crash was in fact identical to the symptoms I had described in my crash statement which was written <u>two years before Neil's crash</u>.

I have given endless thought to the reasons why PZ acted so strangely immediately prior to the crash, and ultimately came to the conclusion that either the main spar cracked as in the case of the Zlin that replaced PZ two years later, or maybe the flaps were not raised from the rear cockpit prior to the roll. But from the feel of the aircraft and Neil Williams's description of how the replacement aircraft reacted, I'm almost certain that PZ had a cracked main spar. The port wing was recovered a short distance from the rest of the aircraft.

World Aerobatic Champion Neil Williams, being the exceptional pilot that he was, managed to prevent the wing of his Zlin from folding completely by rolling the aircraft inverted, thus reversing the stresses on the cracked spar. He descended inverted until just above the ground, he then flicked the aircraft over again and subsequently crash landed. This extremely skilful manoeuvre by Neil undoubtedly saved his life, and although the aircraft was written off, he escaped with a few bruises and suffering from shock.

Two or three years after my crash in the Zlin it was officially stated that the main spar in all the Zlin 526 aircraft had a dangerously short life, and the manufacturers, Moravan Aviation, fitted a gas tight nitrogen filled main spar with a gauge to the front cockpit that would illuminate should the spar crack. PZ, the aircraft I crashed in had been used by the England aerobatic team for many months, and as such had undergone considerable positive and negative "G" loading, which I believe could also have been a contributing to factor my crash. We shall never know.

So it was that the early Zlin's earned themselves a bit of a bad reputation. James Black, who was also a member of the British Aerobatic Team, experienced the first crash in a Zlin used by the team. He was injured but survived the accident. James told me later that he had suffered severe concussion and couldn't remember anything at all about the crash. A few weeks later I flew with James as safety pilot in Papa Zulu when he was still stumping around on crutches. Fortunately he recovered fully and was able to continue with his flying career. Following James's crash arrangements were made for the British Aerobatic Team to use Oxford Air Training School's Zlin 526, and Neil Williams won the European Aerobatic Championship in PZ the same year.

Then came my crash in PZ, and not long after my crash, the replacement Zlin was written off with Neil Williams at the controls. (As described above). Later, a fourth Zlin crashed flown by Neville Browning who was a famous aerobatic display pilot, he crashed in his own Zlin and was killed. So altogether four Zlin's crashed whilst carrying out aerobatic manoeuvres. Three of these Zlin's including PZ were used by the British Aerobatic Team and flown to their maximum 'G' limitations.

PART TWO.

CHAPTER 43.

New Beginnings.

My story continues from the point where, after two years in hospital, I had reached the stage when I was to be discharged from the care of the Nuffield Orthopaedic Hospital in Oxford and become a day patient.

Although I had made considerable progress during the first ninety-six weeks of hospital life, I seemed to have reached a stage when, in spite of continuous therapy, I still needed crutches to walk. I began to seriously doubt if I would ever recover sufficiently to pass a commercial pilot's medical again.

Finally the day came when I said goodbye to the Nurses and Sister who had looked after me so well. From now on I would only return to the Physiotherapy Department as a day patient. Now, living in the caravan, I set myself daily walking tasks around the airport buildings, gradually increasing the distance each day in order to keep me up to the limits of my endurance. It was probably just as much a psychological battle as a physical one. Efforts to stay upright failed frequently, and I found myself performing the sort of antics associated with ones first attempts at roller skating before winding up face down on the deck. It was during one of these little walks that I came face to face again with Sheila Scott, who, as previously mentioned in earlier chapters, I had flown with many times. For some unknown reason Sheila never visited me once during the two years I was in hospital, and now we came face to face outside the main entrance to the PPL section. When she saw me she stopped dead in her tracks, and without saying a word she turned away quickly and made off in the opposite direction. It upset me at the time, we had been quite good friends for many years and I could never make out why she did that. Maybe Sheila was one of those people who cannot face illness or disability, or maybe she was superstitious and thought I would bring her bad luck. I wanted to ask her why she walked away from me, but as things turned out our paths never crossed again.

On another occasion when I was out exercising, something rather wonderful happened that I will never forget. I fell down with a bump trying to negotiate the steps into the basic training building. A beautiful little girl, who was certainly no more than four or five years old, happened to be standing all on her own a few yards from where I fell. She raised her little hands in distress…

'Oh my goodness' she cried and hurried over to help me.

When I finally managed to stand up, this lovely little girl collected the few coins that had spilled out of my trouser pocket, handing them back to me and said…

'There you are, you really must be more careful' and started to brush the dust off my jacket with her tiny hands. I will never forget that charming little soul. That simple encounter left me in high spirits for the rest of the day.

I knew that before long I would have to find work of some kind. Up to this point CSE had continued to pay my full salary, which they in turn recovered from the insurance company. But the time was fast approaching when I would be signed off from medical treatment altogether, then the insurance payments to CSE would cease, and consequently my salary would no longer be paid. I realised that I was unlikely to be fit enough to pass a commercial pilot's medical for some considerable while, and decided to concentrate on making myself useful to Oxford Air Training School in other ways.

During the latter part of my stay in the Nuffield, I had written a lengthy précis about Basic Flying Training. The document, titled "Synopsis of Flying Training", included a rather ambitious project for the expansion of the section I used to be in charge of. I gave the document to my boss in the hope that some of my ideas could be used at Oxford. The manuscript included my personal views on all aspects of flying training together with detailed drawings for a purpose built 'Air Park', and designs for several items of ground training equipment that could be used as aids to pre-flight briefings. I also included a chapter on the psychological aspect of pilot training, a subject which I considered was grossly neglected in the flying instructor's training syllabus.

Then came one of the saddest moments of my career as a flying instructor. It was late afternoon when Rex Smith visited me in the caravan. He said that he and Lord Kildare the Chairman of CSE, were both very impressed with my "Synopsis of Flying Training", and that there were parts of it that they could use at Kidlington. Then he said that there was a far more important matter that he needed to discuss with me. It was then that he said….

'I am sorry to tell you that the Directors of CSE have decided that you will never be allowed to fly for CSE again.'

I stood in silence looking out of the caravan window, unable to bring myself to face Rex, my eyes started to fill with tears. Then I heard myself say…

'I understand Rex,' which wasn't true at all.

In those few seconds my whole world fell apart. For over twelve years I had lived, breathed and literally loved Oxford Airport.

I think that Rex was also upset because he didn't say another word, he just gave my shoulder a squeeze and left.

I stood motionless whilst the full implication of the Director's decision sank in. The reason all this had come as such a shock was that I had always relied on the words Rex said to me when he visited me for the first time in hospital a few days after the crash…

'Concentrate on getting well Ray, don't worry about anything, there will always be a job for you on the flying staff at Oxford.'

I trusted him and thought of those words almost every day during the two years I was recovering in hospital. In fairness to Rex I have to say that he denies making that promise. I know Rex would never lie to me, and I think that he may have unwittingly said those words of encouragement when he visited me shortly after the accident. Under such conditions things are often said to try and comfort those who are badly injured and in terrible pain. In fact I think anyone who saw me in those early days after the crash, never dreamed I would recover sufficiently to be able to fly again anyway.

Rex and I had been friends since the days when he used to instruct on the Tiger Moths in a part time capacity at Kidlington in early 1957. I had flown at Oxford for eleven years, more often than not voluntarily working seven days a week, and I had enjoyed helping with many aspects of developing the basic training flight at Kidlington. Even when I was recovering in the Nuffield Hospital, Rex Smith had asked me to re-design the interior of their recently attained flight training block on Carlisle Airport. I had a small portable drawing board set up on my bed in order to complete the task. The one thing that had kept me going throughout those years in hospital was the challenge of getting well enough to fly for Oxford Air Training School again.

Having received the bad news, my mind turned to Valerie and the effect all this would have on our relationship. We had been given permission to site our caravan on Oxford Airport because of my job as Flight Manager and CFI of basic training, a job that I no longer held. Valerie was employed by CSE and held a very good secretarial job. The complications that would arise from this situation were very depressing. Having received the bad news, I waited for Valerie to return home from work, wondering what her reactions would be when I told her.

We had decided not to get married, our lives together had always been happy and neither of us really felt the need for a permanent commitment. Valerie was an attractive young lady with no shortage of admirers. Pessimistic thoughts took over my mind as I pondered the sort of life I could offer her in the future? My brain was still full of morbid thoughts when Val burst through the door full of the joys of spring; she gave me a big hug, and asked me what sort of day I'd had. Within seconds Valerie had me wondering why the hell I had felt so worried. Almost laughing at my despair she said…

'Don't worry about it Ray, CSE isn't the only company in the world worth working for, just think of it as another challenge, and you'll come through just like you always do. The main thing at the moment is for you to get fully recovered.'

The trouble was that I felt CSE was the only company I wanted to work for.

The next day I was attending the outpatient's clinic at the Nuffield when I bumped into Linda my physiotherapist. She greeted me with….

'Surely you are not still using two walking sticks are you Ray?'

That did it. I was so annoyed with myself that I threw one of my sticks on the ground in front of her and hobbled off! It was not long before I regretted my actions. I began gyrating around my remaining walking stick like a circus act for days, determined never to use a second walking stick again. I paid heavily in terms of unnecessary pain for that act of stupidity, and it was some time before I was able to maintain some resemblance of stability and dispense with the second stick.

Determined to get fit and regain my professional licence was one thing, but I needed to get something lined up that would bring in some money in the meantime. Optimistically I started to apply for various jobs that were advertised in the 'Daily Telegraph.' I managed to get an interview with a helicopter charter company who were advertising for a Chief Executive to run their business based somewhere in the Midlands. When I arrived in London to be interviewed by the agents employed to head-hunt a suitable candidate, I discovered that the company they represented was Pilkington Helicopters Ltd., I knew Mike Pilkington well having been invited to some of the parties at his flat in Woodstock long before my crash. Sadly it was Pilkington's hangar that I had written off when I crashed on top of it in the Zlin! When I told the interviewer of this, the meeting was understandably terminated there and then.

Another interview I attended was for the position of Sales Representative for a pharmaceutical company that manufactured and sold "FITNESS PILLS" to the medical profession. But when they saw me stumble into their offices, pirouetting around my walking stick whilst desperately trying to reach the nearest chair, the interview terminated with. 'We'll let you know.'

Living on the airfield did help to boost my morale. Pilots would sometimes see me sitting at the window of the caravan as they taxied past and give me an encouraging wave, or more often than not a rude gesture! Every day at least two or three of the chaps would pop in for a chat which always cheered me up.

Rex took pity on me and offered me a part time job working in the Ground School. I appreciated his kindness and did it for a short while, but ground school work was definitely not the job for me. I was thankful for the work, but in no way was I ready to give up my fight to return to flying.

I had in fact been airborne a couple of times since the accident. The first occasion happened when I was allowed home to convalesce for a couple of days between operations on my legs and ankles. It was on February 8th 1969 when I was brought back to the airfield as a stretcher case. At the time I had been in hospital for thirty-two weeks, and my surgeon, Mr Morgan, suggested that a couple of days away from hospital life would help boost my moral. Both legs were in straight-leg plasters from the tips of my toes to the top of my thighs.

Assisted by a two strong lads from the hangar staff, Valerie took me over to the flight line where I was lifted out of the car and placed onto the starboard wing of Cherokee G-AVGE. I had to be hauled backwards into the pilots seat as it was the only way I could get my unbending legs through the cockpit door. The seat had been pushed fully back so that my encased feet and legs remained clear of the rudder controls. Eddie Claxton, who had replaced Bill Jordon as overall Chief Instructor, climbed into the right-hand seat and stared with a certain amount of misgiving at the grinning bundle of plaster and bandages sitting next to him.

He took off and kindly flew me around for a few minutes before returning to the circuit and landing. It was a wonderful feeling to actually be in the air again, the flight was certainly the moral booster I needed. After that flight I returned to hospital for many more months and a further six operations.

The next time I flew was on the 29th June. Although I still had both legs in plaster, I was able to stump around for a few yards. My left forearm was still supported by a splint, but with the aid of a normal underarm crutch and a gutter-crutch, I was able to wobble up to the aeroplane looking like a wonky old four-legged table. The same procedure was adopted to get me into the cockpit of Cherokee G-AWTL, but this time it was a nostalgic and very special occasion. My old friend Nils Bartleet, who had been in the Zlin with me when it crashed, was at the controls. Now fully recovered from the accident Nils was back instructing at Kidlington. Flying with my old chum again for the first time since we narrowly escaped death, was a very emotional experience.

1970 arrived. Exactly one hundred and five weeks after the crash I was finally signed off from medical care altogether. My surgeon had warned me that it was very unlikely that I would ever be without pain, and he was absolutely right. Anyway, I succumbed to the idea that "What cannot be cured, must be endured". The road to fitness had been slow and painful, and time was creeping on. More determined than ever to pass my aircrew medical I decided to start making moves in order to see what the future held for me.

Valerie arrived at the caravan one lunchtime with a copy of the "Flight International" magazine, and pointed out an advertisement for an Experienced Instructor to take over the responsibilities of Chief Flying Instructor at Halfpenny Green Flying Club.

'All very well' I said, 'but how the hell can I possibly apply for a Chief Instructors job when my aircrew medical, Commercial Pilots Licence and all my examiners ratings have expired?'

Valerie, replied in her usual optimistic manner…

'Don't be a defeatist, we can address that problem when the time comes. I'll telephone Halfpenny Green Flying Club this afternoon and see if I can get you an appointment.

'But even if I did pass a medical, and even if I did get my instructors rating back, what about you Val?, you have a very good job on the airport, you can't give that up.'

'Oh yes I can' she said, 'and what's more we don't have to look for a house, we can take this one with us.'

I was asked to make a formal application in writing, and within a few days a date was arranged for me to be interviewed the following Saturday by Mr Ted Gibson, the Managing Director of Halfpenny Green Airport,.

For the first time in my life I became apprehensive. What sort of impression would I make as a potential Chief Flying Instructor, limping into the interview room supported by a walking stick and having no licence or current qualifications?

Although the whole thing seemed ridiculous, I eventually convinced myself that it was at least worth having a go.

Having arrived at the gates of Halfpenny Green Airfield my first impressions were very favourable. The aerodrome seemed to be well maintained. There was a very nice clubroom and bar situated upstairs in the old RAF watch tower and a smaller room on the top to house the air traffic control facilities. The main office was situated in one of the old administration buildings skirting the perimeter track, but as far as I could see there were no briefing cubicles, flight planning or lecture rooms. However the overall potential for development and expansion seemed to be very good.

Having had a brief look round, I limped back to the main office building and tapped on a door bearing the sign of "Airport Enquiries".

I was greeted by an attractive young lady who introduced herself as Elizabeth, Mr Gibson's secretary. I was shown into a small, almost empty room where I waited for a few minutes. Eventually the young lady returned and said…

'Would you like to follow me sir?'

Absolutely! … I would have followed her anywhere.

We came to an open door at the far end of a corridor and, in a voice that was almost a whisper, she announced…

'Mr Blyth for you Mr Gibson.'

I entered a rather stark office that still retained its original issue of MOD furniture. A standard grey RAF type filing cabinet, two straight backed wooden chairs, a large picture of an Avro Anson on the wall and a standard MOD grey metal desk with a wicker wastepaper basket beneath. The man sitting behind the desk was about fifty years old, with slightly greying wavy hair and bright blue eyes surmounted by large bushy eyebrows. I also noted that his generous nose was considerably darker red than the rest of his complexion.

'Ted Gibson' he said gripping my hand in a firm handshake. 'Sit down old boy, and tell me all about yourself….How about a cup of coffee before we start, what do you say ?'

Before I could say anything he picked up the phone and ordered two coffees.

I immediately felt at ease with "Ted" as he insisted I called him. We had a lengthy chat and I told him everything about my flying career to date, even to the point that I had no licences, no medical and no current qualifications. When I had finished I sat back in the chair and waited for Ted to find some excuse to show me to the door. Instead, to my astonishment he said…

'I already knew everything you've just told me.'

His friendly face beamed from ear to ear as he told me with pride that anyone who was to be considered for the prestigious position of CFI at Halfpenny Green, was thoroughly investigated before being invited to attend for interview…

'I know your boss Rex Smith very well indeed' he said, 'I just couldn't understand why one of Oxford's CFI's would find it necessary to apply for the job of Chief Instructor with us, so I telephoned Rex. He speaks very highly of you, and I appreciate your honesty in telling me everything about yourself.'

Ted went on to explain that he was a Director of the Airfield Operating Company registered as Bobbington Estates, and that he had also been the CFI of Halfpenny Green Flying Club for many years. He was now looking for someone with the right experience and qualifications to take over the pilot training at Halfpenny Green and bring the club up to the standard required by the Ministry of Defence to tender for pilot training contracts. He also said that having been recommended by Rex Smith he considered I was the right man for the job, and he was prepared to wait for me to pass my medical examination and re-gain my previous qualifications.

It was like a dream. I just couldn't believe that this man was prepared to hold the job open for me whilst I regained my qualifications; there must have been many more suitably qualified applicants after this prodigious job. It was as if my "Guardian Angel" had taken pity on me at last and conjured up a situation especially tailored to suit my present circumstances.

Val and I celebrated that evening with a few drinks, but the job was by no means in the bag. I was certain that I could regain my qualifications, and pass the flying tests, but the CPL medical was the one thing over which I had very little control.

Full of enthusiasm, I decided to take the bull by the horns and apply for the renewal of my CPL medical and commercial pilot's licence straight away. Val suggested that I should wait a while, but I had made up my mind. The following day I applied to the Central Medical Establishment for a date to attend a CPL medical.

Within a short while I received a reply to say that a date had been set for me to attend a medical examination in London a few days hence. I was both excited and nervous, sometimes feeling reasonably confident but other times convinced that I would fail. The worst scenario would be for the medics to write me off altogether. I frequently reminded myself of Bader's words to me when he visited the Radcliffe Hospital… 'NEVER GIVE UP OLD BOY.' So that was it, with a certain amount of self-inflicted bravado I told myself that, come what may, I'll pass the bloody medical if it kills me!

We arrived outside the Central Medical Establishment Building in London a few minutes early. I paid the taxi driver, arranged to meet Valerie in the foyer of CME later in the afternoon, and reluctantly handed her my walking stick.

'I won't be needing this' I said tongue in cheek, and staggered off towards the main entrance.

This was the second time in my career as a pilot that I had attended an aircrew medical at the Central Medical Establishment. The first had been traumatic enough, but at least I was in full working order. This time I faced the same stringent medical with parts of my body being held together with screws and bolts!

The door was opened by a smartly dressed commissionaire who took one look at me and asked if I needed any help. That upset me for a start!

'No thanks' I said indignantly, 'I have an appointment for a Commercial Pilot's Medical.'

The attendant looked surprised and directed me to the reception room, which happened to be up a couple of flights of stairs, and unfortunately for me there were no lifts.

'This is not a good start' I thought, 'I'm going to be in a state of collapse before the medical examination even begins.'

I was in agony by the time I reached the top of the first flight of stairs and leaned against the banister for a few seconds before I attempted to tackle the next flight. I glanced back down the stairs and noted with some embarrassment that the commissionaire was peering suspiciously up at me from the foyer. Eventually I hobbled into the room marked "Aircrew Medical Reception".

It was a bit off-putting to see several other chaps in the waiting area all looking fit enough to enter the British Triathlon Championships, whilst I arrived looking as if I had entered the London Marathon and finished a year later.

After filling in a lengthy form, we were each given a small glass receptacle to pee in, and trooped off to the allotted cubicles to do our stuff. There were the usual strained grunts from those finding it difficult to perform, and a few exclamations of relief. As I limped back into the room clutching my steaming sample, one of the other lads who had been staring at me said...

'Are you OK mate?'

'Yes, why?' I snapped.

'Nothing really, I just thought you looked a bit…..'

I didn't wait to hear his derogatory remarks, and hobbled off.

Cardiogram, Audiogram, Chest X-ray, Eye Test, all seemed to present no problems, although you never know exactly how well you have performed in each department until the end of the medical when you are interviewed by the head surgeon who pronounces you dead or alive.

Then came the bit I was dreading most of all...

'Come in Mr Blyth…take your clothes off please and jump up on to the couch.'

I was wearing orthopaedic shoes that had built-up heels specially made to compensate for the limited movement I had in my ankles. But do you think I could undo the shoelaces? I fumbled away until the doctor, who I must say was a splendid chap, said...

'Let me give you a hand.'

Once the shoes came off the doctor looked a little surprised when I announced that I couldn't stand up without holding on to something. I explained that my ankles had been set in plaster whilst in a downwards-pointing attitude, and I now had limited movement in them.

I was leaning precariously against the examination couch, wondering how the hell I was going to haul myself onto it, when the doctor took my testicles in his hand and said..

'We might as well get this over first,' and asked me to cough.

So there I was, embarrassingly hanging on to the examination couch, knowing full well that if I let go of the bloody thing I would fall over backwards and more importantly I would probably have my testicles ripped off by the doctor who was now holding them firmly in his hand.

'On the couch then.'

The doctor turned away from me to write something on my report, so I made one desperate effort to mount the table-high couch and failed miserably. I managed get one leg onto the plastic covering with my arm wrapped round the top, but when I tried to drag myself up the plastic sheet began to slip off.

As I slid under the couch and onto the floor with a thump, the Doctor swung round to see what had happened.

'My goodness, we are having trouble' he said.

I must have been bright red with embarrassment and began to think that I may as well go home right now. Finally, with more than a little help, I laid down on the examination couch exhausted, thinking that the rest of the examination could only be a formality, I must have failed.

'Your notes from the Nuffield Hospital say you were involved in a plane crash Mr Blyth, I believe you suffered multiple injuries?'

'Yes sir, that's correct.'

'Twenty-seven major fractures eh?'

'Yes sir,'

Thank God he had my hospital notes, otherwise I'm sure that the medical would have been terminated there and then. He continued…

'Now lets see, bend your left knee for me please…is that the best you can do?'

I nodded.

'Thank you'… 'Now bend your right knee'… 'Hmm, that's not very good is it?'….

I tried to get the leg to bend a little more, but it refused point blank to move another fraction of a degree. The doctor however had other ideas and gave it a helping hand.

'Shiii…Phew…' My stifled reaction to the pain sounded like a high-pitched sneeze.

'Sorry old lad, did that hurt you?'

'Not a bit sir.'

The doctor smiled.

I began to think that this bastard is some kind of sadist!

Perspiration began to trickle down the sides of my face as the doctor continued with his vigorous examination. We went through a similar procedure with every joint in my legs, ankles, feet, toes, arms, hands, fingers, and my neck. Most of the joints moved reasonably well, some were a bit stiff, but my ankles had very little movement in them at all, and the big toe on my right foot was solid and refused to move altogether.

Reflexes were checked, heart and lungs listened to, the only response from the doctor was an occasional unconvincing 'Hmm.'

Eventually we got to the point where every movement and limitation of my limbs had been carefully examined, measured and recorded. By this time I was convinced in my own mind that I had botched the medical, so I asked the doctor for his verdict. He continued to scribble copious notes on my medical record without saying a word, rather like an executioner calculating the length of drop needed to snap a neck. Finally he removed his glasses and stared at me for a couple of seconds…

'You will have to wait until you are interviewed by the Air Commodore. He will make the final decision based on the medical reports submitted by all the specialists you have seen today.'

He must have seen the despondent look on my face as he continued…

'Cheer-up old boy, you're not dead yet!'

Life for me had been on hold for such a long time. My determination to fly again had been the main driving force affecting my recovery, now I could do no more and my future was down to one man who would make his decision before I left the building.

I waited outside the Chief Surgeon's office for what seemed hours whilst other aircrew chaps were called in to hear a verdict that would affect their lives forever. Eventually, with my heart pounding, I was called in to see the Air Commodore.

'Sit down Mr Blyth.'

The Air Commodore was a distinguished grey-haired gentleman in civilian clothes. He had a pile of medical reports on his desk together with several large envelopes that I recognised immediately as the type that contained x-rays.

'Well you have been in the wars, I'm surprised you want to start flying again, hasn't the accident put you off?'

'Not at all sir, in fact its been the only thing that's kept me going for the last two years. Flying is my life sir, I honestly don't know what I'd do if I couldn't fly again.'

I shut up at that point. Perhaps I was overdoing it, but I was speaking the truth. I'd go down on bended knee and beg for him to pass me if I thought it would do any good.

The Air Commodore looked very concerned.

'Hmm. Well now, let's see.'

He started to turn over the sheets of paper from the top of the pile in front of him.

'I've looked through all these reports appertaining to your medical examination, and I must say your surgeon seems to have done a pretty good job on you.'

He paused for a while, the suspense was sheer agony.

'I'm prepared to allow you to fly again as a Commercial Pilot providing you first fly with one of our Aviation Doctors who is himself a pilot. He will assess your limitations and capabilities. We may have to restrict you to aircraft without toe brakes, but we'll wait and see.'

I was completely stunned.

The Air Commodore stood up, shook my hand, and wished me good luck. The medical was at last over.

In the taxi back to King's Cross Station the stress of the day gradually caught up with me. It was the culmination of two years mental and physical torture, and whilst I was telling Valerie the good news I broke down.

A few days later I flew to Stanstead with John Mercer in a Twin Comanche to be tested by the Flying Doctor who put me through my paces in no uncertain terms. The two main points he concentrated on were the use of toe brakes, which I managed to overcome by sliding my feet up the rudder peddles so that I could use my heels to apply independent braking, and asymmetric flight to ascertain that my legs were strong enough to hold the aircraft straight with rudder in the event of one of the engines failing.

I returned to Oxford happily with no medical restrictions on my commercial pilot's licence.

There was no stopping me now. I completed one hour refresher flying with Capt; Ken Fillingham. Two hours thirty five minutes instrument flying with Capt Colin Beckworth, and one hour, ten minutes flight instructors renewal test with CAA examiner Capt; Arthur Blackburn, regaining my commercial instructors rating, and CAA examiners rating within a total of five days and a total flying time of four hours forty five minutes.

Ever since the day of the crash my determination to fly again was always foremost in my mind. But without the skills and devoted care of my surgeon, the nurses and my dear indefatigable physiotherapist Linda, who looked after and encouraged me during those long years in hospital, I could never have made it. I will remain indebted to them all for the rest of my life. But now it was time to get settled into a new job

The date was the 22nd April 1970. I had for so long been concentrating solely on recovering from the crash, and revalidating my licences, that the realisation of actually saying goodbye to Oxford Air Training School hadn't really sunk in. Kidlington Airfield had been like a second home to me. I would be leaving the place where all my dreams about flying had come into fruition. The sudden realisation that I would be leaving all my friends and colleagues was devastating.

I sat in the caravan staring dismally out at the airfield, waiting for my 2pm appointment with Rex to arrive. My thoughts drifted back to the many ups and downs I had witnessed during my happy years at Oxford Airport. I had worked hard with a small, but very enthusiastic nucleus of instructors under the leadership of Rex Smith to help build O. A. T. S. into the world renowned flying school it had now become. I would soon be saying goodbye to all of them and leaving the place that had been the centre of my life for thirteen years. Added to this was the saddest thing of all, by moving to the Midlands I would no longer be able to see my little son on a regular weekly basis. Suddenly the prospect of working for Halfpenny Green no longer seemed such a big deal.

Ted Gibson had agreed for me to commence my employment with Bobbington Estates (The operating company) as from the first of May, that gave me a few days to tie things up at Oxford.. Gibson also gave me the good news that he had found a suitable site on the airfield for us to locate our caravan.

Finally the time for the formal interview with my boss arrived. The meeting was quite short. Rex handed me the official letter that spelt out the Directors decision not to allow me to return to flying duties with CSE. He made the point that if ever I needed a reference or advice in the future, I need only get in touch with him. We had been friends for many years, and this final and formal interview was difficult. I looked at him but I just couldn't bring myself to say anything. I shook his hand, turned away quickly and left the office. It had without doubt been the saddest day of my aviation career. But one cannot see into the future, and as things turned out I had a further 8,000 hours flying ahead of me.

Valerie handed in her notice much to the annoyance of her boss, who tried to persuade her to stay on working at Oxford. I also suggested to Valerie that she should keep her job at Oxford at least until we discovered how things worked out with my new job. But Val insisted that she wanted to move over and join me as soon as possible.

The following day Ted Gibson telephoned me again to say that accommodation had been arranged for me to stay at the Anchor Hotel in Kinver as from the 1st May, and that the Directors had kindly agreed for me to stay there at the Company's expense until our mobile home had been transported to HG.

On the 25th April, I was surprised when Rex Smith called in to see me. For a moment my hopes soared thinking that maybe I had been reprieved. But that was not to be. He asked if I would like to fly one of CSE's aircraft over to Halfpenny Green the next day to collect a radio engineer who had been working for a few days on a private aeroplane based at HG. This was fortunate as it gave me the opportunity of having another look around the Green before I actually started working for them.

The following morning I set off from Oxford in Cherokee G-AVLS at 9.30am in clear skies and excellent visibility bound for Halfpenny Green. Having been one of the company's pilots for so many years, it seemed weird having to sign an indemnity form before taking the aeroplane. Forty-five minutes later I arrived overhead HG. It was quite exciting looking down on the ex world-war-two airfield. All its runways, hangars and buildings looked in quite good shape from the air.

Although I had been a CFI at Oxford, my job had been limited to the command of one section of the school. In my new job I would be in charge of all the flying at Halfpenny Green. The sight of this very smart little aerodrome bucked me up considerably, and when I returned to Oxford Airport that evening I felt keen to get cracking with the challenge of making a new career for myself.

On the last day of April 1970, I awoke with mixed feelings again. I had decided to travel to Staffordshire a day earlier than planned so that I would be ready to start my new job at 9am sharp on the 1st day of May as arranged. The previous evening I had seen Eddy and told him that I was moving away to start another job. To my relief he was not upset at all, in fact he was quite excited about me starting to fly again bless him. The distance from Halfpenny Green to Brackley was not too great, and I would still be able to see him quite albeit not so regularly, even so I found it heartbreaking to say goodbye when the time came for me to leave the little chap.

By 10 o'clock I had packed a few things to take with me, and prepared to leave Oxford Airport for the last time. I was just about to throw my suitcase into the back of the Jag, when I noticed a number of chaps hurrying towards me from the direction of the Flight Ops. building. It turned out to be my great friends Nils Bartleet, John Mercer, Brian Murphy, and Johnny Johnson who, although we had said our goodbyes the previous rather hectic evening in the bar, came out to wish me all the best in my new job.

I drove out of the airport gates recalling the excitement I once felt when I entered Kidlington Airfield for the first time more than a decade earlier.

I arrived at Halfpenny Green aerodrome, at around 1pm, the sun was shining brightly and I was quite impressed with the immaculate appearance of the main entrance. There was a large, beautifully painted sign bearing the name 'HALFPENNY GREEN AIRPORT' together with a tall Flag pole and a red and white "lift-up" barrier. The old RAF guardroom also appeared to be freshly painted gleaming white. Just past the guardroom was a well sign-posted roundabout that indicated directions to The Fire Station, Maintenance Hangar, Flying Club, Restaurant, Workshops, Re-fuelling Bay, Air Traffic Control, Main Reception Office, visitors Car Park and in bold red letters the Emergency Services Rendezvous Point.

Having parked my car, I entered the administration block and knocked on the door marked Airport Director. Ted Gibson was apparently away for the day, so his secretary kindly offered to accompany me to the village of Kinver and introduce me to Arthur, who was the proprietor of the Anchor Hotel where I would be staying for a while.

The Anchor was a delightful little "Old English type" hotel situated by a stream. All the rooms had oak beamed ceilings, and there was a welcoming log fire roaring away in the bar. The Manager turned out to be a delightful chap, who I would guess was in his late sixties. He welcomed me to his hotel and showed me to the very cosy bedroom which was to be mine for the next few days.

Whilst I was driving Elizabeth back to the airfield I invited her and her husband to the hotel that evening for a meal. I thought it would be an excellent way of finding out more about the flying activities of the club I was about to become responsible for. Elizabeth accepted my invitation, so I arranged to pick them up at 7pm from their home in Bridgnorth. Elizabeth explained that she would be on her own as she was not married.

That evening I had difficulty in finding her house and arrived a few minutes late. I noticed that there were three attractive young ladies peering out from the bedroom window. Two of these turned out to be Elizabeth's teenage daughters, obviously curious to see the chap who was taking mum out to dinner.

We spent a delightful evening chatting about the club, and how the owner, Mr Marsh, was keen to upgrade the training facilities at Halfpenny Green so that the company could tender for government sponsored pilot training contracts.

I was a little concerned to learn that my new boss, Ted Gibson, had been known to fly occasionally after a lunchtime session in the bar, probably a habit inherited from his wartime days when it was not unheard of to have the odd glass or two before going into action. I liked Ted very much, and it occurred to me that, as his newly appointed CFI, I could be in the unenviable position of trying to prevent my boss, who was also the Managing Director, from flying whilst under the influence of alcohol, a thought that worried me considerably.

It was late when I dropped Elizabeth back at her home, it had been an enjoyable evening and I had learned a lot about the activities of Halfpenny Green Flying Club.

Unfortunately when I returned to the Anchor Hotel it was closed and locked up. Stupidly I had left my key on the dressing table in my room and was now locked out. Reluctantly I knocked on the door and waited. A small dormer window, just above the main entrance door, squeaked open and a feminine voice whispered…

'Are you the pilot that's staying here?'

Apologetically I said that I had left the keys in my bedroom and was locked out.

'Hang on a minute and I'll come down and let you in.'

Moments later the door opened, and there stood a most attractive young lady about nineteen years old, dressed in a mini night-dress and slippers. My immediate thoughts were: 'Raymond old son, this is undoubtedly your day!'

I followed her into the entrance hall, feeling very guilty, heaven knows why. She, told me that her name was Jean, and asked me to excuse the way she was dressed. I was more than pleased to forgive her, and began to wonder what on earth would happen next. Jean had a very slim figure; her pretty doll like face was framed by long jet-black hair almost down to her waist.

'Granddad's in bed' she said, 'You must be Ray, he told me about you, I love aeroplanes, you must tell me all about your new job.'

Well, let's be honest, I'm as human as the next man, and flying was the last thing I had on my mind at that particular moment!

'Would you like a nice hot drink before you go to bed Ray, or should I call you Mr er ?'

'Ray will do fine' I said 'but I don't want you to go to any trouble making drinks at this time of night.'

She insisted that it was no bother, and said if I liked she would bring the drink to my room. I couldn't believe this was happening to me. A few minutes later, there was a light tap on the door of my bedroom, and there she stood holding two mugs of steaming hot chocolate. She giggled and tip-toed into the room.

Jean explained that she was staying at the Hotel for a few days with her grandparents who were the owners of 'The Anchor' before returning to the Lucy Cavendish College in Cambridge. She spoke in a whisper, explaining that her Grandad, Arthur, and his wife were asleep in the next room.

Cripes! This was now becoming a bit of a nightmare. I could just imagine Arthur knocking on the door, and entering to see Jean in her flimsy nightdress sitting on my bed drinking hot chocolate.

I reminded myself that flying instructor's should be prepared to take the odd risk now and then, and this seemed a cracking time to prove the point! But that, dear readers, is another story. Suffice to say that the following morning I came down to breakfast feeling somewhat guilty, and trying to look as nonchalant as possible. I enjoyed an excellent breakfast of eggs and bacon, served by Grandad!

May the 1st 1970 fell on a Friday; this gave me a full day to settle into my new surroundings before the weekend, the Club's busiest days.

Immediately on arrival at the airport, I was invited into the Managing Director's office for a chat and the proverbial cup of tea. Ted briefly told me about the Club's activities, the aeroplanes they owned and other aircraft that they had unlimited use of in the form of hire contracts with their owners. Apparently all the club aircraft were maintained and serviced under contract to Air 70 Ltd., an independent aircraft maintenance company operating in one of Halfpenny Green's hangars. I asked about the club facilities, and was told that the Halfpenny Green Flying Club had, in his opinion, the finest facilities of any private aero club in the country. When I asked if I could see these facilities, Ted said I had already seen them. He was of course referring to the member's bar and restaurant on the first floor of the Air Traffic Control building. When I asked to see the actual training facilities, he simply said there were none, which came as a bit of a shock.

Gibby, as Ted also liked to be called, went on to explain that the flying training side of things operated from the corridor in the reception area. Chairs were available for members to make themselves comfortable whilst waiting to fly, and bookings were taken by the receptionist through the small window, rather like the ticket office on a railway station. I couldn't believe what I was hearing.

'Surely there are briefing cubicles and a flight planning room. Or is there a general lecture room that can be used for everything?' I asked.

Ted shook his head.

'No we don't bother with things like that Ray. We're a flying club; with the best social facilities of it's kind. Flight planning is done on the back of a fag packet here Ray, you'll soon get used to it.'

'I doubt that' I said, 'what about the MOD contracts you hope to tender for, this place doesn't stand a dogs chance in its present state?'

Ted just laughed, and said..

'That's your job old boy.'

'Thanks.'

At that point the telephone rang in his office, a loud female voice with a plumb-in-mouth tone at the other end addressed Gibby as "Darling". At that point I was asked to pop off and familiarise myself with the airfield.

I left Gibson's office slightly taken aback. Having previously been instructing for one of the finest flying training schools in Europe, I knew there would be some disappointing comparisons, but I never expected Halfpenny Green Flying Club to have no ground training facilities at all.

On my way out to the airfield I tapped the small window of the reception office and was greeted by the rather aloof face of a quite attractive receptionist. I introduced myself and asked her if I could take a look at the student pilot's training records, only to be told that, as far as she knew, there was no such thing. It soon became obvious that the social facilities at HG Flying Club were second to none, and the flying training set-up was crap!

At that moment a tall slightly greying middle aged man entered the reception area and introduced himself as Mike Edwards. His deportment was that of a very fit and well dressed gentleman.

Having introduced myself, I asked Mike if he was a member of the flying club. You could have knocked me down with a feather when he told me that he was in fact employed full-time as a QFI at Halfpenny Green.

I just couldn't believe that neither Gibson nor his secretary had mentioned anything about another full-time instructor. Until then I had been under the impression that all the instructors, other than Gibson himself, were employed on a part time basis at weekends.

I apologised to Mike for not seeking him out earlier, and explained the fact that I had no idea he even existed! We continued our chat over a cup of tea in the airports excellent restaurant. Apparently Mike had instructed at Halfpenny Green Flying Club for several years. He was a Commercial Pilot with single and multi engine instructor ratings, and he was also a

CAA Authorised Examiner. I asked him if he had served with the Royal Air Force at any time? He told me that he had joined the RAF in 1937, two years before the outbreak of World War Two. He flew Spitfires and became a Flight Commander during the Battle of Britain, retiring from the RAF in 1946 .

Obviously I was delighted to have Mike on board, and asked him why he hadn't been offered the job of CFI at HG? He told me that it had been made quite clear to him that the Directors were looking for someone who already had considerable experience as a CFI in an airline training environment, and was also qualified to train flying instructors.

Mike obviously had thousands of

hours experience as a flying instructor, and was a great asset to the club, but from what I could make out, he was treated abominably.

I advised Mike to bide his time as I intended to change things around considerably.

It was no surprise to me that most of the part time instructors turned out to be personal friends of Ted Gibson. They seemed to be decent enough types, but they had become a law unto themselves as far as instructing was concerned, coming and going as they pleased.

As there was no office at my disposal, I sat down quietly in the club bar to sum up the situation and make a few notes. There was an immense amount of work to be done. Apart from the aeroplanes themselves, there was nothing that could be remotely described as pilot training facilities at HG, and even worse, the students progress sheets that Ted apparently kept in his office, were not filled in properly, if at all.

Within a few days I called all the part time instructors together and told them that I intended to display advanced bookings on a flight ops board, and part time instructors will be required to make out an availability sheet at least one week in advance, informing us of the days and times they would be available to instruct at the club, if required. From this information I would be able to make out an advanced flying programme showing the allocated takeoff times of each of the day's bookings, together with the instructors and student's name, and the registration of the aircraft to be used. The ops board would be temporarily situated just inside the entrance to the office building until the proper training facilities had been approved and constructed. This procedure (which should have been adopted years ago) will ensure continuity of training for the students, and also make it easier to plan the maintenance schedules for individual aircraft in advance.

This made sense of course, and they knew it, but I had thrown a spanner into their all too convenient strategy of turning up when they felt like it.

Somehow the flying club seemed to have muddled along happily with virtually no systematic control over the training side. Having said all that, the club members seemed contented enough with the status quo. Also it has to be said that Halfpenny Green Aerodrome had become "World Famous" due to the outstanding work of the race committee who organised the Goodyear Air Races each year. But the flying training methods at HG were chaotic.

The Directors wanted me to attain CAA approval for HGFC, and this meant that practically everything on the flight training side would have to be reorganised. I could see that I was going to be as popular as a pork chop in a synagogue with the so-called management committee. I could also sense that I was being viewed with suspicion by some of the club members. I suppose they liked things as they were, and didn't relish the idea of any changes being made.

One incident occurred during the first few days of my employment that certainly wasn't called for and upset me immensely.

Having not been out of hospital all that long, I still experienced bouts of considerable pain and had quite a serious limp. I didn't think anyone would take much notice of this, but sadly I was wrong.

I had just visited the offices of Air 70 and was hobbling back towards the main building when I passed a group of club members chatting away outside the control tower. I said good morning to them and got a rather disgruntled mumbling as a reply. As I reached the door of the reception office I heard one of them say...

'Surely that's not our new CFI, he's a bloody cripple.'

I turned to see the piss-taking look on their grinning faces. I was incensed and decided to go back and sort the buggers out there and then. But when they saw me coming they walked swiftly away from me on to the perimeter track.

Earlier that morning I had been flying the Aztec and the ignition keys were still in my pocket. Without further thought, I hobbled over to G-AXAX, dragged myself into the cockpit, and started the engines. I called the tower for take-off clearance stating that I was going to stay in the circuit for a low run and break, followed by a full-stop landing.

As soon as the wheels left the runway I raised the undercarriage, levelled out at 50 feet and raised the flaps. Keeping the engines at full throttle so that the airspeed built up rapidly, I looked back and saw they were now standing motionless on the peri track looking up at me. Within seconds I was screaming down straight at them. Fortunately for all concerned they threw themselves to the ground as I pulled up from zero feet into a steep climbing turn and rejoined the circuit.

Landing back on the runway I came to a standstill opposite to the air traffic control building, there was no sign of the morons I had just flattened. The controller shouted down from his balcony that Ted would like me to see me in his office.

The whole thing had been over in less than five minutes. I knew that I had set a bloody awful example and would more than likely be fired on the spot, but at least I felt good about it. I had been to hell and back during the previous two years, and the last thing I needed was to be treated like some form of low-life by those sneering bastards.

I stumped into the corridor of the main office and knocked on Ted Gibson's door.

'Come in.'

I stepped into the office.

'Christ Ray, what the bloody hell was that all about?'

I explained what had happened. Ted looked surprised, shook his head and said …

'The bastards asked for that Ray, but you know probably more than anyone, that sort of flying is not on, so perhaps I could persuade you not to do that again old boy?'

Luckily for me that was all that was said and I never heard anything more about it, neither did I encounter anymore sneers from club members.

Not long after I had started work at Halfpenny Green, a pleasant young gentleman who introduced himself to me as Ken Bishop, asked if I was settling in OK. He seemed a friendly sort of chap and I told him that there was a lot to be done if Halfpenny Green ever hoped to be up-graded. He was an inquisitive type, and during our conversation he asked me how I liked the club-type atmosphere as compared to instructing for a large commercial flying school. Diplomatically ignoring the incident in the Aztec, I said that there seemed to be more emphasis on the social side at HG and by comparison the flying training aspect of the club was a bit of a shambles, adding as a joke that it was very nice to be addressed as 'Ray' instead of the more formal 'sir' which was sometimes the case when training airline sponsored students.

Obviously I had said the wrong thing. Ken took my joke as some kind of criticism and retorted…

'Sir, you'll be bloody lucky, I'm the Chairman and *even I* am not addressed as sir.'

I assumed by his remarks that Mr Bishop was the Chairman of HG's Board of Directors, and that being the case I said that I would like to discuss several important matters with him. His reply was quite aggressive...

'If you wish to speak to me about any matters concerning flying training you will have to make an appointment to see me at the next meeting, and you will be invited in at a convenient time to discuss any problems you may have.'

I thought that was a bit pompous and later mentioned my conversation with Mr Bishop to Mike Edwards. He laughed and told me that Ken was neither a member of the Board or a member of staff. He was in fact the Chairman of the members committee.

Mike spoke of the numerous ups and downs he had experienced with the committee. Most of them were private pilots who had initially been taught to fly by Mike, and now as members of the so called "management committee", were not beyond telling our instructors what they may or may not do. All this, for some strange reason, appeared to have the backing of Ted Gibson, who was quite happy to allow these chaps to govern social matters and control the flying activities of the club. This was surely an awful way to run a business. A committee made up of club members, who have no financial interest in the club's business at all, were actually in charge of its flying activities. The committee governed everything, even to the point of recommending the charges made for tuition and aeroplane hire. Mike warned me not to rock the boat saying...

'They will try to get rid of you as well.'

Altogether this had been a disappointing start to what I had originally thought was going to be a very pleasant and challenging job. Perhaps I was expecting too much from a small flying club. Oxford had been the only flying business I had been associated with in the past, and I had been with them from the days when they were a small club with just two Tiger Moths, to the time when they became the largest privately owned professional flying school in the country. Either way, if I was expected to build HG up into a CAA approved training school, I had no intention of being answerable to a part time management committee who had no financial interests in the company.

I went straight over to see Ted Gibson and suggested that we dissolve the so-called management committee forthwith. Ted went red in the face and told me to calm down, adding...

'Mr Marsh (The owner of Bobbington Estates) would never hear of changing the existing system, it has always been this way since the club was formed.'

I asked Gibson why he didn't tell me that I would be answerable to a members committee when he interviewed me?

Gibson avoided the question, he was obviously annoyed, but so was I, and I had made up my mind to sort the matter out there and then. If the things remained unchanged, then I would have no alternative than to walk away from the situation and find another job.

'I'm sorry Ted, but if you don't want to talk to our Chairman about this, then I will. Have to speak to him myself. Perhaps you could arrange for me to have an interview with Mr Marsh as soon as possible please, preferably today?'

Gibby, not at all happy with my sudden outburst, was also suffering from one of his all too frequent hangovers. He lifted a jaundiced eye and muttered...

'You'll do no good Ray, why cause a fuss? You've got a nice little number here.'

I was smouldering…Nice little number my arse, how can any business expect to be financially viable when it's being controlled by a bunch of chaps who are probably only interested in providing low cost flying for themselves? Come what may, I was not going to be put off…

Ted reluctantly lifted the receiver and spoke to Mr Marsh's secretary, who later telephoned back with an appointment for me to call in and see our Chairman at his home at 8.30pm that evening.

This was obviously an awful way to start a new job. But I always have, and always will hate committees, and I was damned if I was going to be told how to do my job by one.

I arrived at the gates of Mr Marsh's property at eight thirty precisely. Although it was quite dark I could see by my car headlights that this was indeed a beautiful old mansion.

A tall, immaculately dressed, middle aged man answered the door. I first took him to be Mr Marsh, but as soon as he addressed me I realised that he was a member of the household staff.

'Do come in sir, Mr Marsh is expecting you.'

I was shown into an oak panelled study with a large open fireplace from which glowing embers omitted the welcoming smell of burnt pine logs.

'I will inform Mr Marsh that you have arrived sir.'

Moments later I was joined by Mr Marsh, a very distinguished looking gentleman who welcomed me with a broad smile and outstretched hand.

'I have been looking forward to meeting you Mr Blyth, no doubt you will be flying me around in our Aztec from time to time' he said.

I was offered a glass of brandy and invited to sit down in a most comfortable leather chair. After a certain amount of small talk I was asked how I felt about working for Bobbington Estates, and my opinion concerning the future development of Halfpenny Green Airport.

Replying to his question I initially explained how I interpreted my terms of reference within his Company. I said that I had been given to understand that my main task was to upgrade both the facilities and the instructional standards at Halfpenny Green Flying Club in order for it be approved by the CAA to tender for both MOD and CAA pilot training contracts.

Mr Marsh seemed quite happy with my appraisal of the situation, and went on to ask me if I had any immediate problems that he could help me with. This of course was the real reason I had asked for the interview. So I took a large swig of his excellent brandy and came straight out with it.

'I would like permission to invalidate the management committee sir.'

There was a long period of silence. Then Mr Marsh, who looked a little surprised, said…

'I presume you have a very good reason for such a request?'

I thought: 'you bet I have' …. but I obviously couldn't address him in that manner..

'Yes sir I do. With respect I cannot see how on earth any business can be expected to remain on a secure financial footing when its operation and overall policy is governed by a part time management committee. The Halfpenny Green Management Committee consists of a group of men who are not employed by this Company. They may indeed be successful businessmen in their own right, but as far as aviation matters are concerned, they are at best a bunch of keen amateurs with no financial interest in HGFC or its parent company Bobbington Estates. My personal opinion is, if this company is to expand and make its mark in the world of professional pilot training, it will never come to fruition whilst it is controlled by a committee made up of club members.'

Mr Marsh's expression changed to one of displeasure, although he had listened carefully to every word I said without interruption. There followed another rather uncomfortable period of silence. Then, whilst topping up my glass with more of his superb brandy he said…

'I should point out that Bobbington Estates employ a firm of accountants, who keep a very crucial eye on the financial aspect of the club's business. Furthermore, as far as the quality of the members who serve on our committee is concerned, many of these gentlemen are personal friends of mine, who run very successful businesses of their own.'

I could see that I was getting into a bit of a tricky situation. The last thing I wanted to do was insult any of Mr Marsh's friends. Nevertheless I had a perfectly justifiable argument and decided to stick to my guns.

'I agree that our accountants would obviously foresee and possibly avert any major financial disaster, but would they be able to detect whether or not the decisions made by the committee were always in the best interests of the company? Surely such matters should be submitted directly to you for approval by our own management team.'

Finally, with tongue in cheek and fortified by the effects of the brandy, I put forward one further question, and asked Mr Marsh how many of his friends who served on our committee allowed their own businesses to be run solely by a committee of unpaid non-employees?

From the expression on Mr Marsh's face, I gathered that he probably thought I had overstepped the mark. So, that being the case, I decided to finish the evening off in style by saying my final non-rehearsed piece, and if that resulted in putting the lid on it for me, well so be it.... I very carefully placed the empty brandy glass on the small occasional table by my chair and said...

'In the end sir, it all boils down to this. I was under the impression that I had been employed to take over the aviation activities of this company, re-organise and expand its training facilities, standardise the instructional methods of our staff pilots, and generally up-grade Halfpenny Green Flying Club to a professional status. Having previously been employed in a very responsible position by one of the world's finest flying training schools, I refuse to be told how to carry out my job by a committee of part time amateur aviators.'

I wanted to make sure that Mr Marsh was aware of the sincerity of my argument, and kept eye to eye contact with him throughout. Nevertheless the thought quickly passed through my mind that I could be packing my bags again tonight and heading back to Kidlington.

Mr Marsh looked first at his watch, then at me.

'Do you want to dispense with committees altogether?' he asked.

Before I could answer he went on to say.

'I expect that you are aware of the "Goodyear Air Race" which is always held at Halfpenny Green. Well, we have a very special sub-committee that organises this event. It takes weeks and weeks of planning, including liaison with the police, the CAA, the BLAC, the RAF aerobatic teams, and the Royal Aero Club of Great Britain. Also the car parking and catering for many thousands of people on its own is a mammoth undertaking.'

He paused to take a sip of Brandy. So I hastened to take the opportunity of agreeing that there should be an *"entertainment's"* committee, I also said that a member of the permanent flying staff should always be present during entertainment committee's meetings in order to advise. But I still insisted that anything at all that involved the use of company aircraft, and the airport facilities, should always be monitored and agreed by the head of the companies aviation matters, i.e. Mr Gibson or myself.

I was asked how Ted Gibson felt about dissolving the management committee. I answered truthfully and said that in my opinion Ted would prefer the status quo, and off load as much responsibility to a management committee as possible. But now that I was here to help him, he would probably see things differently.

I must admit that I was surprised when Mr Marsh finally said…

'Very well, I agree with you. I think that it is time we moved on, and I also think you are the man to take the lead. Are you happy to deal with the finer points of abolishing the management committee and setting up a new committee to deal solely with the Goodyear Air Race and social activities?'

I obviously agreed, in fact nothing could have given me greater pleasure. Mr Marsh accompanied me to the door and said...

'I will get in touch with Mr Gibson first thing in the morning and inform him of my decision. Ted as you know is a Director of HGFC as well as being the Airport Manager. He has a lot on his shoulders, that's why he has employed you to take over all aspects of the flying side.'

We shook hands, and I left the warm comfort of the Marsh residence and drove back to my hotel in Kinver feeling quite pleased with myself.

The next morning I told Mike the good news. He couldn't wait to see the faces of some of the committee when they were told. So I said if he would like to come to the next meeting when I announce the fact that I intended to dissolve the management committee, he would be more than welcome to do so. We decided not to let the cat out of the bag, and to say nothing until the actual meeting took place. In the past they had given poor old Mike a pretty tough ride, telling him what he may or may not do. Most of these chaps were taught to fly by him, and owed what little they knew about aviation to his patience, hard work and understanding.

Gibby called me in to his office the following morning and readily agreed to say nothing until the changes were officially announced at the next committee meeting.

There was also another nasty little problem that I would have to sort out, involving the method used by certain examiners to test students at HG for the issue of their private flying licences.

As previously mentioned, Mike Edwards was a fully qualified CAA Examiner. But Gibby, in his old capacity as CFI, seldom allowed Mike to carry out any tests, preferring to do the tests himself. Apparently one of the part time instructors who served on the BLAC committee had somehow managed to secure an examiners rating for himself without actually being employed full-time in aviation. Gibby was very friendly with this chap and allowed him to come in at weekends and test some of the students for licence issue. (Another case where part time staff seemed to rule the roost). I was informed that this gentleman had taken it upon himself to adopt the totally unethical practice of passing students who had just failed their FHT (Final Handling Test) without the further recommended training being carried out. By doing this of course, he had undermined the authority of the initial examiner who had just failed the student. So I had to prepare myself for yet another confrontation if this ever happened again.

Mr Marsh sent a letter to me outlining the points discussed at our meeting. They included his agreement to abolish the Management Committee and replace it with an Entertainment's Committee. He concluded by saying that I had his consent to convert the ground floor of the Air Traffic Control building into a flying school if I wished to do so, and if I needed to convert any other premises on the airfield, I was to contact him direct for the necessary permission. This was really great news.

I mentioned all this to Gibby, who said that it would be a good idea if I set up my own office in the control building straight away so that I could work without interference from the rest of the staff. I chose a small room overlooking the airfield and converted it into a comfortable little pad of my own, equipping it with an ex-service desk and chair, an electric fire, a filing cabinet and the small portable drawing board I had brought with me from Kidlington.

I prepared scale drawings of a few selected buildings on the airfield that I thought could be refurbished and used for flying training purposes. There were many things to consider. First and foremost mandatory training facilities for CAA course approval would have to be set up to house a functional flight operations room that would become the nerve centre of all flying training carried out at the school. Other rooms would have to be designed to accommodate a flight planning facilities, briefing cubicles, lecture room, instructors office and a pilot's rest room. Finally there was the question of finding a suitable building for conversion into living accommodation to sleep and feed a minimum of thirty resident students. All the above were obligatory requirements for MOD pilot training contracts, unfortunately Halfpenny Green had none of them at that time.

The only permanent flying staff was Ted Gibson, Mike Edwards and myself. So I would have to try and find a nucleus of reliable part time instructors capable of passing the RAF Central Flying School Flight Test. Later, if all went well, I would take on more permanently employed instructors together with flight Ops staff, a cook, and a full time cleaner.

Obviously one of the problems associated with tendering for military and CAA pilot training contracts was that all facilities have to be set up and ready for inspection before contracts could be awarded. The initial cost to set up these facilities would be significant, and unfortunately there was no guarantee that a contract would be awarded.

I aimed to have everything inspected and ready for the Summer of 1971. Another very important aspect would be to ensure that the flying requirements for the club members continued satisfactorily, including the all important plans for the 1971 Goodyear Air Race.

Halfpenny Green Flying Club owned five Piper Cherokee 140 aeroplanes and one Cherokee 180 together with a Beagle Pup approved for aerobatics and spinning. All club aircraft were fitted with VHF radios, and most of them were equipped with radio navigational aids. There were also several interesting privately owned aircraft that I hoped to get my hands on later.

The social side of the club was undoubtedly second to none. Almost every night there was some excuse or other for a first class "hooley". Later I was to be caught out badly after one of these sessions which unfortunately coincided with Valerie's arrival at Halfpenny Green.

The site for our caravan had been cleared and made ready, and all that had to be done was connect it up to the water mains, sewerage and electricity services which the airport maintenance staff kindly offered to do when the van arrived a few days later.

As luck would have it, our mobile home was delivered and had been set up on site the same evening as an impromptu party developed in the club bar. Valerie arrived with the van and decided to wait at home and greet me on my return from work. Unfortunately I had too much to drink and was somewhat late leaving the party. When Val came out from the caravan to greet me, her smile turned to a look of horror when she opened the door of my car. I rolled out onto the ground and was helped to my feet by Ted Gibson's secretary Elizabeth, who had kindly offered to drive my car to the van as I was incapable of driving. The fact that she was a stunning blonde didn't help matters, and my unorthodox arrival took some time to live down!

The first few weeks in my new job passed very quickly. The weather remained good, so I was able to carry out some instructional flying with a good cross section of the club members. It became blatantly obvious that there had been little, or indeed no attempts made to standardise the training methods used by the instructors. So, with the intention of rectifying the situation, I arranged an early meeting for all the instructional staff.

The meeting went quite well to begin with, but when I explained that, as CFI, I would be carrying out standardisation flight checks with all of them, the atmosphere changed. One of the part-timers, who also happened to be the examiner who had taken it upon himself to pass students who had just failed their GFT without dual revision, seemed to think he was above any such standardisation checks, saying…

'If we can't instruct by now we might as well give up and go home.'

I explained that I was not complaining about their quality of instructing which, judging by the students I had flown with, appeared to be pretty good. I merely wished to make sure that our methods were standardised, i.e. we all taught exactly the same manoeuvring speeds and also produced the same blackboard layouts for our pre-flight briefings.

Whilst I was at it I said that I couldn't believe that instructors were not filling in the student progress sheets properly, and from now on I expected to see information about how the student coped with the lesson he had just taken. And not just the word "Satis".

The same instructor complained again and sarcastically said that he didn't have time to write a book about each of the students he flew with. So I suggested that he should indeed go home as he had previously suggested, so that he could give the matter serious thought, and if he didn't wish to comply with the methods I intended to adopt, then he needn't bother to come back.

Having explained that the reason I had been employed was to turn HG into a CAA approved flying training school, the atmosphere in the meeting brightened up a little.

Within a few months the schools facilities were brought up to standard and the accommodation block completed. Part of the confusion re instructional standards turned out to be the club using several differing printed checklists for the same type of aircraft. Virtually none of them kept to the recommended speeds set out in the aircraft manufacturer's handling notes. The differences were not great, or in any way dangerous, but they were obviously confusing to the students. I also noticed that Mike Edwards seemed to have been the only instructor to carry out fully developed spinning details which were a mandatory part of the private pilot syllabus in those days.

The first serious problem I had with a member of the part time staff occurred a few weeks later when I was having lunch. Mike Edwards came over to see me in a bit of a flap and told me that earlier in the day he had flown with a student for the purpose of taking his flying test. (GFT). The candidate apparently messed up on his practice forced landing procedure and consequently failed the test. The student was informed that he would have to have further dual training in forced landings before applying for another test. Later the same morning when Mike returned from a training flight with another student, he saw the young lad that he failed earlier, sitting in the cockpit of a Cherokee with a part time instructor. Mike immediately checked the flight sheet, expecting to see that the lad was booked out for dual practice forced landing training as recommended, only to find that he was about to take his flight test again with the part time examiner without further PFL training as recommended. As previously stated this was not the first time that this examiner had undermined the authority of Mike Edwards who was understandably bloody furious. I asked Mike if there was any chance of stopping the aircraft before it took off, and was told that he had positioned his car in front of the dispersal area so that the Cherokee couldn't move out.

That was the end of my lunch. I followed Mike to the dispersal area, wondering what sort of job I had taken on with this lot.

The examiner who was also the instructor that had complained about standardisation training a few weeks earlier, was now out of the aircraft and running towards us as we approached the dispersal area. As soon as we were within earshot he started mouthing off saying he was going to report Mike to the CAA for parking a car in front of an aircraft with it's engine running. I must admit he certainly had a valid point. I invited the two fuming instructors to step into the office so that the dispute could be settled out of sight and sound of club members and students. But the irate self opinionated examiner refused and continued to hurl abuse at Mike. I tried to calm the chap down, asking him if he had read Mike's recommendations on the student's progress sheet. The answer I got was implausible ...

'I don't take any notice of what he says, that bastard fails everyone.'

I started to say something but he continued to talk over me…

'You needn't start mouthing off Blyth, coming here with all your fancy high-fluting commercial pilot training methods, no-one's going to take any bloody notice of you here mate.'

That was enough for me, there was obviously no way that I was going to calm this chap down, so I told him, that as from that moment his employment as a part time instructor at Halfpenny Green was terminated and asked him to leave the airfield, adding that I would take steps to try and have his CAA examiners authority revoked. I had to step back rather smartly as the chap took a swing at me and missed. Mike, who was an extremely fit man and no small guy, moved forward, and changed the chaps mind for him before he had another go. Throwing the company's headset to the ground he left the airfield shouting abuse at the pair of us.

Fortunately that was the last I saw of him. This annoying confrontation left me keener than ever to get rid of the management committee and anyone else who tried to provoke trouble. The success of any training organisation obviously depends on a keen efficient staff operating in a happy environment.

There seemed to be no limits to the extraordinary behaviour of some of the club's private pilots. For instance I remember walking past a chap swinging the propeller of a 'Minicab' just outside one of the hangars. The aircraft had the traditional type of undercarriage, and although chocks had been placed under the main wheels, there was no-one inside the cockpit. I offered to swing the prop for him so that he could sit inside and control the revs when the engine fired, his reply was a bit negative

'I own this aircraft and I've started it this way for years. It's not one of the clubs aeroplanes.'

No words of thanks, kiss my arse….nothing. He was correct in assuming that it was none of my business, nevertheless it was a dangerous thing to do. Anyway I wished him the best of British luck and continued on my way. But it just so happened that this was his unlucky day! Suddenly there was an almighty cracking noise that sounded exactly like a short burst of machinegun fire. I swung round to see the Minicab up on its nose against the hangar doors with bits of wooden propeller flying everywhere. The owner was rolling over on the tarmac some yards away from his machine. By the time I reached him he had picked himself up and was limping back towards the aeroplane. Reaching into the cockpit to turn off the master switch he looked back at me and said…

'I suppose you've come to gloat.'

I ignored his remarks and helped him to right his aircraft, which had obviously started with the throttle set too far open and jumped the chocks. He was lucky to have escaped being chopped into pieces by the prop. I couldn't help feeling sorry for the chap, and took him back to our caravan where Val made him a nice cup of coffee.

The following morning, Ken Bishop called in at my office tell me that a management committee meeting had been arranged for 8pm that evening and I was formally requested to attend. He added that I would not be permitted to sit through the whole meeting, but if I cared to wait in the club bar, I would be called in when they reached the part of the agenda that concerned me. I asked if it would be alright for Mike Edwards to accompany me, but my request was refused in no uncertain terms.

' Why not?' I asked.

'Just be there' he said, slamming the door as he left.

The self important attitude of these buggers was beginning to get up Raymond's nose in no uncertain terms. If they were supposed to be there for the good of the flying club they could have fooled me! To make things worse, shortly after Ken left my office, Jeff Webster, the head of the South Staffs Sky Divers, our resident parachute club, popped in to see me.

Jeff, a really likeable chap, asked me if I had been informed of the repeated complaints Ted Gibson received about low flying aircraft passing over a house near to the airfield.

'He's threatening to report the matter to the authorities if nothing is done about it.'

The person concerned lived in a large house situated about one hundred yards on the far side of the airfields Northern boundary, smack in line with our 34 runway.

'His house is practically on the runway, what else did the man expect' I asked?

'That chap would complain about noise from the sea if his property was anywhere near the coast' Jeff replied.

Apparently Ted Gibson refused to see the man, so I promised Jeff that I'd go and see him before the matter got completely out of hand. In fact there was no time like the present, it was already early evening, and probably a good time to catch him at home. His name was Mr Holland, a dental surgeon at the local hospital. Jeff knew the man fairly well, and suggested that he should come with me to make the appropriate introductions. I decided to strike whilst the iron was hot, so we set off in Jeff's car there and then. On the way he told me all about the repeated threats and constant complaints Ted Gibson had received from Holland. It was unfortunate that Ted chose to ignore the man, which probably made things a lot worse. But on the last occasion, Holland said he was going to make moves to try and get the airfield closed down altogether. What with one thing and another, It seemed to me that Halfpenny Green Airfield was a wasps nest of problems.

Passing through wrought iron gates we continued up the drive towards a magnificent old house set in immaculate gardens. Everything had gone wrong for me that day and I'd had just about enough. These people needed to be educated about the law relating to low flying aircraft, which states that an aircraft shall not fly less than 500 feet over persons or property etc., without special dispensation from the CAA. One exception to that rule was for aircraft taking off or landing. After all Holland made the choice of buying a property that was actually bordering the airfield's perimeter. In my opinion they wouldn't stand a chance if they took us to court for low flying .

As we approached the entrance to the house, I noticed that Jeff was looking decidedly apprehensive. I tugged at the doorbell chain and was bemused by the sound of church-like chimes that echoed somewhere inside the house. After all the squabbling that had taken place earlier with the instructors, I was more than ready for an argument with this Mr Holland character.

The door creaked open to reveal a middle aged lady, eloquently dressed with slightly greying hair, she was absolutely stunning. Her appearance caught me off guard completely and all former aggression immediately evaporated.

'My name is Ray Blyth, I've recently taken over as head of flying at Halfpenny Green Airfield and my colleague here is Mr Webster who is in charge of the parachute club. I wonder if it would be convenient for us to have a word with Mr Holland please?'

When she spoke her voice was both warm and cultured with a slight accent that I found difficult to place. She said her name was Michelin and her husband, Norman, was not in at that time, although she was expecting him home at any moment. We were invited into a lavishly appointed sitting room and offered a glass of mulled wine, which I for one was more than willing to accept. Moments later I heard the sound of Holland's car crunching its way up the gravelled drive.

Norman Holland was a large, distinguished looking man with grey curly hair, long bushy sideburns and a ruddy complexion that made him a fitting character for any of Dickens's novels. He was smartly dressed in a black suit with just the right amount of shirt-cuff showing. He also sported a bright red waistcoat with crested brass buttons, his black leather shoes were polished to a mirror finish that would be the pride of any sergeant major.

After formal introductions he asked how he could help me. Fortified by the large helping of mulled wine, I pointed out that I had called to see him in connection with his continuous complaints about the airfield, and therefore it was probably more a matter of what I could do to help him. Holland let rip with a deep-throated laugh, and said...

'Splendid....My dear fellow, what a delightful thing to say, you do surprise me, no-one from the airfield ever wants to help me, quite the reverse in fact.'

I hated continual complainers, yet, rather against my will I was beginning to warm towards this idiosyncratic gentlemen. He continued...

'I am forever being disturbed by noisy low flying little aeroplanes that seem to make a point of zooming as close as they can to my house, which incidentally is rented to me by the National Trust and costs a fortune to maintain. It seems to me Ray, that the way some of these fellows fly, they are deliberately trying to annoy me. Surely they should stick to the rules of the air, and not pass over my property at less than 500 feet, should they not?'

I had to admit to myself, but certainly not to Norman Holland, that there were certain individuals at the flying club who might just go out of their way to try and upset him by buzzing his house. However, I pointed out that aircraft flying into or out of an airfield are exempt from the 500-foot rule, otherwise how could they possibly take-off or land? Also as his premises actually adjoined the airfield boundary, and his house was smack on the extended centre line of runway three-four/one-six, it was reasonable to expect aeroplanes to pass over his house considerably lower than 500 feet when using that runaway for taking off or landing. I added that I would look into the situation in case anyone was deliberately flying dangerously, and also promised to write a suitable order in the hitherto non-existent "Pilot's Order Book".

Holland was not particularly happy, but I think he realised that I was correct in my assessment of the situation. So, not to be completely out done, he went on...

'How about this then?...Not many days ago a parachutist made a spectacular landing on the top of my greenhouse, totally demolishing the blasted thing. OK, I admit accidents do happen, but what annoys me more than anything is that I have complained to the Manager of Halfpenny Green Airport on numerous occasions, and to date have never received a reply. Therefore I am exceedingly pleased, and somewhat surprised to see you dear boy.'

Under the circumstances Norman Holland impressed me by his amiability. He looked me in the eye continuously whilst speaking to me, never once did I get the slightest impression that he may be exaggerating. He was genuinely concerned, and under the circumstances I believed he probably had cause for complaint.

In order to deal with the complaints generally, I suggested that we set up a resident's "Airfield Consultative Committee" consisting of Mr Holland and selected members of the local village who could meet at regular intervals with myself representing the airfield, and Jeff Webster representing the parachute club. These meetings would be a good way of ironing out most of the complaints on the spot, and would also keep local residents informed of various activities planned to take place at the airfield. Norman Holland was delighted with my idea, and suggested that the ACC should meet three times a year, with emergency meetings called if necessary.

We left with the Holland's waving goodbye at the door.

'That went well' I said.

Jeff just laughed and said...

'You were going to be brutal in there Ray... what happened to all that aggression?'

It had been a long and somewhat tedious day, but it wasn't over yet.

At 8pm I arrived at the club bar. The steward informed me that the committee meeting being held in Bobbington Estate offices had commenced, and the Chairman, Ken Bishop, had left a message to say that there may not be time for the committee to see me this evening as they had a heavy agenda. Mike sat at the bar with me.

'Typical', he said, 'they'll mess you about just to let you know who's the boss.'

'We'll see about that' I replied.

I waited in the bar for over an hour with no word from the meeting. I finished my pint, got up, and said to Mike...

'Come on old boy, if they don't want to see us, we'll go and see them.'

Mike downed the remains of his pint and as he followed me out of the bar he said...

'I bet you even money Ray that the steward is on the telephone to them right now telling them all he overheard of our conversation.'

As far as I was concerned this had been a pretty bloody day up to now, and I was keen to get the whole thing over and done with.

I knocked hard on the door of the Estate's boardroom but to no avail. I knocked again even harder.

'If they didn't hear that they must all be deaf.' I could hear them talking, but still no-one came to the door. I winked at Mike.

'Come on mate, I've had enough of this crap.'

Half expecting the door to be locked, I tried the handle and it opened. We entered the dismal blue atmosphere of a smoke hazed room, the stark light from the fluorescent tubes lit up the astonished faces of eight men seated at the boardroom table.

'Good evening gentlemen. I hope you will excuse me interrupting your meeting, but I think I have been kept waiting long enough don't you?'

The room became extremely quiet. I looked at the two rows of angry faces waiting for someone to speak. Ken Bishop, almost choking on his cigar, said rather abruptly…

'You have no authority to barge in here like this Ray, this is a serious meeting. I would be obliged if you would kindly wait outside until we are ready to see you', adding, 'I'm afraid Edwards is not on our agenda to attend this meeting.'

I'd had all I could take. To everyone's obvious disapproval, I pulled up a chair and sat down at the boardroom table, beckoning Mike to do the same. I could see no purpose in prolonging this meeting and decided to get straight to the point…

'Seeing that you are too busy to see me gentlemen, I can save you a lot of time and effort this evening by informing you that I am dissolving the management committee altogether. I would like to thank everybody around this table for your past efforts but as of this moment you are all redundant!'

You could have heard a pin drop. For a few seconds the room was in total silence whilst the eight men stared at me in disbelief, I'm sure they expected me to laugh and say it was some sort of joke. But the expression on my face didn't change. Agitated shuffling and mutterings broke the silence. One of the committee said…

'He can't do that, who the bloody hell does he think he is for Christ sake?'

I decided to put their minds at rest.

'I should explain gentlemen, I have discussed this matter thoroughly with the Chairman of Bobbington Estates, Mr Marsh. He agrees with me that Halfpenny Green Flying Club is about to enter a more professional stage in it's development, and as such it's future operations cannot be governed by a committee made up of non-employees. The Chairman appreciates all the work you gentlemen have done for HGFC over the past years, and will be writing to each of you personally in due course.'

Understandably everyone looked a bit shocked and upset, but no-one could argue with the logic of this decision.

Bill Todd introduced himself rather curtly, and asked if I had any idea of the immense amount of work that the committee put into organising the "Goodyear Air Race" each year.

Bill's intervention gave me the perfect opportunity of putting forward the suggestion I had discussed with Mr Marsh…

'I am fully aware of the extreme hard work and highly professional standards your Air Race sub committee has applied to organising the Goodyear Air Races. I have discussed this with Mr Marsh and we would like to change the status of the Management Committee to that of Entertainments Committee in order for you continue planning the Goodyear Air Races, and also deal with any other social events that take place on the airfield. But from now on policy matters and operational matters including the use of company aircraft, will be dealt with by the permanently employed management team, in other words Mr Gibson and myself.

This provoked a lengthy discussion that ended with most of the people around the table agreeing with my proposal. I said that it would also be essential for a member of the permanent staff to be present at these meetings in order to iron out any problems relating to the use and availability of the company's facilities. They reluctantly agreed, so I said that the person representing the permanent staff at their meetings would be Mike Edwards. Judging by their faces, this seemed to upset one or two people, although none of them said a word. Bill Todd was proposed, seconded and duly elected as Chairman of the newly formed entertainment's committee.

Of course there had to be the proverbial fly in the ointment. One member of the now redundant management team stood up, slammed his briefcase closed, and said he might as well f… off if this was all the appreciation he got after years of work. He also added that this is what he expected from a bloody jimmy-jump-up from Oxford Air Training School. I tried to console him by saying that his past efforts were indeed very much appreciated by the Directors of Bobbington Estates, and he would be more than welcome to serve as a member of the newly formed committee. But my words seemed to fall on deaf ears. As he left another guy who was bursting to put in his two-penneth headed for the door shouting…

'You have no right to come to Halfpenny Green lording it over everyone. This is a club, not a f------g commercial flying school.'

I knew I would have to face up to some flack about Oxford, but the arrogance of those two guys was something else. I politely wished them good luck with their future flying, and hoped that when they cooled down they would remain members of the flying club.

After the somewhat eruptive initiation into the throws of becoming Chief Instructor at HG, things finally began to settle down and fall into place. Those that had served on the committee purely for their own benefit eventually faded into the ether. The new entertainment's committee were a great bunch of chaps who met regularly and did an excellent job. The few chaps that organised the Goodyear Air Race were irreplaceable, they had years of experience organising this monumental event, and there was no doubt in anyone's mind that the air race could never have gone ahead in August 1970 without their valued expertise, hard work and enthusiasm.

Our relationship with Norman Holland improved considerably. The consultative committee met regularly, and although the meetings sometimes became a little heated, everyone seemed to abide by the final decisions that were made. Norman in fact proved to be a great help to me, all the villagers took notice of him and treated him like their village "Squire", seldom daring to disagree with him. I felt that we were finally getting somewhere towards gaining the good will of all the local residents.

CHAPTER 44.

Changes of Ownership.

The weeks passed and all was well. Everything fell into place and my staff all worked hard to bring the whole thing into line for the beginning of seasonal contract work from The Ministry of Defence. Then something happened that I was totally unprepared for.

I was summoned to the main office and informed, in the nicest possible way by the Company Chairman Mr Marsh, that Bobbington Estates had been sold lock stock and barrel to Mr Nat Somers, the owner of Southampton Airport. The deal included the sale of the complete airfield, the Club, and the Flying School. The existing tenancy agreement with Air 70 Ltd who maintained our aircraft would be allowed to run its course, and Mr Somers was due to take over as from Monday of the following week!

This certainly came as a shock to everyone including Ted Gibson who knew nothing about the discussions that had taken place. Strangely enough I had noticed a Navajo aircraft arrive on the airfield several times over the previous few days. On each occasion Mr Marsh had greeted the Pilot personally and taken him off in his chauffeur driven car. But I never suspected that negotiations to sell the airport were in progress.

The change of ownership left me fingering rapidly through the back pages of 'Flight International' to see if there were any suitable vacancies I could apply for should Mr Somers decide to dispense with my services.

Monday arrived, and things began to happen extraordinarily quickly. At 9.30am as I was taxying out with a student in one of the company's Cherokees, I noticed the Navajo that I had seen on previous occasions was parked in dispersal. Three gentlemen carrying briefcases emerged, they were greeted by Ted Gibson and escorted to the offices of Bobbington Estates.

One hour later, when I returned from my instructional detail. Mike met me at the aeroplane and told me that I was required to report to the Estate Office immediately. As I entered the main building, I noted that our receptionist Mandy appeared to be crying. Ted's secretary Elizabeth met me outside the office door looking pale and very upset, she whispered 'good luck Ray.'

I didn't need to guess what was coming. With gathering apprehension I knocked on the door and entered.

Three smartly dressed businessmen stared at me, not a smile amongst the lot of them. The tense atmosphere confirmed my suspicions that something very unpleasant had just taken place. Two of the men occupied the seats on either side of the window, the third sat at Ted Gibson's desk, but there was no sign of Ted.

The man sitting at the desk peered over his half-moon spectacles and said...

'Good morning Mr Blyth. My name is Somers. I have just bought this airfield, and you with it I'm afraid.'

I had a nasty feeling that I wasn't going to like what was coming next!

Mr Somers introduced me to the other two gentlemen, who turned out to be his accountant and his company's solicitor. There being nowhere to sit at that time, I stood there in front of the desk rather like a serviceman who had been brought before his commanding officer on a charge of misconduct. The first irrelevant thought that crossed my mind was the remarkable resemblance between Mr Somers and the film actor Alastair Sims, they were almost identical to one another.

Mr Somers shuffled a few papers around on his desk, giving me the impression that he was trying to find suitable words to terminate my employment contract. But I was soon to learn that this man never fumbled his words, he was always direct and straight to the point. His next sentence floored me completely...

'How would you like to be the Airport Manager Mr Blyth?'

I wasn't at all sure what he meant, Mr Gibson was the Airport Manager here. Perhaps he was offering me a job at some other airport. So I said...

'You don't mean Halfpenny Green Airport do you sir?'

Somers glared at me over his spectacles again.

'Well I certainly didn't mean London Airport' he said.

'But what's happened to Mr Gibson?'

I saw the expression on Somers's face change, and immediately wished I hadn't asked that question.

'We seem to be getting off to a bad start Mr Blyth. Will you, or will you not accept the responsibilities of Airport Manager at this airfield, it's a simple enough question that requires a simple answer, yes or no?'

I thought for a moment whilst Somers continued to glare at me impatiently.

'Yes sir, I will accept the job. But I would like to point out that I have never previously undertaken the responsibilities of an airport manager. In fact I have only been in charge of flying training here and also at Oxford. Also, I would like to ask you if I take over as Airport Manager will this cause any grief to Mr Gibson? If so I would rather not accept the job.'

Mr Somers stood up and started to put documents into his briefcase.

'Mr Gibson has already left, he will return in a day or two to empty his desk, in the meantime this will be your office. With effect from this moment, you are the Airport Manager, and I will notify the authorities to this effect. Mrs Elizabeth Wardrobe is now your secretary, and I have no doubt she will help you all she can. You can still oversee the flying, but your main task will be to administer the day to day running of this airport. We will discuss salary at a later date.'

With that the three of them shook hands with me, and, following a word with Elizabeth, returned to their aeroplane.

Feeling completely stunned, I stood at the window of Gibby's Office, staring out at the Navajo as it taxied along the perimeter track towards the duty runway. The whole thing had been over in a flash. I could hardly believe what had happened. Elizabeth appeared at the office door with a cup of much needed coffee.

'Hello Boss' she said smiling.

After a while I learned that there had been an almighty row before Ted Gibson left. The receptionist Mandy, obviously thought the world of Ted and was very upset. She didn't take kindly to me becoming the Manager, and I'm sure she thought that I had something to do with Ted's departure, which in fact was the last thing I wanted and was as much of a mystery to me as it was to her.

I told Mike what had happened. He seemed both surprised and pleased, as there had always been a clash of personalities between himself and Ted Gibson. Patting me on the shoulder he said...

'Well done mate.'

I told him to forget the congratulations, as I had no intention of being the Airport Manager for long. I had only accepted the position as a breathing space, rather than have a stranger telling us how to run things. Flying had been my ambition since childhood, and I had no intention of giving that up.

Over the next few weeks I gained great respect for Mr Somers, whom I soon found out was a very successful businessman and an exceptional pilot. He had been a test pilot at one stage of his career, and also won the Kings Cup Air Race in 1949 flying a Miles Gemini. However, his similarity to Alastair Sims, especially in his portrayal of Mr Scrooge, became even more evident when, in order to save paper, he insisted on us replying to his correspondence by typing on the reverse side of the letters we received.

A couple of weeks after being made Airport Manager, I was approached by Mr David Clement, Executive Director of the resident aircraft maintenance company "Air 70 Limited". He asked me what my reactions would be if Air 70 put in a bid to purchase the flying club and flight training side of the business from Nat Somers. David also said Air 70 would not be interested in purchasing the club unless I stayed on to expand and run the flying aspect of the business. This of course was exactly the sort of thing I hoped would happen, because Nat Somers had shown little interest in expanding the flying side, and managing the airport, as far as I was concerned, was all office work and very little flying.

After a considerable amount of haggling, Somers finally accepted an offer made by Air 70 to purchase Halfpenny Green Flying Club. I was taken on the staff of Air 70 as CFI and Chief Pilot. That left Halfpenny Green without an Airport Manager, so I was very pleased when Nat Somers appointed Elizabeth Wardrobe to fill the vacancy. At last, after the many ups and downs of the past weeks, I was now free to carry on with the business of expanding and developing the flying side of Halfpenny Green.

The time consuming and specialised work of preparing for the 1970 "Goodyear Air Race" was undertaken and very satisfactorily carried out by the same chaps that had always organised this major event. .

Many thousands of spectators from all over the country descended on Halfpenny Green each year to watch the air race. Car parking, the provision of extra public toilets, outside catering, and special arrangements for ambulance and medical facilities were all major concerns that had to be organised. In addition to the race itself, the RAF 'Red Arrows' always put in an appearance, together with various other teams, and solo aerobatic displays. Bill Todd had the unenviable task of race coordinator, and Barry Tempest was responsible for arranging the various flying displays.

A few weeks before the race took place, Barry telephoned me to ask if I would like to take the opportunity of advertising the flying club with a fly past of club aeroplanes whilst the commentator said a few words over the public address system advertising the club's activities. I agreed providing our very tame little fly past didn't have to follow the Red Arrows! Barry laughingly saw my point, and offered us a spot right at the beginning of the aerial display sequences, allowing us a slot time of ten minutes from take-off to landing. On the actual day of the race everything went as planned, and the race was a great success. But there were a couple of close calls that occurred prior to the day of the race that could have been fatal, and I have to admit that the first of these incidents was entirely my fault.

I decided to limit the Club's display to a simple formation of three Cherokee aircraft. As the RAF Red Arrows were performing later in the day, we decided to call ourselves 'The Green Toothpicks.'

The pilot's flying the aircraft would be myself, Mike Edwards and John Curd who was an ex S/ldr and one of our part time instructors. I would lead in our only PA-28-180, whilst Mike and John, who were experienced ex RAF instructors, would be flying the two PA-28-140s.

Obviously we were very limited in the type of display we could put on with three essentially non-aerobatic aeroplanes, so we decided to work out a simple sequence made up of low level formation passes in front of the crowd whilst the commentator said a few words about the activities of the flying club.

On the day everything was perfect, but I nearly came to grief during a practice run a couple of days earlier. The aerial sequence was for us to take-off in vic-three formation, changing to echelon starboard during a right-hand climbing turn after take-off. The turn was continued to line up with the display line for a low pass whilst still in echelon starboard formation. Then during the second climbing turn to the right we changed to line astern formation with another low-run. Finally, for the last pass, we would climb to eight hundred feet, change back to a vic-three formation in the turn and dive down steeply to gain speed and carry out a low-run down the display line. On the R/T call 'break', the two outer aircraft would break steeply left and right, whilst the leading aircraft pulled up into a near vertical wing over. This would be followed by a stream full-stop landing. The timing of this little display fitted our allocated time precisely. I used our Cherokee 180 G-AVSA for the lead aircraft as it gave me a little more power for the wing over that would commence from a few feet above ground level.

It was during one of our practices that things went dangerously wrong. All three of us were experienced in formation flying, so little went wrong on that score. But after our first practice session, Mike mentioned that he thought I was leaving the command to 'Break' a little late. He was flying on my starboard wingtip in the number one position and apparently my late call caused him to pass uncomfortable close to the airfield's NDB aerial. Everything else seemed to be OK. So after a quick cup of tea we decided to go up and run through the sequence again. This time I would call break just before we came to the intersection of the runway and the display line. The R/T call to break would carry two preparatory warnings ….i.e. 'Break… Break… GO.'

So off we went to practice the sequence again. All went well up to the completion of the low pass in line astern. We climbed out to the right changing back to the vic-three formation and completed a steady climbing turn that brought us up to 800 ft. facing the airfield. Then it was down into a steep dive towards the display line. We roared low over the grass, and as we approached the intersection I called…

'Break… Break… Go.'

At the extreme periphery of my vision I saw the underside of my two colleague's aircraft as they broke away steeply to the left and right. Then I made the mistake…. for a split second, I looked back at Mike to see that he was well clear of the NDB aerial. But in that split second my aircraft had edged a few degrees to the left of the display line and was heading straight for the Air Traffic Control building. When I looked to the front the whole building completely blotted out my forward vision, and I could see the occupants of air traffic rushing to escape the impending disaster. I'm not certain of the range but my aircraft was extremely close to the control tower and slightly below the level of the balcony. I hauled back on the control column as hard as I could convinced that I would hit the top of the building. The excessive 'G' loading inflicted on this poor little aeroplane must have been on the limits. At the same second there was an almighty BANG! as the aircraft struck something and slued sideways whilst travelling almost vertically upwards. I fully expected Sierra Alpha to roll on to her back minus a wing or something and dive straight into the ground.

I had already experienced one near-fatal crash in my life that put me in hospital for two years, and I was in no way suffering from the delusion that this could never happen to me again, so I was fully aware that this could well be the one stupid mistake that would cost me my life. The airspeed was decreasing rapidly as I eased the control column forward. The Cherokee appeared to be responding normally to the controls. Adrenaline pumped through my veins like an express train, and I could hear hysterical voices shouting in my headphones. With the aircraft's speed dangerously low, I managed to hold her in a straight and level attitude. Then as the speed built up I very gently eased the control column around to check the response from the ailerons and elevators. Amazingly Sierra Alpha reacted normally. My mouth now parch dry, I glanced nervously at the control surfaces and they appeared to be undamaged. As I eased Sierra Alpha into a very shallow turn to the left I could hear David Smith our Controller calling me urgently…

'Sierra Alpha, I say again you've struck something on the top of the tower.'

I pressed the tit and said...

'I had noticed!'

Having ascertained over the R/T that no-one in the control tower had been injured, I was now struggling to control my own destiny. My heart was still banging away in my ears, and my hands were trembling as I approached to land. Air Traffic informed me that the wheels appeared to be undamaged and I prayed that everything would hold together when I touched down. I decided to land on the grass beside the runway to lessen the risk of fire should the undercarriage fold up.

To cut a long story short, after making a very cautious landing, I returned to dispersal, closed down, and got out to examine the aircraft. I found that I had in fact hit anemometer mast taking the top four feet off the substantially constructed shaft. Somehow the propeller had just missed the mast by a fraction, and the mast had gouged a dent the size of a cricket ball in the leading edge of the starboard wing. I thanked God that I had not injured anyone in the Air Traffic Tower. I had been incredibly stupid to allow my concentration to be distracted for the split second it took to look back at Mike.

The second thing that went wrong before the 1970 Goodyear Air Race, could have been catastrophic. It happened a few days before the actual race took place. The local television station telephoned the race coordinator and asked him if he could stage a simulation of the race ending for the purposes of the TV news programme.

It was arranged for a camera team to come over that evening, and every effort would be made to muster up enough aircraft to make the recording look realistic.

The aircraft taking part in the Goodyear Air Race included a wide range of aeroplanes types ranging from the slowest Tiger Moth and Tipsy Nipper, to the much faster twin engine aircraft.

Every aeroplane in the actual race would be been handicapped according to its scheduled performance. In a perfect situation with all the pilot's flying accurately and all the handicap times being spot-on, every one of the forty or so aircraft in the race would arrive over the marked winning line on the airfield runway at the same time. Although this was very unlikely to be the case during the actual race, this is exactly what the TV people wanted us to simulate for their cameras.

Allowing for the over-exuberance of the pilots, I could see this simulated finish being a short course in death! However it seemed to be the wishes of the Goodyear race organisers, and our company Chairman, to go ahead for the purposes of promoting the forthcoming race.

As far as our company's aircraft were concerned, I arranged for the instructors and the more experienced club pilots who wanted to take part, to fly the club's aeroplanes. Mike would fly the Twin Comanche, and I would fly the Aztec. In order to make the simulation look more authentic, Bill Todd, the official race coordinator, decided more aircraft were required, so he contacted all the private aircraft owners that hangared their aircraft at Halfpenny Green and asked them if they would like to take part. No doubt keen to see themselves on television practically everyone of them agreed.

It was the day of the simulated race, scores of club members and private aircraft owners together with ten or so aircraft that had been invited to take part from other airfields had arrived at Halfpenny Green. In all I believe there were about thirty aeroplanes waiting to take part.

Bill Todd, himself a pilot and the race organiser, gathered all the pilots and the television crew in the clubhouse for a detailed briefing. The idea was that the faster aircraft would hold-off at given altitudes and locations furthest from the field, whilst the slower aircraft would stay closer in at lower altitudes. All the aircraft would be holding to the West of the airfield. Bill, flying a Piper Arrow, would liase with aircraft that had R/T, and when all were ready to start their run in, he would inform Air Traffic Control who would in turn fire a green Verey-Light. As soon as the Verey-Light was fired, all the aircraft were to head for the finishing line retaining their allocated altitudes throughout. The key words being KEEP A GOOD LOOKOUT for other aircraft. Engine start-up time was given, and would be confirmed by a flashing green light from the controllers Aldis lamp. Non-radio aircraft would move out first directed by a ground marshaller, the remaining aircraft would be co-ordinated by Air Traffic Control R/T.

When it came to any questions, I suggested that fewer aircraft should be used and made the point that all aircraft, having passed the finishing line, should climb straight ahead to 2,000 ft. before turning to rejoin the circuit from the dead side of the duty runway. Mike made the point that he too would be happier with less aircraft taking part in the simulation, and a specified height separation should be enforced. The Duty Air Traffic Controller said the whole thing was a potential disaster and should be scrubbed altogether. Several other pilots stated their concern at the safety aspect of thirty aircraft all rushing for the same lateral point at the same time. But this was dismissed by the coordinator, and we were told once again to keep a good lookout and "act sensibly". With that we left the briefing room, most of us with a strong feeling of apprehension.

It had been one of those warm, damp summer afternoons, when bright hazy sunshine gave way to frequent heavy showers of short duration. The television cameramen were setting up their equipment in the centre of the airfield whilst we sat in our aircraft waiting for the signal to start engines. Suddenly the heavens opened up, and hailstones the size of marbles bounced off aircraft wings and all over the airfield. The storm lasted a few minutes then passed as quickly as it had begun, leaving the cameramen drenched, and the poor old pilot of the Tiger Moth looking miserably uncomfortable in his open cockpit aeroplane.

The Aldis lamp flashed an intermittent green, and within seconds the airfield echoed to the roar of aircraft engines. I noted that the Minicab pilot was again swinging the prop of his aeroplane with no-one in the cockpit, nothing untoward happened, God must have been on his side!

Several large puddles glistened on the steaming taxiway as we moved out. Take-off went surprisingly smoothly, with each aircraft allowing sufficient time to avoid the prop-wash from the aircraft ahead.

The storm clouds having rolled away, we climbed into a crystal blue sky to orbit overhead our allocated locations until all aircraft were in position. Bill Todd's voice crackled into my headset asking if there was any aircraft not ready to start the run in. The only reply was someone who muttered something about only having two out of three u/c lights showing, but carry on anyway!

A green star flickered brightly overhead the tower. I rolled out of the turn heading towards the airfield and commenced descending to my allocated height of 300 ft. I didn't see any of the other aircraft until I was about two miles from the perimeter-track... Then all hell broke lose as about twenty or so aircraft appeared all at once, screaming down towards the runway, swerving round each other at low level like dodgems at a fairground. Holding 300 ft I continued towards the finishing line, the Tiger Moth was well in front of the others and was just about to pass over the airfield perimeter-track when some crazy twit flying a Piper Navajo streaked down out of the blue and passed directly underneath the Tiger Moth, there could only have been a few feet between the two aircraft. The Navajo then pulled up sharply in a steep climb leaving the poor old Tiger Moth to pass straight into its slipstream. I watched as the biplane rolled steeply to the left, it's port wing tip could have only been inches from the grass before rearing up like a bucking bronco. Somehow the pilot, Derek Gouk, managed to keep the aircraft in the air. At that second a red Verey Light shot up from the tower causing aircraft to peel off in all directions, how the hell a midair collision was avoided I'll never know. The Tiger Moth staggered round the circuit at low level and managed to land safely on the grass area between the two runways. Aware of aircraft zooming in behind me, I kept clear of the circuit until most of the chaps were down safely. When I finally landed and taxied in to dispersal, I saw Mike dealing in no uncertain manner with the maniac that had been flying the Navajo. Elsewhere pilots stood in groups laughing about the fiasco they had just taken part in, and I wondered if they realised how near they had been to witnessing a major catastrophe.

All went well on the actual day of the race. Our short aerial display advertising the flying club was a success, and needless to say the Red Arrows put on a magnificent show. The race was won by the smallest aircraft taking part, a Tipsy Nipper. Judging by its extremely early arrival, I am willing to bet that the handicap for this tiny aeroplane had been badly miscalculated.

Fortunately, due to the fact that I had been responsible for the organising and flight training of several hundred cadets over the previous eleven years, I was known amongst the employees of the contracts department at the Ministry of Defence, and shortly after submitting our first tender to train cadets at HGFC, I received a telephone message to say that the tender had been accepted, and providing the facilities we had recently installed passed an inspection by the MOD, we were in line for an initial contract to train a small number of cadets during the late Summer of 1970. This meant that I would have to employ extra instructional staff. It was a bit of a chicken and egg situation, but in the end I finished up with a compliment of four full-time QFI's, and a further three part time instructors. In order to prepare the chaps for the forthcoming visit by the "trappers" from the RAF Central Flying School Examining Wing, I held ground school lectures for all our instructors, and flew with them again to ensure that we were standardised to the patter recommended by CFS. Our pre-flight blackboard briefings were also exactly the same as the 17 layouts used to train instructors at RAF Central Flying School.

Following an inspection of the aircraft and our newly completed training facilities, the school was approved for short course training. On the 23rd of June 1970 we were all tested on our knowledge of the ground subjects and flight tested by the RAF Examining Wing, and everyone passed with flying colours.

With Air 70 at the helm, I was now answerable to a new Board of Directors. They consisted of the Chairman Mr Collis, who was the major shareholder, Mr Clement Senior a share holder, and his son David Clement who was now our Managing Director and the only Executive Director working full-time at the airfield. Our Chairman Mr Collis was also the Chairman of 'Collis Radio' in partnership with 'Phillips Radios Ltd.'

Maurice Collis, was a heavily built man, well over six feet tall, his eyes were similar to that of an oriental person, and the majority of his left ear was missing. Although he looked more like a "Mafia" leader, he was in fact an absolute gentleman. His accountant, who was also employed full-time at Halfpenny Green, always referred to him as "The Godfather".

Not long after Air 70 had taken over the flying school I received a telephone call from Mr Collis inviting Valerie and myself over to his house in Wolverhampton for dinner. During the evening I was politely, but very systematically questioned about my previous experience in the aviation industry and my personal plans for the future. Although it was never mentioned at the time, it came as no surprise some weeks later when I was offered a seat on the Board of Directors. I accepted of course, and I telephoned my old boss Rex Smith to tell him the news. His words to me were…

'Well done Ray, but be very careful old son. Directors can sometimes be left holding the can when things go wrong.' A few days later Rex telephoned to ask if I would be interested in working for CSE again. I would have accepted his offer like a shot, but unfortunately the job did not involve flying. The successful applicant would be based in Hong Kong. Rex made it very clear that at this stage he was not actually offering me the job, but merely finding out if I would be interested. He went on to explain that whoever took the job would be interviewing potential Nippon Airline Student pilots in a selection capacity. The appointment would last approximately two years. I asked Rex if I was offered the job could I be employed back on the flying side at Oxford after the two year contract in Hong Kong expired. But he would not commit himself either way. So

I had to say sorry, having fought for over two years to get fit enough to fly again, I could never consider a full-time ground job. Rex understood my reasons, but I think that conversation put the lid on my flying for CSE again.

As expected, my promotion to Director of Flying for Air 70 brought very little extra in the way of remuneration, but it was an opportunity to gain experience, and career wise I seemed to be moving in the right direction.

It soon became evident that in order to bring the operational staff up to its full compliment, we needed to employ one other person to work in Flight Ops. This position carried with it very important responsibilities, so we needed to make absolutely sure that we employed a person who was reliable, trustworthy and efficient, with considerable experience in office and accounts procedures, the person we employed would also have to be flexible and not be opposed to occasionally working unsociable hours.

I wrote a suitably worded advertisement that appeared in all the local newspapers, inviting responsible persons with typing, shorthand, and book keeping skills to apply for a vacancy in flight Ops at Halfpenny Green Airfield, adding that an interest in aviation would be an asset as some flying may be involved. That did it, we had literally hundreds of replies.

David, my new Managing Director was a nice enough young chap, but as he seemed to have very little to do other than sit in his office, I asked him if he would mind carrying out the initial interviews and preparing a short list of suitable applicants for the Ops. job. He agreed, and although we had stacks of replies, he found it quite easy to narrow them down to three or four potentially qualified applicants. David moved out from his old office in the Air 70 maintenance hangar and claimed an office for himself opposite to mine in the base of the Air Traffic Control building. I was a little bit annoyed about this, as office accommodation overlooking the airfield as his did, was earmarked for the instructors who definitely needed to keep an eye on the airfield activities. But seeing as he was now my boss, there was very little I could do about it.

On the day that the interviews were due to take place, I was not down to fly until late morning, this gave me time to continue constructing the urgently needed "Aircraft Movements Board" that I had taken upon myself to design and assemble for the Ops room. Computers didn't exist in those days, and in the absence of a copying machine I had to complete the details of the board's huge backing sheet by hand. With the aid of hundreds of letraset transfer sheets, and allowing for up to ten aircraft operating over a seven day per week period, the board had to be divided up into ten separate hourly bookings (8am to 6pm) per day for each aircraft. That amounted to drawing 700 hourly sectors, each requiring eight letraset transfers. So altogether I had the formidable task of applying 5,600 separate number transfers by hand. It was a job that called for a considerable amount of concentration and lots of patience, so I didn't really need to be interrupted.

Across the corridor from me I heard the first interviewee being ushered into David's office. After about half an hour I heard the same person leaving. Dave appeared at the door and said that he was not happy with the applicant as she was rather scruffy in appearance and didn't seem too keen about working at weekends. The only question she asked David was, how many days holiday would she get?

The next applicant was half an hour late, which in itself would have been enough for me to get rid of her. I could hear David mooching about in his office, obviously getting quite impatient. Eventually the person turned up apologising because she got lost on her way to the airfield. David managed to dispose of her in record time, appearing once again at my office door asking if I would like to do the next interview. But whilst he was chatting to me the next person arrived. She was about forty-five years old, and gave the impression of being a rather motherly sort of person. David spoke to her at length, then brought her into my office. I quite liked the woman, she seemed to have an extremely pleasant personality and had all the qualifications we required for the job, also, she was free of dependant children and was not worried about working at weekends or in the evenings. David still had one more applicant to interview, but I was pretty certain that we had already found the right person for the job.

I had just settled down to the grind of paperwork again, when I heard Mandy bring our final applicant down to David for her interview. After a while David knocked on my door once again, this time without entering, probably because he thought I was getting a bit hacked off at being interrupted. I opened the door, and the vision that stood before me defies adequate description.

A tall, slim, exceptionally attractive young lady with curly blond hair that extended below shoulder length, stood smiling at me. She was immaculately dressed in a very revealing short skirt and tight fitting white blouse with very expensive looking lace up knee-high suede boots. The only way to describe her accurately is to say that she was absolutely gorgeous. I invited her in to my office and asked her to sit down on the one and only chair. David introduced her as Mrs Carol Greenwood, adding that she had all the qualifications we required: 'And more' I thought.

When Carol spoke it was obvious that she had been well educated and I was immediately impressed by her charm and warm cultured voice. Whilst David was enthusiastically babbling away about the job, I was troubled by the thought that he may offer her the job without first talking it over with me. I honestly couldn't understand why this beautiful young lady, obviously quite capable of earning a very considerable salary as a model, had applied for a job with us. I asked Mrs Greenwood how long did she think it would be before she became bored with working behind a flight operations desk and decided to look for alternative employment, pointing out that the last thing we wanted was to train someone who would probably let us down. But Carol stated quite categorically that this would never happen. There was another problem nagging at the back of my mind that I could never actually confront her with. I was pretty certain in my own mind that she would never get much work done because she would undoubtedly be pestered by all the male staff and young student pilots trying to chat her up.

I decided to ask Carol one or two more questions during which time she told me that she was happily married, and they had no plans for starting a family at that time. She was not at all worried about working at weekends, or working overtime in the evenings. She had apparently worked as a secretary to a blind solicitor, which I thought must have been some considerable task. She was currently handling all the accounts and paperwork for a large tyre company based in Bridgnorth. Carol also stated that she was looking for a more interesting job, and she had been attracted to our advertisement because of the job description and the opportunity to fly occasionally. She also said that she had never smoked, which was certainly a plus as far as I was concerned.

I was convinced that she would probably turn the job down when she was advised of the salary, but she just smiled and said "Great".

Well that left me somewhat snookered, so I said that in fairness we would have to see the other applicants short listed and we would be in touch. David looked at me as if I was mad. But I terminated the interview and that was that. As she left the office I couldn't help thinking what a bloody lucky guy her husband was. Well I am human after all!

Having seen Mrs Greenwood to the door, David rushed back into my office like an excited schoolboy…

'What do you think Ray?'

'I think she is the most beautiful woman I have ever seen David. But, I also think that she is definitely not the person for the job in Ops.'

Poor old David looked shattered.

'WHAT?.... Why the hell not?' he snapped.

I explained that I thought she would be pestered by staff and students trying to chat her up and never be able to concentrate on her job. But I could see my words were falling on deaf ears.

'Well Ray my friend, I hate to say this but when it comes to a split decision, I'm the Managing Director, and you're not, so that rules your vote out mate, and as far as I'm concerned Mrs Greenwood gets the job.'

All I could say was...

'Thank God you don't select the flying staff.'

Mike Edwards had also seen Carol leaving the building. He came up to me moments later grinning all over his face.

'Who on earth was that gorgeous creature that just left the office Ray?'

I was not smiling.

'That's the new Ops. secretary.'

Mike thought for a moment then said...

'Hell, nobody will want to do any work with her around.'

'My sentiments entirely.'

Carol started work and began training under the guidance of Mandy. She became efficient at the job in a remarkably short time. And it soon became clear that no-one stood a chance with her. She had some indefinable way of saying keep your distance without actually saying a word. She was well liked by all the staff and everyone showed her great respect.

The accommodation block, kitchen and students dining room, were also up and running, with recently appointed Mrs Price at the helm in the kitchen. Mrs Price, who was no chicken bless her, was a real character. She amused everyone by coming to work on a motor scooter dressed in a fur coat, head scarf, goggles and slippers. Mrs Price however was worth her weight in gold. She was an excellent cook, and kept the students quarters spotless.

The MOD sent us three batches of ten students over a period of six weeks, each batch we given four weeks to complete the course. We were encouraged by the fact that they were all keen lads, everyone of them passed the course with no outright failures. When we had undertaken large numbers of cadets at Oxford, it was sometimes very difficult to get the courses completed on time, especially if long periods of bad weather or poor visibility persisted during the twenty-eight days allocated for each course. Fortunately we were very lucky with the weather during our first season of training contract students at Halfpenny Green.

The 1971 Goodyear Air Race was very successful and went off without a hitch. But towards the end of the year changes in our Board of Directors took place. Two of our Directors, Dave Clement and his father, disagreed over certain matters with our Chairman and subsequently resigned from the board of Air 70 Ltd.

Mr Collis lost no time in asking me if I would take over as Managing Director. I was uncomfortable with the sudden change in our management structure, but under the circumstances I felt obliged to accept the appointment, mainly to try and hold the rest of the company together. All this time of course Bobbington Estates, the company that actually owned the airfield, was still in the possession of Nat Somers.

Over the months that followed we trained several hundred students under contract to the MOD. Many of these lads went on to become pilots in the services. One of the chaps, Cadet Bingham, joined the RAF soon after we had taught him to fly, the last I heard of him many years later was he had risen to the rank of Wing Commander and was in charge of a VC10 squadron.

Now that the flying club and the aerodrome were operating as financially independent companies, it was necessary for the flying club to pay the airfield operators for hangarage and landing fees. This was to be expected of course. But when I decided to add night flying to the curriculum, Nat Somers went into overdrive. He sent me a letter to say that Bobbington Estates owned the portable battery operated runway lighting, and he intended charging the flying club an hourly charge for their use. The rate he proposed charging for the lights was extortionate, and in fact Air 70 had bought the lights in the first place. Also, and this was the bit that really got me going, Nat insisted that Bobbington Estates should provide a security man to stand on duty outside our hangar and lock it up after night flying. We were already renting the hangar from Bobbington Estates and our own employees always attended to locking up after flying. The hourly rate Nat intended to charge us for the services of this person was preposterous. The air traffic controllers overtime naturally had to be paid for by the club, but again this was to be charged at an hourly rate far in excess of anything the club could afford. In the end the total charges the club were required to pay the estates for night flying more than doubled the cost we would normally expect to pay.

Under the circumstances, I had to postpone my plans to introduce night flying training until I could hopefully sort out a more reasonable deal with Nat Somers, and there was little hope of that. I made an appointment to see

470

him when he next visited the airfield. Knowing him to be the sort of person that never backs down, I entered his office with considerable apprehension and was greeted with…

'What's up with you?'

Addressing him as sir, I kicked off like a bull in a china shop …

'How the devil can I put on night flying with the sort of ludicrous charges you intend making? I'm finding it hard enough to run this business profitably as it is. If it had been anyone else that sent me that letter I would have thought they were taking the piss…'

I waited somewhat apprehensively for Nat to reply.

Nat leaned back in his chair, his facial expression never changed whatever you said to him. He glared at me over the top of his half rimmed spectacles for a moment, looking ever more like Alistair Sims, and said…

'Sit down Raymond and tell me exactly what your night flying costs are, and why you inexplicably think I can help.'

I showed Nat the detailed costs I had calculated for night flying to take place at Halfpenny Green, adding that it was ridiculous for us to pay for a man to stand outside the hangar throughout the night's flying programme in order to lock the doors after flying had ceased, especially as we already rented the hangar from the estates and our own security staff locked up the hangar at the cessation of flying every day. I also pointed out that Air 70 had purchased the runway lights in the first place and we shouldn't have to pay anything for their use. Whilst I was going at it full steam I complained about the controller's overtime charges being more than treble the amount they should be for night flying.

At that point I shut up and waited to be verbally slaughtered by Mr Somers.

Nat frowned at me, his eyes never losing contact with mine, then to my utter astonishment he calmly said…

'Raymond you're gradually learning, I admit you were thrown in at the deep end when Gibson left. I'm sure that by now you appreciate that the aviation business is not just about flying aeroplanes. I had wondered if you would have the nerve to tackle me about this, and I'm pleased that you did.'

He carefully studied the figures I had placed on his desk, then he said…

'I can find nothing wrong with your calculations or reasoning.'

He paused to think for a moment, then continued…

'I will do away with our security man altogether but your company must take full responsibility for making sure the hangar is securely guarded when night flying is taking place.'

He scribbled something on his note pad, then leaning across his desk towards me he said...

'If I reduce our charges for night flying facilities by 70%, will that suit you?'

It certainly did, in fact you could have knocked me down with a feather! Nat went on to ask me if I was happy working for Air 70, and as I left his office he said...

'Good luck young man, and next time you come to see me try a calmer approach.'

It was the first, and in fact the only time I actually saw him commit himself to a brief smile. I suppose I do have a habit of going at things rather like a bull in a china shop, but that's me I'm afraid.

We set everything up to get night flying training started at Halfpenny Green, but there was one funny incident that occurred after we applied to the CAA for approval, and their Airfield Inspector turned up to evaluate the runway lighting.

The portable battery operated runway lights were no problem to set up, they simply had to be charged up and set out on the white painted markers each side of the runway. As it was a portable lighting system we had to use the old type AAI's (Angle of Approach Indicators), which were set up on either side of the runway threshold. The Red, Green, and Amber beams were set to remain visible to a pilot during his final approach to land using a three and a half degree angle of approach. If the aircraft was too high the pilot would see two amber lights, too low and he would see two red lights, and when he was correctly established on the glide slope two green lights would be visible to him. One AAI had to be set up at three degrees angle of slope, whilst the other AAI on the opposite side of the runway was set at three and a half degrees. The difference between the two angles would give the pilot an indication of whether or not he was tending to fly high or low.

The rather old AAI's at HG were recovered from under a pile of debris at the back of a hangar, and had not been used for several years, therefore Mike and I had to spend a considerable amount of time setting them up and flight testing them. When we were satisfied that they were working correctly they were locked into position ready for use.

The day finally arrived for our facilities to be approved by the CAA. The inspector turned out to be the same chap I had worked with on several occasions over the years when I was flying at Kidlington. He was a Scotsman, known to everyone as Jock of course..

Jock turned up at the airfield with three friends, two middle-aged men, and a young woman. It turned out that this would be Jock's last night inspection before his retirement from the Civil Aviation Authority, and he asked me if I minded his friends sitting in the back of our Aztec whilst he carried out the airborne part of our night inspection. Although this was unusual, I couldn't see any harm in taking them providing he, as the authority's inspector, authorised the flight and his friends signed the obligatory indemnity forms.

As it was not dark enough to commence the test for a while, Jock and his friends retired to the Bar.

Donald Swan, one of my valued part time instructors, was also on duty that night. Don was a real old stager who spent most of WW2 in the RAF flying Hampden Bombers. No matter what happened, Don never seemed to be perturbed, he was also renowned for smoking a Sherlock Holmes type of pipe.

As darkness fell over the airfield, I stood in the tower chatting with our controller about the fourth coming night inspection, when Don entered the tower. Having ushered me out of the control room onto the balcony for a quiet word he said...

'I thought I had better forewarn you old chum, our esteemed Ministry Inspector is as pissed as a newt in the club bar.'

Don sucked hard at his pipe stifling a laugh. All I could say was...

'What the hell do we do now?'

Outside I could hear Mike running up the engines of the Aztec in preparation for the flight whilst I was faced with the daunting question of whether or not to cancel the inspection. Jock was not actually going to fly the aircraft so I could continue with the flight providing I considered him to be compos mentis enough to carry out the inspection.

I entered the club bar and saw dear old Jock sitting at the bar with his back to me, downing what appeared to be a large glass of whisky. Both he and his friends were indulged in very noisy conversation and laughter. I decided to play it deadpan.

'We're ready if you are Jock.'

'Splendid'...

Apart from very rosy cheeks Jock appeared to be OK.

We signed out in the Ops room where Mike and Don stood obviously trying to hide their amusement. I gave them a wink and said...

'We're off, see you in about half an hour.'

After a considerable amount of waffling, I managed to secure our noisy passengers into their seats at the rear of the aircraft, whilst Jock strapped himself into the front seat. We taxied out, completed our checks, and took off. Jock said he would like to take a general look at the airfield lighting from directly overhead before flying the circuit and checking the AAI's. We levelled out at 2000 ft. and circled the airfield a couple of times. Jock was wearing a headset, which was just as well as our passengers were laughing and screaming loudly in the back.

'Have you seen enough Jock?'

There was no reply. I repeated the question, but still there was no reply. I looked to see if Jock's headphone jack had accidentally been pulled out of the socket, and was surprised to see that my examiner was slumped forward fast asleep!

I have to admit I really liked Jock. Over the years that I had known him he had always been a very methodical and highly efficient inspector. When I was employed at Kidlington Airport, Jock had made many inspections of the aerodrome throughout all its many stages of development, and never once did the slightest non-standard detail escape notice. This was his very last aerodrome inspection before taking retirement, and there he was bless him, with his spectacles just managing to cling on to the tip of his nose, slumped forward in his seat, oblivious to everything around him. I nudged him gently to no avail. I wanted to wake him without causing him any embarrassment so I decided that one way to do this without him realising that I had seen him asleep, would be to close both throttles abruptly, cutting out the sound of the roaring engines completely. This I did. It had two unforeseen effects. The passengers in the back let out blood curdling screams, this in turn startled Jock back to consciousness and he too felt entitled to a sharp AAH! Trying to avoid any unease, I quietly said over the headphones…

'Your passengers seem to be very nervous old chap, are they OK?

By the time everyone had settled down we had started our first run down the glide slope. This time Jock managed to stay awake.

'Looks great Ray, just one more circuit and we can land.'

Those were the words I was hoping for. I breathed a sigh of relief. Being inspected by a Ministry official, who is pretty much oblivious to what's going on, is not the most exciting thing in the world to do. But it was not quite over yet.

Turning on to the final approach to land, I was pleased to see two bright green lights from the AAI's, and a further three green lights confirmed that our undercarriage was securely down and locked. Whilst descending down the glide-slope I took a quick glance at Jock to see if he was watching my efforts. He was out of it again. Then, with no warning at all, a BLINDING WHITE FLASH lit the cockpit brighter than daylight itself partially blinding me. Its split second appearance seemed like a ball of vivid white light directly in front of the cockpit.

'What the hell was that?' I shouted putting AX into a full power climb.

My alarmed voice caused Jock to regain consciousness. He jumped up and having seen nothing he nervously asked what was happening, at the same moment someone from the rear seats casually asked...

'I take it we are allowed to take flash photographs, aren't we?'

We passed our inspection, and obviously nothing was ever mentioned about Jocks last evening's work for the Civil Aviation Authorities.

Soon after we started our night flying courses at Halfpenny Green, our Chairman called a special meeting of the Directors and announced that in his opinion the airport charges we were paying Bobbington Estates were far too high. I expected him to say that he was going to pull out, but he amazed everybody by proposing that Air 70 Ltd. should consider purchasing Bobbington Estates from Nat Somers and run the whole shooting-match ourselves.

After a long discussion about available finances, I was asked to make the initial approach to Mr Nat Somers and find out if he would be interested in selling.

A meeting was arranged for me to see Mr Somers at his offices in Southampton Airport. Nat, not the sort of chap to appreciate beating about the bush, seemed very pleased when I got straight to the point and asked him if he would consider selling Halfpenny Green Airport to Air 70. He replied...

'Certainly Ray, I will sell you Bobbington Estates, providing you can come up with a reasonable offer.'

I shuddered to think what Nat would consider to be a reasonable price. Whilst we were chatting, Nat asked me if I would care to join him for lunch, which I thought that was very generous of him. However, Nat remained in character and lunch turned out to be a cheese roll and a cup each in the staff canteen at Southampton Airport, which I ended up paying for!

After weeks of very complicated negotiation, Bobbington Estates was sold to Air 70 Ltd.

On the afternoon that all the documents were signed, Mr Collis called a Directors meeting and announced...

'Gentlemen, we are now the owners of an airfield, what shall we do with it?'

Our terms of reference as Directors had to be altered slightly, I wound up with overall control of the flying training and operational side of the airfield.

My first thoughts were the possibility of a working liaison with Oxford Air Training School. I telephoned Rex to tell him the latest news with reference to HG Airport, and asked him if he would be interested in Halfpenny Green being used as a satellite airfield for I/F training. Rex seemed quite pleased with the suggestion, and said he would get back to me in a day or so when he had given serious thought to the matter. Eventually we came to an excellent agreement whereby Oxford's students would fly over to HG with their instructors to practice NDB holds and approach procedures etc. This would help to relieve the already over crowded airspace at Kidlington. I agreed to provide a suitable briefing room for the use of Oxford's instructional staff, and a block landing fee was approved for all CSE aircraft.

The above arrangements necessitated a fully qualified Approach Controller to be on duty at all times when Oxford aircraft were practising NDB procedures. Fortunately our Senior Air Traffic Controller was in possession of all the ratings required to satisfy the obligatory requirements set out by the CAA. I also employed a trainee air traffic controller to work under the supervision of our SATCO.

A few months into our agreement with Oxford Air Training School things went badly wrong. Our Chief Controller, who up to then had been a very reliable person, suddenly decided to nip out to the local shop in the firm's car without permission, leaving the airfield during his "on duty" period. At the time of his indiscretion, Oxford aircraft were practising NDB holds and letdown procedures at the airfield. I just happened to pop up the tower to see how things were going, and discovered the unqualified trainee controller giving instructions to one of Oxford's aircraft in the holding pattern.

I reprimanded our SATCO when he returned from his shopping spree, and informed him that if this happened again I would have no alternative than to terminate his employment. Unfortunately the man didn't take my remarks seriously and did exactly the same thing a few days later. So I gave him one month's pay and dismissed him on the spot.

There was worse to follow…and the term 'Out of the frying pan into the fire' comes to mind. I managed to find a suitably qualified controller at short notice and engaged him to start work the following week. Our new

SATCO, I'll call him Sid, turned out to be the greatest oddball I have ever had the misfortune to meet!

Halfpenny Green Aerodrome was promulgated in the 'Air Pilot' to remain open during the hours of daylight, stating that there would be no air traffic control facilities available from 18.00hours without prior arrangements.

Many of the aircraft that visited Halfpenny Green in the evenings were non-radioed, and pilots simply observed the indicators displayed in the signals area in conjunction with the windsock to ascertain which runway was in use. One evening, when it was time for Sid to end his shift, there were still a number of privately owned aircraft flying around in the local area. I just happened to be looking out of my office window when I saw our recently employed controller turn the landing direction 'T' in the signals area so that it indicated the opposite direction to the surface wind and the runway in use. I rushed outside and told Sid to turn the 'T' back to its original position so that it showed the correct runway in use. To my surprise he refused point blank to do so and said....

'I'm not going to do anything of the sort, the bloody students should know by now that it's wrong to take notice of the 'T' if the airfield signals area indicates that the airfield is closed.'

I pointed out that although that may be the case, there was no reason to deliberately turn the landing indicator onto the reciprocal heading of the duty runway. It was a pointless and very dangerous thing to do, especially as it could be very misleading to young student pilots. His aggressive reply was beyond belief!

'That's bollocks..., if they don't know the law it's their bloody fault. Let the stupid bastards learn the hard way if they think they know it all.'

Resisting a great temptation to deck him, I ordered him to turn the runway indicator so that it showed the runway in use, adding that if he didn't do so, I would. He stood there glaring at me as I walked away from him. I had just passed through the flight Ops door when I heard several loud bangs and the sound of breaking glass. To my horror I turned round to see Sid wielding a shovel, using it like an axe and smashing the signals 'T' up altogether. The sound of breaking glass was the electric light bulbs that lit the 'T' at night being smashed to smithereens. I ran out to stop him, he turned towards me snarling and lifted the shovel as if he intended to strike me with it. I shouted...

'What the hell are you doing man? For Christ sake put that bloody shovel down.'

He threw the shovel in my direction, calling me all the foulest names he could muster up, and finally drove off in his car like a lunatic, wheels spinning and tyres screeching. Thankfully he never returned to the airfield and that was the last I saw of him. When I looked at the controller's 'Aircraft Movements Log' that he used to record all the daily aircraft take-offs and landings, I found that Sid had scrawled the most amazing rubbish across the pages ie…

08.15hrs… *Checked the surface of the runways. Didn't see any rubbish. Pity'*

08.50hrs... *Copied out the Met Forecast. The duty instructor could do this, Lazy bastard.*

09.00hrs…*Edwards came up to the Tower for the Met, I hate his guts.*

My early days as an Airport Director were not exactly enthralling. Most of the problems were easily rectified, but there was one peculiar set-up that had been allowed to develop within the maintenance set-up long before I was employed at the Green, in fact I didn't discover what was going on until I was made a director of the airport.

The Chief Engineer employed by Air 70 Aircraft Maintenance Company lived on his own quite near to the airport and had been allowed to collect the mail from the airport mail box on his arrival every morning. Presumably this set-up occurred because both he, and the mail arrived before anyone else every morning. To my astonishment I found out that he then proceeded to open and read all the mail, confidential or otherwise, before the receptionist arrived at 8.30am. It was then collected from the engineer's office by the receptionist who, because the mail had already been opened, could also read it before handing it on to the secretaries of the appropriate departments, i.e. the Estate manager's office, Flying Club, Maintenance Manager, and the various Directors. A situation that beggars belief!

I discovered what was happening when I walked into the engineers office a few days after I had been appointed Group Managing Director, and caught him reading a confidential letter concerning staff salaries. He had the gall to pass me the letter saying…

'I suppose you had better take this with you.'

I asked him how he came to open all the companies mail, and he said it was part of his job and he had always done it. I informed him that he had no authority whatsoever to open any of the companies letters, and from now on the mail would remain unopened until the my secretary arrived and dealt with it accordingly. The Chief Engineer, who was a rather sullen character at the best of times, glared at me for a moment, then let rip with a string of abuses, calling me a f…...g C… and to F… off out of his office.

Needless to say he was interviewed later in the day by our Chairman, and dismissed on the spot.

He was replaced by Mr Charlie Luck, a highly qualified aircraft mechanic who took over as our head of engineering. He was not a young man by any means, but his licences read like an encyclopaedia of aircraft types. Charlie was well liked by everyone, and controlled his staff with all the efficiency and experience he had gained as an ex RAF Chief Engineer. At last most of the problems I inherited when I took over the Green had been ironed out.

A de Havilland Dove G-AMZN, landed at the airfield one morning, and there was a bit of a kerfuffle between the pilot and a gentleman that arrived in a car to meet the aircraft. Ultimately the pilot left the airport in a taxi. A couple of days later I received a telephone call to say that the Dove, formerly operated by an aerial survey company, had been repossessed by a finance company when it landed at Halfpenny Green.

The Dove was temporarily parked along side our maintenance hangar until arrangements were made to have it repositioned. In the meantime, outstanding landing and parking fees would be paid by the finance company concerned.

A few days later I received another telephone call from the Director of the finance business asking if I knew of a suitably qualified pilot who could deliver the Dove to Coventry Airport for them. The words "suitably qualified pilot" could be interpreted in my favour, so I didn't hesitate…

'I would be happy to do the job myself.'

Actually I had never even seen inside a Dove, so this was my chance to do so. I was technically qualified to fly the aircraft on the private section of my commercial licence, but I didn't have the Dove as a type endorsement on my CPL, which meant I couldn't fly it for hire or reward. As I was not carrying passengers and not receiving separate remuneration for the flight, I was in fact legally qualified to "have a go" so to speak.

I asked Mike Edwards if he had ever flown a Dove, he thought for a moment then said he was sure he probably had at some time or another, so I invited him to do a couple of check circuits with me before I left for Coventry. We climbed aboard and entered the cockpit. Inside we were met by an array of unmarked circuit breakers and switches that covered most of the forward section of the cockpit roof, they were not labelled so we assumed they had something to do with the special photographic equipment installed by it's previous operators. The problem was we couldn't find the main Ground/Flight switch. So in the absence of handling notes or a check list, we sat there like a couple of prunes for ages trying this and that, but nothing seemed to work. In the end we had to go rather sheepishly to Charlie Luck, our Chief Engineer, and ask for his help.

With Charlie on board, it wasn't long before we had both engines running smoothly and were ready to taxi out. I sat in the left seat, Mike occupied the right hand seat and our engineer stood behind us whilst we carried out a couple of practice circuits.

Things didn't go too well to start with as I got the tip of the starboard wing caught up in a small bush that was situated on the grass verge alongside the hangar doors. Unfortunately half the bush sprang back behind the wingtip, so we had to close down and cut some of the twigs off the bush before we could proceed. It goes without saying, this didn't impress my Chief Engineer.

I quizzed Mike about the rotate, flap and undercarriage speeds, but his reply seemed a little vague…

'Not sure old chum, it's been some time since I flew one of these.'

Finally we got airborne, and with helpful suggestions from Charlie Luck, who incidentally nearly went ballistic when I pushed the propeller levers into fine pitch far too quickly during the down wind checks, we successfully completed a few circuits and landings. We swapped seats at one stage so that Mike could log some more P1 time on the aeroplane. In the end, as neither of us got the opportunity of flying an aeroplane like this very often, I decided that we should both take the Dove to Coventry, and tossed a coin to see who would fly in the left seat. Luckily I won.

Charlie left us to it, wishing us the best of British luck as he left the aeroplane. Everything went according to plan on the way over. I climbed her to a safe height, and practiced a couple of stalls in the approach configuration, then feathered a prop and flew around on one engine for a while. Finally, after restarting the engine we joined the circuit at Coventry, and landed. Ben McLeod, who was one of our instructors, arrived in a Cherokee 140 and flew us back to Halfpenny Green.

During the flight back Mike asked me how many hours I had logged on the D.H. Dove, I had honest and told him that I'd never been inside one until today. Mike grinned and said ….'Neither had I.'

On one of the rare occasions when I took a day off from flying, I decided to pop up to the Club Bar for a lunchtime drink. I had just ordered a pint of beer, when I overheard one of the Club Members, who jointly owned the Tipsy Nipper aircraft hangared at HG, saying that it was impossible to loop the little aeroplane because of its lack of engine power. I knew they were talking crap because ten years previously I had flown Oxford's Tipsy Nipper G-ARDY on numerous occasions whilst piling in the hours to qualify for an instructors course. One of the Nipper's greatest selling points was that it was stressed for aerobatics.

I stupidly butted into their conversation to point out that the secret was to scale down the radius of the loop to suit the aeroplane, with the backwards pressure on the stick just sufficient to keep the pilot's bum securely on the seat.

No, they wouldn't have it. As far as they were concerned, the Tipsy Nipper definitely couldn't be looped. When I said I had flown many an aerobatic session in that type of aeroplane, I was immediately given the opportunity of proving my point.

Fortunately I hadn't even taken a sip of my beer, which was still waiting patiently on the bar for me to consume. Moments later I was being helped into the tiny cockpit of the Nipper, wishing I'd never opened my big mouth.

I had not flown this type of aircraft since my crash in the Zlin at Oxford, and was having a certain amount of difficulty actually getting into the thing. My legs didn't bend all that well any more and one had to almost double oneself in half to squeeze into the tiny cockpit. In fact the Nipper, being a tricycle undercarriage aeroplane, was so small that it would easily tip back onto it's tail skid if you didn't lean far enough forward when climbing aboard.

Anyway, there I was scrunched up in the cockpit, whilst one of the owners was flicking the prop over rather like a model aeroplane. Eventually it started, and we were off.

I climbed over the airfield to gain sufficient height for a couple of loops, wondering if anyone had nicked my pint. At two thousand feet, I levelled out, completed the pre-aerobatic checks, and selected the duty runway as a reference point to keep straight on. As I lowered the nose of the Nipper to gain speed, I must admit I did wonder if this particular aeroplane had any peculiarities of its own. Fortunately it didn't. In a flash my mood changed from apprehension to euphoric pleasure. A succession of tiny loops brought us down to 1,500 ft, two slow rolls, (When the engine spluttered and all but stopped), a barrel roll, and one last loop brought us back into the empty circuit for a full stop landing. Point made, I was allowed to drink my pint, which miraculously still stood on the bar untouched. Having seen my short demonstration in the Nipper, Derek Gouk, who owned G-ANKK, a very pretty bright yellow Tiger Moth, approached me in the bar and asked if I would be interested in teaching him basic aerobatics in his Tiger. I was delighted. Although it had been many years since I had flown a Tiger Moth, my Irving jacket, flying helmet and goggles had always hung on the back of my office door in hopeful anticipation of such an occasion.

Every Sunday morning for the next few weeks when weather permitted, the unmistakable sound of the Gypsy Major engine could be heard whilst Derek and I looped and rolled this beautifully immaculate aeroplane in the clear blue skies over the open Shropshire countryside.

Derek was already capable of performing a few aerobatics, his biggest problem apart from "Scooping" out of the last quarter of a slow roll, was 'hammer heading' when attempting a stall turn.

Roughly speaking, a stall turn is a manoeuvre used in flying to turn quickly on to a reciprocal heading by putting the aircraft into a vertical climb, and applying full rudder in the direction of the intended turn just before the aircraft stalls, sometimes a little opposite aileron is required to stop the further effect of rudder causing the aircraft to roll. The aeroplane then falls away sideways in a sort of cartwheel action, the throttle is closed as the nose falls past the horizon and the aircraft ends up in a vertical dive and recovers facing in the opposite direction to its original heading. To carry out a good stall turn the pilot's timing is critical.

The following Sunday we taxied out and took off in the comforting warmth of the morning sun. The little Tiger Moth, always a pleasure to fly, purred away in its own inimitable way as we climbed out to the East.

'OK Derek, lets see if we can iron out these stall turns old chap. Show me a stall turn to the right so that I can figure out what you are doing wrong.'

Derek religiously carried out his pre-aerobatic checks, finally making sure that we were not over a built up area with no other aircraft around to get in our way.

'Here we go.'

Derek applied full power easing the Tiger into an almost vertical climb. I watched him in the small front cockpit mirror. He was looking left and right to check the wings were in the vertical position relative to the horizon, (The fuselage is slightly forward of the vertical due to the angle of incidence). But Derek left the application of full rudder a little too late and the aircraft, pointing vertically upwards, started to tail slide finally winding up in a vicious hammerhead stall.

'Hmm, I can see your problem …...'

My voice broke off as Derek hauled back viciously on the stick to recover from the ensuing dive, forcing my goggles to slide down over my mouth. I started again…

'I can see where you're going wrong, you're allowing the speed to drop too low before you apply rudder, and you'll pull the bloody wings off if you haul back on the controls like that! I'll give you a demonstration of how it should be done, follow me through. I have control.'

I was pleased to find that I hadn't lost my touch with the old Tiger. Derek then made several attempts at stall turning to the right, gradually improving his technique with diminishing amounts of prompting from me. Then came the time when we needed to practice stall turns to the left, which in the case of the Tiger Moth, is against the propeller torque, (i.e. the propeller turning anti-clockwise as seen from the cockpit). Without going into a lot of technical detail, suffice-to-say it is much more difficult to stall turn to the left than it is to the right in a Tiger Moth.

We were flying at 3,000 feet and a thin layer of stratus cloud had formed about 2,000 feet below us, but we were still in clear blue skies. I took control once again to demonstrate another stall turn, this time to the left. Checks complete, we started our stall turn pulling up positively into the near vertical attitude.

'This time we need to apply full rudder to the left, and a little earlier than we did to the right, about five knots faster.'

Kilo Kilo started to cartwheel beautifully over to the left. The engine was still at full power as the aircraft paused for a split second against the torque. Things couldn't have been going better for a good clean stall turn when, with no warning what-so-ever, the engine stopped and with little or no forward airspeed the propeller stopped turning. Somebody, (It was me), said 'Oh Shit.' Apart from that we hung practically stationary for a moment in utter silence, the propeller black and motionless against the vivid blue sky. It was make your mind up time, forced landing or attempt a re-start?

Tiger Moths are always started by hand swinging the propeller as electrical starters are not fitted. The only method of attempting a re-start in flight is to dive the aircraft absolutely vertically until the airspeed is sufficient to start the propeller wind-milling. Success usually depends on three things. First and foremost you need to have sufficient height to attempt a re-start, at least 1000 feet of vertical dive is needed to turn the prop. Secondly, you need the guts to hold the aircraft screaming down in a vertical dive, and thirdly, if the engine doesn't start when the propeller starts to windmill, you will have dived off valuable altitude and probably thrown away any chance of making a successful forced landing. So you need to make your mind up pretty quickly before losing too much valuable height.

I was taught to fly on Tiger Moths, and part of the training in those days was to deliberately stop the engine and carry out at least one dive start before passing your private pilot's flight test. But that was in the early 1950s, and it had been over twenty years since I had attempted a Tiger Moth re-start. Nevertheless good training produces immediate and correct reaction to situations that could become dangerous.

Instinctively I thrust the Tiger Moth down into a vertical dive. When you dive an aircraft vertically it always feels as if you have passed through the vertical and are diving slightly inverted. I felt Derek trying to pull against me on his controls in an attempt to recover from the dive whilst the propeller was still at a standstill.

'I have it Derek, I'm re-starting the engine.' I shouted.

Derek released his grip. Obviously in the days when it was mandatory to practice engine re-starts in the Tiger, we always carried out such practices over our airfield so that we could make a 'dead stick' landing if the engine failed to re-start.

We careered vertically downwards, the wind screaming through the wing struts. In seconds we had flashed through the thin layer of stratus cloud and I was horrified to find that we were heading straight down over a built up area. How the hell we had drifted that far in such a short time I'll never know. The airspeed was almost up to 165 mph, which is the VNE (Velocity Never Exceed) limit for a Tiger Moth, and the prop hadn't budged an inch. I remembered that the propeller usually started to turn during practices when assisted by inertia during the pullout from the vertical dive. The ground was getting uncomfortably close when I initiated the recovery as severely as I dare without overstressing the airframe. The aircraft, objecting to the manner it was being handled, juddered violently on the verge of a high-speed stall. Suddenly the prop rotated through half a revolution, stopped for a split second, then turned again this time the engine bursting into life. As we climbed away, Derek's voice came over the headphones...

'Can we pack up for today Ray?'

I agreed, a nice cup of hot tea would be more than welcome.

Every Sunday during the summer months on Halfpenny Green Aerodrome I was awakened at around 7am by loud cries of...

'One thousand and one, one thousand and two, one thousand and three, PULL'

Our mobile home was sited next door to the South Staffs Skydiving Club. The members would practise their drills enthusiastically from 7am until it was time for them to fly off and enjoy themselves by attempting to commit suicide! at least that's the way I thought of it.

The parachute club hired a beautiful old 1930s Dragon Rapide aeroplane together with its owner Chris. I used to look on enviously as this lovely old aeroplane taxied out time and time again throughout the day to take its cargo of parachutists up to ten and sometime twelve thousand feet for their "Free Fall" parachute jumps.

Captain Jim Crocker, a serving officer in the Green Jackets, acted as the parachute club's Chief Instructor at week-ends. Crock was a great character, full of enthusiasm and an inspiration to the members of the parachute club. Soon after I met him we became great friends and frequently met up in the club bar for a few beers after the cessation of flying on Sunday evenings. It was during one of these evenings when I mentioned to Crock that I was having a lot of problems with a farmer whose land boarded the Southeast corner of Halfpenny Green Airfield. I had written to this gentleman asking if he would consider trimming the height of one of his trees that stood less than fifty yards from the threshold of runway 34. But the farmer, Mr R. refused my request.

Whenever the prevailing wind was appropriate we used runway 34, which also happened to be our longest runway, for the purposes of night flying. The tree in question was nothing special, just a nondescript run of the mill half dead hulk that, due to its height, necessitated us displacing the threshold markers of the runway by several meters, effectively shortening the useable length of the runway. We never gave the farmer any cause for complaint, his house was a mile or so from the airfield and our aircraft never had cause to pass directly over any of his buildings. I was very concerned that one of our students could accidentally clip the top branches of that tree when landing at night. But in spite of the fact that we offered him compensation, Mr R. refused point-blank to trim the tree.

Jim Crocker seemed unusually interested when I told him of the farmer's stubbornness, but I thought no more about it. The following Monday morning I received a telephone call from one very irate "farmer of the parish".

'Somebody's cut my f.....g tree down to the roots, I'll have you in court for this.'

No amount of talking would convince Mr R. that I knew nothing about it. The following Sunday I mentioned the matter to Captain Crocker. There was a twinkle in his eye when he said...

'Well I'm buggered, must be some sort of clandestine operation, top secret stuff old boy.'

Fortunately for us the matter was never taken to court.

Sadly later in the year there was a very upsetting parachute accident when the lads from the South Staffs Sky Diving Team attempted a twelve parachute free-fall link-up. It was a glorious day with blue skies and virtually no wind. I had popped over to the caravan for a spot of lunch and was sitting in our tiny garden watching the Dragon Rapide as it droned overhead the airfield at a considerable altitude. I saw the parachutists leave the aircraft and start to link up to form a circle during their free-fall, at the same time the Rapide began its usual steep gliding descent back to the airfield. I could actually hear the bodies whistling through the sky as they descended at great speed linked together in a perfect circle. With them was a very experienced sky-diving cameraman filming from inside the circle of men. At a predetermined altitude the circle broke, and the white canopies of twelve parachutes snapped open in all directions. The cameraman for some reason delayed opening his chute and was still in free-fall. I watched him as he continued earthwards, his arms and legs stretched out to keep himself in a stable attitude. He streaked down towards the ground with no sign of his parachute being deployed. A couple more seconds and it was obviously too late. My stomach turned over as I heard his body hit the ground with a muffled thump and bounce up to a height of several feet. It was a horrendous sight that remains etched in my memory forever. Having never seen the conclusions of the accident report, I can only assume that the poor chap must have misread his altimeter.

The following weekend I witnessed probably one of the funniest, although potentially extremely dangerous, accidents I ever saw. The owner of the Tipsy Nipper aircraft hangared at HG airfield, inadvisably decided to swing the propeller of his aeroplane with no-one in the cockpit and no chocks under the wheels. I can never understand why anyone should attempt anything quite so dangerous when there is always someone around to give them a hand.

Anyway, this chap was swinging the prop, when the engine gave a loud bang and spluttered into life. The throttle had apparently been set too far open, the brakes failed to hold, and the aircraft started to move forwards. The chap who had been swinging the prop, started to run round the aeroplane with the obvious intention of trying to reach the cockpit and close the throttle. But the Tipsy Nipper was gathering speed rapidly, and it became obvious that the poor chap was never going to make it. This type of aeroplane has a handhold at the end of each wing-tip to assist manoeuvring the plane around inside the hangar. The pilot just managed to grab the handhold on the port wing and hung on for dear life. Within seconds both the aircraft and the exasperated pilot were twirling around in circles, the pilot not daring to let go! There were women and children picnicking in the public enclosure quite close to the aeroplane who seemed oblivious to the danger they were in. Within seconds the poor chap was being dragged around so fast that his feet were beginning to lose their grip, and no-one could get near enough to assist him for fear of being struck by the propeller. Whether by accident, or design, the guy finally let go of the wing and sat down with a plonk, obviously very dizzy and disorientated. Fortunately for all concerned the aircraft was facing away from the public area and careered across the airfield hopping up and down like a demented frog. Finally after a king-sized bounce it dived into the ground, snapping its wooden propeller and bending the nose wheel, finally coming to rest with it's tail stuck up in the air. Human nature being what it is, there was a roar of applause from the spectators, as the pilot, who must have been emotionally bruised if nothing else, ran over to inspect the damage to his aeroplane.

CHAPTER 45

Fly into Danger.

During the Autumn I was approached by ITV and asked if we would be interested in allowing them to use Halfpenny Green Aerodrome in a feature film they were making called, "Fly Into Danger". The film would be shown as a series on children's television and would consist of 6 Episodes. They estimated that filming on the airfield would be completed in a period of about two weeks. Provision of a Stunt Pilot for two or three scenes would also be required. The Director of the film was Jonathan Wright-Miller and the Producer was David Foster. The series was planned to be broadcast starting on the 31st May 1972.

Our company would receive suitable remuneration plus excellent free publicity for Halfpenny Green Airport. I would also get the opportunity of stunt flying again. I agreed to allow the filming to take place, and a contract was drawn up. It turned out that the choice of title 'Fly into danger' couldn't be more apt as far as the pilots who had to take part were concerned.

The main character in the film was played by Sue Holderness, who was about nineteen years old at the time. Three professional stunt pilots were contracted to fly in the film, they were Barry Shaw, Peter Smith and myself. I had never met the other two chaps before filming commenced, but we soon realised that we would be relying very much on each other's aerial skills and sense of timing if we were to avoid a serious accident, and by the time the filming had been completed, the three of us agreed that we deserved a medal for attempting some of the crazy things the Sequence Coordinator asked us to do.

The film company very kindly provided a small monitor screen in our flight Ops room so that our staff could see what was happening during the filming. There were several static cameras dotted around the airfield that were permanently left running throughout the day, even when no scenes were actually being filmed. This caused considerable amusement amongst those that were watching the monitor as every now and then various members of our ground staff would inadvertently wander in front of one of these cameras without realising they were performing on screen in the Ops room. Eventually they would see the camera and sheepishly creep off on tip-toe looking very embarrassed.

Once filming started, I had to give Sue Holderness a rough idea of how the controls operated so that she would appear to be doing the correct things when filmed in close-up.

When I actually flew the aeroplane and Sue was supposed to be at the controls, I had to wear a long black wig. It doesn't take much imagination to guess the sort of remarks I had to tolerate from members of my staff.

There were three aircraft involved in the scenes shot at Halfpenny Green. They were a Britten Norman Islander flown by Barry Shaw, a Tiger Moth flown by Peter Smith, and a Cessna 150 flown by me.

I won't go into all the details of the plot, but at one stage in the film Sue Holderness, the "Goodie", is sitting in the cockpit of a C150 parked inside the hangar, when she is informed by a mechanic that the "Baddies" were about to take-off and escape in the twin engine Islander. The script said that Sue starts up the engine of the 150 and gives chase commencing her take-off run from inside the hangar, narrowly missing the doors as the engineers are trying to open them. She emerges from the hangar at high speed, sees the Islander about to take-off, turns through about 45 degrees and tries to head off the Islander. Great story line, but not so great for Barry and me who had to do the flying.

The Air Sequences Director, a large, garishly dressed chap that wore a Stetson most of the time, walked along the perimeter track with his arms wrapped affectionately round the shoulders of Barry and myself, explaining what he wanted us to do in the first flying scene of the day. He spoke with a broad American drawl…

'OK Ray boy, what I want you to do is start up inside the hangar and head full pelt for the doors.'

I must have looked shocked, as he continued…

'Don't worry boy, we'll have em open just wide enough for you to get through by the time you reach em…..Barry old son, you start your take-off run on the runway when the guy in Air Traffic gives you the nod, I'll be on the blower to inform him when I want you to start your take-off run.'

Barry and I looked at one-another. The Director pointed to me and said…

'Then Sue, that's who you're meant to be old son… when you see the Islander moving down the runway, you head straight at it, narrowly missing his goddam tail, you can do that can't yer son?'

Before I could say a word he continued…

'Then, I want yer to keep going, taking off across the runway.'

He turned his head and addressed Barry…

'As soon as you get off the ground Barry, yer turn hard left to pass back over the airfield tower. Get the goddam wingtip as close to the ground as possible so everyone thinks it's sure to crash…. Then Sue, that's you again son,' he said pointing at me, ' you pull up into what I believe is called a stall turn immediately after take-off to give chase, I want you both to fly back very low over the airfield so we can get a couple of ground to air shots of the Islander with you right up its goddam arse. Now do you guys have any trouble with that?'

We both stood silent for a moment. The man was obviously off his rocker. I had a thousand questions, but decided to keep it down to one small piece of advice…

'I would just like to point out that there is no way that a light piston engine aircraft could pull up into a stall turn just after take-off.'

The director went red in the face, obviously very irritated by such a minor point.

'That so?'

He scratched his head…

'Son of a bitch, …you sure boy? … That kinda throws a spanner in it son, we gotta get round it somehow….surely.'

I countered by saying that anyone who knew anything about aeroplanes at all would know that stall turning a C150 from take-off just couldn't happen. That did it, I thought he was about to explode. He stopped dead in his tracks and looked at me as if I was some strange obnoxious creature that had just crawled out of the ground.

'Just a minute boy, just one cotton pickin minute, yer wanner spoil the goddam thrill the kids er goner get from this here film?'

It was little use arguing, so I took his point and resolved to try and find a way round the problem. Barry and I sat on the grass outside ATC. When we stopped laughing, we got down to seriously discussing how we could accomplish the anticipative requirements of the Director. In the end we agreed that the chase sequence would have to be filmed in a series of separate shots from various angles and edited together to make it look as if it was one continuous scene. We had a word with the Director, he agreed with our suggestions and soon after we started flying.

The first part of the sequence where I start my take-off run in the Cessna from inside the hangar, was filmed in slow motion, so that it looked as though I almost clipped the doors at high speed when the film was played back at normal speed. I still had to make it look as authentic as possible during the second shot when I was on the ground and turning to chase the Islander. So I practiced taxying as fast as possible whilst turning with one wheel off the ground. With sufficient speed I was able to maintain control of the angle of bank with the ailerons and rudder, although it took several shots from different camera angles before the Director was satisfied. Just missing the tail of the Islander at ninety degrees to its take off heading was a bit dodgy, and after several heart stopping attempts, we had to film the "Just Missing" bit in reasonably slow motion, even so the C150 was nearly blown over sideways by the slipstream of the Islander. We saw this played back in their control caravan at the correct speed and in my opinion it looked quite impressive. The next shot cut to the Islander just lifting off the runway, which was also filmed separately.

We broke for lunch, which gave us another opportunity to discuss the stall turn immediately after take-off sequence. The only way I could think of making this look authentic was to film the Cessna taking off across the runway at normal take-off speed, the scene would then cut to another camera angle, during which time I have climbed to about a thousand feet, circled round to face the direction of take off and dive down to just above the ground gaining as much speed as possible. Passing close to the repositioned camera I would then pull up into a stall turn to the left with sufficient speed to complete the manoeuvre safely. The two shots carefully edited together should give the appearance of the take-off and pull up into a stall turn as one continuous manoeuvre. But before I attempted this I would need to practice the sequence at a safe altitude to make sure that I wasn't going to finish up six feet underground at the recovery stage of the stall turn.

The Air Sequences Director, with whom I seemed to have developed a rather prickly relationship, agreed with our evaluation of how the stall turn should be filmed. But he then went on to say that I would have to fly the whole sequence twice, as he wanted me to carry a cameraman on the second occasion for air to ground shots. I made the point that I was not too keen to attempt a low level stall turn with the extra weight of a cameraman and his equipment on board for two reasons. First, the extra weight would certainly alter the performance of the Cessna, and second, the aeroplane only had two seats which meant that the cameraman would be sitting next to me holding a bulky camera with a full set of aircraft controls in front of him.

The Director looked flabbergasted and said....

'How's that ? Just run that past me again Mister?'

'I think it's unsafe to carry a cameraman when I attempt a low level stall turn.'

'Son-of-a-bitch, how'd yer come by that crap idea ?' he snarled.

I couldn't believe this character. I'm sure he thought I was deliberately trying to sabotage his aerial sequences.

'Well, first of all it will add extra weight, and secondly he will be too close to the controls for safety.'

The Director seemed to be a bit of an actor himself, and didn't save himself when it came to exercising his mouth. He gave an incredulous false gasp, and went on....

'Stop me if I'm wrong here boy, yer telling me yer plane's too goddam under-powered to carry two guys? What sort of ship's that?'

The argument went on at length. Eventually we agreed that the sequence would first be shot with me on my own. Having calculated that the aeroplane would remain within its max AUW of 1600lbs carrying the cameraman and his equipment, I would then complete a high level practice with the extra weight on board.

The practice flight with the cameraman was carried out at 3000 ft. with the altimeter wound back to zero to simulate the ground level. The result showed that I could pull up vertically from an altitude of six feet, stall turn to the left and recover with 25 to 30 ft. ground clearance providing I commenced a steady pull-up travelling 145mph, which was 5mph below the aircraft's VNE speed.

With the film unit positioned in the centre of the airfield, I started the Cessna's engine and moved out.

I was taking off on the grass area at ninety degrees to the duty runway to simulate the take-off after passing behind the Islander. As I started the take-off run I could see the crash wagon with its blue light flashing away at the far corner of the airfield. I lifted the Cessna off the grass just before crossing the tarmac runway and climbed away.

'Would you come back and do that again Victor Xray, the cameraman was not happy with the shot.'

The call from Air Traffic was not the first or the last I was to receive asking for a repeat performance, in fact they called for a second run on just about everything they filmed. Retakes coupled with the regular rest breaks enforced by their union, made progress very slow, and frequently very irritating.

Eventually the time came when the film unit was ready to film the low level stall turn, and Air Traffic gave me a call…

'OK Victor Xray they're ready for you to commence your run, the surface wind is 350 at 05 knots.'

I had positioned the aircraft at an altitude of one thousand feet just south of the airfield. One last check to make sure the area was clear of other aircraft, and down we went. I kept a small trickle of power on and dived steeply towards the southern boundary of the airfield. It had been made clear that the Director wanted a clean stall turn, and not a "half-hearted wing-over"….. bless him!

As the ground rushed up to meet me I prayed that for once the cameraman had his camera set up correctly and was rolling. The airspeed was 150 mph, bang on the VNE. We ripped over the airfield at zero feet flashing past the cameraman, who had his back to me ready to shoot the pull-up. As I pulled VX up into a vertical climb the airspeed decayed rapidly. Suddenly the controller's voice burst into my eardrums….

'It's a scrub Ray, the cameraman fell over on his arse as you whipped past him!' I replied with a single word…. 'Brilliant.'

Eventually we did get it right. I was shown a playback of the shot, and even the Director was pleased.

After a short brake, I returned to the aircraft to see if the door had been removed ready for the cameraman. A tubular structure had been assembled inside the cockpit to hold the camera rigidly in position during the next filming sequence. The cameraman chosen for the flight, having watched my earlier performance, didn't look too happy. But he was a sensible chap and listened carefully to the briefing I gave him about the procedure and the dangers of getting mixed up with the control column in front of him.

During a practice run at altitude, the cameraman never touched his camera once, he just clung to the sides of his seat and turned rather pale. The stall turn that had already been filmed from the ground was a sort of cartwheel movement to the left. Unfortunately the camera on board for the airborne shot was sitting on the right hand side of the aircraft, so looking out to the right, all he was going to film was a lovely shot of the sky as we wheeled over, but that was what our pedantic Director insisted on.

In the end it took three attempts before the cameraman could be encouraged to let go of the seat and operate the camera successfully. The

Director threw a fit when I told him my long black wig had been sucked off my head and fluttered down somewhere over the open countryside. He reprimanded me with…

'Yer didn't have to wear the goddam wig fer that shot Mister.'

There was another sequence when the Cessna was supposed to have a tyre burst on one of the main wheels whilst the aircraft was being shot at. One of their technicians said he could fix something to the tyre that could be set off electronically to burst the tyre as I touched down. I flatly refused to allow that to happen as the rim and possibly the oleo leg would dig into the ground and wreck the aircraft completely. Instead I simulated a tyre burst by careering across the runway after landing with the port wheel off the ground.

Altogether the filming lasted about a week. My last job was to carry out a close fly-past at a guy who had been bravely filming various sequences from the top of a 150 ft. portable tower. I was told to fly as close as possible to the poor chap, and after the shot had been filmed the cameraman told me that he was convinced he was going to die, and would have refused point blank to do the shot a second time if the first attempt had been a failure.

Later I saw the Tiger Moth impressively doing its stuff over the airfield for another part of the story, and I couldn't help wondering if the pilot had gone through the same sort of verbal onslaught from the short fused Director as I had.

It was very amusing to see the film when it was finally broadcast on ITV some months later. Our Company was well paid for the use of the airfield, and I received a very pleasant letter from the Film Director.

Sadly in my private life things were once again becoming very complicated. My downfall was that I seemed to fall in love too easily. With me it was never a matter of simple indiscriminate promiscuity, I always managed to get myself deeply involved without realising the misery and shattering consequences it would cause. I suppose most people have gone through similar traumas in their personal lives. Many of the pilots I knew seemed to be addicted to this kind of dilemma, and in my case life was continuously complicated and painful as I seemed to get myself into one predicament after another. It was not long after moving to Halfpenny Green Aerodrome that I found living with Valerie and her daughter Laura was becoming heartbreakingly intolerable. Laura, who was now twenty-four years old, was a very attractive young lady, and life soon became very complicated. In fairness to the three of us it was a situation that obviously couldn't go on for much longer.

CHAPTER 46.

Lost in a Thunderstorm.

He was one of those sort of chaps that you couldn't help liking, but from the point of view of him being a qualified PPL member of the club, you could happily have done without him. To save any embarrassment I will simply refer to him as Mr Peter T. Practically everything dear old Peter did went drastically wrong. He was certainly not a dimwit, far from it. He ran his own very successful engineering company, although I cannot for the life of me remember exactly what line of engineering he was in. Peter completed his private pilot's course and passed his flying test with average ability, but he was dangerously unpredictable, accident prone and on occasions, absent minded beyond belief.

I can recall three rather unpleasant incidents that I found myself in, all of them unintentionally instigated by Mr T. The first occurred shortly after he had qualified for his private pilots licence.

It was late one Summer's afternoon when he took off in Cherokee G-ATTF for one hours flying in the local area. The weather at the time was not bad, although the met forecast mentioned the possibility of occasional showers. I was entering up my students record sheets for the day when one of my instructors popped his head round the office door to tell me that there was a nasty looking storm brewing up a few miles East of the airfield. He mentioned that he was concerned about Peter because he had not returned from his planned one hour flight in the local area and was already twenty minutes overdue. I checked with Air Traffic, but they had heard nothing from Tango Foxtrot since it took off and left the circuit. Apparently they had been trying to make contact with Peter to warn him of the approaching storm, but no transmissions from the Cherokee had been received.

I peered through the office window, the sun was still shining on the

495

airfield, but over to the East the sky was as black as night. Peter had only recently passed his PPL test and to date had insufficient first pilot hours to qualify for the commencement of an IMC course, which in very basic terms meant he was not qualified to fly in bad weather conditions.

Moments later Carol called me from Ops to say that the Senior Air Traffic Control Officer at Birmingham Airport was on the telephone and wanted to speak to me. It turned out that his Approach Controller had picked up a light aircraft on his radar that seemed to be wandering around dangerously close to the Birmingham Control Zone, and he asked me if we had anyone airborne in the Birmingham area. I told him that we had one aircraft airborne at that time who was overdue on his flight time, and had only been authorised to remain in the local area. The SATCO at Birmingham went on to say....

'If it is your chappie up there, he's circling round very close to a large active cumulonimbus cloud and we are unable to raise him on any of our frequencies.'

He was obviously worried that it may be a student pilot who was in danger of both entering the active thunderstorm and Birmingham Control Zone. I gave him the registration of the aircraft we had airborne at that time. Convinced that it was Peter that had got himself lost, I spoke to the Birmingham's Approach Controller and said I would take-off in G-AVSA and look for him. I arranged with the controller to work their frequency and if necessary enter the Birmingham Control Zone under radar surveillance. If Peter had violated their airspace without them being able to contact him, I would try to find him visually and guide him out of their zone.

I booked out quickly and rushed out to Sierra Alpha, our Cherokee 180. In the distance I could hear the threatening rumblings of the approaching thunderstorm. Within minutes I was airborne heading East and calling Birmingham Radar. They answered immediately...

'Hello Sierra Alpha, reading you fives, that was quick! We have you on our Radar, steer zero eight five, not above two thousand feet, on QNH 1012 millibars. Your chap is still circling, unfortunately the Cu-Nim is between you and him. I have no height information and there are no other aircraft in that area at the moment.'

Not exactly overjoyed by the news of the thunderstorm being between me and the other aircraft, I acknowledged Birmingham's instructions and continued heading towards their zone. If it was Peter out there, perhaps he would have enough sense to stay out of the storm and find somewhere safe to land.

I was beginning to pick up a considerable amount of static on my headset from the thunderstorm that loomed up like a black giant ahead of me, when Birmingham Radar called me again...

'Sierra Alpha, this is Birmingham Radar, the other aircraft is now in our control zone and appears to be heading West which will take him straight into the storm. He is in your twelve o'clock position, range four miles. You are clear to enter the Birmingham Control Zone, remain on altimeter setting 1012mb not above 2000 feet. There is nothing to conflict with you at the moment other than the unidentified aircraft.'

I acknowledged the controllers instructions, and after a short pause, he called me again...

'I will probably be losing you both in a moment due to heavy clutter on my screen caused by the storm.'

By the time I acknowledged his second call I was being bounced around violently by severe turbulence. Visibility was poor, and it was difficult to judge exactly how far ahead one could actually see.

The turbulence was beginning to build up when an exceedingly brilliant flash of lightening, accompanied by a crash of thunder almost caused me to jump out of my skin! Conditions were worsening by the second, the chances of finding the other aircraft in this visibility, especially not knowing what height he was flying at, were not good. Also, now that Birmingham were unable to see us properly on their radar screen, there was an ever increasing danger of an air collision. Common sense screamed at me to give up the search and turn back. But somewhere out there a light aircraft was in trouble, and the odds were that it was Peter.

A couple of minutes passed, then something caught my attention. A pinpoint of light momentarily appeared out to my right. Still being thrown around by the storm, I turned SA in the general direction of where the light had appeared. Seconds later there it was again, a small pinpoint of light that appeared every few seconds, unmistakably identifiable as the flashing strobe light of another aeroplane moving slowly away to my right. There was no sign of any navigation lights so it was difficult to calculate the other aircraft's possible heading. I called Birmingham, they answered, but the extremely noisy static in my headphones made it impossible to read their transmission. I throttled back slightly, more by instinct than for any other reason. Slowly, through the torrential rain, the grey shape of an aeroplane began to materialise. Fortunately it was heading roughly in the same direction as me. Easing closer I could now read the registration letters....G-ATTF. It was Peter alright and he was obviously in considerable trouble.

With practically no outside reference he was attempting to fly solely on instruments. The turbulence was throwing him around all over the place, and I was very much aware that he could suddenly turn and collide with me before I was able to attract his attention.

I pulled alongside TF keeping as far out as I could without losing sight of him. As I eased in closer alongside Peter, I could see he had his head well down in the cockpit studying the instruments. I tried calling him on the Halfpenny Green approach frequency to no avail. If he would just look out of the cockpit for a second he would see my navigation lights. He was beginning to lose height fast and began turning away from me. Then he suddenly climbed steeply and I lost him in the swirling mist of the cloud. I raised the nose of SA in an attempt to regain visual contact but I couldn't see him. The situation was now extremely dangerous Peter had no idea that I was in close proximity to him, and he could be losing control altogether. Retaining the same heading I flew on for a minute or so, straining my eyes searching for the other aeroplane. Birmingham Control were still unable to read me so I decided it was time to head back to base. I was about to turn on to a Westerly heading when suddenly there was Peters aircraft about a hundred and fifty yards ahead of me moving from left to right. Instinctively I pulled up and banked steeply passing about 200ft over TK. As I passed overhead I saw Peter look at me.

It took a few seconds to bring my aircraft close alongside TF. Peter's ashen face stared at me. I lifted a finger in a teacher like "Come here" movement to indicate that he was to follow me. He nodded, and I pulled ahead sufficiently for him to follow without us losing sight of each other. Fortunately he was able to use my aircraft as a lateral reference to keep straight. I checked the direction indicator with the compass for the umpteenth time, and headed West. Five minutes later we were out of the storm and I was able to inform Birmingham that I had managed to find TF who was now following me home.

Understandably Peter was very shaken up when we landed. He told me that he got lost, and switched on his ADF which had been tuned in to Halfpenny Green's NDB. But Peter had not received any training in the use of ADF and was totally unaware that one of the major errors of this particular radio navigational aid was that the needle will invariably point to an electric storm if there is one within range of the instrument. So Peter must have followed the ADF needle which took him straight in to the centre of the thunderstorm.

Months past and Peter qualified for his IMC and Night Ratings, but not before causing me a couple more problems on the way. Mr T was a scatterbrain to say the least. In fact there were times when I thought he was suffering from serious neurotic imbalance.

In the merry month of May, Peter hired Cherokee G-AZMX to take a friend of his on a flight to Sleap Airfield. Just before dark we received a telephone call from him to say that he had made a heavy landing at Sleap, and the CFI there would not let him take-off to return to Halfpenny Green without first having the aircraft inspected by a qualified aircraft engineer, in the meantime he was returning home by train.

The next day, after an exchange of telephone calls between our chief engineer Charlie Luck and one of the engineers at Sleap, Charlie said he was prepared to authorise a one-off flight for me to bring MX back to Halfpenny Green providing I was happy to fly it. So later that day I was dropped off at Sleap Airfield with the intention of bringing MX back to the Green.

The mechanic at Sleap accompanied me on my external pre-flight checks MX. The undercarriage was undamaged, and the propeller had not struck the ground. Everything appeared to be all right. So I climbed aboard and after giving the engine a good run-up taxied to the holding point of the duty runway with the intention of taking off. But first the pre take-off checks had to be carried out, and as most pilots do, I talked them through as I carried out each of the checks…..

Trimmers set for take-off.

Throttle friction nut tight.

Mixture control set to rich.

Fuel on. Primer locked. Fuel pump on, and sufficient fuel for flight.

Flaps set for take-off.

Engine and flight gauges reading correctly. D.I. synchronised with the compass and un-caged. Altimeter set to the QFE. Pitot Heat off. Rotating Beacon on.

Harness secure.

Door closed and locked.

I gave the engine a final mag-drop test to make sure all was well.

One last check of the flying controls for full and free movement, and I would be ready to go.

I rotated the control column from side to side and checked the ailerons for full and free deflection to the right and left. I pushed the control column forward and looked back at the tail to check the position of the elevators, which were as they should be, full deflection down. Then, pulling the control column fully back to check the elevators came up, I noticed that somehow they didn't feel right. There wasn't the usual positive stop when the control column reached the end of its backward traverse, instead I noticed there was a second little bump that produced a very slight kick-back of the control column. I looked back again at the tail surfaces expecting to see the elevators fully up, but to my surprise they remained hanging down. I stopped the engine, applied the control locks, and jumped out to take a look at the elevators. It should have been impossible to move them whilst the locking pin was in place, but to my horror they were completely loose and moved freely up and down without the control column moving a fraction.

The realisation that I had just narrowly escaped certain death made me feel quite sick. The aircraft would either have careered off the end of the runway or maybe just manage to get off the ground and then porpoise up and down until it crashed.

The engineer came running out to meet me as I taxied back into the dispersal area. I said...

'There is something radically wrong with the elevator cables, they seem to be disconnected to the variable instance tail-plane. Perhaps you'd take a look for me?'

He gave me a disbelieving look, but after I demonstrated the problem he removed the inspection panel to find out exactly what had happened.

'Bloody hell, I've never known that to happen before....The elevator cables are completely off their pulleys, that's a bloody lucky escape you've just had mate.'

A couple of hours later the cables were reinstated and I was airborne on my way back to the Green in MX. The thought of what might have happened if I had taken off earlier was still running through my mind. It was of course a great lesson in the importance of completing your checks thoroughly every time. Mr T was indeed lucky when he was not allowed to take-off.

Thanks to Peter T, Mike and I had a third rather dicey experience when we flew out in our PA28-180 G-AVSA to collect an aeroplane that Peter inexplicably decided to leave at Shobdon Airfield for no apparent reason. He had hired Cherokee G-ATTF the previous day, but failed to return it to Halfpenny Green for reasons best known to himself, and travelled home in a friends car. It was too late to collect the aircraft when we got the message, as Shobdon was about to close for the evening. So our aeroplane had to remain there overnight.

Mike Edwards was not a happy man because Tatty Fox, as he called it, was the aircraft he usually used himself for basic training purposes, and he had a full days programme booked on it for the following day.

It was a very cold morning in late April, when Mike and I set off early for Shobdon in Sierra Alpha. The visibility was good, and the cloud base was about fifteen hundred feet.

The met indicated that we could expect an occasional shower or two throughout the day, other than that, nothing serious was forecast by the met office.

It was a straight forward in and out job. We landed at Shobdon, collected the keys of Tango Foxtrot from the club, checked the aircraft over and set off on the flight back to base.

We decided to climb in formation through the murk and enjoy flying home in clear blue skies above cloud. But that didn't happen, we broke cloud at 2000 feet and there was another layer above us. It was only a short flight back to the Green, so with Mike in the lead we decided to fly between the layers remaining in a fairly open formation

After a while, the two layers of cloud appeared to merge and things began to look a bit gloomy. The flight time remaining was about fifteen minutes, so there was no point in climbing through the second layer. Mike signalled to me to close up so that we could continue flying in formation.

It gradually got darker and darker inside the cloud. We had our navigation lights on, and both our ADF sets were tuned to HG's NDB. Our aircraft were being buffeted about considerably and I stayed well tucked in to Tango Foxtrot, as the last thing I wanted to do was lose sight of Mike's aeroplane.

Mike's voice crackled out over the R/T as he called Halfpenny Green requesting their present weather. They answered immediately….

'Hello Tango Fox, we've been trying to call you, we are experiencing a heavy snowstorm, and visibility is down to less than half a mile, over.'

Mike acknowledged the message, informed them that Sierra Alpha was in formation with him, and that we were IFR at 2000 feet estimating overhead the field in five minutes time.

Mike looked across at me and circled his hand, which meant that we would go into the holding pattern over Halfpenny Green Airfield using their NDB. Seconds later he called me on the R/T…

'Sierra Alpha from Tango Fox, is your ADF still working?'

Being very close in to Tango Fox I had not taken my eyes off his aircraft to check the instruments. I gave a brief glance at the ADF, confirmed that the needle was wandering and not locked on to the HG beacon...

'Tango Fox from Sierra Alpha, the ADF seems to be OK, but I think that HG's NDB has gone off the air.'

We were using Halfpenny Green's approach frequency, so the controller had overheard our transmissions and called us immediately…

'Tango Fox, I've checked the NDB monitor in the Tower, and it appears that it has indeed stopped working, I've sent someone down to check, standby one I'll call you back.'

Mike permitted himself a curse over the R/T. We knew we were close to the airfield so we commenced an orbit to the right whilst we waited to hear from HG. It was now snowing hard making visibility even worse, and ice was forming on the leading edges of our wings. I thought we would probably have to divert to Birmingham Airport and let down there. Tango Foxtrot was not equipped with ILS (Instrument Landing System) and Sierra Alpha was, so if we did divert to Birmingham I would have to take the lead so that we could go down the ILS together, but on second thoughts I doubted that Birmingham Approach would be happy about that.

'The ADF's working again Ray.'

It was Mike's voice. A quick check confirmed that my ADF needle was now locked on to HG's beacon and coding HG in Morse. It was at that point the explanation for its short failure came over the radio….

'Tango Foxtrot from Halfpenny Green, we're sorry about that, our beloved Chairman Mr Collis, apparently walked over to the ADF hut, thought something had been left running by mistake and, not realising what it was, turned the NDB off to save electricity!!' Mike permitted himself another slightly more enthusiastic curse over the R/T.

Snow was still falling profusely on the airfield, and our troubles were by no means over. We confirmed our altimeter setting with Air Traffic, who told us that they already had a total ground cover of snow and visibility was considerably less than half a mile.

The needle of the ADF swung round as we passed overhead the beacon. We had descended to fifteen hundred feet. Mike said he would descend to one thousand feet and attempt an NDB approach, whilst I completed a race-track pattern hold over the beacon.

I heard Mike call beacon outbound, then base turn complete descending to OCL. I waited and waited, it seemed an age before the next message crackled over the RT this time from Air Traffic…

'Tango Fox I can hear your engine, have you landed?'

Bloody hell; I thought, it must be bad if Air Traffic can't see the duty runway.

Mike acknowledged that he was down, then called me…

'The cloud base is about two hundred feet Ray. I was just able to make out the edges of runway 34 as there is a slight depression in the snow where the verges are. If you stay on an accurate back-bearing from the NDB, you can just see Mary Crump's house at about fifty yards range, good luck mate.'

I smiled at Mike's reference to Mary's house as we had spent one or two splendid evenings there. I carried out the same pattern as Mike. It was still snowing hard, but fortunately there was practically no turbulence. One tends to get a bit tense when the instruments show you are down to five hundred feet and you're in IMC conditions.

At two hundred feet I began to get glimpses of the ground. I strained to see ahead, but it was a complete whiteout. Although I was well aware of the low altitude, it still came as a shock to see the tops of hedges and a tree appear just a few feet below.

I managed to get a brief glimpse of Mrs Crump's cottage before passing over the airfield boundary fence that was just peeping out of the snow. The next positive identification I made was the three zigzagging tyre marks in the snow from the wheels of Mike's aeroplane. Sierra Alpha touched down and slithered to a halt. I sat there looking around and could see absolutely bugger-all other than the snow-covered ground and thick snow falling all around. For a moment I wondered if I was in fact on the airfield.

Air Traffic sounded pleased to hear that I had landed, informing me that Mike had so far not appeared in the dispersal area and to be careful I didn't hit him up the chuff whilst taxying. I had one advantage over Mike, I could at least follow his slowly disappearing tyre tracks to dispersal.

It goes to show that even the simplest job like setting off in reasonable weather to collect an aeroplane from an airfield only forty miles away, can turn out to be hazardous.

I just hoped that Mr T wouldn't cause us any more problems when he flew in our aeroplanes.

Things moved on at the Green and we managed to secure larger contracts with the MOD to train CCF Cadets. This made it necessary to employ more instructors to cope with the extra work. I was more than happy to employ my old friend Nils Bartleet again. For the past two or three years Nils had been flying for a company that mainly dealt with freight and most of his flying was at night. He was between jobs at the time so he came to

Halfpenny Green to give himself a break from commercial flying and enjoy a summer of instructing again.

Our Chairman Mr Collis diversified his financial interests and bought a Fridge Freezer manufacturing company in Scotland that had recently gone into receivership. At the same time a wealthy industrialist, Mr Tom Silk appeared on the scene. He joined the Flying Club and began taking flying lessons. At the time these two unrelated events were seemingly of no consequence to the operation of Air 70 Ltd, but with the passing of time they both had a significant effect on the future of Halfpenny Green Airport and Bobbington Estates.

During the Goodyear Air Race held at Halfpenny Green on the 28th August 1972, Prince William of Gloucester and his passenger Vyrell Mitchell crashed in their Piper PA-28R Arrow and were killed. As Managing Director of the airfield at the time, I was elected to be one of the air race judges and sadly witnessed the crash which occurred shortly after they had taken off. Two PA-28R aircraft had been allotted exactly the same handicap time and took off simultaneously. Arriving at the pylon designated as the scatter point, G-AYPW piloted by Prince William, was seen to bank very steeply at low level and hit a tree which severed the port wing tip and aileron. The aircraft then rolled over and crashed inverted on to the road and burst into flames a few hundred yards beyond the aerodrome boundary. Both pilots died on impact.

I personally clocked up another 305 hours flying during 1972, most of it was straightforward instructional flights. But there were one or two flights that turned out to be quite interesting.

Every now and again, we advertised "Trial Flying Lesson Gift Vouchers" in the local newspapers, selling quite a few over the Christmas period. Also people gave these vouchers as birthday presents. One such gentleman who had received a TFL gift voucher, arrived at the airfield one beautiful Summer's morning to fly with me. In spite of the pleasant weather the chap was dressed in a raincoat with a thick woollen scarf wrapped around his neck and a Trilby hat perched on the back of his head. He looked rather like a 1930's film version of a private detective.

Trial flying lessons were planned to give the recipients a short ground briefing followed by half an hours flying in the local area. Then, if they were quite happy, we would let the person hold the dual controls whilst we flew the aircraft back to the airfield. This particular chap, whose name in my logbook is recorded as Mr G. Armitage, refused to remove his hat during the flight, so he sat there in the cockpit with the headphones wrapped over his, now crumpled, Trilby hat. It was more than obvious that Mr Armitage was far from happy about receiving a trial flying lesson as a birthday present.

After a rather pointless briefing, I took off with George (I think that was his Christian Name) clutching the seat and staring straight ahead with hypnotic intensity. I couldn't get him to relax or look down at the ground at all. In fact he never looked at me either. He showed no interest in the scenery, instruments, or anything else other than the sky directly in front of him. I chatted away trying to put the chap at his ease but all I got from him was an occasional grunt of acknowledgement.

If something a little out of the normal ever happens, you can bet your life that it will occur when you least expect it. I suppose in forty years of flying I had about five or six incidents that caused me some concern. So on average you could say that I had a stroke of bad luck about once every seven or eight years, which under the circumstances of being a flying instructor, is not at all bad. This was going to be one of those days.

We were flying along at about two thousand feet, and I was doing my best to glean some sign of interest out of my passenger, when suddenly, without the slightest warning, the engine stopped. Things went a bit quiet in the cockpit although the propeller continued to windmill. To my amazement George was totally oblivious to the situation and continued to stare straight ahead, still clutching the seat with a deathlike grip. His general attitude worried me considerably and rather than taking the risk of him panicking, I said nothing to him about the engine failing. I trimmed the aircraft into a glide whilst heading for an area of open countryside. A rapid investigation produced no obvious reason for the failure. There was no sign of carburettor icing, temperatures and pressures were normal and there was plenty of fuel in both tanks. I changed petrol tanks and switched the fuel pump on but the wind milling prop remained lifeless. Our position was midway between Worcester and Stratford-upon-Avon. I had already set up RAF Pershore's approach frequency on my number two transceiver as I would be passing close to their control zone and intended giving them a call. Although we were too far away from Pershore to attempt a landing there, I decided to give them a quick call on the RT, carefully avoiding the word 'Mayday' as I thought my passenger would probably throw a fit…

'Pershore this is Cherokee Golf Alpha Zulu Mike Xray out of Halfpenny Green, we are at present five nautical miles West of Worcester with two persons on board. We have an engine failure and are committed to make a forced landing, over.'

Pershore acknowledged my call in a flash and said they were alerting the rescue services in the area to standby, they also asked me to remain on frequency as long as I could whilst they tried to identify me on their radar. My passenger must have heard my radio transmission to Pershore through the side-tones of his headset, but he didn't bat an eyelid. Perhaps he thought it was another aircraft making the call or maybe he just wasn't listening.

Fortunately there was a reasonable field within gliding distance that appeared to be long enough to land on. Half the field had been ploughed along it's length leaving a narrow green strip that I took to be grass. Pershore came back on the radio again to let me know that they had identified us on there radar. I told them roughly where I was going to attempt a landing and they kindly wished me good luck.

Emergency landing checks were completed during which time George sat rigidly in his seat, mesmerised and silent. The man was like a statue.

We were down to 600 feet and turning in towards the field I had selected for the landing, when I advised Pershore I was about to land. They informed me that they still had me on radar, and the emergency services were on their way.

With flaps down and the airspeed reduced, the propeller stopped wind-milling altogether. At that point George turned to look at me with his mouth wide open but said nothing. I told Mr Armitage we were going to land and asked him to make sure his harness was done up very tight.

We glided in to land on the grass section of the field with deeply ploughed furrows to our right. Just before touching down we passed a chap sitting on a tractor ploughing the field with his back towards us. Although I didn't want to frighten the farmer, the narrowness of the strip forced me to pass quite close to him. We skimmed past him about ten yards to his left and thumped down on the rough surface of the field. It's difficult to believe all this, but George was staring straight ahead again and never uttered a sound. Moments later as we rolled to a standstill the tractor passed us, and to my amazement the chap at the wheel ignored us completely and carried on ploughing as if aircraft landing on his field was an everyday occurrence!

Once the aircraft came to a halt, George suddenly snapped into life...

'I enjoyed that' he said as he followed me out of the cockpit.

Then, looking a bit puzzled for a second he said...

'I seem to be a bit disorientated, where did I park my car?'

I explained to George that this was not Halfpenny Green Airfield and we had had an engine failure. He stopped dead in his tracks, turned as white as a ghost and murmured.

'F… me.'

As we walked across the field towards the farmhouse, the tractor had already turned at the end of his run and was passing the aircraft again. The driver stood up for a moment whilst the tractor was still moving, and stared at us, then shaking his head, carried on ploughing without so much as a wave.

A mouth-watering smell of freshly cooked stew filled the air as we approached the farmhouse. A middle-aged lady wearing a headscarf over partly concealed hair curlers answered the door. She too showed no surprise at seeing me in my flying overalls with a headset slung round my neck.

'Hello dear' she said as if she had known me for years.

'I'm afraid we have just had an engine failure and had to land our aeroplane in your field. Do you think I could use your telephone please?'

My words invoked no element of astonishment on her face at all. She simply smiled and said….

'Of course you can, and I expect you could do with a nice cup of tea dear?'

I turned to introduce Mr Armitage, but George was nowhere to be seen. In fact I never saw him again, he must have headed for the farm gates and hitched a ride back to the airfield to collect his car without a word to anyone.

In the farmhouse I was directed to a room where an elderly gentleman was immersed in reading his newspaper. I said hello to the chap and asked if I could use his telephone.

'Mornin' he said pointing to the telephone.

I was halfway through making a call to the police, when the old chap suddenly lowered his paper and shot up out of his chair. He stumbled towards the window and shouted….

'Bugger me Martha, there's a bloody aeroplane in our field.'

Moments later the distant sound of approaching sirens broke the peaceful silence of the farm. The fire engine followed by an ambulance and a policeman on a motorcycle streaked into the farmyard. The final indignity was when one of the firemen, who looked totally hacked off, yelled back to one of his colleagues…

'It's alright mate, nobody's hurt, the bloody thing's not even damaged.'

Eventually our engineers arrived and discovered the cause of the engine failure to be in the fuel system. On the spot repairs were carried out and in an amazingly short time the engine was running again.

I thanked my hosts for their kind hospitality, took off passing the man on the tractor who once again ignored me completely, and flew the aircraft back to base. But when MX was on the base leg of the circuit at Halfpenny Green it started spluttering and banging again. Our fire engine and crash crew were already standing by, but fortunately the engine provided sufficient power to make a safe landing. It was taken into the maintenance workshops and worked on for a couple of days before finally being released back to service.

The day to day routine at Halfpenny Green continued much as usual. I had a great staff working for me. Carol Greenwood was now my secretary. We worked very well together, but I began to notice that some days she came to work looking very tired and unhappy. One morning Carol failed to turn up for work. She hadn't telephoned in to let us know she wouldn't be coming in, and that, for Carol, was very much out of character. Her friend that worked in Ops tried to contact her on the telephone, but there was no reply. By mid afternoon there was still no word from Carol, and I began to worry in case she had had an accident on her way to work.

I had an hour and a half gap in my flight schedule, so I made a note of Carol's address and decided to drive the short distance to where she lived and find out if she was in trouble.

On arrival I peered through the tiny window of her cottage and saw Carol sitting with her head in her hands, a partly eaten meal was still on the table. Carol was obviously very upset and probably a little embarrassed to see me. It was then that I learned of Carol's failing marriage and that she had split up from her husband the previous evening. I talked with her for a short while and said that it was probably a storm in a teacup and they would be back together in no time. She was such a lovely natured person, it was sad to see her in such a grievous state. Carol cheered up a little, thanked me for coming over to see her and said she would be back at work the following morning.

At that time, heaven knows I had my own problems at home. This led to me spending most evenings in the club bar.

One morning Ben McLeod tapped on the door of my office and asked if I minded him popping in for a personal chat. As he was one of my instructors, I thought he probably had a personal problem that he wanted to discuss with me, so I asked what I could do to him? His reply was quite a shock …

'I don't suppose you will remember too much about what happened in the bar last night boss, and I hope you won't mind me saying that I reckon, if you're not careful, you are going to get yourself into a lot of trouble.'

'What's the problem' I asked, feeling very apprehensive about what might be coming next.

'Your secretary was in the club bar last night and when you came staggering out of the gents toilet you came face to face with her in the corridor.'

I was beginning to feel very uncomfortable and wondered what on earth I had done.

'Well Boss, without saying a word, you staggered up to her, clasped her head in your hands and kissed her smack on her lips.'

My heart sank, what a bloody stupid thing to do.

'Then what happened?'

'Nothing really boss, she looked a bit surprised, and left the club.'

After listening to Ben, I sat at my desk feeling disgusted with myself. There was no two ways about it, I had to go over to flight ops straight away and apologise to her for my stupid behaviour, hoping that she wouldn't find it necessary to give up her job. Carol had proved to be a great asset to the flying school. I learned later that her father and mother had held a very responsible positions with the well known Pilkington family. As such Carol had been treated as one of the family and was educated by private tutor with the Pilkington children. She was not only a sophisticated young lady, but very beautiful, and we were lucky to have her working for us. Whatever she must have thought of me now didn't bear thinking about.

When I entered the Ops office with considerable trepidation. Carol was sitting at her desk with her back towards me. I put my hands gently on her shoulders and said...

'I'm terribly sorry about what happened last night.'

Carol didn't turn to face me but simply whispered...

'It's alright, I didn't mind.'

I suppose that incident changed my life forever. Carol was at least ten years younger than me, and I never dreamed for one moment that she would ever look twice at me, yet somehow I allowed myself to fall hopelessly in love with her.

To this day I find it hard to believe that we have become inseparable. I can remember the very instant I dared to even think that, just maybe, Carol would consider marrying me. I was waiting for her in the car as she came out of her little cottage and closed the garden gates. She was dressed in a rusty coloured two piece suit, her curly golden hair fell loosely over her shoulders and she was smiling at me with the full soft lips that I have grown to love so much. When she came and sat next to me in the car I asked if she thought she could ever find it in her heart to marry me?

It seemed like a miracle when Carol simply said of course I will, I would love to spend the rest of my life with you.

Then came the very sad and distressing time when I had to face Valerie. When we first got together we agreed that neither of us wanted to commit ourselves to getting married again. Even so, we had spent over seven years together. Val had remained a devoted friend throughout the traumatic years I spent in hospital recovering from the crash. Without her regular visits and Laura's cheery letters, recovery would have been far more difficult to endure. Now I had to find some way of telling Valerie that it was all over. Heaven knows she never deserved to be treated this way. But things had been going wrong for some time. If we had stayed together we would probably have made each others lives a misery, and there was nothing I could do to change what had already happened.

Naturally I was confronted by Carol's father who made it quite clear that he was very concerned about his daughter's future. We had a real heart to heart talk and he took me at my word when I promised him that I would look after and love Carol for the rest of my life. From that day on Bill became the best friend I ever had.

Carol and I decided to live together straight away and rented the Old Vicarage in Claverly, a picturesque village about two miles from the airport.

And now, as I write these words, Carol and I have been together for forty wonderful years. I still awake each morning to see the person who, to me, is the most beautiful lady in the world lying next to me. Her soft hair golden hair may bare a few traces of silver, but to me she will always be the most loving creature God created, and above all, she is my soul mate.

CHAPTER 47.

Times of change.

In the world of aviation things never stay the same for very long. But it still came as a complete shock when our Chairman Mr Collis suddenly announced that due to certain changes in his financial affairs he found it necessary to sell Air 70 and Halfpenny Green Airfield. Nobody other than Mr Freeth, who was the resident accountant on the airfield and a personal friend of Mr Collis, had the slightest inkling that this was likely to happen. I learned later that the income from the joint ventures on the airfield had been transferred to Mr Collis's recently purchased freezer manufacturing company to try and keep it afloat.

This would be the fourth change of the airfield's ownership in the short time I had worked at Halfpenny Green, and it was once again my unfortunate task to inform all our loyal and hard working employee's that the company was going to be sold, and there was a possibility that they may be made redundant.

An advertisement was placed in 'Flight International' offering Bobbington Estates and Air 70 Ltd. for sale as a going concern. The advert attracted several potential buyers and obviously left everyone that worked on the airfield feeling insecure.

Mr Tom Silk, a very wealthy industrialist who also happened to be one of my PPL students, said he would be interested in purchasing the airfield and asked me if I would mind arranging an informal meeting for him to discuss the matter with our Chairman.

Negotiations between the two men lasted several weeks, and at times led to very heated arguments. At one stage things got so bad that the two men refused to meet each other, and I had to act as a "go between" carrying messages to and fro, desperately trying to keep the peace between the two men. I hoped the aerodrome would be sold to someone who would continue to back me in developing the business into a professional Flying Training School. The last thing I wanted to see happen was Halfpenny Green becoming a free for all with several resident flying clubs all competing against one-another.

In the end, after much wrangling, Halfpenny Green aerodrome and Air 70 were sold to Mr Silk. He renamed his newly acquired asset "Midland Aviation Centre" and I was offered the position of Managing Director of the new company. I accepted the position and also managed to get Mike Edwards a seat on the board, he certainly deserved it.

Tom Silk turned out to be an exceedingly difficult person to work with. Although he was undoubtedly a very skilful entrepreneur, he knew precious little about the laws appertaining to operating an airport or the intricacies of running a flying school, and made it quite clear from the start that he resented taking any advice from me or anybody else.

I think the fact that Tom was experiencing difficulty in the early stages of his flying training was causing him considerable embarrassment. There was no need for this, students who take a long time to go solo often turn out to be very good pilots.

Tom blamed his lack of flying skill on to the efficiency of his instructors, and it wasn't long before he and I fell out badly.

When I was appointed Managing Director of Halfpenny Green Airfield, I made absolutely sure that my service agreement was carefully worded, and Tom realised he would have a problem getting rid of me. However, Tom was used to getting his own way with everything, and I think he decided to try and make things so uncomfortable for me that I would resign of my own accord. It wasn't long before I learned how devious this man could be.

One morning a middle aged man who I had never seen before in my life, suddenly turned up in the Flight Ops Office unannounced and proclaimed to everyone's astonishment that he was the newly appointed manager in charge of all flying activities on the airfield. I will call him Captain S. In truth I don't think he had ever been in the cockpit of an aeroplane.

Captain S. acted quite strangely and tried to ignore me completely refusing to discuss his appointment or produce evidence of his terms of reference. Straight away I thought that this was some kind of practical joke. Nothing at all had been said to me about employing another commercial pilot. Surely if Tom had employed someone in a senior position within the company, I, as Managing Director, should have at least been informed and preferably been present at the interview.

Before getting the chap thrown off the airfield altogether, I thought I'd better telephone Tom and find out what the hell was going on, fully expecting to be informed that it was indeed a huge joke. But that was far from the case. Tom said he considered that I had more than enough to do looking after the pilot training side of the business, and Capt S. had been appointed as Chief Pilot and head of commercial flying.

This was ridiculous, Midland Aviation Centre was not approved by the CAA as a commercial operation, it had no Air Operator's Certificate, and no Operation Flight Manuals. In fact the whole business of operating commercially had not been approved or even discussed by the directors. Neither Tom or the man claiming to be Captain S. had any idea of what was involved to set up a CAA approved commercial operation. Presumably they thought it was just a matter of jumping into any old aeroplane and carry fare paying passengers to wherever they wanted to go! (The CAA would have been delighted!)

Tom insisted that Capt S. was a very experienced commercial pilot. But as far as I was concerned the man was completely wacky. He refused to produce any means of identification, he refused to show me his pilots licence or his log books, and appeared to know nothing at all about aviation. How he had bluffed Silk into giving him a job as Chief Commercial Pilot I will never know, I wouldn't have employed him to sweep the hangar floors! Whilst I was talking to Tom on the telephone in my office, Captain S. stomped around the reception office and ostentatiously ordered my staff to remove all the flight training bookings from the Ops board. That was enough for me, I ordered the man to leave, or words to that effect! and threatened to have him thrown out if he didn't leave immediately.

I contacted CAA licensing, they had several Mr S.'s on record but none seemed to fit the description of the man Tom had employed.

I didn't see Mr S. again that day, but the crunch came at ten o'clock the following morning when the telephone rang and the manager of our local pub informed me that someone professing to be in charge of Halfpenny Green Airport had arrived in the bar very drunk wearing nothing but pyjamas and slippers!

Tom refused to speak to me on the telephone, so I assumed that Capt S had disappeared as suddenly as he had arrived. But a day or so later he turned up at the airfield reeking of alcohol and asked for the keys to all our aircraft. My staff made sure that the chap never got anywhere near an aeroplane, and I had him thrown off the airfield. A lot of unpleasantness between Tom and myself followed. In my opinion S was an alcoholic and in desperate need of medical help. I made frequent telephone calls to Toms office in West Bromwich in order to try and sort out this ridiculous state of affairs. Eventually, and after a very heated meeting between the two of us, Capt S disappeared off the scene for good. As far as I could ascertain he didn't have a pilot's licence of any kind and had obviously been paid to annoy me in the hope that I would resign my position with the company, but it didn't work.

Things came to a head one morning when our aircraft were grounded due to inclement weather conditions. Tom arrived in his Rolls Royce and parked outside the main door of the flying school. The cloud base was less than 500 ft. and the visibility at ground level was less than a mile.

I was in our classroom lecturing to a number of cadets when Tom burst in and demanded that I made out a flight plan in order to fly him to RAF St. Mawgan. I explained that our aircraft were obviously grounded because of the weather conditions which were below company limits, adding that flying light aircraft in these conditions was tantamount to suicide. Tom flew into a temper in front of the students and members of my staff, stating that I didn't know what I was talking about. I said...

'Tom, if you carry on like this one day you will kill yourself, and I'm going to make bloody sure that you don't take me with you.'

My remarks must have come close to giving my boss apoplexy. He was absolutely furious, and accused me of being yellow, threatening to terminate my employment as Managing Director of Midland Aviation there and then if I refused to take him to St. Mawgan.

We all say things we don't really mean when tempers flare, and somehow I managed to keep calm whilst Tom strutted out of the room saying if I hadn't got the guts to take him he would find someone else to fly with him.

My fellow instructors, and several members of the Ops staff had witnessed Tom's outburst and were aghast at his ranting and raving.

I had no intention of letting any of my instructors take a risk. I knew that if he ordered a non-instrument rated pilot to go with him in these conditions it would more than likely end up in a fatal accident.

My licenses covered me to fly in adverse weather conditions, even so I knew I would certainly be pushing my luck.

I telephoned RAF St Mawgan who informed me that their conditions were appalling and very similar to those at Halfpenny Green. They estimated the cloud base to be around 150 ft. and said all their aircraft were grounded at the time. Their Approach Controller agreed to give me radar assistance down to their promulgated limits, after that, if I was not in sight of ground I would have to overshoot from the approach.

I should have refused to fly even if my job was threatened, but I was determined to teach my boss a lesson he wouldn't forget, so against my judgement I decided to give it a go.

The track distance was over 200 miles, which meant we would be airborne just under two hours.

I stumped out of the briefing room, the constant pain from my injured legs reminded me in no uncertain terms of the consequences that could occur through giving way to Tom. Our Aztec was unserviceable at the time, and the only aeroplane's available were all single engine Piper Cherokees. I decided to take the 180 G-AVSA, and asked Tom to pre-flight the aircraft whilst I made out the necessary flight plan.

As we were taxying out for take-off Tom had another go at me…

'You're forty-two now Ray? Too old to instruct, I'll give you a job working in one of my factories.'

I didn't bother to reply.

We took-off and entered solid cloud at 150 ft. climbing out on course. Levelling out at 3000 ft. we were still in cloud. I was sitting in the instructors seat on the right hand side of the cockpit and although I could see the flight instruments clearly enough I only had the VHF /VOR set plus the ADF and the engine instruments on my side of the instrument panel. It was however difficult to see the subscale reading of the slightly recessed altimeter on the left hand instrument panel.

I told Tom to set the altimeter subscale to 1013.2mb, adding that if his life ever depended on anything it certainly relied on him setting the subscale accurately to any subsequent reading I would tell him to set.

Established on track, I called London Information to inform them of our details and in-flight conditions. By this time we were experiencing moderate turbulence and Toms former aggressive attitude had changed completely. He had become very quiet and was wriggling about uncomfortably in his seat, probably trying to avoid being airsick. Whenever I spoke to him he replied with a nod or a short grunt. Finally, after about an hours flying with no sight of the ground since take-off, Tom suggested that we turn back. I told him that with the cloud base being almost down to ground level, there was no chance of landing back at Halfpenny Green and I intended to continue to St. Mawgan where we could at least be given a QGH let-down. Tom's initial aggressive attitude had subsided completely, he obviously had no idea of what was going on or where we were. Again and again he asked me if we were lost, and continued urging me to turn back.

Ninety minutes had passed, and the turbulence increased considerable until we were being thrown around like a ping-pong ball in a goldfish bowl. We had not seen the ground since leaving the airfield, and although we were working the appropriate radar stations, flying in those condition in a single engine aeroplane with limited instrumentation and a cloud base of around 150 ft., was not the most ideal set of circumstances.

I switched over from London Information and called St Mawgan's approach. It was a great comfort to hear the controller's voice. He asked us to make a couple of small changes in our heading to confirm radar identification. When St. Mawgan's controller finally said he had positively identified us on Radar, I could see that Tom was a little more relaxed. I pointed out to him that the flight was far from over and the tricky bit was still to come. St. Mawgan approach informed me that all their aircraft were still grounded and they had no known traffic in the area. Their estimated cloud base was 200 ft. on their QNH which I asked Tom to set on his altimeter, adding once again that our lives depended on him setting the subscale accurately.

I requested a QGH let-down which was accepted, we were advised that their break-off altitude was 500 ft. on their QFE, and the QGH would terminate at that point, after that I would be on my own! We carried sufficient fuel to divert to RAF Chivenor which was our planned alternate, but there was a strong possibility that the weather would be just as bad at Chivenor as it was at St Mawgan. The approach controller passed their QFE which, once again, I made sure Tom set accurately on the subscale of our one and only altimeter. The talk-down commenced. We completed the outbound leg, turned inbound and started our descent passing through 900 ft. 800 ft. 700 ft. and 600 ft. without a glimpse of the surface. At 500 ft. still with no sight of the ground, the controller advised us that we were spot on the extended centre line and had one mile to run to the threshold, with that the QGH ended. I squeezed on a little power raising the nose of the aircraft slightly to maintain my approach speed and reduce the rate of descent. We were still in solid cloud at 300 feet. I was about to apply full power and abort the approach when Tom suddenly shouted that he was getting intermittent glimpses of the ground. With less than half a mile to run to the runway threshold I continued to descend to 200feet. At that point I saw the runway approach lights flick past just under our starboard wingtip followed be the runway numbers. We were completely in the clear at exactly 100feet. I closed the throttle and the wheels rumbled onto the runway. The controller asked me to remain on his frequency for taxying instructions, adding that he could hear my engine during the latter part of the approach, but didn't actually see me until we broke cloud a few hundred yards before touching down. I wouldn't mind betting he thought that I was the biggest pratt living to be flying in those conditions, and he would be was right.

We took a taxi from St Mawgan to Torquay. Tom reached his meeting on time, but typically, never uttered one word of thanks to me.

I was invited to sit through the meeting that Tom had to preside over, and I have to say that I was more than impressed by the brilliant business expertise he displayed during the conference, he was indeed a brilliant businessman.

Fortunately the weather front passed through by late afternoon, leaving us with clear skies for our return trip to Halfpenny Green. So the journey home was made with Tom at the controls.

The incident reminded me of a similar state of affairs that occurred during a flight from Oxford several years earlier. A twin engine charter aircraft took off from Kidlington in bad weather conditions and ultimately crashed at its destination airfield. The investigation revealed that the pilot had been under considerable pressure from his passengers to get them to their destination on time for a meeting. An attempt was made to land in very limited visibility which resulted in a fatal crash. The pilot was killed, and only one passenger survived to tell the tale. I'm pretty sure that most charter pilots at some time or other during their career, are subjected to pressures from their passengers. I admit that I should never have taken off from Halfpenny Green that day. I did so to retain my job as MD, and also protect any other member of my flying staff from being threatened with the sack if they refused to carry out the flight. As it happened I was lucky, and I swore I would never take such a risk again.

The situation between my Chairman and myself never relented. In the end I made the decision to try and find suitable alternative employment. But before that happened both Tom and I managed to get ourselves entangled with a more serious and rather strange state of affairs which we both could have done without.

CHAPTER 48.

The Downman Affair.

My office telephone rang and Carol informed me that a gentleman was on the outside line asking to speak to the person in charge of flying, and whoever it was calling didn't wish to give his name. My first thoughts were that someone was telephoning to complain about noise from one of our aeroplanes passing over his property. Carol put me through and the male voice at the other end spoke with a strong Irish accent...

'Good morning to you sir, would I be speaking to the man in charge of the airfield?'

I asked how I could help him and he enquired if I knew my boss Tom Silk on a personal basis, which I thought was a rather strange question. I asked the caller his name and enquired again in what respect I could help him. His reply alerted me to thinking that perhaps I was speaking to some kind of eccentric, or maybe an enraged associate of my boss.

'My name is Downman, and I'm sorry to trouble you on this delightful morning. How well do you know your bosses secretary, I believe her name is Mrs G------?'

Although the question was straight forward enough, there was a tone of cynicism in his voice and I told him that the best thing to do was telephone our head office and speak to my Chairman personally. The caller completely ignored what I said and continued asking me personal questions about my boss that were certainly nothing whatever to do with me.

In the end I told the chap that I had nothing more to say to him, and slammed the receiver down.

Although Tom was anything but a friend of mine, I felt obliged to inform him about the telephone call immediately. I tried to get through to him but his secretary said he was too busy to speak to me. This didn't surprise me at all, so I simply said she should tell him that I telephoned because I was concerned that he may be in some sort of personal trouble, and left it at that. Tom telephoned me back within seconds.

'What the hell's up now Ray, can't you deal with anything without my help?'

I ignored his sarcastic remark and told him of Mr Downman's interest in his secretary. Tom's response was predictably aggressive and ended by him slamming the phone down before I could reply. I thought little more of all this until Tom telephoned me the following morning and for once in his life sounded like a long lost friend.

'Now listen Ray, we've got to get this crackpot off our backs, he's obviously some sort of maniac and if he contacts you again, tell him you're going to report him to the police.'

'What's it all about Tom? Surely you should be the one to report the matter to the police, it's got nothing to do with me. '

Tom's attitude changed in a flash.

'Just do as you're told Ray, telephone the police and do it now.'

His remarks terminated the discussion. So I contacted the police and gave them as much information as I could.

I received a number of weird telephone calls over the following weeks. The caller's calm, smarmy voice would always comment on the weather before enquiring about my bosses movements. On one occasion when I said I was unwilling to cooperate with him, he threaten me with violence from his "Organisation". The police were soon involved at a high level, and because the rapid call tracing system that exists nowadays had not been invented at that time, a recording device was wired into the telephone in my office so that I could record all conversations I had with this guy.

The telephone calls persisted, I had no idea what this chap wanted, and for some reason his attitude towards me became threatening...

'Good morning Mr Blyth, what a lovely morning it is to be sure….. now how are you keeping? I presume that you are in good health at the moment, LETS HOPE IT STAYS THAT WAY.'

The sound of this man's sarcastic voice began to give me the creeps.

'I understand that you're Mr Silk's Chief Pilot Mr Blyth and that suits us very well. My organisation will be asking you to do us a little favour very shortly, so we will. Take my advice Mr Blyth, do as you are instructed and no harm will come to you. I think perhaps we will need to prove our sincerity …. We'll have to see.'

Writing about it now seems too strange to be true. But unfortunately all this really happened. The year was 1972, and to the best of my knowledge there had not been any reports of IRA cells or organisations of a similar nature active in this country, and I must stress that as far as I'm concerned I personally never found out who or what this so-called organisation was about, although I'm sure by the way the police reacted they must have known much more than they were willing to tell me.

I attended several meetings at West Bromwich Police Station, each time I handed in the recordings of my latest telephone conversations with Downman. Before long a couple of plain clothes gentlemen called in to see me at the airfield. Having produced proof of their identity, they proceeded to ask me if I would be willing to co-operate with the authorities in apprehending Downman and whoever else was involved. Although I had no idea what I was letting myself in for, I agreed to help. Tom never made any attempt to disguise the fact that he was a very wealthy man, quite the opposite in fact, and I could only assume that all this was probably something to do with a very unpleasant blackmail attempt. But I didn't realise was serious this was until early one morning Downman called me with a brief message…

'Good morning Captain, what a lovely day it is to be sure… It seems that we are not being taken too seriously … a sad mistake Mr Blyth to be sure… Anyway, to prove our sincerity we have a little surprise for you sir…. A BOMB HAS BEEN PLACED in the Air Traffic Building on Halfpenny Green Airfield that will explode very shortly.'

With that the phone went dead. For a second I was stunned, my office was situated in the air traffic building, surely this must be some kind of stupid joke. This was 1972, and I for one had never heard of bombs being placed in any public buildings in this country. I didn't really believe the man, but it certainly wasn't worth taking any chances. I telephoned the special branch number that had been given to me by the police, and reported the bomb threat. I was told to evacuate the building immediately and await the arrival of the emergency services.

With the help of my colleague Mike Edwards, we moved all the staff out of the building and into the offices of Bobbington Estates as quickly as we could. Mike then positioned himself at the airfield gates to stop anyone else from entering whilst I, convinced that this was a hoax, did my best to try and locate the whereabouts of the so-called bomb.

There were several rooms in the air traffic control and so many nooks and crannies in the building that I didn't know where to start. I searched the ground floor offices very briefly including my own. First to arrive on the scene was Sergeant Kirkham from the local police station at Kinver. I knew Bill Kirkham quite well, and he was the sort of chap that didn't mince his words...

'The best thing you and I can do is get the hell out of here Ray and let them what knows what they're doing deal with it' he said.

There was one remaining area on the ground floor of the air traffic building that I thought was worth taking a quick look at. The old boiler room was the only part of the structure that could be accessed from outside without actually entering the main part of the building. The boiler was no longer in use and the room was used as a junk store. Sgt Kirkham decided to search around the outside of the building whilst I had a very quick look inside. There was lots of rubbish strewn all over the floor. I rummaged around quickly and was just about to leave when I heard something that caused the hair on my neck to stand up. Click Click Click Click, the sound appeared to be coming from behind an old battered Crown & Anchor table top that had been propped up on its side against the back wall. Heart thumping, I eased the top of the board from the wall and there it was. A crumpled black bag about twice the size of a shoe box with a small amount of wire protruding from the top.

I called out to Sergeant Kirkham...

'Bill, I think I've found it.'

Bill's distant reply echoed across the airfield....

'Have you got a F.....g death wish or something? for God's sake get the f--- out of there Ray.'

As I rapidly left the boiler room, an Army vehicle, that turned out to be from a bomb disposal unit based in Birmingham, parked about 100 yards from the Control Tower. I informed the officer in charge that everybody had been evacuated from the building and indicated whereabouts I had discovered the suspicious package. He thanked me and ordered me to leave the area immediately.

Twenty minutes or so later there was a loud explosion. The door of the boiler room together with lots of debris flew into the air in a cloud of black smoke. Sergeant Kirkham grinned...

'You were right' he said, 'it was the bomb.'

Shortly after this event I was collected in a police car and whisked off to West Bromwich Police Station again where I was introduced to Superintendent Peter French, the officer in charge of the case. I asked the superintendent what this was all about, but he said they didn't know for certain, but I'm sure they knew more than they were prepared to tell me. He enquired if I would be willing to help the police by agreeing to cooperate with Downman who was now becoming a threat to peoples safety. Agreeing to help the police was one thing, but cooperating with Downman was another. Not overjoyed by the request I hesitantly agreed to help providing I was afforded some form of protection by the police.

The next telephone call from Downman, was short and not so sweet! It came as a shock when he informed me that he knew I had a young son named Edward who lived with his mother in Brackley Northamptonshire. He went on to say that if I didn't carry out the instructions he gave me to the letter, I wouldn't see Eddy again. He didn't wait for a reply and just rang off. I telephoned Eddy's mother immediately to find out if anything had happened to my son, fortunately he was ok. How in hells name did this guy get that sort of information about my family? It must have been through someone who knew me very well. I informed the police straight away. They told me not to worry and assured me that Eddy would be taken care of. Brackley was a long way from where I now lived, and I was not at all happy about him getting involved in all this cloak and dagger stuff. Apparently Tom's children had also been threatened, so he must have been receiving telephone calls as well.

I was airborne the next time Downman telephoned. One of my instructors took the call and had the phone slammed down in his ear for his trouble.

D. called again later and after remarking on the weather as he nearly always did, he said he would shortly be giving me the map reference of a field that I would be asked to fly to and land in. What was that all about? surely the authorities would never expect me to carry this out.

Two or three days past with nothing further from D. Then at nine o'clock in the morning Downman called again and read out a map reference, stating that this was the field I would be expected to land in. Further instructions would be passed to me in due course. I started to ask him if he seriously thought I would be daft enough to follow his instructions but he slammed the telephone down.

Mike and I poured over a large map in the flight planning room. The six figure reference given to me by Downman turned out to be located in the middle of the Irish sea. Later I received another brief telephone call altering the map reference to a position close to the West coast of Northern Ireland. There followed a series of brief telephone calls to pass instructions on what to do and how to identify the chosen field. For some obscure reason I was instructed to fly at sea level along a certain stretch of the coastline shortly before reaching the field I was to land in. After landing

I was to taxi towards some trees on the Northern edge of the field where I would be met by someone who would take charge of a package I would be carrying. I was reminded in no uncertain terms of the consequences should I deviated from these instructions.

All of this seemed to be very amateurish, but the bomb in air traffic and the threat of harming my son left me in no doubt that it was far from a joke. I couldn't risk anything happening to Eddy, so when the Superintendent in charge of the case asked me if I would cooperate with them and make the flight, I had little choice. It was obvious to me that if I had to land in Ireland and come face to face with these bastards, they would see to it that I didn't take-off again.

A time was set for me to take-off for Northern Ireland carrying a package. I was told by Downman that I was to be the sole occupant in the aircraft, and the take-off from Halfpenny Green would be observed!

A few minutes before the scheduled take-off time, Tom came screeching through the airport gates in his Jenson and disappeared into one of the hangars. I rushed out to see why he was in such a panic, and he told me that someone had followed him all the way to the airfield from his offices in West Bromwich. He said he had received a telephone call from someone threatening to shoot him if he didn't comply to their instructions. I asked Tom what it was that these people had on him, but he told me it was nothing to do with me. Under the circumstances, this whole affair was very much to do with me.

The aircraft had been fuelled up, and I was just signing out when a man appeared in ops, showed me his police identification badge and asked me if I was still happy to go. Happy was not the word I would have chosen, but I was keen to get the whole thing over and done with. I asked him if I could be armed in some way, but he laughed and said it's a bit late for that, and in any case the idea of me being armed was totally out of the question. It may have been a joke to him but I certainly couldn't see the funny side. I felt sure that I was being set up for something, and what ever it was I wasn't going to like it. The man in the suit continued...

'Don't worry, although you will fly out of here on your own, we have cleared it for you to land at RAF Cosford and pick up one of our chaps, his name is Detective Inspector Bob Snee, he is there now waiting for you, he has the package and he'll look after you Mr Blyth.'

I breathed a sigh of relief: 'Thank God for that.'

It was the 19th May 1972. I took off in G-AZMX and landed at RAF Cosford ten minutes later to pick up the D/I. We took off immediately and flew for a further three hours across the Irish sea, over flying the Isle of Man and on to Northern Ireland. As instructed by Downman we flew at low altitude alongside a mile or so of very high cliffs. I was quite nervous about this and couldn't make out why we had been instructed to fly low until we noticed a solitary figure standing on the cliff top looking at us through binoculars. I asked Bob if the man was one of his chaps, and he said as far as he knew nobody from his section was out there.

'That's done it' I said, 'If that guy is one of Downman's lot he will have seen that there is more than one person in the cockpit.'

We climbed to a thousand feet and continued to the specified field where we had been instructed to land. Bob carried a small briefcase and instructed me to fly low across the field as slow as possible, under no circumstances was I to land. I'm sure he was armed and I began to wonder what exactly he intended to do.

'I'm going to drop this briefcase out Ray, as soon as I've dropped it let's get the hell out of here.'

The field Downman had selected for us to land in was enormous, easily large enough to land a light aeroplane in. Bob had great difficulty opening the door wide enough to get the briefcase out because of the slipstream. Anyway with a lot of effort he managed to push the briefcase out through the gap. As we passed low over the surface I banked over steeply to see the briefcase flutter down into the field, I also I saw a single figure standing by the edge of the wood looking up at us.

Bob explained that the case contained nothing but a note that stated the field was too small to land in, requesting who ever collected the case to telephone me when I landed back at the Green. My first thoughts were what will happen to my son Eddy, these bastards are certainly not going to be overjoyed with what we had done, the field was obviously big enough to land in. Moments later as we were climbing away I noticed a military helicopter flying very low heading straight for the same field. I asked Bob if that was anything to do with us? All he said was probably.

On our return journey we had to land at Newtownards Airfield to refuel before crossing the sea again. We were greeted by the local club's Chief Flying Instructor who couldn't have been more offensive if he tried.

'You bloody private pilots are all the same, you get decent clubs like ours a bad name flying around at zero feet like bloody idiots breaking all the regulations in the book.'

He was literarily snarling his words out at Bob.

'Belfast Area Control have been on the blower, you've been reported for low flying, they've got your registration and they followed you on radar so its no good denying it. They said you are to telephone them immediately if you land here, I wouldn't like to be in your shoes matey.'

Bob simply showed his warrant card to the nasty little bugger and said a few curt words that shut him up like a clam. Bob telephoned the SATCO at Belfast Airport, and a few words cleared the matter up instantly.

All the way back I worried about my son Eddy and what this Downman character was likely to do next. He was obviously not going to be overjoyed, and I was bound to be the one that would take the brunt of his anger.

When we landed back at Halfpenny Green someone had already been on the telephone and left a message with Mike to say… 'Tell Blyth he's a dead man.' It didn't end there, Eddy had to be escorted to and from school by the Northamptonshire police, and I got tangled up in more intrigue with the so-called 'organisation', enough to fill a small book in fact. Suffice to say that my son and his grandparents had a very frightening experience, but it all ended without any harm being done to any of them To this day I never found out exactly what it was all about, or if anyone was apprehended on the field in Northern Ireland. I think someone may have been arrested when I was persuaded by the police to set up a meeting with one of Downman's associates outside a public house called "The Stew pony".

In the end I never received one word of gratitude from the authorities or Tom Silk for risking my neck in an investigation that really had nothing at all to do with me.

CHAPTER 49.

The British Schools of Flying.

14th of September 1973 turned out to be one of the happiest days of my life. Carol and I were married at Bridgnorth Registry Office. It was a very quiet and private affair, at least it was until we left the registry office and walked out onto the street. Suddenly three aircraft in tight formation screamed over the building no more that a few feet from the rooftops. It was my lot at it. I prayed they wouldn't return as some well-wisher would be sure to get their registration letters and report them for low flying. As it happened they had enough sense to buzz off quickly. I found out who the culprits were later, all of them very experienced ex RAF chaps that took the risk of being caught low flying. They meant well bless them, and I must admit we thought it was great.

We continued to live at the old Vicarage in Claverly for the time being, but after the Downman affair which had dragged out for months, we decided to start looking for suitable employment elsewhere.

I took the liberty of telephoning my ex boss, the Chairman of CSE Aviation Rex Smith, who was now also a Director of the CAA. I told him about all the escapades that had been going on at Halfpenny Green Airport and asked him if he would be kind enough to let me know if he heard of any pilot vacancies in the future that he thought I would be suited for. A few days later Rex telephoned me to say that he had been having a conversation about me with a Mr Robert Pascoe.

Apparently Bob Pascoe ran the Ipswich Flying School and also owned flying clubs on Southend, Biggin Hill and Shoreham Aerodromes. Mr Pascoe had spoken to Rex about grouping all his flying clubs together under one heading and registering them as The British Schools of Flying.

He told Rex that he hoped to provide a very high standard of training for private pilots in a similar vane to the professional pilot training school at Oxford. Rex had given him my name and kindly inferred that I was the ideal person to set up and run the schools for him. Rex suggested that I should give Bob Pascoe a telephone call and take it from there. It was exactly the sort of job I was looking for. I thanked Rex very much and said I would let him know how I got on.

I contacted Pascoe's Secretary and made an early appointment to meet him at Ipswich Airport. On the day of the appointment I arrived at his office spot on time and was told that Mr Pascoe was out and she didn't know what time he would be back. I waited for an hour and he didn't show up. I and was so annoyed that I left a message to say he wasn't the only one that had to keep appointments and left. I was pretty sure that would be the end of it, but the next morning Pascoe's secretary telephoned to make another appointment and said that Mr Pascoe had been unavoidably delayed. He was still very keen to see me and another appointment was made.

But this time "Sods Law" took a hand and I spilt a whole cup of coffee from a flask down the front of my spotlessly white shirt just before entering the gates of Ipswich Airport. Bob Pascoe of course was immaculately dressed, whilst I entered his office looking more like a tramp! Fortunately Bob saw the funny side when I explained what had happened.

I was very impressed with Pascoe's plans for operating a number of flying clubs and grouping them together under the heading of the British Schools of Flying. He said that Rex had spoken well of me, suggesting I would be the chap to set the whole thing up.

I introduced P, as he liked to be called, to Carol and told him that at the moment she headed up flight operations at HG. Straight away P suggested that Carol should join his team as my secretary.

Having agreed to work for Mr Pascoe we left his offices and drove the short distance to Felixstowe to take a look at the housing situation. We discovered a lovely little two bedroom maisonette for sale, built over the garage belonging to the property. The building was situated on the seafront just a few yards from the beach. The sitting room had a huge French Window that opened up onto a balcony with unobstructed views of the sea. Apart from the sitting room the maisonette had two good sized bedrooms, a bathroom and a lovely little kitchen, all in immaculate order. Another surprise was that a second stairway led to a flat roof with a safety rail, just right for sun bathing. All for the price of £10,000. We put down a deposit on the premises before setting off on our return journey to Halfpenny Green feeling very happy indeed.

Halfpenny Green had been my first command of a complete airfield complex, and in that respect I was sorry to leave. But under the circumstances I had no regrets giving three months termination of contract to Tom Silk.

Typical of the man, he never contacted me or acknowledged my letter in writing for several weeks. I had the impression that maybe he hoped I was trying to pull off some kind of bluff. When he did finally telephone me he said you can go now if you like. But I said that I preferred to work out the full three months as per the wording in my contract, I never saw or spoke to the man again.

The words I had spoken to Tom months earlier when we flew to St Mawgan in that appalling weather ... 'Tom, if you carry on insisting to fly in weather like this you will eventually kill yourself,' sadly came true. In fairness I do not know the exact details of the accident, and it may not have been Tom's fault at all, but a few years after I left the company, he crashed his aircraft into woods near St Agreve in France, killing himself and his lovely wife. I was very sorry indeed to hear of that terrible tragedy.

It was depressing to say farewell to all the staff that worked so hard for me at the Green. They had been a great team. In particular I was sorry to say goodbye to Mike Edwards. He was not only an excellent instructor, but he had been a true friend.

My time at Halfpenny Green had provided me with valuable experience that would stand me in good stead during my continuing career in aviation. At the Green I had been responsible for the aerodrome and all its associated companies including the club, the flying training school and the aircraft maintenance unit. I had re-designed the complete flying training set-up, installed runway lighting and commenced a night flying programme. Fortunately I had also been given the opportunity to set up the infrastructure in order to gain CAA approval and successfully tender for very valuable MOD flying training contracts which ultimately quadrupled the companies financial turnover and showed a good profit margin.

So that was that. Time to move on. I was soon to find out that this meant I had to start the whole procedure all over again.

Carol and I arrived at Ipswich Airport on the first of December 1973. I signed a service contract as Principle of The British Schools of Flying, and Carol was employed as my PA.

My new boss, Bob Pascoe, showed me around the substantial brick built structure of the main airport building. The ground floor consisted of a large number of rooms, most of them empty, there was also a huge reception area with an impressive staircase leading to the upper floor. Upstairs was even better. Originally intended as a hotel, there were about twenty study/bedrooms each with its own en-suite toilet/shower room, excellent accommodation that would be used for future residential students. The whole building was in first class condition. Bob told me there and then that I had his approval to re-design the internal layout of the building in order to provide first class flying school facilities.

I was introduced to a man known to all at Ipswich Airport as "Chippy". Chippy was a smashing little chap, ex navy and, as I was soon to find out, a highly skilled carpenter that was capable of turning his hand to almost any other type of building skill. Over the next few years we were destined to get along extremely well together.

Bob then showed me my office which was situated at the opposite end of a long corridor to his office. It was sheer luxury. I had never seen an office like it. A large room beautifully carpeted complete with an en-suite bathroom. A very posh curved desk occupied the centre of the room, and a large window overlooked the airfield. I was overwhelmed by all this but, there had to be a down side somewhere, and I very soon found out exactly what it was.

I left Carol to set up my office with the books, paperwork and various other items I had brought with me, whilst I wandered over to the flying club building that was at present situated between the main airport building and the aircraft maintenance hangar.

My first impressions were not favourable, it was a bit like peering into the murky shadows of a second-hand furniture store. The windows looked as if they hadn't been cleaned for months. A wooden table which had one of it's legs propped up by a few magazines occupied the centre of a long room. There were a few filthy old armchairs scattered around the place with various items of clothing dumped on them. The walls were covered with out-of-date maps, and a headset, supported by a nail, hung from an open cupboard door.

I could hear loud music pumping out from behind a closed door labelled 'ENQUIRIES' at the far end of the room. I knocked on the door but nobody answered. I knocked again, this time considerably louder, but again there was no response. Finally I opened the door and, through a haze of blue cigarette smoke came face to face with a middle-aged woman who frowned at me through horn-rimmed spectacles.

'Yes?' was her greeting.

'Good morning, is this the Ipswich Flying Club?' I asked.

The woman ignored my question completely.

'You'll have to wait if you want to see John, he's flying at the moment and I don't know when he'll be down' was the abrupt reply. She continued....

'Do you want an application form for a student's licence?...Have you passed your medical yet?

I was a complete stranger to this woman. If I had been someone hoping to join the club and learn to fly, she could have easily put me off the idea altogether.

I replied to her second question...

'Yes I have passed my medical, in fact I've passed several medicals over the years.'

My reply seemed to agitate her.

'What *do* you want then?' She asked curtly.

'My name is Ray McKenzie-Blyth and I have recently been appointed Principle of the British Schools of Flying ...and you are?' I enquired.

The woman looked startled, a forced smile spread across her face changing her demeanour completely and she replied with a suspiciously refined accent.

'Oh how very nice to meet you, I've heard so much about you, I'm the chief instructor's wife and I look after the office side of things.'

'Not for long' I thought.

So this was it. I could see that there were changes to be made, and the sooner the better. I couldn't wait to tell Carol about this lot!

During my first few weeks of employment I was called upon to make decisions that were not altogether popular with some of the existing staff. As a result the CFI and his wife left, leaving Carol and myself to run the flying club as a temporary measure. As soon as replacements were found, Bob Pascoe asked me to prepare a capital budget and a two year advanced cash flow prediction so that his accountants could negotiate an adequate loan from the company's bank to set up his group of flying schools for the sole purpose of obtaining MOD pilot training contracts similar to CSE's commercial pilot training school.

This was quite a task as the "capital required" part of the budget had to incorporate the cost of setting up the high standard of training facility necessary to pass a CAA inspection at each of the companies four schools based at Ipswich, Southend, Biggin Hill and Shoreham airfields. Where necessary I would have to redesign and cost any new building work needed.

Ipswich Airport, where the company had it's head office, was leased to Bob Pascoe by Ipswich Borough Council, and all the facilities operating on the airfield i.e. air traffic control, aircraft maintenance, fire and crash facilities etc, were staffed and operated by the newly registered company "The British Schools of Flying".

The buildings on Ipswich Airport formed an excellent basis for constructing a first class pilot training unit. Unfortunately, when I flew over to take a look at our flying schools based on the other three airfields, I was not at all impressed. After a long discussion with Bob Pascoe, we decided to keep the flying club at Southend operational and closed down our facilities at Biggin Hill and Shoreham.

Once again I set up the small portable drawing board I had used so many times in my days at Oxford and Halfpenny Green, and began to draw up plans to convert the existing buildings on Ipswich Airport. Cash flow predictions had to include the assumption of an income from MOD contracts, this made things difficult because money had to be spent improving the premises so that they could be inspected and approved by the CAA before we were even allowed to submit any tenders to the MOD for pilot training work, so the cash flow predictions had to be presented on a sliding scale to allow for the "chicken and egg" situation of whether or not we were awarded a pilot training contract in the first twelve months. Calculations also had to allow for the provision of a minimum number of flying staff who had to be flight tested and approved by RAF Central Flying School to train students under a ministry contract.

Within two weeks I managed to complete the unenviable task of working out a capital budget and running costs together with a predicted forecast of the income for the first two years of operation. This was ultimately taken to London and submitted to the company's bank.

One fine morning Bob Pascoe entered my office grinning from ear to ear.

'The bank manager has smiled upon your budget Ray, and given it his seal of approval. Building work starts as from today.'

Apart from the resident CFI there had been one other full-time instructor working at Ipswich when I joined the company. He was an ex RAF instructor who appeared to be very disillusioned about the potential transformation of the school. He made no effort to disguise his feelings and moaned about everything I asked him to do. Having seen the pathetic conditions under which he had been working at Ipswich, I was not too surprised at his attitude. He mooched about as if everything he was asked to do was too much trouble, and I began to think that I would have to let him go, but after a short sharp flare-up one morning, Bill Moxon's attitude changed completely and I soon discovered that he was an excellent instructor who, like myself, preferred to work in an efficient and disciplined atmosphere. Later Bill revealed that he had been one of the RAF pilots chosen to fly a Spitfire when they made the "Battle of Britain" film. Lucky chap.

Bob Pascoe owned a London registered company called Lonmet Ltd. Lonmet was the parent company of all Mr Pascoe's businesses and also the UK main agents for Cessna Aircraft sales based at Ipswich Airport. This meant that the British Schools of Flying always had new Cessna aeroplanes at their disposal. All the company's aircraft were maintained by our own maintenance section based at Ipswich. This was a first-rate unit set up in a large hangar near to the main airport buildings. The Chief Engineer was a highly qualified chap by the name of Mr Jack Squirrel. I soon found out that Jack was an exceptional engineer, and a man that I could rely on and trust implicitly to keep all the schools aircraft in tip-top condition.

By the beginning of Summer 1974 we were ready to go. We had set up the school in the main building, which now housed Bob's office suite, my office, the company Secretary's office, a first class operations room that Carol was in charge of, and a flight planning room that was as good as any RAF equivalent I had seen. There were also five briefing cubicles, a large lecture room, and flight instructors offices. A restaurant with full kitchen facilities adjoined the main airport reception area. The upper floor of the building consisted of twenty beautifully furnished study/bedrooms all with en-suite facilities.

When we had successfully completed the move of the school set-up into the new facilities, I drew up some more plans for Chippy to convert the old club hut into another lecture room with special facilities for night flying, including a briefing room and a radio procedures trainer.

The Air Traffic Control building at Ipswich was equipped with CRDF homer facilities. The only runway lighting available was the old type of goose-neck paraffin flares and no angle of approach indicators. Therefore the airfield could not be used for night training purposes. This didn't matter too much as we used our base on Southend Airport to train our night rating students.

The new airport facilities had been inspected by the relevant authorities and declared fully operational in February. We were now ready to commence contract pilot training and were approved by the CAA for short courses.

Bob and I got together to fill in the tender forms and sent them off to the MOD. There followed a nail biting few weeks waiting for the results. To my great relief our tenders were accepted by the RAF and MOD for training ATC and CCF cadets as well as Air Traffic Control students who had to complete a mandatory 30 hours pilot training during their controllers course. Our first intake of resident students was scheduled to arrive in June 1974.

After a session of interviews, I employed a further six first class flying instructors, three of them ex RAF QFIs. I standardised the school's briefing and instructional procedures, and everyone passed their CFS flight check in May 1974. I followed this up with regular standardisation meetings for the instructional staff, so that any problems or discrepancies could be ironed out satisfactorily on the spot.

Once again I relied implicitly on Carol who was now running the flight operations set-up at Ipswich Airport. On average the school received twenty-five contract students a month. At the same time we continued looking after our valued flying club members at week-ends and in the evenings. The following Winter I started night flying, instrument rating and aerobatic rating courses.

Also I made full use of my F.I.C. rating and started instructor courses during the shoulder months together with twin engine training in BSF's fully airways equipped Aztec and twin Comanche.

So that was that. The school had been set up to everybody's satisfaction within the first six months of our employment with BSF.

The Ministry of Defence contracts division were satisfied with the standard attained by all the students they sent to us. We soon gained a very good reputation, and when the school at Halfpenny Green failed to complete their allocation of ATC students within their contracted period in 1974, I received an urgent telephone call from the MOD asking if we could take over HG's contract and train the remainder of their students in addition to our own. For some reason after I left Halfpenny Green, they failed to cope with the number of students allocated to them within the time stipulated in their contract with the MOD. That was very sad, because it meant the end of contract work at the Green for some time to come. We took on the extra students formerly allotted to HG, and managed complete their training successfully within their initial contract period.

My job as the Principle of the British Schools of Flying was incredibly demanding and also very enjoyable, it was a great relief to be away from the daily anxieties and threats of my ex boss and the so called "organisation" which never made any sense to me.

Unfortunately I hadn't heard the last of Downman. One afternoon in late April it all kicked off again when I walked into flight Ops having just landed, and our switchboard operator rushed up to me looking very upset.

'I've just received a telephone call from some irate bloke with an Irish accent who asked to speak to you. When I said you were not in your office he just went mad and yelled out ….Well tell that bastard now that I've found out where he is, he's as good as bloody dead… He then slammed the phone down in my ear. He didn't say who he was and he certainly didn't sound as if he was joking Ray.'

My heart sank. Surely all this wasn't going to start up again. We had moved to Ipswich Airport thinking that would be the end of it. Carol was obviously upset, so there was only one thing to do.

That evening I made an appointment to see the Chief Inspector at Felixstowe Police Station and told him about the telephone call from Downman. It was obvious that the inspector didn't believe me, so I said that he could obtain confirmation from Supt: French at Police Headquarters West Bromwich. At that point he surprised me by turning quite aggressive and said …

'It's no good crawling in here like a scolded cat. You shouldn't get yourself mixed up in those sort of situations.'

I left the police station feeling bloody annoyed to say the least. At the request of the police I had laid myself and my family open to considerable risk, come close to being blown up, and now, having gone to the police for protection, all I got from them was abuse.

About ten o'clock the following evening a police constable knocked on our door and said his inspector had asked him to call around to see if everything was alright. I can only assume that his boss had contacted special branch and found out that I was telling the truth.

Fortunately I heard nothing more for a while, then on the 17th of March, I was in for more trouble than I bargained for.

It all started when I was flying in G-BAZR, a Cessna F150L. I was carrying out a flight test on student pilot Prior for the issue of his private pilots licence, when something very unexpected occurred. We had reached a stage in the test where I asked the student to demonstrate a short field landing. Mr Prior flew the first part of the circuit perfectly, extending the down-wind leg to give himself a longer approach. We were just passing low over the threshold of runway 14, when a man suddenly ran out onto the runway about fifty yards in front of us and hurled an object straight at the aeroplane. Instinctively I grabbed the controls applying full power and swerved the aircraft to the right narrowly avoiding the missile and the bloody idiot that had thrown it. Our airspeed was only a couple of knots above stalling speed at the time so it had been a very tricky situation. If I had attempted to pull up sharply and fly over the intruder, the aircraft would almost certainly have stalled, so with the airport buildings and the control tower to the left of the runway, I had no alternative but to attempt a shallow turn to the right narrowly missing the madman gesticulating in front of us. The Air Traffic Controller immediately called me on the RT and said he had witnessed the incident, and instructed the crash crew to try and apprehend the man on the runway.

Having recently received a death threat over the telephone from 'D', I naturally connected the two incidents and asked our controller to contact the police straight away in the hope of getting someone out here as quickly as possible to deal with the situation.

It had been a split second decision and the avoidance action taken necessitated passing low over a metal fence that separated the airfield from an adjoining field belonging to the council. There was just one other person who witnessed the incident standing near to the fence on the opposite side to the airfield, and I saw him waving his arms as we passed overhead.

By the time we re-joined the circuit and landed, the madman that had been on the runway was nowhere to be seen. The crash crew said that the man had jumped the fence and legged it towards a council estate on the far side of the adjoining field. Half an hour later the police arrived on the scene to take statements from myself, my student Mr Prior, and the Air Traffic Control Officer who had witnessed the incident. The police, who were obviously very keen to find out who it was that had been stupid enough to run out onto an active airfield and hurl an object at an aeroplane attempting to land, said they should have little trouble in tracing the perpetrator.

The second person who I had passed over in the adjoining field whilst taking avoiding action, turned out to be the groundsman who was marking out white lines for a football pitch. So the police officer decided to wander over and ask him if he had witnessed the incident. I should explain that the football pitch was in fact situated inside the original perimeter boundary of Ipswich Airport. But the council had fenced off a section of the airfield for use as a sports field, the boundary fence running parallel to runway 14 just a few metres to the right of the runway.

We heard nothing further for about a week. Then, to my utter amazement, I received a summons to attend the magistrates court at Ipswich to answer a charge of contravening section three rule five of the Air Navigation Order. I was being charged for passing less than 500 ft over a groundsman in the adjoining field whilst I was taking avoiding action to miss the pratt that ran out a few yards in front of me when we were about to touch down.

It took a while for it all to sink in. I just couldn't believe that anyone in their right mind could come to the conclusion that the action I had taken was a deliberate attempt to break the law, when in fact I had obviously avoided a very serious, and probably fatal accident.

I contacted BALPA for legal assistance, but although they were the association originally set up to assist professional pilots, they didn't want to get involved. My boss Bob Pascoe put me in touch with a very good firm of solicitors in Ipswich. When I went to see them the lawyer who was to act for me said that it was an open and shut case in my favour, especially as the relevant section of the Navigation Order stated that "Aircraft taking off and landing, or in a state of emergency, were exempt from the 500 ft. rule".

I duly attended the court and my case was heard by a female magistrate who obviously knew nothing about the Air Navigation Order or aviation in general. Having heard all the witnesses statements, I was sure the case would be dismissed, especially when the police informed the court that they had interviewed a man who had admitted running onto the runway and throwing a missile at the aeroplane whilst it was attempting to land. I couldn't believe it when the magistrate glared at me across the bench and said...

'Do you admit to flying less than 500 ft. over a section of the airfield that had been sectioned off by the council and was being prepared as a football ground?'

I started to explain that I had no choice, but was interrupted sharply by this pompous woman who said...

'Just answer yes or no.'

Of course I had to say yes.

'In that case I find you guilty of dangerous flying and you must pay the sum of £400.'

The clerk of the court quietly advised her that there was no such offence in the statute book and the case had to be referred to as flying in a manner contrary to the ANO section.....etc...etc.

'Well what ever it is, I fine you guilty and you will pay the court the sum of £400 plus court costs' she said.

This was clearly unjust as the order she referred to plainly states that the 500 ft. rule does not apply to aircraft in an emergency or aircraft taking off or landing. At the time of the incident I was in fact in the process of landing, and the action taken was my immediate response to an emergency!

To my disbelief I was told later that the police were not taking any action against the chap who actually admitted running on to the runway, because it was a civil matter. My solicitor also found out that the man's house was situated directly under the approach path of runway 14, and that he had been arrested some years earlier for dragging a private pilot out of an aeroplane in dispersal and physically attacking him. Prior to that he had served a prison sentence for GBH.

So that was it. I had been found guilty of flying less than 500ft over one man in an otherwise empty football ground that adjoined the airfield, to avoid killing the maniac that had run out onto the runway directly in front of me and thrown an object at the aeroplane.

Bob Pascoe, who was furious about the outcome, asked me if I was going to appeal against the sentence. I said I would like to appeal, but £400 was a lot of money at that time, (Well in excess of £2,000 in today's money) and an appeal could cost a hell of a lot more if I lost. So perhaps I should seek legal advice before taking the case to be heard before a judge. Bob generously said that he would personally pay anything over the original fine of £400.

At the time the incident occurred I was representing the CAA as one of their appointed flight test examiners, so I decided to contact the CAA for their legal assistance. I couldn't believe it when I was told that their legal department were in fact responsible for bringing the charge against me in the first place, and they would be acting as the prosecution at the court of appeal. The bunch of --------!

Unbelievably I had to wait two agonising years before my appeal was finally heard by Judge Richards at the Crown Court in Ipswich. The hearing lasted two days. Most of the first day was spent with the two QC's arguing the nuts and bolts of the Navigation Order and whether or not I could be sent to prison if the appeal went against me.

The CAA sent one of the captains from their examining wing at Stansted to give evidence for the prosecution. He arrived looking very impressive in his captain's uniform and never once made eye contact with me throughout the two days of the hearing.

The QC instructed to act for the CAA was obviously very experienced and also probably one of the highest paid barristers in London. I was obviously in for a rough time.

On the second day of the hearing, details of the event were read out by my QC. He also read out the two prohibitions to the 500 ft rule. (a) Taking off and landing, and (b) An action taken by the pilot in an emergency. Pointing out that in this case both of these exemptions applied. He then continued by questioning me in detail about the evasive action I had taken in order to avoid a fatal accident.

The QC acting for the CAA was not only a man of law, but could just as equally have been a great Shakespearean Actor. Whilst questioning me, he swaggered up and down the room, vicariously grasping his flowing robes in a manner frequently seen in film dramas depicting a gripping courtroom scene. He opened his performance with...

'I believe I am right in saying you are a Private Pilot Mr Blyth, are you not?'

'No sir, you are not right.'

'What are you then?'

'I'm an instrument rated Commercial Pilot, Flying Instructor and CAA Flight Test Examiner.'

'You fly little aeroplanes I believe. Tell me Mr Blyth, if you're that good, why aren't you flying commercial airliners?'

'Because I prefer to train commercial pilots, and without the likes of me there would be no airline pilots....Sir.'

'So that gives you the right to contravene the Air Navigation Order does it *mister* Blyth?' he said, emphasising the word mister.

His sarcastic, arrogant manner of talking down at me was beginning to get me annoyed and before I could stop myself, I blurted out in a loud voice...

'Can I ask you a question Sir?'

The QC looked surprised and glanced swiftly at the Judge for his intervention, but Judge Richards said nothing. So I quickly continued with my question...

'What on earth do you think would make an examiner break off in the middle of a flight test, take over control of the aeroplane from his candidate and in full sight of Air Traffic Control beat up a groundsman working in the next field, and then ask the Air Traffic Controller to call the police? What makes you think that anyone in his right mind would do such a stupid thing as that, Sir?'

Again the QC, now red in the face, looked at the judge again for some form of intervention.

There was a brief silence before Judge Richards leaned forward towards the CAA's QC and said....

'Well….answer the man.'

The QC, obviously infuriated muttered…

'Well… er … we shall see.'

I began to feel a lot more comfortable, the Judge seemed to be on my side.

At that point the QC acting on behalf of the CAA seemed to have had enough of me and called for the Aviation Authority's Captain to take the stand…

'Tell me Captain, in your professional capacity as a very experienced pilot, do you think that the defendant flew his aeroplane in a safe and sensible manner?'

'No Sir I do not.'

'Why not Captain?'

'Any pilot knows it is dangerous to attempt a turn at slow speed just above the ground. I would have pulled up over the man on the runway.'

The QC smiled graciously at his star witness.

'Thank you Captain.'

Suddenly the Judge unexpectedly intervened….

'Before you leave the stand Captain, when I was learning to fly my instructor sometimes took over the controls when I was being taught to land, and would carry out what we used to call a "split-arse low level circuit" so that I could have another crack at the actual landing without having to waste valuable time flying all the way round the circuit. Did you ever come across that sort of thing when you were being taught to fly?'

The CAA Captain looked surprised, and after some hesitation he answered…

'Yes my Lord it can be done by an experienced pilot'

I couldn't believe my luck. Judge Richards was obviously an ex RAF pilot, and certainly knew what he was talking about.

The Judge removed his spectacles, and continued…

'And do you consider yourself experienced enough to carry out such a manoeuvre Captain?

'Yes my Lord, I do have considerable flying experience.'

'Really. And how many hours in command do you have Captain?'

' 2,100 hours, my Lord.'

The Judge leaned back in his chair and looked at me.

'Tell me Mr Blyth, or should I say Captain, you are a Captain aren't you?

'Yes my Lord.'

' Well tell me Captain Blyth, how many hours in command do you have?

'5,638 hours my Lord.'

'And you are an instructor?

'Yes my Lord.'

'And you are a CAA appointed examiner?'

'Yes my Lord.'

Judge Richards stared at the CAA captain and addressed him rather sharply...

'Well there you are, Captain Blyth has more than twice your experience, he is also a very experienced flying instructor who has trained RAF and commercial airline pilots, would you say that he has more than adequate flying experience to carry out the manoeuvre in question?'

The CAA pilot looked very uncomfortable and mumbled a reply...

'Speak up Captain I cannot hear what you are saying'

'Yes your Honour I suppose he has.'

At that point the QC acting for the CAA jumped up and asked for me to be returned to the box for further questioning. His first question was the one I had expected from the beginning of the hearing...,

'Mr Blyth, you said in your statement that something was hurled at the aeroplane by the person that ran onto the runway did you not?'

'Yes Sir.'

'Would you tell his Lordship the exact words you used in your statement to describe what you thought the object was?'

'I thought it could have been a hand grenade my Lord.'

My remarks brought on a wonderful stage performance from the CAA's QC. He pretended to look amazed, held his hands in the air and turning to the judge laughingly said...

'A hand grenade my Lord.'

At this point the QC acting on my behalf stood up and addressed the Judge asking for the case to be continued in-camera, whilst a classified statement from the West Midlands Crime Squad was read out.

Before the hearing my QC had written to Supt. French and asked him if he would be prepared to give evidence about the 'D' affair if required. He apparently replied by sending a written statement that could only be read out in a closed court.

When the court was reconvened, my QC started to summarise the proceedings on my behalf when the Judge interrupted and made the following statement...

'I have no intention of wasting any more of the court's time on this case. I find for the appellant.'

Bob Pascoe, who had been sitting in court with me throughout, patted me on the shoulder and said...

'It's all over Ray, you've been cleared old boy.'

What a relief. I was overjoyed. This case had been hanging over me for two years. It was like a heavy weight being lifted from my mind.

Making one final effort to spoil my day, the CAA's QC stood up and asked the judge to apportion half the court costs to me. But Judge Richards was having none of it. He simply said...

'Certainly not, the CAA has plenty of money, let them pay the full costs. This case should never have been brought to court in the first place.'

I was overjoyed.

The two years that passed between attending the magistrates court and the appeal court had been extremely busy. As previously stated, we were awarded our first government contract in June 1974. I had learned long ago from my instructing days at Oxford and Halfpenny Green that flying training programmes carried out under limited term contracts were a completely different ballgame to training individual members of the public to fly. The necessity for absolute standardisation of your instructors was paramount, and with MOD cadet contracts you were committed to a rigid time clause that stated students should complete their 30 hour flying training within 28 days. This meant that flying instructors were often called upon to fly for exceptionally long periods without the protection of compulsory breaks or time off. A situation that, in the case of airline pilots, is prevented by law.

For example, the commercial airline pilot invariably has a second pilot on the flight deck to share the work load. He can fly for sustained periods on autopilot without having anything to do other than make the mandatory R/T calls and occasionally update his navigational aids. If he's lucky he can sit there enjoying the flight, chatting with his co-pilot and drinking the occasional cup of tea brought to him by a member of the cabin crew, (I speak from experience). He is however protected from fatigue by law, and has to adhere to mandatory rest periods and days off.

On the other hand the poor old flying instructor, who probably taught these chaps to fly in the first place, has no such protection. His work load consists of teaching students of various nationalities, temperaments and ability to fly, covering such lessons as, straight and level flight, turning, climbing, descending with power, gliding, practice forced landings, recovering from incipient spins, recovery from stalls in various flight configurations, R/T procedures and circuit training. After further consolidation exercises he continues to teach his students map reading, navigation, and flying on instruments. In cases where there are no ground school facilities available, the flight instructor has to lecture to his students on Met, Aviation Law, Principles of Flight, Flight Planning, Airframes and Engines etc. So you can see that with three or four students allocated to him, he has his work cut out to complete this training in 28days. After which he will receive a new batch of students. In good weather conditions, the job can usually be done without any problems. But if the flight programme is delayed by inclement weather conditions, which in this country is frequently the case, the instructor can be called upon to work seven days a week, sometimes up to ten or twelve hours a day to ensure that the pilot training programme is completed within the time period stipulated in the contract. My point is that flying instructing is not the "Piece of cake" that some people seem to think it is.

Both airline flying and pilot training can be stressful, and lives depend on the skill, judgement and ability of both professions. But unlike his colleagues on the airlines, the instructor is _not_ protected in law by mandatory rest periods or limited on duty time, leaving unscrupulous bosses, who are usually not flying types themselves, to pressurise their flying staff into working dangerously extended hours. This could be alleviated by employing one or maybe two extra flight staff that could be financially balanced when submitting the tender for a large contract. At the time I commenced writing this book, there was still no law to protect instructors from being pressurised into flying ridiculously long hours.

On a lighter note I remember one occasion when we were extremely busy, and I suffered from severe toothache. One of our flying club members, Mr Love, was a dental surgeon who ran a practice in Ipswich. I knew him very well as I had recently been training him to fly twin engine aircraft. It happened to be a Sunday, I was in absolute agony and scheduled to fly all day, at about midday I asked Carol to telephone Mr Love at his home to see if he could recommend something for the pain. He did better than that. He drove over to the airport with his wife who was a dental nurse. I had just landed when they arrived. Mrs Love injected the anaesthetic and her husband extracted the tooth in my office whilst my next student was carrying out his pre-flight checks. The offending tooth having been removed, I was back in the air without my student being any the wiser.

Fortunately I had a great bunch of instructors working for me who, in my opinion, were second to none. They worked extremely long hours for a standard monthly salary with no overtime pay. Like most flying types they flew because they wanted to do nothing else, it was everything to them and they were happy in the knowledge that they were employed throughout the year and not just on a part time basis during the summer months. We also had a very strong flying club membership that I made sure was never neglected. Obviously in the winter months flying was sometimes restricted for days on end due to poor weather conditions. But the lads were safe in the knowledge that their jobs were permanent. Overall the BSF became a very efficient and lucrative business.

CHAPTER 50

The Good, the Bad and the Unpredictable.

The good.

Most of the time my day to day flying experiences were enjoyable. Occasionally they were exceptionally so. My logbook tells me that it was the first day of July 1974 when a very unexpected incident occurred.

I was about to grab a quick sandwich and a cup of tea when I spotted a chap I recognised booking in at the Ops desk and paying his landing fee. Harry was an ex student of mine from way back in 1968. I joined him in our restaurant and in no time we were chatting about old times over a cup of tea. Harry told me that he was now earning his living as a freelance aircraft salesman, and that he had sold one or two aircraft to my old friend Peter Clifford who was still running an aircraft sales business at Kidlington. Harry went on to say that he had flown quite a number of interesting types of aeroplane, and bet me that I would be interested in the aircraft he had just arrived in. I asked him what sort of aeroplane it was, and he suggested that I should pop outside and see for myself.

I quickly downed the remains of my cup of tea and stepped outside onto the dispersal area. There were several visiting aircraft parked on the grass, but one in particular instantly caught my eye…

'Don't tell me you arrived in that' I said pointing to the Lake Buccaneer at the far end of the flight line.

Harry grinned.

'That's right' he said 'Come over and take a look at her.'

It was a simply gorgeous little seaplane, beautifully painted in sparkling white with glowing red streamline markings. The aircraft was obviously amphibian with a neat little retractable undercarriage for landing on airfields. It's single "Pusher" engine was perched on a pedestal above and behind the cockpit with the propeller facing rearwards.

' How in hell's name did you get your hands on that?' I asked.

'Like to have a go Ray? I've got special permission to land on the lakes at Walton-on-the-Naze for a photographic session with publishers of Flight International.'

I didn't need to be asked twice. My students were on solo cross countries, so I informed Ops where I would be, and within minutes I was strapping myself into the delightful cockpit of G-BBGK. Since I had taught him to fly at Kidlington six years earlier, Harry had qualified as a flying instructor. So he kindly allowed me to sit in the pilot's seat for a conversion flight on to sea landing aircraft. This time it was my ex-student teaching me, and what an excellent instructor he turned out to be.

The first unusual thing I noticed when I sat in the cockpit was the position of the throttle, which instead of being in the centre of the lower section of the instrument panel, was suspended from it's quadrant in the roof of the cockpit.

Taxying and take-off checks complete, we were soon airborne, climbing into blue skies heading for the lakes at Walton. I had flown well over one hundred types of aeroplane by then, but this was certainly one of the most exciting little aeroplanes I had had the privilege of flying.

On the way over Harry explained the method of determining an approach and landing on water. The main points of observation were, taking into account the surface wind velocity, the size and direction of the waves, and if possible advanced knowledge of the direction and state of the tide. Obviously, if you had not landed on that particular stretch

of water previously, a low run was essential in order to observe any obstacles that may be floating on the water or high structures that could interfere with the approach.

When we arrived over the Naze, the waters appeared to be as smooth as a sheet of glass and there was virtually no sign of a significant surface wind. Harry briefed me on the speeds recommended for the approach and the extension of flaps etc.. He then demonstrated the first landing I had ever experienced on water.

I was surprised by the bum-kicking thump that occurred when the aircraft touched down on the water. I had imagined it would be more like a soft, smooth "slither" onto the surface, but it was anything but. Once settled on the lake the Buccaneer decelerated very quickly. Taxying was very similar to a boat but using the slipstream from the propeller over the rudder surface for steerage.

We taxied back to the down wind area of the lake, and Harry demonstrated a take-off. Again I was taken aback by the necessity to hold the control column hard back until the aircraft came partly out of the water and skimmed over the surface on what he described as "getting up on the step". After that you either throttle back a little and skied along happily, or continued on full power lifting the aeroplane out of the water at around 45 knots, then it was flaps up as we climbed away to make another circuit and landing.

It was now my turn to have a go. I taxied back to the far end of the lake again, swung round into the direction of take-off, selected a point on the horizon to keep straight on and eased the throttle to the fully forward position. Holding the control column back as far as it would go, we were very soon up on "the step". Then easing the stick forward slightly, we accelerated like greased lighting over the water. As the IAS increased to 40kts, a further light backward pressure on the control column lifted the aircraft off the water and we were airborne.

After letting me make a few circuits, a small motor boat appeared on the scene, and Harry asked me to taxi over to it as it carried the photographer from "Flight International" magazine. Arrangements had been made for photographs to be taken that would appear in the next issue of "Flight".

So it was, on the 1st July 1974 that I had my photograph taken standing up in the cockpit of a Lake Buccaneer, gently floating on the lakes at Walton. The photographs that appeared in full colour on the back cover of "Flight International" some weeks later, are now securely glued on to the appropriate page of my log book.

From there Harry allowed me to fly the aircraft back to Ipswich, we did a couple of stalls at 3000 ft. then joined the circuit to land. It had been a most enjoyable experience that I would never forget. I investigated the possibility of having seaplane training section at Ipswich, but unfortunately legislation was difficult at the time and the idea was shelved.

The Bad.

Every now and again one would experience a few anxious moments, usually when you least expected it.

It was earlier during the Winter of 1974 that I commenced training Neil Pascoe, the bosses son, for his twin-engine rating. Sometimes, if I was carrying out a charter flight in the companies Aztec, I would take Neil with me for the experience. On the 21st March Mr Ken Nunn, Managing Director of a building contractors and one of our regular customers, telephoned our company to ask if there was any possibility of him being picked up from Birmingham and flown back to Ipswich. As I was taking Neil for a lesson in the Aztec that afternoon, it made sense to combine the two and collect Mr Nunn at the same time. I was informed by flight Ops that Ken Nunn would be at Birmingham Airport at 5pm.

I took off at around 4pm and Neil flew the Aztec most of the way, leaving me to join the circuit and land at Birmingham. When we arrived there was no sign of Mr Nunn. Earlier the met forecast showed that there was a likelihood of the winds increasing in strength, so I decided to get an update from the met office at Birmingham whilst we waited. I was told that a strong wind warning had been issued for East Anglia with winds gusting up to 45kts.

Mr Nunn finally arrived in a taxi obviously suffering from an over indulgent business lunch he had attended with his colleagues. Within twenty minutes we were airborne again with Ken secured safely in the back seat. Due to the forecast winds I flew the journey back in the left seat in case we encountered landing difficulties when we reached Ipswich.

With a strong tail wind I calculated that our ground speed would be in the region of 170mph, but as things turned out the wind was obviously considerably stronger than forecast.

It was getting dusk as we passed over Cambridge and also the turbulence was becoming quite severe. We started a slow descent from 3000 feet to 1000 feet. As we were being thrown around a bit, I turned to look at Ken Nunn in the rear seat. He was flat out in dreamland and totally oblivious to all that was going on around him.

The turbulence increased to a point when it was difficult to hold the control column steady. I could have engaging the autopilot but refrained from doing so as I prefer to retain control over an aeroplane myself in these conditions. I called Ipswich Approach Control for a weather update, and they informed me that they were attempting to lay a flarepath for me, but there was one hell of a wind and several of the goosenecks had gone out. I asked what surface wind speed readings they were getting. There was a long pause, then the answer came through...

'We're disregarding the marked runways and attempting to lay a line of flares directly into wind between runways 26 and 32. Our surface wind reading at this time is 290 degrees, gusting erratically between 50 and 55 knots.'

This was storm force winds, that the met forecast had not predicted earlier. I checked and both Southend and Norwich reported similar conditions. Neil asked what my intentions were?

'We've got to come down somewhere so I suppose, if the flarepath is laid dead into wind and we're landing on a grass airfield we should be OK providing we can see what's left of the goosenecks, and when we turn into wind on the final approach our ground speed will probably be down to 5 knots, not far short of flying backwards. Better wake up our passenger in the back Neil, I don't want Ken to be asleep when we attempt a landing.'

The violent turbulence made it difficult to set the sub-scale on the altimeter to the airfield QFE. Descending to 800 ft. we whipped over the airfield at a ground speed that must have been close to 280 miles an hour. I could see the green ident beacon on the top of air traffic but little else. Neil said he caught a glimpse of a few flares, and several appeared to have blown over and set light to the grass. A 180 degree medium turn left us almost out of sight of the lights of Ipswich town. Ipswich Airport's NDB was serviceable and working, so we began a slow, and very turbulent approach in the direction that the ADF needle indicated.

Wheels down and locked, I struggled to hold the aircraft level at 500feet, and never allowed the airspeed to drop below 150kts, knowing full well that we would drop like a brick as soon as I started to bring the throttles back. I also noticed from the odd light or two that past beneath us that we appeared to be almost stationery.

Eventually, after being severely thrown around for what seemed an age, we could just make out the green ident beacon on the top of the tower coding IP in Morse. Then very slowly we came close enough to make out a few flares burning on the ground. All the time during our approach air traffic repeatedly called out the surface wind speed which was fluctuating and at one stage recorded a questionable 85kts. on their anemometer.

Air Traffic Control at Ipswich did not have approach radar, neither did the airfield have portable angle of approach indicators, therefore letting down during the final stages of the approach to land was a bit tricky, especially whilst we were being thrown around like a rat in a piss-pot.

I gradually eased the aircraft down to 100feet, then as we passed the lights of the control building at what seemed to be a walking pace, the wings started to tip violently from side to side. Neil relayed our airspeed throughout the approach, his final call was 100kts as we touched down surprisingly gently abeam a patch of burning grass and stopped within a few yards. It was difficult to keep the aircraft from lifting off again. Most of the flares had either been extinguished or had flipped over setting fire to small patches of grass. Debris was flying around everywhere.

Obviously I had no intention of turning crosswind to taxi to the hangar as advised, and suggested that the crash crew got out to us pronto to secure the aircraft in its present position. When I shut the engines down, the noise from the roaring wind was alarming. The airport fire engine arrived alongside followed by Ken Nunn's chauffer driven Rolls Royce. It took two ground staff to hold the cabin door open against the howling wind. Ken, who had remained asleep most of the time, squeezed through the partly opened door, crawled out on to the wing with great difficulty and ended up face down on the airfield. Having locked the controls both Neil and I decided to slide off the wing on our backsides. After a long struggle the ground crew managed to secure the aircraft with multiple steel corkscrew ties and strong ropes, and a vehicle that used to be the station crash truck was parked across the front of the aircraft as a wind brake

The following morning I checked the surface winds with the nearby USAF base at Woodbridge, and their Met Officer informed me that they had recorded winds of 45 kts with frequent gusts up to 60 kts. (Approx 50 to 70mph)

The unpredictable.

The next bit of excitement occurred on the 4th May when I was confronted with a critical and somewhat unusual situation.

I was airborne from Ipswich in Piper Twin Comanche G-AVUD, an aeroplane that the British School of Flying had recently hired from an aircraft leasing company operating out of Biggin Hill. With me was Mr Edwards who was undergoing twin rating training. Eddy Edwards was already a competent FAA single engine flying instructor with several hundred hours experience.

The weather that day was good with a forward visibility of about ten miles, a cloud base in excess of 2000 ft. and there was very little surface wind at that time.

Ed had had several previous lessons in the Comanche, covering all the upper air work including asymmetric flight. Today was his first time on the circuit flying a twin engine aircraft.

After a couple of demonstration circuits we made a full-stop landing and taxied back to the holding point of runway 08. Having completed the take-off checks I asked Ed to fly a circuit himself whilst I observed his handling of the aeroplane.

We obtained clearance from Air Traffic Control and lined up on the duty runway. Ed opened the throttles smoothly keeping the aircraft perfectly straight down the runway during the take-off run. He had just raised the undercarriage when the aircraft gave a sudden lurch and banked to the right. My student went to adjust the pitch controls, but I could see that the manifold pressure gauges were completely out of synchronisation, the port engine was showing 24"boost and the starboard engine's pressure was totally off the clock. The aircraft was also yawing severely to starboard and beginning to lose height. Ed was struggling.

I informed Ed that I was taking over the controls. He didn't answer me but immediately held his hands up to signify acknowledgement of my instruction. I realised that we had lost all power in the starboard engine. Adjusting the starboard throttle made no difference, the fuel selectors were on main tanks, the fuel pumps were still on, the mixture controls were fully rich and the ignition switches were all on. I began closing the starboard engine down and feathered the propeller to reduce the drag, at the same time increasing the power on the port engine to maintain height. I was able to hold the aircraft straight with the use of considerable left rudder pressure. We were extremely low passing over the Ipswich industrial site which was just on the opposite side of the road to the airport.

I was in the process of trimming the rudder pressure out when the port engine also began spluttering and losing power. Ed looked across at me and yelled out...

'Shall I give out a mayday call.'

I told him to go ahead. The starboard prop now fully feathered had stopped altogether, and I was fighting a losing battling to keep the port engine running.

We were bloody low now, I didn't have time to look at the altimeter, but at a guess I would say less than 500 ft. above the factory roofs. To the left were huge chimneys and ahead of us were miles of built up residential area.

This necessitated going against the rule book and everything I'd been teaching about asymmetric flight. I had no alternative than to turn gently towards the dead starboard engine banking away from the buildings in front and to the left of us whilst the port engine was also back-firing and surging with the throttle, mixture and pitch levers fully forward.

Losing height we were dangerously near the ground by the time I had UD heading down wind on a diagonal path towards the airfield. I could see the fire engine racing towards us as the port engine gave one final surge and stopped completely. The flaps were up but the undercarriage remained lowered. We clipped the hedge of the boundary fence collecting a few twigs and leaves with us as the stall warning hooter blared out and the aircraft started to buffet. She dropped the last few feet and hit the ground with one hell of a thump, coming to a standstill about ten yards inside the airfield boundary. As the crash truck drew up alongside us Ed and I looked at each other, our shocked expressions promoting a spontaneous laugh...

'Shit Ray, that was bloody close' Ed said grabbing me by the shoulder and giving it a friendly shake.

The problem we had experienced was solved by Jack Squirrel our Chief Engineer when he discovered that, although the job had been signed up as complete and inspected, the company we hired the aircraft from had not carried out a mandatory modifications to the injectors on both engines earlier in the year and they had become gummed up. It must have been at least a ten million to one chance that both engines packed up during the same flight and within seconds of one another. But they did.

CHAPTER 51.

Ten Seconds from Death.

If you're lucky, a pilot can fly for a lifetime, accumulate thousands of hours in command and not incur any serious problems. In the forty years I was flying I suppose I had about five or so real hairy moments, which averages out at about one every eight years of flying. The majority of those arse-gripping moments seem to have occurred in 1974, and one of these was the most terrifying flight I ever experienced.

Most of the aircraft used for pilot training at the British Schools of Flying were "Cessna Aerobats". These sturdily built two-seat, high wing monoplanes were ideal aeroplanes for basic training purposes including elementary aerobatics.

Like all training aircraft, these robust little machines had to take quite a lot of hammering from student pilots, especially during the circuit and landing element of their training. But during my period of instructing at Ipswich, I never came across any serious problems with the Aerobat, except on one memorable occasion, and at the time that single incident was the closest I ever came to ending my life!

Two of my most experienced instructors, Brian Rampling (Rampers) and Bill Moxon, (Both ex-RAF QFI's) had come to me on separate occasions complaining about XB's excessively violent wing drop during the stall.

Stalling, as most of you will already know, in simple terms is when an aeroplane doesn't have sufficient airflow over its wings to maintain lift and can no longer fly. The stalling lesson is taught to student pilots so that they can not only recover from a fully developed stall, but also recognise the symptoms of an impending stall and take the necessary action to prevent a full stall occurring.

A wing drop at the point of stall occurs if one wing actually stalls slightly in advance of the other wing, thus causing the aircraft to roll over during the stall. It is not unusual for this to happen with most aeroplanes, but apparently in the case of XB the wing drop was reported to be extremely violent, occurring about three or four knots before the normal stalling speeds as stipulated in the aircraft's manual. Furthermore this characteristic had only recently developed with XB and was reported as gradually getting worse. "Rampers" said that with this particular aeroplane there was no chance of bringing about a nice gentle stall at the beginning of a student's stalling lesson in order to give him confidence......He went on to say...

'A few knots before the stall should occur, the bloody thing adopts all the aerodynamic characteristics of a house brick. It rolls over on to its back and throws itself violently towards the ground just when you're trying to point out that there will be a gentle buffet before the stall occurs! The last time this happened I was flying with Cadet Peterson, it frightened him so much that he let go of the controls, and grabbed hold of me.'

Ramper's tone of voice was very convincing, so I agreed to take XB off the flight line and ask our Chief Engineer Jack Squirrel to take a look at it.

After a couple of days, Jack turned up in my office, sat down on the edge of the desk and said...

'This Xray Bravo aircraft.'

He paused for a moment taking a long suck at his empty pipe, which crackled like the remains of a schoolboy's milk being sucked through a straw.

'This Xray Bravo, I can't find anything wrong with the aeroplane at all boss.'

He stared at a piece of paper he held in his hand.

'I've checked everything that I can think of that could cause this problem, but there seems to be nothing obviously wrong. I did however make a very small adjustment to the ailerons, but apart from that the rigging checked out as it should be. Perhaps you would like to give it a whiz round and let me know what you think?'

Later that day I took XB up to six thousand feet and put it through its paces. I stalled the aircraft from a straight glide, I also stalled it at various power settings, and again off a couple of steep turns. On every occasion when the aircraft was a couple of knots above the makers published stalling speed, the left wing dropped violently and she flicked over into an almost inverted nose down attitude. Even anticipating the wing drop with the use of right rudder didn't stop it. On one occasion I used too much rudder and XB flicked into a spin to the right. The recovery was normal. So I concluded that it was impossible to stop this vicious wing drop, even with the application of opposite rudder and applying full power. The fact that Jack and his team could find no obvious technical reason for XB's behaviour worried me. All the possible causes put forward by myself and my instructors turned out to be of no avail after Jack had carefully investigated every suggestion.

We continued to fly the aircraft for a short time with a flight restriction notice pinned to the front of the A/Cs flight sheet restricting the aircraft to dual flying only.

Eventually XB was taken to the maintenance unit for its annual C of A (Certificate of Airworthiness) check. The aircraft had to be stripped down completely, everything would be meticulously checked, overhauled and re-assembled. Then it would be inspected by a CAA approved inspector (Jack), before being cleared for its Test Flight which has to be carried out by a CAA approved flight test Pilot, (In this case me) and finally released to service.

A few weeks later the office telephone rang, Jack was on the line asking me if I would carry out a C of A flight test on XB. It was early morning, the skies were clear blue, and there was a chill in the air.

'How about now?' I said.

Jack agreed and said he needed about an hour to load the aircraft to its max flight test weight. This is done by calculating the pilots weight, then, to bring it up to its max test weight, ballast in the form of plastic covered bags full of sand are securely strapped inside the aircraft.

Jack asked me how much I weighed, so I told him about 140lbs. There was a slight pause before he replied...

'Bollocks,' and invited me to come over and be weighed on the scales he kept in his office before he commenced loading the aircraft with ballast.

I entered Jack's office to find him smiling at me from behind his desk with a mug of steaming hot tea in his hand.

'140lbs my arse Ray,' he said pointing to a rusty old set of bathroom scales standing in one corner.

'All the paperwork is on my desk Ray and if you wouldn't mind I'd like you to check over the C of G (Centre of Gravity) calculations before you take-off.'

Much to Jack's amusement, the scales read 160lbs. I sat down at the desk with him and entered the "Pilots Weight" on to the weight and balance form. We chatted for a while about the work that had been carried out on the aircraft during it's C of A check, and once again Jack confirmed nothing out of the ordinary had been discovered that would account for XB's vicious behaviour. He added that in all probability the fact that the aeroplane had been stripped down and re-assembled, may have somehow rectified the problem, stranger things have happened he said!

'That's a bit nearer the mark Boss,' Jack was grinning at the figure I had inserted in the box marked "Pilots Weight".

We checked the aircraft manual together one final time to ensure the correct amount of ballast had been used and correctly distributed in order to bring XB up to it's maximum take-off weight, and that our C of G calculations were correct. Jack said he would have the aircraft ready for the test and on line in about fifteen minutes, so I wandered back to the Flight Ops Office to check that everything was ready for another busy day's flying programme at the school. On the way I called into the instructor's crew-room to have a chat with the lads before the days flying started, but the room was empty, most of them had already commenced briefing their students. Others were on the flight line preparing to start up and move out.

I did however catch up with Rampers as he was signing out in Flight Ops. I mentioned that I was about to flight test XB, and asked if he had had any further thoughts about its behaviour during the stall, but Brian could add nothing to our earlier ideas on the subject. Grinning from ear to ear he wished me the best of British luck, and went off to join his student on the flight line.

After a brief look at the morning's mail, I donned my flying overalls. picked up my headset, and returned to Flight Ops to book out. I asked Carol for Xray Bravo's flight sheet. Passing them to me she said…

'I hate that aeroplane, I'm sure it's not safe.'

Carol had never said anything like that before, I think it was because she had overheard various conversations about Xray Bravo that probably made things sound a lot worse than they really were.

Jack appeared at the Ops door.

'I've been trying to get you on the phone boss, she's is ready for you.'

Xray Bravo stood outside the maintenance hangar gleaming in the sunlight. As usual the engineers had made sure that the aircraft was spotlessly clean and polished ready for its C of A air test and ultimate release to service. Jack handed me the standard Flight Test Schedule form for aircraft up to 6000lbs maximum all up weight, and once again explained how he had distributed the additional ballast. Then, handing me the aircraft keys he said...

'See you later Ray, lets hope we've cured the bloody problem once and for all.'

With that he strolled back to the hangar.

Standing by the aeroplane I fingered through the ten page test schedule reminding myself of the various elements of the test and what exactly had to be recorded. I filled in the first few items before starting the all important pre-flight external checks......

Operator.	British Schools of Flying.
Maintenance Organisation.	Lonmet Engineering.
Aircraft Registration.	G-BBXB
Aerodrome.	Ipswich.
Flight Test Report Number.	0147.
Flight Date.	09/10/74
Pilot and licence no.	McKenzie-Blyth. R. — 48710.
Observer.	N/A
Aerodrome Temperature.	I glanced inside the cockpit at the OAT gauge and entered + 2.
Q.F.E.	The altimeter at zero feet showed 997mb. I made a note so that I could verify this with Air Traffic Control later.

A pale autumn sun shone down from a crystal clear sky, and in the still of a crisp morning I could just hear the faint drone of an aircraft as it left the circuit.

External Checks next. This long and detailed inspection of the exterior of the aeroplane is a very important preliminary to any flight. CAA accident reports were full of unnecessary catastrophes where aircraft and pilots have sometimes come to an untimely end by skipping through checks. i.e. Starting up the engine before removing the towing handle and destroying the propeller, an engineer getting beheaded because the pilot didn't call "clear prop" before engaging the starter, and a fatal crash caused by attempting to take-off with external control locks still in place. Being as this was XB's first flight since it's C of A renewal I made doubly sure that every item on the check list was carefully covered.

I sat in the cockpit with the engine running smoothly, all the internal, pre-start, and initial engine checks were complete without any problems showing up. The radio checks on both tower and approach frequencies were satisfactory and the altimeter setting I had recorded earlier turned out to be "Spot on". We were ready to go.

On the way out to the holding point of runway '26' I was checking that the brakes and gyro instruments were all functioning correctly when I recognised the dulcet tones of Cliff Barnet, who was one of our instructors and a great friend of mine, asking Air Traffic Control for permission to position his aeroplane overhead at 2000 ft. and carry out a practice forced landing.

Take-off checks complete, I turned Xray Bravo to see if the approach was clear and saw Cliff on the final stages of his practice forced landing. Then, as I had become accustomed to expect from Cliff, he flashed his landing lights at me as he neared the threshold of the runway. It was a long standing joke, each of us considered the other to be as blind as a bat. The joke started a couple of years previously when Cliff caught me examining a wiring diagram with the aid of a large magnifying glass, and he always wore glasses for flying himself. From that time onwards we used to put on our landing lights whenever we saw each other in the circuit in the pretence of avoiding a mid air collision. Cliff was a great character with a great sense of humour, all his students loved him dearly. It was a very sad day when several years later he tragically lost his life in a flying accident whilst working for 'Flight International' magazine as their light aircraft columnist.

I lined XB up behind Cliff's aeroplane and waited for him to clear the runway. Acknowledging the controller's instructions for take-off clearance I opened up the throttle of XB. It was 10am on the ninth day of October 1974, and the beginning of the most terrifying flight of my life.

As we climbed away from Ipswich Airport I called control and told them I was clearing to the South. The reply came back crisp and clear acknowledging my call and advising me to continue listening out on Southend Approach frequency 128.95mcs.

It really was a beautiful day. The sky was completely clear and the visibility was endless. Below, the River Orwell threaded it's way through the countryside like a slender silver-blue ribbon. I was filled with a feeling of complete peace and freedom. But there was a flight test to be completed and several more instruction flights booked for my attention throughout the rest of the day.

The take-off had been normal with a slight tendency to swing to the left, and the stall warning had not been triggered. I established radio contact with Southend Approach and informed them of my present position and the range of altitudes I would be operating at. They confirmed they had me on radar and there was no conflicting traffic.

Level at 1,000 ft. I was ready to start the timed climb. Flight conditions matched up to those required, we were well clear of any hilly ground that could possibly effect our true rate of climb. The en-route cruising speed was 105mph at the start of the climb reducing to 80mph when the climb was established and the aircraft was trimmed. From then on the altitude, indicated airspeed, engine instruments and outside air temperature had to be noted and entered onto the schedule at 30 second intervals.

Turning the page of the test schedule, I glanced down to see Harwich Docks and a thin white trace of foam on the dark blue sea that marked the path of a Pilot Boat racing out to a D.F.D.S. Seaways Liner waiting off shore for the pilot to take her into the docks. At six thousand feet the timed climb was complete, with no obvious problems showing up.

Eventually I came to the section of the test schedule that dealt with the aircraft's behaviour during the stall.

This was the area that had given us problems previously and needed to be checked out thoroughly. I somewhat overcautiously decided to carry out the next section of the flight test from nine thousand feet.

We had passed over the long green sweep of the Suffolk coastline and were two miles North of Felixstowe. I called Southend to update them on my position and altitude and told them I was about to commence stalling and spinning tests for the next thirty minutes or so. They acknowledged my call and said they still had me on their Radar with no conflicting traffic.

Pre-Stall checks complete, I entered the first stalling sequence with flaps retracted.

The sequence was textbook with the controls becoming sloppy and ineffective, the stall warning sounding out loud and clear, a moderate buffet occurred followed by a quite gentle stall.

'Brilliant, we've cracked it' I thought.

I had recovered with use of power and climbed to regain height whilst entering the results on to the test schedule. The next stall using take-off flap produced similar results with no wing drop. The full flap stall that followed did bring about a marked wing drop, but no more than normally expected. Also stalling with flap and power resulted in a textbook recovery. Perhaps the vicious wing drop experienced before the C of A check had been a rogue problem that had developed and disappeared for no apparent reason.

Next was the dive to VNE speed (Velocity never exceed). Once again the aeroplane responded perfectly with no unusual behaviour. I filled in the eleven boxes on the sheet relating to the VNE test.

Happy as a honey bee in a bed of roses, I climbed the aircraft back to nine thousand feet in order to commence the spinning tests.

Note   Perhaps I should explain for those who have never experienced the ominous excitement of this manoeuvre, a spin is brought about by bringing the aeroplane into the stalling attitude, and just before the airspeed decreases to its stalling speed the pilot deliberately yaws the aeroplane by applying the abrupt use of full rudder. This causes one wing to stall more deeply than the other, the net result being that the aeroplane heads for the ground whilst spinning on its axis. Technically the aircraft is pitching, rolling and yawing at the same time. (I hope experienced pilots will forgive me for oversimplifying the true aerodynamic principles of a spin for the purposes of not getting too technical).

Having levelled XB out at nine thousand feet I meticulously carried out the pre-spin checks. I was still over the sea and outside controlled airspace with no other aircraft in sight.   For no reason in particular, I decided to initiate the first spin to the right. Closing the throttle I raised the nose of XB quite steeply in order to make sure we entered a good positive spin. Just before the stall I applied full right rudder and held the stick hard back. As expected, XB flicked over to the right. Almost inverted, she creaked and groaned for a couple of seconds, then dropped sharply into a nose down attitude and commenced spinning like a top. I noted that the airspeed stabilised at 45mph and the rate of descent was extremely high, all as expected. After three complete turns I checked the throttle was still closed, positively applied full opposite rudder to the direction of the spin (In this case left rudder), and centralising the control column eased it slowly forwards until the autorotation stopped, then immediately centralising the rudder I eased XB out of the resultant dive. Full power was then applied as the nose of XB lifted above the horizon and the aircraft adapted the normal climbing attitude, the carburettor heater control being returned to the cold position.

She responded beautifully. It was a good positive recovery with no problems at all. 'Well that's a relief' I thought, 'Just one more to do, this time to the left then I can return to the airfield for circuits and the final part of the test.'

We were down to seven thousand five hundred feet, so I climbed back to nine thousand and completed my pre-spin checks again.

I held back for a couple of minutes whilst a light twin engine aircraft passed about four thousand feet below me. I watched it until it crossed the coast heading inland, then, after one final area check, I closed the throttle fully and raised the nose of XB to commence another spin, this time to the left. The attitude I selected was rather steep so the airspeed decreased rapidly. Then, just as I was about to apply full left rudder and commence the spin, it happened. Faster than I could think XB snapped over onto her back with the most ferocious shudder and hung there inverted for a couple of seconds, then she dipped and rolled over again so that we were in a steep nose down attitude. I continued to hold the stick hard back and the rudder was already in the full left position. Suddenly the aircraft pitched up violently, rolled over again and flicked into a vicious spin to the left, pitching rolling and yawing at a rapid rate. I counted two complete turns and decided it was time to effect an early recovery as the speed of rotation was really winding up and the ROD (Rate of descent) indicator showed that we were dropping like a stone towards the sea far below us. I made sure the throttle was fully closed and started the standard spin recovery procedure. With the ailerons in the neutral position I attempted to apply full rudder in the opposite direction of the spin, (i.e. right rudder). To my horror the bloody thing was jammed absolutely solid and wouldn't budge!

My first reaction was one of disbelief... 'this can't be happening, perhaps I hadn't applied enough pressure to move the rudder in the first place, lets have another go.' Summoning up all the energy I could, I literally stood up on the right rudder pedal, trying to force it to move with every ounce of strength in my body, but XB's rudder was locked solid. It didn't take a great deal of intelligence to sum up the seriousness of the situation. The aircraft was hurtling down towards the sea, the rudder control locked solid, and if I didn't do something very quickly I would most certainly be killed. If I allowed myself to panic I would have lost before I even started, also I couldn't jump out because we didn't carry parachutes in this type of aircraft.

Within seconds I had tried everything I could think of. Stick fully forward, stick fully back, rocking the throttle, lowering flap, even the application of in-spin and out-spin aileron, all the while desperately trying to force the right rudder pedal forward, but it remained jammed solid and XB wasn't going to recover without full right rudder.

The spin was tightening up, causing the aeroplane to rotate extremely fast. It was difficult to keep a clear head with an alternating whirl of sea, coastline and sky in front of me. I was absolutely terrified, and struggled desperately to think clearly. Something was preventing the rudder from moving, and at best I had seconds to identify the problem and if possible rectify it. These thoughts rushed through my mind simultaneously in a split second. The control column was completely slack and ineffective in my hands. With difficulty I levered myself into a position where I could see the pedals beneath my feet. The rudder was fully over to the left, but other than that I could see nothing wrong. I was beginning to become disoriented, my mind was in turmoil as XB fell rolling from the sky. 'Where the hell was the horizon? What was preventing the rudder from moving? ....think...for God sake THINK.' As we plummeted towards the sea, the fully deflected rudder transmitted turbulent airflow patterns over the control surfaces, causing a vibration inside the cockpit that felt as though we were riding at great speed over an endless cattle grid. I must have been very close to total panic now, looking everywhere in desperation to find something that would prevent the aircraft from crashing.

At that point my terror stricken eyes focused on the co-pilot's seat, something was wrong and my brain was struggling to tell me what it was. By absolute chance I suddenly realised the ballast weight that had been strapped to the co-pilot's seat was missing, and there on the floor, firmly jammed under the right rudder pedal of the co-pilot controls, I could just make out the distorted shape of a half-filled plastic sandbag. Somehow, probably assisted by the 'g' force during recovery from the previous spin, it had slipped out of the harness straps and onto the cockpit floor.

I tried to reach the ballast weight but was prevented from doing so by the safety harness holding me firmly in my seat. Without a second thought I turned the locking mechanism and banged the quick release catch. God almighty what on earth is happening now?....Centrifugal force instantly propelled me sideways across the cockpit, my body hit the co-pilots door with some force. I finished up with my head in a downward position and my legs spread across the instrument panel. I was lucky that I didn't burst through the cockpit door and out into oblivion.

All the above happened in less than a minute, but each second seemed an eternity as the aircraft continued hurtling down towards the sea. Grabbing the harness I had just released myself from, which was now flailing around the cockpit like a snake, I blindly groped around for anything else I could use to haul myself down and reach the ballast weight jammed under the rudder.

Time was running out, I felt sure we would hit the sea at any second. Seizing the plastic ballast sack with both hands I tugged with every ounce of strength God had given me to free it from under the rudder but it didn't budge. Then with one last frenzied effort of desperation I seemed to gain super-human strength and somehow dragged the bag from under the rudder, tearing the thick plastic sides of the bag as I did so. I was upside-down under the instrument panel when I saw the freed rudder pedals kick back, and I'm not exactly sure what happened next. Miraculously the spinning seemed to have stopped abruptly when I pulled the sandbag free, the horrendous vibration stopped immediately, and at that point a terrific screaming noise developed. XB was no longer rotating but descending vertical in a nose dive.

My troubles were far from over. Still partly under the instrument panel, I was desperately trying to clamber out through the network of wires and control levers above my head, when suddenly I was rammed back down still further by a tremendous 'g' force acting on my body. The reason being that the aircraft's elevator trim had been set for straight and level flight at 100kts, but we were now travelling at an airspeed that must have been off the clock, so the position of the trimmer forced the elevators up and Xray Bravo nosed up into an almost vertical climb. It may not have been much of a 'g' force by modern jet flying standards, but when you're not strapped in, almost standing on your head, and suddenly become three times heavier than normal, it does have a certain undesirable effect. By this time I felt sure I was about to die. XB was now climbing steeply without power and consequently losing airspeed rapidly. I was still struggling to get back into my seat when momentarily things became very quiet and I simply floated out from under the instrument panel with no effort at all. I had no idea what attitude the aeroplane was in because I couldn't see out of the cockpit, but I was absolutely sure the bloody thing was about to stall again! and I was right.

I had almost regained an upright position when, sure enough XB dropped her left wing in a most vicious stall again. This time three things were different. We were very low, I was not strapped in, and the only plus was she didn't spin because the rudder was presumably in the neutral position.

As this bastard of an aeroplane rolled over onto her back again, I fell around in the cockpit like a rat in a cement mixer! This time I succeeded in kicking the compass and snapping it off its bracket. I saw the sky where the sea should be and the sea where the sky should be. The free ballast weight that had caused all the trouble was spewing sand all over the cockpit, then, half empty, it hit the windshield, dropped onto the top of the instrument panel and stayed there. Fortunately after a short but very enthusiastic struggle, I managed to regain control, the altimeter set to the local QNH was reading 700 feet.

It was some time before I did anything other than fly around trying to calm myself down and gain some resemblance of composure. We had started the spin at nine thousand feet and lost no less than eight thousand three hundred feet during the attempted recovery. The whole thing could only have lasted about one and a half minutes, but it seemed much longer. My heart was thumping in my ears. My headset lead had snapped off at the jack-plug, and the compass was missing altogether.

I circled for a while, eventually rolling out in the general direction for Ipswich. I have to say its times like these when a chaps mind turns to religion and a few words with God didn't seem out of place.

As the wheels rolled softly on to the grass runway at Ipswich Airport, I breathed a sigh of relief. I taxied up to the maintenance hangar, stopped the engine and sat there for a while. Eventually I made my way into Jacks office clutching the half empty remains of the ballast sack.

Jack seemed busy with his never ending paperwork and didn't look up to see who it was, so I walked up to him and slammed the leaking sandbag down on his desk as hard as I could. Poor old Jack jumped so much that I swear his bottom must have left the seat of his chair. His pipe fell from his mouth as he shouted…

'GOOD GOD MAN'…

I glared at him as he continued…

'What the hell's up Ray?'

I pointed to the ballast weight…

'That's what's up Jack, the bloody ballast weight, and if I had any energy left I'd shove it up your arse.'

Jack straightened his glasses, retrieved his pipe from the floor and stuffed it back into his mouth.

'How do you mean, what's gone wrong old chap ?'

I sat down on the corner of his desk and quietly told him in great detail all that had happened during the flight test. He listened in silence not once interrupting to ask a question. As I came to the part where the rudder became jammed his expression changed and he was obviously very concerned. When I had finished talking there was a long silence, then Jack, in typical form, said,…

'It's a pity you had to break the compass off its bracket, they're quite expensive.'

I was about to strangle the old bugger when I noticed the usual mischievous grin on his face.

'You cheeky ….. ' but Jack interrupted me saying…

'Sit down and have a nice cup of tea.'

We had a long discussion about the incident and finally agreed that we were both at fault. Jack for not securing the ballast weight correctly, and me for not noticing it before starting up.

As I left Jack's office he called out…

'You know we will have to do the whole test again.' He stabbed the air with the stem of his pipe as he spoke in order to emphasise his point.

'WE?' I said.. 'Are you coming next time then?'

Jack never answered.

Later that evening, I sat quietly at home and cast my mind back to 1968 and the terrible crash that nearly killed Nils Bartleet and myself. On that occasion neither of us had had time to become frightened because the whole thing was over in split seconds. But today had been different, the incident I experienced in XB, from the initial spin to recovering from the final hammerhead stall, had lasted something in the region of two or three minutes, certainly long enough to realise that death was imminent. I can say without any fear of contradiction that nothing, absolutely nothing is more terrifying than being that close to death.

Loading the cannons, assisted by Bill my father-in-law

Myself and Carol exercising the horses at Belan with our little dog Kimbo in the foreground

Myself with Jonathon Seagull.

The entrance to Belan courtyard.

Belan Dock

One of the exhibits in the dockyard museum

Top. Llandwrog airfield when first taken over by the author.
Centre. The same airfield six months later.
Bottom Left . CAMCO hangar with one of Air Atlantique's DC 111s.
Bottom Right. Our Rapide in Air Atlantique colours.

Two views of Caernarfon Airport taken in 1995

Carol with the aircraft we used for barnstorming

Taken on a pleasure flight over Caernarfon Castle

Father Christmas pays a visit to Caernarfon Airport
(L to R. Carol, Robin Welshman and Ray)

Mike Collett, Chairman of the Air Atlantique group of companies

G-AIDL at the Blackpool Air Display

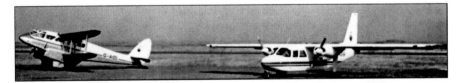

We used both the Rapide and the Bitten Norman Islander for pleasure flying

This picture of passengers waiting to fly, emphasises the popularity of our flights over the mountains

Now retired, Ray with his mate Teddy　　**Cassie when we bought 'Hen Blas'**

Our 'Barnstormer' caravan

**Aerial view of Carol's Gift shop and Café in Aberdaron
(The premises are marked inside the white square)**

Top Left. 1961. O.A.T.S.'s Tipsy Nipper **Top Right.** Allan Hughes's Nord.
Centre Left. Author's Observatory in Brackley from the cockpit of a Tiger Moth
Centre Right. The Author and Swiss Aerobatic Champion Frank Versteegh in
Mirror formation, this photograph was taken from a TV screen during a BBC News
Broadcast.
Bottom Left. Belan with airfield in background. **Bottom Right.** BN2's Cockpit

CAROL

CHAPTER 52.

The Ultimate Assessment.

It was the 30th December 1974, the day when I sent my son on his first solo flight.

As mentioned earlier in Chapter 17, the first time I took my son flying was in a Tiger Moth, he was just seven months old. During his childhood Eddy flew with me on numerous occasions in many different types of aircraft. Even before his little legs could reach the rudder pedals, I used to sit him on a large cushion and strap him into the right hand seat so that he could hold the control column and fly the aeroplane straight and level.

I commenced his official PPL training shortly before he was seventeen years old. Right from the start I was pleased with the intuitive manner he handled the controls. Helped by his previous flying experiences with me throughout his childhood, he reached a safe solo standard within six hours of starting his official course training.

It was just four days after Christmas, a cold, frosty morning with clear blue skies and excellent visibility, when Eddy walked out onto the dispersal area to pre-flight the aeroplane ready for another session on the circuit with me. A light breeze, that bore the delicate fragrance of a Winter's day, caused the faded windsock to stir gently on it's mast. The weather was perfect for a first solo, although my son had no idea of my intentions when I joined him at the aircraft, Cherokee 140 G-AVLG.

It was Eddy's second official session on the circuit. He had done well with his landings and also been taught never to attempt to rectify a bad landing, but to open up and go round again. He had also been shown what to do in the event of an engine failure shortly after take-off. All that was needed now was a few more consolatory circuits.

Once more I closed the throttle at 300 ft. to see how he would handle an engine failure after take-off. I smiled inwardly as Ed immediately lowered the nose and turned the aircraft no more than fifteen degrees out of wind in order to select an area in which to attempt a safe forced landing. Obviously he realised it was a practice, and made a point of telling me that he would have checked for obvious causes of the failure if he had time. I nodded and told him to climb away and continue with the circuit.

Ed completed three perfect touch-and-go circuits, landing smoothly each time. On the fourth approach I asked him to make a full-stop landing and taxi back to the holding point of the duty runway. I never say anything to my students about going on their first solo until the time actually arrives for them to do so. I waited for Ed to complete his take-off checks at the holding point, then when he looked at me and said he was ready to go I said…

'OK old chap, I'm getting out and sending you on your first solo.'

I could see from his face that this came as a shock to him. I'm sure he had no idea that he was ready for his first solo, but like the many hundreds of first solo's I had sent previously, I knew he was safe to fly off on his own. The temptation to do a few more dual circuits because he was my son, never entered my head. I have learned from experience that if you delay sending a student on his own when he has reached a safe enough standard, his flying frequently deteriorates quickly and major problems can develop.

'Listen to me carefully Ed, your life could depend on what I am about to tell you. When you take-off the aircraft is obviously going to be lighter without me on board, therefore you will find that the aeroplane will become airborne quicker and climb slightly steeper than previously. Secondly, when you round out to land and close the throttle, the aeroplane will float for a longer period of time without my weight on board, so don't be caught out by this. Hold her steady in the level attitude just above the ground and wait for her to sink, then co-ordinate the backward pressure on the control column as the aircraft sinks so that she stalls just above the ground and settles smoothly onto the runway. Now, do you have any questions?'

Eddy looked quite confident, and I detected a slight smile on his face. He was ready to go. I informed Air Traffic of a first solo, and asked for "Charlie One to standby". (A code we used to alert the crash crew of an impending first solo landing without alarming the student).

I patted my son on his shoulder and told him to pick me up if he sees me walking back to dispersal after he had landed, adding, if you are not happy with the approach or the landing, open up and go round again. With that I jumped out, secured the harness of the right-hand seat and closed the door.

I stood by the runway and looked at my son sitting alone in the cockpit. Suddenly he became my little boy again! ... Dear God keep him safe.

Ed checked the cockpit door was locked, glanced at me for a second and raised his hand. I knew he was perfectly safe to fly solo, yet for a second I felt like jumping back in the cockpit with him. I had once been asked to teach a fellow instructor's son to fly when he came to Oxford on a Cadet Scholarship. I could never understand why his father didn't want to teach him, and I always said if my son wants to fly, I'll teach him myself. But now the full responsibility of what was about to happen became only too clear.

Up to that time I had completed more than 5,000 hours instructing and confidently sent well over one hundred students on their first solo's. Every one of them landed safely. I knew that Eddy was equally as good as any of them, yet, because he was my little boy, I felt worried.

I saw Ed put the hand mike to his mouth to ask control for take-off clearance. He taxied on to the runway and moved a short distance forward to check that the nose wheel was perfectly straight. Then the engine noise increased to a deafening roar causing the little aeroplane to shudder as Eddy opened the throttle smoothly to full boost. The brakes were released and Lima Golf began to roll purposefully down the runway. I watched the aircraft accelerate keeping perfectly straight, she lilted off smoothly and my son was flying solo for the first time in his life.

Rooted to the spot, I watched for a while as the Cherokee grew smaller climbing away into the distance. I walked quickly to the boundary hedge close to the threshold of the runway. Then looking back at the little Cherokee I saw it's red and white fuselage catch the sun as it hummed its way round the circuit. I listened as the engine reduced power when Eddy levelled the aeroplane out on the crosswind leg at 1000 feet. I watched him turn down wind, and in the few anxious minutes it took my son to fly the circuit my mind returned to the day Eddy was born and I held him in my arms for the first time. I had been partially responsible for giving that little boy life on this planet, and the last thing I wanted, dear God, was to be wholly responsible for taking it away.

But Eddy was experiencing that feeling of complete liberation from worldly problems for the first time. It will be a while before he and his aeroplane fly as one, that can only come with experience. But when this does eventually happen, and he ventures high above clouds tinged by the crimson signature of the sun, he will at last understand his father's tales of tranquil scenes of transcendental beauty that only pilots can comprehend.

I watched the aeroplane as it hummed it's way along the down wind leg of the circuit, I was up there with him in spirit, a thousand questions were running through my mind.... Is there anything I haven't told him?..... What if the engine stops now?..... I wonder if he will remember to apply carburettor heat on the base leg?..... Will he remember to lower flap?......

Lima Golf was turning on to the final approach to land. I moved closer to the bushes so that Eddy would not be distracted if he saw me watching him land. I could see the final stage of flap had been lowered but the aircraft was a little too low. Then I heard the comforting sound of increased power being applied as Eddy squeezed the throttle forwards and raised the nose to reduce the rate of descent whilst retaining a constant approach speed.

The red and silver aeroplane swished passed low over the boundary fence, the engine back firing a couple of times when the throttle was fully closed. The landing was as good as any I had seen, and as the wheels rumbled onto the grass runway I breathed a fathers sigh of relief. First solo's are always stressful moments for instructors, but when it's your own son it's nerve-racking!

I could see Eddy grinning from ear to ear as he taxied back to pick me up. I opened the cockpit door and shook him firmly by the hand...

'Well done Ed, that was a cracking landing.'

It had officially been my day off. So after Eddy signed in and I had written up his progress sheet, it was straight to the club bar for a congratulatory snifter.

Later, on our way back home, we were stopped by a police patrol vehicle that had been following us for a couple of miles. I jumped out of my car quickly, leaving the windows wide open to dispel the possibility of any alcoholic fumes, and walked briskly up to the police car.

'Anything wrong officer?' I said.

'Did you know your near side brake light isn't working sir?'

'I'll get it fixed straight away.'

'Very well sir, see that you do.'

The end to a perfectly special day.

CHAPTER 53.

Full Circle.

1975 turned out to be a very successful year for the Ipswich branch of the British Schools of Flying.

The total time flown by the school's aircraft was well in excess of 6000 hours. Apart from our regular private students, we received MOD contracts for 130 cadets throughout the year. I personally clocked up another 665 hours instructing during the same 12 month period. (Not a lot by airline standards, but a hell of a lot from an instructing point of view when most my flights were about an hour in duration, and the circuit training I did that year probably incorporated something like 2400 take-off's and landings.) My total flying for the year also included 109 GFTs (Flight testing students for the issue of their pilots licence), and twelve TRE flights (Flight testing Commercial Pilots for the inclusion of an additional aircraft type on their professional licence.)

Towards the end of the year I was fortunate enough to get my hands on a beautifully equipped C 402 twin engine Cessna aircraft. Once again the circumstances leading up to this were rather similar to that of the Dove mentioned in chapter 43.

On the morning of the 21st of November, my boss received a telephone call from the Managing Director of a well known aircraft finance company enquiring about a Cessna 402, registration G–BAWZ that had been parked in the dispersal area at Ipswich Airport for two or three weeks. It turned out that the aircraft had been repossessed by the finance company, and they were requesting permission for the aircraft to remain at Ipswich until it was re-sold.

Whilst on the telephone the caller asked if it could be arranged for a suitably qualified pilot to run up the engines and periodically fly the 402 round the circuit to ensure that the aircraft remained in good working order. An arrangement with reference to charges made for parking plus an additional fee for serviceability flights was agreed.

Minutes later Bob popped into my office to enquire if I had ever flown a C 402, to which had to reply that I hadn't. Bob grinned and said...

'Doesn't matter, how would you like to fly the aircraft parked outside your office window ?'

I have never yet missed the opportunity of flying a different aircraft type, so there was only one answer to Bob's question...

'Not half.'

Bob explained the arrangements made with the finance company and said he had put my name forward to be added to their insurance so that I could fly the aircraft occasionally until it was sold.

'Great' I said, 'Who's going to check me out? I've never been inside the cockpit of a 402.'

'Well now's your chance old boy, nothing to it, with your experience you should be capable of flying it without a dual check' was Bob's sanguine reply.

'OK' I said, 'I'll take a look at it boss, are there any handling notes or a check list?'

'They're probably in the aeroplane, anyway you don't need all that stuff Ray, it's just another aeroplane, pick the keys up from my office and take a look at it......Let me know if you need any fuel.'

With that Bob left me wondering what the hell I had let myself in for, it's not a good idea to fly a new type without some kind of check list or handling notes, nevertheless I must admit to feeling rather excited.

The 402, compared to our Aztec, was considerably bigger with wingtip tanks and a long pointed nosecone. The entrance was in two sections, the top half opening upwards and the lower half dropped down containing the entrance steps.

I entered the luxuriously appointed cabin with its executive type layout, and made my way up to the cockpit. Peering through the narrow door my first thoughts were: 'Blimey! it's like the flight deck of a ruddy airliner.'

Several rows of switches lined the cockpit roof above the pilot's windscreen. The flight instruments were pretty much standard and the marvellous array of avionics included a radar screen and just about every type of navigational aid available. There was also a multitude of switches and circuit breaker panels that, in the absence of a pilots check list or a set of handling notes, I would need to study carefully.

I soon sorted out where the trim controls for the rudder, ailerons, and elevators were situated, and a standard central pedestal contained the throttles, mixture and pitch controls.

Special attention had to be paid to the fuel levers and cross feed controls, if I got those wrong it could prove to be fatal. The control column itself looked very businesslike with R/T and intercom buttons and an electric trim-override rocker switch. There was another switch that I later discovered operated the PA system. The four switches protected by a clear plastic "lift-up" hood on the main panel were clearly marked Port and Starboard and were obviously the ignition switches. But where the hell was the master override switch and engine start buttons?

Eventually I found out where everything was situated, so I turned the master switch on. Immediately a multitude various coloured lights winked at me from all quarters of the instrument panel and the electrically operated gyro instruments started to hum as they wound up.

Three bright green lights next to the undercarriage control switch signified that the wheels were securely locked down. The fuel flow gauges, RPM, boost, temperature and pressure gauges were easily sorted, but there were still a few dials and switches that I needed to identify. It was a bit difficult sorting things out in the absence of handling notes, and at that time computers hadn't been invented. After a while I was satisfied that I knew where everything was. I had asked Bob if he would like to come with me on the first flight, but he declined my offer stating he was too busy.

I selected the auxiliary fuel tanks and started the engines allowing them to tick over at 1000rpm for a while. Then, when I had double checked that everything was as it should be, I tested the radios and obtained taxi clearance from the tower.

This was it. I released the park brakes and taxied out on to the airfield to test the steering and braking systems. All was well. The run-up, magneto, pitch control and slow running checks were all within the usual limits and presented no problems, so in the absence of a pilots check list I carried out a standard twin engine pre-take-off check similar to the one I had first memorised at Oxford many years ago .

With the aircraft positioned crosswind at the holding point, I sat there searching the cockpit for anything that I may have missed during my checks. The main fuel tanks had been selected before the run-up, the engines were running smoothly and the Ts and Ps were in the green. I looked back into the passenger cabin one last time and closed the cockpit door. I was ready to go.

Take-off clearance obtained from control, I lined up on runway 08, and began to advance the throttles smoothly to full power. The acceleration was very impressive, far in excess of our Aztec. I had no difficulty in keeping her straight down the runway and in seconds I could feel that she was ready for lift off.....what a beauty!

As we climbed away I selected the u/c lever to up. Immediately the green lights went out and the rumble of the undercarriage being retracted was very audible. Gear up, Flaps up, boost and RPM adjusted, I trimmed the aircraft to climb at 140kts. The ROC was showing 1250fpm. By this time we were just passing through 1500 ft.

I left the circuit for a while and climbed up to 5000 ft. in order to try a couple of stalls, so that I could ascertain safety approach and landing speeds. I was very impressed with this beautifully smooth aeroplane, and would enjoy flying it from time to time until it was finally sold. The ASI was calibrated in kts. and the clean stall occurred at 98kts. (112mph) with no signs of a wing-drop. I stalled her again in the approach configuration with gear down and flaps extended. This time there was a noticeable pre-stall judder and a slight wing-drop at 85kts. (97mph) but nothing at all to get excited about. The stall warning horn sounded about 4kts. before the stall in both cases. The cruising speed at the settings I was using was 217kts. (250mph). After a while I returned to the circuit and completed an overshoot procedure. It was now time to land. I came down the approach at 110kts. (126mph), and rounded out at 90kts. (103mph). In the absence of any handling notes the speeds I used may have been a little high, but I'd sooner be safe than sorry. Everything seemed to work out perfectly and the aircraft kissed the ground as if she was showing me how easy she was to land.

I recorded the speeds and settings I used on the back page of my current log book. Once again it had been great to get my hands on an aeroplane type that I had never flown before. Like most pilots I know, the more complicated an aeroplane is. the more I enjoy flying it, with or without handling notes!

After lunch I asked Carol if she would like to come with me in the 402 for a quick circuit and landing. She jumped at the chance, so I flew the aircraft again later that afternoon with Cassie sitting next to me in the co-pilot's seat.

It was just as well I flew the aircraft when I did, as the following morning we received a telephone call from the finance company to say that the aeroplane had been sold, and a pilot would be collecting it later in the day.

One of the great things about being a flying instructor is that every now and again one comes across an ex student who has had an exceedingly successful career in aviation. In my case this usually happens when I least expect it. For instance it was the end of our contract pilot training season, our last course had been completed on time, and I was hoping to enjoy two days off with Carol and her parents who had come to stay with us for a few days.

On my first day off I was still in bed when the telephone rang at about o'clock in the morning. It turned out to be my boss Bob Pascoe who was going berserk...

'Get over here as quickly as possible Ray. Three Directors from Fisons Chemicals Ltd. are impatiently waiting to be flown over to Belfast for an important meeting.'

I wasn't very impressed with the situation when Bob told me that the flight should have taken off ninety minutes earlier and the part time charter pilot who was scheduled to take the flight, had failed to turn up.

I washed, shaved and got dressed as quick as I could and set off for the airport. On arrival I was met by Bob Pascoe and three gentlemen who were hopping mad, and very anxious to get to Belfast as soon as humanly possible. Fortunately Bob had already made sure that the Aztec was fully fuelled, so I grabbed my flight case from the office and commenced the pre-flight inspection whilst Bob boarded the passengers and secured their baggage in the luggage locker.

Before I knew it, I was doing exactly the thing that I vowed I would never do again after that episode with Tom Silk and the flight to St Mawgan. I was climbing up through thick cloud, with no flight plan and three very disconcerted passengers complaining non-stop in the seats behind me.

Having had a quick word with London Information, I continued climbing through cloud on a North-westerly heading, trying to work out a more accurate course whilst being thrown around in turbulent conditions. (Unfortunately GPS hadn't been invented in the 1970s). I had no idea of the cloud heights or upper air winds as I had been literally pushed into the aircraft the moment I stepped out of my car at the airport.

With the help of my Jeppersons Flight Manual, I was trying to determined which radio aid frequencies I needed, whilst my infuriated passengers continued nagging away at me.

'What time will we arrive at Belfast Captain?

'Why wasn't the aircraft ready when we arrived?'

No explanation was good enough. I tried to explained that I wasn't the pilot scheduled to fly with them and I had come in at the last moment on my day off especially to take them to Ireland. But they weren't listening, and who could blame them?...

'Where are we now Captain?'

I would loved to have told them that I hadn't got a clue... but as thins were, it was best left unsaid. My passengers continued...

'Can you relay a message to the driver waiting for us at Belfast Airport? and best of all...

'I hope you don't expect us to pay for this flight.'

Their continuous whining was dangerously distracting my concentration, I was flying on instruments in turbulent IMC conditions, and in the end I had to tell them politely to button up, otherwise I would have to turn the aircraft around and return them to Ipswich Airport. That seemed to do the trick, but I felt as popular as a pork sandwich at a Muslim's wedding breakfast.

Finally I was in radio contact with Belfast Approach, and two hours after our hurried take-off we touched down safely at Belfast Airport. But as we decelerated down the runway the brakes failed completely. I said nothing to my passengers as the runway was long enough to slow down sufficiently and turn off without difficulty. Air Traffic acknowledged my problem and directed me to a safe area, at the same time sending transport out to collect my passengers and take them to the terminal building where a Fisons car was apparently waiting for them. I was informed that they would meet me back at the airport late the following morning for a return flight to Ipswich. It was at this point I realised that I had no overnight baggage of my own, not even a toothbrush.

Fortunately Fisons had kindly arranged for one of their sales representatives, a young man by the name of Brian, to look after me and take me to a hotel in Belfast where they had booked the original pilot in for the night. I arranged for the brake problem to be sorted out, then set off with Brian for the city centre.

There was considerable rioting and political turmoil in Northern Ireland during that period, and my escort drove me around some of the worst hit areas of Belfast so that I could see the extent of the damage. It was an amazing sight, far worse than I expected. Several buildings had been totally destroyed, many others were completely boarded up.

I was frisked by police when I left the airport and again by security staff when I arrived at the hotel.

That evening Brian picked me up from my hotel and, accompanied by an extremely nice doctor friend of his, we visited a couple of nightclubs in Belfast. I was generously entertained, so much so that I have no recollection of returning to the hotel or going to bed that night.

The following morning I was picked up from the hotel and taken back to Belfast Airport. Having first checked with the aircraft maintenance company that repairs had been carried out to the hydraulic braking system of Lima Papa, I submitted a flight plan to Belfast Control for my return journey to Ipswich.

Whilst I was standing in the flight planning room a voice behind me said...

'Hello Ray, what are you doing in this neck of the woods?'

I turned round to see John Richardson, the very first student I trained to fly when I qualified as an instructor in the 1950s.

John still looked much the same as he did all those years ago, so I asked him what he had been up to since he learned to fly at Kidlington. I certainly didn't anticipate the answer he gave me...

'I was sponsored by the RAF to attend university when I completed my flying training with you. I managed to continue flying by joining the University Air Squadron and eventually joined the RAF when I graduated. In time I flew fast jets. Then I was posted to Central Flying School on an instructor's course. Ultimately I attended the Empire Test Pilot's School at Boscombe Down. I retired from the RAF as a Squadron Leader, and at the present time I'm employed by Hawker Sidley as a member of their Test Flying Team.'

What a wonderful career this lad had made for himself, and to me he still seemed the same young cadet who had done so well at Oxford when I taught him to fly.

As my passenger's were not due to take-off until midday, I spent the morning with John who showed me around the Hawker Sidley Hangar and later took me for a short wiz round in a HS 125 which I enjoyed immensely.

Before we parted I learned that John also held a Civil Flying Instructor's Rating and Flight Examiners Ticket. Apparently he married a young lady who he had taught to fly many years earlier, and she had since become a commercial pilot, and was now working for the CAA as a Flight Operations Inspector. He showed me a photograph of her, she was certainly a cracking little number!

I was now 47 years old, and listening to John's accomplishments since I taught him to fly, made me feel as ancient as Old Father Time himself. So much water had passed under the bridge since we last met, yet to me it all seemed like yesterday.

The return flight to Ipswich was without incident. My passengers were well behaved and thanked me for looking after them. I returned the compliment.

There is a postscript to this story. A few years later I received a letter from the licensing branch of the CAA informing me that their inspector, Captain Richardson, would be arriving to carry out my annual flight check and also inspect the flying school that I was running at that time. Captain Richardson turned out to be the "cracking little number", John's wife, who I imagine would have been around fourteen years old when I taught her future husband to fly. So, there I was being pompously advised on how things should be done! by a young lady who had been taught to fly by an ex student of mine over twenty years ago. Now that's what I call a "Full Circle" of events!

Whilst I was employed by the British Schools of Flying, I had a rather embarrassing experience that took place one afternoon on Ipswich Airfield. It relates to a previous event referred to earlier in the book at the end of chapter 15, when I was visited in hospital by Paul Reed, one of the flying instructors from Oxford who planned to become a flying missionary in Africa. Whilst I was still a bedridden patient in the Radcliffe Hospital, Paul arranged to take me to a church service in Oxford. The task was accomplished with the help of another flying instructor from Kidlington. Having obtained permission from the Sister, they wheeled me out of the ward and dumped me, complete with wheelchair, onto the back of an open truck, tied me securely to the sides of the vehicle and drove off at brake-neck speed to their local church. When we arrived I was frozen stiff, my hair stood up on end, and I was wheeled into the church looking like a scarecrow in striped pyjamas. Paul also gave me a small bible which I cherish to this day.

Seven years later I spotted Paul again when he landed at Ipswich Airport. I recognised him immediately when he got out of the 'Beech Kingair' he was flying. I was delighted to see him, and when he had attended to his disembarking passengers I walked over to him and said...

'Hello Mate, long time no see, how are you keeping old boy?'

He looked at me as if I had just dropped out of the rear end of a horse!

'Not too bad' he said picking up his briefcase and heading towards the administration building.

'How did the missionary position work out.' I asked.

He stopped dead in his tracks and glared at me as if he wanted to kill me, then started walking again.

'Remember that day you took me out in the back of the truck?' I said forcing a smile in an attempt to break the ice.

His pace quickened.

'I've still got the testament you gave to me' I added.

By this time he had almost broken into a run, whilst I, still suffering from the effects of my crash, hobbled behind like Quasi-Modo, desperately trying to keep up.

'Are you in a hurry old chap?' I asked.

He entered the control tower and slammed the door in my face.

He was obviously upset about something. I was also quite hurt by his change of attitude towards me and decided, if he wanted to behave in that manner, he could get stuffed and I'd stay clear of him.

I saw Paul later from the window of my office when he went out to his aeroplane. He was cautiously looking around as if he expected someone to attack him....very strange.

After he had taken off again, I wandered over to the pilot's reporting office to take a look at the landing sheets and find out who the miserable sod was working for these days. But when I read the entry under "Pilots Name" I began to feel sick, it wasn't Paul Reed at all. I thought back to the short conversation we had.

Capt John Hendrie must have thought I was a raving poof!

In general terms things were ticking along nicely at the school. Business was good and because of our excellent facilities and high standards of instruction, the company enjoyed a very good relationship with the contracts division of the MOD.

It was around February 1976, when the bombshell dropped. Ipswich council suddenly announced that they would not be renewing the lease of the airfield to our operating company, Lonmet, when it expired in 1979. The land they said, was now earmarked for building a large residential housing estate.

This came as one hell of a shock to all of us. Bob Pascoe and his solicitors did everything in their power to encourage the council to reverse their decision, but it was hopeless and nothing could be done. Bob said that, with over two years of the lease still to run, anything could happen. But that was of little consolation to me. My future plans to convert BSF into a commercial pilot training school extended far beyond two years, and even if we were lucky enough to find another airfield to lease, it would never have all the buildings and facilities needed to set up the type of residential flying school we were running at the present time.

I felt desperately sorry for Bob. He, and all his staff had worked extremely hard to make the British Schools of Flying a great success. Then out of the blue a situation had developed over which we had no control, and there was nothing we could do to prevent it from happening.

At the time this occurred we had just received application forms from the MOD to tender for training another yearly intake of cadets. In my opinion, Bob then made the biggest mistake he ever made. He told me that he intended to make the most out of the time we had left on the airfield by submitting a pilot training tender to the MOD charging treble the amount we were paid for the previous year's contract, both for the flying training and accommodation costs.

I had personally been involved in tendering for Ministry of Defence flying contracts whilst working for several companies over the previous fifteen years. I knew the chaps at MOD that dealt with these tenders, and I also knew there was no way in this world that they would even consider the sort of increased charges Bob intended to submit. I tried to warn him but Bob would take no notice. He simply went ahead and submitted the tender forms without further consultation.

Three days later I received a telephone call from a man in the contracts department of the MOD in London. For several years I had dealt successfully with the same chap, we knew each other on a Christian-name basis, and the conversation I had with him went something like this. (For obvious reasons I will change the name of the man at the ministry and call him John)

'Hello Ray, this is John at MOD contracts, have you seen the tender sent in by your boss?'

'Yes I have John, and I know what you're going to say.'

'It's a printing error, surely?'

'I'm afraid not.'

'He's bloody mad!..... The tender is in now and there's little I can do. It's a shame we have always had excellent results from the cadets we sent to you Ray.'

'I did warn him John, but he won't listen to me, I'm really upset about it.'

'Well, obviously it's up to him what he decides to tender. I certainly can't guarantee anything, but if you tell him to telephone me within the next half hour and say it was a typing error, I will allow him to re-submit another tender which I am willing to consider along-side those submitted by other schools. As I say Ray, I can't guarantee anything, but if he doesn't agree to call me you don't stand a cat-in-hells chance of getting any cadets at all this year.'

I said I would try to get Bob to reconsider, and the conversation was terminated. I went straight to Bob's office and told him exactly what John had said, adding that he was bloody lucky to get a second chance. Bob's stubborn attitude was sickening...

'They are trying it on Ray, they can't do without us, he'll soon ring back begging us to take his cadets.'

I tried my hardest to get my boss to change his mind but it was hopeless. Consequently a few days later we received a letter from MOD contracts branch to say that our tender had been rejected and no cadets would be allocated to the school in 1976.

Bob was shaken by this and asked me to telephone MOD and tell them it was a clerical error. But I refused, I had my dignity and in any case it was obviously too late, the cadet training programme for the coming season had already been allocated. As far as I could see that was the end of BSF. After so much hard work had been put in by myself and all the other loyal members of our staff, it seemed a criminal shame to throw it all away by sheer greed.

Without pilot training contracts there was no way in this world that the school could exist in its present form. Consequently I made up my mind there and then that I would leave the company.

Sadly I had to tell Bob Pascoe that I would be looking for another job. He was obviously upset, and I can tell you that I wasn't very happy either. Bob was not particularly liked by everyone because of his obstinate attitude, but he had always been a good boss as far as I was concerned, and if I could have seen any long term future for the company and its employees, I would have stayed.

I considered getting out of aviation altogether. Not because I wanted to stop flying, far from it, but I was beginning to feel the long term effects from the crash, and I wondered how long it would be before I failed the stringent six-monthly aircrew medical. But there was one big problem, what sort of job would I be happy doing having spent the majority of my working life in the freedom of the skies?

CHAPTER 54.

The beginning of a new era.

I was intrigued by an advertisement that appeared in the "Times" newspaper. The position advertised carried a very interesting and unusual job description. It read as follow:-

> A unique opportunity has arisen for a person
> with entrepreneurial qualities to develop
> a Napoleonic Fort into a first class Maritime
> Interpretative Centre. Applicants should have
> an imaginative flair, and those short listed
> for interview will be required to demonstrate
> their ability to design and create new projects.
> The successful candidate should be capable of
> writing his own job specification and will
> be required to reside in the Fort.
> A salary in the region of £ ------ is envisaged.
> Apply Box No…

I showed the advertisement to Carol, and we both agreed that, although the position advertised was poles apart from anything I had attempted in the past, there would be no harm in applying for an interview.

Professionally prepared Curriculum Vitae's were not an option in the 1970s, and even if they were, I would still prefer to write my own CV and attach a more personal note to convey a sense of imagination and responsibility.

I knew that I would undoubtedly be competing against applicants with more suitable maritime backgrounds, so I made a point of emphasising the project design aspect of my previous employment. I concluded by assuring the recipient of my enthusiasm, and that I looked forward to discussing the position further if selected for interview.

About ten days later I received a very important looking letter bearing a London postmark and marked "For the personal attention of Capt. R. McKenzie-Blyth."
Excitedly I opened the letter and read out the contents to Carol...

'Dear Mr McKenzie-Blyth.

Thank you for your letter dated the 25th April 1976 in answer to our advertisement in the Times Newspaper.

We are a firm of solicitors acting for the Trustees of Glynllifon Estates, Llanwnda, North Wales. Belan Fort, to which our advertisement refers, is an important section of the above estate, which is owned by The Hon: Robert Wynn, son of Lord Newborough, (7th Baron).

I would very much like to see you whilst I am in London next week. I will be staying at the Connaught Hotel, Mayfair, Hyde Park, Piccadilly, and could meet you in the saloon bar at 11.30am on Monday next the 2nd May. If the above appointment is inconvenient please contact my secretary at the above telephone number. I am enclosing a few details concerning the location and a limited history of Belan Fort for your perusal.

Yours sincerely, Alan Hilton, Director.'

When I looked at the map showing the location of the Fort, I became even more interested in the job. The Fort itself was situated on the Northern shores of a small peninsular that protruded into the Eastern entrance of the Menai Straits. The whole peninsular was part of the grounds belonging to the Fort and, although not mentioned in the advertisement, a disused, second world war, airfield appeared to be included in the area earmarked for development.

The letter I received from Mr Hilton did not ask for any designs at this stage, but having seen the site I was immediately bursting with enthusiasm and just had to get some creative ideas down on paper.

I spent hours designing an imaginative brochure showing Belan Fort as a Maritime Interpretative Centre, and as the disused airfield seemed to be inside the site boundary, I suggested that the aerodrome could be re-licensed and designed as an Air Park offering pleasure flights over the beautiful mountains of Snowdonia.

On the morning of the 2ⁿᵈ May I took a train from Ipswich to London, and after a short taxi ride I arrived at the Connaught Hotel a few minutes early. There was a distinguished looking gentleman sitting on his own at a small table in the saloon bar. He saw me enter the room and came over to me straight away to see if I was the person he was waiting to interview. Within minutes we were chatting enthusiastically as if we had known each other for years.

Mr Hilton explained that the position to be filled was rather extraordinary, in that the whole project from concept design through to completion and opening to the public would be the responsibility of the successful candidate. This would include dealing with the authorities for planning consent, designing and converting the interior of the boathouses around the Fort Dock into museums that would display many valuable artefacts belonging to Lord Newborough and the Wynn family. These exhibits would have to be sorted out and presented in a secure environment in a manner that would describe the history of the Fort from the time it was built and manned by an army of Newborough Volunteers over two hundred years ago, to the present day. It would also be the responsibility of the person appointed to design restaurant facilities within the Fort building and oversee their construction and furnishing. The job would include all aspects of marketing the project, security of the Fort, and the overall control of permanent and seasonal staff. Finally, the successful applicant would become an advisory member of Lord Newborough's board of trustees, and report his progress to the board at regular intervals. Mr Hilton also expressed that a great deal would depend on the persons capability for designing imaginative projects in order to keep Fort Belan in the forefront of major attractions in North Wales.

I was able to chat to Mr Hilton with complete ease. I explained that my wife held a very important job at the moment and that she was capable of handling company accounts as well as all aspects of office duties and staff control.

I presented the initial ideas that I had drafted out for the project without really knowing what the job was all about. Mr Hilton seemed to be very impressed, especially with my concept of including the old disused airfield into the overall project. I was not surprised to learn that there had been over 200 replies to their advertisement and he still had a few more applicants to see from those short listed. He assured me there and then that I would be one of the candidates selected to attend the final interview at the offices of Glynllifon Estates within the next week or so.

I returned home to Carol very excited and full of enthusiasm. It was obvious that the person appointed to manage this very important project would have massive responsibilities, and if selected, Carol would be the ideal person to work with me. If I had to give up flying this was certainly the sort of assignment that I would really enjoy.

Both Carol and I were invited to attend for interview the following week. I noted that the idea of presenting my thoughts for the project in the form of a brochure had caught on, as the letter stated that those being interviewed should bring written ideas on how they envisaged the project could be handled and developed.

The Glynllifon Offices were situated a few miles South of Caernarfon in a beautiful old gatehouse within the boundary walls of the Newborough Estate.

We were made very welcome on arrival by Miss Yarnold, who was secretary to Mr Richard Rutherford the Land Agent for Lord Newborough.

To begin with Mr Rutherford took us in his car to visit Belan Fort.

There was an impressive two mile private drive that led from the main gates on the seafront road at Dinas Dinlle to the entrance of the fort. At the end of the road we drove over a causeway that flooded at high tide turning the fort area into a small island.

We passed through the imposing outer gates of the fort ramparts and crossed over the drawbridge into the main courtyard. It was like being transported 200 years into the past. The courtyard was surrounded by a beautiful quadrangle of charmingly constructed cottage-like buildings that were an integral part of the fort itself. Although it was the most miserable weather, dull and pouring with rain, both Carol and I instantly fell in love with Belan.

Richard Rutherford explained that most of the single storied buildings in the courtyard had been used as barracks for a private army known as the Newborough Volunteers. Other rooms included an armoury, gunpowder store and stables. One section of the building had an upper floor that was initially used as the officers quarters. Part of the courtyard buildings were now used by Lord Newborough and his family on occasions when they visited the fort, and another section had been beautifully converted into living quarters for whoever was successfully appointed to do the job I had applied for.

A sentry walk surrounded the fort on top of the main outer walls with fully serviceable cannons positioned at strategic points, and on the far side of the Northern ramparts one could hear the sea pounding away against the huge boulders protecting the fort walls.

We past through a small postern gate situated in the Eastern wall, crossed over a sizeable grass area where three huge cannons were situated pointing out to sea, and entered the old Fort Docks. One end of the dock opened out onto the Menai Straits, and on the three remaining sides were stone built eighteenth century boat sheds, a workers cottage, an old forge and other buildings, all just begging to be sympathetically reinstated.

Everything about Belan Fort was intriguing, and the possibility of actually living and working here was incredibly exciting. But the work would be very demanding, and whoever undertook this task would bear the great responsibility of preserving the ambience and historic importance of this beautiful old place in his designs for any future developments.

The visit had to be cut short as we were due to return to the estate office for the final interview.

We waited in the secretaries office for a short while before being invited into a room where several distinguished looking gentlemen were seated at a large boardroom table.

Mr Hilton, the gentleman that had interviewed me in London, introduced us to Lord Newborough's son, The Hon Robert Wynn. We were told that Robert was the sole beneficiary of the Estate's Trust and the rest of the gentlemen were members of the Board of Trustees that looked after Roberts financial interests. The Chairman of the trust, Mr Bill Williamson, was a gentleman farmer and a principle magistrate. The rest of the Trustees included Mr Raymond who was managing director of a large firm of accountants in Chester, Mr Wynn-Griffith a Director of Nat West Bank, Mr Brooks a Director of a London firm of stock brokers, and finally Mr Hilton, who was Chairman of a large firm of solicitors in the Wirral. All in all a pretty impressive bunch of chaps.

We were told that only two persons had been selected to attend with their wives for the final interview. There followed a multitude of questions about our previous experiences and the positions we had held with other companies etc. Everyone seemed very pleased with us, so much so that I thought we were certain to be offered the job. I was however asked if I had any maritime knowledge, and of course I had to answer that I had not. We were finally asked to wait in another room whilst the Trustees interviewed the second couple. It was at this point I learned that the other candidate selected for the final interview was a recently retired Naval Captain.

After what seemed an age we were invited back into the boardroom, sincerely thanked for our interest in the position advertised, and told that the job had in fact been offered to the Naval type and his wife. As we left the room the Chairman said…

'I would like you to keep in touch with me Mr Blyth, if a further position arises within the Belan Estate Trust, we would be more than pleased to see you again.'

After days of excitement and anticipation, we had to accept that our dream was no longer on the cards, and having seen Belan Fort in its romantic setting by the sea, with the Snowdon range of mountains as its backdrop, we were literarily heartbroken not to have been offered the job. We felt so sad that we hardly spoke a word during the long drive from Wales back to Felixstowe. One thing was for certain, neither Carol or I would ever forget Belan.

In the back of my mind I clung to the Chairman's final words. Perhaps a miracle would occur one day and we would be able to work and live in that wonderful old fort. But it was just a dream that hung on a very fine thread of hope.

The following day, back at the airfield, Jack, our chief mechanic, asked me if I had recently read "Flight International" magazine. I said that I hadn't and asked him why it was so important.

'Well' he said, 'I reckon the best Chief Flying Instructor's job in the UK was advertised last month, it would suit you down to the ground boss.'

I accompanied him back to his office in the hangar. Jack fumbled through a stack of magazines on the top of his filing cabinet and produced the relevant copy of Flight. Flicking through to the back pages he turned to the situations vacant section, drew a large circle around one of the advertisements and passed it to me. It read...

> Chief Flying Instructor required to take over
> flying training at the Channel Islands Flying
> Club in Jersey. A salary commensurate with the
> responsibility of the above position, plus the
> provision of a rent free house will be offered
> to the successful applicant.
> Applicants should have held a previous
> CFI's position, have considerable experience
> in all aspects of pilot training and also be
> qualified to train flying instructors.
> Apply in writing …

As the advertisement was a few weeks old, I was pretty certain that the interviews would have already taken place. So in the hope that I wasn't too late I telephoned the Jersey Flying Club and spoke to a Mr Clucas who was the Chairman of the J.F.C. Management Committee. I explained who I was and gave him a short description of my previous experience. He seemed very pleased that I had contacted him and said that the interviews for the position of CFI at Jersey were due to take place very shortly and suggested that I send a letter of application off to him straight away. In the meantime he would make arrangements for me to be interviewed with other candidates who had already been short-listed.

I was still feeling very disappointed at not getting the job at Fort Belan. It would have been a wonderful challenge and a job that I would have accepted gladly even if it meant I would not be doing any more flying. Even so, I was pleased to have another interview in the pipeline, and Chief Flying Instructor at Jersey Airport was certainly not to be sniffed at.

I sent off my CV to the directors of Jersey Flying Club. Four days later I received a very nice letter from Mr Clucas acknowledging the receipt of my application and inviting me to attend an interview in The Grosvenor Hotel London the following week.

Six days later, I arrived at the London's Grosvenor Hotel and was directed to a small room where two other applicants were anxiously waiting to be interviewed. I didn't recognise either of them, and after a brief good morning, not a word was spoken.

Minutes later the door opened and the first chap was cordially invited in for his interview. About twenty minutes later the second applicant was ushered in whilst the first chap, now displaying bags of charm and grinning from ear to ear, left the Hotel.

The second interview seemed much shorter, and the applicant left the room looking just as miserable as he did when he entered. So I assumed the position had been offered to the first candidate, and interviewing the rest of us would be a mere formality.

Two distinguished looking gentlemen introduced themselves as Mr Ted Clucas, the Director of Flying at Jersey, and Mr Ray Lock who was a member of the Management Committee and also a Senior Controller at Jersey Airport.

After a warm greeting, I sat down fully expecting to be asked to run through my previous experiences as a CFI. But instead I was flabbergasted when Ted Clucas's opening remarks were…

'Well I think it's just a matter of how much do you want to be paid isn't it Ray?'

I must have looked a little stunned because he continued…

'Don't worry old boy, we know all about you, we have spoken to Rex Smith the Director of Flying Training at the CAA, I believe he used to be your boss at Oxford, and we also had a word with Mr Somers the Director of Southampton Airport who I believe was your Chairman when you were the Managing Director of Halfpenny Green Airport. Both men spoke very highly of you. As far as we're concerned you're the man for us, so let's cut out the bullshit and get down to the details.'

That remarkable and rather unorthodox interview is how I became the Chief Flying Instructor of the Channel Island Flying Club at Jersey Airport.

I felt very sad at leaving the British Schools of Flying and saying goodbye to Bob Pascoe, but under the circumstances I had little choice. The facts were, that even after a fair warning from the contracts department at the MOD, Bob had refused to lower his tender to a more reasonable rate which quite possibly would have assured BSF substantial pilot training contracts for the remainder of their tenancy at Ipswich Airport.

At the end of our last day with The British Schools of Flying, Carol and I were about to get in our car and leave the airport for the last time when one of the club members asked us to pop upstairs into the residents hall. We were astounded to see the place packed. All the staff and members of the club were assembled there waiting to give us a send off we were unlikely to forget. It was a pretty lively evening during which time we were presented with a beautiful oil painting of an RAF Chipmunk, inverted at about 2000 ft. over Ipswich Airfield. The aircraft registration markings on the Chipmunk were the same as one of the aircraft I had flown in the RAFVR with No 6 AEF many years previously, and a local artist had been especially commissioned to do the painting. I had been a little curious when Chris Brown, our Air Traffic Control Officer at Ipswich, had asked to look at my service logbook some weeks earlier. At the time he said his hobby was collecting service aircraft numbers.

I was due to commence my employment with the Channel Islands Flying Club on the 1st June 1976. This meant that we only had a few days to put our house on the market and pack everything we possessed ready to be shipped over to the Channel Islands. Neither of us had been to the Channel Islands previously, so we had no idea what to expect. All we knew was that a house had been provided for us, and I was expected to take up my job as CFI on the first of the month.

Having arranged for a furniture removal company to collect our belongings from Felixstowe and travel with us on the ferry to the Channel Islands the following day, we spent our last night at a hotel in Bournemouth. The next day we drove to Weymouth and boarded the ferry.

It was at this point that we began to feel a little nervous, wondering what awaited us on our arrival. It was a beautiful day although the sea was a little choppy. After nine hours at sea we arrived at St. Helier docks at 9pm.

A wonderful welcome awaited us at the quayside. Ray Lock, accompanied by a team of volunteers from the flying club, were there to greet us and help us move into the house we had not yet seen.

It was well past midnight by the time our helper's left and we settled down to sleep on a mattress that had been placed on the floor of one of the bedrooms. The fact that it had been pitch dark when we arrived meant that we virtually had no idea where the building was actually situated. When we awoke the next morning we discovered that we were the very first tenants in a brand new three bedroom flat that had been built as an extension on the top of a brick built barn. Beneath the flat, the barn itself had been very tastefully designed with a double arched frontage for the purpose of housing farm implements.

We soon discovered that our small plot of land was situated on a cliff top with a steep winding pathway down to a beautiful little bay with smooth golden sands. On either side steep inaccessible cliffs protruded well out to sea, and the only access to this little cove was through the garden of our flat which in effect meant that we had our own very private beach.

The first morning we were there the farmer who owned our flat came round to introduce himself. He was a very friendly man who lived with his wife and daughter in a their large farmhouse just a few hundred yards from our flat. The farm mainly produced Jersey Potatoes, and we hadn't been there long before he kindly gave us two large sacks of new potatoes. I don't think we had ever tasted such lovely spuds in our lives.

We soon discovered that the Channel Island Authorities were extremely efficient. One of the first things we had to do was apply for a work permit. This was no problem as the job of Chief Flying Instructor on Jersey Airport was classed as "State Employment". In fact Carol and I obtained Jersey passports, a Jersey car tax, Jersey number plates for our car and work permits all from the same office in a single morning. Efficiency at its best.

The next couple of days were spent getting the flat straightened out before I started my first day's employment as CFI.

The Jersey Flying Club itself was a beautiful single storey brick building that housed first class bar and restaurant facilities. It was certainly the finest private flying club I had set eyes on up to that time. I was pleased to see Richard Blair, an old friend of mine who had previously been one of my instructors at the British School of Flying, and was now employed as a QFI at Jersey. On my first day he flew me around the island and showed me the training area used by the club, which was positioned well clear of the Jersey control zone. In addition to Richard Blair there were a couple of other well qualified instructors that worked for the club full-time, and a further two or three part time instructors.

The flying training facilities however were crap. They consisted of a huge room situated above the ground floor of the maintenance hangar. In the centre of this hall-like room sat a sizeable table, larger than two full size snooker tables and obviously used for flight planning maps, cups of tea, magazines and practically anything else that came to hand. A few chairs were scattered randomly around, and a circular table stood in one corner bearing an extra large business dairy that was apparently used as the sole method of recording advanced flight bookings. It was obvious to me that all the prestige of the Jersey Flying Club had been centred on the social side of things. So once again it was back to square one!

The large room described above was of adequate size to be sub-divided into several sections in order to form a flight training unit capable of passing the critical eye of the flight standards division of the CAA. Over the next few evenings I sat at home designing and drawing a scale plan to sub-divide the existing room to house a service type Ops room, a couple of briefing cubicles, a proper flight planning room, and a small ten-seat lecture room. The mandatory instructors room and CFI's office could be housed elsewhere. I submitted this plan together with a full explanatory report to the Jersey Airport Management Committee in the hope of convincing them that the club would operate far more efficiently and receive the CAA's blessing if they adopted my ideas. Fortunately a few days later the Chairman Mr Ted Clucas told me that the committee were pleased with my recommendations and agreed unanimously to have the work carried out over the less busy winter months ready for the following season.

Later I was invited to meet the Jersey Airport Management Committee, who turned out to be a splendid bunch of chaps, a mixture of wealthy businessmen and a couple of senior air traffic controller's who I imagine were also quite wealthy.

One of the first tasks I was asked to perform was to look into the charges made by the resident engineering company that serviced the clubs aeroplanes. The committee were under the impression that the costs incurred for maintenance were extortionate. The investigation didn't take long, and I soon found out the charges were very reasonable, about 15% below the average charges made by aircraft maintenance companies on the mainland. My report certainly surprised the committee and undoubtedly pleased the manager of the maintenance company.

The next practice that needed to be eradicated made me less popular than snot on a ham sandwich! I discovered that qualified pilots were simply allowed to hire the clubs aircraft and pay for the flight time they estimated was correct without any reference to the aircraft's tachometer reading or take-off and landing times recorded by air traffic control. So without there being anyone employed by the club to record start-up and shut-down times, pilots made up their own times. Obviously I couldn't accuse anyone of dishonesty, but this practice alone must have cost the club thousands of pounds per year. Imagine this method of payment existing in any other form of business scenario, it would mean that customers would be allowed to make up their minds how much they paid for any item or service they purchased. As far as I was concerned if the committee expected me to be responsible for operating a profitable flying school, this practice had to be eradicated forthwith. The same estimated times had apparently been recorded in the aircraft engine and airframe log books. This was not only illegal, but dangerous, and could mean that engines were in fact operating well over the legal time limits permitted between checks, a practice that could also put pilot's lives at risk. Before I could rectify the situation I had to face the wroth of the management committee who accused me of mistrusting the honesty of club members. I had to inform them, with the greatest respect, that the flying section of Jersey Flying Club was definitely losing money by this practice, and also operating illegally as far as the CAA was concerned. I asked the committee, as businessmen themselves, would they trust their customers to pay whatever they thought was a reasonable amount for the services they provided. There was much mumbling and grumbling around the table until I asked them to consider this...

'If everyone was so honest, why should it make any difference to them if their flight times were recorded accurately by a member of the staff?'

Also members were not paying for their flights on the day they flew. Most of them paid when they felt like it.

Thank heavens it was finally agreed that I should go ahead and re-organise anything I thought necessary to get the school on a proper footing.

Shortly after I introduced the new system, the secretary that worked part time in the club decided she had too much work to do and resigned. I could think of no better person to replace her than Carol as she certainly knew exactly how to run a professional flight operations room and could scale down her ideas to suit the Jersey Flying Club. The Chairman formally interviewed Carol and she was immediately employed as secretary.

I instructed at Jersey almost every day of the week, and in that respect I enjoyed the job very much. All the navigation flying and set cross country exercises were carried out over France.

One of the main problems during the summer months at Jersey was the long delays experienced at the runway holding point due to scheduled airline traffic. Some controller's were more cautious than others and would make light aircraft wait five or more minutes for commercial aircraft to land. On several occasions I was made to wait as long as fifteen minutes for an aeroplane that was on a straight in approach and was so far away that it was literarily out of sight when I was ready for immediate take-off.

There was one controller at Jersey that certainly had it in for club aircraft. One day when I was returning to Jersey with a student on a cross country exercise over France, my student gave a position report north-west of Mont Saint Michelle. The controller kept on asking him for his position, and he repeatedly gave it to him. We were in perfect VFR conditions, well clear of Jersey control zone and there were no other aircraft working the approach frequency at the time. It got so bad that I hardly had time to speak to my student without being interrupted by this over zealous controller requesting our position. Finally he said...

'I can't see you on the radar are you lost or something?'

I bloody near exploded! He was well known for giving students a hard time. He seemed to do his best to un-nerve them and make their lives a misery when he was on duty.

Anyway, it was a hot day and I'd had more than enough crap from this smart-arse in the past. So I pressed the tit and said...

'If you can't see me on your radar its not my fault, try looking out of the bloody window I haven't disappeared altogether, I can clearly see Jersey Airport and I would be obliged for your gracious permission to join the circuit and land.'

My remarks didn't go down too well, he started to fume over the RT and transmitted all sorts of threats about reporting me to the CAA for incorrect R/T procedure etc. He obviously had no idea that I was a commercial pilot with a CAA examiners rating, but he was certainly about to find out. Anyway, I advised the controller that I would come up to the tower and have a word with him when I landed. I shouldn't have allowed myself the pleasure of that outburst, but I was bloody mad and he could do what the hell he liked, I intended to have him.

Finally after landing, we took the Southern exit and I parked the aircraft outside the air traffic building and closed down. I staggered up the unending internal steps of the control tower as fast as my injured legs would allow me. I had heard of multiple complaints from pilots and students about this controller's supercilious attitude towards non-commercial flights, and it was my intention to sort things out even if it cost me my job. He must have seen me coming because the door was locked when I got up there, and no amount of knocking produced a reply. In the end I was asked by a security officer to leave the tower and telephone the approach controller if I wanted to speak to him. I was quite upset at the time and said…

'I don't want to speak to him thank you very much, I just want to deck him.'

I said that as more of a joke than anything, but my comment didn't go down too well with the security officer. I was reported to the airport manager, a nice chap who seemed to understand and simply said, that as no harm was done he'd forget about it. I was also hauled up in front of the Chairman of the Jersey Flying club, who eventually laughed it off and told me to try and calm down! Anyway, after that episode, I never heard that particular controller on the R/T again. It turned out that he was due to retire within a few days of the incident, so that was the end of the matter.

Apart from that incident I enjoyed flying with the Jersey Flying Club, and whenever an opportunity presented itself I would visit the other islands in the group, which brings me to an amusing incident that happened the first time I landed on the aerodrome at Alderney.

It was the 30th of June, I was asked to take a Cherokee over to Alderney and pick up three chaps who had been on the island for a weekend's golf. I had never landed on the island before and didn't know much about the airfield. It was only a twenty minute hop across the sea, but when I took off from Jersey I noticed that there was quite a strong crosswind blowing from the North. The regulations for flying into Alderney Aerodrome stated that aircraft must be able to maintain R/T communication with Jersey Zone, Guernsey Approach, and Alderney Tower. Within a few minutes I had Alderney in sight and changed frequency from Jersey Zone to Alderney on 112.2mcs requesting a straight in approach on 03, a grass strip which was the nearest runway into wind.

The controller informed me that the surface wind was 360 degrees at 15kts with occasional gusts up to 25kts., and cleared me to land. The threshold of runway 03 was quite near to the cliffs, so there was a strong possibility of encountering turbulence on the approach. Well that turned out to be the understatement of the year! The runway was only 400 or so metres in length so I lowered the first stage of flap and commenced a standard powered approach. Suddenly, about half a mile from touchdown, we hit one hell of a downdraft that caused the aircraft to sink down below the level of the cliff tops and I momentarily lost sight of the airfield. With the throttle fully open and the nose of the aircraft raised to climb, I had just started to initiate an overshoot when we hit an equally violent up-draught that tossed us up over the cliff edge on to a very low, short final approach.

Having narrowly missed hitting the cliff top, the landing wasn't too good either, and we bounced down the runway like a tennis ball. At that time in my career I had accumulated over 5000 hours instructing on light aircraft, God alone knows why I didn't correct the bounce with a short burst of power, but I didn't. I cursed every bloody bounce and finally came to a halt opposite three chaps sitting on the grass staring at me in astonishment.

I booked in and apologised for alarming the controller who said that I had completely disappeared from his view behind the cliff before reappearing in a staggeringly high nose attitude and flopping down on the runway, which wasn't much of a compliment! There was another pilot in the office who had just landed in one of Aurigny Airline's Britten Norman Trislanders. When he finally managed to stop laughing he slapped me on the back and said...

'Join the club old boy, you're not the only chap to arrive here like that.'

Having paid the landing fee I asked the chap in reception if he knew where the passengers were that I was supposed to collect and fly back to Jersey. To my embarrassment he said that they were the guys that were sitting on the grass and just witnessed my unfortunate arrival!

I walked over to the three men and said...

'I believe that I have to fly you gentlemen back to Jersey?'

One of them asked me if I was the pilot that had just landed in the Cherokee. I obviously had to own up, whereupon all three stared at me in horror. One young man who later introduced himself as John Corbin said...

'You must be f...... joking mate, have you passed your test yet?'

Before I could think of a suitable reply another chap commented that he'd sooner risk his neck swimming back, adding that he couldn't swim either. This was not a good start to my first charter flight since arriving at the Channel Islands. I sat on the grass with them and explained that the extraordinary landing had been caused by a sudden down-draught at the cliff edge, and that in fact I was the Chief Instructor at Jersey. The smart bastard that had made the previous derogatory remark piped up again and said…

'If you're the CFI what the hell are the other instructors like?'

Their breaths smelt strongly of alcohol and by the glazed look in their bloodshot eyes it had obviously been a lively weekend in which golf had probably played a secondary part.

In the end I was able to get them laughing and eventually into the aeroplane. On the flight back John Corbin, who had elected to sit in the front with me, mentioned that he had always wanted to learn to fly, but never got round to finding out more about it.

John turned out to be an extremely wealthy young man. He spoke fluent French and knew just about every influential person in Jersey on a Christian name basis.

Within the next few months I taught John to fly, and shortly after gaining his licence, he decided to buy his own aeroplane. John came to me for advice, so I contacted my old friend Peter Clifford who still operated his own aircraft sales company on Kidlington Aerodrome. Peter enjoyed the reputation of being one of the most reliable and honest men in the business. In fact my father had purchased a Hawk Moth Major aeroplane from Clifford Aviation Ltd. in the 1960's.

Peter came up with a fully airways equipped Piper Warrior in pristine condition and low engine hours. John purchased the aeroplane straight away and hangared it at Jersey. I checked him out on the Warrior and flew over to France with him on several occasions. One of these flights turned out to be a bit complicated.

It was during the exceptionally hot Summer of 1976 when a strict ban on the use of hose-pipes was in force throughout the Channel Islands. We met up at Jersey airport at 7am so that John could practice circuits in his newly acquired Piper Warrior before the main flow of commercial traffic started to dominate the circuit. John suddenly came up with a cracking idea and suggested that as it was early morning we could leave the island and fly over to France for breakfast. So after a couple more landings we left the Jersey circuit and set course for Dinard.

As usual we had to report to customs on arrival. John seemed to be well acquainted with most of the customs officers at Dinard and chatted away in French for several minutes to one of them. The officer appeared to be very friendly and passed us through customs without the usual formality of filling in arrival forms etc. We left the airport, boarded a taxi and set off for a lovely little café in the centre of Dinard that John had visited many times in the past. The taxi ride was hairy to say the least. The driver tore around the streets like a maniac, tyres screeching at every bend and at one point where the road ahead was blocked, he took a short cut by driving at great speed the wrong way down a one-way street. Eventually, by the grace of God, we arrived at the café feeling somewhat shaken.

After a truly excellent breakfast and an interesting walk around the streets of Dinard, we returned to the airport. (Thankfully not in the same taxi).

When we walked into the reception area we were met by the same customs officer who had passed us through earlier in the day, but this time he seemed very upset and started shouting at us. Unfortunately my knowledge of the French language is restricted to 'open the window and close the door' so I couldn't understand a word he said, but by the look on my friends face we were obviously in trouble. John started to argue with the officer who eventually called one of his colleagues over who turned out to be his boss. I asked John what was going on and he told me that they were annoyed because we had left the airport without filling in the necessary paperwork. I started to mouth off at them when the chief customs officer, who spoke fluent English said...

'You are in serious trouble, why did you leave the airport without permission ?'

I tried to explain that we were given permission to leave by the other officer who knew John well and allowed us to forgo the paperwork.

That did it, and an awful shouting match developed between John and the two customs officers. All this was in French. John turned to me and said that the officer denied letting us through when we arrived. I forgot that one of them spoke English and blurted out...

'The lying bastard.'

With that the boss removed a pistol from his holster and ordered us into his office. I asked John what was happening...

'That wasn't a very wise thing to say Ray. I think we are about to be arrested.'

Finally, after being searched and generally made to feel extremely uncomfortable, we filled in the necessary forms and were allowed to continue our flight back to Jersey. I came across the same customs officer a couple more times when I landed at Dinard with no intention of leaving the airport. Even so he always made a point of glaring at me suspiciously.

The routes I used for various cross country and flight navigation training were interesting, particularly the longer map reading exercises. For instance we would fly from Jersey to St Malo from there to Granville, then North to Cherbourg and round the peninsula to head South to Bayuex, then take up an Easterly heading again to Le Havre and sometimes on to Dieppe before heading West and returning to Jersey.

Our Aircrew Medical Officer at Jersey, known to all as Doctor Jack, bought himself a twin engine Piper Comanche. I was called upon to carry out his twin conversion training, and from then on we spent several exciting afternoons on the circuit whilst Doctor Jack tested my nerves by attempting to fly straight into the ground without rounding out before touchdown! I also remember my first medical renewal with Jack. As a friend he suggested that I popped over to see him out of surgery hours so that we could also have a chat about flying. I was sitting in his consulting room when he said...

'We'll get you checked over first Ray, then we can have a chat over a cup of tea. Take your cloths off and lay down on the couch.'

I took him at his word and stripped off completely whilst Jack left the surgery for a moment. I was laying there completely starkers when his secretary walked in with two cups of tea... screamed... and ran out again. Not the best thing to happen when you are about to have your blood pressure taken!

In contrast to Jacks flying into the ground, a Czechoslovakian pilot who was a Captain for a local company that operated Dakota aircraft from Jersey, came to me to be checked out on light single engine aircraft which he obviously hadn't flown since Pontius was a pilot. He smartened my reactions up a bit by attempting to land a Cherokee twenty feet above the runway, apparently judging his round-out height to be the same as the Dakota.

Carol and I loved living by the sea and working together at Jersey Airport. But I have to say that all the time we were living on the island our thoughts frequently returned to Belan Fort and the intriguing job that I had applied for and unfortunately been turned down. It had been a very special opportunity, for which I would have willingly given up flying, the sort of job that occurs once in a lifetime and only then if one was extremely lucky.

I couldn't get over the dream of living in that old Napoleonic Fort, and the challenge of developing a maritime interpretive centre. Although the opportunity had passed, I still bought books of maritime interest, famous sea battles and the Napoleonic wars. Carol and I would often chat away in the evenings imagining how it would have been to live in the fort, and the sort of projects we would have undertaken. Being short listed for that wonderful job, and then being turned down, was for us, like winning the football pools, and losing the ticket!

Finally, overcome by my enthusiasm, I wrote to the Chairman of the Board of Trustees conveying my interest and enquiring about the progress they were making. Although I knew it was a waste of time, I found it impossible to get Belan out of my mind. Carol felt exactly the same, the experience of visiting the fort and seeing what could have been, left us both feeling drastically unsettled.

The fact of course was that we now had responsible jobs at Jersey Airport, and were very lucky to be there. We soon became friendly with many of the club members and were frequently invited to various parties that took place on the island.

On one occasion Carol and I were invited to a private party given by one of my female student pilots who's husband was also a member of Jersey Flying Club. I will refer to them as Alan and Diana.

We arrived at about eight in the evening and were warmly welcomed into their lovely little cottage which was situated just a short distance from where we lived. Obviously being the first to arrive we sat with our hosts for a while chatting about life on the island and enjoying a glass of punch. After a while, as no other guests had appeared, I asked if we had made the fatal mistake of turning up too early. To my surprise Diana replied...

'Oh it's just the four of us, we thought it would be cosier this way.'

Now I'm not a complete fool, and I had noticed that Alan was paying more than a little attention to Carol. My wife was young and very beautiful, a fact that had not escaped the notice of most males that frequented the flying club, and I began to wonder if this was going to turn out to be one of those parties that Carol and I always avoided like the plague. But Alan and Diana seemed a pleasant enough couple, and after we had chatted for a while I dismissed the idea that it was a set-up. Then Diana, who had been flashing herself around a bit, made the first suspicious move.

'Come and see what you think to our den, it's more comfortable up there.'

We followed Diana up a spiral staircase on to a small landing that led into a luxuriously carpeted room. There were two or three sofas scattered around covered with what appeared to be real leopard skins. In one corner of the room was a small but very well appointed bar. In fact the room was rather like a miniature night-club, with dim lighting and soft music playing through hidden all-round speakers.

We sat there for a while talking about things in general, and sipping one of Alan's so-called champagne cocktails, which incidentally looked like a glass of water with a small jungle growing out of it, when I began to feel decidedly odd. I knew for certain that one glass of punch and a glass of champagne would never have that effect on me. Looking across the room at Carol I could see that something was wrong. I asked her if she was alright, and she said that she felt sick, even in the dim light of the room I could see that her face was deathly white. It was blatantly obvious that our drinks had been spiked and I was bloody fuming.

Alan said he would show Carol to the bathroom and walked out with her, that didn't go down too well with me so I struggled to get myself up from the sofa in order to stop him. At the same time Diana was calmly standing at the bar pouring out more drinks. In spite of feeling very dizzy I eventually managed to get to my feet and told Diana that Carol and I would have to leave. I was swaying around having a hell of a job to remain standing when she threw her arms around my neck and started thrusting her tongue down my throat. She said that we couldn't leave in the state we were in, and we could stay the night. But I had other ideas. Having struggled to get away from the clutches of Diana, I eventually found the bathroom where I saw Carol being violently sick. Alan had his arm around her. I was helping her towards the door when Diana came up to me again and said…

'There's no way you can drive your car like this Ray, anyway I've taken the car keys out of your pocket so you can't drive.'

That really set me off. I was trying to hold Carol up whilst threatening to put one on Alan. Wisely Diana relented and handed over the keys. How she got them out of my pocket in the first place I'll never know. By this time poor old Carol was just about out of it. I struggled to get her into the car, and drove off, obviously in no condition to drive. In fact I was in such a state that it took me over an hour to find our house which in fact was less than a mile away.

Next morning Carol and I felt like death. God alone knows what they put into our drinks. I telephoned the flying club to say we were both sick, then went back to bed. Around midday the doorbell rang. It was Diana holding a huge bunch of flowers. She was obviously very upset and apologised to Carol. As far as we were concerned it was all over and done with, but we didn't feel too good for several days.

A few weeks later something happened that altered our lives completely. I was walking across the tarmac outside the clubhouse when one of my instructors shouted out from the office window to inform me that there was someone on the telephone who wanted to speak to me rather urgently. I cursed because I had a student waiting to fly with me in the Fuji.

You could have knocked me down with a feather when I realised that the person on the telephone was no less than Mr Bill Williamson, the Chairman of the Board of Trustees for Lord Newborough. I will always remember the conversation that followed word for word for the rest of my life.

He asked if I was still interested in the job I had been interviewed for at the Fort several months earlier. I asked him if he meant that another job had arisen at the Fort? Mr Williamson said no, it's not another job, it is exactly the same job you originally applied for, to take over the complete development project and live at the Fort. I felt myself going weak at the knees. Somehow my dream had miraculously come true. But first I needed to know what had happened to the Naval Captain who was originally appointed to do the job? In confidence Mr Williamson told me that, as it turned out, the man didn't fit in at all well. He had little imagination, foresight or ability for the job, and by mutual agreement he was leaving. I accepted the job there and then but had to explain that I would have to honour my terms of employment and serve a full three months notice at the Channel Islands Flying Club. Mr Williamson continued...

'Excellent, we are glad to have you on board Ray, we will be writing to you within the next day or so to confirm your appointment and also arrange a mutually convenient date for you to meet with the directors in London.'

He concluded by asking me to relay his best wishes to Carol.' And that was that.

My eyes filled with tears of excitement as I flew down the stairs from my office and into the flying club to tell Carol the unbelievable news. We were both so excited that we clung to each other for a few seconds, then made fools of ourselves dancing around the car park with joy. That night we had little sleep. We drank endless cups of tea and talked well into the early hours about our future life at Belan Fort.

But now I had to break the news and face the wroth of Ted Clucas the Director of Flying at Jersey. I felt very uncomfortable about leaving the

Channel Islands Flying Club after only five months and all they had done for me. But in fairness Belan was a job that I had applied for before starting work at Jersey, and it was the only job in the world that would have made me leave the Channel Islands Flying Club.

Ted Clucas was furious, and rightly so. He said he felt like punching me on the nose after all they had done to make us comfortable. I could only agree with him and apologised profusely.

I worked the full three months notice at Jersey Flying Club, and the time finally arrived for us to re-pack our belongings and travel joyfully back to our new home in North Wales.

CHAPTER 55.

Belan.

We left the island with mixed feelings. I was ecstatic about my new job, but on the other hand it was highly possible that my flying days were over. Unfortunately we had to leave all our furniture and belongings on Jersey for a few days because we were unable to arrange for it to be transported on the same day as we crossed the channel. Clear skies and little wind made the crossing back to England very enjoyable.

Having lived on an island that was only fifteen miles across at it's longest point, the drive from Weymouth docks to Caernarfon North Wales seemed like a never ending journey. Our future employers had agreed to pay for our accommodation in the Royal Hotel Caernarfon for a few days until our furniture arrived from Jersey.

We reported to the Estate Office at 9am on our first day and were warmly welcomed by Lord Newborough's land agent Mr Richard Rutherford. He accompanied us to Belan where we were introduced to the two existing members of the fort's permanent staff, Wilf the Gardener and a man who, for reasons that will become apparent later, I will call Mr J the General Maintenance Man. I was told that these two gentlemen were now under my jurisdiction and would report to me daily for instructions. The gardener lived in a nearby village, and the maintenance man resided in a small cottage which was part of the fort dock complex.

We had already been shown the rather prestigious section of the courtyard buildings that was now our private residence. Richard suggested that it would probably be a good idea if we spent our first day familiarising ourselves with the layout of Belan and it's eight hundred acres of land, and at the same time we could sort out one of the many vacant rooms in the fort complex that we would like to use as an office. With that, Richard said...

'Well it's all yours now Raymond, if you need any help or advice you know where my office is. I'm sure you'll find the job very interesting and I wish you both the best of luck.'

With that he drove off over the drawbridge and out through the main gates leaving Carol and I standing in the courtyard of this beautiful old fortress feeling slightly overwhelmed and blissfully happy.

The only thing we had been told about the history of Belan was that it had been built in 1775 by the first Lord Newborough to defend North Wales against possible attack by the Spanish, and that a private army known as the "Newborough Volunteers" had been engaged to defend the fort during the Napoleonic Wars. So, with this minimal amount of knowledge, Carol and I set off to discover as much as we could about the more intimate details of the fort and its environs.

The fort was built on the Southern shores of the Menai Straits. Entrance to this fine bastion was gained through huge ironclad doors in the outer wall which was approximately twenty feet high and ten feet thick. A sentry walk along the top of the wall completely surrounded the fort. Having passed through the outer gates, one had to cross a drawbridge spanning the moat and on through a gated archway in an inner wall to enter the main courtyard.

The courtyard had a large central lawn bounded by a gravel pathway and well kept flower beds. The buildings that surrounded the courtyard were originally constructed to form a strong military garrison, but now appeared as beautiful old-fashioned cottages on all four sides of the courtyard. The buildings along the Western side of the quadrangle were now divided into two sections. One half was to be used by the son of Lord Newborough, the Hon. Robert Wynn, on the occasions when he visited the fort, and the other half was our new home. On the opposite side of the courtyard were any number of intriguingly old fashioned rooms that were now available for me to use as facilities in the design of a maritime interpretive centre.

At the Northern end of the courtyard there was a thirty-foot high lookout tower that housed a permanently lit lantern to assist sailors whilst navigating the Menai Straits in adverse weather. On the face of the Southern wall of the tower there was an intriguing vertical sundial, the like of which I had never seen. To the left of the tower base we found the old garrison bakery which I noted had had the interior of the oven filled with concrete for some reason. To the right of the tower was the powder room, which housed large wooden chests that were lead lined and used to hold the black powder (Gunpowder) for the fort's beautifully maintained cannons.

There was an archway at the base of the lookout tower with a flight of wide steps leading up to the main North facing cannon battery that was strategically placed to overlook the Menai Straits and the Island of Anglesey.

The view from inside Belan's lookout tower was truly breathtaking. To the East the Snowdonia range of mountains stretched as far as the eye could see, their peaks capped with snow. To the Northeast, about five miles farther along the Menai Straits, the towers of Caernarfon Castle could clearly be seen. To the South there was a causeway that flooded at high tide causing the fort to become a small island. Two miles beyond the causeway, the derelict runways of an old RAF aerodrome could be seen. RAF Llandwrog had been constructed during the early stages of the 1939-45 war, and the remains of one or two old gun emplacements were just visible, partly hidden amongst the extensive range of sand dunes to the North West of the airfield.. Finally, to the West of the fort there were fine views of Caernarfon Bay, Llanddwyn Island and the Southern coast of Anglesey.

Carol and I were stunned by the silent tranquillity of the place. Only the lapping of waves on the beach at the base of the ramparts, and the occasional cry from seagulls that glided peacefully overhead could be heard.

A narrow tunnelled path passing through the fort's huge outer wall at the Northeast corner of the courtyard, led to a small Postern Gate. On the far side of the gate there was a sizeable mowed green with three huge cannons strategically positioned to overlook the narrow entrance of the Menai Straits.

At the Eastern extremity of the green, a ten foot high stone wall with iron-clad entrance gates surrounded the fort docks. Passing through the gates we entered the dockyard to discover yet another vista of bygone days. From the moment we arrived it had been like stepping into the past and finding ourselves back in the eighteenth century. I learned later from documents that I uncovered in the Caernarfon Town Archives, that this wonderful old dockyard owed its existence to the youthful exuberance of the 2nd Baron Newborough who added it to the forts adroitness in 1824. The actual harbour was 150 metres long and 30 metres wide. It was a tidal dock that dried out completely at low tide, and at high tide the water was approximately 2 fathoms deep.

There were many very interesting examples of how the dockyard operated in the 1800s. For instance in the North Western corner of the yard there was a Chain Burning Stores which was still fully operational and used to burn the rust from ships anchor chains and coat them with pitch, bringing them up to a standard that was as good as new. I found out later that this was the only one of its kind in the world still in use. In the opposite corner of the yard stood a twenty feet high, hand operated crane, geared to lift several tons.

Terraced buildings along three sides of the dockyard consisted of three large boatsheds, a dock cottage, a carpenter's workshop, and a beautiful old Forge in full working order. The South Eastern end of the dock opened out on to the Menai Straits, and at the opposite end was another line of cottage type buildings that included the dock office and other rooms that were full of maritime paraphernalia. The three large boathouses mentioned above were filled with interesting and highly valuable objects from the past. There was also a considerable amount of junk that needed sorting out. There were several interestingly constructed rowing boats and a very valuable punt gun in one of the boatsheds. A beautiful old yacht named "The Ladies Boat" was almost hidden from view by marker buoys of all shapes and colours, anchors, fenders, lots of coiled rope, hundreds of cannon balls, and an old Victorian Dog Cart.

The main boatshed contained a carved and beautifully painted stern-board preserved from the wreckage of an old galleon. A really valuable forty foot clinker built paddle steamer, complete with its brass boiler and fully serviceable steam engine occupied the centre of another boatshed.

It was exciting to discover all these fascinating relics from the past, they must have been worth million's of pounds, and were just waiting to be sorted out, properly protected and presented in an atmosphere of "times past" for the general public to enjoy and admire. I could hardly wait to get started on my new, exciting job.

Having taken a good look at this unique fort with its inimitable dockyard, I realised more than ever that I had undertaken one of the most interesting and challenging tasks I could wish for. It would be a mammoth task, but for me it was indeed a dream job.

I presume my predecessor, the naval captain, had been selected for the job because of his connections with the Royal Navy. No doubt the fact that Lord Newborough himself had been a Naval Officer during world war two also had some bearing on the final decision to employ the Captain in the multifaceted position of designer, development manager and custodian of the Belan Fort project. Probably the reason it had all gone so wrong for him amounted to the fact that he was incapable of imaginative thinking. I was informed that he had confined himself to his quarters for twenty-six weeks and done precisely nothing.

The original plan had been for the fort to be opened to the public as an interpretive centre during the Whitson holidays at the end of May 1977, which gave the Captain just over a year to have the project up and running. In fact six months had past and absolutely nothing at all had been done.

The man's inability to come up with any acceptable ideas for sympathetically transforming the fort from the historic home of the Newborough family into a first class tourist attraction without losing the existing charm and wonderful atmosphere of the place, obviously put the lid on it for the poor chap, and he had to leave.

The problem that I inherited from the situation as it now stood was humongous, because the Trustees still wanted Belan to be ready for opening to the general public on the date originally planned, which only gave me six months, less than half the time allocated to my predecessor, to get everything done from scratch.

In all fairness the Board of Trustees asked me if I thought that I could complete the task in six months. I said that providing there were no lengthy hold-ups with policy decisions, I was sure I could complete the task on time. With that the trustees gave me a very generous budget to accomplish the task, and I was guaranteed that I would not encounter any interference with my work whatsoever.

There was indeed much to be done in the next twenty-four weeks. Having converted one of the small rooms in the courtyard into a two sectioned office, Carol and I got cracking on the very demanding and most interesting task of converting Belan Fort into a Maritime Interpretative Centre.

There followed much burning of the midnight oil. I started by preparing a large 'countdown' graph in the form of a wall chart that showed in detail all the work that had to be carried out and the time allocated to each task, starting with day one and ending on the planned opening date in May 1977.

As far as I was concerned it was imperative not to lose the existing charm of Belan by the use of modern-day configurations. I concentrated on keeping my designs in sympathy with the charming structures that existed. Within the first couple of weeks I had drawn up detailed plans for converting the interior of two sections of the courtyard buildings into an old fashioned teashop and a separate Welsh Crafts gift shop.

Costs for everything obviously had to be worked out in detail. By assuming an entrance fee structure and estimating a nominal visitor potential, I prepared an initial budget and cash flow chart for the first twelve months together with a forward budget and predicted cash flow over the next five years. I submitted everything to the Trustees who immediately gave me permission to get the work underway.

Fortunately Belan had escaped the restrictions of a listed property, so the only legal obligation that I had to address before work could start, was to contact the planning authorities in Caernarfon and obtain their permission for Belan's change of use. Surprisingly permission was granted almost immediately without any setbacks.

Having sorted out the contents of the boat sheds, it was back to the drawing board to design the layout of the museums. Again I strove to retained the character of the buildings and preserve the old world atmosphere that existed. As many of the exhibits were very valuable, I designed a ships type barrier rail with an integral alarm system that would activate if anyone crossed over into the exhibit areas.

It was essential to get all the structural work completed by skilled craftsmen, so I contacted the National Trust and obtained the names of companies that had been employed to carry out work on historic buildings. Eventually I decided to employ Sadlers Bros to carry out the work. I couldn't have made a better choice, they turned out to be really first class craftsmen whose work was beyond reproach.

As well as providing an old fashioned tea room for visitors to the Fort, Carol planned to cater for larger corporate functions. Two of the existing rooms in the courtyard buildings were conveniently situated so that one could be converted into a cosy little tea shop, and the other larger room could be used for the occasional function. Both rooms adjoined the original kitchen.

Whilst the interior of the tea room and kitchen were under construction, I designed a bar-like serving counter using beautiful old carved panels and oak pillars that were in keeping with the age of the fort. The kitchen itself was a very quaint part of the fort because it had originally been built inside a larger room. The inner room had a multi-pane bay window with old "bulls-eye" type glass that overlooked the inside of the larger outer room thus conveying a nostalgic atmosphere of past times.

Carol was brilliant, we worked as a team, there was no way that I could have completed these tasks without her. She carried out all the secretarial duties, arranged all the on-site meetings, catered for the Trustees when they stayed over during their monthly meetings, and kept me going with endless cups of hot tea whilst I was busy designing the layouts and supervising the work being carried out. Carol had her own ideas on how she wanted the tea rooms to look, and we often worked well into the night discussing ideas that would enhance the elegance of the fort. When the gift shop and tea rooms had been completed, Carol went to great lengths in order to obtain exactly the right furniture to compliment the old fashioned beauty of the tea room.

We did, however, encounter one unexpected setback, more of a shock really. It occurred about eleven thirty one night in early December, no more than a few weeks after our arrival at Belan. Outside it was a jet black night with a storm brewing up from the Northeast. We were enjoying a cosy evening in front of a log fire that crackled away in the homely atmosphere of our quarters. Whilst the wind howled around the courtyard, we recalled Lord Newborough's warning that sometimes the winds off the sea at Belan could be quite scary. So, with that in mind, we ignored the blustering storm and settled down to watch the TV.

After a while the wind increased to a thunderous rumble and kicked up such a hullabaloo around the fort that it was impossible to hear the television. I said to Carol that I had better take a look outside and see if the gale was causing any damage.

The switches that controlled the lights in the courtyard were situated by the main entrance inside our house, and as I went to switch them on I noticed that water was pouring in under our door. Before risking opening the door I decided to play safe and take a look through the hall window. At first it was difficult to see because the lights were shrouded in a swirling mist. Then it became frighteningly clear, the courtyard was completely covered by the sea. Foam sprayed everywhere whilst small white crested waves lapped against our front door. I shouted to Carol to come and take a look. For a few seconds we stood there speechless. It was nothing short of a nightmare, what the hell do we do now?

The time was close to midnight. I tried to telephone for help but the lines to the fort were down, (mobile phones hadn't been invented). Strangely enough the electricity was still working without so much as a flicker.

We barricaded the bottom of the door as best we could with towelling, cushions and whatever else we could find. Then Carol and I grabbed anything that was light enough to carry and took it up the stairs for safety. Water was still pouring in under the door, so I told Carol to remain up stairs in the house whilst I attempted to find our maintenance man who lived in one of the dock cottages.

Having donned the small amount of rainwear I possessed, I climbed out of the sitting room window, lowered myself into the water and started to wade through about six inches of churning sea water towards the dockyard. Eventually, struggling against a literarily screaming wind, I managed to reach the maintenance man's cottage and banged on the door. But he flatly refused to assist me in getting further help. So the only option left for me was to try and get in touch with Richard Rutherford, who I assumed must have been used to this sort of thing happening at the fort in previous years. But the problem was Richard lived several miles away and the phone lines were down at the fort. With no other alternative I had to attempt the rather hopeless task of starting my car and driving out to get help.

Getting to my car proved to be difficult as part of the supporting walls of the draw-bridge had collapsed which left a short gap between the end of the bridge and the roadway. Eventually I managed to get to the garage which had been built on slightly higher ground and the sea water was only a couple of inches or so deep at that point. The engine started without problems at the first press of the starter button.

Optimistically I drove down the slope into the shallow waves. The wind buffeted against the side of the car and the rain was so fierce that the wipers had little effect. I was expecting the trouble that greeted me when I reached the causeway because it always flooded during a normal high tide, and this certainly wasn't a normal tide. Six foot marker posts were permanently secured along the section of road that flooded to guide vehicles across in daylight if the tide was shallow enough. On reaching the causeway I was greeted by the sight of small waves maliciously thrashing away between the marker posts, with foam spewing from their tops. With dipped headlights I occasionally caught glimpses of the concrete road beneath the waves and guessed the water to be about a foot deep, perhaps just low enough to get across. I decided to give it a go. I edged along the road slowly in first gear, slipping the clutch to keep the engine running at high revs in the hope that it wouldn't stop. Halfway across the causeway it happened…. the engine spluttered and stopped. After one attempt on the starter I realised that the engine was never going to start as things were. Water had probably shorted out the plugs or the distributor, probably both. I had no other choice but to get out of the car. I remembered that I had a can of Quick-Start somewhere in the boot and, as stupid as it seemed, decided to see if I could use it to restart the engine. It was a struggle to stop the door from being torn off it's hinges by the wind which was gusting at great strength from behind the car. It opened with a whack, dragging me out of the car with it. I found myself standing in bloody cold water that was well above my ankles, but somewhat shallower than I had estimated. I had no torch but could see reasonably well by the reflected beam of the headlights. Having retrieved the can of Quick-Start from the boot, the next problem was to hang on to the fiercely vibrating bonnet once it was open. Fortunately there was a small maintenance light that came on automatically when the bonnet was lifted, so I was able to see the engine reasonably clearly. Gripping the shuddering bonnet with one hand I optimistically sprayed the plug leads and the distributor head and anything else that looked electrical with copious amounts of Quick-Start and slammed the bonnet down quickly. I would have betted certain vital parts of my anatomy against the possibility of that engine starting again, and I would have lost them… I pressed the button, and bingo, the engine started instantly and continued running. My guardian Angel must have been at hand! It was nothing short of an absolute miracle. Good old Jaguar, good old Quick-Start, and good old Guardian Angel!

Finally, after a very hairy drive along flooded roads, during which a section of the exhaust system was torn off, I reached the seafront village of Dinas Dinlle and came across a telephone kiosk that was standing in a few inches of sea water with it's door wide open. Unbelievably the telephone receiver, suspended by its cord, was swinging like a yo-yo well outside the kiosk door. By now it was the early hours of the morning. I didn't know exactly where Richard's house was situated but I did have his telephone number. Someone must have been watching over me that night because amazingly the phone actually worked and I was able to make a reverse charge call via the operator to Richard's house. It was gratifying to hear a friendly voice. Obviously Richard was very concerned and said he would bring help and get to the fort as soon as he possibly could.

The tide was receding as I returned along the seafront road on my way back to Belan. I could now see that the road was covered with masses of shingle and small boulders which explained how I lost part of my car's exhaust. By the time I reached the causeway the road was just clear of the water. Carol, bless her heart was still struggling to prevent water from entering the house.

It was a long night. By sunrise the water had receded from the courtyard, dead rats, mice and some half dead creatures were strewn all around the fort. I suddenly realised the danger I had been in the previous evening when I saw about fifty or more large slates from the rooftops sticking at various angles in the courtyard lawn like a knife throwing circus act, and when I went over to the dockyard cottage to see if Mr J and his family were ok, an enormous hole about six feet deep had appeared in the ground where I had previously walked up to my knees in seawater the previous evening. This huge cavity was caused when part of the path outside the dock cottages collapsed into the main sewer sometime after I passed over it.

Both Carol and I were convinced that flooding must have occurred at the fort in previous years. But I was assured by everyone that this genuinely was the first time that the sea had encroached into the fort during the 200 years of its existence. I was going to write to the manufactures of Quick-Start praising the efficiency of their product, but somehow I didn't get round to it.

Most evenings I studied maritime books about the history of sea battles during the napoleonic wars. Impressed by an illustration that depicted the dire circumstances in which the crew of a galleon ate, slept, and fought, I decided to build a full scale replica of part of a gun deck that would simulate those terrible conditions in which men were expected to work. I discussed my idea with our builder Mr Sadler. He was very interested and asked me to prepare detailed scale drawings of a cutaway version of the gun deck so that his team of skilled carpenters, who were already working at Belan, could construct the display in one of the boatshed museums.

They produced a brilliant full scale model and I installed two of the fort's medium sized cannons onto the gun-deck together with a small table, a powder keg and the ram rods used for loading the cannons. With the aid of one of my books I rigged the cannons myself and had special equipment installed so that visitors could hear a simulation of a galleon sea battle by pressing a button mounted on a stand in front of the diorama.

I had to have all the notices describing the various exhibits colour coded and written in both Welsh and English. It was very important that the description written in Welsh, being the first language in North Wales, always appeared above the English version. Caernarfon Council's Translation Unit wrote out the Welsh version of the notices for me so that I could send them off to be engraved onto two-toned boards. This was quite successful with one exception. A few weeks after we had opened the fort to the general public, I was told by one of our welsh speaking visitors that six of our "**Keep off the grass**" signs erected around the lawns in the courtyard, had been translated into Welsh that read "**Stay out of the hay**".

All the other exhibits were displayed neatly throughout the boat sheds, each with a full explanation of its use and approximate age. I had discovered a giant sized replica of a catapult, that must have weighed several tons, in the corner of one of the boatsheds. The original catapults of this design were made to hurl huge rocks at the walls of castles in order to break them down and gain entry. I discovered however that this particular catapult was made in 1904 by Sir Ralph Payne-Gallway to win a bet with the Hon Frederick Wynn, saying he could hurl a 6lb stone clean across the mouth of the Menai Straits. Although the catapult was on wheels, we found that it was virtually impossible to move as the boatshed floors were made up of thousands of cobbles cemented into the ground, and the wheels of the catapult would not roll over them. So we repainted the catapult where it stood and left it there.

The formidable punt gun was also presented to Frederick Wynn by Sir Ralph as a gift together with a horse-drawn carriage. The punt gun itself was like a long narrow cannon about seven feet in length, with a muzzle aperture 6" in diameter. It was mounted on the flat deck of a vessel similar to a normal punt. Fort records described an occasion when the gun killed 140 ducks with a single shot whilst hunting on the nearby Foryd Bay.

I could find no records at all of how the dog cart arrived at Belan.

Carol and I spent a day at the Craft Trade Fair in Llandudno and placed orders for items to be sold in the Fort Gift Shop. We also placed a significant order with the famous Portmeirion Potteries. North Wales has hundreds of small businesses manufacturing a wide range of goods especially for the tourist trade, and Carol ordered a wide variety of these products to sell in our gift shop.

I thought it sounded better if the name of Belan Fort was reversed to Fort Belan and, with the Trustees permission, I re-registered the operating company under the new name. Long before the fort was due to open I liased with the press so that various items of interest could appear in the local newspapers about the fort being prepared to open its doors to the public. These short news items attracted a lot of attention from the local trade of commerce as well as local individuals, and we were approached by several people who were interested in promoting their own businesses within the fort complex.

Mr Potts, a very skilled engineer now retired, contacted me to ask if we would be interested in him setting up his miniature railway on Belan land so that he could offer short steam train rides around the sand dunes near to the fort. I thought this was an excellent idea that would certainly be a popular added attraction. Having obtained permission for this from the Trustees, approximately two miles of railway track was laid and the miniature railway was up and running profitably by our second year of operation. Also Mr Jack Reaverly, who owned a well known local pottery, contacted me to enquire if he could rent a suitable room within the fort courtyard for him to install a small kiln and potter's wheel. Visitors to the fort could then be given the opportunity of turning a pot for themselves. He would then fire the pot for them and send it by post to their home address. This seemed to be an excellent idea which was ultimately brought to fruition and operated very successfully. A third person who ran an antique book business in Caernarfon, said he would be very interested in renting premises for the purposes of selling maritime associated books. So we fixed him up with a small room close to the museums in the dockyard.

With the help of a local printer we prepared our first glossy brochure. "Welcome to Fort Belan". It had to be printed in both Welsh and English. But the most difficult problem was to chose which of the many beautiful photographs of Belan to include.

Carol advertised in "The Lady" magazine for seasonal staff to work in the gift shop and the tea room. I also needed to employ reliable and trustworthy staff to sell entrance tickets and be on security duty at the main entrance gates situated at the far end of the two mile drive to Fort Belan.

There were of course hundreds of other jobs to do. All the exhibits were carefully prepared and set up in the museums, plans had to be drawn and submitted to the planning authorities for the construction of bus and car parking areas etc. Finally we had everything set up and ready for opening to the general public on the originally planned date, the 1st June 1977.

On the day of opening, the Fort was crammed with visitors. Also the press, and local TV were present when the owner, The Hon Robert Wynn flew in by helicopter and landed on the green to officially open the fort. It was a great day. Carol and I received congratulations from Lord Newborough and the Trustees for all the hard work we had put in to the design and preparation of various facilities and most of all for managing to open the fort in time for the 1977 tourist season.

The first season was very successful with over 20,000 visitors to the fort. Carol and I enjoyed working and living at Belan immensely, in fact we adored the place. During the tourist season we worked seven days a week. Carol and her staff of five young ladies, most of them students on summer vacation from Bangor University, worked extremely hard. The girls were given full board and lived in specially prepared staff rooms situated on the upper floor over the tea room. They were an excellent team that enjoyed working together and loved living in the fort.

In addition to generally overseeing the fort's maintenance and smooth operation, I spent every spare minute thinking up and preparing new projects for the following year. Fortunately I was able to leave the daily running of the tea room and the gift shop including all the ordering of supplies etc. to Carol's valuable expertise. She had a natural way with people, and when necessary she could encourage her staff to work diabolical hours without the slightest grumble from anyone. In fact everybody that worked at Fort Belan seemed to be happy and loved working with Carol as their boss.

I applied to the Ministry of Defence for permission to fire the three large cannons, 2x 32lb & 1x 24lb, situated on the green between the main fort building and the dockyard. The idea was for this to be carried out as a demonstration firing that would take place at a set time, two days per week, limited to the months of April through to September.

Before a licence could be granted, the first essential was to make sure that the cannons themselves were still in good order and safe to fire. This necessitated the barrels of the three cannons being "non-destructive tested". The work was carried out by a special weapons testing company acting on behalf of the Ministry of Defence. When the cannons had been tested and certified "Safe to Fire", I had to provide a special powder room for the storage of gunpowder which also had to be inspected and approved by the MOD. This was no problem as we were able to use the original Fort Armoury for the purpose. Obviously regulations were very strict and involved having a special lead lined powder chest made and fitted inside a concrete bunker within the store. Other cabinets that would contain timed detonators and coils of fuse wire were housed in the armoury. The door to the explosives room had to be reinforced and secured with two very expensive locks manufactured by Chubb.

The existing wooden bases of the two largest cannons needed to be replaced. Although, from their general outward appearance, the bases looked simple enough to construct, they were in fact very complicated. I prepared 19 "Plan and Elevation" drawings for the wooden components, 10 scale drawings depicting the special metal components, and a further twelve detailed "General Assembly" drawings. Also eight new wheels had to be made from hardwood and fitted to newly made axles by means of metal axle pins.

Once again I gave the construction work to Saddler and Sons who constructed everything in their workshops in Shrewsbury. Several weeks later Mr Saddler's men arrived at Belan with the bases and a large crane. I was delighted to see that the huge cannon barrels, that weighed several tons each, fitted perfectly into their new bases.

Obviously, if the cannons were to be fired in front of the general public, I would have to obtain a licence from the Ministry of Defence to actually fire them.

The MOD inspector informed me, that because of possible danger to the public, I would not be allowed to fire the cannons in the normal way by lighting a fuse at the breech. Instead I would have to find a method of using detonators to ignite the gunpowder from a safe distance.

I decided to consult Lord Newborough, himself a retired naval officer and a great character who was renowned for firing cannons, both legally and illegally!

Lord Newborough was a very uncompromising individual who stood little nonsense from anyone. I remember during my first couple of days at Fort Belan, seeing my immediate boss, The Hon Robert Wynn, talking to a man dressed in a scruffy old raincoat with a flat cap on the back of his head. The man was up to is eyes in muck rodding out the sewer drains in the fort courtyard. Our resident maintenance man, who had previously been given instructions to rod the drains, was nowhere to be seen. So I walked over to see what was going on, thinking the man rodding the drains was a council worker. I soon realised that the elderly gentleman in the flat cap and filthy overalls was no less than The Hon Robert Wynn's father, Lord Newborough himself.

On another occasion I had given Mr J the job of rubbing down and painting the window frames of the dock cottages. A couple of days later when I set out to see how the work was progressing, I discovered that the work hadn't even been started, and there was no sign of the man anywhere. Eventually I found him outside the main gates of the fort polishing Robert Wynn's car. It soon became clear that my earlier assessment of this man being useless and a bit of a creep, was spot-on, and I was surprised to learn that he had been employed by my predecessor, the Naval Captain, without producing any references.

Anyway, to get back to the firing of cannons. Obviously it was illegal to fire real cannon balls willy-nilly throughout the countryside, so I consulted Lord Newborough for advice on how to prepare and fire cannons for demonstration purposes. He showed me how to make special cannon balls from the lengths of thick tar-coated rope that he had stored in the fort's powder room. They had to be exactly the right size to form a good compression when rammed into the muzzle of the cannon. Obviously one had to be particularly careful when handling gunpowder in reasonably large quantities. For demonstration purposes his Lordship recommended I should use three pounds in weight of black powder for each charge. The amount had to be weighed out precisely and carefully poured into a clear plastic freezer bag that contained one of the timed electrical detonators. The bag was sealed with special tape and gently pushed down the muzzle of the cannon making sure that the two leads from the detonator were twisted together and long enough to remain protruding from the muzzle. Next he placed the tight fitting rope cannon ball into the muzzle and using the cannon's ramrod, he rammed the ball hard down onto the charge, ensuring that the wires from the detonator remained exposed at the muzzle. A suitable length of fuse wire (About twenty metres) was attached to the now separated detonator wires and reeled out. When ready to fire the extended fuse wires were simply connected to the positive and negative terminals of a six volt battery which resulted in a mighty explosion that could be heard for miles around.

Having been taught how to do this with maximum safety by his Lordship, I was checked out by a MOD inspector, and after all the safety regulations concerning the storing of black powder and detonators was met, I was issued with the much coveted "Licence to Fire Heavy Duty Ships Cannons".

From then on I fired the cannons as a demonstration to the tourists that visited the fort every Wednesday and Sunday at 3pm throughout the summer season. When fired, the guns went off with such a tremendous explosion that we received dozens of irate calls from people who lived as far as five miles away on the Island of Anglesey, complaining that their windows and doors vibrated violently.

The most dangerous problem for me personally was if one of the detonators failed to go off, leaving three pounds of compressed gunpowder with a live detonator inside the cannon that had to be removed. On the odd occasion when this did happen, I always waited for a safety period of at least five minutes before attempting to extract the charge. Then, standing or rather trembling directly in front of the cannon, I had to remove the ball and charge together with the faulty fuse by means of a long pole with a large metal "corkscrew type" extractor on one end. If the charge had gone off whilst being removed, I would have been blown arse over head across the Menai Straits without touching the water!

These things had their funnier moments of course. I remember one weekend when my boss The Hon Robert Wynn who occasionally fired the cannons when he visited the fort, said he would like to give a short demonstration to the visitors about the dangers of gunpowder. He addressed the audience through a loud-hailer and started by explaining that gunpowder would only explode if compressed into a container of some sort. To prove his point he poured a somewhat generous amount of black powder onto a tin plate, and with the words...

'It will only burn with a gentle pink flame.'

He put a match to the gunpowder. There was a blinding flash and Robert disappeared behind a thick cloud of smoke, seconds later he emerge spluttering and coughing, his face totally blackened. A forced grin revealed brilliant white teeth as turned to me and said under his breath...

'Have I lost my eyebrows?'

The highly amused crowd of on-lookers gave Robert a rousing cheer which didn't go down too well, he looked at me indignantly and snapped...

'Carry on Raymond....F... the cannons.'

At the end of each season the British Tourist Board presented a 'Project of the Year Award' to the most interesting new tourist attraction. Entrance was open to any tourist related businesses, but was restricted to first time projects only.

I prepared a detailed dossier that included the history of Belan, information about the fort and its museums, the dock, the old forge and chain burning store, details about the history of the cannons and our firing demonstrations. I also included many pages of coloured photographs and a copy of our 1977 brochure together with copies of all the press cuttings concerning the initial opening of Fort Belan as a tourist attraction. The whole lot was parcelled up and sent off to the British Tourist Board as our entry for the 1977 awards. Some weeks later I received a letter from the Tourist Board to say that although we had not won the main award, they considered our project to be outstanding and had decided to award Fort Belan a special "Certificate of Commendation". My boss Robert Wynn kindly suggested that I should receive the award at the presentations to be held at the Tourist Board offices in London. But Fort Belan belonged to Robert and I insisted that he was the rightful person to receive the award. Needless to say our Trustees were delighted. Robert was a great man to work for, I had great respect for him, and we got along extremely well.

My flying licences were still all current, so after our first successful season at the fort, I decided to pop over to RAF Mona where the North Wales Flying Club operated, and hire an aeroplane to take Carol up for an aerial view of the Fort. The visit turned out to be quite amusing.

The impressive airfield was in current use by the Airforce as a satellite of RAF Valley. The North Wales Flying Club operated from a small hut on the airfield and only flew at weekends.

A very polite young man at the reception desk asked if he could help me. I said that I would like to join the club and hire one of the club's aeroplanes for an hour. The young man looked at me suspiciously. He enquired where I had been flying previously and asked to see my licence and logbook. Having produced the items requested the young man stared at them for a while then disappeared into another room with 'Director' clearly marked on the door.

Minutes later I was sitting in the director's office drinking a cup of tea and being asked by a very pleasant middle aged gentleman if I would be interested in becoming the Chief Flying Instructor of the North Wales Flying Club on a part time basis. The director, a retired policeman, told me that he was very keen to see the general flying standard of the club upgraded to attain CAA short course approval.

I was a little reluctant at first, but having gained permission from the Hon Robert Wynn, I agreed to act as their CFI at weekends during the winter months only.

I telephoned Peter Bond head of aircrew licensing At the CAA and arranged to have my examiners rating transferred to Mona so that I could test a backlog of four students who had been waiting to take their flight tests and written examinations for some time.

The tests turned out to be very disappointing, all of them lacked a basic standard of airmanship. Their general flying was atrocious. None of them had learned the aircraft checks or carried a check list. None of them were capable of carrying out a reasonable short field landing, or knew how to recover from fully developed spin. Only one chap passed the written part of his examinations, sadly the other three came nowhere near.

It was the old story all over again. I also found out that some of the flying instruction had been carried out illegally by members of the club's so called "Management Committee" who were not flying instructors.

I said what had to be said and immediately became very unpopular. There was much muttering in the Welsh language that unfortunately I didn't understand. The students that had failed their flying tests complained bitterly to the committee Chairman and refused to fly with me again. So, with only seven hours fifty minutes instructional flying time at Mona, I resigned as their part time CFI and had no more to do with their club.

Going back to the first few weeks we lived in the Fort, Carol and I decided to buy a little dog. An advertisement in the local paper offered puppies free to a good home. The house where the puppies were living was way up in the mountains, and when we arrived to select a puppy there was only one left, a cracking little female Labrador/Sheepdog cross. It was easy to see why no one else had chosen her. She looked very ill, her little eyes were watery and she was not at all steady on her paws. It was love at first sight. That little puppy may have been the last one of the litter to be chosen for a new home, but I can assure you that she turned out to be the most intelligent and loving little creature ever to be created on God's earth.

We promised the owners that we would give her a good home and that she would be much loved. It was obvious that she was very ill so we immediately had her checked out by the local vet. He told us that she was suffering from Distemper and was in very poor health. We nursed her through her illness and "Kim" grew up to be the most lovable little dog anyone could wish for.

Kimbo, as she was frequently called, had a wonderful life at Belan. She was allowed to roam free throughout the eight hundred acres of land belonging to the fort and never once wore a collar during the whole sixteen years of her life.

I've owned several dogs over the years, loved them all, but none were as intelligent as Kim. She spent every day playing on her own in the two mile stretch of sand dunes surrounding the fort and frequently swam in the Menai Straits.

Her favourite pastime was to come out with me in the car to shoot rabbits at night. Amazingly Kim could retrieve from day one. It was as if she had been trained for years, yet I never once had told her to 'fetch' or 'drop', it just came naturally. She always sat next to me in the front of the car looking out for a rabbit to be caught in the headlights. Invariably Kim spotted a rabbit long before I did, she would thrust her nose forward on the windscreen as if to say 'There's one dad.'

I was licensed to use firearms on the eight hundred acres of Belan land, and carried a twenty-two calibre bolt action rifle with a telescopic sight for the job. The second I lifted that gun up to take aim, Kimbo would stop panting and hold her breath until I fired the shot, then she would leap out through the open window of the car to retrieve the rabbit, sometimes two or three hundred yards away, proudly bringing it straight back to the car door and dropping it at my feet. The funny thing was if I missed the target. She would remain in her seat and glare at me as if to say 'What the hell are you doing?'

Another remarkable thing about Kim was her sense of timing. Every Wednesday and Sunday she somehow knew it was cannon firing day. At five minutes before the cannons were due to be fired, she would come bounding in over the drawbridge and stay close at Carol's feet until cannon firing was over. Then off she would go to play in the sand dunes again.

Kim also loved to play "hide and seek" inside the fort. Carol only had to say, 'do you want to play hide and seek,' and she would sit down immediately with her ears pricked up, whilst I went off to hide and Carol counted up to ten, then, without another word from Carol, she would scamper off to find me. I could hide anywhere in the fort but Kim would always sniff me out. It was so funny, I could hear her getting nearer and nearer, nervously peering round corners and behind doors waiting for me to jump out. Then when she found me she would make a fuss of me and dash back to Carol to begin the game all over again. I adored that dog, there must be a heaven for such lovely creatures.

Before the fort had completed its first year as a tourist attraction. my attention naturally turned to the old RAF Llandwrog Airfield which was an inclusive part of the land belonging to the fort.

I discovered that one of the old tarmac runways was still serviceable, although not in a very good condition. So the idea came to me that during the summer months we could offer pleasure flights over Snowdonia to tourists when they visited Fort Belan.

There were of course major setbacks to this idea that somehow would have to be overcome before we could legally operate an aeroplane for the purposes of carrying fare paying passengers. The main one being the aircraft we used would have to be owned by a commercial operator that held an Air Operators Certificate (OAC) and officially based at a CAA licensed Airfield. Llandwrog was far from becoming a licensed airfield and Belan didn't own an aeroplane of any description.

But where there's a will there's a way. I soon discovered that our parent company Glynllifon Estates, had already leased the disused airfield to Keenair Services of Liverpool for use as a satellite landing strip which they hardly ever used. This made me think….Maybe I could come to some amicable arrangement with Keenair Services.

In order to carry out pleasure-flying the aircraft used had to be operated under the jurisdiction of an approved company that provided mandatory maintenance services, and the aircraft type used for pleasure-flying would have to be specified in the company's Operations Manual. Also a suitably

627

qualified commercial pilot with the aircraft type endorsed on his licence had to be named in the company's ops manual.

I knew that Keenair Services were operating commercially from Liverpool Airport and asked our Trustees if they would permit me to approach Keenair's Chairman with a view to discussing the possibilities of a joint agreement between our two businesses in order to provide pleasure-flying at our airfield. The Chairman of our Trustees agreed that this would be a good idea if I could pull it off. But as it turned out, it wasn't as easy as I thought it would be.

Keenair's Chairman, Mr Jim Keen was very mindful of the fact that I had been a commercial pilot and flying instructor for many years and that I was also reasonably well known for developing the British Schools of Flying. I'm sure Jim thought that Glynllifon Estates had employed me to remove Keenair Services from Llandwrog and take over the development of the airfield for Lord Newborough. I had great difficulty in convincing Jim that this was not the case, and we could work together without it having the slightest effect on his use of Llandwrog Airfield. Also he could make a significant amount of money.

The deal I put to Jim was this. Keenair could provide the aeroplane, probably a Cherokee 180 or a Cessna 172, plus the fuel, and I would provide a commercial pilot. The hourly rate Keenair Services would charge Belan for the aircraft would be twice the hourly rate he charged for flying training, and I would fly the aircraft as a commercial pilot free of charge. As Liverpool Airport was obviously the licensed base for all Keenair's aircraft, and his fully licensed maintenance unit was also based there, this would overcome the problem of Llandwrog not having a maintenance unit or being a licensed airfield. We were of course in the 1970s and legislation has changed considerably since those days. In order to do this legally of course, I would have to become one of the named pilots in Keenair's Operations Manual and Llandwrog Airfield would also have to appear in his flight Operations Manual as an authorised satellite for the purpose of pleasure flight operations.

This arrangement meant that the aircraft used for pleasure-flying would make Jim Keen twice as much money than it would if it were used as one of his many training aircraft, and he would not have to pay me as the pilot. Therefore as the saying goes, the idea was watertight and potentially very profitable.

In the end Jim overcame his suspicions about me and agreed to my proposals. By the time we had made all the necessary arrangements it was almost the end of the 1977 season. In fact we only flew for twelve days using G-AVGK a Cherokee 180. But in that short time I carried out 144 flights, carried 432 passengers and both the directors of Keenair Services and the Trustees of Fort Belan were thrilled with the results.

Unfortunately there was one very unpleasant incident that occurred a short time after the fort had been opened to the public. The resident maintenance man finally overstepped the mark and was caught collecting entrance money from tourists who arrived by boat and not handing the money over to his employer. He was interviewed by me in the presence of my boss and given instant dismissal. He became very aggressive, threatening me, the Hon Robert Wynn and Lord Newborough's land agent Richard Rutherford with violence. He refused to leave the cottage which went with the job. The electricity to the premises was eventually cut off by the electricity board. He attempted to re-connect it himself which resulted in his wife being electrocuted when she tried to switch the cooker on. A few days after that he frightened me to death when he purposely fired his shot gun very close to my head one night in the pitch dark just outside my quarters where he had waited for me. This resulted in the police confiscating his guns. A court case ensued and it turned out that the man had several previous convictions for robbery and causing grievous bodily harm. All this made me wonder why my predecessor had taken him on at Belan without insisting on references of any kind.

I interviewed, and finally took on an excellent fellow who was experienced in all aspects of the building trade and had once worked in his father's building business. He had first class references, and ultimately turned out to be a very skilled craftsman and a great friend.

The pleasure-flying operation proved to be financially sound, although it was totally different to the sort of flying I was used to. The scenery in North Wales was beautiful. I never tired of flying over the mountains and castles, but having spent most of my flying career training student pilots, I soon found that carrying pleasure flight passengers was a totally different kettle of fish!

The Cherokee only had three passenger seats, one of them being the seat next to the pilot, which meant that passengers sitting in the front had a full set of controls facing them. An arrangement that almost proved to be fatal on more than one occasion.

I was carrying two small boys in the rear seats of the aeroplane whilst their father sat in the front next to me. Having made sure that all my passengers were safely strapped in, we were taxying out to the runway holding-point when I became a little worried about the advice the father was giving to his children...

'Now then lads, when we take-off hold on very tight, keep your eyes closed and don't look down.'

The children had been quite excited, but were obviously a little perturbed by their dad's remarks. He then went on to say...

'If you don't like it the pilot will bring you down straight away, don't worry boys lots of children get frightened.'

The children had obviously been looking forward to their first flight in an aeroplane, but their dad was beginning to put the fear of God into them. I assured the lads that there was nothing at all to be afraid of, but their father never stopped spouting out ridiculous advice to his children. It was quite obvious to me that he was the one that was getting worked up about flying, and his constant yacking was upsetting the children.

As soon as we lined up on the runway, the man became very quiet and I noticed that he was gripping the sides of his seat. I told him to relax and assured everyone that it was best to look out and enjoy the scenery.

We had just taken off and were low over the sea when the man let out a frightful scream and grabbed the control column in front of him with both hands. He was trying to pull back on the control column with all his strength. I tried to push against him, at the same time realising that if he suddenly let go we would be into the sea. I had seconds to make up my mind what to do whilst the man continued screaming his head off. There was only one action I could take. Gripping the wheel with my left hand and jamming my left elbow into my chest so that it couldn't be forced back any further, I hit the man as hard as I could with a backward swipe of my clenched right fist. The punch unfortunately caught him in the neck. He immediately let go of the controls, gurgled a bit and stopped screaming, then he slumped over to the right hand side of the cockpit.

As I banked the aircraft over to make an emergency landing, I could hear one the children in the back crying, no doubt terrified by their father's screams. With the aircraft safely back on the ground, I shut the engine down and released the safety lock of my passengers door. I apologised to the man for hitting him and offered to refund his money, but he refused to speak to me. He quickly left the aeroplane and hurried off to his car, his children following close behind sobbing their hearts out. Before I could get out of the aircraft, the man had driven off with his children. My ground assistant said that he had noticed that the man was upset, and tried to speak to him, but he was ignored completely. Expecting to hear more and possibly be involved in a court case, I telephoned the police about the incident. They sent an officer over to the airfield later to take a statement from me. But luckily no further action taken.

After that incident I never felt happy about carrying passengers in the front of an aircraft with dual controls. Many years previously I had experienced a student freezing on the controls during a spinning lesson. But he was a training pilot and instantly responded to my abrasive commands.

There was one other serious incident that occurred during a pleasure flight some years later.

A car drew up with a man, his wife and a small baby on board. The person selling the flight tickets said that there would obviously by no charge for the baby, but carrying a baby was their responsibility. The family boarded the aircraft. The mother and her baby sat in the back. The child, who appeared to be about four or five weeks old, was obviously too young to occupy a seat of it's own, and had to be held in its mothers arms.

The husband was safely strapped into the front seat next to me. Everyone seemed to be quite happy until the aircraft left the ground. We were about one hundred feet into the air when there was a bloodcurdling shriek from the back of the aircraft. I guessed the woman had started to panic, so I commenced a gentle turn in order to return and land straight away. The airfield at the time operated a air/ground radio advisory service, so I pressed the transmit button to relay an emergency return to land message. Unfortunately all the controller could hear was the high pitched screams of my passenger and naturally wondered what the hell was going on.

Things then got considerably worse. The woman, who was sitting directly behind her husband, leaned forward, grabbed him round the neck and attempted to pull the poor chap backwards. Now, whilst flying at about three hundred feet, I was doing my best to get the aircraft safely back on the ground as quickly as possible. Suddenly the woman released her grip from her husbands neck, undid her safety belt and caught hold of the locking device in an attempt to open the door. Her poor husband, hampered by the restrictions his own harness, was trying to pull her hand off the door and calm her down.

As we landed on the runway the crash truck drew up alongside the aircraft. The driver had also heard the screams during my attempted radio transmissions and was obviously wondering what he was going to find inside the aeroplane.

When we came to a standstill I turned to look at the woman who was now crying hysterically, but there was neither sign nor sound of the baby. The man hurriedly left the aircraft leaving his wife to scramble out behind him. Both of them totally oblivious of the fact that there was no sign of a baby. The husband remained on the tarmac trying to console his blubbering wife, whilst I, hardly daring to think what had happen to the child, began searching the cockpit. Surely the baby would be crying if it was still in the aeroplane. Suddenly I became aware of a small foot kicking away on the floor from under my seat. The baby was totally silent, it's little eyes wide open staring at me. His mother must have allowed the baby to drop to the floor when she unfastened her safety harness whilst we were still in flight. Presumably the child had rolled forward under my seat when the brakes were applied after the landing.

At that point I felt very sorry for them, but my sorrow soon turned to anger when the husband turned to me and calmly said...

'She gets like this in the car sometimes. We are going to fly off to America soon, so I took her on a pleasure flight to see how she would react to flying.'

I could have murdered the man for not warning me of his wife's potential neurotic behaviour. Fortunately the child was unhurt, and I heard nothing further.

A year or so later a rather unusual incident occurred when I was in the circuit at Caernarfon Airport returning from a thirty-minute pleasure flight over the mountains.

At the time we were using runway 26 on a left-hand circuit. We were down to about 500 ft. and banking left to turn onto the final approach. Suddenly there was an almighty bang that sounded like something striking the side of the cockpit with considerable force.

Having landed and the passengers had disembarked, I examined the left hand side of the fuselage. At first I couldn't see any damage at all. Then, on closer inspection, I discovered a small hole in the fuselage in line with the pilots seat. There appeared to be lead splattered around the hole, and the only conclusion that I could make was that a rifle bullet had struck the aeroplane. I called the police who, with the help of their forensic expert, confirmed that it was a .22 calibre bullet that had struck the aircraft. What remained of the bullet was apparently wedged in a vertical metal strut that was level with the pilot's armrest.

Using a police map of the area, I pointed out the approximate position of the aircraft when I heard the bang. One of the policemen immediately said he had a good idea who it was that fired the shot. They could never prove it of course, because the bullet had been completely shattered, but the chap they had in mind was always complaining about aircraft noise to the police. He also held a firearms certificate, and was licensed to keep a .22 rifle on his property.

I don't know how many times the person concerned had taken a pop-shot at us, but this time he was lucky. I must say it was a bloody good shot. If the bullet had hit the aircraft half an inch fore or aft of the strut, it would have struck me. This was surely another incident that could be credited to my humourless guardian angel!

Keen to find other ways of attracting visitors to Belan, I discovered that there was a very impressive 45ft passenger vessel that offered tourists pleasure trips up and down the Menai Straits from their quayside mooring just outside Caernarfon Castle. I contacted the owner Mr Tony Freeman and asked him if he would be interested in offering a service from Caernarfon Castle to Belan Dock for tourists who wanted to visit the Fort Belan. He was delighted with the idea, and very soon he was bringing boat loads of visitors to the fort.

After a couple of successful seasons, Tony decided to sell the boat and purchase a floating restaurant that was moored near to Caernarfon Castle. He asked me if I would be interested in purchasing the vessel and ultimately operate the cruiser business from our docks at the fort. Obviously this was a matter for the Trustees, so I promised to put the idea to them at the next meeting.

Trustees meetings were always held in one of the beautiful old rooms at Belan that had been converted into a boardroom. The exquisite 30ft. table had been specially made out of several old quay-heading boards that had once been used in the fort docks. The ten magnificent chairs that surrounded the table bore the Newborough coat of arms in full colour, and at one end of the room there was a huge and equally impressive sideboard.

Our Trustees would arrive the evening before the meeting, spending the night in the Fort's many comfortable bedrooms. Ravishing breakfasts prepared by Carol were laid out on silver trays for his Lordship and the Trustees to help themselves when they came down from their rooms in the morning. Myself and Lord Newborough's agent Richard Rutherford also attended the Trustees meetings as advisories. There was always a warm atmosphere at those meetings. To this day I always associate the smell of cigar smoke and pine-logs burning on an open fire with those happy times.

The Trustees agreed in principle to purchasing the boat and I was asked to negotiate a price and prepare an estimated forward cash flow for the operation of the cruiser during the first twelve months of the coming season should we purchase the vessel. Eventually we bought the Menai Cruiser business and set up a separate operating company registered as "Menai Cruises". Both Richard Rutherford and myself became Directors of the new company. The next thing was to employ a Skipper suitably licensed to operate a vessel carrying fare paying passengers. Fortunately this problem was overcome immediately as the existing skipper agreed to work for us on a seasonal basis.

The cruiser weighed thirty tons, this meant that the existing cradle we operated on Fort Belan's main slipway was not robust enough to carry that sort of weight. With the help and considerable expertise of our maintenance man Roy Organ, we constructed a special heavy-duty carriage that would run on the existing rails of the slipway situated on the sea-facing side of the dock cottages.

With the help of as many men as I could muster up at the time, we managed to drive the cruiser onto the partly submerged boat cradle at high tide and commence the gradual process of winching her out of the water. Everything progressed smoothly until the boat was completely out of the water and about halfway up the slipway. Suddenly there was an an ear-splitting crack followed by a loud screeching noise, and thirty tons of cruiser started to roll slowly sideways off the cradle.

Roy immediately slammed on the brakes of the winch. It was a heart stopping moment alright, the two main securing ropes had snapped and there was little we could do other than watch the vessel as it gradually tipped over. Eventually, after lots of creaking and groaning, she came to rest against the rear walls of the dock cottage at an angle of about 30 degrees.

Fortunately the slipway had originally been constructed to carry much narrower boats, and the location of the rails allowed plenty of room for the Belan boats. The Menai Cruiser by comparison had a much larger beam, and therefore was closer to the cottage walls, which turned out to be very fortuitous.

Other than a few minor scratches, no damage was done. It took a couple of back-breaking hours and the use of two large hydraulic jacks to restore the boat to her upright position and secure it once again to the cradle. By the time we had finally hauled her into the boathouse, daylight was slowly melting into the darkness of night.

The addition of male and female Peacocks enhanced the gardens of the fort, although the noise they made first thing in the mornings certainly took some getting used to. We named the birds Henry and Claira. Henry was a beautiful creature, he would strut around the fort courtyard as if he owned the place. Both birds became very tame and soon commenced breeding. During the eight years that she was with us, Claira constructed very rough nests out of a few scattered twigs and invariably laid her eggs in the most precarious of locations. One year the most amazing thing happened.

Claira would disappear for short periods, so we assumed that she had gone off to build a nest and lay her eggs. Most mornings she would turn up in the courtyard to be fed, then slip away unobserved. I tried to locate where she had built her nest but my efforts were unsuccessful.

It was on one of our cannon firing days. I had just completed the cannon firing demonstration, and as usual the explosions had caused quite a lot of excitement amongst the spectators that had gathered on the green, some were laughing, others looked a bit shocked. The extremely loud bangs could be quite frightening, in fact one year we had an elderly lady pass out completely and had to be taken off in an ambulance. Anyway, on this occasion I was in the act of replacing the protective wooden bungs back into the muzzles of the cannons, when I spotted dear old Claira, our female peacock. She was crouched down under the 32-pounder cannon I had just fired. Amazingly she had built her nest between rocks no more than three feet from the muzzle of the cannon. On closer inspection I found that two of the eggs had already hatched out, so she must have been sitting on her nest totally undisturbed during several of our twice weekly cannon firing demonstrations. The deafening noise from those explosions shook the windows of houses miles away on Anglesey, and must have been devastating for that poor bird. The devotion that little Claira had shown to her chicks was truly remarkable.

On the third year we were at Fort Belan I entered into a contract with a riding school so that horse riding could be offered as an additional facility for visitors to the fort. The riding school provided three horses and a young lady riding instructor. There were already beautiful old stables and a tack room at the rear of the courtyard buildings, so we were able to provide stabling and grazing land for the horses.

At the end of the season we offered grazing and stabling facilities for the three horses throughout the winter months. This turned out to be great fun for Carol and myself as the owner of the riding school left two saddles and all the tack so that we could exercise the horses ourselves throughout the five months when the fort was closed to the general public.

There were a couple of embarrassing moments that occurred during the first Winter we looked after the horses. We had been taught to ride by the owners and were reasonably competent up to the "Rising Trot" stage, anything more advanced than that was certainly far too ambitious for me to tackle. However, Carol and I had decided to take the horses out along the sand dunes. We had been out together several times just ambling along through the dunes and along the seafront at a walking pace. The horse that I always rode was named Ginger, and Carol rode a horse named Topper which she promptly renamed Dobbin because he was clumsy and seemed to trip over just about everything that lay in his path. Dobbin was stocky and looked very much like a lovely old carthorse bless him. Ginger on the other hand was more frisky, I always thought he had a mischievous look in his eyes, and he took great delight in frightening me to death. We loved them both very much.

On this particular occasion we were ambling along enjoying ourselves when suddenly a poor little rabbit, obviously suffering from Myxomatosis, ran out from the sand dunes and crashed headlong into a large rusty sheet of corrugated iron that was partly protruding from the sand. The loud bang spooked the horses and they took off straight up an extremely steep sand hill, prancing and kicking like mad bulls. Poor old Carol and I clung on to our horse's necks for dear life until they finally calmed down and came to a standstill. Fortunately for us nobody was around to witness our moment of sheer panic, and after regaining our composure we walked the horses back to the stables.

The second incident occurred some time later. I was all togged up like a toff ready to set off with Carol for another meandering horseback adventure! Due to the leg injuries I sustained in my aeroplane crash years earlier, I could only mount a horse by standing on a stool or a chair. On this occasion I managed to struggle aboard by standing on the low wall that skirted the fort moat. I was making myself comfortable in the saddle when I spotted a couple of trespassers meandering around about hundred yards outside the main gates to the fort. It was the perfect opportunity for me to show off and act like the "Lord of the Manor". Determined to look the part I made sure that my slightly oversize riding hat sat squarely on my head, straightened my back and with an amiable prod on the stirrups Ginger and I set off over the drawbridge and out through the fort gates. Another squeeze on the stirrups brought Ginger to a gentle trot and me to the nervous limits of my riding skills. Over exaggerating the rising bit of the rising trot, I thought: 'this should impress em.' My intentions were to trot up to the intruders and say something like …

'I say you chaps, do you know you're trespassing on my land?'

I should have known better! We were almost up to the trespassers when old Ginger, enjoying the freshness of the morning, decided to sport himself to a bit of a gallop. He dug his hoofs into the turf and took off like a bloody rocket.

Struggling to stay on the horse and retain some air of dignity, I hung on to Ginger's mane with one hand, and streaking past the intruders I managed to raise my hat and shout a very, high pitched 'Good Morning,' before disappearing into the sand hills with my arse taking an uncontrollable hammering from the saddle!

I returned to the fort minutes later white faced and shaken, vowing never to straddle another bloody horse as long as I lived. Carol of course couldn't stop laughing.

'Serves you right' she said, 'that'll stop you from trying to show off.'

I must admit it was easy to get carried away sometimes. Riding horses, firing the cannons, flying around Snowdon, and occasionally taking a trip in the fort's cruiser was rather like enjoying a multi millionaire's lifestyle, without the accompanying bank balance! But I never lost sight of the fact that the job carried with it an enormous amount of responsibility.

I was always looking for new and appropriate ways of marketing the facilities at the fort. Then one morning I received a letter from Chris Jackson, the Managing Director of Colwyn Bay Zoo, asking if I would be interested in forming an advertising consortium to promote ten of the most popular attractions in North Wales. This was a brilliant idea because it meant that the ten most popular attractions in North Wales would hand out leaflets to all their visitors featuring the details of the other nine attractions. In my opinion we couldn't get a more effective means of promoting our businesses to people who were already on holiday in this part of the country.

The idea took off immediately. We called ourselves "North Wales Ten Top Attractions" (TTA), and by the time we went to press our consortium incorporated… Fort Belan (which included the pleasure flights and cruises), Colwyn Bay Zoo, Caernarfon Castle, Llechwedd Slate Mines, Llangollen Canal Museum, Porth Madog Potteries, North Wales Woollen Mills, Portmeirion Village, Bodmin Gardens and the Festiniog Steam Railway. Several other companies tried to join the consortium once we were established. But we kept to the ten attractions that initially agreed to take part.

The ten attractions formed a committee made up of a Director or General Manager from each of the attractions that met once per month to discuss marketing strategy and various promotional ideas, also the consortium re-designed new brochures and hanging cards for the following season. All ten attractions delivered TTA promotional material to the Tourist Information Centres and caravan parks in their area, as well as handing a TTA leaflet to every customer that visited their own attraction, this guaranteed maximum distribution of our advertising throughout North Wales. We also ran schemes offering special discounts to tourists who visited three or more of the TTA.

Each attraction took it in turn to take on the a yearly responsibility as Chairman of the committee. When it was my turn I found that there was a lot more work attached to the job than I ever imagined. The secretarial duties were shared by the offices of Colwyn Bay Zoo and Llechwedd Slate Mines. Records showed that the formation of Ten Top Attractions increased the numbers of visitors to each attraction by over 20%.

One of the magical things about living at Belan was enjoying the sight and sounds of a multitude of bird life. It was wonderful to see the seagulls carrying out their aerial manoeuvres against a backdrop of blue skies and snow crested mountains. I think most pilots have a great affinity with our feathered friends. One can only marvel at them and wish that we could fly with a fraction of their skill.

Occasionally people would bring a sick bird to us at the fort in the hope that we could help them in some way. I will always remember with unbounded affection a young seagull that had fallen sick with suspected Botulism poisoning. I found him one morning on the shores of the Menai Straits just a few yards in front of the fort's main cannon battery. He was very ill and staggering around too weak to fly. I carried him home and made a comfortable nest for him inside a large open-topped box. We named him Jonathon after the character in Richard Bach's book 'Jonathan Livingston Seagull.'

Jonathon had all the symptoms of Botulism, a form of toxin poisoning frequently found in birds and animals. I had come across this vicious form of poisoning previously with seagulls, and unless something is done in the early stages of the illness, the bird soon dies.

I found that the best form of treatment was flush out the birds system.

The method I used was to give the poor creature a teaspoon full of cod liver oil in order to clear the bacteria through his system as quickly as possible. Jonathan was very frail, so in order to administer his medicine I allowed him to peck me, and whilst he was endeavouring to sever my finger, I squirted an eye-dropper full of oil into his mouth. By the end of the second day I could see from the droppings in his home made nest that the oil was beginning to pass through his system. By the end of the third day he became quite hungry and was obviously feeling much better. After a few more days of hand feeding, Jonathan was strong enough to walk around on his own again.

Most of the Herring Gulls I had rescued prior to Jonathan remained aggressive. But for some reason this little chap was totally different. Before long he became much stronger and seemed to be quite content just walking around the courtyard. Eventually Jonathan took to following two or three feet behind me wherever I went within the confines of the fort. In one corner of the fort courtyard there was a small enclosure originally built to house his Lordship's dogs, but no longer in use. The area was completely enclosed by a high stone wall. So Jonathon had the old kennels to himself during the daytime when the fort was open to visitors. He seemed to be happy waddling around in there and never attempted to fly at all. Our little dog Kimbo was never a threat to Jonathan, she wandered around totally ignoring him.

As time went by Jonathon became more and more used to me handling him. For instance, if on occasions I sat him on the kitchen table in our house to feed him one or two tasty morsels, he would always be extremely careful not to peck my hand. Afterwards he liked to nuzzle his little head against my face and drop off to sleep for a few minutes.

He let me examine his 35" wingspan carefully without making the slightest fuss. As far as I could tell there was nothing that would prevent him from flying off whenever he chose to do so. It seemed strange to me that this naturally wild creature never attempted to fly. I tried walking as fast as I could whilst he followed me, but Jonathan merely spread his wings out fully and hopped along to keep up with me without lifting off.

Having taken care of him for a couple of weeks, I thought it was time for Jonathan to return to the wild for his own good, but I needed to get the little chap flying properly first.

Early one morning when there was a light off-sea breeze, I decided to try and get him to fly by launching him into the air from the battlements that overlooked the foreshore. I felt quite sad as this could be the last few moments I would spend with Jonathan and I may never see him again. Worst of all was the realisation that he could crash on the foreshore without making any attempt to fly.

I picked my little friend up holding his folded wings gently against his warm soft body and kissed him on the top of his tiny head, then, pointing him towards the sea, I launched him into the sky as cautiously as I dare. My heart almost stopped as I watched Jonathan drop like a stone. He left it to the very last second before spreading his magnificent wings, then, just skimming the waves, Jonathan headed off gracefully towards the Isle of Anglesey. I watched him for a few seconds with tears in my eyes. Then I made my way slowly back down the steps from the gun battery towards the courtyard. Saddened by the thought of not seeing my little friend again, I instinctively turned to see if he was following me, but of course he wasn't there. Glancing at the empty enclosure where Jonathan had spent so much of his time, I turned into the courtyard and suddenly realised that Jonathan had beaten me to it, he had turned back and was waiting for me on our doorstep. With hands on my hips I towered over the little fellow...

'As much as I love you Johnny old chap, this just won't do.'

Jonathan stayed around for a day or two, then one morning he wasn't there. I looked for him everywhere but he had finally decided to set off into the world on his own again. I searched the skies for him continuously, but although I saw plenty of gulls flying around I knew that none of them was Jonathan.

But the story didn't end there. A couple of weeks later the most bizarre thing happened. I had driven the two miles from the fort to the airfield in order to commence the day's pleasure-flying, and was walking around the aircraft carrying out the external checks, when I noticed two gulls land on the grass a few yards in front of the aeroplane. One of the gulls looked a little wary and remained at a safe distance, whilst the other gull started to walk towards me.

That little waddle with the occasional hop and a flutter was unmistakable. How Jonathan found me at the airfield I'll never know. But there he was, my diminutive little friend had popped over to see me, no doubt to introduce his girlfriend. I didn't attempt to pick him up as I wouldn't want to embarrass him in front of his young lady, that would never do. After strutting around with his head tilted to one side to look up at me with his bright yellow eyes, he waddled back to his little mate and together they took off, circling once just a few feet overhead before climbing away into the distance. There was little doubt I had just had the honour of a wild bird visiting me to say goodbye and thanks for helping me. I hoped he would return sometime, but it was the last time I saw Jonathan.

Mr Don Barnshaw, the gentleman who assisted me and sold the pleasure flight tickets, had seen the seagull many times previously when it was recovering at the fort. He said he would never have believed the bird visited me at the airfield had he not seen it with his own eyes. It was like a wonderful little miracle.

I must just mention a short, but rather funny story about poor old Don Barnshaw. When cars arrived at our caravan, Don's job was to issue tickets to the fort and at the same time try to sell the occupants a pleasure flight. I was sitting quietly in the caravan whilst Don was chatting to a couple of ladies that had just drawn up in their car. All of a sudden I heard a terrorizing scream that obviously came from one of the young ladies. I rushed out to see what had happened and found Don apologising profusely to one of the ladies. Eventually the car screeched off leaving Don looking very embarrassed. Apparently he had leaned into the car window to explain the various flights that were featured on the brochure he was holding, when suddenly his false teeth shot out landing squarely on the woman's lap! Hence the scream!

CHAPTER 56.

Space City.

One of the most important components of my job was to retain tourists interest in the fort by updating existing, or adding new, interesting aspects to the fort's facilities every year.

To my way of thinking, Belan would always be a diminutive but extremely important citadel in a land of huge Castles. As such it would remain the sort of attraction that would be visited by people who were already on holiday in Wales, but I wanted Belan to have something that people would make a special trip to see whether on holiday in or not.

I started assessing the problem by thinking laterally, or as they say "outside the box".

I asked myself the following question...What entity or event would be significant enough to attract visitors in their million's from all over the world? It was quite a problem. It would have to be something really unusual, something out of the ordinary, in fact it would have to be something "*Out of this World*".

Having given the matter considerable thought it occurred to me that there was only one event that would undoubtedly attract the attention of everyone in the world, and that would be an alien spacecraft landing on this planet. I admit it was a ridiculous thought as there was no likelihood of this ever happening. But just for a moment imagine what would occur if that did happen. Apart from world-wide panic, people would flock into the area in their million's. Now, however unlikely, or however stupid the initial idea seemed to be, I had planted a seed in my mind that certainly warranted further interpretation. The question was therefore, how could I link the two main elements, fiction and serious fact, of this scenario to bring extra tourists to Belan?

After a lot of thought I hit on a closely related idea that I was convinced would attract thousands of visitors not only to Belan but to North Wales in general. It would also be an all year attraction as opposed to a seasonal attraction.

My idea was to construct and conceal a huge "Flying Saucer" out of sight in the sand dunes near to Belan. My reasoning was as follows…

Remember it was 1979 when I came up with this idea, and it seemed almost inconceivable that it was only at the beginning of this very same century when Orville Wright achieved man's first flight in an aeroplane, and a mere 66 years later Neil Armstrong stepped out on to the moon's surface. The fact that million's of people throughout the world turned on their television sets to witness the moon-landing as it actually happened, demonstrated the overwhelming public interest in space travel. Believe it or not, in 1979 there was not one scientifically related tourist attraction in the United Kingdom *solely devoted* to man's incredible headway into space travel.

We were in the midst of a scientific revolution, and my idea was to take full advantage of these "greatest-of-all-time" achievements by constructing a facility that would function as a living, growing institution, devoted exclusively to the latest space technology and research. In other words a space museum. Its amenities would be constantly up-dated to display in detail the very latest developments in space flight and astronomical research.

I soon became very enthusiastic about the idea, but before proposing such a project to the Board of Trustees, who on the face of it might think I was totally mad, I needed to carry out a considerable amount of research and prepare a convincing presentation.

My initial idea would be to build a structure that would recount the history of space flight from the first Russian "Sputnik' to the present day, using astronomical and technical exhibits, photographs, and working models.

I kept to my original thought's of constructing a "Flying Saucer" as an appropriate building to house the exhibits. In my opinion the "Saucer" would provide a sound basis for very impressive and striking advertising. Indeed what could be more intriguing than a mysterious silver space craft lurking amongst the sand hills with the mountains of Snowdonia as a backdrop.

I wrote to Sir Patrick Moore, who, as stated in an earlier chapter, I knew from my younger days when I was a member of the British Astronomical

Association. I explained my ideas and asked Patrick for his advice. He kindly invited me to dinner at his home in Selsey where we discussed the matter in great detail. Patrick was very helpful and offered to give me his full support. He also agreed to let us use his name in any forthcoming advertising.

'Its about time this country took a greater interest in the development of space travel,' he said, 'and I wish you every success with your imaginative ideas.'

Patrick also furnished me with a number of interesting contacts that I would find helpful later in the development of the project.

After showing me around his excellent observatory, Patrick asked me to help him see off the best part of a bottle of fine single malt whisky, and entertained both me and Woody, his dear housekeeper, by playing several tunes on his Xylophone. He also typed out a short note confirming his willingness to assist in the project if needed. The whole evening was very enjoyable and one I will never forget.

For my initial presentation I drew out scale plans for the saucer shaped facility. A scale model of the dome shaped roof of the saucer building was prepared for me by a company that produced professional industrial models for the car industry etc. At the same time I contacted a friend of mine who was the director of an advertising company called "Treasures of Britain". I explained my ideas to him and said that I was preparing a "future projects" presentation called "Space City", which I intended to put forward to the Belan Trustees, and asked him if he could come up with a suitably impressive frontispiece for the presentation document. He was very enthusiastic about the idea and said that the project lent itself to a most imaginative and creative advertising programme.

A few days later my friend returned with a beautifully designed placard prepared by one of his artists. The Card was about 15"x 12". The background was matt black. At the top of the card the words SPACE CITY had been spray-painted in large futuristic silver lettering that faded into pale blue. Immediately below the lettering was a painting of a saucer-shaped spacecraft that was very mystically portrayed. In smaller letters arched above the saucer were the words.. *"it's out of this world"* and at the base of the saucer leading out from a ray of light emitted from the saucer it read ...

Take a glimpse into the future.
See in detail all about the NASA Moon landings.
See future plans for space travel.
'The Most Fantastic Tourist Phenomenon' (Patrick Moore)

644

All this was airbrushed on to the black background to produce the most mystical effect.

I presented my initial ideas for the new project to the Trustees in the form of a carefully prepared 35 page document accompanied by my drawings, the letter of interest from Sir Patrick Moore, and the advertising placard prepared by Mr Brunton. Having made my presentation to a stunned and rather silent collection of entrepreneurial executives ......I suffered a lengthy period of stunned silence! ......Then to my surprise there was a spontaneous applause. I glanced at my colleagues sitting around the boardroom table and everyone of them was clapping enthusiastically. The Chairman, Bill Williamson spoke first...

'Well done Ray, you have obviously put a lot of hard work and research into this very interesting presentation. I would now like to hear comments from the rest of the board.'

Everyone was very complimentary including Lord Newborough's land agent Richard Rutherford, which surprised me as he usually put up an argument about anything I suggested. But most of all I was very keen to hear the comments made by Mike Wynn-Griffith who was also a Director of Nat West Bank, and Alan Hilton who was the solicitor for the Trust and Lord Newborough's Estate.

Fortunately for me both of these gentlemen were very complimentary about the project I had put before them. Bill Williamson summed up by saying that I had permission to take the project one stage further by carrying out a detailed feasibility study and a full structure plan for the development of Space City.

The Trustees fully appreciated that Carol and I worked together at Belan as a joint management team. Carol worked extremely hard during the season supervising our female employees, running the restaurant and gift shop operation as well as dealing with the considerable amount of secretarial work needed to run the fort operation. Apart from flying the aeroplane and firing the cannons, my side of the job dealt with overseeing the operation as a whole including the pleasure cruiser, and sorting out the many day to day problems.

The fort was closed to visitors during the winter months, but there was still an enormous amount of work to be carried out by the permanent staff in preparation for the coming season. The end of year accounts with preparatory budgets and forecast cash flow for next season, stock taking for the shop and restaurant, general maintenance of the fort and the museums, boat maintenance, the preparation of the gardens ready for the Spring, attending various trade fairs to purchase new stock for the gift shop, all these jobs, plus looking after two lovely horses, had to be completed by Carol and myself with the much valued help of our permanent maintenance man, and a part time gardener. So having to include the detailed design of a complicated new project to my list of winter jobs meant that we would frequently be working well into the night, and I have to say, we enjoyed every minute of it.

It was two years before I finally had everything in place to make a fully detailed presentation of the Space City project to the Trustees. Based on a five year phased development plan my new presentation included several additional facilities.

I made a scale model of the interior of the saucer shaped museum, the dome roof of the model could be removed to reveal the various sections, and each section had tiny models of the exhibits they were planned to contain. My intention was to have a minimum of twenty-five separate displays housed within the saucer's dome. I drew the displays in detail, costed each display separately, and also made a scale model of each item using the excellent modelling media 'PlastiKard.'

I then contacted the Kennedy Space Centre in the USA. They were very interested in the project and offered to help us when the time came. Their PR Executive mentioned in his letter to me that the directors of Kennedy Space Centre were keen to generate more world interest in their various developments. He said that they would be able to send me many hundreds of photographs for display purposes and also donate certain obsolete items to our museum. I contacted and received offers of help from NASA's Ames Research Centre, NASA's Goddard Flight Centre, and NASA's Johnson Space Centre. Also the Chief Administrator of NASA Research Centre in Cleveland Ohio said he would be willing to provide regular updated reports on the progress of NASA's planned space flight programmes, providing our facilities were deemed to be appropriate.

Next, having thought up another idea for having a spaceship that would simulate a complete journey around all the planets in the Solar System, I designed a mechanism that would seat around thirty visitors and rotate and tilt around two axis points whilst simulating visits to the planets by means of the latest NASA films being observed on a back-projection screen through the nose cone of the spaceship. I made outline drawings of the craft and passed my ideas to an engineering company who worked out the cost of manufacturing the device for me. I also wrote to NASA about my idea, and the head of their Audio Visual Dept in Alaska State Library replied offering me incredible support for the whole project. He said that they could make up a suitable film for us to use in the simulator from cuttings held in their existing film stock.

It took some time for the Russian Space Agency to answer my letter, but in the end they also offered various photographic exhibits for free.

Another part of the development that I had in mind was to provide a star theatre for the visitors. Having done some research into the matter I decided to contact the world renowned optical company "Goto" who had their head offices in Tokyo. They sent me details of their latest very impressive Multi-Image Planetarium System together with scale drawings for a suitable facility to house their smallest projector. The planetarium would show outer space programmes such as 'Journey into the World of Tomorrow' etc. Goto also sent me full particulars and photographs of the planetarium to include in my presentation document to the Trustees.

Intriguing items could be sold in the Flying Saucer's Gift Shop, which included numerous astronomical books, slides and commemorative stamps, framed space photographs, Starlog 'T' shirts, space flight commemorative coins, 56 different spacesuit badges for all the Gemini, Apollo, Mercury and Columbia space flights, boxed space suits for children, junior scientists experimental kits, scale model spaceships and a multitude of space related games and posters. All these items were not on sale in this country at that time and we were offered the sole agency for most of those products.

Finally I added an Observatory to my list of facilities. I was quite at home with this aspect of Space City, as I had already built my own telescope and observatory many years previously. I came to the conclusion that the "Goto 16 inch Cassegrain Reflector" with a power driven equatorial head would be the ideal telescope for the job. The inclusion of an observatory would extend the use of our project into providing interesting night observations and lectures not only for interested tourists, but also for study purposes by professional bodies such as Bangor University.

Obviously I realised that the cost of all this would probably promote mass heart attacks amongst our Trustees. So I set about finding various means of financing the project over a five or six year staged development plan, building the saucer first, then constructing the rest of Space City at staged intervals.

I made a few preliminary telephone calls to several commercial banks and financiers without giving too much away at this stage. Although most of them were very curious to find out exactly what I was up to, none of them showed any enthusiasm about financing tourist orientated businesses at that time.

Then I contacted Charterhouse Japheth the well known merchant bankers. The gentlemen on the other end of the telephone was very pleasant, and when I explained that I was seeking to expand an already popular tourist attraction with a new facility that would occupy an area of approximately 40,000 square feet, he immediately transferred me to one of his directors. Three days later I attended an interview at the offices of Charterhouse to discuss the Space City project.

To say that I was nervous would be a gross understatement. The director that interviewed me questioned me about every item on the plans and asked to see details of all the free backup material on offer from NASA. Several hours later, feeling quite exhausted, I thought that was it. But we had hardly started. He studied my estimated capital budget for about ten minutes in absolute silence, giving me occasional glances that I interpreted as: 'this guy doesn't know what the hell he's talking about.' I began to feel very uncomfortable when he looked up suddenly and said...

'Have you done any of this sort of thing before?'

I replied by saying it was probably obvious that I wasn't an accountant, but I had prepared the figures as a guide for my Trustees to look at, hoping that they didn't die of shock!

He gave me a brief smile and picked up the five year forecast cash flow that I had sweated over for days. Another period of silence ensued. In the end I felt so nervous that I was sure I would eventually be carted off to hospital with some kind of seizure.

Finally he scooped all my paperwork together, tapped them on his desk to straighten the sheets out, and tucked them into the file I had given him.

'Considering that you are certainly not an accountant, I am impressed with your presentation. I find the project most interesting although I think your capital repayment plan is somewhat optimistic. I happen to know one of your Trustees very well, in fact Mike Wynn-Griffith is a friend of mine. Has he seen your ideas yet?'

'No sir'

'Does he know you're here?

'No sir.'

'Right, I'll say nothing until you have presented this feasibility study to your Trustees, I would like to discuss the matter with Mr Wynn-Griffith but you can tell him that we would most likely be interested in providing capital assistance, which at this stage I would estimate could be in the region of three to five million pounds' (In 1979 that was one hell of a lot of money in 1979). He continued…

'I'm sure you appreciate there would have to be certain securities in place, and we would probably look for a part share in the equity of an independently set-up company. But all this would be up for discussion with your Trustees and their accountants.'

He stood up, handed back the file, shook hands and wished me good luck. That was it.

I left the building feeling exhausted and very excited. But now I had to face the Trustees, my premature actions in seeking financial support could go either way.

The day of the Trustees meeting arrived. I set up the scale models I had made together with all the brochures, information and sample goods sent to me from America as a special display in my office at the fort together with all the technical information from Goto. Everything was there for the members of the board to study in detail.

The meeting came to the final item on the agenda which read "Future Projects".

With a feeling of considerable trepidation I explained to the Trustees that I had expanded my plans for a single "Flying Saucer Museum" to a much more ambitious project that would occupy 40,000sq. ft. of the Belan land at present under my jurisdiction.

I handed out copies of my presentation outlining the plans and the cost of the project to each of the Trustees, sat down and waited for the explosion.

'Good God'… 'Bloody hell'… were the first spirited comments that echoed around the boardroom.

This initial outburst was followed by lots of muttering noises that emerged through the blue haze of cigar smoke in the boardroom. Having seen the illustration on the cover of the document, their was a quick rustling of pages as everyone quickly turned to the page headed "Cost and Phased Development". I watched the faces of the seven intellectual businessmen as they studied the pages of the document…

'Well I'm…..' Mike Wynn-Griffith's eyebrows nearly shot off the top of his head.

'Charterhouse eh? well done Ray, I would never have thought…'

He stopped short and continued to study the rest of the document. Finally coffee was brought to the table and the Chairman addressed me with rather mixed feelings.

'Well I wouldn't want the bloody thing in my garden Ray, but I have to congratulate you on the hard work you have put into this very detailed document.' He turned to Wynn-Griffith… 'What do you think Mike?'

Mike, a Director of Nat West Bank, scowled at me over his reading glasses…

'Well you might have overstepped the mark a bit Ray.. contacting Charterhouse, nevertheless old boy, well done. I'm all for taking the project to the next stage.'

Richard Rutherford, who was obviously unimpressed, stared hypnotically at the table, but he brightened up a little and nodded in agreement when Mike had rebuked me for contacting Charterhouse without first consulting the board.

I stood up and explained that with such an expensive project, I thought it was my job to seek some form of alternative capital investment before dumping that responsibility in the laps of the Trustees. I then invited the board to see the demonstration I had laid out for them in my office.

We all trooped across the courtyard to my office where the Trustees enthusiasm was boosted further by the detailed model layout and documentary proof of support from NASA etc.

A few days later Mike Wynn-Griffith and Alan Hilton our solicitor had a meeting with the directors of Charterhouse, whilst I set about the problem of obtaining planning permission from the local council. I was convinced that the planning authorities would welcome a project that would not only bring more employment to the area, but would also attract more tourists to North Wales.

I set up a meeting with the Chief Planning Officer to visit Belan and look at the model of 'Space City' so that he could see for himself the terrific backing we could expect from the American Space Agency. My boss the Hon Robert Wynn was in attendance together with our solicitor Alan Hilton.

The Chief Executive of the council arrived with the Chief Planning Officer and two other members of the planning committee. He immediately announced that he didn't have much time as he had an important appointment to attend elsewhere. I also noted that he made a point of not shaking hands with anybody.

The Chief Executive peered at the model layout of Space City and, looking at the Hon Robert Wynn remarked curtly…

'You stand to make a lot of money out of this I suppose?'

Robert ignored his rather pointed remarks and went on to introduce me as the Manager of Fort Belan who will now outline our plans to develop this additional attraction on grounds belonging to the fort.

I gave them a full and detailed presentation of our plans which lasted about thirty minutes, during that time I noticed that the Chief Executive seemed totally uninterested and repeatedly glanced at his watch. There followed a mumbled conversation amongst the councillors in Welsh, which, as invited guests of the Hon Robert Wynn I considered to be extremely bad manners. All the councillors at that meeting spoke fluent English, yet chose not to do so.

The first chap to address us in the English language was the Chief Executive. He thanked us for our hospitality and said he was impressed with the presentation but he doubted if the narrow winding road from the A499 leading to the Fort would be wide enough to take the possible increase in traffic, and that the road couldn't be widened because it was situated between the sea front and a row of private dwellings. He concluded that although the council was keen to promote small Welsh businesses in the area, Space City in his eyes was an enormous project and did not fit into the infrastructure planned for this area.

With the exception of the Chief Planning Officer, they all hurriedly adjourned to their cars and sped off. The CPO however stayed to take a further look at the various models and study the plans in greater detail. Finally he said that he was very intrigued with the concept of Space City. He thought that if it was allowed to go ahead it would most certainly prove to be very popular and certainly boost tourism in the area. Before he left he wished us every success with our project and said he would forward the forms for outline planning permission to us straight away.

Although we were pleased with the CPO's enthusiasm we were stunned by the Chief Executive's remarks.

As I expected, our planning application was refused. It was rejected on the grounds that the service road leading to Fort Belan was insufficiently wide enough to take any extra traffic. I could never prove it, but I am sure that the Chief Executive pressurised the CPO and his planning committee into this decision. But the fight had only just begun.

When Lord Newborough learned of the council's reasons for rejecting our planning application, he generously offered to donate a suitable area of land to the council so that they could construct a new wider road from the A499 to the gates of Fort Belan. Robert and I felt sure that this generous offer would be accepted by the planners because the council had been unsuccessful in purchasing this land from Lord Newborough previously, and now he offered the land to them as a gift.

The council once more refused us planning permission for Space City.

This time on the grounds of cost. They stated that even if the ground was donated, they could never afford the cost of constructing the road.

I researched the availability of EEC grants, and discovered that money was made available to councils to assist in approved schemes that promoted tourism. The application for these grants had to be made direct from local authorities, so I wrote a letter to the Chief Executive for Gwynedd asking him if he would consider applying for an EEC grant to construct a new road for better access to Fort Belan.

Having waited several weeks, I finally received a letter from the Chief Exec's Office thanking me for my earlier correspondence. It went on to say that Gwynedd Council were already seeking financial assistance from the EEC that would be spent elsewhere in the county and in our case they had no intention of seeking grant aid to construct a new road to the fort as planning permission for expanding the complex had already been refused.

The Trustees were extremely annoyed and disappointed by the council's decision. As far as I was concerned it was heart breaking. I had been working for two years designing a project that would have been ideal for the local area and tourism in North Wales generally. Advertised nationally, it would have brought thousands of visitors to North Wales on daily visits as well as holidays. Organised bus trips, school visits, and regular visits from universities to use our observatory and planetarium would have been a good thing for tourism in North Wales. Although it had the blessing of the Chief Planning Officer, it was downed by the Chief Executive of Gwynedd, who already had the reputation of being prejudiced against the development of English projects in North Wales.

In desperation I wrote to His Royal Highness the Prince of Wales, furnishing him with full details of how our plans to build 'Space City' had been turned down completely out of hand with no further comeback by the short-sightedness of the council. I explained that the project would cause no visual offence as it would be constructed on our own land completely obscured by the sand dunes. I mentioned that both NASA and the Russian Space Agency were very enthusiastic about the project and keen to assist by displaying their technology. The project would obviously be of immense benefit to the local area, offering full-time employment and generally boosting tourism in North Wales. I also pointed out that the council was eligible to apply for a EEC grant in order to construct the road. Finally I enclosed a copy of the letter I had received from the Chief Executives Office saying that in our case they had no intention of applying for an EEC grant.

Within a few days I received a reply from Buckingham Palace thanking me for my letter. It stated that the Prince found the project most interesting but normally he would not interfere in council matters, however in this particular case I may hear from his office again at sometime in the future.

I was instructed by the Trustees to submit a formal appeal against the council's decision which I did. Not only was it turned down, but I was incensed by the final paragraph in the planning authorities letter, which read… 'Any further applications for development at 'Fort Belan' that would be likely to increase traffic to the fort would automatically be turned down on the grounds of an inadequate service road'.

For Carol and I it was the beginning of a very disturbing period in our lives. On Friday the 13th of May 1983 I was shocked to learn of the death of my father. He was in his early eighties and was not suffering from any long term illness, he suddenly died from a stroke after climbing the stairs to his flat. Carol and I drove over to the police station in Sawbridgworth to collect Dad's personal belongings, then on to his flat to make all the necessary arrangements for the funeral and cremation. It was a distressing time.

A few days after Dad's cremation, his ashes arrived at Fort Belan by post. My dear friend Robyn Welshman, who was selling pleasure flight tickets for me that year, brought the package containing my father's ashes to me in the fort. Not knowing what it contained, he plonked the parcel on the desk and said…

'Parcel for you boss.'

I knew immediately what it was and I said to him…

'That's my dad in there Robyn.'

His jaw dropped…

'I'm so sorry Ray, I had no idea.'

Robyn and I drove down to the airfield with Dad's ashes. Carol, who knew what my plans were, stayed behind in the fort.

I climbed into G-AVGK and Robyn passed my fathers ashes to me.

'Well this is it Pop.' I said as I strapped the tiny urn into the co-pilot's seat.

Dad had flown this very aeroplane himself a few years earlier. He also loved Belan and spent hours just wandering around the grounds enjoying it's peace and quietness.

With tears streaming down my face, dad and I took off together for the last time. I talked to him all the while as we climbed up towards the fort.

653

I said, Goodbye Dad, kissed the side of the urn and gently distributed my father's ashes over Fort Belan from one thousand feet. I could see Cassie down there on the Ramparts of the fort and knew she would be in floods of tears. When I landed back at the airfield Robyn was anxiously waiting for me. I climbed out of the cockpit and Robyn put his arm around my shoulder and said...

'Come on Ray, there's a nice cup of tea waiting for you in the caravan.'

But first I drove back to see Cassie. She came up to the car her eyes full of tears. That was the end of dear old Pop... The realisation that I would never see him again was hard to take. His death left a great void in my life. I felt sure that he would have approved with the method I chose to distribute his ashes, because he enjoyed flying and loved Belan so much.

In the absence of planning permission for Space City, I had to come up with an idea for an added attraction that could be incorporated at Belan and hopefully not meet any resistance from the planning authorities.

I read an article in the local newspaper about someone who was desperately trying to find a home for his two fully grown pet Lion's. He had apparently received a court order for the Lion's to be removed from his premises, and if suitable accommodation could not be found within a specified period, the poor creatures would have to be destroyed.

A Lion House could easily be constructed within the outer walls of the fort, and would no doubt be an added attraction for our visitors. I contacted the person concerned and was invited over to his premises to take a look at the animals concerned. They appeared to be in excellent health, and after a long discussion with the owner I agreed to put the matter to our Trustees and seek their permission to take the matter further. The owner telephoned me later to say the deadline for having his Lion's destroyed had been delayed subject a decision by our Trustees.

I drew up plans for the construction of an adequately sized lion house and showed them to Chris Jackson, who was the Managing Director of Colwyn Bay Zoo. Chris said he thought my proposed plans had a reasonable chance of being accepted by the various regulatory bodies involved, but warned me that adult Lion's weren't the easiest animals to look after.

I planned to construct the building between the outer and inner walls of the fort using matching stone to blend in with the existing features. The next step was to submit my proposals to the Trustees at our next meeting in a few days time.

On the morning of the meeting I detected a strange atmosphere amongst the Trustees who for some reason seemed to avoid speaking to me before the conference started. I mentioned this to Carol, but she said I was over sensitive and imagining things.

As in previous management meetings, various matters concerning the trust's tenants and various other negotiations unrelated to Fort Belan were early items on the agenda to be discussed in detail. Then it was time for the midday break, and the Trustees stretched their legs wandering around the grounds of the fort whilst the large boardroom table was being prepared for lunch. Usually at this point, I would be approached by various Trustees who would be interested to know how things were going at the fort and what had I got up my sleeve to surprise them at this meeting etc. But it was obvious that everyone purposely avoided speaking to me. I did however overhear the Chairman of the Trust, Bill Williamson, say to Mike Wynn-Griffith, I feel dreadful, this is the worst thing I have ever had to do.

When the meeting resumed, the next item on the agenda was headed, <u>Fort Belan. New Projects.</u> I was waiting for the Chairman to ask me to put forward my plans for the coming season, but instead he looked at me and said...

'I think perhaps we should have Carol in for this Ray, would you mind asking her to join us?'

I collected Carol from Robert's kitchen where she was preparing coffee. I said that I was sure we were going to get the sack, but couldn't for the life of me think why. Carol and I had worked so hard during the eight years we had been employed by the trust. During the summer months we worked at least 10 hours a day, seven days a week, and during the Winter we worked enthusiastically preparing the fort complex for the coming season, organising and overseeing the general maintenance of the fort and dockyard buildings, attending trade exhibitions, ordering new stock and planning new projects for the coming season. Thanks to Carol our accounts were immaculate and accurate to the penny, the business was making an excellent profit...So if we were to be dispensed with, whatever could have gone wrong?

Back in the boardroom we were asked to take a seat whilst our Chairman told us why he needed to talk to us. This is what he said...

'I'm sure you both appreciate that all businesses have to expand in the long-term in order to survive, especially in the tourism market, unfortunately the attitude of the local planning authorities have prevented us from doing this. You Ray, and the board of Trustees have done all we can to try and persuade the local authorities to change their strategy with reference to the restrictions they have placed on road widening, unfortunately without success. Therefore in consultation with Robert the Trustees have come to the joint, and most regrettable decision to sell Fort Belan and invest the capital elsewhere. I know that I speak for everyone around this table when I say we could not have employed two more conscientious, hard working and friendly people to manage and expand this business for us. Your work has been exemplary.'

Everyone at the meeting murmured their agreement with the Chairman's remarks and at last condescended to look us in the face.

Carol and I were completely devastated. Everything that we thought about, planned for, even dreamed about had been shattered in the few seconds it had taken Bill Williamson to tell us of the trusts decision.

For me it had been a dreadful year. My father had died, the two years I had spent designing Space City had been rejected by the council, and finally our precious jobs had come to an end which also meant that we would very soon have nowhere to live.

I was completely shattered and found it difficult to say anything, it was such a shock to me that tears rolled down the cheeks of my face and I just sat there in silence. Everyone in the boardroom looked upset and very sorry for us. Carol bravely held back her tears until we were in our house.

Having been told that Belan would be closed down and sold, we were asked to leave the boardroom whilst the Trustees discussed the details of our redundancy.

The old cliché "The bottom dropped out of our world" was never more true than it was for Carol and myself. For us Belan had never been, just a job, it was our whole life. We worked, dreamed, lived for and loved that beautiful old place.

My thoughts turned immediately to the poor chap that owned the Lion's. I telephoned him straight away with the bad news. I had built up his hopes of saving those beautiful creatures, and now I had to give him the news that would almost certainly result in the demise of his pets. He thanked me for trying, and I could tell by his voice that the poor chap was in tears, I felt like a criminal.

Moments later Robert Wynn came over to our quarters. He put his hand on my shoulder and said…

'We would like you both to rejoin us in the boardroom.'

The discussion that took place was very complicated, but it was clear that the Trustees were determined to show their appreciation for our accomplishments over the last eight years. In fact the net result was almost unbelievable.

First and foremost the ten year lease with Keenair Services for the hire of a suitable aeroplane to operate within Keenair's AOC for pleasure-flying was legally transferred to me, and we were also given the caravan that was used for the pleasure flight office. We were aloud to keep the company van that had a very professional looking "Pleasure Fights" advertisement painted on the sides. Finally we were given a large sum of money that could be used to purchase a small house, or used as a deposit on a more expensive property.

The income from the pleasure flight operation was in fact worth considerably more to us than our joint salaries had been, at the same time I would only be flying during the Summer season, the rest of the time we could do as we pleased. I telephoned Jim Keen immediately informing him of the change. He sounded quite annoyed that he had not been informed of the changes made by the Trustees. But when he realised that his existing sublease of the airfield from the Trustees would not be affected and our joint flying arrangements would continue, he was quite happy.

Also Robert Wynn said he had no objection to us continuing to live at the Fort until we had found a place of our own.

With the exciting new prospect of having our own flying business and buying our own house, the shock of losing our jobs at Belan became a little easier to bear. But Carol and I knew in our hearts that wherever we went, there would never be another place as beautiful and peaceful as our beloved Fort.

We immediately started to look for a suitable house to purchase within commuting distance of the airfield. We must have scoured through hundreds of house details sent to us by local agents. Most days were spent driving around searching for the sort of house we would both be happy with. But after living in Belan it was never going to be easy.

One day Carol was mulling through a stack of house details in an agents premises in Porthmadog, when she spotted the details of a lovely old farmhouse situated halfway up a mountain. As soon as I saw the price I told her to forget it, we just couldn't afford such a place. Carol kept the details, and every time we were anywhere near that house Carol would insist we made a detour onto a very narrow 'B' class road so that we could gaze up the mountain at the large white house she wanted us to take a look at. Carol must have asked me a hundred times to telephone for an

657

appointment to view the farmhouse which incidentally was named "Llwyn Beddw". I tried to discourage her by saying you'll only upset yourself if you fall in love with the place because there was just no way that we could afford that sort of money.

In the end I gave in and we made an appointment to meet the owners and take a look at the house. We drove through the farm gates and proceeded to climb up the steep track towards "Llwyn Beddw". Here and there huge boulders peeped out from areas of tall grass leaving one in no doubt that this house was indeed situated on the side of a mountain. We parked the car and as I leaned over another gate to lift the latch I was startled to see two fully grown Lhama's peering at us inquisitively, literally within *spitting distance!* We cautiously made our way past them, and were met at the front door by the owner, a very friendly young man who invited us in to meet his wife.

One had to stoop low to enter as the door was only about five feet high. The entrance led into the warm atmosphere of a farmhouse kitchen with white stone walls and splendid old oak beams. Whilst his wife set about making us a cup of tea, her husband Martin showed us around the property.

The kitchen was in fact split-level, the lower section being used as the dining area, whilst the upper section was the true kitchen where a large solid-fuel 'Aga' burned away happily. In addition to the Aga, practically every type of built-in appliance including a large electric cooker were neatly housed in the upper section. The cooking area was about two feet higher than the dining area. Access between the two was provided by three semi circular polished stone steps. A lengthy low-level serving bar constructed of primordial bricks with a polished slate top unobtrusively separated the upper and lower levels. The thickness of the farmhouse walls was made visibly evident by the depths of the windowsills which were about two feet in depth. Several wicker baskets and strings of onions hung down from the beams.

We followed Martin through a small latched door into a large oak-beamed room. For a moment I stood completely overwhelmed by the warm atmosphere and tranquillity that seemed to exist in this lovely old room. I glanced across at Carol and I could see by the look on her face that she felt exactly the same way.

The main feature of this room was the biggest inglenook fireplace I had ever seen. It was constructed of welsh quarry stone with an old and very weathered tree trunk supporting the stone chimney breast. A log fire crackled away in the huge cast-iron dog grate, filling the room with the portentous odour of burning pine-logs. I thought that nothing would ever replace Fort Belan as a home for Carol and myself, but I was wrong, the perfect alternative home for us was staring me in the face. The problem now was could we afford to buy it?

Martin showed us around the rest of the house. There were four charming bedrooms and a beautiful little bathroom, all with beamed ceilings, and one of the bedrooms would be perfect to use as a study. "Llywn Beddw" had been built in the seventeenth century. It stood in two acres of land situated just over one thousand feet above sea level. A freshwater spring, situated a few yards further up the mountainside, fed water by gravity directly into a collection tank, and from there it was automatically supplied to the house by an electric pump. The views to the West of the property were astounding. The sea was only two miles away, and from the sitting room window you could see Fort Belan, the Airfield, Caernarfon Castle and on a clear day it was just possible to make out the coast of the Isle of Man on the horizon.

We sat by the fire and chatted for while over a cup of tea. Then, however stupid this may sound, to my surprise I heard myself saying that we would purchase Llywn Beddw and asking Martin how soon would he be able to vacate the house?

The expression on Carol's face was an adorable mixture of surprise and utter delight when she realised that, by hook or by crook, I would find a way of purchasing "Llywn Beddw" for her. That night, whilst the wind whistled around the fort, we cuddled up together and once again planned our exciting future.

To my surprise we had no trouble in arranging a suitable mortgage and whilst we were waiting for the contracts to be exchanged, the Trustees kept their word and allowed us to continue living at Fort Belan. It was quite an exciting time for us, because we not only had a fabulous house of our own to look forward to, but we were also going to start our own pleasure flying business in North Wales. We registered our company as "Snowdon Pleasure Flights".

My flying instructor's ratings etc. had been allowed to lapse, but for the time being that didn't matter as I still had a current Commercial Pilots Licence with all the essential endorsements needed to carry out flying for hire and reward.

We purchased new furniture for the house and stored it in the room that used to be our office at the fort.

When contracts were exchanged for the purchase of our new home, Martin asked us if we minded taking care of his Lhama's for a few days whilst he fenced off a field at his new premises, and of course we readily agreed.

As "Llywn Beddw" was only a few miles from the Fort, Carol and I used our van to transport most of our worldly goods to the farmhouse, but we did have to hire a "Man with a Van" to deliver our three piece suite, welsh dresser and a couple of beds.

The day we moved in, Mr Jones, the "Man with a Van", arrived about midday carrying our precious items of furniture. He was full of praise and admiration for the location of our house and it's magnificent views, but his enthusiasm for our new house diminished as the afternoon progressed. The first thing that displeased him was when he discovered the doors had to be taken off in order to get our three piece suite into the house. Finally, with the doors removed, we managed to stagger through the entrance and down a couple of steps carrying the large chairs. It took some time to manoeuvre the settee into the correct angle in order for it to pass through the narrow entrance into the sitting room. Mr Jones leaned against the wall wiping the perspiration from his brow. He was not a young man, all the lifting and struggling was beginning to get the better of him. But there was worse to come. He was entering the front door for the umpteenth time when I heard one hell of a thump.... Poor old Jones had walked full-tilt smack into the beam above the low entrance door. He swayed backwards holding his head in his hands swearing profusely. (In Welsh and English!) It must have been a nasty shock for the poor old chap, he staggered over to the opposite side of the garden path and slumped up against the low wooden fence. I started to walk towards the house in order to fetch him a glass of water when I heard a loud ….'Splat'.... followed instantly by a pitiful yell. I turned to see that Mr Jones had decided to console himself by talking to the large male Lhama. Unfortunately the Lhama hadn't taken too kindly to Jones and ejected a charitably sized gob smack into the poor chap's face!

Jones glared at me in despair. I couldn't help noticing a thin trickle of blood and a generous portion of spit running down his weathered old face. Finally, having dabbed his forehead with his handkerchief, the old fellow uttered a few words in English…

'I can tell you in all honesty Mr Blyth, this is the last bloody time I come anywhere near this place.'

He was a lovely old chap, and we really liked him. I helped him into the house and sat him down whilst Carol made us all a most welcomed cup of hot tea. We paid him generously for his efforts. Finally we watched him as he clambered in to his van and drove off down the mountain, never to see him again.

Not long after moving into our new home, we added another member to the family, a lovely little Siamese kitten who grew up to be quite a character. He was a thoroughbred cat who's registered name was so long and unpronounceable that we decided to call him "Percy". Within no time Percy and our dog Kimbo became inseparable, they were always larking about and getting into mischief, in fact a few years later their antics were comparable to that of Bonnie and Clyde!

CHAPTER 57.

Barnstorming.

So once again flying was to be my full-time occupation, but on this occasion it was going to be our own business. The pleasure-flying season had in fact commenced a few weeks before we moved from Fort Belan into our new home. This gave us time to set up everything in the flight caravan that we had inherited from the Trustees. The caravan was already connected to the water supply and mains electricity at the airfield, and being quite a large van we were able to use two thirds of the floor space as the pleasure-flight sales office. The van also housed a small kitchen area and a chemical toilet compartment. A standard BT telephone was connected to the van, with a further direct line telephone to the old Air Traffic building which was now manned part time by a member of Keenair's staff. The control tower itself was of the standard RAF wartime pattern which was now a derelict shell. A rather primitive shack similar to a flat topped greenhouse had been erected on the roof of the old tower to house the controller and his minimal transceiver equipment. The remaining one third of our caravan was partitioned off to form a miniature Flight Ops. Room. I was rather proud of our little Ops. room because it housed much more than the detailed requirements laid down by the CAA for the provision of A to A flight operations. When the CAA inspector, Captain Tony Trowbridge, visited us he gave our set-up a glowing report and approval was instantly granted.

Keenair Services, supplied me with a 180 Piper Cherokee G-AVGK, and also provided "Avgas" from their aviation business at Liverpool Airport. In return I agreed to pay Keenair Services a very reasonable hourly wet-hull rate.

By a most amazing stroke of bad luck, tragedy struck yet again. It happened two or three days before we moved into our new home whilst we were still living in our previous quarters at Belan. I had just come down the stairs from our bedroom in the fort when I heard a strange rumbling noise. At first I thought it was the sound of an approaching jet aircraft, but the noise increased and the walls of the fort started to tremble. The next possibility that crossed my mind was perhaps the large boiler that heated the whole of the fort was severely malfunctioning. By the time I got to the door, the walls were fairly rocking and the rumbling noise sounded like continuos thunder. I opened our front door and stepped out into the courtyard to see Wilf, our gardener, running for all he was worth over the drawbridge and out through the fort gates.

In a matter of split seconds the ground was rocking violently, and my mind went into overdrive....Had a war started and an atomic bomb exploded somewhere miles away? Was this the end of the world? I was joined in the courtyard by Carol who looked as white as a ghost.

'Whatever is it?' she said as the rumbling slowly began drifting away.

The vibrations that had been rocking the fort gradually died down. I can't remember who first came out with the correct hypothesis or even how we found out, but the fact was the area had just experienced a moderate earthquake measuring 5.2 on the Richter scale. Apparently the epicentre was located somewhere close to Porthmadog and several buildings had been damaged with chimney's falling and gable-ends of houses collapsing. Radio Wales warned people living in Gwynedd to expect severe after-shocks, and sure enough we experienced one or two nerve-racking moments, but none as severe as the original quake.

The following morning as I was taxying our aeroplane from the grass dispersal point in front of our caravan to the refuelling area, the nose of the aircraft suddenly pitched down. There was a loud bang followed by a noise that sounded like a short burst of machinegun fire. The aircraft came to a sudden halt with one blade of the propeller stuck vertically into the ground. I switched everything off and jumped out quickly to see what had happened.

The taxiway from the caravan to the perimeter track was made up of firm ground that had been used by aircraft regularly since the airport was constructed at the beginning of the Second World War. The nose wheel had apparently passed over a section of ground that suddenly opened up into a shallow hole. We could only put this down to the earth being disturbed by the severe shaking of the earthquake the previous day, and had now given way under the weight of the aeroplanes nose wheel which sank several inches into the ground allowing the propeller to strike the surface and stop the engine. Further examination showed that the prop had struck a submerged rock which was buried just below the upper surface of the ground. Both tips of the propeller blades were bent to an angle of about ninety degrees.

When this sort of thing happens it not only means that the propeller has to be replaced, but the engine also has to be dismantled and checked for damage. This was one hell of a thing to happen right at the start of operating our new business. Jim Keen was not at all pleased. He arranged for Golf Kilo to be road transported back to his maintenance unit at Liverpool Airport for repairs. Five days later he supplied me with a Cessna 172. The five days of waiting for another aeroplane to arrive were indeed anxious times. The pleasure flight season is very limited, and every day without the aeroplane we were losing customers. The problem was that although Keenair Services were not short of aircraft and could have replaced Golf Kilo straight away, Jim Keen did not at first believe that the cause of the bent prop was due to land subsidence. I'm sure he thought that I had been responsible in some way, that being the case it would have made our contract null and void. In the end Jim flew over to Caernarfon and looked at the ground where the accident had occurred. Not only could he see that the ground had given way, but also the regular six or seven slots where the propeller had carved itself into the ground before striking the submerged rock.

With the C172 on site we decided to move things around so that the aircraft was permanently positioned on part of the old concrete perimeter track.

During our first season, 1984, Snowdon Pleasure Flights carried 2,568 passengers in the Cessna 172's three passenger seats. The flights lasted between 10 and 30 minutes, depending on the particular flight the customer required. The following season we carried 2,772 passengers. When I first started pleasure flying I was surprised by the number of passengers who had never been up in an aeroplane before. I have no exact figures but at a reasonable guess I would say that seven out of ten people said they had never flown before.

There was no permanent refuelling facility at Caernarfon Aerodrome, so Jim Keen used to deliver fifty gallon drums of fuel by air which we hand pumped into five gallon drums and stored in the old RAF hangar. When my aeroplane needed refuelling, I would pump the fuel from the drums straight into the aircraft via a filtered funnel. Later Jim bought a 500 gallon tank mounted on a four wheel trailer with a hand pumping device attached. Although this was still quite strenuous to operate, it was a great improvement on lifting the heavy drums.

On occasions sheep from a neighbouring field would get through the airfield wire netting security fence and wander onto the runway. With the help of Kimbo, who was part sheepdog, we soon rounded them up and drove them back to the field where they belonged.

Every now and then, when I returned the aircraft back to the hangar at the end of a day's flying, Kimbo would hop into the seat beside me and come along for the ride. Frequently members of the public would park their cars on the roadway near to the perimeter track to watch me taking off and landing. One evening, when I taxied the aircraft back to the hangar, I sat Kimbo in the pilots seat with a headset and microphone placed on her head. As we taxied past the onlookers I ducked down well out of sight so that it looked as if Kimbo was the pilot. We stopped abeam the hangar and I popped up to see the spectators staring in absolute amazement at the aeroplane. I don't know whether they really thought the aeroplane was being controlled by a dog or not, but it was amusing to see the look of astonishment on their faces.

It is illegal to fly kites or model aeroplanes near to an active airfield although not everybody is aware of this fact. The Eastern boundary of Llandwrog Airfield actually bordered on to a large caravan park that was directly in line with the touchdown point of runway 26. The owner, a great friend of mine, kindly posted several large notices around the site informing his customers of the law relative to kite flying. In the main things ran pretty smoothly until one day I landed and was surprised to see that there was a length of cord attached to the starboard wheel, with a further fifty feet or so of cord trailing behind the aircraft with remains of a kite attached to it. Obviously I was very concerned about this, because if the cord had been wrapped around the child's hand, it could have resulted in dreadful injuries. I was just about to contact the owner of the caravan park when a very irate, red faced man about forty years old, came running through the main gates of the airfield shouting out and gesticulating wildly.

'Are you the bloody maniac that was flying that aeroplane?' he demanded.

I informed him that I had just landed and discovered a kite attached to the aircraft's undercarriage. Expressing my urgent concern, I enquired if the child flying the kite had been injured?

The man virtually exploded and screamed out...

'I was flying that bloody kite and you're going to wind up in court for low flying mate.'

I asked the chap whereabouts he was when the aircraft collected his kite.

'On the lawn right outside my bloody caravan mate' he snapped poking his finger into my chest. I asked him if he had read the notices forbidding kites to be flown on the campsite and that according to the Air Navigation Order kites may not be flown within a 5km radius of any airfield. With that the enraged character turned even nastier.

'Don't quote the bloody Air Navigation Order to me lad,' he said wagging his finger under my nose, 'I'm a very senior officer from Scotland Yard and you're going to lose your lic……….'

I interrupted the supercilious tongue wagging bastard there and then…

'You can take me to court any time you like, and it will do you no good, even if you're the chief bloody constable, you obviously haven't got a clue about the ANO, and what's more I can take you to court for contravening the safety of aircraft and others who were on the camp site. If you want to play with kites, you should do it somewhere else *SIR.* '

Promising me that I would hear more about the matter, the chap grabbed what was left of his kite and stormed off the airfield threatening that I hadn't heard the last of the matter.

Later I found out from the campsite owner that the so called "very senior officer from Scotland Yard" was in fact a Police Constable from Brentwood Police Station.

'He's a real bolshie bastard Ray, always complaining about something or other, but his little son is really cut up about losing his kite.'

I felt sorry for the lad and asked the campsite manager to give the lad a kite from the campsite shop which I would pay for. I never heard anything further about the incident.

I had to smile to myself. It was unlucky to collect a kite when landing, but the chances of it being flown by a copper must have been a million to one!.

Obviously pleasure flying and aerial photography was a totally different job to instructing airline students and private pilots, but I enjoyed every moment, and apart from the beautiful scenery and the many varied weather conditions we encountered, I was entertained daily by the never ending amusing antics of our passengers. Let me explain…

Pleasure flight passengers come in a variety of interesting types. Tall, short, slim, fat, enormous, old, young, quiet, mouthy, giggly and sometimes bloody rude. They arrive in all sorts of condition. Sober, drunk, cheerful, miserable, frightened, excited, and in some cases have to be accompanied by a police officer or a security guard. The smells they leave in a restricted cockpit can vary from pleasantly perfumed, to an odour that fits the description of "Eau de Cologne and Winkles". Passengers attitudes can range from happy to obnoxious. When they clamber into the cockpit with you it's a gamble as to what one is going to be faced with throughout the flight.

The remarks made by passengers frequently take some beating! and either make me laugh or bore me fartless. Here are a few examples of what they say, together with the sort of replies they sometimes get from me :-

Passengers remark.	Reply from Pilot
'Don't crash will you pilot?' …	*I'll do my best.'*
'How long have you been flying?'…	*'Several weeks.'*
'I expect it's like driving a car?' …	*'Absolutely.'*
'It seems as if we are standing still.'	*'We are.'*
'I once went up in a real big aeroplane..'	*'I must have your autograph!'*
'How many times have you crashed?' …	*'Countless.'*
'Don't loop the loop!' ….	I'd usually pretend not to hear that remark.
'I hope you can land this thing. Is there much of a bump when we land?'	*'Well let's put it this way, if you have false teeth or are wearing contact lenses, take em out before we land!'*
'This is not as good as flying in the big stuff'….	*'Don't worry, if we crash its exactly the same!'*

I must say that most of the passengers I have flown with are extremely nice people, who generally enjoy their flight immensely and many of them were quite amusing without having any intention of being so. Once again they seem to fit into several different categories. For instance:-

There are the nervous types, bless them, who try to cover their apprehension by an exaggerated display of confidence. I call these types "The Whistlers". They approach the aircraft nonchalantly whistling a totally unrecognisable and tuneless ditty, just a series of haphazard notes. Then, having stumbled awkwardly into the aeroplane, they replace their tuneless whistling by a rendition of equally haphazard and unrecognisable words, something like this:-

'Pum pum de do diddy do pum perpum pum' etc.

This performance would gradually die away when they discover that they have no idea how to fasten the passengers seat harness, but would rather die than suffer the indignity of asking for help. Sometimes a chap in this predicament would have a quiet word with himself...

'Let me see now, ah this is... no it isn't, pum pum do de do do pum...' and so on.

When I ask these types if they need any assistance they will invariably say...

'No its quite alright, I've done this hundreds of times before, I just don't seem to be able to...er.' And they carry on fiddling away with no idea what they're doing. In the end they give up and either pretend they have succeeded by holding the ends of their seat harness, or they condescend to ask for help by saying... 'This is different to the ones I'm used to.'

The next category are those that like to show off with their knowledge. They come under the heading of "Smart Arses". Here are a couple of examples of what I mean.

We've just taken off and are climbing away when the passenger looks down at the runway and asks...

'Was this once an airfield?'

I usually reply by asking him what he thinks it is now? (In the nicest possible way of course).

The other type of smart arse is the chap that shouts at you as loudly as possible so that his fellow passengers can admire him, for example this is the sort of information I am regularly told...

'I'm a pilot, aerobatics and all that stuff you know!'

I am always interested in this remark if the person is genuine, and I ask them where they did there flying training. But often the reply is a little disappointing...

'Taught myself mate.....radio controlled model aeroplanes ....much more difficult to fly than the real thing.'

'Is it really, how do you work that one out?'

The crap answer always came back that the controls are reversed when the model is flying towards you. In order to shut these boring types up, I usually say that I also used to fly model aeroplanes myself, and if that doesn't work, a short sharp "involuntary" forward movement of the control column when in flight is guaranteed to produce a quick gasp, followed by silence!

One thing I really loved doing was flying with children. Naturally they are always excited and their little faces light up when they climb aboard. Some children were very observant, noticing everything that went on in the cockpit. I used to play a game with some of them when I took them up in our Cherokee 180. The elevator trim control was a crank handle situated in the roof of the cockpit. The pilot frequently needs to turn the trim handle several times during a flight. These adjustments could also be made by pressing a small rocker switch situated on the control column. If the pilot used the rocker switch, the handle in the roof would automatically turn on its own. Sometimes I would see an inquisitive little pair of eyes looking up at the trim handle apparently turning on its own. Eventually the small person sitting next to me could not resist asking me what the handle was for and why did it turn on its own? I would explain roughly what a trimmer handle was for, and tell them that I had to turn it from time to time. They would usually tell me that they saw it moving on it's own. Then I would reply ….

'Did it really? I've been told by other pilots that sometimes it turns on its own, although I've never seen it. They say it's the ghost of an old wartime pilot flying in the cockpit with us who turns the handle for fun.'

Usually the child never takes his eyes off the trimmer from then on. I would keep my hand cupped over the small trimmer switch on the control column so that no-one could see it, then, pretending my attention was drawn to something outside the window I'd squeeze the switch a couple of times. The trim handle in the roof would turn on its own and the child would yell out…. ' LOOK IT'S MOVING ON ITS OWN AGAIN.' I always looked up too late to see it. After repeating this a few times the parents in the back seats would occasionally get excited as well. I never let on how I did it, and when the flight was over the children would rush off to tell everyone about the "ghost in the aeroplane".

Some passengers are really entertaining to watch, and with a little help from me, they can become even more entertaining, they are the "Camera Types".

I remember an elderly gentleman who climbed aboard armed with a very old "Brownie Box Camera" suspended from his neck by a piece of string. I asked him if there was anything in particular that he would like to photograph. Surprisingly he replied…

'Yes, I would rather like to photograph my car, it's in the airport car park.'

Not all that ambitious bless him, but in the end he never took a photograph of his precious Ford Sierra or anything else because he clutched the base of the seat with both hands and was too nervous to let go.

On another occasion a well built man, who must have weighed around twenty stone, squeezed himself into the front seat next to me. Breathing heavily he announced that he would like to take a few photographs of Caernarfon Castle. He was carrying an expensive looking camera complete with a zoom lens attachment that was almost the size of a small cannon. We took off and headed towards Caernarfon. There wasn't much room for movement as I was already crammed in tight against the left side of the cockpit. He had been briefed before we took off not to touch any of the controls, but as he shuffled about trying to get himself comfortable, he grabbed the dual control column in front of him to pull himself forward. I reacted quickly, but not fast enough to prevent the aircraft pitching up sharply. I shouted at him to let go, at the same time I had to push hard to counteract the man's strength. He suddenly let go and for a split second we pitched down which caused the man to grab the control column again. With the aid of one or two old fashioned profanities, I convinced the guy to keep his hands well away from the controls and calm down. During all this excitement I noticed that a strong smell of something nasty began to fill the cockpit.

When we arrived overhead Caernarfon, the man tried to point the huge zoom lens of his camera at the castle, but there was insufficient room between himself and the cockpit window. Before I could say a word he released his safety belt and launched himself sideways towards me until he was just about sitting on my lap.

With little room to move I banked the aircraft over to give him a clear shot of the castle, at the same time preventing the aircraft from turning by the appropriate use of top rudder. This of course necessitates the aircraft to fly out of balance. I had warned him of this effect, but my enthusiastic photographer tried to remain upright and banged his head on the door. Unfortunately he was clutching the camera's trigger at the time and I could hear the shutter clicking away automatically, obviously taking numerous pictures of the cockpit floor.

The second attempt should have been much better as I explained to my agitated friend for the second time, that the only way to hold an aeroplane in a sustained bank for photographic purposes without the aircraft turning, was to fly out of balance which is why the aircraft tends to slip sideways. Once again we approached the castle, whilst the profusely sweating camera-man prepared himself to take another photograph. I banked the aircraft over, applied sufficient rudder to prevent a turn, and held it there waiting for the telltale "click" of the camera. I waited, and waited and waited as we slowly drifted over the castle, but the chap seemed to be hypnotised and did nothing. Involuntarily I blurted out...

'For f... sake press the bloody button!!!!'.

The castle drifted away and I finally released the pressure on the rudder. As the wing shot up... "click"... too late, he had taken a picture of the clear blue sky! Unfortunately his pleasure flight had run out of time. He looked so fed up and miserable that I felt sorry for the poor chap and decided to do one more orbit of the castle. But this time the camera remained silent. The set-up seemed perfect so I asked him why he hadn't taken the photograph?...

'I'm going to be sick!'

Fortunately he grabbed the sick bag just in time.

One day I took a passenger flying who told me his lifetimes ambition was to take photographs of the summit of Snowdon from the air. He sat in the back of the aircraft with his wife who was very quiet and appeared to be a little nervous. The man himself seemed to be overjoyed and commenced clicking away with his camera from the second we started taxiing. The Snowdon flight was the most expensive trip we did. It took about thirty minutes to complete which included an orbit around the summit, returning to the airfield via the Llanberis Pass. We had just started climbing out towards the mountains when there was one hell of a bust-up in the back seats. His wife, who up to that point had been as silent as a mouse, was letting rip at her husband mercilessly. She called him every kind of stupid "B" she could think of. Then it was his turn and he started on her...

'Its your fault you silly cow, you should have told me.'

After the outburst things died down until we reached the summit, when all hell broke out again. Then, on the way back to the airfield, not a word was spoken. I was wearing headphones and couldn't hear exactly what they had been arguing about. So I tried to strike up a friendly conversation with them, but that certainly didn't work, I just received a grunt or two in reply. It turned out that in the first instance he had been taking pictures of the airfield with the lens cap on whilst we taxied out. Then, to top it off, as we flew over the summit of Snowdon he lined his camera up to take a photograph and found he had run out of film altogether. When we landed his wife had the cheek to suggest that we should refund the money they had paid for the flight.

There are other types who are in a category of their own, I'll call them "The Rubbernecks". I have only come across a few of these types, but they all appear to have little control over their neck muscles, in fact they act as if their necks were made of sponge rubber. Providing they sit next to you, these types are instantly recognisable and once identified they are great fun to play with. If you have good peripheral eyesight, and fortunately I have, you will be able to identify a rubberneck without looking directly at him. As soon as you open the throttle to take-off...his head goes right back and his mouth pops delicately open! Close the throttle the head wobbles forward and the mouth will snap closed. It works best if they are totally relaxed, but if they fall asleep they could become a danger to themselves. I've spent many a happy moment squeezing the throttle open and closing it again, whilst my passenger gently nods away totally unaware of what I'm up to. A touch of rudder, and their heads wobble sensitively from side to side. Subtle co-ordination of throttle and rudder can produce a rolling effect, a sort of drowsy orbit. It's all jolly good fun!

Every now and again one gets the distasteful type of passenger that breaks wind uncontrollably from take-off to landing, With three passengers aboard, the perpetrator is seldom identified, especially if all the passengers are female. So I assume, having issued each other with verbal disclaimers, they walk away from the aircraft blaming me. Worse still, the passengers who are boarding for the next flight, glare at me in disgust.

Some passengers are so overwhelmed by the magic of their first-time flight, that they completely forget to use their camera altogether, others persist in using flash photography whilst photographing through the perspex window which I'm sure must reflect back and ruin their artistic efforts.

The next group of passengers are more annoying and come under the heading of the "Confidence Givers".

It goes something like this. A family of four would board for a flight and one of them, usually the man, would set out to strike terror into the hearts of the rest of the family...

'Now there's no need to be nervous, and don't let the idea of crashing enter your head...we're not going to do that are we Mr Pilot?'

Then, as we commence the takeoff run he starts again...

'Don't look down whatever you do...you'll shit yourself.'

After that the advice giver invariably turns pale and remains quiet throughout the flight until we are coming in to land, then he kicks off again...

'We're landing now, it seems a bit fast but I think the pilot knows what he's doing…oh and don't forget to keep your mouth closed or you could bite your tongue off when we hit the ground!'

These characters really annoy me. They are obviously close to hysteria and do their best to frighten the crap out of everyone else, what's the point of that when they have paid good money to see the beautiful scenery that North Wales has to offer?

On one occasion a chap climbed aboard wearing a tracksuit. Unbeknown to me he was wearing wet swimming trunks underneath. When he vacated the aeroplane the seat he had been sitting on was literally saturated. Obviously we couldn't expect anyone to sit on a soaking wet seat, so we borrowed an extension lead from Air Traffic Control and dried the seat out with the use of Carol's hair dryer.

Then there was the case of "Sod the sick bag, get the pilot instead".

Returning from the mountains we were 500 ft. above Crib Goch one afternoon when I noticed the young man sitting next to me was sweating profusely and generally fidgeting around in his seat. From experience I knew this was usually the forerunner of air sickness. I tapped him on the shoulder and pointed to the sick bag situated in the side pocket of the cockpit door. The lad nodded but left the bag where it was. We continued to descend on our way back to base whilst my front seat passenger was distinctly turning a delicate shade of green. As the guy seemed to be doing nothing about it, I reached across, pulled out the sick bag, opened it up and put it on his lap. At this point his father, who was sitting behind me said…

'He doesn't need that bag pilot, he's never been sick in his life.'

The lad, who was about sixteen years old, sat there for a while contemplating the sick-bag, then he turned to me as if to say something and threw up with considerable gusto, hitting me square in the face!

I had copious amounts of what appeared to be "Chicken Supreme" in my eyes, mouth and dripping off my chin. It had splashed all over the instrument panel and down the front of my shirt. I was bloody fuming and, as if that wasn't bad enough, his father piped up again and said laughingly…

'I expect you're used to this sort of thing aren't you pilot?'

I was close to blowing a gasket, and it didn't end there. When we landed I noticed the boy had somehow avoided getting anything on himself, so when I climbed out of the cockpit covered in vomit, all the waiting passengers must have thought that I had been sick….definitely not a good advertisement. I drove home, had a bath and changed my clothes. During that time several of the waiting passengers had asked for their money back and left. I didn't get as much as sorry from the father or his son.

Thankfully most of the thousands of passengers I have carried in light aircraft throughout the forty plus years of my flying career, behaved themselves impeccably and were a pleasure to fly with. In some cases my heart went out to them.

One day a strange little car drew up alongside our caravan and a young man in his mid twenties wound the window down and asked if I would take him for a flight over Puffin Island. I said that it was no problem as it was one of our advertised flights, but it would be a bit expensive if he intended to go on his own with no-one to share the cost of the flight. He said...

'I don't mind paying the full cost but I do have a bit of a problem...I haven't got any legs.'

He also told me that he didn't have artificial limbs either. The poor chap had been run over by a train when he was much younger. His legs had been amputated from the hip leaving nothing for artificial limbs to be attached to. I was in a bit of a quandary as to how to handle this problem as the chap didn't have anyone with him in the car to help. Somehow I had to get him to the aircraft which was on the far side of a fence. There was no gate as such and passengers had to negotiate a simple stile before boarding the aircraft.

'You can carry me, I only weigh seven stones' he suggested.

I considered the risks. I didn't want to disappoint the young man, neither did I want to be prosecuted for causing any harm to him if we fell over. He was very keen and obviously wanted to make this flight, so I said ...

'I should warn you old chum, if I attempt to carry you to the aeroplane it will probably be a bit of a wobbly journey with the odd chance that we won't make it in one go! You see the problem is that although I do have both my legs, I damaged them badly in an aeroplane crash years ago, and neither of them work very well.'

'Lets give it a try' he said gamely. 'Plonk me on the wing and I can pull myself into the cockpit backwards.'

That was good enough for me. The man showed great spirit and I would do my best to get him on board. I picked him up and was surprised at how light he was. He hung on to me with his arms around my neck and we made it in one go. That courageous young man really enjoyed his flight, and it was a privilege to fly him. When we returned I made sure he didn't pay a penny.

It wasn't always in the aeroplane that minor traumas occurred. I was taxing back towards dispersal after a short pleasure flight, when I noticed that Carol was standing by the door of the caravan looking very upset.

When my passengers had disembarked, Carol came up to the cockpit door looking very serious.

'What one earth has happened? I asked...

'It's Kimbo, you're not going to be too happy Ray.'

The second I heard Kim's name I thought she had been knocked down and killed by a customers car.

'Good Lord, she's not dead is she?'

Carol continued to look very uncomfortable. ...

'She's not dead, she's been bonked!!!.'

'Bonked? What do you mean, *bonked*?'

Kimbo hadn't been spayed when she was a puppy, but she was now eight years old and we thought too old to start having puppies. As far as I was concerned it didn't matter whether she was too old or not, it was certainly the last thing I wanted to happen to her. I wondered how the hell such a thing had happened without anyone noticing? Carol told me that she was talking to a man and his wife about the various flights available. They had a little dog on a lead standing with them and whilst the couple were discussing which flight to take, Kimbo, who was on heat at the time, slid silently up to this handsome young canine, and bingo it was love at first sight, they were locked in sexual activities without anybody noticing. Carol was the first to see what was going on and shouted at Kimbo who staggered back into the caravan dragging the poor male dog still locked to her and obviously in considerable pain.

When they finally separated, the owners of the dog were apparently very apologetic. I could see the couple standing by the caravan looking apprehensively at me. Apparently Carol had said that I would be furious when I found out what had happened and they were now considering whether to fly with me or not! I wasn't exactly over the moon about it, but I was considerably relieved to know that my little friend was OK and had not been knocked down. The matter was rectified that evening with a visit to our local Vet who gave Kimbo an injection that put an end to the possibility of her being pregnant.

Our caravan had a direct telephone link with the chap in the control tower, but there were occasions when the air/ground advisory service was not available because the one and only operator had to have a day off. At such times Carol could tell what I was doing by listening in to the Caernarfon control frequency on the small radio receiver we had installed in our caravan. In order to meet the requirements laid down by the CAA, the airfield had to have a fire tender of some kind, so Keenair Services supplied us with a rather clapped out 1940s fire engine. It was a bit of a hit and miss arrangement as Phil Hudson, who Keenair employed as the air/ground Radio Controller, also stood in as the mandatory fireman and was expected to operate the fire engine in emergency cases. When Phil took his day off, a part time fireman from the Caernarfon Fire Service sometimes stood in for Phil, but there were several occasions when he didn't turn up and there was neither a radio advisory service or fireman on duty!

There was one occasion that I will never forget, it was the time when Carol took it upon herself to react to a situation that she really wasn't prepared for.

It was late one Summer's afternoon when gusty wind conditions made it totally unsuitable for pleasure-flying. Phil, our radio operator, took advantage of the situation and decided to take his one day off per week. Carol and I were sitting in the caravan chatting to a friend of ours when the telephone rang. The local coastguard station were on the line asking if I would take part in a search for a small fishing vessel that had gone missing in the Caernarfon Bay area. When I lived at Belan I became a member of the coastguard as an observer. Later, when they realised I was operating a pleasure-flying business, I was asked to assist with the occasional aerial search. Alan Hughes, the chap we were chatting to when the phone rang, was also a pilot, so I asked him if he would like to come with me on the search, two pairs of eyes are certainly an advantage in such situations. He readily agreed and we were airborne in no time. The wind was gusting strongly from the West. Fortunately our one and only runway happened to be East/West so there was no problem with the take-off. Immediately we were airborne, *WHAM*, the turbulence hit us like a giant fist. A cloud base of five hundred feet prevented us from climbing to a decent observing height. Below us the sea was raging in a frenzied turmoil of white foam and we certainly felt sorry for any poor devil that was in trouble in a sea like that.

About forty minutes later Holyhead Coastguard came up on the R/T with the good news that the search had been called off as the boat had been discovered mooring up in the harbour and no persons were missing. I changed frequency back to Caernarfon so that Carol, who was listening out on her air-band receiver, would know that we were returning to the circuit. She couldn't reply of course as her radio was only a receiver. What I didn't appreciate at the time was that the surface wind had swung round about 80 degrees giving us a very high crosswind component on our one and only runway.

I soon realised what had happened when I caught sight of the windsock. It was a calibrated 15kt. sock which now stood out horizontally as straight as a gun-barrel indicating that we had a very strong Northerly surface wind, well over fifteen kts. I told Alan we may have to divert to RAF Valley, but we would give it a try here first. We were flying in a Cherokee 180 that had a specified maximum cross wind component of 17kts. I was well experienced in this type of aircraft as I must have had more than 4,000 hours in command instructing on Cherokees at that time, so I felt competent to at least have a shot at landing and knew exactly what to do if anything started to go wrong. We joined the circuit and decided to assess the wind by carrying out a low level overshoot. Immediately it was obvious that the wind was considerably more than 17kts. I was steering 315 degrees to maintain a constant run down the centreline of the 270 runway. We completed another short, low level circuit, turning onto the final approach at half a mile. The turbulence at low level was brutal, buffeting the aircraft up and down like a fairground swish-back. In order to maintain a constant track down the extended centreline of the runway, I decided to use a combination of wing-down and crabbing methods during the approach, I also lowered half flap (Not the standard recommended procedure for these conditions) which I intended to dump just before the stall onto the runway to ensure the aircraft stayed firmly on the ground without lifting a wing and ground looping. I was glad to have Alan aboard, I needed both hands on the control column once the throttle was closed. I instructed Al to dump the flap immediately I gave him the signal. All the way down the approach the turbulence stayed with us as we tracked sideways towards the runway. Alan gripped the manual flap lever with both hands as we crossed the threshold. I closed the throttle, kicked as hard as I could on the left rudder pedal and shouted to Alan to dump the flap. The nose swung to the left, the further effect rolling the aircraft level as the wheels thumped the runway. We were down. I applied the brakes and even with full right aileron and a touch of left rudder the starboard wing was attempting to lift and the aircraft was trying to weathercock into wind.

It was at that point I saw my wife, dear old Carol was staggering towards us, she must have run over two hundred yards carrying the heavy duty fire extinguisher we kept in our caravan. She had obviously seen us struggling with the strong crosswind bless her, and being the only other person on the airfield, rushed out to help us with a fire extinguisher should a catastrophe have occurred.

One Summer's day when we had been particularly busy, I was about to taxi out with three passengers on board for a flight over Snowdon, when I heard the pilot of a visiting aircraft inform control that he was on final approach to land on runway 26. As we had to backtrack the same runway I decided to close down and wait until the visiting aeroplane landed.

Looking out of the cockpit window I could see that the aircraft, a Beagle Pup, was obviously far too high to land, and unless the pilot lost height by side slipping, he would have to overshoot and go round again. To my surprise the pilot did neither and opted to continue his approach. The aircraft touched down about three quarters of the way down the runway going like a bat out of hell. I expected the pilot to open up immediately and go round again, but instead he attempted to stop. Clouds of blue smoke emerged from the tyres as the brakes were vigorously applied. Then, realising that the aircraft could never stop before crashing through the barrier fence and hitting the sea wall, the pilot slammed on full power in an attempt to take-off again, but the aircraft was no longer travelling fast enough to lift off safely in the remaining few yards of the runway. It was like watching a horror movie in slow motion! The aircraft literarily staggered off the ground in an extremely high nose attitude, then, almost hovering at about fifty feet, it began to roll over to the left and head down towards the area where we were parked.

The only exit door in our aircraft was on the passenger's side, so I ordered the person sitting next to me to vacate the aeroplane and I followed him out. At that moment the Beagle Pup skimmed past the nose of our aircraft in a shallow banked attitude with it's left wingtip inches from the ground. It hit the ground and crashed through the wire mesh perimeter fence on the southern boundary about fifteen yards from where we were parked, leaving most of its undercarriage wrapped up in the fence. It continued to skid across the road in a shower of sparks, clipped a stationary car and careered on through a second fence taking a couple of posts with it. The aircraft finally finished up facing back towards the airfield with its tail stuck up in the air.

Within seconds I had reached the wreckage, there was a strong smell of petrol fumes and I could see people inside the cockpit struggling to get out. Wrenching the hatch open I leaned inside. At that point the pilot who had managed to release himself from his safety harness, shouted 'get out of the way' and took a half-hearted swing at me. I tried to help him but he pushed past me and ran into the field. I'm sure he had no idea what he was doing. Having turned the fuel cock, master switch, and ignition switches off, I helped the three remaining passengers from the wreckage.

In the distance I could hear the comforting sound of the airfield fire engine as it headed down the road with it's siren blasting away. I was checking to see if the passengers had any obvious injuries when the pilot re-appeared. He saw me talking to his passengers, so I told him that as far as I could tell they seemed to be alright. Then, to my surprise he told me to piss off and mind my own business. This really annoyed me so I said...

'You left your passengers strapped in the wreckage with the fuel and the electrics turned on, and I hope you're not going to try and turn your cock-up of a landing into an act of bloody heroism mate.'

The confrontation ended abruptly as the fire engine approached the wreckage, and in spite of the seriousness of the situation it was at this point a rather funny "Keystone Cops" incident occurred that really made me laugh.

The condition of our clapped-out fire engine just about ticked all the mandatory boxes required in those days to attain CAA approval as an authorised fire appliance, but only just. In fact it was more of a much treasured antique than anything else. On the day of the accident the vehicle was driven by Phil Hudson, who was ambiguously employed in the multi capacity of Air Traffic Controller, Aircraft Refueller, Fireman, Tea Maker and General Dog's Body.

As the fire engine rattled its way towards the crashed aeroplane, it passed over the tangled remains of the barbed-wire fence that had been destroyed by the crashing aeroplane. In so doing it ripped the exhaust pipe and silencer from the bottom of the fire engine which immediately started to sound like the rapid fire of a 12.7mm machine gun. At that point Phil slammed the brakes on, leapt out of his cab and, completely ignoring the crashed aeroplane, started swearing profusely at the top of his voice...

'Cor look at the bloody mess that f.....g fence has made of my fire engine, I'd just put a new f-----g exhaust on there last week....Bastard fences never ought to be allowed near aerodromes.'

Phil gave the broken silencer a hefty kick sending it whizzing across the field towards the road. It didn't end there, Phil's tantrum about the damage to his fire engine caused the pilot of the Beagle Pup to kick off again. It seemed so funny I just doubled up. The argument between Phil, the pilot and his passengers that had now joined in, was still going on when the local Police, Ambulance and Town Fire Brigade arrived. I left them to it and returned to my aircraft where my passengers were patiently waiting for me. Later the police took a statement from me as one of the eye witnesses.

During my career in aviation I have had the privilege of flying with some very interesting people. For instance one afternoon an elderly gentleman turned up on his own and asked to be taken for a flight, preferably over the sea for a "bit of low flying" if that was allowed.

I asked him why he wanted to do this instead of flying over the more scenic mountains. The reply he gave me was certainly unexpected…

'I was a flight engineer in one of the Lancasters of 617 squadron during the Dam Buster Raid, and I would love to fly low over the water again just for old times sake.'

Ken Smith was the flight engineer in a Lancaster Captained by P/O Rice when they bombed the Mona Dam on the 17th May 1943. Obviously I was delighted to meet Ken and it was a privilege to fly with him. His dear old face lit up as we skimmed the waves along the coast of Anglesey and out over Caernarfon Bay. When we landed Ken, then 75 years old, couldn't stop thanking me. He was adamant about paying for the flight but I wouldn't accept a penny. Later he sent me photocopies of the relevant pages in his logbook and aloud me to borrow a very interesting scrapbook that he had put together during World War Two. In 1995 I received a Christmas card from him, which is now glued to the rear cover of the current log book.

One Summer's afternoon a mini bus turned up at the airfield. The sides of the vehicle were painted with lovely flowers and seaside scenes. It arrived with eight or ten little children on board together with their carer and a nurse. Some of the children were as young as three or four years old. The bus was from the "Sunshine Club". The sad news was that all the children on board were terminally ill with cancer.

It was absolutely heart breaking to see their pale, excited little faces when they saw the aeroplane they were going to fly in.

Sadly one little chap named Charlie was completely blind. He was just five years old and didn't have very long to live. The nurse said that Charlie was mad about aeroplanes and had only recently lost his sight. I strapped his fragile little body in the front seat next to me, and once we were airborne I let him hold the control column. I showed him how the aeroplane would climb if he eased back on the wheel, and how it would dive if he pushed it gently forwards. His little face lit up.

'You have a go on your own Charlie.' I said.

I was astonished by the way that child confidently moved the control column, and although he couldn't see, he put the nose of the aeroplane back exactly on the horizon each time I told him to fly level. I have to admit that tears streamed down my face, and I had a job to speak to the little fellow at one stage because of the huge lump in my throat. Charlie beamed from ear to ear and couldn't wait to tell his pals that he had really flown the aeroplane himself. I asked the nurse if there was any hope for him. She said...

'I'm afraid not, this is probably the last time he will be able to come out on one of these trips with us.'

I had to walk away from her. I know God is not to blame, but it's hard to understand why these things happen to such young and innocent children.

On a lighter side I once had to take a police sergeant up on a fairly turbulent morning to get an aerial view of premises that they had been tipped off would be raided that night. During the flight the cockpit filled with a rather obnoxious smell. He was a big strapping fellow, and when we landed he apologised profusely and said he had been so nervous that he had messed his pants!

Sometimes the most unexpected things happened. For instance, one afternoon I was sitting in the pleasure flight caravan enjoying the proverbial cup of tea, when an Army Captain suddenly burst in through the door and announced that he was commandeering the aeroplane and me with it for military purposes! He was obviously quite serious and made it very clear that he didn't expect any trouble from me. I must admit I was quite enthralled with the whole thing and within minutes we were airborne in our Piper Cherokee flying very low at his request over the sand dunes near to Fort Belan. Apparently this was serious stuff. A large and very important army exercise had been taking place in North Wales during the last few weeks, and part of the action had suddenly moved to the small peninsular that jutted out into the Menai Straits, the very same piece of land that included Fort Belan. A small section of men acting as part of the invasion forces had arrived by sea and apparently gone to ground somewhere in the sand hills. The Captain flying with me said his men were dug in close to the airfield and it was his intention to find out exactly where the "enemy" were and radio their position to his Platoon Commander.

I entered into the spirit of the thing wholeheartedly and told him I had served my national service with the army and later flown as a pilot with the RAFVR in my younger days. This seemed to please him immensely.

We headed towards the Northern tip of the peninsular at low level.

'There the bastards are' he shouted pointing to a bunch of chaps crouched down in the sand dunes.

He asked me if I would fly as low as possible over them…

'Absolutely, right away sir, I'm all for that.' I replied.

We peeled off to dive straight down at the "enemy". Several more chaps appeared that had been well camouflaged nearby and opened fire on us with light machine guns… We were so close that, apart from seeing the flashes, I could clearly hear the crack of their guns as we skimmed over them.

'I hope that's blank ammunition they're using old boy.' I said.

The officer nodded, obviously not amused at being addressed as old boy. He radioed the position of the "enemy" to his troops whilst we returned to the airfield and landed.

Later I saw a column of men being marched out of the sand dunes with their hands on their heads. The Captain returned to our caravan shortly afterwards as pleased as punch with the days proceedings. He paid for the flight, thanked me for entering into the spirit of things, and said…

'One of the "enemy" Sergeants was a bit upset at being captured, and complained that you were too low and flying illegally. So I said nothing's illegal in war Sergeant, and told him to keep his mouth shut.'

One never knew what to expect during a Summer's pleasure-flying. Heart attacks, vomiting, screams of fear, joyous laughter, tears, sarcasm, and praise were all experienced during the years I operated pleasure flights over Snowdonia.

Flying mentally handicapped people was very rewarding. For instance I will never forget one young lady that I took for a short pleasure flight over Caernarfon Castle. She sat in the back of the aeroplane with her carer. Her contorted facial expression portrayed a mixture of hate and mental agony. With the greatest respect to the poor girl she was distressingly ugly. We were flying along the coast in smooth air, and as we approached the castle I looked back to see if everything was OK. I can tell you now, I got the shock of my life. Gone was the girl with the agonising looks. In her place was a beautiful young lady, totally relaxed and smiling happily as she gazed out of the cockpit window at the scenery below. I would never have believed the miraculous change in this young girl's face had I not seen it for myself. My heart went out to her, it is these sort of rewarding experiences that really makes the day worthwhile.

CHAPTER 58.

Snowdon Mountain Railway.

Snowdon Pleasure Flights legal set-up was such that our "Barnstorming" operation had to be limited to licensed fields. There were exceptions to this rule, but one had to obtain written permission from the CAA for special clearance, and all our flights were subject to the rules set out in Keenair's Flight Operations Manual.

At the beginning of our third pleasure flying season, Jim Keen told me that he could no longer afford to lease Caernarfon Airfield from Glynllifon Estates. This was extremely bad news for Carol and me because our pleasure flying and aerial photography business depended entirely on operating under the jurisdiction of Keenair's Air Operators Certificate. Although my written agreement with Keenair Services still had several more years to run, I would be out of business immediately Keenair pulled out from Llandwrog Airfield.

Jim and I had become great friends, and he asked me if I could help with the problem of finding another operator to purchase the remaining period of his lease. I said I would try my best to help, but in so doing I would obviously be cutting my own throat. I didn't hold out much hope of finding anyone who would consider purchasing the few years remaining on the lease when many thousands of pounds needed spending on Llandwrog airfield before it could be licensed by the CAA to operate commercially.

Jim agreed to hire an aeroplane to Snowdon Pleasure Flights for the rest of the season, after that, if he had failed to sell the remainder of his lease, Keenair Services would have to pull and face the legal consequences.

Needless to say both Carol and I were deeply upset about our pleasure flying business coming to an untimely end. I was now faced with two major problems. Firstly, if Keenair Services pulled out, I would be left with no aircraft contract, no covering AOC, and the airfield would not have a licensed operator. Secondly, if I was successful in finding another company willing to purchase the remaining period of the lease, they would almost certainly wish to carry out the pleasure-flying themselves.

Anyway looking on the infinitesimal bright side of things, we were still in business for one more season. I could only hope for a miracle to occur that would change the disastrous situation as it now stood.

The problems that confronted Carol and me were massive. What was going to happen to the airfield, and more importantly, what was going to happen to us when Keenair Services ceased to honour the P/F agreement that had been made over to us as part of our redundancy package?

The way ahead looked bleak. The last thing I wanted to do was move to another area and return to flying instructing. We had made sufficient profit during our first two pleasure-flying seasons to continue paying our mortgage for a further year, so time, albeit limited, was on our side, perhaps something would turn up.

I scanned all the aviation magazines in the hope of finding an answer to my problem and wrote to several friends and contacts I had in the aviation world, all without success.

Then, one morning whilst reading our local newspaper the "Caernarfon and Denbigh Herald", I noticed an interesting item about the operators of Snowdon Mountain Railway Ltd. The article praised the success of the little steam railway that took thousands of tourists to the summit of Snowdon each year. It also said that they were now in the process of changing some of their steam engines for diesel locomotives, which I personally thought was a great shame. Then something caught my eye. The article went on to mention that Snowdon Mountain Railway's parent company, Cadougan Properties Ltd., were interested in extending their interests in the tourist trade and were looking to purchase other unusual businesses connected with tourism in North Wales.

The substance of this article immediately gave me an idea which I thought was at least worthy of a telephone call. First I made a few enquiries and found out that Cadougan Properties was in fact one of this countries largest property and business developers with their head office in the West End of London.

Initially, I decided to contact Snowdon Mountain Railway Ltd. (SMR) to find out more about their parent company's plans to expand their interests. I spoke to their Managing Director Mr Derek Rogerson who was most helpful. I told him that the lease holders of Llandwrog Airfield were looking to relinquish the lease, and explained the predicament that this left me in with Snowdon Pleasure Flights having to close down. I asked Mr Rogerson if he thought Cadougan Properties would consider taking over the lease and perhaps develop the airfield into a tourist orientated Air Park. I gave him brief details of my experience in the flying world and the responsibilities of my more recent position as Project Development Manager at Fort Belan. Mr Rogerson seemed quite enthusiastic and said that their parent company could very well be interested. He suggested that I leave it to him to have a chat with his board of directors in the first instance, and that he would contact me in a day or two to let me know their reactions.

A few days later Derek telephoned me to say that the directors of Cadougan were indeed interested in my ideas and would pay me a visit at the airfield in a week or two.

Cassie and I started to get very excited. It was at least a pinpoint of light at the end of a very long dark tunnel.

Not long afterwards Derek telephoned to say that two directors from Cadougan would meet me at the airfield the following morning. I must admit I started to panic a bit. Although I had prepared a document with my ideas for developing Llandwrog Airfield, I had hoped to meet them in the offices of Snowdon Mountain Railway and feared they would arrive to see little to enthuse them other than an old caravan and a partly derelict airfield with one marginally serviceable runway and a few dilapidated world war two buildings.

I was nervously waiting for them to arrive when I saw an enormous and very expensive looking black car heading towards the airfield. It stopped just inside the main gates and two young men, who I estimated were in their mid thirties, got out of the car and stood for a while looking at the airfield. Eventually they turned and walked towards me. We shook hands and I invited them into our modest little caravan to meet Carol and join us for a cup of coffee. (We considered it wise to upgrade from tea on this auspicious occasion!)

It soon became evident that these gentlemen were very adroit characters. They wasted no time with small talk and went straight into giving me a very thorough third degree. They asked me personal questions about my past managerial experience in the aviation business, the positions I had held, how long I was employed by each company and the reasons for leaving. As they were not too familiar with the aviation industry, they wanted to know exactly what my work had entailed. They showed particular interest in my duties as project manager for Fort Belan. Then came the million dollar question. How did I envisage the integration of Llandwrog Airfield with tourism in North Wales?

I pointed out that the geographical location of the airfield with its entrance gates being adjacent to the seafront with beautiful sandy beaches and the Mountains of Snowdonia as a backdrop, made it the ideal site for development within the tourism industry. By adopting a phased development strategy, Llandwrog Airfield could eventually be designated by the CAA as "Caernarfon Airport" and become a unique Air-Park for visiting pilots and tourists alike. The attraction could offer its visitors such facilities as pleasure flights over the castles and mountains of North Wales, an interesting Museum depicting the history of the airfield during the 1939-1945 war, a Flying Club, Restaurant, Craft Shop, and eventually aircraft refuelling and maintenance facilities.

I could tell that the two men were interested in my ideas. They wandered around the airfield on their own for a while and then left, saying that they would be talking things over with Mr Rogerson who would contact me again in the near future.

The next thing that I heard from Derek was that Cadougan Properties would be sending their "Aviation Expert" to assess the situation. I was quite pleased about this because if he was an aviation expert he would see the potential of Llandwrog, also there was a good chance that I already knew him.

In due course an appointment was set up and once again Carol and I anxiously awaited the arrival of "The Man from Head Office".

Sadly when the guy turned up I took an immediate dislike to his exaggerated air of authority. I chatted with him for some time, explaining my ideas etc., but he seemed more interested in creating an impression on me than listening to what I was saying. He strutted around the caravan looking at the wall-maps showing the P/F routes and aerial photographs of the castles. Then he said he would like to look at the aeroplane. I said he was more than welcome, but it was of little relevance as the aircraft was on hire and would shortly be returned to Keenair Services. He sat in the pilots seat for a while messing around with the controls and twiddling the elevator trim handle backwards and forwards. I'm not sure if this was meant to impress me or not, but I was beginning to have my doubts about the authenticity of this guy who proclaimed to be Cadougan's "Aviation Expert". He seemed to be missing the point altogether. My small mobile flight office and one hired aeroplane had little to do with the purchase of the airfield lease and the potential development of Llandwrog Aerodrome. In the end I was convinced that this man knew very little about the aviation industry.

My future and that of Llandwrog Airfield were at stake here, and I didn't want to rock the boat too much at this stage, but I had to know exactly what this chap was up to. So I decided to ask him, in as friendly a way as possible, what his qualifications actually were. He appeared to be offended by my question, and replied…

'I'm here to appraise the business potential of this airfield and also assess your capabilities as a pilot and potential manager for one of Cadougan's Properties, that should be sufficient to satisfy your curiosity.'

He was wrong I had one more question for him…

'I fully understand what you're saying old boy, but what exactly are your qualifications?'

He was obviously furious and blurted out…

'I'm a qualified pilot myself and a friend of the Directors.

My years of experience as a flying instructor, instinctively told me that this guy's knowledge about flying was zilch. So I made out to be impressed and said…

'I'm sure our paths must have crossed previously, I used to train commercial pilots at Oxford Air Training School, perhaps we met there, where did you do your Commercial Pilot Training?'

'I'm not a commercial pilot, I have well over a hundred hours flying experience as a private pilot.'

His reply didn't surprise me at all. Nothing to be ashamed of I'm sure, but I would have thought that the directors of Cadougan Properties, who were considering whether or not to invest in a civil aviation project, would have sent someone more professionally qualified than a private pilot to assess the potential.

So here was I, a fully qualified commercial pilot instructor and CAA examiner, being assessed by a chap who's only qualification was a recently acquired PPL. But facts are facts and I had to go along with that.

Several weeks later Derek telephoned me again to say his board of directors were agreeable to purchasing the remainder of the Llandwrog Airfield lease from Keenair Services Ltd., providing that the actual owners of the aerodrome, Glynllifon Estates, were willing to extent the lease to ninety-nine years. That being the case I would be offered employment as Managing Director of a new company to be named "Snowdon Mountain Aviation" which would be a subsidiary of Snowdon Mountain Railway Co.

Ltd. If these arrangements went ahead, I would be expected to supervise the development of Llandwrog Airfield to a fully licensed airfield which they hoped would eventually be designated as "Caernarfon Airport". All details with reference to pleasure-flying and the tourist side of the development would be discussed at a later board meeting.

It couldn't be better. We would be able to continue living in our home in the mountains, and Llandwrog Airfield would have the financial support it needed to be reinstated into a first class aerodrome. Once again Carol and I could celebrate the beginnings of another adventure, but our celebrations were premature.

Jim Keen was only too pleased to sell the lease on, but the problem laid firmly in the hands of Glynllifon Estates who were not happy about extending the lease.

Cadougan Properties were certainly not interested in laying huge sums of money to develop the aerodrome with only a few years to run on the existing lease.

Derek Rogerson and myself attended several meetings with the solicitors and accountants from both Glynllifon Estates and Cadougan's Properties Ltd. But my old bosses the Trustees of Glynllifon Estates would not budge and refused to extend the lease of the airfield.

I was devastated by their decision and wrote a long letter to the Chairman of Lord Newborough's Trustees saying how disappointed I was not to be in a position to develop the airfield that I had previously run on their behalf. I said that the decision of the trustees not to lease the airfield to one of the biggest business development companies in Great Britain was a grave mistake as the proposed plans to renovate Llandwrog Aerodrome into a fully licensed commercial airfield that would ultimately be designated as Caernarfon Airport would increase the value of their property enormously.

Fortunately Cadougan Directors were still interested in backing a tourist-orientated Air Park in North Wales. Although we knew it would be a hard slog to find another disused airfield and obtain planning permission to turn it back into an active airfield, Derek and I began our search. It was indeed a heart-breaking task, especially when the perfect airfield was right on our doorstep. But we tried.

The nearest we came to finding a possible site was Penrhos, an ex wartime fighter airfield. But unfortunately part of the airfield was already rented out as a residential caravan site. In the end we realised that it would be a hopeless task to try and proceed further, and gave up the idea.

Just a few days before Christmas I received a telephone call from my old boss, The Hon Robert Wynn, who was the sole beneficiary of the trust and in effect personally owned Llandwrog Airport. He said that his Trustees had changed their minds and were now willing to lease Llandwrog Airfield to Cadougan Properties for a period of 99 years, adding…

'You and Carol can now enjoy your Christmas.'

And what a wonderful Christmas present that was.

CHAPTER 59.

This time from Scratch.

The Directors of Cadougan Properties decided that their recent acquisition of Llandwrog Airfield should be a financially independent subsidiary of Snowdon Mountain Railway (SMR). Intrinsically a new operating company was registered in the name of 'Snowdon Mountain Aviation Ltd.' (SMA) and I was designated to become the Managing Director of the newly formed company. I was happy to learn that my immediate boss would be the man who had become a great friend, Mr Derek Rogerson, the Managing Director of Snowdon Mountain Railway Ltd.

Carol assisting me at the airfield from day one. In fact we were the only employees on the airfield during the first few weeks. The arrangements were that our joint salary would be equivalent to the average annual net profit we made when we ran our own pleasure-flying business.

Taking over an airfield that was unlicensed and last used as an auxiliary landing strip by Keenair Services, was not as simple as it would first appear. Previously we were able to run our pleasure-flying business using a Keenair Service's aeroplane that operated under the auspices of their Air Operators Certificate based on Liverpool Airport. Now that Keenair no longer leased the aerodrome as a satellite to their business at Liverpool, Llandwrog was completely unlicensed. As such Snowdon Mountain Aviation Ltd. could not legally operate pleasure flights from the airfield until it became fully licensed by the CAA. In addition to the airfield licence we would need to be granted an Air Operators Certificate.

Carol and I decided to set up our small office on the first floor of the old RAF control tower. The room was sparse, just four plain walls, two metal desks, a couple of chairs, and a serviceable telephone. The building was connected to the mains electricity, and there were derisory toilet facilities on the ground floor.

We arrived on day one armed with Cassie's typewriter, my small drawing board, a stack of plain paper, a telephone directory (No computers or mobile telephones in those days), an electric kettle, a couple of mugs, and the all important milk sugar and tea. Our task was to convert a derelict world war two airfield into a CAA licensed Airport, and to form an approved operating company for the use of commercial aircraft. This was one hell of an assignment and we were starting from scratch. But Carol and I had worked successfully together on many projects and looked forward excitedly to the new challenge ahead.

My previous working relationship with CAA Flight Operations Inspector Capt Tony Trowbridge proved to be invaluable. He was the first person I contacted for advice, and straight away he sent me all the mandatory Civil Aviation Publications relating to the licensing of airfields and the writing of an Operations Manual which enabled me to get started.

We had to carry out a tremendous amount of work on the airfield before it measured up to the licensing standards laid out in CAP 168. After hours of planning and designing I contracted the work out to local builders. The existing runway had to be resurfaced in accordance with strict regulations. Threshold displacements had been calculated and marked out on the runways. Security fences were erected and a multitude of the mandatory aerodrome signs were manufactured and erected in accordance with CAA regulations. I drew up plans for the construction of a new Air Traffic Control room to replace the wooden shack previously used by Keenair Services, and contracted the construction work out to Sadlers Ltd. who had previously carried out excellent work for me when I was working at Fort Belan.

The Aerodrome Manual was quite a complicated document to write. It covered every aspect of the airfield in great detail and took me some time to produce. Finally, after considerable scrutiny it was approved by the CAA, and after a full inspection, Llandwrog airfield was fully licensed and approved to operate as Caernarfon Airport.

But the most complex of all the documents I had to write was the company's multi-facetted Flight Operations Manual.

This document took several weeks to complete and ultimately contained three large volumes of valid information detailing every aspect of the company's commercial operation and flight limitations. In addition, all aircraft that were operated commercially by SMA had to be inspected by a CAA Flight Ops Inspector to see that mandatory passenger safety signs, aircraft markings, and safety equipment installed conformed to the regulations set out by CAA flight standards before our Air Operators Certificate was finally issued and we legally licensed to operate.

Looking back now I can hardly believe that all the above was completed within three months from the day we took over the airfield.

Extra staff had been employed throughout the development of the airfield, and by the time the airport was at full strength, we employed a combination of over forty full and part time staff.

In order to get the pleasure flying side operational I initially leased a Cessna 172 from Keenair Services, and on the 29th March 1986 I took off in G-BKLP with our first three passengers aboard bound for the mountains of Snowdonia.

In the fullness of time we had our own flying school, a large refuelling bay, a first class restaurant and a gift shop. As expected, we had many confrontations with the council's planning department before my design for the Air Museum was approved. The local planning inspector, a rather stroppy young lady, insisted that the exterior of the museum should be painted a bright mustard colour instead of the more suitable dark blue we requested. She told me point blankly that if we didn't agree to the mustard colour, she would make sure that our planning application was rejected.

The building was constructed on a site quite close to the entrance gates of the airport, its main theme being based on the history of RAF Llandwrog during the second world war. The addition of the museum successfully made Caernarfon Airport an "All Weather Tourist Attraction."

Later I decided to extend the range of our exhibits and attended several MOD auctions, adding a Javelin, Vampire, Sea Hawk, Anson, Hunter, Dove, Wessex Helicopter, Varsity Simulator and many other items to our exhibits. Also I managed to secure one of the largest collections of beautifully made 1/72 scale model aircraft on permanent loan to our museum from a local professional model maker.

During the first few years of operation, we lacked our own aircraft maintenance facilities. We overcame this by renting a hangar to an outside maintenance company who supplied resident engineers to look after our requirements.

Caernarfon Airport was now featured in all relevant CAA publications including the "Air Pilot", and with the airport being located close to the beautiful Snowdonia range of mountains and bordering the seafront, we soon became very popular with visiting aircraft flying in from all over Europe.

As always Carol was my right hand person. She had been working in the capacity of flight operations manager for several companies over a period of twelve years, and she knew the job inside-out. It was comforting to know I could rely on her implicitly to run the things for me at times when I was away from the airfield and flying. She did everything from co-ordinating the flying programme, organizing the aircraft maintenance schedules with our engineering section, taking care of customer relations and supervising the Ops, restaurant and shop staff as well as taking care of the accounts.

On occasions when the opportunity presented itself, Carol would come flying with me, but our individual responsibilities were such that we seldom had the chance to fly together. However, it was sods law that one of the most horrendous meteorological experiences I ever had whilst flying over mountainous terrain took place when Carol was with me, and it came very close to putting her off flying for the rest of her life.

The North Wales TTA consortium decided to advertise all ten attractions on television, and came to the conclusion that the best way to feature some of the facilities was to film them all from the air. They commissioned a professional advertising agency to make the film who in turn commissioned a helicopter company to take aerial shots for them.

It was arranged that Snowdon Mountain Aviation's section of the film would feature our Cessna 172 aeroplane flying over the summit of Snowdon and peeling off to descend through the Llanberis Pass….. Excellent idea….. or was it?

On the day that filming was to take place, arrangements were made for the helicopter to land at Caernarfon Airport at 6am. The door of the helicopter would then be removed for filming purposes, and after a short briefing we would both take-off and head for the summit of Snowdon. Carol would also fly with me to take the part of a pleasure-flight passenger waving happily from the rear window of the Cessna.

We arrived at the airport at 5.30am. It was a cold, crisp morning with crystal clear skies and virtually no surface wind, perfect conditions for filming. We pushed the aeroplane out from the hangar, checked the fuel and carried out the pre-flight inspection.

Spot on 6am the helicopter arrived overhead the airfield and landed alongside our aircraft. The pilot, John, was very experienced in aerial filming and had carried out work for most of the major British television companies.

Our plan was for the helicopter to take-off first and climb to 4,100 feet, which would give him a clearance of just over 500 feet above the summit of Snowdon. He would hover just East of the peak in an up-sun position relative to my aircraft which would pass between the helicopter and the summit of the mountain. I would then complete one clockwise orbit and peel off to the right descending over the Horseshoe Ridge into the Llanberis Pass.

The cameraman assembled his gyro stabilised camera mount and climbed in. Within a few minutes John had lifted off and was hovering in front of the control tower whilst I taxied Lima Papa to the holding point of 08. We both had our radios tuned to a pre-arranged frequency so that we could communicate with each other during the flight, and Carol, who also had a headset, sat behind me ready to play the part of an enthusiastic tourist.

Although I had marvelled at the magnificent views whilst flying over Snowdonia many times in the past, this morning's sensational display seemed even more amazing than usual. The air remained calm, the crimson sun, still very low over the horizon, cast long shadows across the pink mists that rested between the craggy peaks. Well ahead of us I could see the sun glinting on the rotor blades of John's helicopter, looking for all the world like a silver disc dancing in the illustriousness of the morning sky. Little did I know what awaited us at the summit.

More often than not the air over mountainous terrain is turbulent. The direction and strength of the wind, and the ambient temperatures combined with the instinct gained by constantly flying over mountainous country, can give a pilot advanced warning of what to expect as he approaches the mountains. When flying in mountainous areas, a sound knowledge of the inherent dangers are essential to any pilot wishing to live to a ripe old age. Today everything was beautifully calm as we headed towards the summit. I did however notice a slight nudge on the controls as we climbed through 2000 ft., up to that point we had experienced perfectly still air conditions.

The radio crackled into life as the helicopter pilot announced he was now in position hovering just East of the summit. I acknowledged his call and said that we were slightly below the peak to the West of him and I should pop up into his view in thirty seconds. We passed over Crib Goch, the most hazardous path on the mountain, and levelled out. I could see the helicopter hovering like a tiny dragonfly about half a mile away in our one o'clock position. Passing over the summit I commenced a right hand turn as pre-arranged. Carol, was now waving vigorously from the rear seat window playing her part as the passenger when……. WHAM!… there was a horrifying bang, followed by a tremendous jolt that forced my chin hard down onto my chest. For a split second I thought we had struck something pretty solid with the underside of the fuselage. Then there was a tremendous gush of wind that sounded like an express train rushing past, and the aircraft lurched violently upwards at an incredible rate of climb with the nose of the aircraft pointing slightly down. I gripped the rubber protection strip around the top of the instrument panel as tight as I could to stop my body being forced against the control column which I clung on to with my other hand. Two or three seconds later there was a terrific WHACK that caused the aircraft to shudder and we dropped like a stone. I struggled to gain control whilst the side of the mountain appeared to roar vertically upwards past the cockpit windows. It was a miracle that the main spar of the wings didn't fracture. Fighting with every ounce of strength in my body I tried to control the aircraft that was now being forced viciously down between the mountainous sides of the Horseshoe Pass like a lift with a broken cable. The stall warning horn was sounding all the time and I could hear Carol screaming behind me, but there was absolutely nothing I could do to help her. The aircraft was falling in a completely flat attitude when suddenly it pitched up. The juddering stopped, and stall warning hooter became silent. As quickly as it had begun the turbulence stopped as if it had been turned off by a switch, we were flying in calm air with the controls reacting normally.

For the first time in many hundreds of hours mountain flying, I had apparently flown into what is known as "Clear Air Turbulence" (CAT), one of the most dangerous meteorological phenomena you could ever have the misfortune of encountering. The only thing that had saved us from total destruction was the fact that we had been forced down some 750 feet into the Horseshoe Gap narrowly missing the mountain walls on either side.

As we climbed up again, two conflicting voices were attempting to gain my attention. The first was Carol begging me to return to the airfield. The second was the voice of the helicopter pilot telling me that his cameraman was not happy with the way we suddenly disappeared from sight, and could we do another run without diving so violently?

In spite of poor old Carol's plea to return to the airfield, the job had to be done, and I carried out a second run, this time avoiding the steep slopes of Crib Goch altogether. Everything went smoothly and although the cameraman was happy, Carol was not. She had flown with me when

I carried out spinning and aerobatics in a Cessna Aerobat and Chipmunk without the slightest complaint, but this experience tipped the scales for Carol and she vowed she would never fly with me again. Fortunately with the passing of time she relented, but would never fly over the mountains with me.

When I landed I contacted the Met Office at RAF Valley. The forecaster was grateful that I had called him. He said it was extremely unusual to encounter CAT at that altitude, but having listened to my description of the incident he confirmed that it was Clear Air Turbulence, and said he would ask their Approach Controller to warn aircraft in that area throughout the day.

Clear Air Turbulence is an extremely violent air mass. There is no pre-warning, and it is impossible to detect either by the naked eye or radar, as such it is very difficult to avoid. CAT is caused when massive bodies of air moving vertically at widely different speeds, collide. Normal to severe turbulence can be expected when approaching or entering cumulus cloud, or flying over mountainous regions when strong winds or high surface temperatures are present. But Clear Air Turbulence is totally unpredictable, it occurs without the slightest warning and is extremely hazardous to aircraft. In 1966 BOAC flight 911 broke up in flight whilst experiencing severe turbulence flying down wind of mount Fuji in Japan. Usually these conditions occur at altitudes above 20,000 ft. but as we found out to our consternation, they can occur at much lower altitudes. In my job as a pleasure flight pilot flying over the mountains, I recorded 1,486 flights over Snowdon, during that time I only experienced severe clear air turbulence on that one flight. Since man first started to fly, Snowdon has claimed the lives of literally hundreds of aircrew. Records show that around sixty aircraft came to grief on the Snowdonia Range of Mountains. Most of them were from RAF Llandwrog during world war two, many were probably caused by poor navigation in IMC conditions, but how many of those recorded crashes were caused by the effect of Clear Air Turbulence?

Within the first year of operating Caernarfon Airport we opened up a flying school. Soon SMA was employing a staff of five flying instructors and a small number of ground support staff.

In addition to the C172 I was leasing from Keenair, I purchased a Piper Cherokee 140 from Klingair Ltd. at Donnington. The aircraft was fully equipped for instrument flying. We also started twin rating courses in a Piper Apache G-ARTD loaned to us by Doctor Jones who based his aeroplane at Caernarfon.

Doc. Jones, known jokingly as Doctor Death by the instructors who flew with him, was an eminent Consultant Psychiatrist that practiced in Denbigh Hospital and also lectured at universities throughout the UK. He was a very generous, kind-hearted man who had personally adopted a large family of mentally handicapped children. Together with a full time nurse, these children lived with him in his sizeable house on Anglesey. Not long after I was introduced to Dr Jones, he kindly offered to let us use his Apache for twin engine training at a very reasonable hourly rate. We also agreed to insure and maintain the aeroplane for him.

One afternoon I was looking out of my office window and saw the Apache coming in to land on runway 26. It was more of an arrival than a landing as it bounced heartily from one end of the runway to the other. I was interested to see who the pilot was that had made such an entertaining landing. Amazingly no less than eight children, the doctor and his private nurse emerged from the cockpit of this six seat aeroplane. I hate to think where the calculated C of G was, and how much overweight that aeroplane would have been, both when it took off and when it landed.

I flew with Doctor Jones several times in an attempt to improve his landings and also teach him how to navigate using the radio aids in his aeroplane. I knew that he had been taught to fly at a club on Anglesey, but I never met the instructor who trained him. At times his attempts to land were nothing short of terrifying, so bad in fact that out of all our instructors only Dave Lloyd and myself would fly with him. Having said that, he was a lovely man, and well respected in the medical profession.

There is however a very sad twist to this story. Many years later the psychiatrist's aeroplane G-ARTD finally met its demise.

When this happened I had retired from flying, and my successor, Alistair Lynn-Macrea an ex RAF Squadron Leader, had taken over my position as Managing Director. We met up occasionally for a chat about various aspects of the company he was now running, and I found Alistair to be an absolute gentlemen. Some months after Alistair had taken over from me, I was shocked to learn of his sudden death.

At about 2.15pm on a beautifully clear afternoon, Alistair took off on his own in Doctor Jones's Apache without signing out or saying a word to anyone. Minutes later the aircraft was observed by several people in the area to fly straight into the side of Moel Hebos, one of the Snowdonia range of mountains, striking the rock face about 350 ft. below its 2,500 ft.

summit. Alistair was killed instantly. Apparently one of the witnesses said that there appeared to be nothing wrong with the aeroplane, it was flying at a constant height and heading, the engine sounded normal and it just flew straight into the side of the mountain without making any attempt to avoid the impact. At the inquest it was stated that an examination of the wreckage by the CAA's Accident Investigation Board indicated that the aircraft was functioning normally immediately prior to the crash. It was also revealed that the pilot did have personal problems at the time and there was a possibility that he used the Apache to end his life. It is very sad to think that the crash occurred in an aeroplane belonging to an eminent psychiatrist, a man that maybe could have helped sort out this poor man's problems.

CHAPTER 60.

A Gentleman's Aerial Carriage.

It was during the Winter of 1987 when my association with the Dragon Rapide first began. Carol was browsing through a copy of 'Flight' magazine when she suddenly said…

'Look at this Ray, remember the type of aeroplane you always said you would love to have on our fleet for pleasure-flying? Well there's one up for sale.'

Carol passed the magazine to me and there it was in large black print.

DH 89a DRAGON RAPIDE FOR SALE,
Apply for details to Capt. Hood, c/o Biggin Hill Aerodrome.

It wasn't just the fact that the aircraft would carry more passengers than the Cessna that attracted me, I was certain that the sight of a beautiful old 1930s de-Havilland Rapide aeroplane trundling around the sky would attract more tourists to our airfield for pleasure flights.

I got in touch with Captain Hood who informed me that the aircraft had just completed its Certificate of Air Worthiness inspection and was fully licensed by the CAA to carry passengers.

Antique aircraft are not cheap to purchase and certainly not cheap to operate commercially, so I was well aware that before I could convince my fellow directors that this was the aeroplane for us, I had to back up my enthusiasm with hard commercial facts. At that time there were only two de Havilland Rapide's operating commercially in this country, so it was not an easy task to produce a forward budget and predicted cash flow for the operation of an almost extinct aeroplane.

Finally, after many long and sometimes heated boardroom discussions, it was agreed that I should contact Capt. Hood again and arrange to see the Rapide in company with my fellow directors.

My heart almost missed a beat as the hangar doors at Biggin Hill rolled back noisily, and there she was, one beautiful old de-Havilland Rapide. She was painted silver with dark blue registration letters and trim. I remember thinking how pompous she looked standing there with her nose high in the air. Our directors were certainly impressed with the aeroplane but unfortunately didn't agree to purchase the aircraft straight away. The full story of the wrangling and arguments that pursued are too dreary to include in this book. We almost lost her to another potential purchaser who wanted to take the aircraft to America. But in the end, thanks to the enthusiasm of our financial director, Brian Lever, a price was agreed and Snowdon Mountain Aviation added a Rapide to its fleet of aircraft.

On the 3rd March 1987 I set out to collect de Havilland Rapide G-AIDL from Biggin Hill and bring her back to Caernarfon.

As the weather was bordering on IMC, I flew over to Biggin Hill in our Cessna 172 accompanied by a couple of my staff pilots. The idea was for one of them to fly the Cessna back to Caernarfon and, as the Rapide had no Radio Navigational Aids, and I had never flown, or even sat in the pilot's seat of a Rapide in my life, the second chap could help me navigate around the London Control Zone as I would probably have my hands full getting used to the way the aircraft handled on the journey back to Caernarfon.

Initially arrangements were made with Capt. Hood for me to be checked out on the Rapide by his designated Check Captain. Not that it was a complicated aeroplane, far from it, but I had heard on the grapevine, and soon learned from experience that the DH-89-A could be a handful to land, especially in a strong crosswind.

By the time we arrived at Biggin Hill the weather had deteriorated badly and the surface wind was becoming quite gusty, I was then informed by Captain Hood that his Check Captain for the Rapide had failed to turn up. I realised that with the winds gusting up to 25kts and low cloud forming, this was probably a smart decision on his part. So under the circumstances I had little choice but to fly the Rapide back to Caernarfon without a check ride. I suppose having flown thousands of hours as first pilot in over 100 different types of aircraft, boosted my confidence a little. So I handed the cheque to a very sad Capt. Hood who looked as if he was saying goodbye to a real old and trusted friend. He handed over a briefcase full of airframe and engine logbooks together with all the other mandatory paperwork, shook hands with me and drove off in his car.

I made my way over to the Rapide to inform my mate Dave that we were off. Having searched the briefcase thoroughly I discovered that there was no sign of a check list or handling notes for the Rapide which left me in a bit of a quandary. I thought I had better warn Dave of the situation…

'Sorry Dave there's nobody available to check me out, and I can't find any handling notes or a check list. If you are not happy flying with me you can go back in the Cessna and I'll follow on in the Rapide.'

Dave shook his head and said…

'The Cessna has already taken off and is on its way back to Caernarfon boss. Anyway I'd rather fly back in the Rapide.'

After a thorough external pre-flight check we gave the props a few turns by hand and climbed aboard. The eight passenger seats were upholstered in light green worsted, capped with slip-on white leather covers. It was like a journey into the past, and I could see why they used to call this lovely old aeroplane a "Gentleman's Aerial Carriage". Having made my way up the steeply inclined fuselage towards the flight deck. I poked my head through the opening in the forward bulkhead to enter the cockpit, and was rewarded with that wonderful smell of leather, doped canvas and octane.

I soon found out that there is a knack to entering the cockpit, if you get it wrong you can find yourself in the embarrassing position of having to crawl out backwards and start all over again. So it's right leg first, then double yourself almost in half so that you can enter the cockpit, slide your left leg over the pilot's seat onto the left rudder and wriggle in. I eventually wound up in a sitting position that seemed as if my feet were almost at the same level as my ears, this would improve of course when the tail comes up and the aircraft is in flight.

The cockpit layout was typical of most aircraft of the 30s and 40s. Large black instruments that gave no indication of the aircraft's in-flight limitations. The only navigation instruments were a DGI and a P6 compass, the needle of which was extremely difficult to see. A huge, very businesslike control column of the "Spectacle" type dominated the cockpit, it had a considerable back and forth traverse that came right up to almost under your chin when pulled fully back. A large elevator trim wheel was situated on the left-hand side of the cockpit just below the throttle quadrant. I discovered that the rudder trim was the small crank-type handle that poked out near the base and to the right of the control column. The flaps were operated by a large lever just to the right of my seat. Everything about the controls in this lovely old aeroplane was giant-like. It took a little while to sort out the unmarked switches on the panel to the left of me that also housed the PA system, rows of fuses and circuit breakers. Eventually, after sorting out the fuel system levers and brass handled priming pump together with a few more knobs and switches, I decided to have a go at starting the engines. This proved to be quite straight forward and before long we were up and running, ready for taxi clearance to the holding point of runway 21.

Taxying the Rapide is carried out using the same technique as that used in the Chipmunk. i.e. Release the handbrake, apply full rudder deflection (In either direction) then apply the handbrake until it begins to bite and you can feel he rudder move, continue to apply the brake for a further two notches on the quadrant and set the handbrake in that position. Then using full deflection of the rudder you have individual braking for each wheel at the extreme end of the rudder movement. This coupled with the use of asymmetric power from the engines should make steering whilst taxying quite easy. But not so today! David removed the chocks and jumped aboard. Having been given taxi clearance by Biggin Control, I was shocked to discovered that the left wheel brake didn't work at all! With the handbrake locked fully on the starboard wheel locked and the port wheel continued to rolled freely.

As the weather was deteriorating fast and there didn't appear to be any mechanics on duty when we collected the aircraft from the hangar, I decided to continue taxying. Eventually I managed to reach the end of the runway by turning through 270 degrees or more to the right every time I needed to turn left, much to the amusement of the duty air traffic controller who asked me if I was feeling well. With no port brake, the engine run-up to check the magnetos at the holding point was a bit of a rapid business to say the least, but the mag drop had been OK when the chocks were in place outside the hangar earlier. Finally we were ready. I obtained take-off clearance and pirouetted Delta Lima gracefully onto the runway. The controller, with a certain amount of concerned amazement in his voice, asked me again if everything was OK before finally clearing us for take-off.

Fortunately by carefully juggling the throttles I was able to keep perfectly straight during the take-off run. Eventually she rose elegantly into the air, it was the beginning of a long and lasting friendship between pilot and aeroplane.

Immediately we were airborne I began to get the feel of this lovely old aeroplane. Once the tail was up the view from the cockpit was paramount.

The elevators seemed a little spongy, but the rudder was very positive and the ailerons, although a little heavy, had a good firm feel about them.

As we climbed away from "Biggin on the Bump" as it was affectionately called, my thoughts flashed back to my old friend and course instructor Frank Sturdy. He was killed on Biggin Hill years earlier practising asymmetric flying in a Heron aircraft, it was a sobering thought.

We continued climbing for a while on a North-Westerly heading, said cheerio to the controller and attempted to change frequency to London Information. It was at this point we discovered another problem. The ancient "Mickey Mouse" radio installed in DL must have had some sort of a rubber belt arrangement that changed the digital frequency indicator, unfortunately the tension in the belt had slackened, consequently when the station selector knob was turned the actual frequency changed but the digital indicator slipped and sometimes didn't move at all. As a result of this we had no way of knowing what frequencies we were selecting. Consequently Dave spent most of the flight leaning into the cockpit counting the number of clicks in order to try and select the correct frequency.

Map reading our way round the London Control Zone didn't give us any problems. It was inspiring to look down through the wisps of cloud and see the very heart of London with the silvery River Thames winding its way past the Houses of Parliament and Big Ben.

Not having any performance details readily available, I climbed her to a safe height and slowly brought both throttles back to check the speed at which the aircraft showed signs of stalling. She started to buffet at around 62 mph with flap down, so I decided to add 5 mph to that speed in order to make a safe approach and landing when we reached the airfield. Eventually we crossed the peak of Snowdon and descended towards Caernarfon Airport, only to be greeted by a very nasty crosswind on our one and only 26/08 runway. We could see there were crowds of people waiting to take a look at the Rapide when she arrived, and Dave said that he could see TV cameras set up on the top of the control tower. Carol must have arranged for the Welsh TV News crew to come over and witness the momentous occasion of the "Dragon Returns to Wales". That was all I needed. Having never landed a Rapide in my life, I was to make my first attempt in a howling crosswind with the TV boys all waiting to catch the dubious arrival on camera.

Fortunately by an incredible stoke of luck David had managed to make contact with Caernarfon Tower on our antiquated radio. Our controller informed us that the surface wind was 160 degrees at eighteen to twenty knots, which was almost at right angles to the runway. I chose runway 08 because it did have a very slight headwind component compared to its reciprocal heading. As requested by control we made two low runs down the runway for the benefit of the TV cameras, at the same time I was able to assess the drift, which as far as I was concerned seemed horrendous. Capt. Hood had warned me that using the crab technique of approach with a Rapide in a strong wind could be fatal. Apparently, with considerable wing area, she rolls quite viciously from the further effect of the rudder when you slew the aircraft straight just before touchdown, and you can also run out of aileron control whilst trying to offset the roll. So, not wishing to give the TV reporters too much excitement, I decided to land one wheel at a time using the wing- down technique to keep straight.

With sweaty palms I lined Delta Lima up with the runway and called finals to land. As the old lady rocked and buffeted her way down the approach, the runway for some reason looked a lot smaller than usual. She touched down beautifully on the starboard wheel and was easy to keep straight with the huge rudder. I eased her down onto the port wheel without any trouble…. Great… but it wasn't over yet. Once the airspeed started to decay and the tail dropped, the huge tail fin acted like a weathercock and with no braking on the left wheel I couldn't hold her straight. She swung round smartly into wind and trundled off the runway onto the 'No Taxying' grass area. I heard Dave breath a sigh of relief in the back and say something quite unprintable as we taxied in towards the waiting crowds. Fortunately I was able to make a long radius turn to the right so that I arrived on the perimeter track without having to turn left, or in this case with no left brake, turning 270 degrees to the right! Once on the perimeter track I was able to taxi up to the tower keeping straight by the use of asymmetric thrust from the engines. Apparently the landing looked good because everyone thought I had turned onto the grass quickly to prevent the aircraft from rolling over in the gusty conditions, which I suppose I would have done, but in this case I had no choice and the surface wind did it for me!

We clambered down from the fuselage to be met at the cabin door by reporters and my dear wife clutching a bottle of Vintage Champagne. If it hadn't have been for Carol, who instigated the purchase of the Rapide in the first place, thousands of pleasure flight passengers would never have had the privilege and excitement of flying in our very valuable and much treasured 1930s airliner, an aeroplane that in its day, rightfully earned the title of "A Gentleman's Aerial Carriage".

Once our engineer had rectified the problem with the port brake, and attended to a couple of other minor problems including the radio frequency selector, arrangements were made for the de-Havilland Rapide to be included in our ops manual as well as my pilots licence, and within a few days the aircraft was operating commercially out of Caernarfon Airport.

I never took any liberties with the Rapide, she was an old lady that demanded respect. Her construction being mainly of wood and fabric was a fact that one would be well advised to bare in mind when flying her. But even on the odd occasion when we were caught in severe turbulence, she seemed to take it all in her stride. Sometimes the old lady's mags would play up and she would pop and bang for a while. A bit of coaxing never went astray on such occasions. I felt we had a sort of understanding for one another. I even found myself talking to her, although swearing at her always seemed to make things worse!! (I think old pilots get a bit eccentric and treat their aircraft like an old pal...especially if the aeroplane is the same age as the pilot, which was the case with Delta Lima and myself, we both made our first appearance into this world in the early 1930s.)

To begin with however it was without doubt a love/hate relationship between DL and myself. As the hangar doors opened each morning, there she was, my 1930s aerial carriage glaring down snootily at me as if to say 'What the hell do you want?' and I would ask her....

'What nasty little tricks have you got up your aerodynamic sleeve for me today?'

I admit I did swear at her on occasions, and she's blown a gasket or two at me more than once. But in the end we flew together for over 1,500 enjoyable hours. I suppose it sounds a little stupid, but after a while I truly loved that old aeroplane, and years later when we finally parted I had a huge lump in my throat as she disappeared over the horizon to be based at Coventry Airport.

Although DL was a simple, basic aeroplane to fly, you did have to fly her, no doubt about that. Lose concentration for a moment, especially when taking off or landing in a crosswind, and she would bite. Like most aircraft, she was a completely different kettle of fish to fly when she was fully loaded. Without passengers the Rapide could fly on one engine and just about manage to climb. But fully loaded it was a different matter altogether, in fact it was practically impossible to maintain height if you lost an engine when flying at maximum all-up weight..

During the time I flew Delta Lima I had some interesting moments, but there was one flight I will never forget.

705

Close to maximum weight with a full load of passengers we taxied out to the holding point of the duty runway at Caernarfon Airport potentially bound for a pleasure flight over Snowdon. It was a beautifully clear day with very little surface wind, so I was really looking forward to a pleasant flight over the mountains.

Take-off checks complete I addressed the passengers through the PA system asking them once again to ensure their harnesses were done up tight. Having obtained take-off clearance from control I taxied Delta Lima onto the threshold of runway 26, and opened the throttles smoothly to commence the take-off run. With the tail up we were about three-quarters of the way down the runway and just about to lift off when the starboard engine suddenly started to misfire and lose power. There was only 200metres of runway ahead of us, beyond that there was a six feet high embankment with the sea on the far side. We were well past the point where we could have aborted the take-off, and with the tail up on a conventional undercarriage aeroplane it would have been fatal to apply the brakes and attempt to stop before hitting the embankment. The sudden loss of power caused the Rapide to swing to the right and I had to apply considerable left rudder to prevent the aircraft from ground looping which at take-off speed would have been disastrous, even so the aircraft swung through about twenty degrees to the right, came off the runway onto the grass and headed straight for a five feet high barbed wire cattle fence that ran parallel along the full length of the runway. If the undercarriage caught the fence or hit one of the concrete fence posts we would almost certainly summersault over onto our back. Determined to clear the fence I started to pump the starboard throttle which seemed to keep the starboard engine running, albeit with considerable loss of power. At the last second I hauled back on the control column, and Delta Lima hopped gracefully over the fence clearing it by about five or six feet. We skimmed over the sand dunes for a few yards with the airspeed dangerously near the stall so it was nigh on impossible to raise the nose of the aircraft without stalling. Delta Lima just clipped the top of a large sand hill, bounced up about fifty feet and somehow managed to retain sufficient speed to remain airborne…but only just! Phil Hudson our air traffic controller obviously saw what was happening and hit the crash alarm button.

I struggled to keep her going by vigorously pumping the throttle of the dying engine. The old timer seemed to sympathise with my efforts and staggered along turning very slowly to the right. Considerable left rudder and aileron were needed to prevent the aircraft from rolling over. By flying completely out of balance and juggling with ailerons and rudder I was able to complete the lowest circuit I had ever done, all the time the aircraft was gently buffeting, teetering on the stall with our starboard wingtips just a few feet off the ground. It was impossible to warn the passengers because the PA system worked from a hand-held microphone, to say that I already had my hands full is a gross understatement. Amazingly that marvellous old machine kept flying, almost clipping the Eastern boundary fence, I closed the throttles and the starboard wheel mercifully touched down on the grass undershoot of the runway. I felt a bit shaken up but I had to smile when I heard one of the passenger loudly complaining about the flight being too short and she was going to ask for her money back.

The starboard propeller stopped turning altogether as we rolled to a standstill and the airfield's fire truck pulled up alongside. I informed the passengers that we had experienced a problem with one of the engines. Amazingly it seemed that they were oblivious to the situation and probably thought that bouncing off sand hills and almost scraping the wingtips on the ground were all part of the entertainment. Anyway when I explained what had happened there was a stunned silence for a moment, then someone said 'Lets hear it for the pilot' and they all started to cheer and clap. As the clapping subsided I heard the trembling voice of one of the older passengers asking …

'Can I get out now please?'

All the passengers were offered an alternative flight or their money back. Most of them chose to fly with me later in the Cessna. A short time after the event details of the incident appeared in several pilot related magazines.

Landing an aeroplane with a traditional type of undercarriage is a world apart from landing the modern tricycle undercarriage aircraft that most students are taught to fly on these days. Flying a 1930s or 1940s aircraft is, in my opinion, one hell of a privilege. During my forty-plus years as a pilot I was fortunate enough to fly quite a few old aircraft types. But for me the Mk 9 Spitfire, and the Dragon Rapide, rate as the two most exciting aeroplanes I have ever had the pleasure of flying.

Checking a pilot out to fly the Rapide is something else, and can be a very hairy experience for the poor old instructor!

The value of the aeroplane, and its high maintenance costs were reflected in the appropriate section of SMA's Flight Operations Manual, which stated…

Pilots wishing to fly the company's Rapide must have a minimum of 800 hours in command, a valid twin rating, and at least 100 hours experience flying conventional undercarriage aircraft. Although not mentioned in the ops manual, it was considered essential that the Training Captain destined to carry out the conversion training should have…. Faith in God, considerable courage, a strong will to live, and sometimes a quick change of underwear!

The first pilot I taught to fly the DH-89 was Capt Peter Brooks. Fortunately he was a very experienced flying instructor with considerable "tail-down" experience himself, and I had no problems checking Peter out on the Rapide.

It's not easy to instruct in the Rapide as there is just one set of controls, and worse still there is only room for one person in the cockpit. So the instructor has to stand behind the pilot under training, lean in through the cockpit door, and convey his instructions to the student whilst being totally out of reach of any of the flying controls himself. This can be quite nerve-racking especially when things start to go seriously wrong.

I found the best way to train pilots on the Rapide was to make sure every detail was covered by a thorough ground briefing first. Then demonstrate all the procedures for the upper-air-work and circuit training myself with the trainee pilot standing behind me peering over my shoulder. That would be followed by a in-depth de-briefing session before taking to the air again with my student at the controls and me standing behind him.

I did experience one training flight in the Rapide when things went badly wrong. The chap I was to check out had all the necessary requirements and experience laid down in the company's operations manual. He worked for us part time as a qualified flying instructor, and frequently flew the company's twin engine Piper Apache.

After a thorough ground briefing and demonstration flight, we took to the air again in Delta Lima with my student at the controls. All went along swimmingly throughout the upper air work and, having completed a few stalls and carried out the asymmetric flight sequence, we returned to the circuit to practice a few landings.

The chap could fly the aeroplane well enough, but landing the thing turned out to be a bloody nightmare.

We made numerous attempts at landing, all of them resulting in an overshoot having first careered from one end of the runway to the other in a spectacular series of leaps and bounces. I decided to give the chap one more go at trying to land the Rapide, and if that failed my intention's were to climb the aircraft to a safe height and attempt to change places with him so that I could land the aeroplane myself.

However, on his final attempt he succeeded in touching down smoothly without bouncing. I was just breathing a quiet sigh of relief when the aircraft gradually began to turn to the right whilst we were still running down the runway with the tail wheel off the ground. The Rapide has quite a large rudder which is very effective on the landing run until the tail stalls and comes down, at which point the aircraft can then be kept straight by the application of gentle braking and the use of asymmetric power if needed.

In this case the aircraft left the runway and I could see that the pilot was making no attempt to rectify the beginnings of a ground loop. (This is when the aircraft continues to tighten up the turn, loops round on one wheel, and sometimes sticking a wing into the ground during the process).

I shouted...

'Full left rudder and increase the power on the starboard engine.'

All I could do was shout instructions to him as there was no way I could possibly reach the controls myself. But he wasn't listening to me at all, he just shouted and started to panic.

As the Rapide headed at speed for the airfield boundary fence, my student continued shouting so loudly that there was no way he could possibly hear what I was trying to get him to do. I wasn't strapped in as I had to stand at the entrance to the cockpit. At the last second I braced myself for the inevitable. We struck the wire mesh fence with the undercarriage and the tail shot straight up in the air. There was a loud band and the props stopped turning. I thought for a moment that the aircraft was going to tipple right over onto it's back, but it stayed poised on its nose for a couple of seconds before the tail came down again with a hell of a smack. The airport crash alarm was wailing away in the distance whilst my student released his harness, clambered out of the cockpit, stepped over me and exited the aircraft. Aware of the strong smell of petrol, I scrambled in the cockpit and rapidly turned off the electrics and the fuel. Two members of our crash crew entered the cockpit in a flash. and hauled me out unceremoniously onto the grass. Fortunately there was no fire and no-one was hurt.

The overall damage to the aircraft was surprisingly little. The props needed inspecting but appeared to be ok, the fabric of the lower wings had been badly torn in several places, the undercarriage cowlings were bent and the landing light in the nose of the aircraft was smashed. Our engineers were brilliant and had her back on line again within a few days.

One of my full-time instructors who I checked out on the Rapide without incident was Capt. Peter Lawton. Peter ultimately wrote an excellent description of what it was like to fly the Rapide which was published as the centre piece of the January 1996 issue of "PILOT" magazine.

Many years later when I retired and left North Wales to return to my home County of Norfolk, I was sitting in the garden one Summer's afternoon when I heard the unmistakable sound of Twin Gipsy Queen engines slowly approaching the overhead. I looked up and couldn't believe my eyes. There was dear old Delta Lima plodding along and doing her stuff, probably on her way to an air display at one of Norfolk's airfields. I watched her droning off into the distance until I finally lost sight of her in the summer haze. It was lovely to see her again, but at the same time I had a strong feeling of sadness. I loved that old aeroplane..

CHAPTER 61.

Spitfire.

As I drove from the airfield with Cassie to our little cottage in the mountains, there was no question in my mind that I was the luckiest man alive, being happily married and having a job that to me was the best job in the world. I had achieved just about everything I had dreamed of as a child except for one thing which was now out of the question and long since been filed away in my mind as an unattainable childhood fantasy.

When I was a schoolboy the Battle of Britain raged in the skies over Great Britain. My pal Eddy Baldock and I had volunteered to fly Spitfires for the Airforce and were heart broken when we were turned down by the recruiting sergeant because we were still in short pants! I have often recalled the wonderful imaginary adventures we shared during our childhood days when we flew our scale model Spitfires down King's Lynn High Street and planned to do the real thing together when we grew up. Sadly this was not to be, I am alive and my dearest friend Eddy is dead. Theoretically I should have been killed in 1968 when I crashed in the Zlin, instead I lived. Eddy, having survived fighting in Korea during his two years National Service serving with the Royal Artillery, was killed in a totally avoidable factory accident shortly after his demob, he was just twenty-one. Where's the justice in that? Sometimes I wonder how God makes these choices. There are times when one's faith has to be strong to cope with such questions.

The sun was resting on a crimson horizon behind us as our car made its way slowly up the last few hundred yards of mountain path that lead to our home. I was dreaming of the past when I was suddenly jolted back to reality by Carol who said …

'Ray, what would you like for your birthday?'

I had no idea what brought that on as it was nowhere near my birthday. I always answered that question with…

'Oh I don't know…. A Rolls-Royce, or better still a Spitfire.'

Carol just laughed and nothing more was said.

We all have our dreams, Carol's was to own a small café and gift shop in a seaside village when we retired from flying. She often used to say to me…

'Just think how lovely it would be Ray. We would live above our little shop and in the mornings we would just pop downstairs and open up our own business. I could look after the teashop and you could run the gift shop. What do you think?'

I must admit I was as enthusiastic as Carol about her dreams of the future, living by the sea had always appealed to both of us.

During one of our infrequent days off together, we decided to take a trip down to the southern tip of the Lleyn Peninsular and spend the day by the sea in Aberdaron, a small village about thirty miles South of Caernarfon Airport.

Aberdaron is a very pretty little village that overlooks the Island of Bardsey, an island that was once owned by Lord Newborough my previous employer that also owned Fort Belan. I believe the island is now in the hands of the National Trust.

A stream ran through the centre of Aberdaron village, passing under a quaint little bridge, before babbling over the rocks and weaving it's way out to sea. The beach itself was no more than a hundred yards from the centre of the tiny village. Bordering the stream was 'Hen Blas', a charming old-fashioned gift shop that advertised the additional services of a tearoom within. With Carol's dream in mind, we decided to take a look inside and perhaps glean a few ideas for the future.

The shop was very well stocked with all the usual gifts and seaside paraphernalia, but the thing that really caught my eye was a narrow archway in the middle of the rear wall of the shop that led into a quaint little split-level tearoom with low ceilings, oak beams and a huge inglenook fireplace. It was one of the prettiest tea rooms I had ever seen, and the idea of customers who popped in for a cup of tea having to pass through a tempting array of gifts first, was indeed good sales strategy. The building was built of welsh stone, and there was a real old fashioned streetlamp by the front door that the owner told us was still in working order.

We both fell in love with the place and Carol commented that this was exactly the sort of small business she had in mind for us one day in the future.

We had a friendly chat with the owner who asked if there was any chance of me taking a photograph of Bardsey Island from the air. The Island was easily visible from the nearby beach, and Mr Glyn Harrison, the owner, said that he would like to sell postcards featuring an aerial view of Bardsey.

Our visit to Aberdaron cemented Carols dream of one day owning a café and gift shop firmly in the minds of both of us. In the meantime we enjoyed working together at Caernarfon Airport, and I was in for one very big surprise.

It was a fine May morning in 1988 when Carol and I arrived at the airport at 8.45am. as usual. To my surprise there were several cars in the public car park which, apart from cars belonging to the staff, was normally empty at that time of the morning. I asked Carol if she had any idea why this should be? but she avoided the question, and as we had quite a number of privately owned aircraft hangared at the airfield, I assumed they were probably off to some rally or other that I had not heard about. When I entered the building I was met by a strangely over-enthusiastic burst of "Good Morning's" from various members of my staff.

Looking out of my office window I could see that there were several private owners carrying out pre-flight inspections on their aircraft which were parked on the grass area outside. Convinced that they were off on some pre-arranged day out, I thought no more about it and sat down at my desk to read the company's mail. Suddenly Carol burst into the room and said...

'Come on Ray we're off.'

'OFF' I said.... 'Off where'?

It was then that Carol told me of something she and members of the staff had been planning for many weeks.

'You are going to realise your childhood dream darling, we have arranged for you to fly a Mk 1X Spitfire, it's one of the few still flying that actually took part in the Battle of Britain!

I was speechless. This must be some kind of joke. Any minute now someone's going to come in here with a radio controlled model of a Spitfire or something like that.

It turned out that it wasn't a joke at all. Unbeknown to me, Carol, with the very generous financial help from all my staff and club members, had made arrangements for me to fly ML407, an ex Battle of Britain Spitfire that had been converted into a dual seat aircraft by Nick Grace. Carol had contacted Nick, and somehow managed to get him to agree to allow me

713

to fly it. Only Carol's inspirational nature could have possibly persuaded our staff and club members to assist her in turning my childhood aspiration into reality, and how they all managed to keep their plans a secret from me during those many weeks of planning I will never know. As for me, I was overwhelmed by everyone's generosity and had great difficulty to hide the tears that welled up in my eyes when Carol told me of their plans.

Moments later I was hustled into the rear seat of our C172 with Carol. Eight aircraft carrying staff and club members took off bound for Goodwood Aerodrome.

Our two pilots were Lewis Roberts and Alan Hughes. I never sit in the rear seats of any aeroplane if I can help it. But this was indeed a very special occasion.

The journey was not without incident. Not knowing anything about being taken for a flight to Goodwood Aerodrome that morning, I had consumed too many cups of tea earlier and of course the inevitable happened... before long I was bursting and needed to wee badly. I was OK until I was told by our pilot, that he was temporarily uncertain of our position...In other words we were lost.

I soon realised that there was no hope of me being able to hold out until we landed. The only remedy I could think of to avoid total embarrassment was to use a sick-bag for my untimely needs. The use of a sick-bag for the purposes of emptying ones bladder in the presence of three other people in a very small space calls for a certain amount of dexterity. The problem was solved by the use of a plastic covered aeronautical chart that Carol held up as a screen, whilst I, with some difficulty and a certain amount of dexterity, perched on the edge of the seat and piddled with considerable gusto into the paper bag.

The relief was blissful, but the side effects were horrendous. Embarrassingly all the windows in the cockpit were completely steamed up by the, now humid, atmosphere. I apologised profusely. Alan Hughes saw the funny side and couldn't stop laughing, but Mr Roberts who was flying the aircraft, was not at all amused. I watched him trying to see out of the now opaque windscreen without saying a word, whilst Alan avidly tried to clear the moisture with one of Carols tissues.

The problem of disposing with a soggy bag that was liable to burst at any moment, caused further embarrassment. The sick-bag was unfortunately one of those old fashioned bags that had a greaseproof lining but there was no way of sealing the top. The difficulty now was to find some means of disposing with the contents without further upsetting the crew. Our altitude at the time was in the region of 3,000 feet, so there was no fear of causing any harm by disposing with the contents through an open cockpit window. The trouble was that the two "hatch type" windows were in the front half of the cockpit and I was sitting directly behind our disgruntled pilot.

I remember thinking: 'I taught that young bugger to fly, surely he can show some latitude in his disapproval of his ex instructor's misfortune?'

At my request Mr Roberts reluctantly opened the window and leaned well forward so that I could dispose of the bag. There was one hell of a noise as air rushed past the open cockpit window. I eased forward in my seat to dispose of the bag when SWOOSH....the slipstream sucked the bag of urine from my hand and out of the window before I could do anything about it.

A fine delicate spray of atomised pee swirled round the cockpit like an early morning mist. Fortunately Carol and Alan saw the funny side, but regrettably Mr Roberts did not, he slammed the hatch closed, uttered a few swearwords in welsh, and slumped down in his seat looking even more disgruntled. After that the cockpit went a little quiet for a while. Alan Hughes eventually identified our position and with a slight correction in our heading we continued on course for Goodwood.

Eight aircraft carrying sixteen members of staff and club members had arrived almost simultaneously into the circuit at Goodwood Aerodrome and landed. Twenty minutes later we finally arrived.

ML407 was parked in the dispersal area just in front of the control building. She looked magnificent in her wartime camouflage with RAF roundels on the fuselage and wings.

Carol soon had things organised, and after we had all partaken of an excellent breakfast in the restaurant at Goodwood Flying Club, I was taken over to ML407's dispersal and introduced to Nick Grace the owner.

Nick was a typical flying type. He immediately made me feel welcome and asked how much flying I had done, and what types of aircraft I had flown. I told him what he needed to know, adding that I had dreamed of flying a Spitfire ever since I was a small boy during the second world war when I watched an aerial battle that took place above us in the skies over Norfolk. In fact at this moment I felt just as excited as I had done all those years ago.

Nick was ready to fly, so I donned my flying overalls, climbed into the cockpit of ML407 and strapped myself in.

Just sitting in a Spitfire that had completed almost two hundred sorties during the last war, was unbelievable. Nick stood on the port wing and leaned into the cockpit to brief me on the controls and instruments. The layout was fairly straight forward and not unlike some of the other vintage aircraft types I had flown. It was just a matter of remembering the engine limitations, brake pressures and flying speeds etc. The aircraft was equipped with a CSU (Constant Speed Unit) which made things a lot easier for aerobatics, which I hoped I would be allowed to have a crack at.

Because of the vast amount of engine in front of us, there was literarily no forward visibility at all when the tail was down in the three point attitude. I had read about this many times, but when I actually sat in the cockpit, I began to wonder what sort of a cock-up I would make of the landing. I remembered that a curved approach procedure was used when landing the Spitfire, but I was very pleased when Nick said...

'This aircraft is worth a lot of money Ray, so I'll follow you through during the take-off and landing. Be ready for a swing to the left during the take-off run and climb away at 180mph. Also you need to remember that the elevator trim, it's very sensitive, so be careful when you use it, especially near the ground.'

When Nick Grace rebuilt the aircraft, he retained the second cockpit that had been added to the aeroplane for training purposes during the latter part of its service life. So ML407 now had two complete sets of controls.

Nick climbed in and plugged his headset into the I/C so that we could talk to one another without difficulty. The engine was started up and the chocks were removed. The noise inside the cockpit was louder than I expected. We tested the brake pressure 80lb/sq in; and checked the pneumatic pressure at 220lb/sq in;

Ignition checked, we moved out onto the airfield and headed for the holding point. Like the Chipmunk and Tiger Moth you needed to weave the nose from side to side to make sure the area ahead was clear. As we taxied out Nick completed the checks and called the tower for immediate take-off clearance.

Within no time we were tearing down the runway, it was not as difficult to keep straight as I had expected. Once airborne, Nick raised the undercarriage and shouted down the headphones...

'You have control Ray, climb straight ahead at 180 mph. Level out at 2,000ft.'

I looked out at the starboard wing to see that beautiful elliptical shape that is loved by so many pilots. I was flying a real Spitfire.....I couldn't believe it. I was in a dream world, but bloody soon snapped out of it when Nick's voice brought me back to reality.

'You've passed 2,000ft Ray. Level out now and when you're nicely trimmed turn back towards the airfield.'

I needed to smarten up a bit, at this stage the aircraft was well ahead of me. I levelled out, the trimmer was certainly very sensitive. We were well past 3,000 ft by the time I started a medium turn to the left.

'Tighten it up Ray, we'll be miles away at this rate.'

Nick was right, I'd only been flying a couple of minutes and Goodwood Aerodrome was almost out of sight.

'OK Ray throw her around a bit. Leave the throttle where it is, the CSU will take care of that.'

I was delighted with the immediate response to the slightest movement of the control column, and concentrated on flying the aircraft as accurately as possible. Previous flying experience soon paid off, within no time I felt at one with this beautiful aeroplane.

After a while we returned to the airfield. Control confirmed there were no other aircraft in the area and we were cleared to carry out aerobatics overhead the field.

I completed the checks as Nick called them out to me.

'OK. Ray lets see what you can do, she goes round a loop nicely at about 300mph.'

I eased the stick forward and the speed built up rapidly, coming up to 300mph I eased gently back on the controls and started to push the throttle forward.

'No need for that, leave the throttle where it is, I told you its got a CSU'

Shit! I'd forgotten .

The wingtips were spot on the horizon as we passed through the vertical attitude. I looked back above my head to see the horizon and….. Bloody Hell! A Cessna 152 was smack in front of us. I tightened up the loop to pass under the Cessna as Nick shouted…

'I have it.'

We past about a hundred feet under the Cessna.

I was given control again to have another crack at a loop, whilst Nick had a few abrasive words with the controller.

The loops completed successfully, Nick suggested I finish off with a barrel roll and a couple of slow rolls.

The barrel roll was easy enough, but the first of the slow rolls was far from perfect. I pushed the stick forwards slightly to hold the nose up whilst passing through the inverted attitude as one had to in the Chipmunk and the Zlin, but the Spit didn't need any of that and my actions caused a brief inverted climb. Nick laughed…

'You don't need to do that with a Spit Ray, very sensitive aeroplane this, try again and just barrel it slightly.'

I was enjoying every second flying this wonderful aeroplane, and before I knew it Nick's voice brought me back to reality again…

'Not bad Ray, not bad at all, you seem to know what you're doing, now if you're happy we'll rejoin the circuit and I'll follow you through on the controls when you land'… …adding,…'in case you make a cock-up of it!'

Gear down and locked, flaps applied, IAS 100 mph reducing to 95 mph, the aircraft responded to the lightest touch of the controls. I was familiar with the curved approach technique as I had used this method many times in the past whilst completing short, low level circuits in the Rapide. But with the Spitfire it was the only way to retain visual contact with the runway. I loved every second of the flight, although I must admit I felt very vulnerable when I rounded out and I couldn't see the runway at all. There was very little surface wind and we seemed to float forever. The touchdown was surprisingly smooth, although I had to work hard on the rudder in order to keep straight whilst the aircraft decelerated to taxying speed. When we had cleared the runway Nick took over again and taxied the aircraft back to the hangar. Before closing down Nick pressed the tit and said…

'That landing was surprisingly good. You'll do Ray.'

Sadly, the flight I had always dreamed of and will never forget, was over.

I had a short chat with Nick about ML407 and he told me how he had first come across the machine in a museum in Scotland. It had taken him five years to rebuild her back into its existing immaculate condition. He said that Johnnie Houlton, a New Zealand Airforce flying officer, was flying the aircraft in 1944 when he shot down a Junkers 88 over the Normandy beaches South of Omaha. ML407 carried the letters OU-V during that period.

I couldn't thank Nick enough. I had flown a Spitfire Mk 1X, an event that will stay with me as my most exciting flight for the rest of my life. My ever lasting thanks to Cassie, and all the club members and staff, that contributed to making my childhood dream a reality.

Happily Carol's dream of owning her own business also came true. By the strangest coincidence the little café and gift shop business that Carol had fallen in love with when we had visited Aberdaron years earlier, came up for sale, and we were able to purchase the premises within a few weeks.

Leaving our lovely old farmhouse in the mountains was a heart wrenching experience, but it was a very sensible decision that paid off generously over the next few years. We now lived above our own business in the tiny picturesque village of Aberdaron.

We also owned a small section of the stream that babbled over the rocks alongside the property, together with the stone steps that led down to the water's edge right outside our front door. It was great to be so close to the sea and Aberdaron's beautiful sandy beach, which was less than one minute's walking distance from our door. At night we could lay in bed listening to the sea crashing down on the beach, and in the mornings awake to the call of the seagulls.

Now that we lived on the extreme Western tip of the Lleyn Peninsular, I had to drive thirty miles to the airfield every morning. It was a journey along narrow roads that twisted and wound their way through the steep slopes of the Rival Mountains. The scenery was wonderful with mists and brilliant sunshine, or maybe gales and thunderstorms, no two mornings were the same, it was a journey I never tired of. Obviously our little dog Kimbo and our Siamese cat Percy accompanied us to Aberdaron, and soon became well known to the residents of the village for getting up to mischief.

There was much work to be done to make the café, shop, and living accommodation exactly how we wanted it to be. Carol got stuck in enthusiastically straight away, and I helped on my day's off from the airfield. Finally, when the cafe and shop were opened for the summer season, Carol employed a small full-time seasonal staff supplemented by reliable part time employees all of whom lived in the village.

Carol and I had worked together as a team for over nineteen years, and as far as I was concerned she was virtually irreplaceable. Everybody who had worked at the airport with Carol missed her happy personality, she had a natural way of dealing with both staff and customers, now that she was no longer in charge, it would be a long time before I could carry out my flying duties without worrying about how the ground personnel and office staff were coping.

Finding a capable person to manage the flight operations at Caernarfon turned out to be a nightmare. The person would need to have considerable experience in staff management, book keeping and secretarial work. The job also carried the responsibility of handling large amounts of cash, so in addition to finding someone with the above capabilities, I had to find a person of integrity who had impeccable references.

Unfortunately having employed three persons in succession, and none of them lasting more than a few weeks, I had to employ two persons to replace Carol, one took care of the accounts and secretarial side, whilst the other had to be trained in flight Ops.

The journey by car from the airport to Aberdaron took around 45 minutes in reasonable weather. To breakdown in the mountains in the pitch black of a blustery winter's night long before mobile telephones had been invented, could be quite a harrowing experience. One of the most embarrassing moments of my life occurred on one such night when I was returning home from work. It was a cold, dark midwinter's night, and the roads were covered with a light dusting of snow. I had just gone through the mountain pass and was driving along the most remote area imaginable when the engine of my car suddenly stopped. I got out of the car in freezing conditions and went through all the usual checks to see if I could remedy the problem, but there was nothing I could do to get the engine running. I remembered there was an isolated telephone box about a quarter of a mile further along the road. I had made a mental note of the of the kiosk when I first travelled along this road, thinking that it had obviously been located there for the use of anyone unfortunate enough to break down in such a remote area, never thinking I would have to use it.

I set off up the steep road in the blackness of the evening, it was bitter cold with snow swirling around me, I hoped that maybe a car would come along and stop to give me a lift, but no such luck.

Before long I could just make out the dim light of the telephone kiosk. I always carried my diary which contained all the telephone numbers I was likely to need. Dolydd Service Station was situated about twenty miles North of where I had broken down. Fortunately Emyr, the owner of the garage lived on the premises, and although the garage was officially closed, Emyr kindly agreed to come out straight away.

I set off down the mountain road to the car with the wind still howling around me. It was very difficult to see, but I made it back to the car before the breakdown truck arrived. Within a few minutes of my waiting in the car I could see the lights of a vehicle slowly weaving its way up the road towards me. At that moment the wants of nature suddenly beckoned me, and I decided that I just had time for a quick pee before Emyr arrived. That's when the trouble started. I fumbled around with icy fingers and eventually started to relieve myself by the side of the road. But the truck from the garage turned out to be much closer than I had at first estimated, so with one determined effort I strained to complete the job in hand. But sadly disaster struck... Splat... My efforts were too enthusiastic and I "followed through" in no uncertain terms!

'Oh God no'

Before I could even think what to do under the circumstances, the breakdown truck had pulled up, Emyr was out of the cab and trying to get my car started.

I stood well back! Hopefully out of sniffing distance. After about ten minutes Emyr slammed the bonnet of my car closed and said...

'Its no good Ray, I can't find out what the problem is, I'll have to take it back to the garage, you can borrow my daughter's car to get home tonight and bring it back on your way to work in the morning, I should have your car fixed by then.'

Apart from feeling very uncomfortable, I was beginning to smell pretty foul into the bargain.

'Ok I'll sit in my car then...You needn't worry Emyr, I'll keep the towing rope tight' I said.

'No need Ray, I'll hoist the front end up and you can come back in the truck with me, it's warmer in there.'

My heart sank. Things were getting serious, I wasn't even sure if it was safe to take a step or two. Panic began to set in...

'If its ok with you Emyr I'll ride in my car, use the indicators and all that.' I said.

'Can't do that Ray bach. It's against my insurance policy mate, jump in the cab, we'll be back in no time.'

I was desperate. I hoisted myself precariously into the cabin and squelched down gently onto the seat, smelling putrid.

'Phew, have you trodden in anything nasty mate?' I said, attack being the best method of defence!

'I don't know Ray, one of us has that's for sure.'

Emyr had a quick sniff around the cab. then opened the window.

'What a bloody awful smell, something must have died on the road Ray bach, we can clean our shoes when we get back to the garage.'

The twenty-mile drive back to Dolydd Garage was "eye-watering". I just sat there stinking, and praying that the contents of my pants hadn't seeped through and left a smelly stain on the seat of Emyr's truck.

By the time we arrived back at his house it was getting late. Emyr's wife stood in the doorway with her hands on her hips, obviously the evening meal had been ruined. So Emyr hurriedly put some newspaper on the floor of the car I was about to borrow, and that was that. I wasn't exactly popular when I got home either.

Carol loved having her own Café and Gift shop in Aberdaron. But looking back now we both agree that of all the jobs when Carol and I worked together, one of the loveliest times we had was when we had our own small flying business. Our cosy little caravan set-up met all the requirements for CAA approval, and being located on a quiet airfield just a few yards from the sea, was all we could have wished for. Each morning Carol and I would arrive early at the caravan with our little dog Kimbo. I would start the day by pushing our aeroplane out of the hangar, and topping it up with fuel, whilst Carol took Kimbo down to our dispersal area and opened up the caravan. On warm summer mornings, we would sit outside listening to the sea crashing on the nearby rocks whilst enjoying a nice cup of tea, and a round of hot buttered toast.

Often enthusiastic photographers would make arrangements to fly as early as 6am in order to capture the awe inspiring prismatic effects of the sun rising through the mists and crags of Snowdon, a sight that once seen is never forgotten.

But that all happened a long time ago. CAA regulations have changed drastically since then, and now that Llandwrog aerodrome had become Caernarfon Airport, the operational side of flying became a whole different ballgame with a myriad of flight checks and regulations to be adhered to.

I had my work cut out as MD but I still managed to fit in some instructing and carried out most of the GFT's at Caernarfon. Also as an approved TRE examiner I was occasionally called upon to flight test a commercial pilot for the issue of a new aircraft type endorsement. Apart from everything else I made sure that I continued flying the Rapide and our Britten Norman Islander, sharing the flights with my deputy Capt Peter Brooks.

A red line in my logbook, reminds me of a twin rating test I carried out on a pilot from another flying school on the 24th May 1991. He arrived with his instructor in a Beech Twin 76. I had not flown this type of aircraft previously so, as I normally do in such cases, I flew the aeroplane around the circuit a couple of times myself to make sure I knew where everything was in the cockpit before testing the pilot.

As per standard procedure. I briefed the candidate thoroughly about test he was about to take, and asked him if he had any questions before we took off.

During the first part of the test the candidate flew all the upper air work sequences reasonable well although his lookout was not as good as I would have liked. But when it came to flight procedures in the circuit it was a different matter altogether. After completing a couple of standard "touch and go" circuits. I asked him to carry out a short field landing. This time he lowered the undercarriage and forgot to carry out the rest of his down-wind checks. The final approach turned out to be much too high, so he closed both throttles and elected to glide down the last couple of hundred feet. Having started his round-out about two thirds of the way down the runway with the flaps still retracted, it soon became obvious that there was no chance of him landing without crashing through the barrier and winding up in the sea. As he chose to do nothing about it, I told him to overshoot and go round again. Before I could stop him he left the port engine in tick-over and slammed the throttle of the starboard engine fully forward together with the propeller pitch control for the port engine and pulled back on the control column at the same time. The net result was the aircraft pitched up sharply and rolled violently to the left. I grabbed the controls, the aircraft had in fact partially snap-rolled just over ninety degrees with the wingtip about ten feet from the ground. Instinctively I opened the port throttle fully at the same time reducing power on the starboard engine, stood up on the right rudder and applied right aileron! The aircraft rolled back almost level but yawed significantly to the left heading straight for the control tower. I managed to bank away gently to avoid giving our controller a heart attack or worse.

We climbed away with me still at the controls. My student, (and probably me as well) looking a little ghostlike.

As I raised the gear, my student said…

'Would you like me to try that again, sir?' to which I replied…

'I'd rather you didn't.'

My fellow instructor Peter Brooks, who happened to be in the control tower at the time, told me afterwards that he hit the crash alarm before diving out of the door.

We landed and walked back to the control building where the instructor, who brought the student over to Caernarfon, was waiting for us. Beaming from ear to ear he asked…

'Did he pass Ray?'

'Did you see what just happened…we're lucky to be alive, never mind passing the bloody test!' I said.

He seemed quite put out by my remarks. Anyway I recommended that he gave his student more dual practice with overshoot procedures and general engine handling. Then suggested he could put the lad up with me again for another test. But he never did return and I understand that another examiner was asked to carry out the test. That, in my opinion, showed the ineptitude of the instructor. Sometime later I discovered the G-OADY made a heavy landing causing the nose wheel to collapse, but in all honesty I didn't find out who the pilot was at the time.

A couple of Summer's previously in 1989, I was approached by the current British Aerobatic Champion, Nigel Lamb, who asked if he could hangar his aeroplane at Caernarfon and practice his aerobatic sequences over the airfield during the weeks preceding the British and European Aerobatic Championships. I was more than delighted and said he could keep his aeroplane at Caernarfon free of charge. His practice aerobatic displays would obviously pay dividends as far as we were concerned. In fact it attracted hundreds of visitors to the airfield, which in turn benefited our pleasure-flying activities and increased the number of visits to our museum, gift shop and restaurant.

Nigel and I ultimately became very good friends, we flew together many times, and on one occasion I led the Toyota Team in a "vic" formation flying the Rapide for advertising purposes. We flew along the sea front low level with the Toyota aircraft making smoke. It looked really good and created lots of interest in the airport's activities.

One morning I arrived at the airfield earlier than usual. It was one of those magic mornings when the air was brisk with a hint of spring freshness and the sea sparkled blue as though it were made of azure crystal. Just the sort of day a chap could enjoy a few gentle early-morning aerobatics.

I could see the 'Extra 300' being pushed out of the hangar. Nigel was obviously about to take advantage of such a lovely morning to practice his highly advanced aerobatic sequences. As I was about to enter the office building Nigel beckoned me over.

'Lovely day Nigel' I said 'I expect you're off for an early morning twist-up.'

I was watching him carrying out his usual meticulous pre-flight inspection on the 300 when he casually remarked...

'Like to come with me Ray?'

I had flown with Nigel before in his 'Pitts Special' which I enjoyed immensely. But to fly with the current world champion in his 300 was an offer that no self-respecting pilot in his right mind would refuse, providing he loved aerobatics of course! I hurried back to the office to collect my flying gear and informed Ops where I would be for the next half hour or so.

The panoramic view of snow-capped Snowdonia was breathtaking as we climbed steeply into the clear morning sky. I must admit, although I have taught aerobatics to many students during the time I was an instructor at Oxford, I was experiencing mixed feelings of excitement and apprehension. Maybe, having watched him from the ground, I knew exactly what to expect when Nigel commenced his latest aerobatic sequence!

We levelled off at three thousand feet and Nigel asked me if I would like to have a go at flying her around the sky for a couple of minutes to get the feel of the 300. I was impressed by the aircraft's lightness and response to the slightest touch of the controls. It was indeed a beautiful aeroplane to fly.

Nigel's calm South African drawl came through on my headset.

'OK Ray mate, I have control. Would you like me to show you the sequence I plan to do at this year's championships?'

Tightening my harness until I nearly cut myself in half, I heard my voice agreeing in the side-tones of my head-set. I suppose having had one near-fatal crash, it was the intrinsic strength of the aeroplane as opposed to the capability of the pilot that was nagging at me. Either way I wasn't going to miss out on this opportunity.

'My hands and feet are well clear of the controls Nigel, go ahead mate.'

I had enjoyed watching Nigel practice his latest sequence in the Extra many times in the past few days and noticed how the colossal positive and negative G forces showed on his face when he landed. His eyes were always bloodshot, he looked tired and liked to be left alone for a while to recuperate. I wondered how my 59 year old body would stand up to it all. We were at three thousand feet over the airfield. Nigel had a quick look around to see the area was clear... then all hell was let loose.

The horizon appeared and disappeared from all angles in rapid succession with me inverted and hanging in my harness one second, then being forced out of the seat upside-down with considerable negative G the next.

I recognised the hesitation rolls, tail slides, rolling circles and spins etc., but although Nigel was calling out the various sequences as he performed them, sometimes I had no idea what was actually happening. During one mind-boggling manoeuvre the aircraft started somersaulting, we were literally plunging and tumbling head first at a tremendous rate, and I must admit I was seriously pleased when it stopped!

Throughout the flight I had been subjected to considerable amounts of positive and negative G, red-out's, grey-out's, partial black-out's and been arse over head so many times I lost count. Finally the sequence ended and there we were the right way up serenely flying along straight and level, exactly where we started, overhead the airfield.

Mercifully that was that. Or was it?

'What do you think of that Ray?'

'Lovely' I said, hoping he wouldn't take me too seriously!

'What the hell was that last manoeuvre Nigel ?'

'A Lumcevak' he replied, 'did you like it?'

'Yes ' I replied.

I was lying!

'I'll show you how it's done Ray.'

Oh God, why did I say yes. Before I knew what was happening we did another one that seemed even worse than the first. Then Nigel's dulcet tones sounded through my headset again.

'We'll do one more, this time you can follow me through on the controls, but hold them lightly and don't grip them.'

'OK' I replied.

Don't grip them the man said !!

I put my feet and hands lightly on the controls. I needn't have bothered.

'Here we go Ray.'

The stick jerked violently out of my hand and pushed my right leg hard against the cockpit side, my feet flew off the rudder and I came close to smacking my head on my knees.

Once again the aircraft was somersaulting, tumbling nose over tail seemingly out of control. I remember observing this manoeuvre from the ground when it was performed with "smoke-on", the whole thing looked like a tangled knot of smoke with aircraft parts poking out, rotating and falling vertically from the sky.

Before we landed Nigel had taken me through the full sequence he intended to fly at the next world championships. One particular manoeuvre that fascinated me was the "Salmon Leap" which is a sort of stall turn. The aeroplane commences a vertical climb with full power, and then, by the co-ordinated use of rudder and aileron, the aircraft waggles like a fish leaping out of the water. Eventually the controls are centralised and a stall occurs from the vertical attitude, a controlled tail-slide follows and the aircraft finally topples over, the throttle is closed, and the aircraft is recovered from the ensuing dive.

Nigel didn't let me land the 300. Just as well as I hadn't fully recovered from the "wonderful?!" aerobatic sequences he had just shown me.

It had been an education for me to experience just what can be achieved in a modern day aerobatic aeroplane by someone who has devoted a lifetime to aerobatic flying. Nigel Lamb and I remained friends for many years. I lost contact with him when I retired in 1996. Since then he has had great success flying in the "Red Bull" air races.

During my flying career I have been privileged to fly with three of the greatest aerobatic pilots in the world. Ray Hanna who was the leader of the RAF's premier formation aerobatic team the Red Arrows. Neil Williams, former Empire Test Pilot and twelve times British Aerobatic Champion. And Nigel Lamb, British unlimited Aerobatic Champion eight times from 1986 to 1993. At the time of writing Nigel held the number three position in the World Red Bull Air Races. Also it was my privilege to fly in formation with the Swiss Aerobatic Champion, Frank Versteegh, in an inverted mirror formation for the BBC TV news team in Wales.

Good things are very often followed by bad events. Not long after my flights with Nigel Lamb I heard the terrible news that my best friend and former colleague Mike Edwards had died. I couldn't believe it. A few weeks previously I had spoken to him on the R/T when he called up on Caernarfon's frequency to say hello. He was flying at eight thousand feet on a cross country with a student somewhere down South.

Mike was a World War Two Battle of Britain Spitfire pilot. He worked with me as my deputy at Halfpenny Green for several years. When I left to take up a job as Principle of the British Schools of Flying, Mike gave up his job at the Green to come and work for me again. We were the best of pals and I miss him very much indeed.

I attended his funeral. A large wreath in the shape of a Spitfire was placed on his coffin together with his RAF officers cap. During the funeral ceremony we were told by his brother that Mike had been decorated during the war, and that he was also a Freeman of the City of London. He had never mentioned either of those facts to me in all the years I had known him. We had flown together on numerous occasions and spent many happy evenings supping the proverbial "quick-half". The quick half invariably led to a good thrash that lasted until turning out time. God bless you Michael wherever you are.

The operating company that was formed to run the airport i.e. Snowdon Mountain Aviation, had recently become a Public Liability Company and was now totally independent of Snowdon Mountain Railway Ltd. As such we were now answerable to our shareholders for the profitability and expansion of the business.

My colleague Derek Rogerson, who was also the resident managing director of our parent company 'Snowdon Mountain Railway', had a bee in his bonnet about the income from our café. He always quoted the sales of "Chocolate Penguin Bars" sold at the railway's mountaintop Café as an example. He would say…

'We have the largest sales of Penguin Bars in the country Ray, and the airfield café could be the same.'

I loved old Derek he was a great friend of mine and had it not been for him we would not be running Caernarfon Airport. But he couldn't see for the life of him that his Penguin sales in the café at the top of Snowdon were sold to customers who had no other choice. They had to buy a bloody Penguin because apart from a cup of tea that was all they sold, and the poor sods couldn't just nip back down the mountain for a quick snack. So at the end of every financial year Derek would tell me that I should be selling Penguins, bless him.

On a more serious note, Caernarfon Airport had grown into a thriving business, but it lacked one major section, we did not have our own Maintenance Unit. We had the facilities, a large hangar that we leased out short term to an independent aircraft maintenance company that looked after us very well, but it was extremely costly.

Derek and I would have long, but never heated, arguments on how to cut down on aircraft maintenance costs. Every time I had to explain all the latest mandatory rules and regulations appertaining to aircraft maintenance schedules laid down by the CAA that we had to adhere to by law. The facts were that we just couldn't afford to run our own maintenance unit for the limited number of aircraft we operated. Sadly it soon became obvious to all of us on the board that if this company was to expand further it needed to be taken over by a larger company already operating commercially in the airline business. Preferably with a need to have its own aircraft maintenance unit and radio servicing facilities. This was indeed a very sad and obvious fact that had to be faced.

The day came when I was called to our head office at Snowdon Mountain Railway. All the London Directors were there. Derek looked at me rather sadly and I knew what was coming. There was no small talk. I was put out of my misery quite swiftly…

'We have decided, very reluctantly, to put the airport up for sale, and if

728

you agree we would like to include your continued employment as part of the deal.'

Although we had touched on the subject previously, my stomach turned into a knot. I was not too keen on being sold off like some piece of surplus equipment. I sat there whilst the meeting continued to discuss other matters that concerned the railway. Subdued voices prattled away in the background whilst I had to deal for the umpteenth time with worrying about my future career. The thought of having to find another company to take over my little world was devastating. One thing was for sure, I would never take on another derelict airfield from scratch again.

I certainly didn't relish the thought of breaking the news to my staff at the airport. They were a good bunch, and very loyal to me. At least it was a better situation than the time when Halfpenny Green Airfield was sold and I had to make all the staff redundant, that was dreadful. When I informed my staff of the directors decision to sell the company, I assured them that it would be sold as a going concern, and asked them not to react too hastily as their jobs should be safe. I promised that I would personally do my best to prevent any redundancies. Fortunately my staff trusted me implicitly, and not one member left the company.

When the advertisement appeared in "Flight International" magazine I could have wept. I also realised that my job would almost certainly be on the line when the next company took over. But as far as the airport was concerned, the right purchaser would hopefully continue to expand the company into other areas that the directors of Snowdon Mountain Railway would not consider. ie. (a) Providing a regular scheduled flight service, (b) Installing runway lighting and approach indicators, (c) Installing navigational aids such as a NDB, (d) Building a much needed larger petrol and jet refuelling installation, (e) Resurfacing a second runway, (f) Installing their own aircraft maintenance unit and radio repair section.

The following morning I went to the airfield early saddened by the decision to sell. I strolled across the airfield collecting my thoughts. The grass was still heavy with early morning dew and a light westerly breeze brought with it the fresh smell of the sea. What more could I have done? The place had been derelict when I took it over. Now it had become licensed by the CAA as Caernarfon Airport and was showing a very good annual profit. Perhaps selling a few more bloody Penguins would have dune the trick. Thanks to Carol's hard work and enthusiasm our Café and Gift Shop business in Aberdaron turned out to be a little goldmine, and would support us comfortably without any worries. But flying was still in my blood, and I wasn't going to give it up if I could help it.

Several companies showed an interest in our advertisement, but one application in particular intrigued me. It was sent to us via a firm of solicitors in Jersey. Their letter was short and to the point.

> Dear Sirs,
> We refer to your recent advertisement in Flight International. Our clients are genuinely interested in purchasing Caernarfon Airport and would like to set up a meeting in order to discuss the matter further.
> Yours faithfully...etc..

Our board of directors decided that Derek Rogerson and myself should interview all potential purchasers and report our views to the board so that a shortlist could be drawn up. The minimum acceptable price for the business had been worked out by our company's accountants in conjunction with the firms solicitors, and it was decided to put the sale of the company out to tender so that it could be sold without revealing the actual price paid. Also, whoever purchased the business would have to relinquish "Snowdon Mountain" from the title of the company and replace it with a new company name.

We interviewed several interested parties. Most of them turned pale and made their excuses to escape when an approximate figure for the purchase was indicated. The directors of the North Wales Flying Club based on RAF Mona came to see us, they too made a hasty retreat when we hinted at a possible price.

Then came the big surprise. Two distinguished looking gentlemen, who initially contacted us via their solicitors in Jersey, surprised us by arriving for interview spot on their scheduled time in a Citation 11 executive twin jet aircraft. It was all very mysterious, because the appointment was made in the name of a company that couldn't be traced and no-one had even heard of. They were shown to my office where Derek and myself were waiting to greet them and very curious to find out exactly who they were. We introduced ourselves to a Mr Mike Collett and his Group Managing Director Mr James Foden. We were still no wiser.

Both men were very pleasant characters, but I noticed that Mr Collett did most of the talking. Derek answered detailed questions relative to the financial side of the business, and I was left to explain the operational side.

Strangely enough they didn't seem very interested in the financial aspect, and didn't bat an eyelid when the price we were looking for was mentioned. Mr Collett then directed a question to me…

'Tell us about you're operation here Ray, how did it get started, and what were your future plans for the airfield?'

I explained that Snowdon Mountain Railway had purchased Llandwrog Aerodrome from Glynllivon Estates in January 1986 when it was just a derelict ex-wartime airfield, and described how, with sound financial backing and considerable hard work, we had built the airfield up to become licensed by the CAA for commercial traffic and designated as Caernarfon Airport. I mentioned, amongst other things, that the airport was in need of its own aircraft maintenance unit and concluded by saying…

'We have now reached the stage whereby the airfield needs to expand to its full potential and, in my opinion, this can only be established with a successful commercial aircraft operator at the helm.'

Mr Collett listened carefully to what I had to say, then asked…

'Tell me why you think having your own maintenance unit is so important, surely you could subcontract another company to maintain your aircraft for you?'

At this point I began to think that these gentlemen were millionaires who simply wanted to purchase an airfield from which they could operate their private jet. (How wrong could I be?)

So I went through a lengthy explanation about CAA aircraft regulations, maintenance schedules, C of A checks, 100 hour checks etc. etc.…

'The cost of using an autonomous maintenance company was very expensive for the number of aircraft we now operated as well as being very inconvenient. Precious flying time was wasted especially when a small problem causes an aircraft to be grounded until it can be fitted into the work schedule of an independent maintenance company. That is why I came to the conclusion that this business would function far more efficiently if it were operated by a company already in the aviation business as opposed to a railway company. If, for instance, the purchaser already operated an aircraft charter business and was paying large fees for landing and hangarage, it could be run more cost effectively by operating from it's own airfield with all the facilities it needed.'

Mr Collett smiled…

'Well done' he said. 'Now, do you know who we really are?'

Embarrassingly I had to say that I had never heard of them, and waited for the answer.

'I am the Chairman of Air Atlantique.'

His reply stunned me into utter silence. Air Atlantique was just about the biggest privately owned Air Charter, and Aircraft Maintenance company in the world. With bases at Jersey, Coventry and Malta and God knows where else.

Feeling somewhat embarrassed, I apologised for my lecture on the basic intricacies of aircraft maintenance, to which he laughed and said…

'No need to apologise Ray, I needed to know exactly what your reasons were for selling the airport and Snowdon Mountain Aviation, and I think you have made that quite clear.'

I offered to show them around, but Mr Collett simply said no need, and promised that we would definitely hear from him again within the next day or so.

I saw them to their aeroplane, and watched admiringly as Mike Collett started the two powerful jet engines. That interview turned out to be the beginning of a whole new chapter in my aviation career and the further development of Caernarfon Airport.

CHAPTER 62.

Air Atlantique.

The early morning drive to work from Aberdaron to the airport was enjoyable at any time, but for me the most beautiful time of year was late Autumn. The trees and hedgerows would slowly change their shades of green into a revelation of rich golden reds, and the merest streaks of snow would brush the mountain tops, turning the whole scene into a living portrait of the "Beauty of North Wales".

In 1992 Snowdon Mountain Aviation Ltd. was sold and became a subsidiary of Air Atlantique. and, as The company remained the sole operators of Caernarfon Airport, and was re-registered as Air Caernarfon Ltd. Also an independent aircraft maintenance company was set up and registered under the name of CAMCO Ltd., (Caernarfon Aircraft Maintenance Company). I then became the overall Managing Director of the two companies and continued to work at the airport until I retired in January 1996. But it hadn't all been plain sailing.

Our Chairmen Mike Collett was the sort of chap that knew exactly what he wanted and always made sure that he got it irrespective of anyone else on the board who dared to disagree with him.

I had retained my job as part of the initial take-over deal, and in all fairness Mike really knew nothing about me or the way I operated. As such I had the distinct impression that I was being scrutinized with a certain amount of suspicion.

Initially it seemed that nobody at Air Atlantique's head office had been told that I was the Managing Director of Air Caernarfon, which proved to be somewhat embarrassing whenever I telephoned Coventry to speak to the head of accounts and other departments. For instance Martin Slater, who was the Director responsible for Air Atlantique's massive engineering division in this country and abroad, landed at Caernarfon a week or so after the take-over and wandered around the airfield completely ignoring me. Finally, when I returned from a short pleasure flight in the Rapide, he came over to speak to me and asked if I was the Chief Pilot? He looked astonished when I told him that I was the Managing Director. I explained how I had taken over the airfield when it was derelict and built it up to become designated as Caernarfon Airport by the CAA. Martin apologised profusely and said ...

'I had no idea Ray, they never tell anyone what's going on in this company.'

He went on to explain that he had been sent over by Mike Collett to assess the way that Caernarfon Airport was being run. That annoyed me immensely at the time, but thinking about it later I suppose I had done exactly the same thing when Bob Pascoe had asked me to take a look at the way BSF's flying schools at Biggin Hill and Shoreham were being run. Unfortunately I discovered that they were a total financial disaster, and recommend closing them down.

Now that Air Atlantique was the parent company, I had considerably more paperwork to deal with in the form of weekly, instead of monthly statistics and financial returns from all the operational sections on the airport. From day one I received long faxes from Mike almost every day asking for details about this and that, together with instructions to change things around from one system to another. Mike and I had our differences to start with, and things finally came to a head one day when Mike wanted me to sell the pleasure flying tickets in the museum, instead of the flight office which was close to the aircraft dispersal area. The argument didn't last long, we both got a bit "hot under the collar" and I wound up getting fired! A few days later Mike telephoned me and asked me if I would like to take over the flying club as my own business. I said I would think about it. Then, whilst I was still serving my three months notice, Mike telephoned me again. The conversation went like this...

'Hello Ray. I've decided not to accept your resignation.'
'Hello Mike, I never gave in my notice ...you sacked me.'
'Did I?'
'Yes you did.'
'OK....You sure?'
'Yes'
'Well anyway, I want you to carry on working for me as MD.'
'OK'

And that was it , we never fell out again. Anyone that has ever worked for Mike knows its very unwise to argue with him. Mike and I eventually became very good friends and I worked for Air Atlantique until I retired four years later.

Fortunately all my employees retained their jobs when the take-over occurred. A Chief Engineer and several qualified engineers had to be employed to work in our newly formed maintenance company, CAMCO. I also employed two more full time and two part time flying instructors. By a strange coincidence David Balmer, one of the flying instructors I employed, told me that his very first flight in an aeroplane had taken place many years earlier when he was eleven years old. Apparently his father paid for him go on a pleasure flight with me in a PA 28 180 after they had visited Fort Belan.

The flight must have sparked off his ambition to become a pilot. David, was now a fully qualified flying instructor and joined the staff of our flying school. We became great friends, although he was sometimes a bit of a lively handful at a party!! But that's not the end of the story, David eventually left Air Caernarfon, and some years after I retired I discovered that he joined KLM, and over a period of time had risen to the rank of Line Training Captain.

Peter Brooks and I continued to enjoy ourselves flying the Rapide and our Britten-Norman Islander which Air Atlantique had added to our fleet of aircraft. Later Peter moved to our head office at Coventry working in Air Atlantique's oil pollution control unit. I flew with Peter again as P2 in one of Air Alantique's Dakotas when he qualified as a DC3 Captain.

The airport itself soon took on a new look. All the paint work on our aircraft and buildings was changed to conform with the Air Atlantique colours. Our maintenance unit CAMCO later opened a first class radio and avionics section. Also a huge refuelling station was built to supply both octane and jet fuel.

When I was called upon to designed the refuelling installation for Caernarfon Airport I obviously had to conform to all the safety regulations as laid down by the CAA and fire authorities. My design was approved by the CAA and the cost of construction was approved by my boss at Air Atlantique. I then had to face the bureaucracy, and in this case ignorance of the local planning officer. Having applied for planning permission to build the fuel bay, a young man appeared at my office door one morning. Announcing in grand style that he was from the planning office in Caernarfon, he told me that he had been sent over to inspect the area where we planned to build our fuel installation. As we walked over to the site, we passed our 2000 gallon petrol bowser refuelling an aeroplane that was parked on the dispersal area.

'What's that doing there?' he asked.

Although it seemed pretty obvious, I explained that it was a petrol bowser engaged in refuelling one of our aeroplanes. With a rather over-exaggerated gesture of shock, he stared at it for a moment, then blurted out…

'Mobile tankers are not allowed on airports, you should know better, get it removed at once.'

I laughed at first because I thought he was joking, but sure as hell he wasn't. He started ranting and raving about fire regulations, the dangerous goods act, and warned me that he intended to report me for contravening regulations and breaking the law.

In an effort to try and calm down this supercilious little prick, I explained that petrol bowsers were used at most airfields including London Airport at Heathrow. Now quite red in the face, he pulled a notepad from his briefcase and started to scribble away vigorously…

'Heathrow you say? well I'll soon put a stop to that!'

God help us if these are the sort of chaps that run our councils. Dealing with pompous idiots like that together with mountains of paperwork had become all in a day's work for me, but fortunately flying was always there to lift the spirits and carry me through the rest of the day with a smile.

During the Summer the producers of two of BBC Wales regular television programmes…. 'Get Going' and 'On the Road' approached me to ask if our company would be interested in taking part in the two programmes. One would be about the Airport Museum, and the other about training private pilots, in which we would give their presenter, Arfon Haines-Davies, his first flying lesson.

Naturally I agreed, two half hour television programmes featuring a couple of our main attractions was excellent free advertising that we could ill afford to lose. In addition the company would also receive payment for it's efforts.

The programmes were a success, although I found it embarrassing to see myself trying to act as nonchalant as possible on television.

One of the sequences filmed in the museum took place in front of a 'Vampire' jet trainer aircraft. All the displays in the museum had information placards giving full technical details and the history of each exhibit. These details had been carefully researched by myself to make sure they were absolutely accurate before the placards were printed.

Filming in the museum was a serious business. There was no rehearsal or scripts to adhere to, I just had to show Arfon Haines-Davies around the various aircraft and exhibits in the museum and answer the questions he would put to me. Unfortunately on the day of the filming I happened to be wearing shoes with metal heal caps. The museum was housed in a huge hangar type building, and when I walked from one exhibit to another my footsteps clicked away and echoed around the building sounding, as one of the sound engineers put it, 'rather like the delicate footsteps of a whore!'

We had to make several re-takes, because each time I clanked my way over to the Vampire with Arfon, he would burst out laughing.

The cameraman zoomed in on the placard bearing the detailed history of the aircraft then panned up to me standing on the wing. At that point the interviewer asked me....

'Tell me Captain Blyth, was this type of aircraft ever used for pilot training at RAF Valley here in North Wales?'

I then answered confidently...

'No, not to my knowledge.'

There was a stunned silence whilst the cameras continued rolling and Arfon bent down to pick up the placard. Presenting it to the camera he said...

'I don't want to make these questions too hard for you Capt Blyth, but I believe you wrote these placards, and it says here quite plainly that this actual aircraft was used regularly to train pilots at RAF Valley!'

At that point he literarily exploded into uncontrollable laughter, I was so surprised that I lost my footing and slid off the wing of the Vampire into a heap on the floor, and the bloody cameras remained rolling throughout this cock-up until the Director finally shouted 'CUT.'

We made re-take after retake, because every time Arfon asked me the same question, we both started giggling, and once that sort of thing happens it takes a lot of willpower to get through the shot with a straight face .

Finally when we completed the filming, the Director said he would probably show the "out-takes" on a separate TV programme later in the year providing I didn't object.

The second programme "Get Going" took place a few days later, featuring Arfon Haines-Davies again, this time supposedly having his first flying lesson with me. This also proved to be a bit of a scream as he was terrified of flying. Everything went off reasonably well during the ground briefing etc. But once we got into the air, poor old Arfon, who was suppose to be playing the part of an enthusiastic student pilot, was so nervous he couldn't utter a word, and I wound up talking to myself throughout the flight.

In spite of all the problems, I was impressed with the final results when the programme was shown on TV a few weeks later. The editor must have been a clever chap to put that lot together without showing a sign of a smirk on our faces. Later the producer sent me a VHS copy of both programmes including the sequences that were edited out.

Every now and again something unusual would turn up to break the daily routine. On one of those occasions our Chairman, Mike Collett, and our group Managing Director James Foden, were chatting with me in my office when our receptionist rang through to say that the BBCTV news team were on the airfield and wanted to see me. It turned out that the Swiss Aerobatic Champion Frank Versteegh was going to land at Caernarfon to be interviewed by the BBC, and they would like permission to interview him standing by his aeroplane in the dispersal area. Mike suggested that it would be a good idea if we could get some advertising mileage out of Versteegh's visit.

When he landed in his Extra 300 plane, I went over to greet him and introduce myself. The cockpit canopy opened and this 6ft. 4ins giant of a man climbed out to shake hands with me. I told him that the television news team were on the airfield and waiting to interview him. As we walked towards the main building, Frank pointed at our Rapide standing outside the hangar and said…

'Who's the lucky pilot that flies that lovely old machine?'

I told him that I did most of the flying in the Rapide, explaining that we used the aircraft to take tourists on pleasure flights over the mountains.

Later, when his interview with the BBC was complete, he came over to tell me that he was about to carry out a low flypast for the TV cameras, and said he would love to fly in mirror formation with our Rapide if that was possible. It was a brilliant idea and an excellent advertisement for our company as well. I shot back into the office to ask whether Mike or James would like to fly the Rapide in mirror formation with the Swiss Aerobatic Champion. They both declined and suggested that I should do it.

Frank Versteegh was an out and out perfectionist. He told me exactly what he was going to do and briefed me to take-off in the Rapide, level out at 200 feet and carry out a rate one turn left to head back towards the airfield and complete a low run past the tower at fifty feet…

'Fly absolutely level and perfectly straight Ray, I will position my aircraft quite close over the top of you fully inverted, and don't break formation until I tell you that I'm clear.' he said.

The BBC cameras were in place on top of the Air Traffic Control building as we taxied out to the runway. Checks complete, Frank gave me the thumbs up and I was away. As briefed I climbed to 200 ft. and turned slowly round so as to fly straight and level down the duty runway. I didn't hear a peep out of Frank and was just looking down to see if he had in fact taken off, when a shadow fell over the cockpit of the Rapide blocking out the sunlight. Making sure I didn't move a fraction off the straight and level attitude, I snatched a very quick glance upwards...

'Jesus!!'.... I could see the top of Franks head inside the cockpit of the Extra just a few feet above my head. We flew past the tower, I hardly dare take my eyes off the horizon.

'OK Ray...That's it.'

I looked up again but there was no sign of the Extra 300. As I banked to turn I saw his aeroplane touching down on the runway. That night I watched the BBC news and saw the whole thing again from a very different standpoint. It was very impressive, and damn good free advertising for us.

On another occasion the producer of Cilla Black's TV programme "Blind Date" contacted us and said he would like to organise a pleasure flight over Snowdon as part of a day's outing for the two lucky persons who were the winners of the competition.

The programme features one person who has to choose a partner of the opposite sex to go on a blind date. The catch is that they have to choose their blind date purely by listening to the voices and promises of three contestant's without actually seeing them until the choice has been made. Having selected a partner, the couple finally see each other for the first time, then Cilla Black sends them off together on a "Blind Date" that the organisers have set up prior to the programme. This can sometimes turn out to be very embarrassing, especially if the two winning contestants hate one another on sight, as did happen with the couple who were sent to us for a pleasure flight as part of their winning prize.

We were informed that the "loving" couple would be arriving around midday in a chauffeur driven car together with the Programme Director and a film crew. I expected to see the young lady and her escort holding hands and thoroughly enjoying themselves. But things turned out to be very different. The chap looked like he had just been sentenced to death, and by the look on the girls face she wished she could be the executioner!

The cameras were set up on the airfield, and the director was doing his best to persuade the "young lady" to say something nice about her blind date, when to everyone's amazement she blurted out ...

'I wished I picked anyone but that drip, and what's more I f.....g hate aeroplanes.'

Later, with breath that smelt like a distillery, she told me that she had been out all night with one of the other contestants and was suffering from a king sized hangover.

The poor chap who was supposed to be her partner for the day, was obviously in a very awkward situation. Her behaviour was abominable, and to be perfectly honest she was certainly no oil painting!. I'm sure the young man was more interested in the aeroplane than his date, and who could blame him?

Another row started up because neither of them wanted to sit in the back. In the end the director of the programme decided that the man should sit in the front next to me, whilst the young lady as he called her, sat in the back with the cameraman.

The "lovers" argued throughout the flight, shouting abuse at one another until we landed. They then set off in one of those stretched out luxury cars to "enjoy" the rest of their day out together. God help em! The director looked really hacked off, he apologised for the girl's behaviour, adding they were the worst couple that had ever taken part in the Blind Date programme.

One Saturday afternoon in August 1991, F/Lt Al Hoy popped in to see me. Al was stationed at RAF Scampton and flew with the Red Arrows as Red Two. Prior to joining the Red Arrows Al had been a staff instructor at Central Flying School. He was due to retire from the RAF at the end of the year, and because of my previous connections with the Red Arrows, he had been advised to contact me about organising a four week resettlement training programme for him at Air Caernarfon later in the year..

Naturally I was more than pleased to have Al with us. His ultimate aim was to learn as much as possible about the civilian side of aviation, and in particular how to set up a fully licensed CAA approved commercial operation from scratch.

F/Lt Al Hoy joined us on the 8th October, and after an enjoyable four weeks of delving into the endless mysteries of CAA legislation and the inscrutable mountain of associated paperwork, Al departed on the 5th Nov wondering if leaving the RAF was such a good idea after all! Unfortunately

I never heard how Al did get on in civilian life, but I'm prepared to bet that whatever he did he would have been successful.

Air Atlantique installed permanent runway lighting along our 08/26 runway, which expanded our range of operational hours and pilot training considerably. Looking at other opportunities to increase our range of services, Mike and I agreed that North Wales would be an excellent area to operate the services of aerial advertising, especially during the summer months. Within a week Air Atlantique provided all the equipment for the job and our staff pilots had to be trained in the art of Banner Towing.

Learning how to pick up a banner in flight calls for a high degree of accuracy on the part of the pilot, and training someone to do this can sometimes prove to be a bit tricky.

We decided that our C172 was the best aeroplane for the job, and had the pick-up hook and release mechanism fitted to G-AYUV.

The aerial advertisement is prepared by pegging six-foot letters to a length of specially made netting. The message is then attached to a very long steel towing cable. One end of the cable is attached to a pick-up wire suspended between two very light ten foot high poles that are placed thirty feet apart. (Rather like a tall linen-line) The poles themselves are held upright in a similar manner to that used for erecting tent poles. The procedure for picking up the banner is as follows...

Shortly after take-off when the aircraft is in a low down wind position, the pilot reduces the airspeed, lowers fifteen degrees of flap and releases the towing hook from it's locked position so that it trails out about 100mtrs behind and slightly below his aeroplane. Turning onto the final approach the pilot aims to fly over a position central to the two posts supporting the pick-up wire. When he has passed safely over the airfield boundary, travelling about 10 to 12 knots above the aircraft's stalling speed, he descends to a height about three feet above the pickup wire suspended between the two posts. The pilot has to judge his height accurately so that the towing hook snatches the pick-up wire and the banner which is laid out forward of the posts. The banner then curls up from the ground as the aircraft passes overhead. The pilot is left in no doubt at all when the hook collects the wire from the posts. The aircraft suddenly jerks and begins to slow down rapidly, you have to apply full power immediately and start to climb at a fairly steep angle. To start with you are only lifting the weight of the cable, but a couple of seconds later the banner is lifted from the ground and by that time you certainly need to be flying at maximum power. If the aircraft is too low the towing hook will hit the ground and bounce over the wire, and if you happened to be dangerously low, the undercarriage and the prop could strike the cable after which anything could happen. Being too high of course simply means the hook would miss the cable altogether and you would need to go round again and have another go.

I remember the first few times I picked up a banner I pushed the throttle forwards with so much enthusiasm when the hook collected the banner, that it's little wonder the lever didn't bend! Like most things its easy when you get used to it, but to start with it can be close to terrifying! Another thing you have to remember if you were flying along a seafront or to one side of a town, is to make sure you were heading in the correct direction for people on the ground to read the banner, as all the letters and words appear back to front on the opposite side..

Releasing the banner can be misleading. The idea is to fly over the airfield low, remembering that the banner always hangs several feet lower than the aircraft, then, at the correct moment pull the release handle so that the banner floats down gracefully onto the airfield. It is very easy to misjudge the combined length of the cable and banner. The first time I picked up an advertising banner I flew along the seafront at Dinas Dinlle advertising "Pleasure Flights". I returned triumphantly to the airfield, made a low pass and released the banner just before I was abeam the control tower, hoping it would flutter down onto the grass along side the runway. A high pitched voice from the controller informed me that the banner had in fact come down in the middle of a caravan site adjacent to the airfield! The engineers that recovered the banner said that it had become entangled with the TV aerials of several caravans and the owners were far from impressed!

On one occasion we were commissioned to tow a banner advertising the opening of a new entertainments centre on the seafront at Llandudno. The timing had to be spot on to coincide with the actual opening ceremony. I had special dispensation from the CAA to fly quite low over the sea front. I flew about 2000yds out to sea to begin with so that I could turn and descend to a lower altitude for the run past. As I approached the entertainments centre I could see crowds of people outside the building. Spot on the time planned for the opening ceremony I was flying at about 150feet just off the coast. The aircraft was almost level with the attraction when I saw a couple of rockets go up to an altitude well above me before bursting into a crescendo of red, yellow and green stars.

That was OK, but the next second there were several powerful looking rockets zooming up that appeared to be aimed at the aircraft, eventually bursting with a hell of a bang way behind us. The banner I was towing was quite a length which made it impossible to manoeuvre out of the way as quickly as I would have liked. I had just started a climbing turn away from the display area when a rocket went off with an ear-shattering explosion about six feet in front and slightly below the nose of the aircraft, discharging a number of smaller maroons that exploded under the port wing. That was enough for me, I climbed away and returned to the airfield.

Immediately after landing I telephoned the organisers and asked them what the hell did they think they were playing at? They apologised profusely and said the firework company that carried out the display were under the illusion that it had been agreed for the rockets to be aimed at the aeroplane to give the visitors a bit of excitement. I pointed out that it was me that got all the F…..g excitement, and I didn't take too kindly to the pratt that authorised the display. In the end I thought it prudent not to make too much fuss as I knew from past experience, complaints that resulted in a CAA investigation had a nasty habit of backfiring, and, with my luck, I could wind up answering a charge of low flying again, even if it was authorised.

I checked out two of my pilots for banner towing so that we could take it in turns to carry out the various advertising flights, one of them resulted in quite a surprise.

I was helping Carol in our gift shop in Aberdaron during my day off from the airport, when the door burst open and one of the villagers rushed in excitedly and asked Carol to come out into the street and look at something. It happened to be her birthday and I thought perhaps someone had arranged some kind of surprise for her. They had, it was my lot from the airfield.

When we stepped outside we saw Air Caernarfon's Cessna towing a banner which read "HAPPY BIRTHDAY CAROL". It was quite a surprise for Cassie, and a bit of a shock for me too, I certainly knew nothing about it. It turned out to be David Balmer, one of my instructors, circled the village several times then climbed away into the distance. Moments later several neighbours and friends brought birthday cards into the shop, thus proving that aerial advertising does bring in the results!

My choice of profession was never dull, life was always full of surprises at the airfield, and my much loved staff that worked for me frequently came up with surprises…

One morning I was struggling through the usual paperwork that appeared on my desk with monotonous regularly, when I was distracted by the unfamiliar sound of heavy engines roaring away in reverse thrust.

I stood up to take a look through my office window and got the shock of my life. A C130 Hercules had landed unannounced and was taxying down the centre of our 800metre runway. At that second my telephone rang, our Controller Tom Pritchard was on the line and said...

'The Captain of the C130 that has just landed is asking if you would like to go up for a trip round the local area boss?'

I was astounded, apart from an occasional visit from one of Air Atlantique's Dakota's, I seldom saw any aircraft bigger than our Rapide on the runway at Caernarfon. In contrast the RAF Hercules seemed enormous. I hurried over to the aircraft that was now stationary halfway down the runway with it's engines roaring away. A member of the crew came out to meet me wearing a headset with a long cable that obviously linked him to the flight-deck, and said...

'If you would care to go aboard sir, the Captain has invited you on to the flight-deck.' The Capt., F/Lt Tapsfield, welcomed me on board and explained that because we had allowed him to use our runway for a couple of practice short field landings, he would like to offer me and two members of my staff aboard for a short flight. I was quite surprised, no-one had told me that we had accepted the Herc; for practice landings.

It turned out to be Tom Pritchard, himself an ex RAF Controller, who had set the whole thing up, he climbed aboard to take a seat in the lower section of the enormous fuselage. Later Tom, who nearly always had his camera with him, joined me on the flight-deck to take a few photographs. All my staff at the airfield were second to none, they worked hard, loved their jobs and were a pleasure to work with, which in turn made my job the best job in the world.

It goes without saying the flight was most enjoyable. We droned pleasantly around the mountains for a while returning to the circuit after about half an hour. The landing was incredibly short for such a huge aeroplane. In fact the aircraft came to a halt considerably less than halfway down our 800m runway, a feat rarely achieved in still air by our Rapide!

The Captain was in fact very interested in our 1934 Rapide. Obviously he couldn't close down the C130 so I promised to take him up in G-AIDL if he ever had time to call in and visit us by road or something smaller than a Hercules. Tom took a photograph of me leaving the aircraft, after all it's not every day that a RAF Hercules drops in and invites one up for a flight?

Another pleasant surprise occurred when a chap by the name of Tony Hodgson telephoned me to arrange an IMC rating renewal test. He turned up in a Twin Beech C45 aeroplane that had once been used by an American

General as his personal aircraft during WW2. The fuselage was painted in standard United States Airforce colours with a very colourful naked lady bearing the name "Southern Comfort" displayed on the port side of the nose cone. Over the months that followed I became friends with Tony and was allowed to fly the C45 from time to time. He also owned a beautiful ex RAF Harvard FX301 that was still in military colours, and I was given the opportunity of flying this aeroplane. Such occasions made my job even more enjoyable. Tony asked me if I would like to demonstrate the C45 at Blackpool Air Displays for him whilst he flew the Harvard. But I was already committed to demonstrate our dear old Rapide at the same display.

In the early 1990s there was a shortage of CAA Check Captains for the DH 89. At one stage I was the only authorised Check Captain on this type of aircraft in the country. Clacton Aero Club operated one of the three remaining de-Havilland Rapide's and badly needed a Check Captain. They asked me if I would carry out mandatory flight checks on their authorised captains and become their nominated TRE. (Type Rating Examiner).

The head of CAA Flight Operations approved this and my boss at Air Atlantique had no objection to me carrying out the tests providing Air Caernarfon received payment for my services. So for a while I acted as Clacton Aero Club's TRE and Training Captain on the DH-89-A, Cessna and Piper variants. The question then arose who could carry out my Base and Line Check on the Rapide as I was the only approved Check Captain? The CAA got round this by giving a British Airways pilot, Capt Murphy, a one-off dispensation to test me.

The conditions for the test were far from perfect as the cross wind component on the runway was close to the limits for the Rapide. We had a bit of a laugh during the test when we were on our final approach to land. The wind started gusting up a bit and I asked Capt Murphy what sort of approach and landing he wanted me to do…

'A safe one will do fine Ray.'

After the flight check we popped out to the local for lunch, and this is when I got the shock of my life. During out conversation I asked Capt Murphy what type of aircraft he was flying. His matter of fact answer certainly took me by surprise…

'Well its quite an interesting job really, I spend part of my time as a Check Captain on the Concorde.'

He was a delightful young man, the sort of chap that, had I not have asked him, he would never have mentioned flying Concorde, and I felt quite privileged to have flown with him.

Since those days I believe another two or three Dragon Rapide's have been restored and issued with a public transport C of A. They are of course expensive aircraft to operate, mainly because of the shortage of spares.

When in 1991 I reached the tender age of sixty, I received the shattering news that I could no longer fly single crew aircraft commercially. Sadly this meant my days of flying the Rapide commercially were over. On further investigation I learned that I could still legally continue to fly passengers in the Rapide under the authority of the private pilots section of my commercial licence providing my passengers didn't actually pay for the flight!

I was somewhat flabbergasted by this as I was still in possession of my current commercial pilot's licence, including a current class one medical certificate that had to be regularly up-dated at six monthly intervals, all that had changed was my age. In other words, if I had a heart attack and crashed into the middle of a town, I would be flying perfectly legally providing my passengers hadn't paid for the flight. The obvious question was, how can carrying passengers free of charge make any difference to their safety, which surely must be the main consideration?

At that time Great Britain was the only country in Europe that had this ridiculous rule, every other country stopped pilots operating commercially in single crew aircraft at the standard retiring age of 65. Another point that seemed to be grossly unjust was that a UK licensed pilot who earned his living exclusively by carrying passengers in a single crew aeroplane, was prevented by the State from earning his living when he reached the age of sixty, yet was not allowed to draw his State Pension for a further five years when he became sixty-five.

Hundreds of British pilots complained to the authorities about this ludicrous situation, but the CAA had no intention of changing the regulations to concur with other EU countries. Unfortunately for me it took another ten years before common sense finally prevailed, and the CAA were forced to come into line with other European Union countries. On the 10th March 2006 the CAA issued an amendment to the Air Navigation Order that increased the age of single crew operations from sixty to sixty-five, not that it did me any good, I was seventy five by then!

The concluding five years of my flying career passed quickly, and the day finally arrived when I found myself packing up all the belongings that had meant so much to me over the years. I removed the old flying suit, leather helmet and goggles that had hung on my office door for years and packed them away. The sight of the Gosport Tubes still attached to the ear pieces of my flying helmet brought back vivid memories of learning to fly. It had been more than forty years since I strove to hear the wise words of my instructor as he fought to make himself heard over the noise of the slipstream roaring past the open cockpit of our Tiger Moth.

I emptied the drawers of my desk and carefully packed away the drawing instruments my father had given me for my sixteenth birthday. These reliable old inanimate friends brought back cherished memories of the various projects I had been involved with at Halfpenny Green, Ipswich, Jersey, Fort Belan, Caernarfon Airport and the two exciting years I spent designing Space City.

Everything packed away, I placed the two cardboard boxes in the boot of my car sadly realising that they, together with my logbooks, were the sole remains of a long and treasured career.

A farewell party had been laid on for me by all the staff at Caernarfon Airport. Air Atlantique's Chairman Mike Collett and Managing Director James Foden arrived in the company's Jet Cessna Citation. During the evening Mike Collett made a short speech and said some very nice things about me. In a way it seemed unreal, I couldn't really grasp the fact that my career in aviation was over. It was an evening of mixed feelings, pride, happiness and great sadness. Our air traffic controller Phil Hudson arrived and approached me with a serious look on his face...

'Max sends his apologies, he's very sorry he couldn't attend, but he already had a previous engagement.'

I had to laugh because Max, bless him, was a very friendly little black mongrel dog. He belonged to Phil and was our much loved mascot at the airport, and also a great friend of our little dog Kimbo.

After a three course meal Tom Pritchard made a little speech on behalf of the staff that brought tears to my eyes, and presented me with a beautiful painting featuring a Tiger Moth taking off from a grass airfield. It had been signed by all the staff, including Group Captain Phil Langril who was the ex CO of our at neighbouring airport, RAF Valley. It was a great evening that ultimately faded into oblivion.

The following morning Carol came with me to pick up Mike and James from the hotel where they had stayed the night, and drive them to the airport. We watched them take-off for the last time bound for their offices at Coventry.

It was a gorgeous morning and, like the hundreds of times I had seen them in the past, the Snowdonia range of mountains looked beautiful against a pale blue sky. I planned to take one last flight around the local area with Carol by my side. Nothing fancy, just a steady and rather nostalgic flight in a Cessna 172. We took off on runway 26 and climbed steadily into the morning sky. A short time later as we rejoined the circuit and I looked down with pride at Caernarfon Airport, remembering the derelict place it had been when I first accepted the challenge of building it up to become probably the finest privately owned licensed airport in England. It had become the epitome of all I had strived for. We landed and walked away from the aeroplane holding hands. It was the end of an era.

Ray and Carol retired to Norfolk in 1996. They both love the Norfolk Broads and were lucky enough to buy "The Beehive", a beautiful old thatched house situated on a small peninsular of land located at the junction of Daisy Broad and the River Bure. With water on three sides of the house there was over 100 yards of quay heading including two small harbours incorporated into the property. With magnificent views of the river from all the rooms, Carol and Ray decided to start up a small Bed and Breakfast Business. They ran the business very successfully for over five years, but sadly developers constructed a massive complex of holiday lets on the northern shores of Daisy Broad and the peaceful ambience of the Beehive was lost. Reluctantly they decided to sell the Beehive and buy a small house that was situated on the cliffs at Trimingham. With their garden stretching down to just a few yards from the cliff edge, they enjoyed panoramic views of the sea. A few years later Carol spotted a lovely old Windmill that was for sale. The mill is located on the banks of the river Bure well out into the Norfolk Marshes, a really quiet and peaceful place, and that's where they now live.

Lightning Source UK Ltd.
Milton Keynes UK
UKOW031959030713

213139UK00002B/4/P